CW00376419

ISBN 978-0-260-97026-8
PIBN 10995499

CATALOGUE

MICHIGAN MINING SCHOOL.

HOUGHTON, MICHIGAN.

1890-1891.

HOUGHTON, MICHIGAN.
PUBLISHED BY THE MINING SCHOOL.
1891.

CATALOGUE

OF THE

Michigan Mining School.

WITH STATEMENTS CONCERNING THE INSTITUTION AND ITS
COURSES OF INSTRUCTION.

HOUGHTON, MICHIGAN.

1890-1891.

HOUGHTON, MICHIGAN.
PUBLISHED BY THE MINING SCHOOL.
1891.

PRESS OF
MINING JOURNAL CO. (LIMITED),
MARQUETTE, MICH.

TABLE OF CONTENTS.

	PAGE.
Table of Contents..............................	3, 4
Board of Control..............................	5, 6
Board of Visitors..............................	7
Board of the Geological Survey..............................	7
Officers of the Michigan Mining School and Geological Survey..............................	8, 10
Faculty of the Michigan Mining School..............	11
Catalogue of Students..............................	12-18
Requirements for Admission..............................	19-21
The Course of Instruction..............................	22-24
Outline of the Course of Study..............................	25-32
Departments of Instruction..............................	33-61
Mathematics..............................	33
Physics..............................	34
Drawing	34-38
Mechanical Engineering..............................	38, 39
Mechanics of Materials..............................	40
Summer Course in Shop Practice..............................	40, 41
Electrical Engineering..............................	42
Surveying..............................	43-46
Summer Course in Surveying..............................	43-45
Mine Surveying..............................	45, 46
Hydraulics..............................	46
Mining..............................	46-48
Chemistry..............................	48-51
General Chemistry..............................	48
Qualitative Analysis..............................	48, 49
Quantitative Analysis..............................	49
Technical Analysis..............................	49, 50
Assaying..............................	50, 51
Ore Dressing..............................	51, 52
Metallurgy..............................	52, 53
Crystallography..............................	53
Mineralogy..............................	54, 55
Lithology	55, 56
Petrography..............................	56, 57
Palæontology..............................	57
Stratigraphical and Historical Geology.............	58
Physical Geology..............................	58, 59

	PAGE.
Economic Geology	59, 60
Summer Course in Geology	60, 61
Thesis	61
Organization	62
Regulations of the School	63-65
Location of School, and Map of Portage Lake Mining District*	65-67
Mining Industries of Michigan	66, 67
Expenses	68, 69
Employment	69-71
The Longyear Prizes	72, 73
The Charles E. Wright Scholarship	74
The Norrie Scholarship	75
The Longyear Fund	76
Degrees	76, 77
Graduate Instruction and Degrees	77, 78
Collections	78
Library	79
Reading Room and Periodicals	79-83
Text-Books	83, 84
Examination Questions for Admission	84-90
Buildings	91-95
Basement Plan	92
First Floor Plan	93
Second Floor Plan	94
Third Floor Plan	95
Graduates	96-98
Calendar	99-102

*The plate for the map has been kindly loaned by Mr. B. T. Judkins. of the Portage Lake Mining Gazette.

BOARD OF CONTROL OF THE MINING SCHOOL.

1890-1891.

Term Expires.

JAMES NORTH WRIGHT, Calumet............June 9, 1891.
THOMAS LINCOLN CHADBOURNE, Houghton.June 9, 1891.
Hon. JAY ABEL HUBBELL, Houghton..........June 9, 1893.
JOHN SENTER, Houghton..... ....June 9, 1893.
JOHN MONROE LONGYEAR, Marquette........June 9, 1895.
ALFRED KIDDER, Marquette..................June 9, 1895.

OFFICERS OF THE BOARD OF CONTROL.

PRESIDENT OF THE BOARD OF CONTROL,
JAMES NORTH WRIGHT.

SECRETARY OF THE BOARD OF CONTROL,
THOMAS LINCOLN CHADBOURNE.

DIRECTOR OF THE MINING SCHOOL,
MARSHMAN EDWARD WADSWORTH.

TREASURER AND PURCHASING AGENT OF THE MINING SCHOOL,
ALLEN FORSYTH REES.

BOARD OF CONTROL OF THE
MINING SCHOOL.

1891-1892.

	Term Expires.
HON. JAY ABEL HUBBELL, Houghton	June 9, 1893.
HON. MICHAEL CHAMBERS, St. Ignace	June 9, 1893.
JOHN MONROE LONGYEAR, Marquette	June 9, 1895.
ALFRED KIDDER, Marquette	June 9, 1895.
JAMES RENRICK COOPER, Hancock	June 9, 1897.
HON. PETER WHITE, Marquette	June 9, 1897.

OFFICERS OF THE BOARD OF CONTROL.

PRESIDENT OF THE BOARD OF CONTROL,
HON. JAY ABEL HUBBELL.

SECRETARY OF THE BOARD OF CONTROL,
ALLEN FORSYTH REES.

*DIRECTOR OF THE MINING SCHOOL,
MARSHMAN EDWARD WADSWORTH.

†TREASURER AND PURCHASING AGENT OF THE MINING SCHOOL.
ALLEN FORSYTH REES.

---

*All letters of inquiry, applications for catalogues, admission, etc., should be sent to the Director.

†All communications concerning purchases, bills, etc., should be sent to the Treasurer.

*OFFICERS OF THE MICHIGAN MINING SCH))L AND)F THE STATE GE)L)GICAL SURVEY.

1890-1891-

MARSHMAN EDWARD WADSWORTH, A. B. (Bowdoin College).
A.M., Ph.D. (Harvard University),
Director and State Geologist.
Professor of Mineralogy, Petrography and Geology.

ARTHUR EDWIN HAYNES, M.S., M Ph. (Hillsdale College),
Professor of Mathematics and Physics.

HARRY FREDERICK KELLER, B.S., (University of Pennsylvania),
Ph.D., (University of Strasburg),
Professor of Chemistry, and Chemist on the Geological Survey.

ALFRED CHURCH LANE, A.M., Ph.D. (Harvard University),
Instructor in Petrography and Geology, and Assistant on
the Geological Survey.

EDGAR KIDWELL, A.M. (Georgetown College), M.E. (University
of Pennsylvania),
Instructor in Mechanical Engineering and Drawing.

FRED FRALEY SHARPLESS, S B. (University of Michigan),
Instructor in Ore Dressing, Assaying and Metallurgy, and
Chemist on the Geological Survey.

FRED WARNER DENTON, C E. (Columbia School of Mines),
Instructor in Mining Engineering.

WALTER JOHN BALDWIN, S B. (University of Michigan),
Assistant in Mineralogy.

ARTHUR EDMUND SEAMAN,
Assistant in Mineralogy and on the Geological Survey.

ROBERT IRWIN REES,
Librarian and Clerk.

HENRY GIBBS,
Janitor: in charge of the Chemical Supply Room.

PATRICK ROBERT DILLON.
Engineer and Assistant Janitor.

---

*The first eight officers arranged in order of collegiate seniority.

*OFFICERS OF THE MICHIGAN MINING SCHOOL AND OF THE STATE GEOLOGICAL SURVEY.

1891-1892.

MARSHMAN EDWARD WADSWORTH, A.B. (Bowdoin College)
A.M., Ph.D.(Harvard University),
Director and State Geologist.
Professor of Mineralogy, Petrography and Geology.

LUCIUS LEE HUBBARD, A.B. (Harvard University), LL.B.
(Boston University), A.M., Ph D. (University of Bonn),
Assistant in Mineralogy, and on the Geological Survey.

ARTHUR EDWIN HAYNES, M.S., M.Ph. (Hillsdale College),
Professor of Mathematics and Physics.

HARRY FREDERICK KELLER, B.S. (University of Pennsylvania),
Ph. D. (University of Strasburg),
Professor of Chemistry, and Chemist on the Geological Survey.

HORACE BUSHNELL PATTON, A.B. (Amherst College), Ph.D.
(University of Heidelberg),
Instructor in Mineralogy and Petrography, and Assistant on
the Geological Survey.

ALFRED CHURCH LANE, A M , Ph.D. (Harvard University),
Instructor in Petrography and Geology, and Assistant on
the Geological Survey.

EDGAR KIDWELL, A.M. (Georgetown University), M.E. (University of Pennsylvania),
Instructor in Mechanical Engineering and Drawing.
In charge of the Department.

FRED FRALEY SHARPLESS, S.B. (University of Michigan),
Instructor in Ore Dressing, Assaying and Metallurgy, and
Chemist on the Geological Survey.

FRED WARNER DENTON, C.E. (Columbia College School of
Mines),
Instructor in Mining Engineering and Surveying, and Assistant
on the Geological Survey.

---

*The first eleven officers arranged in order of collegiate seniority.

. WALTER JOHN BALDWIN, S.B. (University of Michigan)
Instructor in Mathematics and Physics.

JOHN FRANCIS ROWLAND JR.. B.S., M.E. (University of
Pennsylvania).
Instructor in Mechanical Engineering and Drawing.

ARTHUR EDMUND SEAMAN,
Assistant in Mineralogy and on the Geological Survey.

ROBERT IRWIN REES,
Librarian and Clerk.

HENRY GIBBS,
· Janitor: in charge of the Chemical Supply Room.

PATRICK ROBERT DILLON,
Engineer and Assistant Janitor.

LEMUEL SEVERANCE,
Janitor's Assistant.

MISS KATE KILLIAN,
Stenographer and Typewriter for the Geological Survey.

FACULTY OF THE MINING SCHOOL.

MARSHMAN EDWARD WADSWORTH, A.M., Ph.D.,
DIRECTOR.
Professor of Mineralogy, Petrography and Geology.

ARTHUR EDWIN HAYNES, M.S., M.Ph.,
Professor of Mathematics and Physics.
Secretary of the Faculty.

HARRY FREDERICK KELLER, B.S., Ph.D.,
Professor of Chemistry.

EDGAR KIDWELL, A.M., M.E.,
Instructor in Mechanical Engineering and Drawing.

FRED FRALEY SHARPLESS, S.B.,
Instructor in Assaying, Ore Dressing and Metallurgy.

FRED WARNER DENTON, C.E.,
Instructor in Mining Engineering and Surveying.

GRADUATE STUDENTS.

NAME.	RESIDENCE.	ROOM.
BALDWIN, WALTER JOHN, S.B. (University of Michigan). Mineralogy, Chemistry, Mining, Ore Dressing.	*Romansville, Pa.*	Mrs. E. M. Hoar's.
HUBBARD, LUCIUS LEE, A.B. (Harvard University), LL. B. (Boston University), A.M., Ph.D. (University of Bonn), Mineralogy.	*Boston, Mass.*	Douglas House.
LAWTON, CHARLES LATHAM, S.B. (Michigan Agricultural College), Mineralogy and Mining.	*Crystal Falls.*	Butterfield House.
LULING, THEODORE WILLIAM, A.B. (University of Cambridge). Mineralogy and Building Stones.	*London, England.*	Mrs. Boxer's.
SHERZER, WILL HITTEL, M.S. (University of Michigan), Mineralogy and Petrography.	*Saginaw.*	Mr. Sherzer's.

CLASS OF 1891.

NAME.	RESIDENCE.	ROOM.
BOSSERT, OTTO HENRY,	*Milwaukee, Wisconsin.*	Mrs. Rice's.
*CHYNOWETH, CLARENCE BARTLETT,	*Houghton.*	Mr. Chynoweth's.
CLOSE, FRED BAGLEY,	*Hancock.*	Mr. Close's.
*COLWELL, ALFRED BUNDY,	*Appleton, Wisconsin.*	Mrs. Brimacombe's.
DENGLER, THEODORE,	*Chicago, Illinois.*	Mrs. Brimacombe's.
DYER, HOLMES HAYWARD,	*Ionia.*	Mr. Trim's.
FINK, EDWARD,	*Milwaukee, Wisconsin.*	Mrs. E. M. Hoar's.
McDONALD, WILLIAM NEAL,	*Houghton.*	Mr. McDonald's.
PALMER, EDWARD VOSE,	*Marquette.*	Mrs. E. M. Hoar's.

*Taking a Partial Course.

CLASS OF 1892.

NAME.	RESIDENCE.	ROOM.
*FULLER, FRED DWIGHT,	*Milwaukee, Wisconsin.*	
		Mrs. S. Gray's.
HONNOLD, WILLIAM LINCOLN,	*Camp Point, Illinois.*	
		Bank Building.
*McCHRYSTAL, JACKSON CARLOS,	*Eureka, Utah.*	
		Mrs. Rice's.
OPPEN, WILLIAM ADOLPH,	*Green Bay, Wisconsin.*	
		Pfeiffer's Hotel.
*ROPES, LEVERETT SMITH,	*Ishpeming.*	
		Mrs. E. M. Hoar's.
*RYGAARD, HANS PETER,	*Marquette.*	
		Sheldon's Block.
TOWER, LOUIS LOVELL,	*Ionia.*	
		Mr. E. R. Penberthy's.

SPECIAL STUDENT.

SEAMAN, ARTHUR EDMUND, Mineralogy and Geology.

Houghton.

Mr. Seaman's.

---

*Taking a Partial Course.

CLASS OF 1893.

NAME.	RESIDENCE.	ROOM.

ABBOTT, AI ARTHUR, S.B.(Michigan Agricultural College),
Holt.
Mrs. P. Didier's Sr.

*BEEN, JOHN THEODORE,   *Skanee.*
Mrs. John Penberthy's

CLUTE, WILLIAM MERRILEES,   *Lansing.*
Miss Nora Kelly's.

CHURCH, GEORGE BATCHELOR,   *Flint.*
Mrs. Alford's.

CRANSON, ROBERT EDWARD,   *St. Johns.*
Mrs. Brimacombe's.

FISHER, JAMES.   *Quincy Mine.*
Mr. Fisher's.

*FRENCH, WILLIAM CUTLER,   *Champion Mine.*
Mr. J. H. Chandler's.

GILLIES, DONALD,   *Lake Linden.*
Mrs. Alford's.

HARRINGTON, FREDERICK LUCE,   *Port Huron.*
Bank Building.

*HOOPER, JAMES HENRY,   *Beaver Mine, Canada.*
Mrs. Brimacombe's.

HOTALING, EUGENE JAY RITTER,   *Chicago, Illinois.*
Mrs. Mac Farland's.

*JAMES, HOUGHTON EDWARD,   *Houghton.*
Mrs. James's.

KIRK, MARCUS EUGENE,   *Sturgis.*
Mr. R. M. Edwards' Office.

*MASON, CLARENCE GEORGE,   *Hancock.*
Mr. Mason's.

MASON, RUSSELL TEEL,   *Boulder, Colorado.*
Mrs. Rashleigh's.

*McCAULEY, JAMES,   *Hancock.*
Mr. McCauley's.

McCORMACK, EDWARD,   *Lake Linden.*
Mrs. Burrows.

---
*Taking a Partial Course.

NAME.	RESIDENCE.	ROOM.

*McCORMICK, EDWARD PATRICK,   *Calumet.*
                                        Mrs. A. Harris's.

McDONALD, ERWIN HUNTINGTON,   *Lyon Mt., N. Y.*
                                        Mr. E. R. Penberthy's.

*McGRATH, MICHAEL,   *Hancock.*
                                        Mr. McGrath's.

*MORALEE, MATTHEW MADISON, Jr.,   *Hancock.*
                                        Mr. Moralee's.

*RIEDINGER, LOUIS EDWARD,   *Marquette.*
                                        Mr. E. R. Penberthy's.

*ROURKE, JERRY,   *Hancock,*
                                        Mr. Rourke's.

SILLIMAN, ARTHUR PARKS, B.L. (University of Wisconsin),
                     Hudson, Wisconsin.
                                        Mrs. Trim's.

SHATTUCK, HORACE VOLNEY,   *Adrian.*
                                        Mr. S. Harris's.

*SULLIVAN, DENNIS,   *Lake Linden.*
                                        Mrs. Burrows's.

TRENGOVE, SAMUEL REED,   *Lake Linden.*
                                        Mr. E. R. Penberthy's.

WATERS, ALBERT LATCHA, S.B (Michigan Agricultural College),
                     Spring Lake.
                                        Mrs. Rashleigh's.

WATSON, JOHN BONE,   *Opechee.*
                                        Mr. E. R. Penberthy's.

*WILLIAMS, BERT HENRY,   *Champion Mine.*
                                        Mrs. Ormsby's.

---

*Taking a Partial Course.

SPECIAL STUDENTS.

NAME.	RESIDENCE.	ROOM.
BUTLER, MARK, Chemistry.	*Milwaukee, Wisconsin.* Mrs. Burrows's.	
CARY, RODMAN HASARD, Surveying.	*Lansing.* Butterfield House.	
CROZE, LAWRENCE LUDGER, Chemistry.	*Houghton.* Mr. Croze's.	
FORBES, DARWIN CARRIE, Chemistry and Assaying.	*Marquette.* Mrs. MacFarland's.	
GLANVILLE, JAMES GUNDRY, Drawing.	*Lake Linden.* Mrs. Burrows's.	
JAMES, IVOR GLENDOWER, Chemistry,	*Houghton.* Pfeiffer's Hotel.	
OSBORNE, DAVID W., Drawing.	*Houghton.* Mrs. Osborne's.	
PARSONS, ALBERT WILCOX, Drawing.	*Adrian.* Mrs. Burrows's.	
REES, ROBERT IRWIN, Mathematics.	*Houghton.* Mr. A. F. Rees's.	
ROSS, GEORGE EDWARD, Chemistry.	*Hancock.* Mr. James Ross's.	
SENTER, HENRY MORTIMER, Chemistry.	*Houghton.* Mr. John Senter's.	
STONE, CHARLES J., Surveying.	*Lansing.* Butterfield House.	
STRINGHAM, JOSEPH, Jr. Chemistry and Mineralogy.	*Saginaw.* Mrs. Brimacombe's.	

*Taking a partial course.

SUMMARY.

Graduate Students.................................... 5
Class of 1891............................. 9
Class of 1892.. 8
Class of 1893................. 43

—————
65

BY STATES AND COUNTRIES.

Canada 1
Colorado... 1
England.. 1
Illinois 4
Massachusetts.. 1
Michigan, Upper Peninsula....... .... 33 ⎱
Michigan, Lower Peninsula............... 15 ⎰ 48
New York... 1
Pennsylvania 1
Utah... 1
Wisconsin 6

—————
65

AVERAGE AGE OF STUDENTS.

First Year..21 years.
Second Year.......................... ....24 years.
Third Year..23 years.
Graduate Students.....................................30 years.
Average Age of all the Students.....................24½ years.

REQUIREMENTS FOR ADMISSION.

Candidates for the regular course will be examined in:

ARITHMETIC AND METRIC SYSTEM: either Wentworth's High School, Ray's Higher, Olney's Practical, Robinson's Practical, or an equivalent.

ALGEBRA, THROUGH QUADRATIC EQUATIONS: either Wentworth's School, Olney's Complete, Robinson's Elementary, Loomis's Elements, Van Velzer and Slichter's School, or an equivalent.

GEOMETRY—PLANE, SOLID AND SPHERICAL: either Davies's Legendre revised by Van Amringe, Wentworth's New, Olney's Revised, Chauvenet's revised by Byerly, or an equivalent.

BOOK-KEEPING—ELEMENTS OF SINGLE AND DOUBLE ENTRY: either Bryant and Stratton's, Mayhew's, the first 62 pages of The New Complete Book-keeping, or an equivalent.

ELEMENTARY PHYSICS: either Gage's or Avery's Elements, or an equivalent.

ELEMENTS OF ASTRONOMY: either Newcomb's Popular or School, Young's High School, or an equivalent.

It would be well for those who are preparing to take the full course here, to give especial attention to the Mathematics and Physics required for entrance, since a thorough knowledge of the elements of these subjects is not only indispensable in entering upon the courses in those subjects, but it is very important in its relation to most of the other subjects; as the courses in Mathematics and Physics form a large part of the necessary preparation for successful work in the other studies of the course.

No student will be admitted as a regular student who has more than two conditions.

No student will be admitted as a regular student at any time after the beginning of the fall term, unless he is prepared on the back work of the class he desires to join, but he may enter as a special student at any time, on compliance with the conditions specified below.

Students who are graduates of high schools or academies of good standing, which have an established course of study covering the requirements for admission to this institution, may be admitted on probation on compliance with the following conditions:

They *must* present a detailed statement of the course of study they have pursued for graduation, such as is usually given in a school catalogue, and a certificate addressed to the Director of the Mining School, stating that they possess a good moral character, and have graduated from the school with a rank of not less than 85 on a scale of 100 in each study required for admission to the Mining School. The certificates *must give* the rank of the student in each study, and *must be signed* by the principal or superintendent of the school in question.

Any abuse of this privilege, by sending any improperly prepared students, will deprive the school sending such students of this privilege hereafter.

Students desiring to enter on certificate, instead of by examination, *must see* that their certificates conform to the above requirements, and only papers which do so conform will be received in place of an examination.

Students desiring to enter for advanced standing must satisfy the Faculty of their proficiency in the preceding studies of the course.

Students from other institutions will be admitted on presentation of a certificate from the proper officers of those institutions; of the *good standing* and *rank* of the students therein; and all studies which *shall be found to be the real equivalents* of the studies of the Mining School course will be accepted in lieu of the corresponding studies here; if the certificates presented shall show that they obtained a satisfactory rank in those studies; provided that the application for the acceptance of their past work as an equivalent for work in the Mining School, shall be made at the time the students in question join the Mining School.

Persons who wish to enter as special students are admitted at any time to take such studies as they may be qualified to pursue. They are required to give a detailed statement of their previous studies; and all special students who intend to enter the regular course subsequently should present the same certificates, in so far as they are able, as those required from all persons entering the regular course for the degree of Mining Engineer.

This gives two classes of students in the undergraduate department of the school: The regular students and the special students. The regular students are those who are candidates for the degree of Mining Engineer, and who have passed an examination for admission, or who have been admitted on a certificate as specified above. They take the full course.

Special students in this institution are divided into two classes:

1st. Those persons who wish to take some subject or subjects only which are taught in the Mining School, and who are not candidates for any degree.

2nd. Persons who are unable to take the full course of study in the school in the specified time, either on account of insufficient preparation, ill-health, or any other cause. As a rule they intend to take a degree, but take four or more years for the work. They are enrolled as students taking a partial course. Any person can pass from the class of special students into that of the regular students by making up the subjects already taken by the class which he wishes to join and by passing the necessary examinations.

No student will be received as a regular student under seventeen years of age, except upon ample evidence of exceptional ability and strength to endure and profit by the labors of the course.

All persons intending to join the Mining School are requested to give early notice of that intention to the Director, stating whether they wish to enter as special or regular students, and whether they wish to enter by examination or by certificate.

THE COURSE OF INSTRUCTION.

The course of instruction for the regular students extends over a period of three years, effecting a saving of time in years by continuing the work through most of the year, and by making the course strictly professional and technical. This institution, like Theological, Law and Medical schools, assumes that the student's preparatory and literary education has been completed prior to his entering upon his professional studies. Like other professional schools, the Michigan Mining School urges all students intending to take their professional studies here, to obtain previously an education of the broadest and most liberal character. This is necessary if the student wishes to fully profit by his studies here, and desires to take that high professional rank that should be the ultimate aim of every graduate. Although not required, the student is advised to obtain a reading knowledge of some of the important modern languages, like German, French, Swedish and Spanish, and he ought to have thoroughly studied subjects that will give him the requisite training in habits of close, accurate and logical reasoning, together with a good command of language, e. g. Psychology, Logic, Rhetoric, Literature, etc. Experience has shown that of two students of equal ability, the one who can give the time to obtain the best preparation, will in the end pass far beyond the one who has had the inferior training. But while it is preferred that students entering should have a liberal education for their own advantage, the School will not repel, but invites and will try to assist in every possible way, all those who have not been so fortunate, and in conformity to this idea, it has confined its requirements for admission to those subjects which are absolutely essential as a preparation for the required course.

The Michigan Mining School is especially organized to afford training and instruction for the following classes:

1. Those who desire a practical professional education in Mining Engineering, particularly graduates of colleges or schools in which a more general or literary education is given.

2. Persons who wish to take certain subjects as an aid to them in their future practical work.

3. Persons who desire to obtain a knowledge of some science,

taught here, for the purposes of general education, or for use in teaching, or as an aid to them in their studies in some other professional course or school.

In preparing the course of instruction the effort has been made to contribute somewhat to the solution of one of the greatest educátional problems of the age: to properly combine scientific or theoretical knowledge with practical training. In pursuance of this object it is intended that the student shall be well grounded in the principles or in the science of all the subjects he studies, while it is further proposed that he shall also have experience and practice in every subject taught, so far as the means and time at the disposal of the school will allow. That is, the student shall have an opportunity to observe and to verify in the laboratory, field, mill or mine, whatever he shall have learned in the class room.

Further, it is intended that the practical work shall here be carried to such an extent that the pupil can make use of it subsequently in his profession after graduation.

In general, the instruction will be given by means of lectures, recitations, and laboratory and field practice, including the inspection of mills, mines and smelting works. Each student will receive individual instruction in the laboratories, and those qualified will be advised and directed in original investigations.

Every facility will be given to students who desire to pursue any subject or subjects taught in the school, provided they enter during the time that subject is taught in its regular course. Such students are enrolled as special students.

In mathematics, physics, chemistry, mineralogy, petrography, geology, drawing, etc., the instruction is so given that any one who desires a knowledge of any of these subjects, as a matter of general education, or as a preparation for teaching, or for any other profession, can profitably study here.

The amount of labor is so great in accomplishing the necessary work of the regular course in this institution in the given time, that every student needs to present himself promptly at the opening of the school year and remain until its close. Every regular student is required to spend seven hours a day for five days each week in laboratory or field work, or in recitation or lecture. He prepares for his recitations in time taken outside of the seven hours a day.

Since the instruction is largely personal, the maximum amount of work that can be done by each student is limited only by his time and ability, while in most of his studies he can advance as far and as rapidly as he is able to do consistently with good work.

Various excursions are taken to the mines, mills and smelting works in the vicinity, on Saturdays or on other days, as occasion may require. Part of these excursions are required and part voluntary, and all students when on these excursions are under the direction of the instructor in charge, and are subject to discipline, the same as when in the laboratories of the School.

OUTLINE OF THE COURSE OF STUDY.

FIRST YEAR.

FALL TERM—FOURTEEN WEEKS.

MATHEMATICS: Higher Algebra, Plane and Analytical Trigonometry. Recitations. Seven hours a week.
> Professor Haynes.

DRAWING: Drawing Instruments and Materials, Plane Geometrical Problems, Projection, Development, Round Writing. Lectures and Work in Drawing Room. Ten hours a week.
> Mr. Rowland.

PHYSICS: Elementary Mechanics, Sound, Heat, Light. Lectures, Recitations and Laboratory work. Three hours a week.
> Professor Haynes.

CHEMISTRY: General Principles and Non-metals, Blowpipe Analysis. Lectures, Recitations and Laboratory work Seven hours a week.
> Professor Keller.

MINERALOGY: Crystallography and Determinative Mineralogy. Lectures, Recitations and Laboratory work. Eight hours a week.
> The Director, Drs. Patton, Hubbard and Lane, and Mr. Seaman.

WINTER TERM—FOURTEEN WEEKS.

MATHEMATICS: Spherical Trigonometry, Mensuration, Analytical Geometry. Recitations. Seven hours a week.
> Professor Haynes.

DRAWING: Intersection of Lines, Surfaces and Solids, Tinting, Lettering, Round Writing. Lectures and Work in Drawing Room. Eight hours a week for six weeks.
> Mr. Rowland.

DRAWING: Topographical Drawing: Making Scales, Plotting, Topographical Signs. Lectures and work in the Drawing Room. Eight hours a week for eight weeks.
Messrs. Denton and Rowland.

SURVEYING: Lectures and Recitations. Two hours a week.
Mr. Denton.

PHYSICS: Light, Electricity and Magnetism. Lectures, Recitations and Laboratory work. Three hours a week.
Professor Haynes

CHEMISTRY: Metals. Lectures and Recitations. Two hours a week.
Professor Keller.

MINERALOGY AND LITHOLOGY: Determinative. Lectures, Recitations and Laboratory work. Thirteen hours a week.
The Director, Drs. Patton, Hubbard and Lane, and Mr. Seaman.

SPRING TERM—SIX WEEKS.

MATHEMATICS: Analytical Geometry. Five hours a week.
Professor Haynes.

PHYSICS: Practical Laboratory work in Experimental Physics. Fifteen hours a week.
Professor Haynes.

CHEMISTRY: Introduction to Qualitative Analysis. Recitations and Laboratory work. Fifteen hours a weeks.
Professor Keller.

SUMMER TERM—ELEVEN WEEKS.

SURVEYING: Plane, Topographical and Railroad Surveying. Lectures, Recitations and Practical Work in the Field and Drawing Room. Five days a week.
Mr. Denton.

SECOND YEAR.

FALL TERM—FOURTEEN WEEKS.

MATHEMATICS: Differential and Integral Calculus. Recitations. Five hours a week.
                                    Professor Haynes.

DRAWING: Isometric and Cabinet Projection, Figuring, Line Shading, Construction Drawing. Lectures and Work in Drawing Room. Four hours a week.
                                    Mr. Kidwell.

PROPERTIES OF MATERIALS: Wrought and Cast Iron, Steel, Copper, Tin, Zinc, Antimony, Bismuth, Alloys. Timber and Lubricating Oils. Lectures and Recitations. Two hours a week.
                                    Mr. Rowland.

CHEMISTRY: Qualitative Analysis. Recitations and Laboratory work. Fourteen hours a week.
                                    Professor Keller.

CHEMISTRY: Reduction and Oxidation. Recitations. One hour a week.
                                    Mr. Sharpless.

METALLURGY: Fuel, Refractory Materials, Iron, Steel and Aluminum. Lectures and Recitations. Four hours a week.
                                    Mr. Sharpless.

PETROGRAPHY: Optical and Microscopic Mineralogy Lectures, Recitations and Laboratory work. Five hours a week.
                                    Drs. Lane and Patton.

WINTER TERM—FOURTEEN WEEKS.

MATHEMATICS: Differential and Integral Calculus, Mechanics. Recitations. Five hours a week.
                                    Professor Haynes.

DRAWING: Machine Drawing, Tracing, Blue Printing, Making Drawings from Models. Lectures and Work in Drawing Room. Three hours a week.
                                    Mr. Kidwell.

MECHANISM: Laws of Motion. Linkwork. Cams. Teeth of Wheels. Aggregate Motion. Miscellaneous Problems in Applied Mechanics. Lectures and Recitations. Four hours a week.

Mr. Rowland.

ELECTRICITY: Electrical Instruments and Measurements. Discussion of Electromotive Force. Current. Quantity, Density, etc. Lectures and Recitations. Two hours a week.

Mr. Kidwell.

CHEMISTRY: Quantitative Analysis. Lectures. Recitations. and Laboratory work. Eleven hours a week.

Professor Keller and Mr. Sharpless.

CHEMISTRY: Stoichiometry. Recitations. One hour a week.

Mr. Sharpless.

MINING AND MINE SURVEYING: Lectures and Recitations. Four hours a week.

Mr. Denton.

STRATIGRAPHICAL GEOLOGY AND PALÆONTOLOGY: Lectures and Recitations. Five hours a week.

Dr. Lane.

SPRING TERM—SIX WEEKS.

MINE SURVEYING AND MINING: Practical work in the mines. Five days a week.

Mr. Denton.

SUMMER TERM—EIGHT WEEKS.

SHOPWORK: Practical work in Pattern and Machine Shops. Five days a week.

Messrs. Kidwell and Rowland.

THIRD YEAR.

FALL TERM—FOURTEEN WEEKS.

DRAWING: Graphical Statics; Analysis of Roof Trusses of various standard designs. Lectures and Work in Drawing Room. Four hours a week.
Mr. Kidwell.

CHEMISTRY: Quantitative Analysis. Lectures, Recitations, and Laboratory work. Thirteen hours a week.
Professor Keller and Mr. Sharpless.

METALLURGY: Copper and Lead. Lectures and Recitations. Two hours a week.
Mr. Sharpless.

ORE DRESSING: Lectures and Recitations. One hour a week.
Mr. Sharpless.

MECHANICS OF MATERIALS: Application of Principles of Statics to Rigid Bodies, Elasticity and Resistance of Materials, Discussion of Beams, Columns and Shafts, Combined Stresses, Testing of Materials. Lectures and Recitations. Three hours a week for seven weeks, and two hours a week for seven weeks.
Mr. Kidwell.

MECHANICAL ENGINEERING: The Steam Engine and Allied Subjects. Lectures and Recitations. Four hours a week for seven weeks, and five hours a week for seven weeks.
Mr. Kidwell.

ELECTRICAL ENGINEERING: Magnets, Electro-Magnetic Induction and Theory of the Dynamo. Lectures and Recitations. Three hours a week.
Mr. Kidwell.

PHYSICAL GEOLOGY: Lectures and Recitations. Five hours a week.
The Director.

WINTER TERM—FOURTEEN WEEKS.

CHEMISTRY: Metallurgical Analysis. Recitations and Laboratory work. Seven hours a week.
Mr. Sharpless.

METALLURGY: Lead, Silver, and Gold. Lectures and Recitations. Two hours a week.

> Mr. Sharpless.

ORE DRESSING: Lectures and Recitations. One hour a week.

> Mr. Sharpless.

MECHANICAL ENGINEERING: The Steam Engine, Steam Boilers, and their Details. Lectures and Recitations. Three hours a week.

> Mr. Kidwell.

MECHANICAL ENGINEERING: Engineering Appliances. Lectures on Pumps, Indicators, Gauges, Planimeters, etc. One hour a week.

> Mr. Rowland.

MINING ENGINEERING AND MINE ACCOUNTS: Lectures and Recitations. Four hours a week.

> Mr. Denton.

HYDRAULIC AND STRUCTURAL ENGINEERING: Lectures and Recitations. Three hours a week.

> Mr. Denton.

ECONOMIC GEOLOGY: Lectures and Recitations. Five hours a week.

> The Director.

ELECTIVES.

DRAWING: Engineering Design. Floors, Trestles, Columns, Shafting, Steam Piping, etc. Lectures and Work in Drawing Room. Six hours a week.

> Mr. Kidwell.

AND

ELECTRICAL ENGINEERING: Motors and their Applications, Storage Batteries, Arc and Incandescent Lamps, Wiring, Electrical Fittings, etc. Lectures and Recitations. Three hours a week.

> Mr. Kidwell.

OR

CHEMISTRY: Technical Analytical Methods. Lectures, Recitations and Laboratory work. Nine hours a week.

> Professor Keller.

Every student who is pursuing the regular course is required to select either the nine hours in Engineering Design and Electrical Engineering, or the nine hours in Technical Chemistry. The selection is to be made with the consent of the instructor and submitted to the Faculty for approval, at the commencement of the winter term.

SPRING TERM—SIX WEEKS.

ASSAYING: Practical work in the Laboratory with Lectures and Recitations. Five days a week, two weeks.

Mr. Sharpless.

ORE DRESSING: Practical work in the Stamp Mill. Five days a week, four weeks.

Mr. Sharpless.

SUMMER TERM—SIX WEEKS.

GEOLOGY: Practical work in the Field and Mines. Five days a week.

The Director and Assistants.

THESES.

Revision of the above course will be made at any time when it is thought that it can be improved, or when the needs of the school demand it, and all the students are expected to conform to these changes whenever introduced.

CLASS OF 1893.

This class will take Determinative Mineralogy and Lithology in the Fall term of 1891, in place of the Petrography, which will be given later, and the subsequent course in Geology will be correspondingly shortened for this class.

The relative proportion of time given to theoretical study and to practice is approximately stated below.

	LECTURES AND RECITATIONS.	LABORATORY, MILL, MINE AND FIELD PRACTICE.
First Year.	464 hours	1111 hours.
Second Year.	490 hours	980 hours.
Third Year.	560 hours	840 hours.

PROJECTED FOUR YEARS COURSE.

In order to be able to give more time to the technical parts of the education of a Mining Engineer, it is proposed to lengthen the course of study to four years. Should this be done it will require all regular students joining the entering class of the Mining School in September, 1893, to take this projected course. An outline of the course is given in table II.

TAI

Algel
n
Physi
Mech:
Topo:
Surve
Chem
Cryst:

Calcu
Drawi
Prope
Chemi
Organ
Stochi
Metall
Miner:
Mining
Shop P

Drawi
Graphi
Mecha
Mecha
Mecba
Electri
Chemic

DEPARTMENTS OF INSTRUCTION.

MATHEMATICS.

PROFESSOR HAYNES.

The course in Mathematics is progressive, and no part can be taken very profitably by the student, unless he has passed in all the required preparatory work and in each successive subject, before entering upon any of the more advanced studies.

In Mathematics, the object sought is to give the student a thorough working knowledge of the subject, so far as it is essential to the successful application of its principles to the practical mathematical work required in the subsequent courses in Mine Surveying, Railroad Surveying, Plane Surveying, and such other practical applications as are found in Mechanical Engineering, Electrical Engineering, Physics, etc.

The course includes, in Algebra—a review of Quadratics, Differentiation, Indeterminate Co-efficients, Formulæ, Logarithms, Loci of Equations and Higher Equations; in Trigonometry—Plane, Analytical, and Spherical Trigonometry, with Mensuration; in Analytical Geometry—the straight line, circle, parabola, ellipse, hyperbola, the transformation of co-ordinates, the plane, and surfaces and solids of revolution. This course closes with the study of the Differential and the Integral Calculus, and their applications to various practical problems in Physics, Analytical Mechanics, etc.

Both in this course and in that in Physics special care is taken to point out and enforce the practical bearing of the subjects under discussion, and it has been found that this adds greatly to the meaning of the student's work, and forms a powerful incentive to thoroughness. However, in both of these courses the fundamental truth is kept constantly in mind, that the most successful practical work is based upon a thorough theoretical foundation. No one acquainted with the splendid achievements connected with mining in the immediate vicinity of this school, which are constantly before its students, as a great object lesson, can doubt the necessity of a knowledge of Mathematics and of Physics in securing these results, and of their eminent practical value in this great industry.

PHYSICS.

Professor Haynes.

Two terms of fourteen weeks each are spent upon the study of General Physics, including the topics of Mechanics, Hydrostatics, Pneumatics, Heat, Light, Magnetism and Electricity; in these two terms regular recitations are required, and the topics are illustrated by the instructor with lectures and experiments. This course closes with a term of six weeks, 15 hours a week of Laboratory work, in which the student is required to do the work under the supervision of the instructor; the experiments being mostly in the domain of physical measurements, including those of Specific Gravity, Heat, Light and Electricity.

The methods of instruction in this department vary through the recitation, in the solution of problems, in lectures and in laboratory work, in such a way as to not only afford the necessary variety, but at the same time to furnish a constant encouragement to the student to become self-reliant both in his methods of thought and in his work.

In the laboratory work of this department each student is required to make a sketch and give a description of the apparatus used in each experiment; to put down his data, computations, conclusions, etc., during laboratory hours, in a note book: and, at *the close of the laboratory work of each day to leave this book with the instructor for his inspection.*

Many new and valuable forms of laboratory and lecture apparatus have been added to the equipment of the Physical Laboratory during the past year, and it will be further increased during the year to come. No student is permitted to take this practical laboratory course who has not passed in the necessary theoretical study and lectures preceding it.

DRAWING.

Mr. Kidwell and Mr. Rowland.

The course in Drawing extends over the entire three years. In planning it, the object kept constantly in view was to give special prominence to such branches of Drawing as are of value to the engineer, hence such subjects as perspective, shades and shadows, etc., have been excluded, and more than the usual proportion of time is devoted to Mechanical and Topographical Drawing.

During the entire course, all drawings accepted by the In-

structors are considered as the property of the school, and are
bound and deposited in the Library. Drawings that are not
satisfactory are returned, and must be made up by the student
in his own time.

The following schedule shows the distribution of work during the three years.

FIRST YEAR.

Description, preparation, and testing of drawing instruments
and materials: graphical solution of plane geometrical problems,
methods of arranging drawings on sheet, tinting, and harmony
of colors. (Warren's *Drafting Instruments and Operations*, supplemented with lectures). Projections: intersections of lines and
surfaces; development of surfaces; elevations; sections; lettering of various kinds, such as Roman, Italic, Gothic, Block and
Round Writing; borders for drawings. Warren's *Elementary Projection Drawing*, with lectures. Topographical Drawing: Making scales; methods of plotting surveys, by protractor and rectangular co-ordinates: topographical signs. Fall Term, 10 hours
per week, Winter Term, 8 hours per week.

Accuracy, neatness, and a thorough understanding of the
work in progress are insisted upon at all times, and no sheet will
be accepted which would not pass in the average drafting room.
The subject of lettering receives considerable attention during
the entire course, as nothing more effectually spoils a good
mechanical drawing or map than the miserable styles of lettering so generally used. Every attempt is made to avoid mere
copying. After the principles given in the text-books have been
thoroughly studied, special problems prepared by the Instructors
are given for solution.

The Topographical Drawing is under the personal supervision of the Instructor in Surveying, and is arranged with
special reference to the practical work in Plane and Mine Surveying. The first sheets are devoted to the making of scales,
and to the different methods of plotting survey lines, the student having previously made the necessary computations from
field notes furnished him. These sheets are followed by practice
in making topographical signs and in filling in the details of a
survey. This course gives the student sufficient skill to plot his
own surveys, and assists him in the making of these surveys, by
teaching him what data are necessary for plotting.

*No student may take this course in Drawing who has entrance
conditions in Mathematics.*

SECOND YEAR.

Isometric and cabinet projection; the theory of construction, drawing, figuring and line shading; tracing and blue printing; the use of bond paper; machine sketching, and the production of complete working drawings from model, or rough sketches furnished by the instructor. A system of recording drawings is also taught. (Lectures and work in Drawing room). Fall Term, four hours per week; winter term, three hours per week.

All working drawings are either traced and blue printed, or are drawn originally on bond paper from which prints are made direct. Each student will be allowed to keep a complete set of prints of all his drawings.

No student may take this course who has conditions in any part of the first year's work in Drawing or Mathematics.

THIRD YEAR.

Graphical Statics—Analysis of Roof Trusses of various standard designs. (Greene's *Roof Trusses*, supplemented with lectures). Fall term, four hours per week.

While the text-book will serve as a guide, the scope of the instruction will not be confined to it. The course is designed to teach not only the modes of determining the forces in the different members of structures, but also the method of designing such members to resist those forces, by the application of the laws previously deduced in the study of Mechanics of Materials. Each student will be required to design a truss, and make the complete working drawings for the same.

No student may take this course who has conditions in any part of the previous two years' instruction in Drawing, Mathematics, or Mechanics.

Designing—Lectures and work in Drawing Room. Winter Term, 6 hours per week.

Prominence is given in this course to the designing of girders, columns, shafts, floors for heavy loads, framing, trestles, etc. Special attention is also given to designs for long lines of steam-pipe, line and counter shafting for various duties, etc. No design is accepted unless accompanied with complete working drawings and bill of materials.

No student may take this course who has conditions in any part of the previous two years work in Drawing, Mathematics, Mechanics, Properties of Materials, Graphical Statics, Mechanism, or Mechanics of Materials.

In addition to the regular course in Drawing, numerous applications of the subject are obtained in connection with the other courses: the students are required to make plats of all their field work in Plane Surveying, to prepare working plans and sections of a mine from their own survey, make a map and profile of a railroad line surveyed by themselves, and to draw sections, diagrams, maps, etc., in their geological field work.

Much personal instruction is given during the entire course. In addition to the regular lectures and recitations, the Instructors are present in the Drawing Room during the hours prescribed for practical work, to give advice and personal instruction to those who need it. The Drawing Room will be open on Saturdays until 4 P.M., to accomodate those who wish to work on that day, and usually one of the Instructors will be on hand to give them any required assistance.

Those who desire to take the course in Drawing only, and devote their entire time to it, may do so, provided the Instructor in charge of the course is convinced of their competency to profit by the instruction. To pursue the course with success, Plane, Solid and Spherical Geometry, Plane Trigonometry, and Analytical Geometry of two dimensions, should have been well mastered. In case these subjects have not been completed, the Instructor in Drawing will prescribe such courses in Mathematics as he considers are necessary, and these will be obligatory on the part of the student.

INSTRUMENTS NEEDED.

Each student upon entrance will provide himself with the following list of instruments and materials, which is given for the convenience of those who may desire to purchase such goods before coming to Houghton.

One 5 inch Alteneder straight line drawing pen.
One 6 inch Alteneder dividers, with bow pen, needle point, and extension bar.
One 2½ inch Ball-Bennet spring bow pen.
One 3 inch Ball-Bennet spring bow dividers.
One 8 inch horn protractor.
One T square, 36 inch blade.
One 8 inch 30°x60° rubber triangle.
One 8 inch 45° rubber triangle.
One dozen German silver thumb tacks, ½ inch diameter.
One bottle Windsor and Newton's prepared India ink.
One bottle Windsor and Newton's Prussian Blue.
One Davidson's velvet rubber, size about ½x½x1½ inches.
One Davidson's velvet rubber, size about 1½x3x½ inches.

One Soennecken's Round Writing Copy Book, and case of
   assorted pens.
Two HHHHH Faber's lead pencils, two HHHHHHHH Faber's pencils.
Six sheets Whatman's Imperial, cold pressed paper, N surface,
   selected best.
One bottle mucilage and brush, or paste and brush.
One medium sized sponge.
One piece of chamois skin not less than one foot square.
Six cabinet saucers, diameter 1½ inches.
One boxwood scale, Rondinella divided.
One box, (12 half pans), Keuffel and Esser's technical colors.
One piece of artists' gum, size about 1½x3x¼ inches.
   A drawing board, two rubber curves, and two sable brushes
will also be required. Owing to liability of getting sizes that
will not answer, these latter should be purchased in Houghton.

The articles called for in this list are necessary for a proper
prosecution of the course, and therefore care should be taken to
get the exact instruments specified, or others of *equal grade.*
Instruments not up to standard will not be allowed in the Drawing Room, as they will not give satisfaction, and will waste the
time of both instructors and students.

MECHANICAL ENGINEERING.

Mr. Kidwell and Mr. Rowland.

The course in Mechanical Engineering during the past year
has been made more exhaustive, and the time devoted to it has
been more than doubled, so that the instruction is now amply
sufficient to give the student a good preparation for actual work,
and to point out the lines of study to be pursued, should he
desire to continue the subject after graduation. The following
is a detailed statement of the course.

SECOND YEAR.

Properties of Materials of Engineering—Lectures on
cast and wrought iron; steel; copper and its important alloys; tin;
zinc; antimony; bismuth; timber; and lubricating oils. Fall Term,
2 hours per week.
   The course includes a full discussion of the various grades of
material, methods of manufacture, forms in which it appears in
the market, their adaptation to the purposes of the engineer,
methods of preserving materials from corrosion, decay, etc. The
course is supplemented by practical work in testing, for details
of which see section on Mechanics of Materials.
   Courses of lectures are also given on stone, cement, concrete,
brick, their properties and general qualities, mode of preparation

and their combinations in construction, etc., for the details of which see sections of Hydraulics, and Economic Geology.

No student may take this course who has conditions in Physics, or first year Mathematics.

MECHANISM—Laws of motion; linkwork, cams; teeth of wheels, with use of odontograph; wheels in trains; aggregate motion; miscellaneous problems in Applied Mechanics, with applications. Determination of proper sizes of pulleys, belts, etc., for particular duties. (Goodeve's *Elements of Mechanism*, supplemented with lectures, and machinery in shops and laboratory). Winter Term, 4 hours per week.

No student may take this course who has conditions in Mathematics, Mechanics, or Drawing.

THIRD YEAR.

THE STEAM ENGINE, AND ALLIED SUBJECTS—An elementary course on the thermo-dynamics of air and steam engines; the relation between the size of an engine, and the work it can do; the mechanics, mechanism, and details of steam engines; valves and valve gears; indicator diagrams, their interpretation, and methods of working them up: the various kinds of boilers, their fittings, and the relative proportions of their various parts: fuel, and heat developed during combustion; condensation and condensers: causes of low efficiency in steam engines, with methods of reducing the loss; the influence of compounding cylinders; testing of engines and boilers (Holmes's *The Steam Engine*, supplemented with lectures and laboratory practice on Saturdays). 4 hours per week first half, 5 hours per week second half of Fall Term; 3 hours per week, Winter Term.

No student may take this course who has conditions in Mathematics, Physics, Mechanics, Drawing, Mechanism, or Properties of Materials.

ENGINEERING APPLIANCES—Lectures on steam pumps, gauges, lubricators, safety valves, steam pipe and fittings, boiler and pipe coverings, belting and packing, discussion of instruments used in testing, such as Prony brake, various kinds of dynamometers, steam engine indicators, speed counters, polar planimeters, etc. (Trade Circulars and testing apparatus in laboratory). Winter Term, 1 hour per week.

A large and very complete assortment of Trade Catalogues from the leading industrial establishments is kept up to date, and is constantly referred to in these lectures. These Catalogues are at the service of the general public, as well as the students.

This course must be preceded by the First Term's work in the Steam Engine.

MECHANICS OF MATERIALS.

Mr. Kidwell.

Application of the principles of statics to rigid bodies; elasticity and resistance of materials: cantilevers; simple, restrained and continuous beams; bodies of uniform strength; riveting; torsion of shafts; combined stresses: designing of beams, columns, and shafts, in wood and metal. (Merriman's *Mechanics of Materials*, suplemented with lectures). 8 hours per week first half, 2 hours per week second half of Fall Term.

Testing of Materials of Engineering—Such as wrought and cast iron, steel, brick, stone and slate. Lectures, recitations, practical work in the laboratory on Saturdays. Each student makes a series of tests in tension, compression, and cross breaking, on laboratory testing machines.

The school is provided with a 100,000 lb. machine fitted for tests in tension, compression, and cross-breaking; and a cement testing machine. Those having materials to be tested should make applications to the Instructor in charge of the Department, and make definite arrangements with him for the precise work which they desire to have done.

No student may take these courses who has conditions in Physics, Mechanics, Mathematics, Properties of Materials, or Drawing.

SHOP PRACTICE.

Mr. Kidwell and Mr. Rowland.

The entire Summer Term of the second year of the course is devoted to shop work. In the Machine Shop instruction is given in chipping, filing, scraping, general vise work, forging and use of machine tools. A course in pipe fitting and some practice in setting shafting will also be given.

In the Pattern Shop a course in bench work, making joints, turning, etc., precedes actual practice in pattern making. All work done in both shops is to blue prints made in the Drawing Room. The shop work is planned with special reference to the needs of the school, and such models of valves, link motions, mechanical movements, etc , as are needed for lecture purposes, will be made by the students.

The equipment of the shops has been carefully selected, and will be increased as fast as the needs of the school require it.

The Machine Shop contains work benches for eighteen students, a 24-inch by 16-foot engine lathe, a smaller screw cutting lathe, two hand lathes, a 34-inch drill press, a 16-inch shaper, a planer of capacity 8x2x2 feet, a Brainard No. 4 Universal Milling Machine, an Ashcroft Oil Testing Machine, a variety of grinding machinery, with a full complement of chucks, taps, drills, reamers, and other smaller tools. A complete set of pipe fitting tools up to 2½ inches is also in stock. A 100,000 lb. tension machine, and a cement testing machine complete the equipment of this shop. The Pattern Shop contains two large wood lathes; jig, circular, and band saws; buffing machines; a full equipment of hand tools and appliances, and work benches for twenty-five students. Each student has a separate work bench, drawer, locker, and set of hand tools, for which he will be held responsible. Any damage to tools or other part of equipment, beyond wear and tear by legitimate use, will be charged to the student responsible for it.

Power for shops is supplied by a 9 in. by 9 in. New York Safety Steam Power Company's vertical high speed engine, driven by a 45 H. P. horizontal boiler in Stamp Mill. The Buckeye automatic engine and other machinery in the Stamp Mill are also available for study. These engines are fitted with all necessary rigging for indicator work, efficiency tests, etc., and the school is well provided with steam engine indicators, planimeters, speed counters, scales and other instruments needed for engine and boiler testing.

To familiarize the students with the operation and care of machinery, each one will be detailed from time to time to fire the boiler, run the engine, clean and oil the machinery, and to perform such other duties as the Instructor in charge may assign to him.

During the Summer term of 1892, and thereafter, persons desiring to take the shop work only, will be admitted as special students, on presentation of evidence that they can pursue the course with profit. Application should be made to the Director or to Mr. Kidwell, not later than June 15th. *No student will be allowed to enter the course after the first week of the summer term.*

No students having conditions in Drawing, Mechanism, or Properties of Materials, may take this course, except those who enter for shop work only.

ELECTRICAL ENGINEERING.

Mr. Kidwell.

The growing tendency toward the more extended use of electricity in mining, both as an illuminant, and motive power for hauling, and operating portable machinery, will require of the Mining Engineer of the future a working knowledge of Electrical Engineering; hence an elementary course in that subject is prescribed for all regular students in this institution.

The instruction will be made as comprehensive as the time available will permit, and special care will be taken to familiarize the student with the fundamental principles of the science. Sufficient ground will be covered to enable him to understand the electrical machinery, appliances, and processes in general use, and give him a good foundation for more advanced work should he desire to devote himself more particularly to Electrical Engineering after graduation.

The preparatory course in Electricity given in Physics is supplemented with the following:

SECOND YEAR.

Electrical Instruments and Measurements—Discussion and measurement of current, electrometric force, quantity, density, resistance and insulation, commercial ammeters, voltmeters, resistance sets, condensers, etc.; power and its measurement. (Ayrton's *Practical Electricity*, with lectures). 2 hours per week, Winter Term.

No student may take this course who has conditions in Mathematics, Mechanics, or Physics.

THIRD YEAR.

Electrical Engineering—Electro-magnets, and electro-magnetic induction, theory of the dynamo, both direct and alternating current, with discussion of the typical forms in general use; motors and their applications; transformers; storage batteries; electrical fittings, wiring, etc. Slingo and Brooker's *Electrical Engineering*, with lectures) 3 hours per week, Fall and Winter Terms.

No student may take this course who has conditions in Mathematics, Physics, Mechanics, Drawing or the preceding year's work in Electricity.

PLANE SURVEYING.

MR. DENTON.

The course in Surveying is designed to be practical and complete as far as regards the ordinary wants of a Mining or Civil Engineer. The course begins with two hours per week in the Spring Term of the first year.

This part of the course is devoted exclusively to the study of the computations necessary in Plane Surveying, and to the making of maps and scales.

Davies's Surveying is used in this work as a text-book. The Topographical Drawing which is in charge of the same instructor, is arranged with special reference to this course, and the two subjects are made to harmonize, and to prepare the student to perform the practical work of the Summer Course in Surveying with facility.

Understanding the computations and the methods of plotting thoroughly, the student is able to appreciate the different methods of collecting data, and can devote his whole attention to them, and to the practical work. To take this course the student must have passed in all the preceeding Mathematics.

SUMMER COURSE IN SURVEYING.

MR. DENTON.

During eleven weeks of each summer, a special course of Surveying will be conducted. Attendance upon this course is obligatory for all regular students completing the first year.

The object of this summer course is two-fold:

First, to give the regular students more thorough and extended practice in the field than it is possible to do while other school work is being carried on. Second, to provide a thorough, practical course in Surveying for persons, other than regular students, who may be desirous of becoming surveyors, or who may wish to obtain practical experience in the subject. There is perhaps no course of study which can be offered by an institution, that will give so quick and profitable returns for the money and time expended by the pupil, as a thorough, practical course in Surveying, since employment at a fair salary can almost always be obtained by a competent surveyor.

In this summer course, study and practical work are combined.

Johnson's "Theory and Practice of Surveying," last edition, is used as a text-book; being supplemented when necessary with lectures. Generally the first hour of the day is devoted to class room work and the remainder to field work.

The subjects studied comprise the use and adjustments of surveying instruments, and methods of surveying.

For field work the students are divided into squads of from two to five men each. Each squad is required to make a certain number of surveys: while each member of the squad has to make from the work done, a full set of notes, computations and maps.

The field work consists of:

1. Exercises in pacing, with a detailed survey of a field by pacing.
2. Practice in chaining distances, and in laying off right angles and parallel lines with the chain.
3. Practice in ranging lines with sight poles under different conditions.
4. Exercises in reading compass bearings.
5. Detail survey of a farm, made by means of compass and chain.
6. Adjustment of the hand level, and practice in its use.
7. Topographical survey on the rectangular plan, with compass, chain and hand level.
8. Adjustment of the transit, and exercises in reading the angles of a triangle by the repetition method.
9. Determination of the true meridian by observations on Polaris and on the sun.
10. Running a close traverse, the angles being determined by repetition, the distances measured with a steel tape, and afterwards corrected for inclination, catenary, and temperature.
11. Running an azimuth traverse around a polygon, the distances being measured by a telemeter.
12. City surveying, laying out lots and streets, and determining the position of house and fence lines.
13. Adjustment of the Wye level, and running a line of levels about one mile in length.
14. Survey of a mining claim, with solar compass, according to Government regulations.
15. Retracing and subdividing of a section of land in accordance with the United States Government field notes.
16. Topographical survey with the plane table, based upon a system of triangulation with the transit.
17. Topographical survey with transit and stadia.
18. Railroad survey. About one mile of road is located, slope stakes set, profiles, maps and cross sections made, and the cuttings and embankments calculated.

The Mining School owns the following set of instruments: one plane table from Buff and Berger—nine transits, three from Buff and Berger, three from Heller and Brightly, two from Fauth, one from Gurley—five Wye levels, two from Heller and Brightly, one from Buff and Berger, two from Gurley—five Burt compasses, five magnetic compasses, fifteen Locke hand levels, six water levels. In addition to these more expensive instruments, the School owns the necessary number of mining lamps, chairs, steel tapes, poles, rods, etc.

Two of the transits are provided with three tripod outfits for mine surveying, and all the transits are adapted to mine as well as surface work.

Persons wishing to join the summer course only, are required to prepare themselves upon the first two books of Davies's Surveying, revised by Van Amringe, in the subjects of Plane Trigonometry, Logarithms, and Mensuration.

Those attending the Summer course should provide themselves with Johnson's "Theory and Practice of Surveying," last edition, a pair of six-inch dividers with pen and pencil attachments, a right line pen, a decimal scale, a large triangle, a T square, medium and hard pencils, and a ten or twenty-five foot steel pocket tape graduated to feet and tenths. These articles are indispensable, but additional drawing instruments will be found convenient.

The furnishing of the surveying apparatus by the Mining School is a considerable expense to the institution, and while losses due to ordinary and legitimate wear and tear of the instruments, are borne by the School, any injuries due to carelessness on the part of the student must be made good by him.

The Summer Course in Surveying will commence each year about the first of July, and all persons who desire to attend are requested to send in their names early to the Director of the Mining School, or to Mr. Denton, in charge of the course, in order that proper provision may be made for them. This course, like all others in the school, is free to any one who is properly qualified, whether a resident of the State of Michigan or not. The course is given in Houghton. Regular students must have passed in all the preceding Mathematics and Plane Surveying in order to take this course.

MINE SURVEYING.

Mr Denton.

Instruction in Mine Surveying is given to the second year students by means of text-books, lectures and recitations. Many practical problems are assigned the students to be solved by them.

A portion of the six weeks spent at the mines during the spring term is occupied in making a Mine survey. Each student is required to make a full set of computations and maps based upon his survey. Students taking this course must have passed in the preceding work in Mining and Plane Surveying.

HYDRAULICS.

MR. DENTON.

Instruction in this course is given with the aid of a text-book, especial attention being paid to the solution of practical problems. The course involves the flow of water through orifices, pipes and canals, and over weirs, the calculation of sizes of pipes and conduits to convey given discharges, the construction of dams, reservoir walls, etc. Water power and water motors are discussed at length. Merriman's "Treatise on Hydraulics" is used as a text-book. In this course are also considered briefly materials—stone, cement, concrete, brick, their properties and general qualities, mode of preparation, and their combinations in construction; structures—masonry construction, theory and practical building of retaining walls, foundations, etc.

Students taking this course must have passed in the preceding courses in Mathematics.

MINING.

MR. DENTON.

The course consists of a series of lectures illustrated by diagrams, photographs, and sketches. The students make full notes of these lectures, and are required to recite upon them at short intervals. The work is arranged to cover, as thoroughly as the time allotted will permit, the various operations that are necessary in mining enterprises.

The following outline of subjects will give an idea of the ground covered.

1st. SURFACE EXCAVATION:

Determination of the amount and character of the material to be removed, methods of excavation, comparative cost and economy of different methods of removing excavated material.

2nd. EXPLOSIVES:

Gunpowder, constituents, manufacture, properties.

Higher Explosives, constituents, manufacture, properties,

precautions necessary, comparative strength, and special advantages, testing.

3rd. DRILLING:

Hand drilling, types of drills.

Machine drills, description, careful study of successful forms of machines, rate of drilling, repairing, cost.

4th. BLASTING:

Theory of blasting, with reference to the calculation of amount of explosives necessary for large blasts; location of holes, charging, tamping, firing by fuse and electricity.

5th. AIR COMPRESSORS:

Conditions of working, types, special study of the Rand and Ingersoll Compressors.

6th. PROSPECTING:

Different methods, deep prospecting, by oil well boring method, by diamond drills. Conditions under which the different methods are applicable, and their cost.

7th. SHAFT SINKING:

Through easy ground by ordinary methods. Study of the methods used successfully in sinking through difficult ground, cost and comparative merits.

8th. DRIFTING.

9th. METHODS OF EXPLOITATION:

Typical methods for narrow and wide veins and beds, including coal mining.

10th. UNDERGROUND TRANSPORTATION:

Tramming, mule and mechanical haulage, construction of cars.

11th. HOISTING:

Inclined and vertical shafts, style of engines, automatic and safety devices, cages, skips, wire ropes.

12th. MINE DRAINAGE:

Adits, collecting water, raising the water with winding machinery, Cornish and direct acting pumps.

13th. MINE VENTILATION AND LIGHTING.

14th. ACCIDENTS AND MINE ACCOUNTS.

In connection with this work, frequent visits to neighboring mines are made, where the machinery and processes described can be seen by the student in actual operation. In order to make these visits of permanent value to the student, he is required to write a description of the mine visited, accompanying his description with sketches, showing dimensions and details of certain pieces of machinery, or other objects, that may have been indicated to him.

During six weeks of the Spring Term of the second year. the class in Mining is occupied in studying at some of the neighboring mines. About two weeks of this time is given to making mine surveys and the remainder to the detailed study of mining operations.

CHEMISTRY.

GENERAL CHEMISTRY.

PROFESSOR KELLER.

The course in General Chemistry extends over the first year. Instruction is given by experimental lectures, recitations, and laboratory exercises. The general plan followed is that of Richter's "Inorganic Chemistry," which is also the text-book used in the recitations. Smith and Keller's "Laboratory Notes" serves as a guide in the practical work. The subjects treated during the first term are the fundamental principles of the science, and the chemistry of the non-metallic elements: a course in blowpipe analysis, preparatory to determinative mineralogy. is given before the regular chemical exercises are taken up. Only two hours a week are allotted to chemistry during the winter term, and they are mainly devoted to recitations on the metals. These recitations are supplemented, however, by informal lectures and illustrated by experiments, diagrams, and suites of specimens from the chemical and mineralogical collections. Laboratory exercises on this part occupy fifteen hours a week during the entire Spring Term: they are designed to form an introduction to Qualitative Analysis.

Examinations are held at the end of each term. and *no student having conditions is permitted to continue any subsequent part of the course in Chemistry.*

QUALITATIVE ANALYSIS.

PROFESSOR KELLER AND MR. SHARPLESS.

The fall term and. if necessary, part of the winter term of the second year, are devoted to a systematic course in Qualitative Analysis. The student having already performed the preliminary experiments. is expected to be familiar with the important reactions of the metals and the acids. He begins by studying their division into analytical groups and then proceeds to the separation and identification of the individual members of each group. After completing this work he is given mixtures, whose composition is not known to him, for qualitative examination. These mixtures are carefully selected and graded; their number depends upon the accuracy and rapidity with which the student accomplishes the detection of the constituents.

With the exception of one class-room recitation on Qualitative Analysis and another on Oxidation and Reduction (with Mr. Sharpless), the instruction is confined to the laboratory. Daily recitations are made there; students are required to keep a complete and detailed record of their work, to write the equations representing the reactions involved in it, and to explain to the instructor the reasons for each operation they perform. Fresenius's Manual is used.

QUANTITATIVE ANALYSIS.

PROFESSOR KELLER AND MR. SHARPLESS.

In Quantitative Analysis students begin their work by learning the necessary manipulation, especially in the operation of weighing. They are then given a number of exercises in gravimetric analysis. Beginning with the determination of a single constituent in salts of known composition, they proceed by degrees to complete analysis of more complex substances. These examples are selected with a view to afford practice in all the principal operations of gravimetric analysis, as well as in the determination of the important basic and acid radicals. When this is accomplished the typical volumetric processes are taken up in order, and these are finally followed by work involving the combined use of gravimetric and volumetric methods.

A complete course of lectures, supplemented by recitations runs parallel to the laboratory practice. The chief book of reference is Fresenius's (the students are required to provide themselves with it); other standard works and the original literature are also constantly consulted. One of the instructors is always present in the laboratory during the regular working hours, and personal assistance is rendered when necessary.

TECHNICAL ANALYSIS.

PROFESSOR KELLER AND MR. SHARPLESS.

To this subject is devoted the time available for Chemistry during the Winter Term of the third year.

Mr. Sharpless offers a course in Metallurgical Analysis of seven hours a week. The object of this course is to acquaint the student with the special methods of analysis that are in use in the laboratories of metallurgical establishments. Special prominence is given to the assay and complete analysis of iron ores, the determination of the impurities—Carbon, Silicon, Phosphorus, Sulphur, Manganese—in pig iron and steel, the analysis of fuel, slag, limestone, etc. The student is taught not only to perform these determinations *accurately*, but also to work as *rapidly* as is consistent with the desired degree of accuracy. Complete sets of special apparatus have been procured and constructed for this work. Detailed printed directions by Mr. Sharpless are used as a guide, and most of the original literature is also accessible.

In addition, nine hours a week, elective with Designing and Electrical Engineering, are allotted to practice in special methods of analysis with Professor Keller. This course includes the analysis of water for hygienic and industrial purposes, analysis of gases, explosives, furnace products, refined copper, etc. A series of lectures supplements the laboratory practice.

The aim has been to make the laboratory appliances and conveniences as complete and ample as possible. The laboratories, lecture, balance, and supply rooms are all on the same floor. The laboratories are furnished with large fume chambers which have a good draught, and are supplied with hot plates, and sand and steam baths. The tables are furnished with sinks—one for each pair of students—and have abundant gas and water supplies. Filter pumps are arranged at each sink so as to provide a pump for each student. The laboratories are supplied with gas, and are well lighted, as well as fully equipped with all the modern appliances needed for chemical analysis.

ASSAYING.

Mr. Sharpless.

Instruction is given in the fire assay of gold, silver, lead and and copper ores; gold and silver coin, bullion, copper "mineral" and slags.

The assay laboratory contains ten large crucible furnaces and eighteen muffle furnaces of the Brown pattern, and sixteen crucible and muffle gasoline furnaces (Hoskins's), the intention being to provide a muffle for each student and so avoid the inconvenience of making one furnace do for two or more persons. The laboratory is provided with a Blake and a Gates crusher, laboratory size, to be run by power, large buck plates, large and small mortars, sets of sieves, etc. The weighing room is supplied with six pulp scales and five button balances, of Troemner's and Becker's make, for use in this department.

Of the two weeks devoted to assaying, almost all the time is spent in the laboratory, lectures and recitations forming a minor portion of the work. 125 to 150 assays are made upon samples differing as widely as possible in composition, and, consequently, in methods of treatment.

Students who desire to pursue this course must have taken one term's work in Quantitative Analysis.

ORE DRESSING.

Mr Sharpless.

The course in Ore Dressing extends over the first, second, and third terms of the third year.

During the first and second terms, instruction is given in the theory of amalgamation and mechanical treatment of ores previous to their smelting.

This instruction is given, for the most part, by lectures, supplemented, when possible, with text-book work and references to the standard literature on the subject.

The ground covered by the lectures includes—

I. Physical properties upon which ore dressing operations are based.

II. Theory of jigging and slime treatment.

III. Hand dressing.

IV. Crushing machinery, jaw crushers, stamps, rolls, pulverizers, etc.

V. Sizing machinery, flat and revolving screens, tables, etc.

VI. Sorting machinery, jigs, settlers, etc.

VII. Typical ore dressing works.

With each mechanical device studied, the theory of its use, its advantages and disadvantages, are discussed, and when possible the machine is examined in the Mining School stamp mill or in one of the stamp mills in the vicinity. When no machines are available for this work, use is made of drawings and photographs, with which this department is well supplied.

During the Fall and Winter terms considerable time is devoted to the examination of dressing plants near Houghton. These examinations are made on Saturdays, but are a part of the obligatory work. Students are required to make careful notes of all observations, make sketches of plants and machinery, and make, to the instructor, written reports of such observations.

During the third term instruction is given in the mining laboratory, in amalgamating and dressing of gold, silver, lead and copper ores.

The mining laboratory is equipped with an assortment of modern crushing, sizing and sorting machines, and is well prepared to treat free-milling and refractory ores by such methods as analysis and mill tests show to give the best results. Students are required to care for the machinery, carry out the dressing operations, and check their results by fire assay. When the work on an ore has been finished, the student makes his report.

This report includes the results obtained by all methods used, whether they are positive or negative, as well as the method which seems to be the most economical for its treatment.

The apparatus at the disposal of a student at present consists of the following pieces: One 650-pound three stamp battery, for wet or dry crushing, furnished with copper plates; one Blake crusher; one Gates crusher; one sample grinder; one pair of rolls; one amalgamating pan; one settler; two jigs; one Calumet separator; one spitzkasten; one Frue vanner; apron tables; screens; precipitating tanks; and settling tanks sufficient to enable the student to check all his results by assay.

It is required that this course be preceded by the first year's course in Physics, and second year's course in Mathematics, and be accompanied by the third year's course in Metallurgy and Assaying.

METALLURGY.

MR. SHARPLESS.

Instruction in Metallurgy is given during the second and third years by lectures and recitations, supplemented when possible by the use of text-books and visits to metallurgical works. The object of the course is to give the student a thorough foundation in the fundamental principles of the different metallurgical processes. In studying each of the metals special attention is paid to the properties of the commercial forms, and to the effects of impurities upon their value for engineering purposes. During the second year fuel, refractory materials, iron, steel and aluminum are discussed; the various ores of iron; the properties of cast iron, wrought iron and steel; the methods by which objectionable elements in the ore may be kept out of the finished product, or their effects neutralized; theory and description of blast furnace and puddling process; puddled, blistered and crucible steel; acid and basic Bessemer steel; and open-hearth steel processes.

During the third year the metallurgy of copper, lead, silver, and gold is studied by lectures and frequent references to the library. It is the aim of these courses to acquaint the student with the best modern American methods in sufficient detail to enable him to make an intelligent choice for the treatment of any particular ore, and also to familiarize him with the modern metallurgical literature.

In connection with these courses frequent visits are made to the smelting works in the vicinity, and each student is required to report upon the observations made by him.

Students taking either of the courses in Metallurgy, must have taken the first year Chemistry and Mineralogy.

CRYSTALLOGRAPHY.

THE DIRECTOR AND ASSISTANTS.

Instruction in this subject will be given by means of lectures and laboratory practice in determining the forms and planes of about eleven hundred glass and wooden crystal models, with recitations upon the same. In connection with the course in Mineralogy the instruction is confined to giving the student the practical knowledge of crystal forms which he needs in his Determinative Mineralogy. The subject is further discussed in connection with the course in Petrography.

MINERALOGY.

THE DIRECTOR AND ASSISTANTS.

For Determinative Mineralogy, there is provided a typical set of all the important minerals, special attention being paid to those of economic value, as well as to those occurring as gangue or rock-forming minerals. Special collections are arranged showing the physical characters of minerals, their pseudomorphs, etc.

These minerals are arranged in drawers labeled, and are at all times freely accessible to the student. Lectures are given upon these specimens, in which their essential characteristics are pointed out, particular attention being paid to the features which will distinguish each mineral from all others in the set.

Besides the typical collection of minerals, there are arranged in a large number of drawers, some fifteen thousand specimens of the same mineral species These are placed in convenient groups, but are unlabeled. These specimens are selected so as to give as great a variety of form, appearance and habitat as possible, in order that the student may be familiar with all the types that he will be likely to meet with in his professional practice. Drawers of these unlabeled minerals are assigned to each student, who is required to determine them and to recite upon them. He is required to do that which the practical mineralogist does: to determine his minerals by the shortest method possible, consistent with accuracy, the method to vary according to the specimen. To this end every method of determination short of quantitative analysis is employed; that is, in each case the crystal form and other physical characters are used, as well as the blowpipe and wet tests, so far as they may be needed.

After the student has studied and recited upon the specimens contained in a sufficient number of drawers of one group, he is then assigned to drawers containing the unlabeled minerals of another group, which have mixed with them specimens of the preceding group or groups. In this way each student is required to determine in his course from 3,000 to 6,000 different mineral specimens. Besides the lecture notes, the student uses Dr. E. S. Dana's "Text Book of Mineralogy."

The result of this work is such that a student not only knows how to determine any mineral that he may meet, but he is also enabled to recognize at sight the great majority of over three hundred mineral species, which he is required to study in this course.

Some twenty-two thousand mineral specimens were added to the mineralogical collections during 1889 and 1890, making this institution second to none in its means employed in giving instruction in practical Determinative Mineralogy. The entire collections number over twenty-seven thousand specimens of minerals.

LITHOLOGY.

THE DIRECTOR AND ASSISTANTS.

Large and complete collections of rock specimens are arranged for the use of the student. The course of instruction here is similar to that followed in the course in Mineralogy. Lectures are given upon the specimens of the typical collection, the method of classification explained, and the distinguishing characters of the different groups, species and varieties pointed out. Special attention is called to the variations and alterations in rocks, and to their local modifications due to their special mode of occurrence in the field. After the study of a sufficiently large number of types has been had, the student has assigned to him drawers containing unlabeled specimens of these rocks, which he is expected to determine and to recite upon, as he has done in his study of the minerals. The course is thus made thorough and practical.

Besides the general lithological collections, there are special collections arranged according to the classification of Rosenbusch, according to geological ages, etc., etc.

There is also a large collection of microscopic sections of rocks, especially to accompany the Rosenbusch collection. For further illustration and study, recourse may be had to the collections of the Michigan State Geological Survey, now numbering between six and seven thousand specimens and an equal number of microscopic sections. These collections are at present deposited in the Laboratory of Economic Geology, under the charge of the State Geologist and his assistants. The lithological collections of the Mining School contains over eleven thousand specimens; over nine thousand having been added

during the past two years. By means of these collections the
student is rendered practically familiar with all the rock varieties he is liable to meet. A student to take this course must
have completed the courses in Crystallography and Mineralogy.

PETROGRAPHY.

Drs. Lane and Patton.

The main object of this course is to enable students to use
the petrographical microscope in the recognition of minerals and
rocks, but much of Physical Mineralogy, and some parts of
Crystallography, are most appropriately taken up in this connection.

The study of this new field of science has, within the past
ten years, been introduced into the leading universities, but is,
so far as we know, only here given as a part of a regular Mining
School course. There is, therefore, as yet no textbook which
covers the field or is adapted to the needs of the class of students
in question. The instruction is consequently through lectures
and laboratory work, with syllabi and tables.

The microscope, besides enabling us to see the structure of
fine grained rocks and divine their origin, finds quite as important a use in attachments, which allow us to determine many
minerals, from their optical properties, more easily and accurately than with the blowpipe. Each student has a microscope, and is
required to measure the various optical constants useful in the
determination of minerals.

Various other means of determining minerals and rocks, in
which the microscope is of more or less help—for example, microchemical reactions and mechanical and magnetic separations—are
also studied. The study of the texture of rocks as seen in thin
sections, which indicates their origin and original chemical
character, and the study of the associations of minerals, occupy
much time. The classification and nomenclature of rocks are
but lightly treated.   ·

Most of the working microscopes were made by Bausch &
Lomb expressly for the school, but all the leading makes, English, French, German and American, are owned either by the
school or instructors, and are available for inspection. There is
also at least one complete set of the more delicate or less

important accessories accompanying Fuess's latest and best microscope, *e.g.*, axial angle attachment, compensator, comparateur, Bertrand's, Calderon's, Abbe's and Sorby's oculars. Bertrand's goniometer, etc. These, as well as Jannetaz's thermal apparatus, Groth's "Universal-Apparat," Wollaston's, Hirschwald's Fuess's and other goniometers, reflectometers, polariscope, pyroelectric dustsprinkler, etc., are used for illustration, demonstration and advanced research. For this latter it will be seen that there is ample equipment, and while the general course is strictly elementary, practical and non-mathematical, the instructors are ready to lend students, who wish more thorough and extensive training, all the help they need. A student to take this course must have completed the courses in Physics, Crystallography, Mineralogy, first year Chemistry and Lithology.

PALÆONTOLOGY.

Dr. Lane.

This course is given as an elementary one. It will begin by a review of the fundamental principles of Zoology and Botany, for use in recognition of fossils. Although details are left out, a personal handling of living forms will be insisted on, so that the knowledge will be real as far it goes.

In Palæontology, certain groups which yield common and characteristic fossils will be treated more in detail. There is a small type collection of living forms and a larger one of fossils, containing over a thousand specimens, for the student to consult. A collection of over fifteen hundred specimens, especially selected to cover the commoner fossils of the whole geological column, will be used to drill the students in recognizing fossils in different states of preservation, in assigning them to their general orders, and in certain cases giving their generic names. The specimens are arranged unlabeled in drawers, for the students to work upon, and pains will be taken to train the eye to recognize resemblances and differences. The practical work will be similar to that pursued in the course in Mineralogy. No particular text book will be required. The library is well supplied with books on the branches covered by this course: and advice on buying books will be given to the students, according to their individual needs.

STRATIGRAPHICAL AND HISTORICAL GEOLOGY.

DR. LANE.

This will be in continuation of the course in Palæontology. The formations which compose the earth's crust will be taken up in their order, and their characteristic life and lithology, their distribution and peculiarities, will be described.

The student will also be expected, without using books for the purpose, to assign a sufficient number of characteristic fossils to their periods, and will be exercised in determining horizons, with the help of Palæontological literature, as the library contains full sets of the New York and other state reports and various special works which may be used for this purpose.

Text Book: Archibald Geikie's "Text Book of Geology", books V. and VI.

Students taking this course must have completed the preceding work in Mineralogy, Lithology, Petrography and Palæontology.

PHYSICAL GEOLOGY.

THE DIRECTOR.

The instruction of Physical Geology is intended to be especially adapted to the needs of the explorer, the engineer, the petrographer, the geologist, the miner, the quarryman, and all others who desire to understand the connection and the structural relations that rock masses have to one another and to the valuable deposits which they may contain. It is intended to treat of the origin and alterations of rocks, general volcanic and earthquake action, metamorphism, jointing, faulting, cleavage, mountain building, eruptive rocks and crystalline schists, the action of air, surface and underground waters and life: the interior condition of the earth, etc , especially in their relations to the problems that the economic geologist, miner and quarryman have to meet. On account of the connection of the Mining School and the Geological Survey, the student has brought before him constantly the various problems that are arising in the practical work in the survey, and their methods of solution.

The course will be given by lectures and by recitations based upon the lectures and upon Dr. Archibald Geikie's "Text Book of Geology", books I, II part 1, III, IV and VII. Students who wish to take this course must complete the preceding work in Physics, Elementary Chemistry, Mineralogy, Lithology, Petrography and Geology.

ECONOMIC GEOLOGY.

THE DIRECTOR.

The instruction in this subject will be given by lectures, recitations, and practical observations in the field and in the mines.

The lectures will treat of the following subjects:

1   Mineral veins and metalliferous deposits: their classification, mode of occurrence, and the theories of their origin, special attention being paid to iron, copper, gold, silver, lead, tin, zinc, mercury and manganese.
2.   Coal, lignite, peat, petroleum, asphaltum and natural gas.
3.   Salt and saline earths.
4.   Materials used for grinding, whetting and polishing.
5.   Gems and decorative materials.
6.   Building stones and road-making materials.
7.   Lime, cement and artificial stone.
8.   Refractory or fire-resisting materials.
9.   Clay, sands, etc , used for pottery, porcelain and glass.
10.   Mineral medicines.
11.   Pigments, dyes and detergents.
12.   Water and water supply.
13   Mineral and thermal springs.

Special attention is given to the instruction of the student in Mineralogy, Petrography and Geology, in order that he may in after years understand the nature of the deposits upon which he may be at work; since disastrous mistakes probably occur in the practice of a mining engineer, oftener through ignorance of the petrographical and geological relations of the ore deposits in question, than from a lack of engineering or metallurgical skill.

The location of the school affords special advantages for the study of Petrography and General and Economic Geology. It is situated in the midst of the vast and ancient lava flows and conglomerates generally known as the Copper-bearing or Keweenawan series, and near the Eastern or Potsdam Sandstone. In the immediate vicinity are to be solved some of the most important and fundamental problems of petrographical and geological science *e.g.* the metamorphism or alteration of rocks, the true age of the so-called Keweenawan series, the relation of the so-called Huronian and Laurentian series, the origin of the iron ore, etc., while almost every problem of Geology finds its illustration in some portion of the Upper Peninsula.

The instruction in the various departments under the charge of the Director is intended to be given so that all those who wish to obtain a knowledge of the subjects as a matter of general information, or to prepare themselves for teachers or investigators, can attend with advantage.

The opportunities for practical instruction in Mineralogy and Geology, particularly in Economic Geology, have been greatly increased by placing the State Geological Survey under the charge of the Director of the Mining School. This arrangement enables skilled specialists to be employed for the mutual advantage of both the School and the Survey. It further brings the student in direct contact with the practical applications of Geology, and with its more important problems under discussion at the present time. Students who wish to take this course must have completed the preceding work in Physics, Elementary Chemistry, Mineralogy, Lithology, Petrography and Geology. Exceptions in the requirements in any of the above courses may be made in favor of special students of age and experience, who would be benefited by such exceptions being made.

SUMMER COURSE IN GEOLOGY.

THE DIRECTOR AND ASSISTANTS.

The summer term of the third year is spent in the field and in the mines, in the practical study of various questions in General and Economic Geology, Mineralogy and Petrography.

In order to increase the usefulness of the Mining School by enabling persons to attend upon some of its courses of instruction, the summer courses in Geology, Shop-practice and Surveying have been established. Attendance upon all these courses is obligatory upon all candidates for a degree in this institution. They are also open to persons who wish to attend them alone. The summer course in Geology will commence in July and continue for six weeks. The course consists essentially in the observation and discussion of observed phenomena of the sedimentary and eruptive rocks, whether metamorphic or not, as well as the associated ores as seen in the Upper Peninsula of Michigan. The work for the most part will be done in the vicinity of the mines, and students will be expected to make maps, notes, sections, diagrams, etc.

As are the other courses in the Mining School, this course is open without charge to any one, whether a resident of Michigan or not. It is hoped that this course will be of practical value to all teachers and others who wish to obtain a knowledge of the field occurrence of minerals and rocks, including ores, as well as to see the various phases of mining. In 1890 the class studied the Lake Superior coast and adjacent islands north and south of Marquette, and the mines and adjacent country about Negaunee, Ishpeming, Humboldt, Republic, Champion and the Gold Range. The next course will be given in the summer of 1892.

Persons desiring to attend the summer course in Geology are requested to prepare themselves by studying some of the larger Geological manuals, such as Geikie, Dana, Prestwich and Phillips. Special attention needs to be paid to the department of Physical Geology, therefore the works of Geikie and Green are preferred. Since the number of persons who can attend a field course in Geology at one time and place is limited, it is requested that all those who desire to join the class shall give early notice of their wishes to the Director. All attending the course should provide themselves with hammers, compasses, specimen bags, streakers, magnifying glasses, small magnets, etc.

Students in the Mining School will not be allowed to take this course until they have completed the preceding courses in Mineralogy, Lithology, Petrography and Geology.

THESIS.

Every student completing the three years course is required to present to the Faculty a satisfactory thesis, embodying the results of an investigation upon some subject related to the studies of that course, before he can be recommended to receive his degree Students intending to graduate in any year are required to select their subjects and present them to the faculty for approval by the first of March of that year,

ORGANIZATION.

The Michigan Mining School is an institution established and supported by the State, in accordance with that liberal educational policy which has placed the University of Michigan amongst the foremost educational institutions of America.

The Mining School is organized under the authority of an act, approved May 1, 1885, portions of which are as follows:

SECTION 1.—*The People of the State of Michigan enact:* That a school shall be established in the Upper Peninsula of the State of Michigan, to be called the Michigan Mining School, for the purpose and under the regulations contained in this act.

SEC. 2 —The said school shall be under the control and management of a board of six members, not less than four of whom shall be residents of the Upper Peninsula of the State of Michigan, who shall be known as the "Board of Control of the Michigan Mining School," and who shall be appointed by the Governor of the State of Michigan, by and with the consent of the Senate *   *   *   *, and who shall serve without compensation

SEC. 5.—The course of instruction shall embrace geology, mineralogy, chemistry, mining and mining engineering, and such other branches of practical and theoretical knowledge as will, in the opinion of the board, conduce to the end of enabling the students of said institution to obtain a full knowledge of the science, art and practice of mining, and the application of machinery thereto. Tuition shall be free in said institution to all bona fide residents of this state, but a reasonable charge for incidental expenses, not less than ten dollars nor exceeding thirty dollars per year, may be made against any student, if deemed necessary, and the board shall not be obliged to furnish books, apparatus, or other materials for the use of students

SEC. 6.—The course of study, the terms, and the hours of instruction, shall be regulated by the board, who shall also have power to make all such rules and regulations concerning admission, control and discipline of students, and such others, as may be deemed necessary for the good government of the Institution and the convenience and transaction of its business

SEC. 7.—No debt shall be contracted beyond or apart from the actual means at the disposal of the Institution. The board may dispose of or lease any property donated to the State for said School, or which may be acquired in payment of debts except of such as is necessary for the accommodation of the school.   *   *   *   *   *   *   *   *

In conformity with the above act, the Michigan Mining School was first opened to students September 15th, 1886.

REGULATIONS OF THE SCHOOL.

Neatness, order and good government in a school of this character are requisite, if the school is to maintain credit and character both at home and abroad. Students that enter this institution are supposed to do so in order to prepare themselves for their profession, and like students in Theological, Law or Medical schools, are pre-supposed to understand what they are here for, to attend strictly to that business, and to conduct themselves as gentlemen. The members of the Faculty have no time to waste on primary instruction, nor in conducting a reform school (which the state has elsewhere provided), as may with propriety be done by non-professional schools. If a man cannot be a man and attend to his duties as he should, this institution has no place for him. It is not obliged to proceed further than to be satisfied that any man's presence is injurious to the School, or that his longer stay is of no advantage to himself: neither is it obliged to deal out repeated warnings, nor even any warning. Methods that are proper, or that are in vogue in academies, normal schools, and colleges, are entirely out of place in a professional school whose students average over twenty-four years of age.

The general rules of the school, so far as they need be announced to the general public, are as follows:

The Faculty have full power to admonish, dismiss, suspend, or expel any student, for cause.

Each member of the Faculty is held responsible for the rooms, apparatus, etc., under his charge, and for the good order and discipline of the students under his charge.

Each instructor is required to be in attendance during the working hours in his department, and he has the power of disciplining or suspending any student from his room, until such time as the case shall have been acted upon by the Faculty.

All absences of students from recitations, lectures, field and laboratory work, are considered as failures in recitations, and are so ranked unless excused by vote of the Faculty, and also made up. Tardiness is considered as a half-absence

Each instructor shall keep a record of the daily work of each student under his charge, and rank him on a scale of 100; and no student shall be permitted to pass who has not obtained an average of at least 75 in his daily work.

Examinations shall be held at the end of every term or, if desired, at the completion of each subject, if falling within the term. The examinations are to be ranked on a scale of 100, and no student passed unless he has obtained a rank of at least 75 in them. ˷

These regulations require that every student, in order to pass, must obtain a class standing of at least 75 on a scale of 100, in all term work, and also in all examinations.

The method of making up deficiencies in daily work varies with the subject, at the discretion of the instructor.

Students having chosen their course or subjects are not allowed to change or drop any of their subjects, except upon petition, and by vote of the Faculty.

The rank of each student is reported to himself, or, if he is a minor, to his parents or guardian, after the close of each term. With this is reported all absences, whether excused or not, and such other information concerning the student as it may be considered advisable to report.

Entrance conditions are to be made up at the beginning of the winter term following In the case of failure, a second opportunity is given at the commencement of the following spring term.

Special regulations have to be made concerning the conditions received during the various terms, owing to the special arrangement of the terms and the work in this institution.

Conditions received in any laboratory work can only be made up at some subsequent time by repetition of the work, when the laboratory is open for work on the same subject. This also applies to Shop-practice, Drawing (excluding Topographical Drawing) and to all Field, Mine or Mill work.

Conditions received on work (not included under the general head of laboratory work) are to be made up as follows:

Conditions received during the fall term in Algebra, Trigonometry, Calculus, Physics, Properties of Materials, Graphical Statics, Mechanics of Materials, Mechanical and Electrical Engineering, Chemistry, Ore Dressing, Metallurgy, Stratigraphical, Physical and Economic Geology, are to be made up at the commencement of the winter term following.

Conditions received during the winter term in Trigonometry, Analytical Geometry, Physics, first year Chemistry, Ore Dressing and Metallurgy are to be made up at the commencement of the spring term following.

Conditions received during the winter term in Plane Surveying, Topographical Drawing, Hydraulics, Physical Geology, Economic Geology and the third year work in Mining, Mechanical Engineering and Electrical Engineering, are to be made up at the opening of the summer term following.

Conditions received during the winter term in Calculus, Mechanics, Mechanism and in second year Chemistry, Mining, Mine Surveying, Mechanical Engineering and Electrical Engineering are to be made up at the commencement of the fall term following.

Conditions received during the spring term in Analytical Geometry are to be made up at the commencement of the fall term following.

Conditions received in the summer term in the theoretical work in Surveying are to be made up at the commencement of the winter term following.

The times at which the above examinations will be held will be assigned by the Faculty at the opening of each term.

In case of failure on the part of any student to remove his conditions at the specified time, he will be allowed another opportunity at the commencement of the next succeeding term in which instruction in the same study is given. If he fails then, he will have to take the course in that subject over again. No work can be taken by any student, when the preceding work upon which he is conditioned is considered essential to its successful prosecution, except upon petition and special vote of the Faculty.

Any of the general regulations of the school may be suspended by the Faculty, in behalf of special students of age and experience, if such suspension seems advisable, to aid said students in their work.

All students are required to observe proper decorum, and to refrain from any conduct that disturbs others, or is injurious to the school.

The attempt of any student to present as his own the work of another, or to pass in his daily work or examinations by improper means, or to falsify in any of his school relations, is regarded as a most serious offence, and renders the offender liable to immediate suspension or even to expulsion.

LOCATION.

The school is located at Houghton, the county seat of Houghton county. The twin towns of Houghton and Hancock lie in the sheltered valley of Portage Lake, an arm of Lake Superior. The climate is bracing and healthful. Although Houghton is in a high latitude, yet one is far less inconvenienced by the cold here than he much further south along the Atlantic coast, or in the vicinity of the lakes. This is due to the dryness of the Houghton climate, a climate which is free from any malaria, hay fever, etc. In general, students coming from localities further south have found health and strength improved by the change. The town has an abundant supply of pure spring water. Houghton is easily reached by rail from Detroit, Chicago, Milwaukee, St. Paul and Duluth (a descriptive pamphlet showing the routes to Houghton can be obtained from the General Passenger Agent, D., S. S. & A. R'y., Minneapolis, Minn.); and by steamer from all the important ports on the chain of the Great Lakes. Within the State, half-fare rates are given to the students of the Mining School by the Duluth, South Shore & Atlantic, and the Mineral Range, and Hancock & Calumet railways.

While the school itself is situated in the Portage Lake copper

district, the access of the Keweenawan copper district on the
north is easy, and there lie within comparatively short distances
the Ontonagon copper district, and the Iron Mining regions of
Marquette, Menominee and Gogebic.

In the immediate vicinity of the Mining School, are situated
the Quincy, Atlantic, Franklin and Huron copper mines, while
within a distance of fifteen miles are situated the Calumet and
Hecla, Tamarack, Osceola and other copper mines, with their
machine shops, smelting works, rolling and stamp mills, etc In
the iron mining regions lie numerous great iron mines, prominent among which are the Cleveland, Jackson, Lake Superior,
Lake Angeline, Champion, Republic, Chapin, Vulcan, Cyclops,
Colby and Norrie.

In addition to the copper and iron, gold, silver, gypsum,
building stones, slate, coal, salt, etc., are numbered among the
mineral productions of the State.

Some idea of the vastness of the mining operations in the
Lake Superior district can be gathered from the following statistics: It contains over sixty-five copper mines, which have produced up to 1890, one billion three hundred and twenty-seven
million seven hundred and ninety-nine thousand four hundred
and twenty pounds of copper, valued at two hundred and forty-
three million seven hundred and six thousand eight hundred
and nine dollars.   The cost sheet of one mine alone is some four
millions yearly, mainly expended in this region. One mine alone
has paid over thirty-five millions of dollars in dividends, or over
three times as much as any other mine now working in the
United States, except one, and over twice as much as that one.

In the iron mining districts about Lake Superior, in Michigan, there was produced in 1890 seven million one hundred and
eighty-five thousand one hundred and seventy-five tons of iron
ore, or nearly one-half of all the iron ore produced in the United
States.

The Michigan iron mines have produced since their discovery
over fifty millions of tons of iron ore.

Michigan is credited by the Director of the Mint with producing in 1889 gold to the amount of seventy thousand dollars,
and silver amounting to seventy-seven thousand five hundred
and seventy-five dollars.

The state of Michigan is also the chief producer of salt and
gypsum in the United States.

The Michigan Mining School has been located in the Upper
Peninsula of Michigan for the same reason that a medical

school should be in the vicinity of large hospitals, in order that it should be associated with the objects about which it treats.

From this location the student of the Michigan Mining School is placed in a mining atmosphere, in which all his surroundings and associations are in conformity with his present and future work. He is thus enabled to see in actual operation some of the most successful and extensive mining operations now conducted anywhere.

The Calumet and Hecla mine is now worked at a depth on the lode of over 4,000 feet, with an extent in length of about two and one-half miles. This mine is operated by fourteen shafts, one of which is a six-compartment shaft, now sunk to a perpendicular depth of about 2,500 feet; and which when completed will be upward of 5,000 feet deep. The aggregate power of the steam plant in use and under construction is some 37,500 horse power, including one engine of 4,700 horse power and eleven other engines of an average of 2,000 horse power each. The stamp mills of this mine contain 18 improved Ball steam stamps, making from 95 to 98 blows per minute, and crushing about 4,500 tons of the rock of the lode in twenty-four hours. The three pumping engines have an aggregate capacity of 50,000,000 gallons in twenty-four hours; while another triple expansion pumping engine, now nearly completed, has alone the capacity of 60,000,000 gallons in twenty-four hours. Besides the two sand wheels forty feet in diameter capable of elevating some 16,000,000 to 18,000,000 gallons of water and 1,600 tons of sand per day, there is nearly completed another wheel fifty-four feet in diameter designed to elevate 30,000,000 gallons of water and 3,000 tons of sand per day.

The smelting works of this mine contain sixteen refining furnaces with an aggregate capacity of 224 tons in twenty-four hours. They also contain two blast and two blister furnaces, etc. All the other appliances of this remarkable mine are commensurate to those above given.

The Tamarack mine has two perpendicular shafts, one over 2,500 feet and the other nearly 3,000 feet in depth.

The other mines, mills, smelting works, etc., are all well equipped for their work, and every assistance is given by their officers and men to aid the students of the Mining School in studying the various appliances, under the direction of the Faculty of the School.

EXPENSES.

Under the act of organization, the Board of Control have made the school entirely free, no charge being made for tuition or incidentals, whether the student was a resident of the state of Michigan, or of the United States, or not: all has been made free to the students from every land. Owing to the fact that the expenses of providing a thorough technical education in any branch, particularly in Mining Engineering, are much greater than those attendant upon a literary education, it is possible that after a few more years, the same tuition fee will be charged non-resident students that is now charged students in most of the technical schools in other states, while there will also be charged to all students the amount allowed for incidentals, as specified in the act of organization. Should this change be made, due and full notice will be given. The supplies in the Chemical and allied Laboratories are furnished the students, and they are required to pay for materials, re-agents, etc., and for the use and breakage of apparatus.

To insure the payment on the part of the student, members of the third year class and special students in Chemistry are required, at the beginning of each year, to deposit with the treasurer of the school a sum of not less than $60 00. All other students are required to deposit $30.00. Any portion of this deposit not used will be returned to the student upon leaving school, or at the end of each year, as he chooses. Further, should the material used by the student exceed his deposit, an additional deposit will be required.

No supplies will be furnished the student from any department until he presents a receipt from the Treasurer showing that the required deposit has been made.

There are no dormitories connected with the school. Arrangements are being made whereby those who desire to do so can obtain board and rooms in private families, and in boarding houses, in Houghton and Hancock, at prices varying from $16.00 to $25.00 per calendar month. $20.00 per month is understood to be the standard or average price. This is to include room, heat and lights, as well as board. Board alone can be obtained now for from $15.00 to $20.00 per calendar month.

The necessary expenses of the student may be estimated as follows for each year:

Board, etc., 10¼ months (@ $16 to $25	$168 00 to	$262.50
Apparatus, chemicals, etc.	25.00 to	60.00
Books and Drawing Materials	25.00 to	55.00
Traveling Expenses (Excursions, Field work, etc.)	10.00 to	60.00
Washing	20.00 to	30.00
Total	$248.00 to	$467.50

EMPLOYMENT.

The question is often asked the officers of the Mining School if they can promise employment to students on graduation. The only answer is, that neither the Mining School nor any other self-respecting institution can make any such promises. The question of employment depends on too many factors to be promised three years in advance. It depends on the demand and the supply, which are liable to vary from year to year, and it also very largely depends on a student's personal "equation." A thorough hard working student with the ability to command the respect of men and to manage them, and to work harmoniously with his fellow officers, will hardly ever fail of obtaining the choicest positions that are open to him, especially after having the practical work and experience about mines, that the graduates of this school have.

Education and training do not give qualities to any man: they simply sharpen and develop those natural abilities that he possesses, hence if he is not by nature fitted for a certain position, he ought not, and will not be likely, to obtain it. On the other hand, whatever may be a man's natural abilities, he will not be likely to obtain a position of any high grade unless he has been educated for it, either in school or outside—the outside education being by far the most expensive kind of education that can be obtained.

Slothful, lazy and inefficient students will not naturally obtain places as readily as the hard-working ones, other things being equal. They certainly will not be so recommended the officers of the Mining School, since a man who cannot be trusted to attend faithfully to his work when engaged in obtaining his professional training is not one whom it is safe to trust with important business and mining interests.

Students need to remember that their conduct, from the day they enter the Mining School until they leave it, has an all important bearing upon their future position and standing.

The Director of the Mining School makes one invariable rule. i. e., to inform all persons desiring students or graduates of this school of the defects, as well as the virtues of the candidates, so far as he knows them, believing that such a course is the only one that is just either to the employer, the student, or the school. When information is fully given concerning the position and the desired qualities of the person to fill it, pains are taken to select the student who is believed to be most suitable for the position.

In order to secure the best future for themselves, students are urged to neglect no opportunities to inform themselves in the practical work of mining, in addition to those opportunities that the school affords.

The graduates are also urged to turn their attention to a field in which success is almost sure to men of ability and energy; to enter the mines or works as miners, foremen, or in some other subordinate capacity, and thoroughly master every detail from the lowest to the highest work.

It is men who have had a thorough education, both in theoretical and practical mining, and who have worked in every grade of work, that are even now sought to take charge of our mines and their allied industries. The future is for the man who is willing to commence at the bottom of his profession and who is conscious of the truth, that on graduation he is only just prepared to begin his work.

The graduates of the school are urged to keep the Director constantly informed concerning their positions, salaries, etc., and also what their desires are, in order that they may be assisted to advance if opportunity offers.

Officers of mines and others desiring surveyors, engineers, draughtsmen, foremen, chemists, assayers, etc, etc., are requested to make their wants fully known to the Director of the Mining School, who will then recommend suitable candidates to them, if he knows of any.

The inquiry is frequently made by persons intending to become students, if they can attend to their school work and earn enough to pay their way at the same time. Such a course is not practicable, as the regular school work, if it is done as it should be, requires the entire available time of any student, however strong and able he may be. As a special student, taking only a few studies, one might be able to procure sufficient work to pay his way. The better way for the needy student is either to attend to his school and his labor alternate years, or else to borrow the means to continue his education, repaying through his increased earning power after graduation.

The salaries obtained upon graduation have been from $540.00 to $1500.00, averaging about $900.00 per year. The lower salaries were obtained by students who had less practical experience with men and with the world in general; these were obliged to spend some time in acquiring a special kind of knowledge that the Mining School cannot give.

So far as known, the salaries increase after a varied time from $900 00 to even $3600.00 or more per year, averaging about $1200. All this, however, is dependent upon the demand and supply, the state of the mining industries at any time, as well as on other factors that need not be mentioned.

PRIZES AND SCHOLARSHIPS.

THE LONGYEAR PRIZES.

Through the liberality of J. M. Longyear, Esq , of Marquette, the following prizes have been offered, as stated in his letter making the offer, which is here appended:

Marquette, Michigan, Nov. 9, 1887.

CHARLES E. WRIGHT, ESQ , MARQUETTE:

DEAR SIR--I wish to offer three first prizes of seventy-five dollars ($75) each, and three second prizes of fifty dollars ($50) each, to be competed for by the members of the senior class of the Michigan Mining School. The competition to be by means of papers on three subjects, written by members of the class and submitted to the Board of Control for examination, in such a manner and at such a time as the Board may determine. I desire subjects selected with a view of producing papers which will be of practical use in developing the mineral resources of the state of Michigan. I should like something which would be of service to the average woodsman or explorer, and suggest the subjects of Practical Field Geology, and the use of the Dial and the Dip Compass in explorations, leaving the selection of the third subject to the judgment of the Board. If this offer is accepted and there are two or more papers on each subject submitted, I will pay seventy-five dollars to each of the writers of the three papers which may be awarded the first prize, and fifty dollars to each of the writers of the three papers which may be awarded the second prizes.

I would suggest, however, that in case only two papers are submitted, that the Board reserve the right of awarding only one prize, in case such action should seem advisable. In case only one paper should be submitted, I should like the Board to exercise its judgment in awarding a prize. It is my desire to publish the papers under the writer's names, in pamphlet form, for distribution among miners, explorers, land owners, and others.

Yours very truly,

J. M. LONGYEAR.

In conformity to the above letter, the Board of Control have decided upon the following subjects and conditions:

SUBJECTS.

1. Field Geology: its Methods and their Applications.
2. The Dial and the Dip Compass and their Uses
3. The Diamond Drill and its Uses.

CONDITIONS.

The conditions under which the prizes are to be awarded are as follows:

The papers for this year are to be presented by September 30th, 1891; and for the following year by September 30th, 1892.

A student may present a paper upon each of the three subjects, which will entitle him to three prizes, if his papers are found worthy.

The dissertations must be written in a clear, legible hand, or type-written, on letter paper, quarto size. The sheets are to be securely fastened together, written one side only, and a margin of not less than one inch left all around, in order that the dissertation may be bound if desired.

The title page is to have upon it an assumed name, and each dissertation is to be accompanied by a sealed envelope bearing the same name. This envelope must contain the writer's true, as well as assumed, name and address, and it will not be opened until the awards have been made.

No prizes will be awarded unless the papers are judged by the committee to whom they are referred to be of a sufficiently high standing to be entitled to a prize; hence there may be awarded all, part or none of the prizes, as the case may be.

These prizes can now be competed for by any students of the school, whether special or regular, without restriction to the graduating class, as was originally specified.

THE CHARLES E. WRIGHT
SCHOLARSHIP.

The Charles E. Wright Scholarship has been founded by Mrs. Carrie A. Wright, of Ann Arbor, in accordance with the conditions expressed in the letter given below:

To the Honorable Board of Control of the Michigan Mining School:

GENTLEMEN.—In memory of my husband, the late Charles E. Wright, and as a token of the deep interest he had in the Michigan Mining School, I desire to give to said school the sum of one thousand dollars.

If said gift shall be accepted, it is to be held under the following conditions, to-wit: It is to be invested as a permanent fund by the Board of Control, to form the nucleus of a scholarship to be known as the Charles E. Wright Scholarship. The income is to be given to some indigent student, by vote of the Board of Control, with the advice and consent of the faculty of said school.

The award is to be made during the first term of the year to some student who has a satisfactory record during the entire preceding year in the Michigan Mining School, and who intends to devote himself to the profession of Mining Engineering or Geological work. The income is to be divided into three equal parts, to be paid during the three terms of the year, and if at any time the conduct or standing of the student receiving the award should become unsatisfactory, the portion then remaining unpaid should be withheld from him and given to some other student, in accordance with the terms of this gift.

(Signed)   CARRIE A. WRIGHT.

THE NORRIE SCHOLARSHIP.

The fund for this scholarship has been given in accordance with the conditions stated below, and it is expected that the income from this scholarship will be available in 1891 and 1892.

This scholarship will be awarded in accordance with Mr. Norrie's requirements as given below:

Know all men by these presents, That I, A. Lanfear Norrie, of the city of New York, hereby give, grant, assign and set over unto the Michigan Mining School, of Houghton, Michigan, and to Peter White, D. H. Ball and J. M. Longyear, of Marquette, Michigan, as trustees, the sum of five thousand dollars ($5,000), lawful money of the United States.

The conditions of this gift, and upon which this fund is to be taken, are, that the said trustees shall invest the same upon bond and mortgage in the village of Marquette, or of the city of Detroit, in the State of Michigan, or in the city of Milwaukee, in the State of Wisconsin, or in the city of Chicago, in the State of Illinois, upon unencumbered improved real estate.

That one-half of the income of said sum of $5,000 shall be paid yearly by said trustees unto the Board of Control for the support of some student whose father has worked in, or in some way been connected with mining operations in the Upper Peninsula of Michigan, who shall be designated by the faculty of said school; and the remainder of said income shall be accumulated and invested as said principal shall be invested, and that this fund with its accumulations shall be the basis of a larger fund to be obtained from other contributions, amounting to at least one hundred thousand dollars ($100,000), to be used for the erection of a dormitory building for the use of such students as shall be designated by said faculty, which building, when erected, shall be under the exclusive control of the corporation or Board of Control of the said Michigan Mining School.

This gift is to the said trustees and their successors forever, for the benefit of the said Mining School. In case of the death of either of the said trustees, the survivors or survivor shall appoint a successor or successors.

When the erection of said building shall be commenced, after the said fund of one hundred thousand dollars is obtained, the sum hereby given, with all its accumulations, shall be paid over to the said Mining School, for the purpose aforesaid.

Witness my hand, the 30th day of January, 1890.

A. LANFEAR NORRIE.

Witness, T. E. O. M. STETSON.

We, Peter White, D. H. Ball and J. M. Longyear, the persons named in the above instrument, accept the trust therein granted, in all respects, and agree to comply with the conditions thereof.

Witness our hands, the 1st day of February, 1890.

PETER WHITE,
D. H. BALL,
J. M. LONGYEAR.

THE LONGYEAR FUND.

This is a fund of $5000 given for the year 1889 by Mr. J. M. Longyear, of the Board of Control, to be the property of the Mining School, to be loaned to students of said school that may be designated by the Treasurer and Director, said students being unable to maintain their connection with the school without such aid. This money is not to be a gift to the student, but he is to pay it back as soon as practicable after graduation. After his graduation, interest will be charged him for the first three years at 5 per cent, and for the following two years at 7 per cent. The money and the interest are to go to the fund, to aid other students in the same way. This method, it is believed, will lead the student to a more manly feeling than a gift outright would produce in him, since it gives him the means of paying for his own education, assists him when he most needs assistance, and enables him to return the money to aid others, at a time when he can best do so. It is believed that it would be better if all funds given to the school for investment and use, should be accompanied by some proviso that a certain portion, at least, of the income shall be paid or set aside, to increase the principal until it shall attain a limit either fixed or left to the proper authorities to determine. Such a method would enable the institution in the future to do much more good, than it would if the income were to be spent entirely each year.

The school is in great need of funds to aid students who are otherwise unable to obtain an education, or to attend this institution. Aid of this kind is frequently sought by able and worthy young men, and all is done that can be with the limited means at the command of the school to aid them.

DEGREES.

Students who entered the regular course in the Mining School during the school year 1889-90, or prior, on completion of a course similar to that given them, as shall be specified by the Faculty, will have conferred upon them the degree of Bachelor of Science,

Such students may afterward obtain the degree of Mining Engineer, by returning to the school and completing the three years course; or else upon application to the Board of Control and Faculty, and upon presentation of satisfactory evidence of two years successful practical work, and of a suitable thesis in some line co-ordinate with their course of study in this school.

The thesis must be on an original investigation undertaken in Mining, Mechanical or Electrical Engineering, Chemistry, Metallurgy, Mineralogy, Petrography, Geology, or in some allied subject that shall belong within the objects of this institution, and it must be approved by the Faculty.

Students who complete the present course of three years and present a satisfactory thesis, will receive the degree of Mining Engineer or Engineer of Mines (E. M.). The thesis must conform to the requirements given above, and must be completed and approved by the Faculty, before that body will recommend that the degree of Mining Engineer, or Engineer of Mines, be conferred upon the student.

For higher degrees see Graduate Instruction and Degrees.

GRADUATE INSTRUCTION AND DEGREES.

Students who are graduates of this or other institutions will be admitted as special students to take any study taught in this school, or to take special graduate instruction.

Those who wish to become candidates for a higher degree will enter under the following terms:

Students who are graduates of this institution, or of others of similar grade, whose course shall be approved by the Faculty, will be admitted as candidates for the degree of Doctor of Philosophy. In order to attain this degree they must pursue for at least two years an advanced course of study in subjects germane to the undergraduate course in this institution, which course of study is to be approved by the Faculty.

One of the years of study may, in special cases, be spent elsewhere, and the work accepted, on sufficient proof of its thoroughness and high character, as the equivalent of one year's work spent here. But under no condition will the degree be given, unless one year at least is spent as a resident worker at this institution.

Students who are both graduates of this or of an equivalent professional school, and also of some college or university whose course of study is accepted by the Faculty, may be admitted to the degree of Doctor of Philosophy, after taking for at least one year an approved course of study at this institution.

The degree of Doctor of Philosophy will only be given in case the student shall have shown marked ability, power for original investigation, has passed a satisfactory oral public examination, and presented a thesis embodying the result of original investigation, which has been approved by the faculty.

Students who are graduates of this or of other institutions having a satisfactory equivalent course, and who shall have pursued here according to the above regulations, a successful course of study, for the degree of Doctor of Philosophy, may at the same time receive the degree of Mining Engineer, if said degree has not been conferred on their previous graduation.

COLLECTIONS.

For the purpose of illustration and study a number of collections have been provided for the use of the students:

Invertebrate Zoological collection.............. 1,000 specimens.
Palæontological collections.................... 2,600 specimens.
Mineralogical collections. ....27,000 specimens.
Lithological and Geological collections........11,000 specimens.
State Geological Survey collections............. 6,500 specimens.

Besides the above, there are collections of palæontological charts, metallurgical, geological and petrographical diagrams, geological models, maps, etc.

Collections of slags, metallurgical products, materials for illustration in economic geology, as well as some exhibition collections, have been commenced, and all persons who can are urged to contribute to the school collections of minerals, rocks, veinstones, ores, slags, metallurgical products, samples of building stones, machinery, tools, etc., and models, photographs and prints of the same, etc.

In the case of the mineral products used in arts and manufactures, it is desired to procure specimens showing the various stages in the processes of manufacture. It is especially important for the school to receive and preserve sets of cores from drill holes, samples of ores from every mine, with specimens of the associated gangue minerals and rocks, as well as of the walls and associated country rocks.

LIBRARY.

The Library of the School contains at present 7,649 volumes besides numerous pamphlets, and additions are constantly made to it. It is proposed not only to have a good reference library for student work, but also one that shall be as complete as possible upon the subjects taught in the school. It is especially desired to have a full set of all reports and works relating to the mining and other mineral industries of the districts bordering on Lake Superior. It is also hoped to make the library valuable for reference, both for practical and scientific men; and it is freely open to all who desire to consult it.

In addition to the school library, the scientific library of the Director is deposited in the school building, and can be used by students and others. This library is especially devoted to Crystallography, Mineralogy, Petrography and General and Economic Geology.

Contributions of pamphlets, papers, maps and books on subjects germane to those taught in this institution are solicited for the Mining School Library. Plans, drawings and engravings relating to mines, mining machinery and metallurgy are desired.

It is hoped to make the library very full in files of the different journals published in the mineral regions; and contributions of present and past numbers of such journals are solicited for the library, to aid in making it a complete depository of materials relating to the history of the Lake Superior region.

READING ROOM.

Connected with the library is a Reading-Room which is supplied with the following periodicals:

Acta Mathematica, Stockholm.
American Chemical Journal, Baltimore.
American Engineer, Chicago.
American Geologist, Minneapolis.
American Journal of Mathematics, Baltimore.
American Journal of Science, New Haven.
American Machinist, New York.
American Naturalist, Philadelphia.
Annalen der Physik und Chemie, Leipzig.
Annalen der Physik und Chemie, Beiblätter, Leipzig.
Annales de Chimie et de Physique, Paris.
Annales Industrielles, Paris.
Annales de la Société, Géologique de Belgique, Liège.

Annales des Mines, Paris.
Annales des Ponts et Chaussées, Paris.
Annales des Sciences Géologiques, Paris.
Annals of the New York Academy of Science, New York.
Annals of Mathematics, University of Virginia.
Archiv der Mathematik und Physik, Leipzig.
Berg- und Hüttenmaennische Zeitung, Leipzig.
Berg- und Hüttenmaennisches Jahrbuch, Vienna.
Berichte der Deutschen chemischen Gesellschaft, Berlin
Builder, London.
Bulletin of the American Iron and Steel Association, Phila-
delphia.
Bulletin of the Philosophical Society, Washington.
Bulletin de la Société Chimique de Paris.
Bulletin des Sciences Mathématiques, Paris.
Bulletin de la Société Française de Minéralogie, Paris.
Bulletin de la Société Géologique de France, Paris.
Bulletin de la Société Mathématique de France, Paris.
*Calumet Conglomerate, Red Jacket, Michigan.
*Calumet and Red Jacket News, Calumet, Michigan.
Chemical News and Journal of Physical Science, London.
Chemiker Zeitung, Cöthen, Germany.
Chemische Industrie, Berlin.
Civilingenieur, Leipzig.
Colliery Engineer, Scranton, Pa.
Comptes Rendus, Hebdomadaires des Séances de l'Académie
des Sciences, Paris.
Connecticut Academy of Arts and Sciences, Transactions,
New Haven.
*Current, Norway, Michigan.
Daily Mining Journal, Marquette. Michigan.
Dingler's Polytechnisches Journal, Stuttgart.
*Diamond Drill, Crystal Falls, Mich.
Education, Boston.
Electrical Engineer, New York.
Electrical Engineer, London
Electrical World, New York.
Electrician, London.
Elektrotechnische Zeitschrift, Berlin.
Engineer, New York.
Engineer, London.
Engineering, London.
Engineering, New York.

*Gift of the Publishers.

Engineering and Mining Journal, New York.
Engineering News and American Railway Journal, New York.
Essex Institute Bulletin.
*Florence Mining News, Florence, Wis.
Génie Civil, Paris.
Geological Magazine, London.
Industries, London.
Iron, London.
Iron Age, New York.
*Iron Ore, Ishpeming, Mich.
Jahres-Bericht der Chemischen Technologie, Leipzig.
Jahresbericht über die Fortschritte der Chemie, Braunschweig, Germany.
Jahrbuch für das Berg- und Hüttenwesen, Freiberg.
Jahrbuch der kaiserlich-königlichen geologischen Reichsanstalt, Vienna.
Jahrbuch der Königlich Preusseschen geologischen Landesanstalt and Bergakademie, Berlin.
Jahrbuch über die Fortschritte der Mathematik, Berlin.
*Johns Hopkins University Circulars.
Journal of Analytical and Applied Chemistry, Easton, Pa.
Journal of the Chemical Society, London.
Journal of Education, Boston.
Journal of the Franklin Institute, Philadelphia.
Journal of the Geological Society, London.
Journal of the Iron and Steel Institute, London.
Journal des Mathématiques Pures et Appliquées, Paris.
Journal für die reine und angewandte Mathematik, Berlin.
Journal de Pharmacie et de Chimie, Paris.
Journal de Physique Théorique et Appliquée, Paris.
Journal für praktische Chemie, Leipzig.
Journal of the Society of Arts, London.
Journal of the Society of Chemical Industry, London.
Journal of Useful Inventions, New York.
Justus Liebig's Annalen der Chemie, Leipzig.
Knowledge, London.
Kritischer Vierteljahresbericht über die Berg- & Hüttenmännische und verwandte Literatur, Freiberg.
*Lake Superior Democrat, Ishpeming, Mich.
*L'Anse Sentinel, L'Anse, Mich.
London, Edinburgh and Dublin Philosophical Magazine and Journal of Science, London.
Lumière Électrique, Paris.

*Gift of the Publishers.

[1] Manufacturer and Builder, New York.

Mathematical Magazine, Washington.

Mathematische Annalen, Leipzig.

Memoirs of the American Academy of Arts and Sciences, Boston.

Memoirs of the Boston Society of Natural History.

Michigan Copper Journal, Hancock, Mich.

Michigan School Moderator, Lansing, Mich.

Mineralogical Magazine and Journal of the Mineralogical Society, London.

Mineralogische und Petrograpische Mittheilungen, Vienna.

Mining Journal, Railway and Commercial Gazette, London.

Mining and Scientific Press, San Francisco.

*Mining and Scientific Review, Denver.

Mining World and Engineering Record, London.

*Montana Mining Review, Helena, Montana.

Nature, London.

Neues Jahrbuch für Mineralogie. Geologie und Palæontologie, Stuttgart.

Nouvelles Annales de Mathématiques, Paris.

Oesterreichische Zeitschrift für Berg- und Hüttenwesen, Vienna.

*Official Gazette of the U. S. Patent Office. Washington.

*Ontonagon Herald, Ontonagon, Mich.

*Ontonagon Miner, Ontonagon. Mich.

Petermann's Mittheilungen aus Justus Perthes' geographischer Anstalt, Gotha.

Philosophical Transactions of the Royal Society of London.

*Pick and Axe, Bessemer, Mich.

Popular Science Monthly, New York.

Portage Lake Mining Gazette, Houghton, Mich.

Proceedings of the Academy of Natural Sciences, Philadelphia.

Proceedings of the American Academy of Arts and Sciences, Boston.

Proceedings of the American Association for the Advancement of Science. Salem, Massachusetts.

Proceedings of the Boston Society of Natural History, Boston.

Proceedings of the Institution of Civil Engineers, London.

Proceedings of the Institution of Mechanical Engineers, London.

Proceedings of the Geologists' Association, London.

Proceedings of the London Mathematical Society.

Proceedings of the Royal Geographical Society and Monthly

*Gift of the Publishers.

Record of Geography, London.

Proceedings of the Royal Society of London.

*Publishers' Weekly, New York.

Quarterly Journal of the Geological Society, London.

Quarterly Journal of Pure and Applied Mathematics, London.

Railroad and Engineering Journal, New York.

Report of the British Association for the Advancement of Science, London.

Revue Universelle des Mines, de la Métallurgie, Paris.

School of Mines Quarterly, New York.

Science, New York.

Scientific American, New York.

Scientific American Supplement, New York.

Sitzungsberichte der kaiserlichen Akademie der Wissenschaften, Vienna.

Sitzungsberichte der königlich preussischen Akademie der Wissenschaften zu Berlin.

Stahl und Eisen, Düsseldorf.

Technologiste, Paris.

*Torch Lake Times, Lake Linden, Mich.

*Transactions of the American Institute of Mining Engineers, New York.

Transactions of the American Society of Civil Engineers, New York.

Transactions of the American Society of Mechanical Engineers, New York.

Transactions of the Manchester Geological Society, Manchester

Transactions of the North of England Institute of Mining Engineers, Newcastle-upon-Tyne.

Transactions of the Royal Society of Canada, Montreal.

Transactions of the Royal Society of Edinburgh.

Transactions of the Academy of Science, St. Louis.

Verhandlungen der k. k. geologischen Reichsanstalt, Vienna.

Washington Philosophical Society, Bulletin.

Zeitschrift für analytische Chemie, Wiesbaden.

Zeitschrift für das Berg- Hütten- u. Salinen- wesen, Berlin.

Zeitschrift der Deutschen geologischen Gesellschaft, Berlin.

Zeitschrift für Krystallographie und Mineralogie, Leipzig.

Zeitschrift für Physikalische Chemie, Leipzig.

TEXT BOOKS.

In 1890-1891 the following text-books were used:

Olney's University Algebra.

---

*Gift of the Publishers.

Davies's Surveying, revised by Van Amringe.
Johnson's Surveying, 1891.
Atkinson's Ganot's Physics.
Peck's Mechanics.
Wentworth's Analytical Geometry.
Peck's Practical Calculus.
Greene's Graphical Analysis of Roof Trusses.
Merriman's Mechanics of Materials.
Merriman's Hydraulics, 1890.
Richter's Inorganic Chemistry.
Smith and Keller's Laboratory Notes.
Eliot and Storer's Qualitative Analysis.
Volhard and Zimmermann's Experiments in General Chemistry.
Fresenius's Qualitative Analysis, London Edition.
Fresenius's Quantitative Chemical Analysis, by O. D. Allen and S. W. Johnson.
Greenwood's Steel and Iron.
Smith's Electro-Chemical Analysis.
E. S. Dana's Text-book of Mineralogy.
A. Geikie's Text-book of Geology.
Williams's Applied Geology.
Peters's Modern American Methods of Copper Smelting.
Kunhardt's Art of Ore Dressing.
Holmes's Steam Engine.
Goodeve's Mechanism.
Slingo and Brooker's Electrical Engineering.

EXAMINATION QUESTIONS FOR ADMISSION TO THE MINING SCHOOL.

ARITHMETIC.

1. (1). Draw a line a decimeter long and divide it into centimeters.

   (2). What is the fundamental unit of length in the metric system.

2. (1). Describe the units of capacity and of weight in the metric system.

   (2). Draw a cubic centimeter, a cubic decimeter.

3. (1). Multiply $\frac{4}{5}$ by $\frac{3}{4}$ and explain the process.

   (2). Divide $\frac{9}{10}$ by $\frac{2}{15}$ and explain the process.

4. Change the common fractions to decimals in question 3, and perform the operations there required.

5. (1). B lost 5 per cent by selling a hektoliter of turpentine which cost $15. For what did he sell it a liter?

(2). If copper sells for 30 cents per kilogram, and the seller makes 40 per cent on the cost, after deducting 10 per cent from his asking price, what was the asking price?

6. (1) Having sold a consignment of goods on three per cent commission, the agent was instructed to invest the proceeds, after deducting his commission of 2 per cent. His whole commission was $265. What amount did he invest?

(2) If copper stock pays 8 per cent on the par value, at what price must it be purchased to pay 10 per cent on the cost.

7. (1) What is the interest of $16941.20 for 1 yr. 7 mo. and 28 days at 4¼ per cent.

(2). What sum of money, invested at 6¼ per cent, will produce $279,815 00 in 1 yr. and 6 mo.

8. (1) A ship's chronometer, set at Greenwich, points to 5 h. 40 min. 20 sec. P.M. when the sun is on the meridian; what is the ship's longitude?

(2) A steamer arrives at Halifax, 63° 35′ west at 4 h. 30 min. P. M ; the fact is telegraphed to New York without loss of time. The longitude of New York being 74° 1′ west, what is the time of the receipt of the telegram?

9. Extract the square root of 58.140625, of .0900316969.

10. Extract the cube root of 10460353203, of .000148877.

ALGEBRA.

Add $a-2b+c$, $4-3b-c+2d$, $4d-3c-a$, $7c-a-d$; and subtract $c-2b+a$ from the same.

2. (1). Multiply $x^6+x^5y-x^3y^3+xy^5+y^6$ by x^2-xy+y^2.

(2). Divide $y^8-2b^4y^4+b^8$ by $y^3+by^2+b^2y+b^3$.

3. (1). Find the factors of $324\,a^4b^2-64b^6$, of y^3+y^2-y-1 and of y^7+1.

(2). Prove that x^m-1 is exactly divisible by $x-1$, m being a positive integer,

4.   (1). What is the sum of $\dfrac{x}{(x-y)(x-z)}$ $\dfrac{y}{(y-z)(y-x)}$ and

$\dfrac{z}{(z-x)(z-y)}$.

(2.) Extract the square root of $4\,a^2+9\,b^2+16\,c^2-12ab$ $-24\,bc+16ac$.

5.   (1). Extract the square root of $30+12\sqrt{6}$.

(2). Solve $\dfrac{y-5}{2}-\dfrac{y-3}{4}+\dfrac{y+3}{5}-\dfrac{y+5}{6}=0$, and explain the transformations necessary for the solution.

6.   (1). Solve $x^2+px+q=0$ and give the conditions under which the roots are real and *unequal*, real and *equal*, imaginary, also when are they equal *numerically* with opposite signs.

(2). What is the sum of the two roots of the preceding equation? What is their product?

7.   (1). Solve $\sqrt{x-3}+\sqrt{3x+4}+\sqrt{x+2}=0$.

(2). Find the values of x and y in the independent, simultaneous equations $x+y=27$ and $x^3+y^3=5103$.

8.   Find the 6th and the 15th terms of $(x-y)^{25}$, reducing the numerical results to their prime factors and not performing the multiplications.

9.   (1). Prove that, if the corresponding terms of two proportions be multiplied together or divided by each other, the result, in either case, is a proportion.

(2). If $a:b=x:y=z:q$, Prove that $a:b=\dfrac{x+z}{y+q}$.

10.   (1). Find the sum of ten terms of the series 1, 8, 5, 7, etc.; Also the sum of the entire series, 27, 9, 3, 1, ⅓, etc.

(2). Under the influence of a force g, assumed to be constant, a body falls to the earth from a height h and rebounds one-half this distance, it then falls again to the earth and again rebounds one-half the last distance fallen, and so continues its motion; find the entire distance fallen and the time of falling this distance.

PLANE GEOMETRY.

Demonstrate the following propositions:

1. The sum of the angles of any plane triangle is equal to two right angles.
2. Show that each angle of an equiangular pentagon is $\frac{6}{5}$ of a right angle.
3. In the same or in equal circles, angles at the center have the same ratio as their intercepted arcs. (Two cases.)
4. An inscribed angle is measured by one-half the intercepted arc. (Three cases.)
5. Two triangles are similar when an angle of · the one is equal to an angle of the other, and the sides including these angles are proportional.
6. When a line is divided in extreme and mean ratio, the greater segment is one side of a regular decagon inscribed in a circle whose radius is the given line.
7. Similar polygons are to each other as the squares described on their homologous sides.
8. The square described upon the hypothenuse of a right triangle is equivalent to the sum of the squares described upon the other two sides.
9. (Problem) Given the perimeters of a regular inscribed and a similar circumscribed polygon, to compute the perimeters of regular inscribed and circumscribed polygons of double the number of sides.
10. (Problem) To compute the ratio of the circumference of a circle to its diameter.

SOLID AND SPHERICAL GEOMETRY.

Demostrate the following propositions:

1. If a straight line is perpendicular to each of two straight lines at their intersection, it is perpendicular to their plane.
2. If two triedral angles have the three face angles of the one equal, respectively, to the three face angles of the other, the corresponding diedral angles are equal,

3. Two triangular pyramids having equivalent bases and equal altitudes are equivalent.

4. The frustum of a triangular pyramid is equivalent to the sum of three pyramids whose common altitude is the altitude of the frustum, and whose bases are the lower base, the upper base and a mean proportional between the bases of the frustum.

5 In two polar triangles, each angle of one is measured by the supplement of the side lying opposite to it in the other.

6. The sum of the angles of a spherical triangle is greater than two and less than six right angles.

7. The area of a spherical triangle, expressed in spherical degrees, is numerically equal to the spherical excess of the triangle.

8. The area of a zone is equal to the product of its altitude by the circumference of a great circle.

9. (Problem). To find the volume of a spherical segment.

10. (Problem). To find the volume of that part of a sphere lying outside of a chord revolved parallel to its diameter and at a constant distance from it.

ELEMENTARY PHYSICS.

1. (1) Upon what property do most of the characteristic properties of matter depend.
   (2) Name three general and five characteristic properties of matter.

2. (1) Name and define the three states of matter.
   (2) Give Newton's laws of motion.

3. (1) Define work and energy, give the formula for the calculation of kinetic energy from weight and velocity.
   (2) Give the laws of freely falling bodies.

4. (1) How prove that the atmosphere has weight?
   (2) What is the object of experiments in the study of physics?

5. (1) Diagram and explain the operation of the hydrostatic press.
   (2) Define specific gravity and describe the experiments necessary to determine the specific gravity of an irregular solid. If the specific gravity of copper is 8.9, what is the

volume, in cubic centimeters of a mass of this metal which weighs 3.2 pounds ?

6. (1) What is the mechanical equivalent of heat ? To what is the heat. of a body due? Do the atoms or the molecules of a body set either themselves or one another in motion?

    (2) Give your idea of force. What is sound? What are the properties of a musical note? Diagram and explain the phonograph and the telephone.

7. (1) Explain the ways in which heat may be transmitted. Give some of its principal sources and effects. Change —40° F. to C. Upon what does the boiling point depend?

    (2) Define light. What constitutes the difference between light and heat? Between the different colors? What is the velocity of light ? Of sound in the air, at the temperature 0° C.?

8 (1) Give the laws of magnets. Give the laws of currents of electricity. Explain Ampère's theory of the magnet. How may magnets be made ?

    (2) Describe the experiments and the results obtained by the use of a galvanometer, a primary coil, a secondary coil, a battery and a magnet. Tabulate the results.

9. (1) Give Ohm's law. Define ohm, volt, ampère. Draw diagrams showing how to connect cells in series and in arc or abreast. If a Bunsen cell has an electromotive force of 1.8 volts and internal resistance of .9 ohm, show how to connect ten such cells to get the greatest current, the external resistance being 100 ohms?

    (2) Give some of the principal uses of electric currents. Explain how such currents are produced by a dynamo?

10. (1) What constitutes the difference between the operation of a dynamo and that of an electro-motor?

    (2) In charging a storage battery, what is stored up in it? What is meant by "the conservation of energy ?"

ASTRONOMY.

1 What is the general structure of the Solar System, and what is the physical constitution of the sun and its surroundings?

2. What is the physical constitution and special characteristics of the inner group of planets, including the moon?

3. What are the physical constitution and characteristics of the outer group of planets?
4. What are the aspects, forms and physical constitution of the comets, meteors and shooting stars.
5. What are nebulæ; new, variable and double stars, and upon what evidences are the views concerning them based?
6. How are stars located in the heavens? What are declination, right ascension. hour angle, latitude, longitude? and what are the six parts of the Polar triangle?
7. Describe the four kinds of time giving the maximum variations between them. How is the longitude of a place determined?
8. What is the general structure of the universe?
9. State clearly the Nebular Hypothesis, and give the evidence upon which it is based?
10. Give the general phenomena of the tides, their causes and laws.

BOOK-KEEPING.

1. Explain the use of day-book. journal and ledger. and state the rules for entering transactions in them.
2. What is a trial balance, and what is the process of making one?
3. Is a trial balance an absolute check? State reasons for your answer.
4. State the rules for crediting and debiting bills payable and bills receivable.

    In addition to questions of the above character, a record of supposed transactions is given to the candidate to enter in the proper manner in the different books. and he is required to make his own rulings.

BUILDINGS.

The main building now occupied by the Mining School was completed by the state in 1889, at a cost of $75,000. The building is constructed of Portage Entry sandstone, with a tile roof. It is heated and ventilated by steam, having two large boilers for heating, and an extra boiler for driving machinery.

The larger part of the site and grounds were donated to the school by the Honorable Jay A. Hubbell, to whom the organization of the school is chiefly due. The building has a large and independent supply of spring water, sufficient for all its present needs.

The main building is 109 feet by 53 feet, with a wing 37 feet by 25 feet. The interior portion of the building has been arranged so as to save the greatest amount of space possible for the laboratories and working rooms, consistent with safety to the structure and proper light. The halls have been reduced to a minimum. The plans of the four floors are appended: The basement floor is used for a Boiler Room, Weighing Room, Metal and Wood-Working Shops, and Assaying Laboratory. The first floor contains the Director's Room, Reading Room, Library, and Laboratories of General and Economic Geology, Petrography and Mineralogy. On the second floor are situated the Mathematical and other Recitation Rooms, together with the Laboratories for Physics, Drawing, Surveying and Mining Engineering. The third floor is devoted to the Chemical Laboratories, Chemical Lecture Room, Chemical Supply Room, Balance Room, etc.

During the Spring of 1889 the Legislature of the State of Michigan appropriated $104,000 for the furnishing of the new building, and for the expenses of the school for 1889-90. Under the provisions of that appropriation the Board of Control has equipped the various laboratories of the building, purchased collections, machinery, books, periodicals, etc.

A well appointed Stamp Mill and Ore Dressing Works completes the buildings belonging to the Mining School.

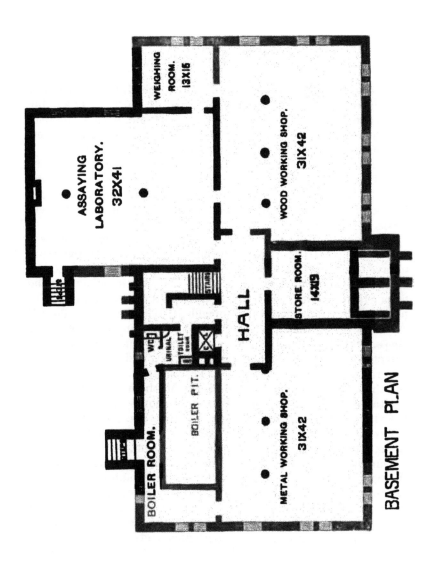

BASEMENT PLAN

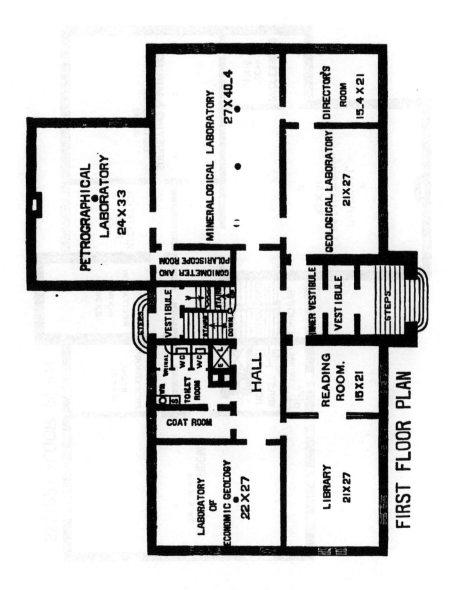

FIRST FLOOR PLAN

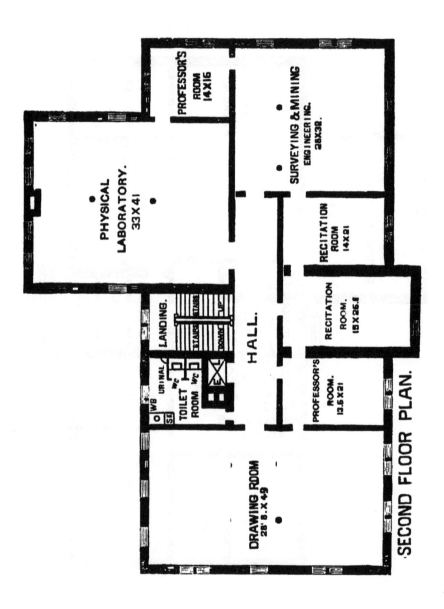

PROFESSOR'S ROOM 14X16

SURVEYING & MINING ENGINEERING. 28X38.

PHYSICAL LABORATORY. 33X41

RECITATION ROOM 14X21

LANDING.

STAIRS

ROOM

HALL.

RECITATION ROOM. 15X26.8

URINAL

WC

TOILET ROOM

WC

WB

SK

PROFESSOR'S ROOM. 13.5X21

DRAWING ROOM 28'8.X49

SECOND FLOOR PLAN.

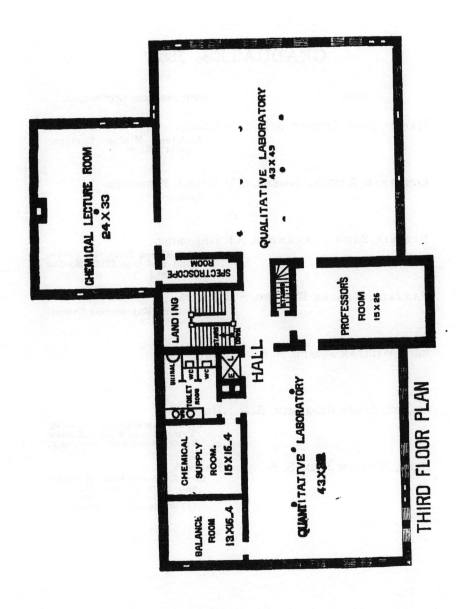

THIRD FLOOR PLAN

GRADUATES, 1888.

NAME.   RESIDENCE AND OCCUPATION.

HARRIS, JOHN LUTHER, S. B........Quincy.
>Assistant Mining Engineer,
>Quincy Mine.

LONGYEAR, EDMUND JOSEPH, S. B.Mesabi, Minnesota.
>Explorer.

PARNELL, SAM'L ALEXANDER, S.B Ishpeming.
>Chief Mining Engineer, Cleve-
>land and Iron Cliffs Mining
>Company.

PARNALL, WILLIAM EDWARD, S B.Ithaca.
>Electrical Engineering,Cornell
>University.

REID, WILLIAM JOSEPH, S. B......Ishpeming.

SEAGER, JAMES BENJAMIN, S. B...Hancock.
>Mining Engineer and Chemist,
>Tyler's Forks Mine and Lake
>Superior Redstone Company.

UREN, WILLIAM JOHN, S. B........Hancock.
>Civil Engineer, Mineral Range
>and Hancock and Calumet
>Railroads, and County Sur-
>veyor, Houghton County.

GRADUATES, 1889.

NAME.	RESIDENCE AND OCCUPATION.

CROZE, WALTER WILFRED JOS., S.B. . . Negaunee.
Chief Mining Engineer, Jackson Iron Company.

FARWELL, PAUL, S. B. . . . . Pueblo, Colorado.
Assistant Chemist, The Philadelphia Smelting and Refining Company.

*FESING, HERMAN WILLIAM, S. B. . . Iron Mountain.
Mining Engineer and Chemist. Hamilton Ore Company.

*HAAS, JACOB, S. B. . . . . Houghton.
Civil Engineer.

HOATSON, JOHN, S. B. . . . . Butte City.
Assistant Mining Engineer and Assayer, Butte and Boston Company.

PRYOR, REGINALD CHAPPLE . . . . Houghton.
Civil Engineer.

---

*See Graduates of 1890 for the second degree.

GRADUATES, 1890.

NAME.	RESIDENCE AND OCCUPATION.

DANIELL, JOSHUA, S. B...........Opechee.
> Assistant Mining Engineer, Tamarack. Osceola and Kearsarge Mines.

DRAKE, FRANK, S. B.............Negaunee.
> Chief Mining Engineer, Schlesinger Mining Company.

FESING, HERMAN WM., S. B., E. M .Iron Mountain.
> Mining Engineer and Chemist, Hamilton Ore Co.

HAAS, JACOB, S. B., E. M.........Houghton.
> Civil Engineer.

HODGSON, WILLIAM ADAMS, S. B...Houghton.

SUTTON, LINTON BEACH, S. B......Palmer.
> Mining Engineer and Chemist, Volunteer Mine.

WAKEFIELD, ARTHUR ALBERT, S.B..Milwaukee, Wis.

CALENDAR.

1890-1891.

Fall Term commences Monday morning, September 15, 1890.

Registration of Students, 9:10 A. M. Monday, Mining Engineering Room, Second Floor.

Exercises commence for the two upper classes, 10 A. M. Monday.

Examinations for admission and advanced standing commence 10 A. M. Monday.

November, Thanksgiving Recess, Wednesday noon until Monday morning.

Fall Term ends Friday evening, December 19, 1890.

Recess of two weeks.

Winter Term commences Monday morning, January 5, 1891.

Winter Term ends Friday evening, April 10, 1891.

Recess of nine days.

Spring Term commences Monday morning, April 20, 1891.

Spring Term ends Friday evening, May 29, 1891.

Summer recess.

Summer course in Surveying commences Monday morning, June 29, 1891.

Summer course in Surveying ends Friday evening, September 11, 1891.

Fall recess.

Fall Term commences Monday morning, September 14, 1891.

CALENDAR.

1891-1892.

Fall Term commences Monday morning, September 14, 1891.

Registration of Students, 9:10 A. M. Monday, Mining Engineering Room, Second Floor.

Exercises commence for the two upper classes, 10 A. M. Monday.

Examinations for admission and advanced standing commence 10 A. M. Monday.

November, Thanksgiving Recess, Wednesday noon until Monday morning.   •

Fall Term ends Friday evening, December 18, 1891.

Recess of two weeks.

Winter Term commences Monday morning, January 4, 1892.

Winter Term ends Friday evening, April 8, 1892.

Recess of nine days.

Spring Term commences Monday morning, April 18, 1892.

Spring Term ends Friday evening, May 27, 1892.

Summer recess.

Summer course in Surveying commences Tuesday morning, July 5, 1892.

Summer course in Surveying ends Friday evening, September 16, 1892.

Summer shop practice begins Monday morning, July 25, 1892.

Summer shop practice ends Friday evening, September 16, 1892.

Summer course in Field Geology begins Monday morning, July 25, 1892.

Summer course in Field Geology ends Friday evening, September 2, 1892.

Fall recess.

Fall Term commences Monday morning, September 19, 1892.

Fall Term ends December 23, 1892.

CALENDAR 1891.

	S	M	T	W	T	F	S		S	M	T	W	T	F	S
Jan.	..	..	..	..	1	2	3	July.	..	..	..	1	2	3	4
	4	5	6	7	8	9	10		5	6	7	8	9	10	11
	11	12	13	14	15	16	17		12	13	14	15	16	17	18
	18	19	20	21	22	23	24		19	20	21	22	23	24	25
	25	26	27	28	29	30	31		26	27	28	29	30	31	..
	..	..	..	..	..	..	..								
Feb.	1	2	3	4	5	6	7	Aug.	..	..	..	..	..	..	1
	8	9	10	11	12	13	14		2	3	4	5	9	7	8
	15	16	17	18	19	20	21		9	10	11	12	13	14	15
	22	23	24	25	26	27	28		16	17	18	19	20	21	22
	..	..	..	..	..	..	..		23	24	25	26	27	28	29
									30	31	..	..	..	..	..
Mar.	1	2	3	4	5	6	7	Sept.	..	..	1	2	3	4	5
	8	9	10	11	12	13	14		6	7	8	9	10	11	12
	15	16	17	18	19	20	21		13	14	15	16	17	18	19
	22	23	24	25	26	27	28		20	21	22	23	24	25	26
	29	30	31	..	..	..	..		27	28	29	30	..	..	..
April.	..	..	..	1	2	3	4	Oct.	..	..	..	..	1	2	3
	5	6	7	8	9	10	11		4	5	6	7	8	9	10
	12	13	14	15	16	17	18		11	12	13	14	15	16	17
	19	20	21	22	23	24	25		18	19	20	21	22	23	24
	26	27	28	29	30	..	..		25	26	27	28	29	30	31
May.	..	..	..	..	..	1	2	Nov.	1	2	3	4	5	6	7
	3	4	5	6	7	8	9		8	9	10	11	12	13	14
	10	11	12	13	14	15	16		15	16	17	18	19	20	21
	17	18	19	20	21	22	23		22	23	24	25	26	27	28
	24	25	26	27	28	29	30		29	30	..	..	..	..	..
	31	..	..	..	..	..	..		..	..	..	..	..	..	..
June.	..	1	2	3	4	5	6	Dec.	..	..	1	2	3	4	5
	7	8	9	10	11	12	13		6	7	8	9	10	11	12
	14	15	16	17	18	19	20		13	14	15	16	17	18	19
	21	22	23	24	25	26	27		20	21	22	23	24	25	26
	28	29	30	..	..	..	..		27	28	29	30	31	..	..

CALENDAR 1892

	S	M	T	W	T	F	S			S	M	T	W	T	F	S
Jan						1	2		**July.**						1	2
	3	4	5	6	7	8	9			3	4	5	6	7	8	9
	10	11	12	13	14	15	16			10	11	12	13	14	15	16
	17	18	19	20	21	22	23			17	18	19	20	21	22	23
	24	25	26	27	28	29	30			24	25	26	27	28	29	30
	31									31						
Feb		1	2	3	4	5	6		**Aug.**		1	2	3	4	5	6
	7	8	9	10	11	12	13			7	8	9	10	11	12	13
	14	15	16	17	18	19	20			14	15	16	17	18	19	20
	21	22	23	24	25	26	27			21	22	23	24	25	26	27
	28	29								28	29	30	31			
Mar.			1	2	3	4	5		**Sept.**					1	2	3
	6	7	8	9	10	11	12			4	5	6	7	8	9	10
	13	14	15	16	17	18	19			11	12	13	14	15	16	17
	20	21	22	23	24	25	26			18	19	20	21	22	23	24
	27	28	29	30	31					25	26	27	28	29	30	
April						1	2		**Oct.**							1
	3	4	5	6	7	8	9			2	3	4	5	6	7	8
	10	11	12	13	14	15	16			9	10	11	12	13	14	15
	17	18	19	20	21	22	23			16	17	18	19	20	21	22
	24	25	26	27	28	29	30			23	24	25	26	27	28	29
										30	31					
May.	1	2	3	4	5	6	7		**Nov.**			1	2	3	4	5
	8	9	10	11	12	13	14			6	7	8	9	10	11	12
	15	16	17	18	19	20	21			13	14	15	16	17	18	19
	22	23	24	25	26	27	28			20	21	22	23	24	25	26
	29	30	31							27	28	29	30			
June.					1	2	3	4	**Dec.**					1	2	3
	5	6	7	8	9	10	11			4	5	6	7	8	9	10
	12	13	14	15	16	17	18			11	12	13	14	15	16	17
	19	20	21	22	23	24	25			18	19	20	21	22	23	24
	26	27	28	29	30					25	26	27	28	29	30	31

Michigan Mining School.

Houghton, Michigan.

1891–1892.

HOUGHTON, MICHIGAN.
PUBLISHED BY THE MINING SCHOOL.
1892.

CATALOGUE

OF THE

MICHIGAN MINING SCHOOL.

WITH STATEMENTS CONCERNING THE INSTITUTION AND
ITS COURSES OF INSTRUCTION.

HOUGHTON, MICHIGAN.

1891–1892.

HOUGHTON, MICH., U. S. A.
PUBLISHED BY THE MINING SCHOOL.
JANUARY, 1893.

PRESSES OF
DARIUS D. THORP
LANSING, MICH.

TABLE OF CONTENTS.

PAGE.

Board of Control... 1
Board of Visitors....................................... 2
Board of the Geological Survey......................... 3
Officers of the Michigan Mining School and Geological Survey   4, 5
Faculty of the Michigan Mining School................. 6
Register of Students, 1891–1892....................... 7–15
Register of Students, Fall Term, 1892................. 16–28
Requirements for Admission............................ 29–34
The Course of Instruction............................. 35–38
Outline of the Courses of Study....................... 39–56
Departments of Instruction............................ 57–113
    Mathematics..................................... 57, 58
    Physics... 58–61
    Drawing... 61–68
    Chemistry....................................... 68–77
    General Chemistry............................... 68, 69
    Qualitative Analysis............................ 69, 70
    Quantitative Analysis........................... 70, 71
    Metallurgical Analysis.......................... 71, 72
    Synthetic Chemistry............................. 72, 73
    Assaying.. 73, 74
    Ore Dressing.................................... 74–76
    Metallurgy...................................... 76, 77
    Mechanical Engineering.......................... 78, 81
    Mechanics of Materials.......................... 81, 82
    Summer Course in Shop Practice.................. 82–84
    Electrical Engineering.......................... 84, 85
    Plane Surveying................................. 86
    Summer Course in Surveying...................... 86–90
    Mine Surveying.................................. 90
    Hydraulics...................................... 91
    Mining.. 91–94
    Crystallography................................. 94
    Mineralogy...................................... 95–99
    Petrography..................................... 100–103
    Lithology....................................... 103, 104
    Paleontology.................................... 105

Departments of Instruction—*Continued.*

	PAGE.
Stratigraphical and Historical Geology	106
Physical Geology	107
Economic Geology	108–111
Summer Course in Geology	111, 112
Theses	113
Organization	114, 115
Regulations of the School	116–119
Location	120
Mining Industries of Michigan	121–123
Expenses	124–126
Employment	127–130
Prizes and Scholarships	131–136
The Longyear Prizes	131–133
The Charles E. Wright Scholarship	133
The Norrie Scholarship	134, 135
The Longyear Fund	135, 136
Degrees and Graduate Instruction	137–139
Collections	140, 141
Library	142
Reading Room and Periodicals	143–149
Text-Books	150, 151
Examination Questions for Admission	152–160
Buildings and Plans	161–166
Basement Plan	163
First Floor Plan	164
Second Floor Plan	165
Third Floor Plan	166
Graduates	167–170
School Associations	171–172
Calendar	173–175

TABLES AND PLATES:

Table I.—Three Years' Course, to face page 39.
Table II.—Four Years' Course, to face page 47.
Plan of Drawing Room, to face page 66.
Mechanical Laboratories and Assay Room, to face page 83.
Tables of Minerals Studied, to follow page 97.
Classification of Rocks, to face page 104.

BOARD OF CONTROL OF THE MINING SCHOOL.

1891-1892.

	Term Expires.
Hon. Jay Abel Hubbell, Houghton	June 9, 1893
Hon. Michael Chambers, St. Ignace	June 9, 1893
John Monroe Longyear, Marquette	June 9, 1895
Alfred Kidder, Marquette	June 9, 1895
James Renrick Cooper, Hancock	June 9, 1897
Preston Carpenter Firth West, Calumet	June 9, 1897

OFFICERS OF THE BOARD OF CONTROL.

PRESIDENT OF THE BOARD OF CONTROL,
HON. JAY ABEL HUBBELL.

SECRETARY OF THE BOARD OF CONTROL.
ALLEN FORSYTH REES.

*DIRECTOR OF THE MINING SCHOOL,
MARSHMAN EDWARD WADSWORTH.

†TREASURER AND PURCHASING AGENT OF THE MICHIGAN MINING SCHOOL,
ALLEN FORSYTH REES.

* All letters of inquiry, applications for catalogues, admission, etc., should be sent to the Director.

† All communications concerning purchases, bills, etc., should be sent to the Treasurer.

BOARD OF VISITORS TO THE MINING SCHOOL.

Sept. 7th, 1891, to Sept. 5th, 1892.

Hon. DAVID AUGUSTUS HAMMOND. CHARLOTTE, *Chairman.*

Hon. PERRY FRANCIS POWERS, CADILLAC.

SAMUEL EMORY WHITNEY, DETROIT.

Sept. 5th, 1892 to September 4th, 1893.

PROF. MORTIMER ELWYN COOLEY, ANN ARBOR, *Chairman.*

EDWARD LEROY PARMENTER, VULCAN.

HUGH BROWN, LANSING.

BOARD OF THE GEOLOGICAL SURVEY OF MICHIGAN.

1890-1892.

Hon. EDWIN BARUCH WINANS,

Governor of the State of Michigan, President of the Board.

Hon. FERRIS SMITH FITCH,

Superintendent of Public Instruction, Secretary of the Board.

Hon. SAMUEL S. BABCOCK,

President of the State Board of Education.

OFFICERS OF THE MICHIGAN MINING SCHOOL AND OF THE STATE GEOLOGICAL SURVEY.

MARSHMAN EDWARD WADSWORTH, A. B. (Bowdoin College)
A. M., Ph. D. (Harvard University).
Director and State Geologist,
Professor of Mineralogy, Petrography and Geology.

GEORGE AUGUSTUS KOENIG. M. E. (Polytechnikum, Karlsruhe)
A. M., Ph. D. (University of Heidelberg).
Professor of Chemistry, and Chemist on the Geological Survey.

LUCIUS LEE HUBBARD, A. B. (Harvard University), LL. B.
(Boston University), A. M , Ph. D. (University of Bonn).
Assistant in Mineralogy, and on the Geological Survey.

ARTHUR EDWIN HAYNES, M. S., M. Ph. (Hillsdale College),
Professor of Mathematics and Physics.

HORACE BUSHNELL PATTON, A. B. (Amherst College),
Ph. D. (University of Heidelberg),
Instructor in Mineralogy and Petrography, and Assistant on the
Geological Survey.

ALFRED CHURCH LANE, A. M., Ph. D. (Harvard University),
Instructor in Petrography and Geology, and Assistant on the
Geological Survey.

EDGAR KIDWELL, A. M., (Georgetown University), M. E. (University
of Pennsylvania).
Professor of Mechanical and Electrical Engineering.

FRED FRALEY SHARPLESS. S. B. (University of Michigan),
Professor of Metallurgy, and Chemist on the Geological Survey.

FRED WARNER DENTON. C. E. (Columbia College School of Mines),
Professor of Civil and Mining Engineering, and Assistant on the
Geological Survey.

WALTER JOHN BALDWIN, S. B. (University of Michigan),
Assistant in Surveying.

CARROLL LIVINGSTON HOYT, M. E. (Cornell University).
Instructor in Mechanical Engineering and Drawing.

ARTHUR EDMUND SEAMAN,
Assistant in Mineralogy, and on the Geological Survey.

ERWIN HUNTINGTON MCDONALD,
Assistant in Surveying.

ROBERT IRWIN REES,
Librarian and Clerk.

JOHN BONE WATSON,
Draughtsman for the Geological Survey.

ALEXANDER CRAIG,
Assistant in the Machine Shops.

———

HENRY GIBBS,
Janitor and Supply Clerk.

PATRICK ROBERT DILLON,
Engineer and Assistant Janitor.

MISS KATE KILLIAN,
Stenographer and Typewriter for the Mining School.

MISS HELEN MARY RYAN,
Stenographer and Typewriter for the Geological Survey.

JOHN BRIMACOMBE,
Janitor's Assistant.

FACULTY OF THE MINING SCHOOL.

MARSHMAN EDWARD WADSWORTH, A. M., Ph. D., DIRECTOR.
Professor of Mineralogy, Petrography and Geology.

GEORGE AUGUSTUS KOENIG, M. E., A. M., Ph. D.,
Professor of Chemistry.

ARTHUR EDWIN HAYNES, M. S., M. Ph.,
Professor of Mathematics and Physics, Secretary of the Faculty.

EDGAR KIDWELL, A. M., M. E.,
Professor of Mechanical and Electrical Engineering.

FRED FRALEY SHARPLESS, S. B.,
Professor of Metallurgy.

FRED WARNER DENTON, C. E.,
Professor of Civil and Mining Engineering.

REGISTER OF STUDENTS

FOR THE SCHOOL YEAR, 1891 1892.

GRADUATE STUDENTS.

Name.	Residence.	Room.
BAILEY, CHARLES EMERSON, A. B. (Marietta College). Mineralogy.	*Quincy Mine, Hancock.*	Mr. Bailey's.
BASADRE, GORGE, E. M. (School of Mines, Lima, Peru). Assaying and Ore Dressing.	*Tacna, Peru.*	Mr. E. R. Penberthy's.
BOSSERT, OTTO HENRY, E. M. Chemistry.	*Milwaukee, Wis.*	Mrs. Rice's.
DENGLER, THEODORE, E. M. Chemistry.	*Chicago, Ill.*	Mr. Cameron's.
FINK, EDWARD, E. M. Chemistry.	*Milwaukee, Wis.*	Mrs. E. M. Hoar's.
JOYCE, CHARLES FRANCIS, S. B. (University of Wisconsin). Chemistry and Assaying.	*De Pere, Wis.*	
LAWTON, CHARLES LATHAM, S. B. (Michigan Agricultural College).	*Palmer.*	Butterfield House.
O'BRIEN, WILLIAM JAMES, A. B. (Detroit College), Chemistry.	*Detroit.*	Bank Building.

CLASS OF 1892.

Name.	Residence.	Room.
COLWELL, ALFRED BUNDY,	*Appleton, Wis.,*	
		Mrs. Douglass's.
ROPES, LEVERETT SMITH,	*Ishpeming,*	
		Mrs. Douglass's.

CLASS OF 1893.

Name.	Residence	Room.
ABBOTT, AI ARTHUR, S. B. (Michigan Agricultural College),	*Holt.*	Mrs. P. Didier's.
CHURCH, GEORGE BATCHELOR,	*Flint.*	Mrs. Alford's.
CRANSON, ROBERT EDWARD,	*St. Johns.*	Rev. W. R. Cross's.
FISHER, JAMES,	*Hancock.*	Mr. Fisher's.
GILLIES, DONALD,	*Lake Linden.*	Mrs. Alford's
HARRINGTON, FREDERICK LUCE,	*Port Huron.*	Mrs. E. M. Hoar's.
KIRK, MARCUS EUGENE,	*Sturgis.*	Mrs. J. Thomas's.
McDONALD, ERWIN HUNTINGTON,	*Lyon Mountain, N. Y.*	Butterfield House.
MASON, RUSSELL TEAL,	*Boulder, Col.*	Keweenaw Club.
OPPEN, WILLIAM ADOLPH,	*Milwaukee, Wis.*	Mr. Penberthy's.
SHATTUCK, HORACE VOLNEY,	*Adrian.*	Mrs. E. M. Hoar's.
SILLIMAN, ARTHUR PARKS, B. L. (University of Wisconsin),	*Hudson, Wis.*	Mrs. Burrows.
TOWER, LOUIS LOVELL,	*Ionia.*	Mrs. Rice's.
TRENGOVE, SAMUEL REED,	*Lake Linden.*	Mrs. Brimacombe's.
WATERS, ALBERT LATCHA, S. B. (Michigan Agricultural College),	*Spring Lake.*	Keweenaw Club.
WATSON, JOHN BONE,	*Opechee.*	Mrs. Brimacombe's.

CLASS OF 1894.

Name.	Residence.	Room.
ASHBAUGH, LEWIS EUGENE,	Hillsdale.	
		Professor Haynes's.
BARSTOW, GEORGE MITCHELL,	Detroit.	
		Mrs. Beard's.
BRULÉ, FRED JOSEPH,	Lake Linden.	
		Miss Kelly's.
BURRALL, FREDERICK PECK,	Battle Creek.	
		Keweenaw Club.
CAMERON, DONALD,	St. Louis.	
		Mr. T. Davey's.
CORRIGAN, JOHN ALEXANDER,	Cleveland, Ohio.	
		Dallmeyer Block.
DURFEE, ELMER WHIPPLE,	Grand Rapids.	
		Mr. Hummel's.
EBY, JOHN HENRY, B. A. (Franklin and Marshall College).	Lancaster, Pa.	
		Mr. Hummel's.
HARRIS, JOHN MORTIMER,	Lake Linden.	
		Mrs. Brimacombe's.
HARVEY, JAMES M., JR.,	Constantine.	
		Butterfield House.
HARVEY, WILLIAM ARTHUR,	Toronto, Canada.	
		Mr. J. E. Edwards's.
JAMES, HOUGHTON EDWARD,	Houghton.	
		Mrs. James's.
JONES, MAURICE LINDLEY,	Benton Harbor.	
		Keweenaw Club.
KAMPE, WESLEY EDWARD, A. B., B. S. (Hanover College).	Madison, Ind.	
		Mrs. Dallmeyer's.
KNIGHT, JOHN ALEXANDER,	Ionia.	
		Professor Haynes's.
KIRCHEN, JOHN GEORGE,	Lake Linden.	
		Miss Kelly's.
LOCKLIN, LEWIS CASS,	North Adams.	
		Professor Haynes's.

Name.	Residence.	Room.
McCauley, James.	Hancock.	
		Mr. McCauley's.
McCormick, Edward Patrick,	Calumet.	
		Mrs. Burrows's.
MacFarlane, George Campbell,	Bay City.	
		Mrs. Rashleigh's.
McGrath, Michael,	Hancock.	
		Mr. McGrath's.
Mason, Clarence George,	Hancock.	
		Mr. Mason's.
Moore, Carlton Franklin,	Marquette.	
		Mr. Sparling's.
Newton, Lee Luke,	Lake Linden.	
		Miss Kelly's.
Parks, Henry James,	Lake Linden.	
		Miss Kelly's.
Peiffer, Philip,	Lake Linden.	
		Mrs. P. Didier's.
Ridley, Frederick William,	Newcastle-on-Tyne, England.	
		Mrs. E. M. Hoar's.
Riedinger, Lewis Edward,	Marquette.	
		Mr. Penberthy's.
Rourke, Jerry,	Hancock.	
		Mr. Rourke's.
Seeley, Burton Tyndall,	Genesee Township.	
		Mr. Sparling's.
Stringham, Joseph, Jr.,	Saginaw.	
		Rev. W. R. Cross's.
Sullivan, Dennis,	Lake Linden.	
		Mrs. Burrows's.
Williams, Bert Henry.	Champion.	
		Mr. Ormsby's.
Wraith, William,	Newcastle, Col.	
		Mrs. Dallmeyer's.

SPECIAL STUDENTS.

Name.	Residence.	Room.
BAWDEN, WILLIAM EDWARD, Mathematics, Physics and Draw- ing.	*Bessemer.,*	
		Mr. Stringer's.
BENSON, JOHN SYDNEY, Chemistry.	*Wardner, Idaho.*	
		Keweenaw Club.
BURNHAM, MATTHEW HOWARD. Mineralogy, Chemistry and Met- allurgy.	*Pasadena, Cal.*	
		Bank Building.
CORGAN, WILL JOHN, Mathematics.	*Ontonagon.*	
		Mr. Chappell's.
CORRY, ANDREW VAN, Assaying.	*Butte City, Montana.*	
		Butterfield House.
CROZE, CHARLES EDWARD, Shop Practice.	*Houghton.*	
		Mr. Croze's.
CROZE, LAWRENCE LUDGER, Mathematics and Chemistry.	*Houghton.*	
		Mr. Croze's.
CROZE, JOSEPH HENRY, Shop Practice.	*Houghton.*	
		Mr. Croze's.
GLANVILLE, JAMES GUNDRY, Drawing.	*Lake Linden.*	
		Mrs. Brimacombe's.
GOODELL, HORATIO STEWART, Shop Practice.	*Detroit.*	
		Mr. Goodell's.
GOTTSTEIN, PAUL, Mathematics and Drawing.	*Houghton.*	
		Mr. Gottstein's.

Name.	Residence.	Room.

McCHRYSTAL, JACKSON CARLOS,
Geology, Chemistry, Metallurgy
and Ore Dressing.

Eureka, Utah.

Mrs. Rice's.

PARSONS, ALBERT WILCOX,
Mathematics and Drawing. *Adrian.*

Mrs. Krellwitz's.

REES, ROBERT IRWIN,
Physics. *Houghton.*

Mr. A. F. Rees's.

ROSS, GEORGE EDWARD,
Chemistry. *Hancock.*

Mr. Ross's.

SCHLICTING, RHINO,
Mathematics and Chemistry. *Lake Linden.*

Mrs. Schlicting's.

SEVERANCE, LEMUEL,
Mathematics. *Lake Linden.*

Mrs. A. Harris's.

WARNER, GEORGE EBEN,
Mathematics and Drawing. *Boulder, Montana.*

Mr. Sparling's.

REGISTER OF STUDENTS

FALL TERM, 1892.

2

GRADUATE STUDENTS

Name.	Residence.	Room.
DRAKE, FRANK, S. B., Mechanical and Electrical Engineering, Geology, Petrography, Mineralogy and Chemistry.	*Portland, Oregon.*	Keweenaw Club.
KAMPE, WESLEY EDWARD, A. B., S. B. (Hanover College), Chemistry.	*Madison, Ind.*	Butterfield House.
STILLMAN, ARTHUR PARKS, B. L. (University of Wisconsin), Chemistry, Geology, Mathematics and Electrical Engineering.	*Hudson, Wis.*	Mrs. Burrows's.

CLASS OF 1893.

Name.	Residence.	Room.
ABBOTT, AI ARTHUR, S. B. (Michigan Agricultural College),	*Holt.*	
		Mrs. P. Didier's.
CHURCH, GEORGE BATCHELOR.	*Flint.*	
		Mrs. Alford's.
CRANSON, ROBERT EDWARD,	*St. Johns.*	
		Mr. Cranson's.
FISHER, JAMES,	*Hancock.*	
		Mr. Fisher's.
GILLIES, DONALD,	*Lake Linden.*	
		Mrs. Alford's.
HARRINGTON, FREDERICK LUCE,	*Port Huron.*	
		Mrs. E. M. Hoar's.
HONNOLD, WILLIAM LINCOLN,	*Camp Point. Ill.*	
		Mrs. Douglass's.
KIRK, MARCUS EUGENE,	*Cincinnati, Ohio.*	
		Mrs. Thomas's.
McDONALD, ERWIN HUNTINGTON,	*Lyon Mountain, N. Y.*	
		Butterfield House.
McDONALD, WILLIAM NEAL,	*Houghton.*	
		Mr. McDonald's.
ROPES, LEVERETT SMITH,	*Ishpeming.*	
		Mrs. Douglass's.
TOWER, LOUIS LOVELL,	*Ionia.*	
		Mrs. Rice's.
TRENGOVE, SAMUEL REED,	*Lake Linden.*	
		Mrs. Brimacombe's
WATERS, ALBERT LATCHA, S. B. (Michigan Agricultural College),	*Spring Lake.*	
		Keweenaw Club.

CLASS OF 1894.

Name.	Residence.	Room.
BRULÉ, FREDERICK JOSEPH,	*Lake Linden.*	
		Miss Kelly's.
BURRALL, FREDERICK PECK,	*Battle Creek.*	
		Mr. Cameron's.
CAMERON, DONALD,	*St. Louis.*	
		Mr. Davey's.
CORRIGAN, JOHN ALEXANDER.	*Cleveland, Ohio.*	
		Dallmeyer Block.
DURFEE, ELMER WHIPPLE,	*Grand Rapids.*	
		Mr. Hummel's.
EBY, JOHN HENRY, B. A. (Franklin and Marshall College).	*Lancaster, Pa.*	
		Mr. Hummel's.
JONES, MAURICE LINDLEY.	*Benton Harbor.*	
		Mrs. E. M. Hoar's.
KIRCHEN, JOHN GEORGE,	*Lake Linden.*	
		Dallmeyer Block.
KNIGHT, JOHN ALEXANDER,	*Ionia.*	
		Miss Jones's.
MASON, CLARENCE GEORGE,	*Hancock.*	
		Mr. Mason's.
McCAULEY, JAMES,	*Hancock.*	
		Mr. McCauley's.
McCORMICK, EDWARD PATRICK,	*Calumet.*	
		Mrs. Burrows's.
McFARLANE, GEORGE CAMPBELL,	*Bay City.*	
		Mrs. Beard's.
McGRATH, MICHAEL,	*Hancock.*	
		Mr. McGrath's.
MOORE, CARLTON FRANKLIN,	*Marquette.*	
		Mr. Sparling's.
NEWTON, LEE LUKE,	*Lake Linden.*	
		Miss Kelly's.
PARKS, HENRY JAMES,	*Lake Linden.*	
		Dallmeyer Block.
PEIFFER, PHILIP,	*Lake Linden.*	
		Mrs. P. Didier's.

Name.	Residence.	Room.
RIDLEY, FREDERICK WILLIAM,	*Newcastle-on-Tyne, England.*	
		Mrs. E. M. Hoar's.
RIEDINGER, LOUIS EDWARD.	*Marquette.*	
		Mrs. Rice's.
ROURKE, JERRY,	*Hancock.*	
		Mr. Rourke's.
SEELEY, BURTON TYNDALL.	*Genesee Township.*	
		Mr. Sparling's.
STRINGHAM, JOSEPH, JR.,	*Saginaw.*	
		Mr. Stringham's.
WILLIAMS, BERT HENRY,	*Champion.*	
		Mr. Ormsby's.
WRAITH, WILLIAM,	*Newcastle, Col.*	
		Mrs. Dallmeyer's.

CLASS OF 1895.

Name.	Residence.	Room.
BARLOW, ROYCE ELWIN.	*Hastings.*	
		Mrs. Trim's.
BARSTOW, GEORGE MITCHELL,	*Detroit.*	
		Mrs. Beard's.
BATES, ARMAND WALTER,	*Ironwood.*	
		Mrs. Dallmayer's.
BEEN, JOHN THEODORE,	*Skanee.*	
		Mr. Lange's.
CALHOUN, CHARLES ANDREW,	*Albert Mines, Albert Co., New Brunswick.*	
		Mrs. Mitchell's.
CAMERON, WILLIAM,	*St. Louis.*	
		Mr. Davey's.
CHANDLER, MARION INEZ,	*Hancock.*	
		Mr. Chandler's.
CLARK, GEORGE CLOUGH,	*Springfield, Mo.*	
		Mrs. Brimacombe's.
COLEMAN, MILTON WATSON,	*Calumet.*	
		Hartmann Block.
CORGAN, WILL JOHN,	*Ontonagon.*	
		Mr. Chappell's.
DAVIS, CARL RAYMOND,	*Helena, Mont.*	
		Mr. Lange's.
DOCKERY, LOVE,	*Love, Miss.*	
		Mrs. Rashleigh's.
DuBOIS, WILBUR FISK,	*Mobile Ala.*	
		Mr. Cameron's.
EMLAW, HARLOW STIGAND,	*Grand Haven.*	
		Mr. E. K. Lord's.
ESSELSTYN, JOHN NELSON,	*Lansing.*	
		Mr. J. Edwards's.
GREEN, FRED TUBELL,	*Berlin, Canada.*	
		Mrs. S. Gray's.
HOLBERT, HENRY HOFFMAN,	*St. Clair.*	
		Mr. Trims's.
HOOPER, JAMES KNIGHT,	*Crystal Falls.*	
		Mrs. Brimacombe's.

Name.	Residence.	Room.
KENT, BAMLET,	Calumet.	
		Hartmann Block.
MARTIN, NICHOLAS JOHN,	Bessemer.	
		Mr. Sparling's.
McDONALD, DONALD,	Calumet.	
		Mrs. Brimacombe's.
McINTYRE, CHARLES,	Lake Linden.	
		Miss Jones's.
MONROE WILLIAM DEARBORN,	Bath.	
		Mrs. Cameron's.
ORR, JOHN FORREST,	L'Anse.	
		Mr. McCurdy's.
PAULL, STEPHEN, JR.,	Calumet.	
		Mr. McCurdy's.
RASHLEIGH, WILLIAM JOHN,	Houghton.	
		Mrs. Rashleigh's.
ROSE, ROBERT SHELDON,	Fon du Lac, Wis.	
		Mr. Lange's.
ROWE, DAVID PRESCOTT,	Chicago, Ill.	
		Mrs. Dallmeyer's.
SLOCK, GEORGE,	Houghton.	
		Mr. Slock's.
UPHAM, WILLIAM ERASTUS,	Duluth, Minn.	
		Mrs. Burrows's.
WEARNE, WILLIAM, JR.,	Red Jacket.	
		Mr. McCurdy's.
WEBB, FREDERICK MERKLEE,	River Edge, N. J.	
		Mr. Lange's.
WOOD, ROBERT JOHN,	Cleveland, Ohio.	
		Dallmeyer Block.
WRIGHT, LOUIS ALDRO,	San Antonio, Texas.	
		Keweenaw Club.
WYCKOFF, FRED CARLTON,	Jacobsville.	
		Mr. Chandler's.

SPECIAL STUDENTS.

————

Name.	Residence.	Room.
BENSON, JOHN SYDNEY, Chemistry and Mineralogy.	*Wardner, Idaho.*	Mr. Livermore's.
CRUSE, JAMES ALFRED, Mathematics and Drawing.	*Red Jacket.*	Mrs. Brimacombe's.
OPPEN, WILLIAM ADOLPH, Chemistry.	*Milwaukee, Wis.*	Mr. Livermore's.
ROSS, GEORGE EDWARD, Chemistry.	*Hancock.*	Mr. Ross's.
SEAMAN, ARTHUR EDMUND, Petrography.	*Houghton.*	Mr. Seaman's.
WATSON, JOHN BONE, Geology.	*Opecher.*	Mrs. Brimacombe's.

SUMMARY.

1891-1892.

Graduate Students	8
Class of 1892	2
Class of 1893	16
Class of 1894	34
Special Students	18
	78

BY COUNTRIES AND STATES.

California		4
Canada		1
Colorado		2
England		1
Idaho		1
Illinois		4
Indiana		4
Michigan { Upper Peninsula	34 }	57
Michigan { Lower Peninsula	23 }	57
Montana		2
New York		1
Ohio		4
Pennsylvania		4
Peru		4
Utah		1
Wisconsin		6
		78

SUMMARY.

Fall Term, 1892.

Graduate Students	8
Class of 1893	14
Class of 1894	25
Class of 1895	35
Special Students	6
	88

BY COUNTRIES AND STATES.

Alabama	1
Canada	1
Colorado	1
England	1
Idaho	1
Illinois	2
Indiana	1
Michigan { Upper Peninsula........ 38 } { Lower Peninsula........21 }	59
Minnesota	1
Mississippi	1
Missouri	1
Montana	1
New Brunswick	1
New Jersey	1
New York	1
Ohio	3
Oregon	1
Pennsylvania	1
Texas	1
Wisconsin	3
	88

AVERAGE AGE OF STUDENTS.

1891-1892.

Special Students	22 years.
Class of 1894	20½ years.
Class of 1893	21½ years.
Class of 1892	24 years.
Graduate Students	24 years.
Average Age of all Students	21½ years.

Fall Term, 1892

Special Students	25 years.
Class of 1895	21 years.
Class of 1894	21 years.
Class of 1893	23 years.
Graduate Students	23 years.
Average Age of all Students	22 years.

REQUIREMENTS FOR ADMISSION.

Candidates who are twenty years of , age and over and who desire to enter the regular course will be examined in :

ARITHMETIC AND METRIC SYSTEM : either Wentworth's High School, Ray's Higher, Olney's Practical, Robinson's Practical, or an equivalent.

ALGEBRA, THROUGH QUADRATIC EQUATIONS : either Wentworth's School, Olney's Complete, Robinson's Elementary, Loomis's Elements, Van Velzer and Slichter's School, or an equivalent.

GEOMETRY—PLANE, SOLID AND SPHERICAL : either Davies's Legendre revised by Van Amringe, Wentworth's New, Olney's Revised, Chauvenet's revised by Byerly, Peck's Manual, or an equivalent.

BOOK-KEEPING—Elements of Single and Double Entry : either Bryant and Stratton's, Mayhew's, the first 62 pages of The New Complete Book-keeping, or an equivalent.

ELEMENTARY PHYSICS : either Gage's or Avery's Elements, or an equivalent.

ELEMENTS OF ASTRONOMY : either Newcomb's Popular or School, Young's High School, or an equivalent.

Or the candidate, if of the required age (twenty years or over), may present a certificate from the superintendent or principal of a high school, academy or seminary in good standing, certifying that the candidate has studied not less than one year in that institution, and has been examined by the superintendent or principal that signed the certificate, and that the candidate has passed in the subjects required for admission to this institution with a rank of not less than eighty-five on a scale of one hundred in each and every study required for admission.

Candidates for admission who are under twenty years of age must either take an examination at the Mining School in all subjects required for admission : or they must present a certificate from the superintendent or principal of some reputable high school, academy or seminary, that they have completed one of the *regular courses* of study in that school and *have graduated,* obtaining a rank of not less than eighty-five in a scale of one hundred in each and every subject required for admission to the Mining School, and that the candidates's rank in all other studies in the school's prescribed course is not less than seventy-five for each and every one.

All pupils admitted on certificate will be placed on probation, and afterwards dropped from the course if on trial they shall be found not to be properly qualified ; and no certificate will be accepted afterwards from the teachers and schools improperly recommending such pupils.

The certificates to be presented shall be in the form given below, and blanks can be obtained on application to the Director, by letter or otherwise.

Students desiring to enter on certificate, instead of by examination, *must see* that their certificates conform to the one required here, and only papers which do so conform will be received in place of an examination.

APPLICATION FOR ADMISSION TO THE MICHIGAN MINING SCHOOL.

Of Mr. ....

Age of candidate..

Name of school..

Name of principal or superintendent........................

Course taken...

I certify that Mr.................................graduated in the...school under my charge; that he was examined in the following studies under my direction and that he obtained the marks set opposite each subject. I further certify that the examinations, to the best of my knowledge and belief, have been conducted fairly and honorably. I also certify that Mr. ....is of good moral character, that his attention to his duties has been ...., and that his conduct has been............................

I also send with this a catalogue or schedule which will show the course of study taken by Mr............... ....in this institution.

(Signed) ....

Subjects.	Rank.
Arithmetic...............................	....
Metric System..........................	....
Algebra through Quadratics........	....
Geometry, Plane......................	....
Geometry, Solid.......................	....
Geometry, Spherical..................	....
Astronomy..............................	....
Book-keeping..........................	....
Physics	....

Required Studies.

Other studies taken to be given here, with the rank obtained:

....

....

....

....

ENTRANCE CONDITIONS.

No student will be admitted as a regular student with conditions in any other subject than Astronomy and Book-keeping. The condition in Astronomy must be made up at the commencement of the winter term after entrance, and the condition in Book-keeping by the commencement of the winter term of the third year.

In case of failure to make up his conditions as required, the student will be dropped from the course and not allowed to continue until the conditions shall have been removed.

It is necessary for those who are preparing to take the regular course in the Mining School to give special attention to the Mathematics and Physics required for entrance, since a thorough working knowledge of the elements of these subjects is not only indispensable for entry upon the advance work in them, but is very important in its relation to most of the other subjects taken, as Mathematics and Physics form a large part of the required preparation for successful work in the other studies of the course.

SPECIAL STUDENTS.

Persons of nineteen years of age or over will be admitted as special students to take such studies as they may be found qualified to pursue, but they will be required to take sufficient work to occupy all the time that is at their disposal for school duties. This regulation will be departed from only for good and sufficient reasons in the case of persons of age and experience.

UNDERGRADUATES OF OTHER INSTITUTIONS.

Undergraduates of any high grade Scientific or Technical School, College, or University, will be admitted on the presentation of a certificate from the proper officers of that institution, stating that said undergraduates have been regularly admitted to said school, etc.; that they have pursued their studies there for a specified length of time; that they have passed upon entrance or subsequently in the school in all the subjects required for admission to the Mining School; that their standing in the institution in question was good, and that they have been honorably dismissed at their own request. If these undergraduates will also present proper certificates showing the ranks obtained in their respective institutions in such subjects as they have taken there, all studies which shall be found by examination or otherwise to be the real equivalents of the studies of the Mining School course will be accepted in lieu of the corresponding studies

3

here, if the certificates presented shall show that they obtained a satisfactory rank in those studies; provided that the application for the acceptance of their past work, as an equivalent for work in the Mining School, shall be made at the time that the students in question join the Mining School.

Owing to the strongly marked professional or practical character of the work done in the Mining School, experience has shown that as a rule the only studies that can be allowed are the theoretical Mathematics, Physics and Surveying, some Chemistry, Drawing and Stratigraphical Geology and Palæontology.

GRADUATE STUDENTS.

Graduates of any high grade Scientific or Technical School, College or University will be admitted to take special graduate instruction or as candidates for the higher degrees (see Degrees and Graduate Instruction), but they must satisfy the Faculty that their previous course has been of a grade entitling them to the privileges they seek. Those graduates who desire to enter upon the regular undergraduate work of the Mining School for the purpose of obtaining the degree of Bachelor of Science or that of Mining Engineer can do so under the same conditions as those given for "Undergraduates of other Institutions."

All persons desiring information upon special points relating to the Mining School are requested carefully to read the catalogue before writing for that information. as the catalogue is prepared with the intention of answering all questions that might be asked by correspondents.

THE COURSE OF INSTRUCTION.

The course of instruction for all students entering upon the First, or Freshman Year, in September, 1893, and subsequently, will be that given in Table II.

The student completing the first three years of that course will have conferred upon him the degree of Bachelor of Science (S. B.), and those who complete the additional fourth year and present a suitable thesis will receive the degree of Mining Engineer (E. M.).

Any student who is prepared to enter upon the course given in Table I prior to September, 1893, or upon the second or third year of that course at the time, can do so, and receive the degree of Mining Engineer on the completion of that course.

The Michigan Mining School, like Theological, Law and Medical schools, assumes that the student's preparatory and literary education has been completed prior to his entering upon his professional studies. Like other professional schools, the Michigan Mining School urges all students intending to take their professional studies here, to obtain previously an education of the broadest and most liberal character. This is necessary if the student wishes fully to profit by his studies here, and desires to take that high professional rank that should be the ultimate aim of every graduate. Although not required, the student is advised to obtain before entering the school a reading knowledge of some of the important modern languages, like German, French, Swedish, and Spanish, and to have thoroughly studied subjects that will give him the requisite training in habits of close, accurate and logical reasoning, together with a good command of language, e. g., Psychology, Logic, Rhetoric, Literature, etc. Experience has shown that of two students of equal ability, the one that can give the time to obtain the best preparation, will in the end ·pass far beyond the one that has had the inferior training.

While it is preferred that students entering should have a liberal education, for their own advantage, the School will not repel, but invites and will try to assist in every possible way, all those who have not been so fortunate, if they have the requisite knowledge and ability to profit by the course, and in conformity with this idea, it has confined its requirements for admission to those subjects that are absolutely essential as a preparation for the required course. So, too, the course of instruction is restricted to those subjects that are considered essential to the practical work of a Mining Engineer, since the School does not concern itself with anything except its legitimate business—*professional or technical education.*

In preparing the course of instruction, the effort has been made to contribute somewhat to the solution of one of the greatest educational problems of the age—properly to combine scientific or theoretical knowledge with practical training. In pursuance of this object it is intended that the student shall be well grounded in the principles or in the science of all the subjects he studies, while it is further proposed that he shall also obtain experience and practice in every subject taught, so far as the means and time at the disposal of the School will permit. That is, the student shall have an opportunity to observe and to verify in the laboratory, field, mill or mine, whatever he shall have learned in the class room.

Further, it is intended that the practical work shall here be carried to such an extent that the pupil can make use of it subsequently in his profession.

In general the instruction will be given by means of lectures, recitations, and laboratory and field practice, including the inspection of mills, mines and smelting works. Each student will receive individual instruction in the laboratories, and those qualified will be advised and directed in original investigations.

Every facility will be given to special students who desire to pursue any particular subject or subjects taught in the school, provided they enter during the time when that subject or subjects are taught in their regular order.

In Mathematics, Physics, Chemistry, Mineralogy, Petrography, Geology, Drawing, etc., the instruction is so given that any one who desires a knowledge of any of these subjects, as a matter of general education, or as a preparation for teaching, or for some other profession than Mining Engineering, can profitably study here.

The amount of labor is so great in accomplishing the necessary work of the regular course in this institution in the given time, that every student needs to present himself promptly at the opening of the school year and remain until its close. Every regular student is required to spend from six to seven hours a day for five days each week in laboratory or field work, or in recitation or lecture. He prepares for his recitations in time taken outside of these six or seven hours a day.

Since the instruction is largely personal, the maximum amount of work that can be done by each student is limited only by his time and ability, while in most of his studies he can advance as far and as rapidly as he is able to do consistently with good work.

Various excursions are taken to the mines, mills and smelting-works in the vicinity, on Saturdays or on other days, as occasion may require. Some of these excursions are required and some are voluntary, and all students that join in them are under the direction of the instructor in charge, and are subject to discipline, the same as when in the laboratories of the school.

It is advised that no student should endeavor to enter the Mining School unless he is interested in the subjects taught and intends to attend strictly to his business, since under these conditions alone will he be allowed to remain.

D	11	12
	—	—
	5	5
	2	2
	....	....
	3	3
D	10	10
	....	....
	4	4
	....	....
	11	11
	—	—
	5	5
	....	....
	6	6
	12	12
	2	2
	4	4
	....	....
	....	....
	....	....
	....	..
	6	6
	....	....
	—	—
	4	4
D	10	10
	....	....
	1	1
	3	3
	8	8
	5	5
	4	4
	....	....
	....	....
	5	5

and

OUTLINE OF THE COURSE OF STUDY FOR THE CLASSES OF 1893, 1894 AND 1895.

FIRST YEAR.

Fall Term—Fourteen Weeks.

MATHEMATICS: Higher Algebra, Plane and Analytical Trigonometry. Recitations. Seven hours a week.

Professor Haynes.

PHYSICS: Elementary Mechanics, Sound, Heat, Light. Lectures and Recitations. Three hours a week.

Professor Haynes.

DRAWING: Drawing-instruments and Materials, Plane Geometrical Problems, Projection, Development, Round Writing. Lectures, and work in Drawing Room. Ten hours a week.

Mr. Hoyt.

CHEMISTRY: General Principles and Non-Metals, Blowpipe Analysis. Lectures, Recitations and Laboratory work. Four hours a week.

Professor Koenig.

MINERALOGY: Crystallography and Determinative Mineralogy. Lectures, Recitations and Laboratory work. Eleven hours a week.

The Director, Drs. Patton, Hubbard and Lane, and Mr. Seaman.

Winter Term—Fourteen Weeks.

MATHEMATICS: Spherical Trigonometry. Mensuration. Analytical Geometry. Recitations. Seven hours a week.

Professor Haynes.

DRAWING: Intersection of Lines, Surfaces and Solids. Tinting. Lettering. Round Writing. Lectures, and work in the Drawing Room. Eight hours a week for six weeks.

Mr. Hoyt.

DRAWING: Topographical Drawing. Making Scales. Plotting. Topographical Signs. Lectures, and work in the Drawing Room. Eight hours a week for eight weeks.

Professor Denton and Mr. Hoyt.

SURVEYING. Lectures and Recitations. Two hours a week.

Professor Denton.

PHYSICS: Light, Electricity and Magnetism. Lectures and Recitations. Three hours a week.

Professor Haynes.

CHEMISTRY: Metals. Lectures, Recitations and Laboratory work. Four hours a week.

Professor Koenig.

MINERALOGY, DETERMINATIVE. Lectures, Recitations and Laboratory work. Eleven hours a week.

The Director, Drs. Patton, Hibbard and Lane, and Mr. Seaman.

Spring Term—Six Weeks.

MATHEMATICS: Analytical Geometry. Recitations. Five hours a week.   Professor Haynes.

PHYSICS, EXPERIMENTAL. Recitations and practical Laboratory work. Fifteen hours a week.
Professor Haynes.

CHEMISTRY: Introduction to Qualitative Analysis. Recitations and Laboratory work. Fifteen hours a week.

Professor Koenig.

Summer Term—Eleven Weeks.

SURVEYING: Plane, Topographical and Railroad Surveying. Lectures, Recitations and practical work in the Field and Drawing Room. Five days a week.

Professor Denton and Assistants.

SECOND YEAR.

Fall Term—Fourteen Weeks.

MATHEMATICS: Differential and Integral Calculus. Recitations. Five hours a week.

Professor Haynes.

DRAWING: Construction Drawing from Rough Sketches and Models. Lectures, and work in Drawing Room. Six hours a week.

Mr. Hoyt.

CHEMISTRY: Qualitative Analysis. Recitations and Laboratory work. Twelve hours a week.

Professors Koenig and Sharpless.

CHEMISTRY: Reduction and Oxidation, Stoichiometry. Recitations. Two hours a week.

Professor Sharpless.

METALLURGY: Fuel, Refractory Materials, Iron, Steel and Aluminum. Lectures and Recitations. Four hours a week.

Professor Sharpless.

PETROGRAPHY AND LITHOLOGY: Optical and Microscopic Mineralogy, Determinative Lithology. Lectures, Recitations and Laboratory work. Six hours a week.

The Director and Drs. Lane and Patton.

Winter Term—Fourteen Weeks.

MATHEMATICS: Integral Calculus. Recitations. Two hours a week.

Professor Haynes.

MECHANICS, ANALYTICAL. Recitations. Five hours a week.　Professor Haynes.

DRAWING: Machine Drawing, Tracing, Blue Printing, Making Drawings from Models. Lectures, and work in Drawing Room. Four hours a week.

Mr. Hoyt.

MECHANISM: Laws of Motion, Linkwork, Cams, Teeth of Wheels, Aggregate Motion, etc. Lectures and Recitations. Three hours a week.

Professor Kidwell.

CHEMISTRY: Quantitative Analysis. Lectures, Recitations and Laboratory work. Ten hours a week.

Professors Koenig and Sharpless.

MINING AND MINE SURVEYING. Lectures and Recitations. Four hours a week.

Professor Denton.

STRATIGRAPHICAL GEOLOGY AND PALEONTOLOGY. Lectures and Recitations. Five hours a week.

Dr. Lane.

Spring Term—Six Weeks.

MINE SURVEYING AND MINING. Practical work in the Mines. Five days a week.

Professor Denton.

Summer Term—Eight Weeks.

SHOPWORK. Practical work in the Pattern and Machine Shops. Five days a week.

Professor Kidwell and Messrs. Hoyt and Craig.

THIRD YEAR.

Fall Term—Fourteen Weeks.

DRAWING: Graphical Statics; Analysis of Roof Trusses of various standard designs. Lectures, and work in Drawing Room. Four hours a week.

Mr. Hoyt.

CHEMISTRY: Quantitative Analysis. Lectures, Recitations and Laboratory work. Thirteen hours a week.

> Professors Koenig and Sharpless.

METALLURGY: Copper and Lead. Lectures and Recitations. Three hours a week.

> Professor Sharpless.

ORE DRESSING. Lectures and Recitations. One hour a week.

> Professor Sharpless.

MECHANICS OF MATERIALS: Application of Principles of Statics to Rigid Bodies. Elasticity and Resistance of Materials, Discussion of Beams, Columns and Shafts. Combined Stresses, Testing of Materials. Lectures and Recitations. Three hours a week.

> Professor Kidwell.

MECHANICAL ENGINEERING: The Steam Engine and Allied Subjects. Lectures and Recitations. Five hours a week.

> Professor Kidwell.

ELECTRICAL ENGINEERING: Batteries, Ammeters, Orthometers, Electrical Measurements, Magnets, Electro-Magnetic Induction and Theory of the Dynamo. Lectures and Recitations. Four hours a week.

> Professor Kidwell.

PHYSICAL GEOLOGY. Lectures and Recitations. Five hours a week.

> The Director.

DRAWING: Designing, Floors, Trestles, Flumes, Steam Piping, Arrangement of Steam Plants. Lectures, and work in the Drawing Room. Four hours a week.

Professor Kidwell.

CHEMISTRY: Metallurgical Analysis. Recitations and Laboratory work. Seven hours a week.

Professors Koenig and Sharpless.

METALLURGY: Lead, Silver and Gold. Lectures and Recitations. Two hours a week.

Professor Sharpless.

ORE DRESSING. Lectures and Recitations. One hour a week.

Professor Sharpless.

MECHANICAL ENGINEERING: The Steam Engine continued, Steam Boilers, Fuel, Steam Pumps. Lectures and Recitations. Four hours a week.

Professor Kidwell.

ENGINEERING: Appliances, Gauges, Lubricators, Safety Valves, Fuel Heaters, etc. Lectures and Recitations. One hour a week.

Mr. Hoyt.

ELECTRICAL ENGINEERING: Motors and their Applications, Storage Batteries, Arc and Incandescent Lamps, Wiring, Electrical Fittings, etc. Lectures and Recitations. Four hours a week.

Professor Kidwell.

MINING ENGINEERING AND MINE ACCOUNTS.   Lectures
and Recitations. Four hours a week.

> Professor Denton.

HYDRAULIC AND STRUCTURAL ENGINEERING.   Lectures
and Recitations. Three hours a week.

> Professor Denton.

ECONOMIC GEOLOGY.   Lectures and Recitations.   Five
hours a week.

> The Director.

Spring Term—Six Weeks.

PREPARATION OF THESIS.

Summer Term—Eleven Weeks.

ASSAYING.   Practical work in the Laboratory, with Lectures and Recitations. Five days a week, two
weeks.

> Professor Sharpless.

ORE DRESSING.   Practical work in the Stamp Mill.   Five
days a week, four weeks.

> Professor Sharpless.

GEOLOGY.   Practical work in the Field and Mines.   Five
days a week, four weeks.

> The Director and Assistants.

wing

12	13	14
7	7	7
3	3	3
13	13	12
...	...	...
8	8	8
5	5	5
4	4	4
8	8	8
3	2	2
4	4	4
...	...	...
...	...	...
...	...	...
12	13	12
...	...	...
4	4	4
11	11	11
...	...	...
1	1	1
3	3	3

OUTLINE OF THE COURSE OF STUDY FOR THE CLASS ENTERING IN 1893.

FIRST, OR FRESHMAN YEAR.

Fall Term—Fourteen Weeks.

MATHEMATICS: Higher Algebra. Recitations. Five hours a week.

Professor Haynes.

MATHEMATICS: Plane and Analytical Trigonometry. Recitations. Two hours a week.

Professor Haynes.

PHYSICS: Elementary Mechanics, Sound, Heat, Light. Lectures and Recitations. Three hours a week.

Professor Haynes.

DRAWING: Drawing-instruments and Materials, Plane Geometrical Problems, Projection, Development, Intersection of Lines, Surfaces and Solids, Tinting, Lettering, Round Writing. Lectures and work in Drawing Room. Ten hours a week.

Mr. Hoyt.

CHEMISTRY: General Principles and Non-metals, Blow-pipe Analysis. Lectures, Recitations and Laboratory work. Eight hours a week.

Professor Koenig.

MATHEMATICS : Spherical Trigonometry and Mensuration. Recitations. Two hours a week.

> Professor Haynes.

MATHEMATICS : Analytical Geometry. Recitations. Five hours a week.

> Professor Haynes.

PHYSICS : Light, Electricity and Magnetism. Lectures and Recitations. Three hours a week.

> Professor Haynes.

DRAWING : Topographical Drawing; Making Scales, Platting, Topographical Signs. Lectures and work in the Drawing Room. Ten hours a week.

> Professor Denton and Mr. Hoyt.

SURVEYING. Lectures and Recitations. Three hours a week.

> Professor Denton.

CHEMISTRY : Metals. Lectures and Recitations. Seven hours a week.

> Professor Koenig.

MATHEMATICS : Analytical Geometry. Recitations. Five hours a week.

> Professor Haynes.

PHYSICS. EXPERIMENTAL. Recitations and Practical Laboratory work. Fifteen hours a week.

> Professor Haynes.

CHEMISTRY : Introduction to Qualitative Analysis. Recitations and Laboratory work. Fifteen hours a week.

Professor Koenig.

Summer Term—Eleven Weeks.

SURVEYING : Plane, Topographical and Railroad Surveying. Lectures, Recitations, and Practical work in the Field and Drawing Room. Five days a week.

Professor Denton and Assistants.

SECOND, OR SOPHOMORE YEAR.

Fall Term—Fourteen Weeks.

MATHEMATICS : Differential and Integral Calculus. Recitations. Five hours a week.

Professor Haynes.

DRAWING : Construction Drawing from Rough Sketches and Models. Lectures, and work in Drawing Room. Four hours a week.

Mr. Hoyt.

CHEMISTRY: Qualitative Analysis. Recitations and Laboratory work. Eight hours a week.

Professor Koenig.

CHEMISTRY: Reduction and Oxidation, Stoichiometry. Recitations. Two hours a week.

Professor Sharpless.

4

METALLURGY: Fuel. Refractory Materials. Iron. Steel, and Aluminum. Lectures and Recitations. Four hours a week.

Professor Sharpless.

MINERALOGY: Crystallography and Determinative Mineralogy. Lectures, Recitations and Laboratory work. Twelve hours a week.

The Director, Drs. Patton, Hubbard and Lane, and Mr. Seaman.

Winter Term.—Fourteen Weeks.

MATHEMATICS: Integral Calculus. Recitations. Two hours a week.

Professor Haynes.

MATHEMATICS: Analytical Mechanics. Recitations. Five hours a week.

Professor Haynes.

DRAWING: Machine Drawing. Tracing. Blue Printing. Making Drawings from Models. Lectures, and work in Drawing Room. Four hours a week.

Mr. Hoyt.

PROPERTIES OF MATERIALS: Wrought and Cast Iron. Steel. Copper. Tin. Zinc. Antimony. Bismuth. Alloys. Timber and Lubricating Oils. Lectures and Recitations. Two hours a week.

Mr. Hoyt.

CHEMISTRY: Qualitative Analysis. Recitations and Laboratory Work. Six hours a week.

Professors Koenig and Sharpless.

Mining and Mine Surveying. Lectures and Recitations. Four hours a week.

Professor Denton.

Mineralogy, Determinative. Lectures, Recitations and Laboratory work. Twelve hours a week.
> The Director, Drs. Patton, Hubbard and Lane, and Mr. Seaman.

Spring Term—Six Weeks.

Mining. Practical work in the Mines.

Professor Denton.

Summer Term—Ten Weeks.

Shopwork. Practical work in Pattern and Machine Shops. Five days a week.
> Professor Kidwell and Messrs. Hoyt and Craig.

THIRD, OR JUNIOR YEAR.

Fall Term—Fourteen Weeks.

Drawing. Lectures, and work in Drawing Room. Four hours a week.

Mr. Hoyt.

Chemistry: Quantitative Analysis. Lectures, Recitations and Laboratory work. Eleven hours a week.

Professors Koenig and Sharpless.

Metallurgy: Copper and Lead. Lectures and Recitations. Three hours a week.

Professor Sharpless.

ORE DRESSING. Lectures and Recitations. One hour a week.

> Professor Sharpless.

MECHANISM: Laws of Motion, Linkwork, Cams, Teeth of Wheels, Aggregate Motion, etc. Lectures and Recitations. Four hours a week.

> Professor Kidwell.

MECHANICAL ENGINEERING. Lectures and Recitations. Two hours a week.

> Professor Kidwell.

PETROGRAPHY AND LITHOLOGY: Optical and Microscopic Mineralogy. Determinative Lithology. Recitations and Laboratory work. Six hours a week.

> The Director, and Drs. Lane and Patton.

STRATIGRAPHICAL GEOLOGY AND PALEONTOLOGY. Lecture and Recitations. Five hours a week.

> Dr. Lane.

Winter Term—Fourteen Weeks.

DRAWING: Graphical Statics; Analysis of Roof Trusses of various standard designs. Lectures, and work in Drawing Room. Three hours a week.

> Mr. Hoyt.

CHEMISTRY: Quantitative Analysis. Lectures, Recitations and Laboratory work. Twelve hours a week.

> Professors Koenig and Sharpless.

METALLURGY: Silver and Gold. Lectures and Recitations. Two hours a week.

> Professor Sharpless.

ORE DRESSING. Lectures and Recitations. One hour a
week.   Professor Sharpless.

MECHANICS OF MATERIALS: Application of Principles
of Statics to Rigid Bodies, Elasticity and
Resistance of Materials, Discussion of Beams,
Columns and Shafts, Combined Stresses, Test-
ing of Materials. Lectures and Recitations.
Three hours a week.
                                   Professor Kidwell.

MECHANICAL ENGINEERING, continued. Lectures and
Recitations. Two hours a week.
                                   Professor Kidwell.

HYDRAULIC ENGINEERING. Lectures and Recitations.
Three hours a week.   Professor Denton.

MINING ENGINEERING AND MINE ACCOUNTS. Lectures
and Recitations. Four hours a week.
                                   Professor Denton.

PHYSICAL GEOLOGY. Lectures and Recitations. Five
hours a week.   The Director.

Spring Term—Six Weeks.

MINE SURVEYING AND MINING. Practical work in the
Mines. Five days a week.
                                   Professor Denton.

Summer Term—Twelve Weeks.

ASSAYING. Practical work in the Laboratory with Lectures and Recitations. Five days a week, two
weeks,   Professor Sharpless,

ORE DRESSING. Practical work in the Stamp Mill. Five days a week, four weeks.

Professor Sharpless.

METALLURGY. Practical work in Methods of Roasting, Smelting, etc. Five days a week, six weeks.

Professor Sharpless.

FOURTH, OR SENIOR YEAR.

Fall Term—Fourteen Weeks.

DRAWING: Designing Columns, Beams, Floors, Trestles, Flumes, Steam Piping, etc. Lectures, and work in Drawing Room. Four hours a week.

Professor Kidwell.

CHEMISTRY: Metallurgical Analysis. Recitations and Laboratory work. Twelve hours a week.

Professors Koenig and Sharpless.

MECHANICAL ENGINEERING: The Steam Engine and Allied Subjects. Lectures and Recitations. Five hours a week.

Professor Kidwell.

ELECTRICAL ENGINEERING: Batteries, Ammeters, Orthometers, Electrical Measurements, Magnets, Electro-Magnetic Induction and Theory of the Dynamo. Lectures and Recitations. Four hours a week.

Professor Kidwell.

ECONOMIC GEOLOGY. Lectures and Recitations. Five hours a week.

The Director.

Winter Term—Fourteen Weeks.

DESIGNING, continued. Five hours a week.
Professor Kidwell.

CHEMISTRY: Technical Analytical Methods. Lectures, Recitations and Laboratory work. Nine hours a week.
Professors Koenig and Sharpless.

MECHANICAL ENGINEERING: The Steam Engine, continued; Steam Boilers, Fuel, Steam Pumps. Lectures and Recitations. Four hours a week.
Professor Kidwell.

ENGINEERING APPLIANCES: Pumps, Gauges, Safety Valves, Feed Heaters, etc. Lectures and Recitations. One hour a week.
Mr. Hoyt.

ELECTRICAL ENGINEERING: Motors and their applications, Storage Batteries, Arc and Incandescent Lamps, Wiring, Electrical Fittings, etc. Lectures and Recitations. Four hours a week.
Professor Kidwell.

MINING ENGINEERING. Lectures and Recitations. Two hours a week.
Professor Denton.

STRUCTURAL ENGINEERING. Lectures and Recitations. Two hours a week.
Professor Denton.

ECONOMIC GEOLOGY. Lectures and Recitations. Five hours a week.
The Director.

Spring Term—Six Weeks.

PREPARATION OF THESIS.

Summer Term—Six Weeks.

MECHANICAL ENGINEERING. Practice in the Testing
Laboratory. Five days a week, five weeks.
Professor Kidwell.

GEOLOGY. Practical work in the Field and Mines. Five
days a week, four weeks.
The Director and Assistants.

Revision of the above courses will be made at any time
when it is thought they can be improved, or when the
needs of the School demand it, and all the students are
expected to conform to these changes whenever introduced.

DEPARTMENTS OF INSTRUCTION.

MATHEMÂTICS.

PROFESSOR HAYNES.

FIRST YEAR.—Fall and winter terms, seven hours a week; spring term, five hours a week.

SECOND YEAR.—Fall term, five hours a week; winter term, seven hours a week.

The course in Mathematics is progressive, and no part of it can be taken very profitably by the student, unless he shall have passed in all the required preparatory work and in each successive subject, before entering upon any of the more advanced studies.

In Mathematics, the object sought is to give the student a thorough working knowledge of the subject, so far as it is essential to the successful application of its principles to the practical mathematical work required in the subsequent courses in Mine Surveying, Railroad Surveying, Plane Surveying, and such other practical applications as are found in Mechanical Engineering, Electrical Engineering, Physics, etc.

The course includes, in Algebra—a review of Quadratics, Differentiation, Indeterminate Co-efficients, Formulæ, Logarithms, Loci of Equations and Higher Equations; in Trigonometry—Plane, Analytical, and Spherical Trigonometry, with Mensuration; in Analytical Geometry—the straight line, circle, parabola, ellipse, hyperbola, the transformation of co-ordinates, the plane, and surfaces and solids of revolution. This course closes with the stud of the Differential and the Integral Calculus, and their applications to various practical problems in Physics, Analytical Mechanics, etc.

Both in this course and in that in Physics special care is taken to point out and enforce the practical bearing of the subjects under discussion, and it has been found that this adds greatly to the meaning of the student's work, and forms a powerful incentive to thoroughness. However, in both of these courses the fundamental truth is kept constantly in mind, that the most successful practical work is based upon a thorough theoretical foundation. No one acquainted with the splendid achievements connected with mining in the immediate vicinity of this school, which are constantly before its students, as a great object lesson, can doubt the necessity of a knowledge of Mathematics and of Physics in securing these results, and of their eminent practical value in developing and maintaining this great industry.

PHYSICS.

PROFESSOR HAYNES.

FIRST YEAR.—Fall and winter terms, three hours a week; spring term, fifteen hours a week.

Two terms of fourteen weeks each are spent upon the study of General Physics, including the topics of Mechanics, Hydrostatics, Pneumatics, Heat, Light, Magnetism and Electricity. In these two terms regular recitations are required, and the topics are illustrated by the instructor with lectures and experiments. This course closes with a term of six weeks of recitation and laboratory work, in which the student is required to do the work under the supervision of the instructor, the experiments being mostly in the domain of physical measurements, including those of Specific Gravity, Heat, Light and Electricity.

The method of instruction in this department combines recitations, lectures, laboratory work, and the solution of problems, in such a way as not only to afford the necessary variety, but at the same time to furnish also a constant encouragement to the student to become self-reliant both in his methods of thought and in his work.

In the laboratory work of this department each student is required to make a sketch and give a description of the apparatus used in each experiment; to put ·down his data, computations, conclusions, etc., during laboratory hours. in a note book: and, *at the close of the laboratory work of each day to leave this book with the instructor for his inspection.*

No student is permitted to take this practical laboratory course who has not passed in the necessary theoretical study and lectures that preceded it.

The equipment of the Physical Laboratory. which was quite recently begun and which is constantly growing, now contains among other pieces for lecture purposes the following:

Mariott's Apparatus.

Savart's Wheel.

Atwood's Machine.

A large Toepler-Holtz Electric Machine.

An Édison dynamo.

5 small Electric Motors,

1 set Natterer Tubes.

2 sets Geissler Tubes.

1 Combined Polariscope and Stauroscope.

1 Combined Projecting Lantern and Polariscope.

1 Lissajou's Apparatus.

2 Singing Flame Apparatus.

1 Tonometer, etc.

The following list embraces a part of the apparatus now contained in the laboratory. for students' use:

5 Earth Inductors.

5 Sliding Coil Magnets.

4 Tangent Galvanometers.

6 Astatic Galvanometers.

4 Single Coil Mirror Galvanometers.

4 Double Coil Mirror Galvanometers.

3 Dead-Beat Mirror Galvanometers.

12 Sets for Kundt's Experiment.

24 Resistance Coils.

12 Calorimeters.

12 Steam Jackets. "Apparatus A."

8 Resistance Boxes, range 1 ohm to 11332 ohms.

5 Spectragoniometers (Geneva).

6 Benson Photometers.

12 Micrometers (ratchet).

13 Spherometers.

6 Pierce's Bridges.

1 B. A. Bridge.

2 Standard Ohms.

1 Cathetometer.

1 Becker Balance.

6 Kohlbusch Balances.

1 Springer Torsion Balance.

3 Marine Sextants.

1 Astronomical Sextant with artificial horizon.

1 Cistern Barometer.

2 Aneroid Barometers.

2 Jolly Balances.

7 Sonometers.

1 "Bradley's Complete Apparatus," range 2-10000 of an ohm to 11111 1-10 ohms.

1 "Standard Resistance Box and Bridge," tested by Professor W. A. Anthony; range from 1-1,000,000 of an ohm to 110 millions of ohms.

DRAWING.

PROFESSOR KIDWELL AND MR. HOYT.

The course in drawing extends over the entire three years. In planning it, the object kept constantly in view was to give special prominence to such branches of Drawing as are of most value to the engineer; hence such subjects as perspective, shades and shadows, etc., have been excluded, and more than the usual proportion of time is devoted to Mechanical and Topographical Drawing.

During the entire course, all Drawings accepted by the instructors are considered as the property of the School, and are preserved for the use of the department. Drawings that are not satisfactory are returned, and must be made up by the student in his own time.

The following schedule shows the distribution of work during the three years.

FIRST YEAR.—Fall term, ten hours a week; winter term, eight hours a week.

DESCRIPTION, PREPARATION, AND TESTING OF DRAW-
ING-INSTRUMENTS AND MATERIALS; graphical solution of
geometrical problems. Descriptive Geometry: Projections
on right and olique planes; intersections of lines, surfaces and solids: plans, elevations and sections   Tinting,
Lettering: Roman, Italic, Gothic, and block letters;
Soennecken's system of Round Writing. Angel's " *Practical Plane aud Solid Geometry*" is used as the text book
in Descriptive Geometry, and the other subjects are
taught by lectures.

After the principles given in the text-book have been
mastered. special problems prepared by the instructor are
given for solution.

TOPOGRAPHICAL DRAWING : Making scales: methods
of plotting surveys, by protractor and rectangular co-
ordinates : topographical signs. This branch of Drawing
is under the personal supervision of the Professor of
Civil and Mining Engineering, and is arranged with
special reference to the practical work in Plane and Mine
Surveying. The first sheets are devoted to the making
of scales, and to the different methods of plotting survey
lines, the student having previously made the necessary
computations from field notes furnished him. These
sheets are followed by practice in making topographical
signs and in filling in the details of a survey. This
course gives the student sufficient skill to plat his own
surveys, and assists him in the making of these surveys,
by teaching him what data are necessary for platting.

Every attempt is made to avoid mere copying. Accuracy,
neatness, and a thorough understanding of the work in
progress are insisted upon at all times, and no sheet will
be accepted that would not pass in the average drafting
room. The subject of lettering receives considerable

attention during the entire course, as nothing more effectually spoils a good mechanical drawing or map than injudiciously selected or poorly executed lettering.

No student may take first year work in Drawing who has entrance conditions in Plane, Solid or Spherical Geometry.

SECOND YEAR.—Fall term, six hours a week; winter term, four hours a week.

ISOMETRIC AND CABINET PROJECTION: Construction Drawing; dimensioning, lettering, and the shading of working drawings; elements of design with regard to the relative proportion of parts of machines; tracing, blue printing, and use of bond paper; production of complete working drawings from the model, on rough sketches furnished by the instructor. Lectures, and work in Drawing Room.

MACHINE SKETCHING: Making working sketches, with all necessary views, sections, dimensions, etc., of pieces of machinery assigned by the instructor. This work must be done by the student outside of class hours, in a book of sectioned paper to be devoted exclusively to this subject and turned in for inspection on the date set by the instructor.

Each student will be allowed to keep a complete set of prints of all his tracings or drawings, on bond paper.

No student may take this course who has conditions in any part of the first year's work in Drawing.

THIRD YEAR.—Fall term, four hours a week; winter term, four hours a week.

GRAPHICAL STATICS: Analysis of roof and bridge

trusses of various standard designs. (Greene's *"Roof Trusses,"* supplemented with lectures.)

While the text-book will serve as a guide, the scope of the instruction will not be confined to it. The course is designed to teach the theory of the graphical analysis of stresses in structures, and leads up to the course in designing given in the succeeding term.

No student may take this course who has conditions in any part of the previous two years' instruction in Drawing or Mechanics.

DESIGNING. Lectures, and work in Drawing Room.

Prominence is given in this course to the designing of girders, columns, shafts, floors for heavy loads, framing, trestles, etc. Special attention is also given to designs for long lines of steampipe, line and counter shafting for various duties, etc. No design is accepted unless accompanied by complete working drawings and bill of materials.

No student may take this course who has conditions in any part of the previous work in Drawing, Mechanics, Properties of Materials, Graphical Statics, Mechanism, or Mechanics of Materials.

In addition to the regular instruction in Drawing, numerous applications of the subject are obtained in connection with the other courses; the students are required to make plats of all their field work in Plane Surveying, to prepare working plans and sections of a mine from their own survey, make a map and profile of a railroad line surveyed by themselves, and to draw sections, diagrams, maps, etc, in their geological field work.

Much personal instruction is given during the entire course. In addition to the regular lectures and recitations, the instructors are present in the Drawing Room during the hours prescribed for practical work, to give advice and personal instruction to those who need it.

Whenever students desire the privilege of working in the Drawing Room on Saturdays or other holidays during the fall and winter terms, arrangements may usually be made with the instructor, the day before, by which such privilege can be granted.

Special Students in Drawing.

Those who desire to enter as special students to take the course in Drawing only or in Drawing in conjunction with some other subject, may do so, provided the professor in charge of the course is convinced of their competency to profit by the instruction. To pursue the course with success, Plane, Solid and Spherical Geometry, Plane Trigonometry, and Analytical Geometry of two dimensions should have been well mastered. In case these subjects have not been completed, the professor in charge will prescribe such courses in mathematics as he considers necessary, which will be obligatory on the part of the student, and determine the number of hours to be devoted to the work.

The Four Years's Course.

An inspection of the table of hours for the four years's course, to go into effect in September, 1893, will show a material increase in the number of hours to be devoted to Drawing. During the first term of the first year, the instruction will be confined to the same subjects now taught in that term, but the increased time will permit more extended work in Descriptive Geometry. The instruction in Topographical Drawing will be made more exhaustive by devoting to it ten hours a week for an entire term, instead of eight hours a week for eight weeks, as at present. The course in Constructive Drawing and Machine Sketching will be expanded, and occupy two terms of the second year, and one term of the third. Graphical Statics will occupy the winter term of the third year. The instruction in Mechanics of Materials, Mechanism, and a portion of the Mechanical Engineering, will also be given during the third year, so that at the opening of the fourth year, the student will be prepared to enter intelligently upon the work of designing, which will be continued through two terms, instead of one as at present.

Equipment.

This Department is well equipped for every branch of the work it professes to teach. The more expensive or rarely used instruments are in stock, and are used by the students as occasion may demand. The drawing tables have been so planned that each student has a private drawer or locker for his instruments and materials and a rack for his drawing board. A printing frame capable of making a blue print 3x4 feet, several frames of smaller capacity, a new slate vat for developing prints, and a drying rack, have been added during the past year. The accompanying plan will show the arrangement of the room.

Instruments Needed by Students.

Each student upon entrance will provide himself with the following instruments and materials, a list of which is given for the convenience of those who may desire to purchase before coming to Houghton:

One 5-inch Altender right improved line pen.

One 5½-inch Altender dividers (pivot joint) with hair spring, pen and pencil points, and extension bar.

One 2½-inch Altender bow pen.

One 2½-inch Altender bow pencil.

One 2½-inch Altender bow dividers.

One 8-inch horn protractor.

One 12-inch triangular scale, divided into twelfths.

One T square, 36-inch blade.

One 8-inch 30°x60° rubber triangle.

One 8-inch 45° rubber triangle.

One each K. & E. Amber curves, Nos. 1820–6; 1820–11; 1820–15.

One dozen German silver thumb tacks, ⅜ diam.

One bottle W. and N. or Higgins's prepared India ink.

One Faber's pencil form wood-cased rubber.

One diam. rubber No. 877.

One piece Artist's gum, ½x1½x3 inches.

Two each Faber's artist's 6 H and 4 H pencils.

One bottle mucilage (or paste) with brush.

One medium sized sponge, fine quality.

One Arksansas stone, about ½x¾x3 inches.

Two cabinet saucers, about 1¾ inches diam.

One piece chamois skin, not less than 12 inches square.

One Soennecken Round Writing Copy Book, and box of selected pens.

A black enameled tin box, 13x8x4 inches, with lock, in which instruments can be kept, is strongly recommended.

A drawing board and two sable brushes will also be required. Owing to liability of getting sizes that will not answer, these latter should be purchased in Houghton.

The articles called for in this list are necessary for a proper prosecution of the course, and care should therefore

be taken to get exact instruments specified, or others of
equal grade. Instruments not up to standard will not be
allowed in the Drawing Room, as they will not give satisfaction, and will waste the time both of instructors and
of students.

CHEMISTRY.

GENERAL CHEMISTRY.

PROFESSOR KOENIG.

FIRST YEAR.—Fall term, four hours a week; winter
term, four hours a week; spring term. fifteen hours a
week.   ·

Transformation, or change, of matter either in form
or in substance, or in both, is the ultimate aim of the
engineer, and more especially of the mining and metallurgical engineer. A thorough knowledge of the properties of matter, then, is the base from which all engineering
designs must be started and brought to a successful end.
The course in general chemistry, dealing with the material
particles in their action upon each other, is so conducted
that the student, from the start, is made an investigator
and not a mere recipient of accumulated knowledge.
Beginning with a course in blow-pipe work, the student
becomes acquainted with the two most important operations of metallurgy—oxidation, and deoxidation, or
reduction to the metallic state, of metallic compounds.
He learns to appreciate the importance of minute quantities and forces in performing a series of changes by
such simple means as a small flame. He proceeds then
to the investigation of the non-metallic elements in their

several states of aggregation—solid, liquid and gaseous. Lectures are intended only to show the student the best mode of manipulation and to explain abstract conceptions, such as affinity, the law of combination by simple multiples, etc. Recitations serve to tell the student whether he has conceived correct notions as the result of his experiments. Richter's *Inorganic Chemistry* and Smith and Keller's *Laboratory Notes* serve the student as textbook and guide in the laboratory work.

Examinations are held at the end of each term, and *no student having conditions in chemistry is permitted to continue any subsequent part in the course until those conditions are removed.*

QUALITATIVE ANALYSIS.

PROFESSORS KOENIG AND SHARPLESS.

SECOND YEAR.—Fall term, fourteen hours a week; winter term, ten hours a week.

The fall term, and, if necessary, part of the winter term of the second year, are devoted to a systematic course in Qualitative Analysis. The student having already performed the preliminary experiments, is expected to be familiar with the important reactions of the metals and the acids. He begins by studying their division into analytical groups, and then proceeds to the separation and identification of the individual members of each group. After completing this work he is given mixtures, whose composition is not known to him, for qualitative examination. These mixtures are carefully selected and graded; their number depends upon the accuracy and rapidity with which the student accomplishes the detection of their constituents.

With the exception of three class-room recitations, on Qualitative Analysis, on Oxidation and Reduction, and on Stoichiometry, the instruction is confined to the laboratory. Daily recitations are made there; students are required to keep a complete and detailed record of their work, to write the equations representing the reactions involved in it, and to explain to the instructor the reasons for each operation they perform. Fresenius's Manual is used.

QUANTITATIVE ANALYSIS.

PROFESSORS KOENIG AND SHARPLESS.

THIRD YEAR.—Fall term, ten hours a week.

The course in Quantitative Analysis is so organized that the student proceeds from the complete analysis of a simple, soluble salt to the separation of the constituents in the most refractory and insoluble mineral body. One or more representative minerals are chosen from each group, sulphides and sulphosalts first, then carbonates, phosphates, silicates, etc. In each analysis those methods only are selected which will give the best results in the shortest time. Thus gravimetric, volumetric and optic methods are given from the start. In order to be a candidate for a degree, a student must have made at least one complete and correct analysis in each of the groups mentioned above.

A complete course of lectures, supplemented by recitations, accompanies the laboratory practice. The chief book of reference is Fresenius's (the students are required to provide themselves with it); other standard works and the original literature are also constantly consulted. One of the instructors is always present in the laboratory during the regular working hours, and personal assistance is rendered when necessary.

METALLURGICAL ANALYSIS.

PROFESSORS KOENIG AND SHARPLESS.

THIRD YEAR.—Winter term, seven hours a week.

The object of this course is to acquaint the student with the special methods of analysis that are in use in the laboratories of metallurgical establishments. Special prominence is given to the assay and complete analysis of iron ores; to the determination of the impurities, carbon, silicon, phosphorus, sulphur and manganese in pig iron and steel; the analysis of fuel, slag, limestone, etc. The student is taught not only to make these determinations accurately (and does not proceed until the results are perfectly correct), but also to work as *rapidly* as is consistent with the desired degree of accuracy. Complete sets of special apparatus have been procured and constructed for this work. Detailed printed directions by Professor Sharpless are used as a guide, and most of the original literature is also accessible.

The aim has been to make the laboratory appliances and conveniences as complete and ample as possible. The laboratories, lecture, balance, and supply rooms are all on the same floor. The laboratories are furnished with large fume chambers which have a good draught, and are supplied with hot plates and steam baths. The tables are furnished with sinks—one for each pair of students—and have abundant gas and water supplies. Filter pumps are arranged at each sink so as to provide a pump for each student. The laboratories are supplied with gas, and are well lighted, as well as fully equipped with all the modern appliances needed for chemical analysis. The balance room is provided with thirteen analytical balances of Becker and Sons' or Troemner's make. A dark room is furnished with a three-telescope spectroscope and the necessary auxiliary apparatus for electric examination. A double set of Hempel's apparatus for the analysis of gases, and Bunsen's endiometric apparatus for the same purpose, are at the disposal of the students.

SYNTHETIC CHEMISTRY.

PROFESSOR KOENIG.

Fall and winter terms: hours according to time at disposal of student.

This course is offered to special students in Chemistry and to those regular students that show marked aptness for chemical work and have completed the work in this department required by the school. The aim of the course is to train the student's inventive faculties. Synthesis represents the real end of Chemistry, while analysis is merely a means toward that end. The former is the basis of all chemical manufacture, and, therefore, the part of the science which to the apt student is most lucrative.

The plan of the course is as follows: The professor

mentions to the student a certain process in which, according to his knowledge or experience, an improvement is possible, such as the treatment of titaniferous iron ores, for example. The student then masters all the available literature on the subject and prepares a plan for attacking the problem by experiment. This plan may be accepted or modified by the professor. As a matter of course, the latter will perform the intellectual part of the work; the student in most cases merely executes his directions, but while thus serving as an adjutant the student will learn how to proceed in a new problem (by himself). Whether such experiments prove practically successful or not is not very material. Negative results are as valuable, generally, as positive ones.

It is thought that this course may lead men to return from business life, in which they have arrived at certain ideas, to this school to avail themselves of its facilities in their proposed experiments, and in their turn bring the school into closer relations with the world of practice.

ASSAYING.

PROFESSOR SHARPLESS.

THIRD YEAR.—Summer term; five days a week, two weeks.

Instruction is given in the fire assay of gold, silver, lead and copper ores, gold and silver coin, bullion, copper "mineral" and slags.

The assay laboratory contains ten large crucible furnaces and eighteen muffle furnaces of the Brown pattern, and sixteen crucible and muffle gasoline furnaces (Hoskins's), the intention being to provide a muffle for each student and so avoid the inconvenience of making one furnace do for two or more persons. The laboratory is provided with a Blake and a Gates crusher, laboratory size, to be run by power; large buck plates, large and small mortars, sets of sieves, etc. The weighing room is supplied with six pulp scales and five button balances, of Troemner's and Becker's make, for use in this department.

Of the two weeks devoted to assaying, almost all the time is spent in the laboratory; lectures and recitations form a minor portion of the work. One hundred and twenty-five to one hundred and fifty assays are made upon samples differing as widely as possible in composition, and, consequently, in methods of treatment.

Students who desire to pursue this course must have taken one term's work in Quantitative Analysis.

ORE DRESSING.

PROFESSOR SHARPLESS.

THIRD YEAR.—Fall and winter terms, one hour a week; summer term, five days a week, four weeks.

During the fall and winter terms instruction is given in the theory of amalgamation and mechanical treatment of ores previous to their smelting.

This instruction is given, for the most part, by lectures, supplemented, when possible, by references to the standard literature on the subject.

The ground covered by the lectures includes:

I. Physical properties upon which ore dressing operations are based.

II. Theory of jigging, and slime treatment.

III. Hand dressing.

IV. Crushing-machinery; jaw crushers, stamps, rolls, pulverizers, etc.

V. Sizing-machinery; flat and revolving screens, tables, etc.

VI. Sorting-machinery; jigs. settlers, etc.

VII. Typical ore dressing works.

With each mechanical device studied, the theory of its use, its advantages and disadvantages, are discussed, and when possible the machine is examined in the Mining School stamp mill or in one of the stamp mills in the vicinity. When no machines are available for this work, use is made of drawings and photographs. with which this department is well supplied.

During the fall and winter terms considerable time is devoted to the examination of dressing-plants near Houghton. These examinations are made on Saturdays, but are a part of the obligatory work. Students are required to make careful notes of all observations, make sketches of plants and machinery, and make, to the instructor, written reports of such observations.

During the spring term instruction is given in the Mining Laboratory, in amalgamating and dressing gold, silver, lead and copper ores.

The mining laboratory is equipped with an assortment of modern crushing, sizing and sorting machines, and is well prepared to treat free milling and refractory ores by such methods as analysis and mill tests show to give the best results. Students are required to care for the machinery, carry out the dressing operations, and check their results by fire assay. When the work on an ore has been finished, the student makes his report. This report includes the results obtained by all methods used, whether they are positive or negative, as well as the method which seems to be the most economical for the treatment of the ore.

The apparatus at the disposal of a student at present consists of the following pieces: One 650-pound three-stamp battery, for wet or dry crushing, furnished with copper plates; one Blake crusher; one Gates crusher; one sample grinder; one pair of rolls; one amalgamating pan; one settler; two jigs; one Calumet separator; one spitz-kasten; one Frue vanner; apron tables; screens; precipitating tanks; and settling tanks sufficient to enable the student to check all his results by assay.

During the past year the School has erected a 7x10 reverberatory roasting furnace. This will enable the students to treat their concentrates and refractory ores, which, heretofore, they have not been able to do.

It is required that this course be preceded by the first year's course in Physics, and second year's course in Mathematics, and be accompanied by the third year's course in Metallurgy and Assaying.

METALLURGY.

PROFESSOR SHARPLESS.

SECOND AND THIRD YEARS.—Second Year: Fall Term, four hours a week. Third Year: Fall Term, three hours a week; Winter Term, two hours a week.

Instruction in Metallurgy is given during the second

and third years in lectures and recitations, supplemented when possible by the use of text-books and visits to the metallurgical works. The object of the course is to give the student a thorough foundation in the fundamental principles of the different metallurgical processes. In studying each of the metals special attention is paid to the properties of the commercial forms, and to the effects of impurities upon their value for engineering purposes. During the second year, fuel, refractory materials, iron, steel and aluminum are discussed; the various ores of iron; the properties of cast iron, wrought iron and steel; the methods by which objectionable elements in the ore may be kept out of the finished product, or their effects neutralized; theory and description of blast furnace and puddling process; puddled, blistered, and crucible steel; acid and basic Bessemer steel; and open-hearth steel processes.

During the third year the metallurgy of copper, lead, silver and gold is studied by lectures and frequent references to the library. It is the aim of these courses to acquaint the student with the best modern American methods in sufficient detail to enable him to make an intelligent choice for the treatment of any particular ore, and also to familiarize him with the modern metallurgical literature.

In connection with these courses frequent visits are made to the smelting works in the vicinity, and each student is required to report upon the observations made by him.

Students taking either of the courses in Metallurgy must have taken the first year's courses in Chemistry and Mineralogy.

MECHANICAL ENGINEERING.

PROFESSOR KIDWELL AND MR. HOYT.

The course in Mechanical Engineering has been made sufficiently full to give the student a good preparation for actual work, and to point out the lines of study to be pursued, should he desire to continue the subject after graduation. The following is a detailed statement of the course:

SECOND YEAR.—Winter term, two hours a week.

PROPERTIES OF MATERIALS OF ENGINEERING:—Lectures on cast and wrought iron; steel; copper and its important alloys; tin: zinc: antimony: bismuth: timber: and lubricating oils.

The course includes a full discussion of methods of manufacture of the various grades of material, forms in which they appear in the market, their adaptation to the purposes of the engineer, methods of preserving materials from corrosion and decay, etc. The course is supplemented by practical work in testing, for details of which see section on Mechanics of Materials.

No student may take this course who has conditions in Physics.

Courses of lectures are also given on stone, cement, concrete, brick, their properties and general qualities, mode of preparation and their combinations in construction, etc., for the details of which see sections on Hydraulics and Economic Geology.

Winter Term, three hours a week.

MECHANISM: Laws of Motion; linkwork; cams; teeth of wheels, with use of odontograph; wheels in trains;

aggregate motion; miscellaneous problems in Applied Mechanics, with applications. Power-transmitting machinery: pulleys, belting, hangers, shafting, clutches, etc., and determination of proper sizes for particular duties. Taught partly from lectures, partly from Goodeve's *Elements of Mechanism* as a text book.

No student may take this course who has conditions ·in Mathematics, Mechanics or Drawing.

THIRD YEAR.—Winter Term, one hour a week.

ENGINEERING APPLIANCES.—Steam gauges; lubricators; safety valves; reducing valves; steam traps; feed heaters and purifiers; steam separators; damper regulators; the various styles of patent grates; steam pipe and fittings; boiler and pipe coverings; rubber, leather and copper belting, etc. Taught partly by lectures, and partly from the various manufacturers's trade circulars.

This course must be preceded by the first term's work on the Steam Engine.

A large and very complete library of trade circulars from the leading industrial establishments is kept up to date, and is constantly re'erred to in these lectures. These catalogues are at the service of the general public as well as of the students.

Fall Term, five hours a week; Winter Term, four hours a week.

THE STEAM ENGINE AND ALLIED SUBJECTS.—(a) An elementary course on the thermo-dynamics of air and steam engines; the relation between the size and the power of an engine; the mechanics, mechanism, and details of steam engines; valves and valve gears; indicator diagrams, their interpretation, and methods of working them up; the various kinds of boilers, their fittings, and the relative size of the various parts; fuel and heat developed during combustion; condensation and condensers; causes of low efficiency in steam engines; the influence of compounding cylinders; injectors, inspirators, and ejector condensers; boiler chimneys. (Holmes's *The Steam Engine*, supplemented with lectures.)

(b) Steam pumps, with discussion of the typical forms in use,—taught by lectures. (c) Instruments and appliances used in boiler testing, such as dynamometers, steam engine indicators, polar planimeters, speed counters, pyrometers, calorimeters, etc. Lectures. (d) Practical work in testing, on Saturdays during winter term.

The department is well equipped with apparatus for work scheduled in (c) and (d). Among the instruments on hand are one Crosby and one Tabor indicator, with full complement of springs, Heath stop-watch, two polar planimeters, Ashcroft revolution counter, Schaeffer and Budenberg tachometer, lazy tongs and other reducing gears, Ashcroft pyrometer, set of ten Green's standard thermometers, Haisler and Barrus calorimeters, water meters, Ashcroft boiler test pump, steam gauge testing machine, etc. There are also on hand a number of cut models of injectors, etc., for illustrating lectures.

The Four Years's Course.

The adoption of the Four Years's Course will enable the work in this department to be made more efficient by extending the lectures over three years, instead of two as at present. The subjects of Mechanism, Mechanics of Materials, Properties of Materials, and the introductory work in Mechanical Engineering will all be given during the first three years, enabling the advanced work of the fourth year to be increased in scope. The increased time available will also permit the introduction of a special course of lectures on Mining Machinery during the winter term, and five weeks extra work in the Testing Laboratory during the last summer of the course.

MECHANICS OF MATERIALS.

PROFESSOR KIDWELL.

THIRD YEAR.—Fall Term, three hours a week.

APPLICATION OF THE PRINCIPLES OF STATICS TO RIGID BODIES; elasticity and resistance of materials; cantilevers; simple, restrained and continuous beams; bodies of uniform strength; riveting; torsion of shafts; combined stresses; computation of proper sizes and proportions of beams, columns and shafts. (Merriman's *Mechanics of Materials*, supplemented with lectures.)

TESTING OF MATERIALS OF ENGINEERING.—Such as wrought and cast iron, steel, brick, stone and slate. Lectures, recitations, practical work in the Laboratory on Saturdays. Each student makes a series of tests in tension, compression, torsion, shearing, and cross breaking, on laboratory testing machines.

The School is provided with a 100,000 lb. machine fitted for tests in tension, compression, cross-breaking and shearing; a Thurston autographic torsion machine, an Olsen 2,000 lb. cement tester, and an Ashcroft oil testing machine. There are also on hand a Henning electric contact micrometer for measurement of extension, an electric micrometer for compression tests, a B. & S. vernier caliper, and several micrometer calipers.

6

Those having materials to be tested should make application to the professor in charge of the department, and make definite arrangements with him for the precise work they desire to have done.

No student may take these subjects who has conditions in Mechanics, Mathematics, or Properties of Materials.

SUMMER COURSE IN SHOP PRACTICE.

PROFESSOR KIDWELL, MR. HOYT AND MR. CRAIG.

Summer Term, five days a week.

The entire summer term of the second year of the course is devoted to shop work. In the Machine Shop instruction is given in chipping, filing, scraping, general vise work, pipe fitting, and use of machine tools. In the Pattern Shop a course in bench work, making joints, turning, etc., precedes actual practice in pattern making. All work done in both shops is to blue prints made in the Drawing Room. The shop work is planned with special reference to the needs of the School, and such models of valves, link motions, mechanical movements, etc., as are needed for lecture purposes, will be made by the students. All articles made in the shops are considered as the property of the School.

The equipment of the shops has been carefully selected, and will be increased as fast as the School requires it. The machine shop contains work benches for twelve students, a 24-inch by 16-foot New Haven Tool Co. engine lathe, a Prentice screw-cutting lathe, two hand lathes, a 34-inch automatic feed Blaisdell drill press, a 20-inch Lodge and Davis drill press, a 16-inch Gould and

MECHANICAL LABORAT
AND
ASSAY ROOM
MICHIGAN MINING SCH
HOUGHTON MICH.

Eberhardt shaper, a Whitcomb planer of capacity 8x2x2 feet, a Brainard No. 4 Universal milling machine, one wet and two dry emery grinders, and several smaller machine tools. The assortment of chucks, taps, drills, reamers, and general tools is very complete. For practice in pipe fitting a separate bench has been provided, and a complete set of pipe tools and fittings up to two inches inclusive is in stock. The Pattern Shop contains two Clement wood lathes, a 33-inch Fay hand saw, Beach jig saw, emery and grindstones, Pedrick and Ayer gouge grinders, a very complete assortment of hand tools and appliances, and work benches for eighteen students. Each student, in each shop, has a separate work bench, locker, and set of hand tools, for which he will be held responsible. Any damage to tools, or other part of the equipment, beyond wear and tear by legitimate use, will be charged to the student accountable for it.

The check system of accounting for tools is used in both shops, thus familiarizing the student with its operation by actual practice. Both shops will be lighted with electricity, furnished by a No. 4 Edison dynamo in the testing room. Power for shops is supplied by a 9x9 inch New York Safety vertical high speed engine, arranged to take steam either from the boilers in the building, or from the boiler in the Stamp Mill. In the Stamp Mill are an 8x12 Buckeye automatic engine, and a variety of milling machinery available for study.

To familiarize the students with the operation and care of machinery, each one will be detailed from time to time to fire the boiler, run the engine, clean and oil the machinery, and to perform such other duties as the instructor in charge may assign him.

No students having conditions in Drawing, Mechanics,

or Properties of Materials, may take this course, except those who enter for shop work only.

Special Students in Shop Work.

Since the summer term of 1892, persons desiring to take shop work only, and devote all their time to it, may, in case there is room for them, be admitted as special students, on presentation of evidence that they can pursue the course with profit. Such special students must be of the age prescribed for entrance, and should have had the equivalent of a high school course. Application should be made to the Professor in charge of the work not later than one week before the course opens in July. *No student will be allowed to enter the course after the first week of the summer term.*

ELECTRICAL ENGINEERING.

PROFESSOR KIDWELL.

The growing tendency toward the more extended use of electricity in mining, both as an illuminant, and as a motive power for hauling, and operating portable machinery, will require of the Mining Engineer of the future a working knowledge of Electrical Engineering; hence an elementary course in that subject is prescribed for all regular students in this institution.

The instruction will be made as comprehensive as the time available will permit, and special care will be taken to familiarize the student with the fundamental principles of the science. Sufficient ground will be covered to enable him to understand the electrical machinery, appliances, and processes in general use, and give him a good foundation for more advanced work, should he desire to devote himself more particularly to Electrical Engineering after graduation.

The preparatory course in Electricity given in Physics is supplemented with the following:

THIRD YEAR.—Fall and Winter Terms, four hours a week.

ELECTRICAL INSTRUMENTS AND MEASUREMENTS: Primary batteries, the various forms of ammeters, voltmeters, bridges, resistance sets, etc., and the methods of using them in making measurements of current, electromotive force, insulation resistance, and in determining faults, etc. Power and its measurement.

ELECTRICAL ENGINEERING: Theory of the dynamo, both direct and alternating current, with description and discussion of the typical forms in general use; motors and their applications; transformers; stage batteries; wiring; fittings; etc. (Slingo and Brooker's *Electrical Engineering* supplemented with lectures.) Discussion of electrical machinery in hauling, hoisting. drilling, and other mining uses. (Trade circulars.)

A 12K Edison dynamo has been set up in the testing room, and is wired to light the mechanical engineering laboratories. There are also a 2HP Sprague motor arranged to drive some of the testing machinery, several Ayrton and Perry ammeters and voltmeters, Beyman Ammeters, storage cells, and a number of other instruments for electrical work.

No student may take this course who has conditions in Mathematics, Physics, Mechanics or Drawing.

PLANE SURVEYING.

PROFESSOR DENTON.

FIRST YEAR.—Winter Term, two hours a week.

The course in surveying is designed to be practical and complete as far as regards the ordinary wants of a mining or civil engineer. The course begins in the winter term of the first year. This part of the course is devoted exclusively to the study of the computations necessary in plane surveying, and to the making of maps and scales.

Johnson's *Theory and Practice of Surveying* is used as a text-book. The Topographical Drawing, which is in charge of the same instructor, is arranged with special reference to this course, and the two subjects are made to harmonize, and to prepare the student to perform the practical work of the summer course in surveying with facility.

Understanding the computations and the methods of plotting, the student is able to appreciate the different methods of collecting data, and can devote his whole attention to them, and to the practical work. *To take this course the student must have passed in all the preceding Mathematics.*

SUMMER COURSE IN SURVEYING.

PROFESSOR DENTON.

FIRST YEAR.—Summer Term, five days a week.

During eleven weeks of each summer a special course of surveying will be conducted. Attendance upon this course is obligatory for all regular students that intend to complete the first year. The object of this summer course is two fold:

First, to give the regular students more thorough and extended practice in the field than it is possible to do while other school work is being carried on. Second, to provide a thorough, practical course in surveying for persons, other than regular students, who may be desirous of becoming surveyors, or who may wish to obtain practical experience in the subject. There is perhaps no course of study which can be offered by an institution, that will give so quick and profitable returns for the money and time expended by the pupil, as a thorough, practical course in surveying, since employment at a fair salary can almost always be obtained by a competent surveyor.

In this summer course study and practical work are combined.

Johnson's *Theory and Practice of Surveying*, last edition, is used as a text-book, being supplemented when necessary with lectures. Generally the first hour of the day is devoted to class-room work and the remainder of it to field work.

The subjects studied comprise the use and adjustments of surveying instruments, and methods of surveying.

For field work the students are divided into squads of from two to five men each. Each squad is required to make a certain number of surveys, and each member of the squad has to make, from the work done, a full set of notes, computations and maps.

The field work consists of:

1. Exercises in pacing, with a detailed survey of a field by pacing.

2. Practice in chaining distances and in laying off right angles and parallel lines with the chain

3. Practice in ranging lines with sight poles under different conditions.

4. Exercises in reading compass bearings.

5. Detailed survey of a farm, made by means of solar compass and chain.

6. Adjustment of the hand level, and practice in its use.

7. Topographical survey on the rectangular plan, with compass, chain and hand level.

8. Adjustment of the transit, and exercises in reading the angles of a triangle by the repetition method.

9. Determination of the true meridian by observations on Polaris and on the sun, and by means of solar attachments to the transit.

10. Running a close traverse, the angles being determined by repetition, the distances measured with a steel tape, and afterwards corrected for inclination, catenary, and temperature.

11. Running an azimuth traverse around a polygon, the distances being measured by a telemeter.

12. City surveying, laying out lots and streets, and determining the position of house and fence lines.

13. Adjustment of the Wye level, and running line of levels about one mile in length.

14. Survey of a mining claim, with transit, according to government regulations.

15. Retracing and subdividing of a section of land in accordance with the United States Government field notes.

16. Topographical survey with the plane table, based upon a system of triangulation with the transit.

17. Topographical survey with transit and stadia.

18. Railroad survey. About one mile of road is located, slope stakes set, profiles, maps and cross sections made, and the cuttings and embankments calculated.

The Mining School owns the following set of instruments: One plane table from Buff and Berger; nine transits, three from Buff and Berger, three from Heller and Brightly, two from Gurley; five Burt solar compasses; five magnetic compasses; fifteen Locke hand levels. In addition to these more expensive instruments, the School owns the necessary number of mining lamps, chains, steel tapes, poles, rods, etc.

Two of the transits are provided with three tripod outfits for mine surveying, and all the transits are adapted to mine as well as surface work.

Persons that wish to join the Summer Course only, are required to prepare themselves upon the first two books of Davies's Surveying revised by Van Amringe, in the subjects of Plane Trigonometry, Logarithms and Mensuration.

Those attending the Summer Course should provide themselves with Johnson's *Theory and Practice of Surveying*, last edition, a pair of six-inch dividers with pen and pencil attachments, a right line pen, a decimal scale, a large triangle, a T square, medium and hard pencils, and a twenty-five foot steel pocket tape graduated to feet and tenths. These articles are indispensable, but additional drawing instruments will be found convenient.

The furnishing of the surveying apparatus by the Mining School is a considerable expense to the institution, and while losses due to ordinary and legitimate wear and tear of the instruments are borne by the school, any injuries due to carelessness on the part of the student must be made good by him.

The summer course in Surveying will commence each year about the first of July, and all persons who desire to attend are requested to send in their names early to Professor Denton, in charge of the course, in order that proper provision may be made for them. This course, like all others in the School, is free to any one who is properly qualified, whether a resident of the State of Michigan or not. The course is given in Houghton.

Regular students, in order to take this course, must have passed in all the preceding Mathematics and Plane Surveying.

MINE SURVEYING.

PROFESSOR DENTON.

SECOND YEAR.—Winter Term, two hours a week; Spring Term, two weeks.

Instruction in Mine Surveying is given to the second year students by means of text-books, lectures and recitations. Many practical problems are assigned the students, to be solved by them.

A portion of the six weeks spent at the mines during the spring term is occupied in making a mine-survey. Each student is required to make a full set of computations and maps based upon his survey.

Students taking this course must have passed in the preceding work in Mining and Plane Surveying.

HYDRAULICS.

PROFESSOR DENTON.

Winter Term, three hours a week.

Instruction in this course is given with the aid of a text-book, especial attention being paid to the solution of practical problems. The course involves the flow of water through orifices, pipes and canals, and over weirs, the calculation of sizes of pipes and conduits to convey given discharges, the construction of dams, reservoir walls, etc. Water power and water motors are discussed at length. Merriman's *Treatise on Hydraulics* is used as a text-book. In this course are also considered briefly materials—stone, cement, concrete, brick, their properties and general qualities, mode of preparation, and their combinations in construction; structures—masonry construction, theory and practical building of retaining walls, foundations, etc.

Students taking this course must have passed in the preceding course in Mathematics.

MINING.

PROFESSOR DENTON.

SECOND YEAR.—Winter Term, two hours a week; Spring Term, four weeks.

The course consists of a series of lectures illustrated by diagrams, photographs, and sketches. The students may make full notes of these lectures, and are required to recite upon them at short intervals. The work is arranged · to cover, as thoroughly as the time allotted will permit, the various operations that are necessary in mining enterprises.

The following outline of subjects will give an idea of the ground covered.

1st. SURFACE EXCAVATION:

Determination of the amount and character of the material to be removed, methods of excavation, comparative cost and economy of different methods of removing excavated material.

2nd. EXPLOSIVES :

Gunpowder ; constituents, manufacture, properties.

Higher explosives ; constituents, manufacture, properties, precautions necessary, comparative strength, and special advantages ; testing.

3rd. DRILLING :

Hand drilling, types ·of drills.

Machine drills ; description, careful study of successful forms of machines, rate of drilling, repairing, cost.

4th. BLASTING :

Theory of blasting, with reference to the calculation of amount of explosives necessary for large blasts ; location of holes, charging, tamping, firing by fuse and electricity.

5th. AIR COMPRESSORS :

Conditions of working, types, special study of the Rand and Ingersoll Compressors.

6th. PROSPECTING :

Different methods ; deep prospecting, by oil well boring method, by diamond drills ; conditions under which the different methods are applicable, and their cost,

7th. SHAFT SINKING :

Through easy ground by ordinary methods. Study of the methods used successfully in sinking through difficult ground, cost and comparative merits.

8th DRIFTING.

9th. METHODS OF EXPLOITATION :

Typical methods for narrow and for wide veins and beds, including coal mining.

10th. UNDERGROUND TRANSPORTATION :

Tramming, mule and mechanical haulage; construction of cars.

11th. HOISTING :

Inclined and vertical shafts, style of engines, automatic and safety devices, cages, skips, wire ropes.

12th. MINE DRAINAGE :

Adits, collecting water, raising the water with winding machinery, Cornish and direct acting pumps.

13th. MINE VENTILATION AND LIGHTING.

14th. ACCIDENTS AND MINE ACCOUNTS.

In connection with this work, frequent visits to neighboring mines are made, where the machinery and processes described can be seen by the student in actual operation. In order to make these visits of permanent value to the student, he is required to write a description of the mine visited, accompanying his description with sketches, showing dimensions and details of certain pieces of machinery, or other objects, that may have been indicated to him.

. During six weeks of the spring term of the second year, the class in mining is occupied in studying at some of the neighboring mines. About two weeks of this time are given to making mine surveys and the remainder to the detailed study of mining operations.

CRYSTALLOGRAPHY.

THE DIRECTOR AND ASSISTANTS.

FIRST YEAR—Fall Term, eleven hours a week, five weeks.

Instruction in this subject is given by means of lectures and laboratory practice in determining the forms and planes of glass and wooden crystal models, and natural crystals, with recitations and examinations upon the same. The instruction is given in connection with the course in Mineralogy and therefore is confined to training the student in that practical knowledge of crystal forms which he needs in his Determinative Mineralogy. Crystallography is further discussed in connection with the course in Petrography. For purposes of instruction in this subject the laboratory is supplied with the following collections:

Crystal Models in Glass............................... 151
Crystal Models in Wood and Plaster................. 2,153
Natural Crystals....................................... 1,800
                                                      ——
                                                      4,104

MINERALOGY.

THE DIRECTOR AND ASSISTANTS.

FIRST YEAR—Fall Term, eleven hours a week, nine weeks; Winter Term, eleven hours a week, fourteen weeks.

For Determinative Mineralogy there is provided a typical set of all the important minerals, special attention being paid to those of economic value, as well as to those occuring as gangue, or rock-forming minerals. Special collections are arranged showing the physical characters of minerals, their pseudomorphs, etc.

These minerals are arranged in drawers, labeled, and are at all times freely accessible to the student.

Beside the typical collection of minerals, there are placed in drawers a large number of specimens of the same mineral species. These are arranged in convenient groups, but are unlabeled. These specimens are selected so as to represent as great a variety of form, appearance and locality as possible, in order that the student may be familiar with all the types that he will be likely to meet with in his professional practice. Drawers of these unlabeled minerals are assigned to each student, who is required to determine them and to recite upon them. He is required to do that which the practical mineralogist does; to determine his minerals by the shortest method possible, consistent with accuracy, the method to vary according to the specimen. To this end every method of determination short of quantitative analysis is employed; that is, in each case the crystal form and other physical characters are used, as well as the blowpipe and wet tests, so far as they may be needed.

After the student has studied and recited upon the

specimens contained in a sufficient number of drawers of one group, he is then assigned to drawers containing the unlabeled minerals of another group, which have mixed with them specimens of the preceding group or groups. In this way each student is required to determine in his course from 3,000 to 6,000 different mineral specimens, belonging to the 301 selected species.

The instruction is based on the sixth edition of Professor James D. Dana's *System of Mineralogy*, revised by Professor Edward S. Dana, 1892, and every student is expected to provide himself with a copy. In addition, or supplementary, to this work there is given a series of lectures and notes by the Director, in which the characteristic features of each mineral, its uses, and the practical methods employed to distinguish each one are pointed out. Especial attention is given to the methods needed in the field and mine, when one can not have recourse to a chemical laboratory. Every effort is made to train the student to close, accurate observation, to reason correctly upon what he sees, and to exercise good judgment in his decisions.

The result of this work is such that a student not only knows how to proceed in order to determine any mineral that he may meet, but he is also enabled to recognize at sight, or by simple tests, the great majority of specimens belonging to the three hundred and one mineral species that he is required to study in his course.

During the summer term of 1892 the entire mineral collection was rearranged to correspond to the sixth edition of Dana's *System of Mineralogy*, with the exception of some modifications that, it was thought, would enable the student to do his determinative work in an easier and better way.

Beside the collections given under the head of Crystallography there are the following for use in the laboratory work in Mineralogy:

Collection illustrating Physical Properties, Pseudomorphs, etc.,		285
Lecture Collection		10,000

Practice Collection		
First Series	2,500	
Second Series	2,100	
Third Series	1,275	
Fourth Series	3,225	
Fifth Series	1,525	17,025
Sixth Series	1,850	
Seventh Series	1,425	
Review Series	3,125	

27,810

In order that the special mineralogical work done in this institution can be better understood by persons seeking information upon this point, and in addition to serve as a guide to the pupil in referring to the lecture specimens, the appended tables are given of the species to be studied in the laboratory work in this course. The system of numbering is that adopted by Professors Brush, of Yale, and Cooke of Harvard; the original-collection numbers increase by ten each time in order to allow of interpolations of new specimens without having to renumber those already in the lecture collection.

The tables only show the numbers of the specimens belonging to the species upon which laboratory work is given, and not those of the other species represented in the lecture collection.

7

FIRST SERIES.—FIFTY-FIVE SPECIES.

Subclass	Group	Species	Pages in Dana's Mineral.	No. of Figures	First and last Illustrations of the Species	No. of Speci- mens.
Native Elements						
Sulphides, Arsenides, and Antimonides						

FIRST SERIES.—*Continued.*

Divisions.	Group.	Species.	Pages in Dana's System.	No. of Drawer.	First and last numbers of the Specimens.	No. of Specimens.
Sulphantimonides, Etc.	Kermesite	{ Kermesite........	106, 107	42	10620–10630	5
	Zinkenite........	{ Zinkenite........	112	42	10640–10650	2
		{ Berthierite........	114, 115	42	10660–10735	7
	Jamesonite........	{ Jamesonite	122, 123	42	10760–10995	28
	Bournonite.......	{ Bournonite	126–128	42, 43	10996–11235	29
		{ Boulangerite	129, 130	43	11260–11350	10
	Pyrargyrite.....	{ Pyrargyrite......	131–134	43	11360–11420	10
		{ Proustite	134, 135	43	11430–11540	22
	Tetrahedrite....	{ Tetrahedrite.....	137–141	43, 44	11580–12000	51
		{ Stephanite	143–145	44, 45	12050–12190	20
	Enargite	{ Enargite	147–149	45	12310–12320	14

PETROGRAPHY.

DRS. LANE AND PATTON.

The main object of this course is to enable the students to use the petrographical microscope in the determination of minerals and rocks, but much of Physical Mineralogy and some parts of Crystallography are most appropriately taken up in this connection.

The study of this new field of science has, within the past ten years, been introduced into the leading universities, but is, so far as we know, only here given as a part of a regular mining school course. There is, therefore, as yet no text-book that covers the field or is adapted to the needs of the class of students in question. The instruction is consequently through lectures and laboratory work, with syllabi and tables, including Lane's *Petrographical Tables* and Michel Lévy's *Tableau des Birefringences.*

The microscope, beside enabling us to see the structure of fine grained rocks and divine their origin, finds quite as important a use in connection with the attachments, which allow us to determine many minerals, from their optical properties, more easily and accurately than with the blow-pipe. Each student has a microscope, and is required to measure the various optical constants useful in the determination of minerals.

Various other means of determining minerals and rocks, in which the microscope is of more or less help,—for example, microchemical reactions and mechanical and magnetic separations,—are also noted. The study of the texture of rocks as seen in thin sections, which indicates their origin and original chemical character, and the study

Class	Group	Subgroup	Mineral			
Deutoxides	Rutile	Rutile		237-290	74, 75	23640-23630	110
		Zircon		432-433	75, 76	23480-23880	58
		Brookite		243, 243	76	23910-24010	15
		Pyrolusite		243, 244	76, 77	24080-24050	68
Hydrous Oxides	Opal	Opal	Precious Opal Fire Opal Girasol Common Opal Resin Opal Semi-Opal Hydrophane Cacholong Opal-Agate Menilite Jasp-Opal Wood-Opal Hyalite Florite Geyserite Tripolite	194-197	77-90	24040-26650	133
		Turgite		246	80	26960-26980	5
		Diaspore		247	80	26900-26960	22
		Göthite		247, 248	80, 81	26940-26450	44
		Manganite		248, 250	81, 83	26450-26570	15
	Limonite	Limonite	Yellow Ochre Umber Bog Ore Pisolitic Oolitic	250, 251	82-85	26680-27060	114
	Bauxite	Wochenite		251	95	26680-27090	15
	Brucite	Brucite		252, 253	95, 96	27700-27090	31
		Gibbsite		254, 255	96	27900-28080	12
		Sassolite		255	96	28080-28080	7
		Hydrotalcite		255	97	28080-28630	15
		Chalcophanite		256, 257	97	28940-28820	9
		Psilomelane		257	87, 88	28880-28870	38
	Wad	Wad	Asbolite Lampadite Bog Man	257, 258		28880-28800	25

Topas { Topas, Pyrophysalite, Pycnite	492–496	816–817	50890–50980	45
Andalusite { Andalusite, Chiastolite	496–498	817, 818	50940–51220	58
Sillimanite { Sillimanite, Fibrolite, Bucholzite	498–499	818, 819	51280–51620	40
Cyanite / Dumortierite	500, 501 / 556	820, 821 / 822	51680–52150 / 52140–52165	54 / 6
Zoisite { Zoisite, Thulite, Saussurite	513–516	823, 823	52170–52560	43
Epidote { Epidote / Piedmontite	516–521 / 521, 522	823, 824 / 824	52560–53000 / 52970–53160	49 / 12
Allanite { Allanite, Orthite	522–526	824, 825	53170–53490	36
Gadolinite	509–512	825	53500–53840	16
Axinite	527–529	825, 826	53650–53880	22
Chondrodite / Ilvaite	529–533 / 541, 543	826 / 826, 827	53840–54000 / 54070–54360	28 / 25
Cerite	550	827	54310–54380	8
Tourmaline { Rubellite, Indicolite	551–556	827–830	54390–55760	153
Staurolite	556–560	830, 831	55770–56110	55
Titanite { Titanite, Sphene, Greenovite	712–716	831, 832	56120–56900	53

Group	Subgroup	Mineral				No.
Serpentines and Talc } { Serpentine	Serpentine {	Baltimorite	675	364, 365	66950–67090	22
		Picrosmine	676	365	67090–67105	14
	Dewylite					
	Genthite					
	Garnierite {	Noumeite	674, 677	366	67300–67380	17
		Garnierite				
	Talc {	Talc	678–680	366–368	67340–68010	71
		Steatite				
		Rensselaerite				
	Pyrophyllite		691, 692	368, 369	68050–68340	25
	Pinite {	Pinite	431, 621	369, 370	68350–68810	74
		Fahlunite	451			
		Chlorophyllite	451			
		Gigantolite	491, 621			
		Gieseckite	455, 621			
		Liebenerite	455, 621			
		Killinite	365, 621			
		Agalmatolite	623, 691			
		Oncite	692			
	Septolite	Meerschaum	680, 681	370	68920–68950	14
	Kaolinite {	Kaolinite	685–687	370, 371	68900–69410	55
		Pholerite				
Kaolin	Halloysite {	Halloysite	688, 689	372	69450–69650	30
		Indianaite	695			
		Smectite				
		Fuller's Earth				
		Bole				
	Allophane		693, 694	372	69690–69900	18
Chrysocolla	Chrysocolla		699, 700	373	69900–70380	49
Hisingerite {		Glauconite	688, 694	374	70090–70570	19
		Chloropal	701, 703	374	70580–70670	12
		Hisingerite	702, 703	374	70700–70790	10
		Neotocite	704, 705	374	70810–70860	5

Hydrous Sulphates.					
	Gypsum	Alabaster / Gypsum	941, 942 944, 945	400 / 400–401	90020–90050 / 90080–90480	12 / 18
	Copperas	Melanterite / Chalcanthite	966, 967 / 968	401 / 401	90080–90750 / 90760–90850	8 / 11
	Coquimbite	Coquimbite / Alunogen	964–966 / 970 / 974	402 / 402 / 402	81000–81180 / 81200–81250 / 81260–81880	10 / 6 / 10
	Alum	Copiapite / Aluminite / Alunite				
Tungstates and Molybdates.	Wolframite	Wolframite / Hübnerite	983–985	402, 403	81380–81550	19
	Scheelite	Scheelite / Wulfenite	985–988 / 989–991	403 / 403	81560–81780 / 81770–81990	21 / 30
Mellates.	Mellite	Mellite	994, 995	401	82000–82050	14
Hydrocarbons.	Paraffin	Hatchettite / Ozocerite	997 / 998, 999	404 / 404	82070–82180 / 82170–82250	10 / 11
	Resin	Succinite / Copalite / Retinellite	1002, 1006 / 1007 / 1009	405 / 405 / 405	82240–82400 / 82420–82500 / 82510–82560	20 / 11 / 6
	Petroleum	Naptha / Petroleum	1015–1017	405	82570	25
	Bitumen	Asphaltum / Elaterite / Albertite / Uintahite	1017, 1018 / 1018, 1019 / 1020 / 1020	405, 406 / 406 / 406 / 406	82590–82910 / 82920–82930 / 82940–82960 / 82970–82990	30 / 7 / 4 / 3
	Coal	Anthracite / Bituminous, or Bituminous Coal / Cannelite, or Cannel Coal / Torbanite / Lignite, or Brown Coal / Jet	1021 / 1021–1024 / 1022 / 1009, 1025 / 1032	406 / 406, 407 / 407 / 407 / 407, 408	83000–83020 / 83090–83110 / 83120–83310 / 83215–83319 / 83320–83970	8 / 12 / 9 / 5 / 50

of the associations of minerals occupies much time. The classification, nomenclature and determination of rocks are given in the course in Lithology.

The general course is strictly elementary, practical and non-mathematical, as the effort is to give the student such facts as he needs in his future work, and to train him in the use of the microscope,—an instrument that is employed now in almost every department of practical life.

It will be seen, however, that the apparatus is ample also for advanced research; it covers all that is found to· be of service in the best petrographical laboratories of Europe and America, and the instructors are ready to lend students, that wish more thorough and extensive training, all the help they need.

A student to take this course must have completed the courses in Physics. Crystallography, Mineralogy, and the first year's Chemistry.

For the purpose of giving the above elementary and advanced instruction the department is supplied, amongst other things, with the following apparatus:

Twenty-nine Bausch and Lomb's Petrographical Microscopes, made expressly for the Michigan Mining School; with Micrometer Eyepieces, Bertrand's Lenses, Quartz Wedges, Undulation Plates, etc.

Four Beck's Petrographical Microscopes with Accessories.

One Fuess's Largest Petrographical Microscope of the latest pattern with all the Accessories; made expressly for this institution.

One Nachet's Largest Petrographical Microscope. with all the Accessories.

One Dick's Petrographical Microscope, with Swift's Objectives and other Accessories.

One Projection Microscope.

One Nachet's Inverted Chemical Microscope.

One Spectroscope.

One Spectropolarizer.

One Sorby's Apparatus for observing the four images given by biaxial bodies.

Two Calderon's Oculars.

Three Bertrand's Oculars.

One Spectroscope Ocular.

One Goniometer Ocular.

One Babinet's Compensator Ocular.

One Michel-Levy's Comparateur.

One Axial Angle Apparatus for measurements in oil.

Two Axial Angle Apparatus.

One Periscope Eyepiece.

One Filar Micrometer.

One Cross-hair Micrometer.

Three Micrometers.

Four Camera Lucidas.

Two Abbé's Camera Lucidas.

One Bausch and Lomb's One-inch Microphotographic Objective.

One Mica Plate Nose Piece.

Many Extra Eyepieces, Objectives, etc.

One Condenser.

One Condenser with Iris Diaphragm.

One Jannettaz's Thermal Apparatus.

One Latterman's Apparatus.

One Fuess's Polariscope with Accessories.

One Groth's Universal Apparatus, with Goniometer.

One Fuess's Application Goniometer for dull crystals.

One Fuess's Reflection Goniometer.

One Hirschwald's Microscope Goniometer.

One Linhof's Reflection Goniometer.

One Total Reflectometer Attachment.

Fourteen Miller's Goniometers.

One Stage Goniometer.

One Bertraud's Micro-goniometer with Special Stage.

One Flask for measuring Index of Fluids.

One Pyroelectric Duster.

One Strong's Chest and Apparatus, for Microchemical Reactions, etc., etc.

Thin Sections of European Rocks and Minerals..... 752

Thin Sections of Geological Survey Collection..... 6,293
                                                  ———
                                                  7,045

In connection with the Lecture Collection of Rocks about two thousand sections are being made this school year, and will be available in 1893.

LITHOLOGY.

THE DIRECTOR AND ASSISTANTS.

SECOND YEAR.—Fall Term, six hours a week.

Large and complete collections of rock specimens are arranged for the use of the student. The course of instruction here is similar to that followed in the course in Mineralogy. Lectures are given upon the specimens of the typical collection, the method of classification explained, and the distinguishing characters of the different groups, species, and varieties pointed out. Special attention is called to the variations and alterations in

rocks, and to their local modifications du
special mode of occurrence in the field.

The object of the course is to give the st
training in the practical determination of j
will enable him to know them in the field an
well as to observe their alterations and mod
subjects that have a very important bearing
vital questions relating to ore deposits.

After the study of a sufficiently large numb
has been had, the student has assigned to hi
containing unlabeled specimens of these rocks,
is expected to determine and recite upon, as he
in his study of the minerals. The course is t
thorough and practical, and adapted to the nee
miner and geologist, giving them a training
can make use of in their future work.

The following collections of rocks are availabl
in this course:

Lecture Collection............................
Practice Collection...........................
Rosenbusch Collection ....
Collection of Michigan Rocks..................
Collection of the State Geological Survey.......

The subjoined classification of rocks will sh
scope of the laboratory work and lectures, as the
tion is given entirely by lectures and laboratory p

	Rhyolite. [Liparite.] Nevadite.	Granite.		Mica Schist. Gneiss.
Phosphorolite.	(Guano.)	Phosphorite. Coprolite.	Apatite.	
Barolite.			Barite. Celestite.	
Selenolite.			Gypsum. Anhydrite.	
Limestone.	Marl.	Chalk. Marl.	Travertine. Marl. Oolite. Pisolite. Limestone.	Limestone. Dolomite. Magnesite.	Marble.	Ophicalcite.
Carbonolite.	Turf. Peat.		Lignite. Torbanite. Cannelite, or Cannel Coal. Bituminosite, or Bituminous Coal.	Asphaltum. Coal. Graphite.	Albertite. Anthracite.

PALEONTOLOGY.

DR. LANE.

SECOND YEAR.—Winter Term, five hours a week, seven weeks.

This course is given as an elementary one. It will begin by a review of the fundamental principles of Zoölogy and Botany for use in recognition of fossils. Although details are left out, a personal handling of the forms of living species will be insisted upon, so that the knowledge will be real as far as it goes.

In paleontology, certain groups that yield common and characteristic fossils will be treated more in detail. There is a small type-collection of living and fossil forms, arranged zoölogically in accordance with the system of Nicholson's New *Manual of Paleontology;* and a larger one of fossils, containing over a thousand specimens, arranged mainly according to horizons, for the student to consult. A collection of over fifteen hundred specimens, especially selected to cover the commoner fossils of the whole geological column, will be used to drill the students in recognizing fossils in different states of preservation, in assigning them to their general orders, and in certain cases giving their generic names. The specimens are arranged unlabeled in drawers, for the students to work upon, and pains will be taken to train the eye to recognize resemblances and differences. The practical work will be similar to that pursued in the course in Mineralogy. No particular text-book will be required. The library is well supplied with books on the branches covered by this course, and advice on buying books will be given to the students according to their individual needs.

STRATIGRAPHICAL AND HISTORICAL GEOLOGY.

DR. LANE.

SECOND YEAR.—Winter Term, five hours a week, seven weeks.

This will be in continuation of the course in Paleontology. The formations which compose the earth's crust will be taken up in their order, and their characteristic life and lithology, their distribution and peculiarities, will be described.

The student will also be expected, without using books for the purpose, to assign a sufficient number of characteristic fossils to their periods, and if the time permits will be exercised in determining horizons, with the help of paleontological literature, as the library contains full sets of the New York and other State reports and various special works which may be used for this purpose.

The text-book used in 1891 and previously was Dr. Archibald Geikie's *Text Book on Geology*, books V and VI.

Owing to this work being out of print during the preparation of the third edition, there is temporarily used Professor Joseph LeConte's *Elements of Geology*, third edition.

Students taking this course must have completed the preceding work in Mineralogy, Lithology, and Paleontology.

PHYSICAL GEOLOGY.

THE DIRECTOR.

THIRD YEAR.—Fall Term, five hours a week.

The instruction in Physical Geology is intended to be especially adapted to the needs of the explorer, the engineer, the petrographer, the geologist, the miner, the quarryman, and of all others that desire to understand the connection and the structural relations that rock masses have to one another and to the valuable deposits which they may contain. It is intended to treat of the origin and alterations of rocks, of general volcanic and earthquake action, metamorphism, jointing, faulting, cleavage, mountain building, eruptive rocks and crystalline schists; the action of air, surface and underground waters and life; the interior condition of the earth, etc., especially in their relations to the problems that the economic geologist, miner and quarryman have to meet. On account of the connection of the Mining School and the Geological Survey, the student has brought before him constantly the various problems that arise in the practical work in the survey, and their methods of solution.

The course in 1891–1892 was given by lectures and by recitations based upon the lectures and upon Dr. Archibald Geikie's *Text Book of Geology,* books I, II (part I), III, IV and VII. As stated under the head of Stratigraphical and Historical Geology LeConte's *Elements of Geology* will be used until the third edition of Geikie's text book shall have been issued.

Students who wish to take this course must have completed the preceding work in Physics, Elementary Chemistry, Mineralogy, Petrography, Lithology and Geology.

ECONOMIC GEOLOGY.

THE DIRECTOR.

THIRD YEAR.—Winter Term, five hours a week.

It is intended to give the instruction in this subject by lectures, recitations, and practical observations in the field and in the mines. The design of the lectures is to cover the following subjects:

I. Metalliferous or Ore Deposits.

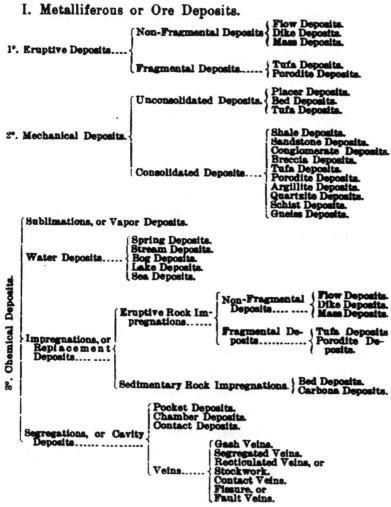

II. Hydrocarbons.

1°. Resins.................
{ Succinite.
Retinite.
Retinellite.
Ambrite.
Copalite.

2°. Paraffins..............
{ Hatchettite.
Ozocerite.
Zietrisikite.
Urpethite.

3°. Bitumens...............
{ Natural Gas.. }Gaseous.
Naptha.......{ Fluid.
Petroleum..
Maltha.. }Semi-Fluid.
Elaterite....
Asphaltum..
Albertite....
Wurtzilite.. }Solids.
Grahamite..
Uintahite...

4°. Peats.................
{ Turf.
Peat.

5°. Coals.................
{ Lignite, or Brown Coal.
(Jet.)
Torbanite.
Cannelite, or
Cannel Coal.
Bituminosite, or
Bituminous Coal.
Anthracite.

III. Salt and saline earths.

IV. Materials used for grinding, whetting and polishing.

V. Gems and decorative materials.

VI. Building stones and road-making materials.

VII. Lime, cement and artificial stone.

VIII. Refractory, or fire-resisting materials.

IX. Clay, sands, etc., used for pottery, porcelain and glass.

X. Mineral, medicines.

XI. Pigments, dyes and detergents.

XII. Water and water supply.

XIII. Mineral and thermal springs.

In 1891–1892 Phillips's *Ore Deposits* was used as a text-book.'

Special attention is given to the instruction of the student in Mineralogy, Petrography and Geology, in order that he may in after years understand the nature of the deposits upon which he may be at work; since disastrous mistakes probably occur in the practice of a mining engineer oftener through ignorance of the petrographical and geological relations of the ore deposits in question, than from a lack of engineering or metallurgical skill.

The location of the school affords special advantages for the study of Petrography and General and Economic Geology. It is situated in the midst of the vast and ancient lava flows and conglomerates generally known as the Copper-bearing or Keweenawan series, and near the Eastern or Potsdam Sandstone. In the immediate vicinity are to be solved some of the most important and fundamental problems of petrographical and geological science, e. g. the metamorphism or alteration of rocks, the true age of the so-called Keweenawan series, the relation of the so-called Huronian and Laurentian series, the origin of the iron ore, etc., while almost every problem of Geology finds its illustration in some portion of the Upper Peninsula.

The instruction in the various departments under the charge of the Director is intended to be given so that all those who wish to obtain a knowledge of the subjects as a matter of general information, or to prepare themselves to be teachers or investigators, can attend with advantage.

'The opportunities for practical instruction in Mineralogy and Geology, particularly in Economic Geology, have been greatly increased by placing the State Geological Survey under the charge of the Director of the Mining School. This arrangement enables skilled specialists to be employed for the mutual advantage of the School and the Survey. It further brings the student into direct contact with the practical applications of Geology, and with its more important problems under discussion at the present time. *Students who wish to take this course must have completed the preceding work in Physics, Elementary Chemistry, Mineralogy, Petrography, Lithology and Geology.* Exceptions in the requirements in any of the above courses may be made in favor of special students of age and experience, who would be benefited by such exceptions.

SUMMER COURSE IN GEOLOGY.

THE DIRECTOR AND ASSISTANTS.

THIRD YEAR—Summer Term, five days a week, four weeks.

Part of the summer term of the third year is spent in the field and in the mines, in the practical study of various questions in General and Economic Geology, Mineralogy and Petrography.

In order to increase the usefulness of the Mining School by enabling persons to take some of its courses of instruction, the summer courses in Geology, Shop-practice and Surveying have been established. All candidates for a degree in this institution are required to take all of these courses. They are also open to persons, not otherwise members of the Mining School, who wish to attend them. The summer course in Geology will commence in August and continue for four weeks. The course consists essentially in the examination and discussion of observed phenomena of the sedimentary and eruptive

rocks, whether metamorphic or not, as well as of the associated ores to be seen in the Upper Peninsula of
Michigan. The work for the most part will be done in
the vicinity of the mines, and students will be expected
to make maps, notes, sections, diagrams, etc.

This course, like all others in the Mining School, is
open without charge to any one, whether a resident of
Michigan or not. It is hoped that it will be of practical value to all teachers and others who wish to obtain
a knowledge of the field occurrence of minerals and rocks,
including ores, as well as to see the various phases of
mining. The classes have studied the Lake Superior
coast and adjacent islands north and south of Marquette,
and the mines and adjacent country about Negaunee,
Ishpeming, Humboldt, Republic, Champion and the Gold
Range. The next course will be given in the summer
of 1893.

The student of geology can study within the limits of
the Upper Peninsula of Michigan the following stratigraphical formations, commencing in the list with the
oldest.

Azoic or Archaean System.............	Laurentian (?) Period	Cascade Formation.
	Huronian (?) Period...	Republic Formation. Mesnard Formation.
	Michigan Period........	Holyoke Formation. Negaunee Formation.
Paleozoic System...	Cambrian Period......	Potsdam Formation. [Keweenawan Formation.] Calciferous Formation.
	Silurian Period..........	Trenton Formation. Hudson River Formation. Niagara Formation. Onondaga Formation. Lower Helderberg Formation.
	Devonian Period.......	Upper Helderberg Formation
Anthropozoic System.................	Quaternary Period.....	Pleistocene Formation. Recent Formation.

THESES.

Every student who is a candidate for the degree of Mining Engineer in either course is required to present to the Faculty a satisfactory thesis, embodying the results of an investigation upon some subject related to the studies of that course, before he can be recommended to receive his degree. Students that intend to graduate in any year are required to select their subjects and present them to the Faculty for approval by the first of March of that year.

Candidates for the degree of Bachelor of Science to be given at the completion of the first three years of the four years course going into effect in September, 1893, are not required to present any thesis.

ORGANIZATION.

The Michigan Mining School is an institution established and supported by the State of Michigan in accordance with that liberal educational policy which has placed the University of Michigan amongst the foremost educational institutions of America.

The Mining School is organized under the authority of an Act, approved May 1, 1885, portions of which are as follows:

"SECTION 1. The people of the State of Michigan enact: That a school shall be established in the Upper Peninsula of the State of Michigan, to be called the Michigan Mining School, for the purpose and under the regulations contained in this Act.

"SEC. 2. The said school shall be under the control and management of a board of six members, not less than four of whom shall be residents of the Upper Peninsula of the State of Michigan, who shall be known as the 'Board of Control of the Michigan Mining School,' and who shall be appointed by the Governor of the State of Michigan, by and with the consent of the Senate (* * * *) and who shall serve without compensation.

"SEC. 5. The course of instruction shall embrace geology, mineralogy, chemistry, mining and mining engineering, and such other branches of practical and theoretical knowledge as will, in the opinion of the board, conduce to the end of enabling the students of said institution to obtain a full knowledge of the science, art and practice of mining, and the application of machinery .thereto. Tuition shall be free in said institution to all bona fide residents of this State, but a reasonable charge for incidental expenses, not less than ten dollars nor exceeding thirty dollars per year, may be made against any student, if deemed necessary, and the board shall not be obliged to furnish books, apparatus, or other materials for the use of students.

"SEC. 6. The course of study, the terms, and the hours of instruction, shall be regulated by the board, who shall also have power to make all such rules and regulations concerning admission, control and discipline of students, and such others, as may be deemed necessary for the good government of the Institution and the convenience and transaction of its business.

"SEC. 7. No debt shall be contracted beyond or apart from the actual means at the disposal of the Inststution. The board may dispose of or lease any property donated to the State for said School, or which may be acquired in payment of debts except of such as is necessary for the accommodation of the school. * * * * * *"

In conformity with the above act, the Michigan Mining School was first opened to students September 15, 1886, and has been made free to students from every land. All are received on the same conditions, no matter where their residence may be.

REGULATIONS OF THE SCHOOL.

Neatness, order and good conduct on the part of the students in a school of this character are requisite, if the school is to maintain credit both at home and abroad.

Students that enter this institution are supposed to do so in order to prepare themselves for their profession, and, like students in Technological, Law or Medical Schools, are pre-supposed to understand what they are here for, to attend strictly to that business, and to conduct themselves as gentlemen. The members of the Faculty have no time to waste on primary instruction, nor in conducting a reform school (which the State has elsewhere provided), as may with propriety be done by non-professional schools. If a man cannot be a man and attend to his duties as he should, this institution has no place for him. It is not obliged to proceed further than to be satisfied that any man's presence is injurious to the school, or that his longer stay is of no advantage to himself; neither is it obliged to deal out repeated warnings, nor even any warning. Methods that are proper, or that are in vogue in academies, normal schools and colleges, are entirely out of place in a professional school whose students average over twenty-one years of age.

The general rules of the School, so far as they need be announced to the general public, are as follows:

The Faculty have full power to admonish, dismiss, suspend, or expel any student, for cause.

Each member of the Faculty is held responsible for the rooms, apparatus, etc., of his department, and for the good order and discipline of the students under his charge.

Each instructor is required to be in attendance during the working hours in his department, and he has the power to discipline or suspend any student from his room until such time as the case shall have been acted upon by the Faculty.

All absences of students from recitations, lectures, field and laboratory work, are considered as failures in recitations, and are so ranked unless excused by vote of the Faculty, and made up. Tardiness is considered as a half-absence.

Each instructor shall keep a record of the daily work of each student under his charge, and rank him on a scale of 100; and no student shall be permitted to pass who has not obtained an average of at least 75 in his daily work.

Examinations shall be held at the end of every term, or, if desired, at the completion of each subject, if falling within the term. The examinations are ranked on a scale of 100, and no student shall be permitted to pass unless he obtains a rank of 75.

It will thus be seen that every student, in order to pass, must obtain a class standing of at least 75 on a scale of 100, in all term work, and *also* in all examinations.

The method of making up deficiencies in daily work varies with the subject, at the discretion of the instructor.

In the case of all foreseen minor absences the instructor in charge of the exercise to be missed should be spoken to before the absence occurs. All absences from town of a day or more must be arranged for previously with the Director or they will not be excused, but this does not relieve the student from handing in to the Faculty the usual petition for excuse.

All excuses for absences must be handed in to the proper officer within one week after the absence shall have occurred; a number of unexcused absences will subject the student to discipline.

All students taking special or partial courses shall be referred to a committee consisting of the Director, the Secretary, and one other member of the Faculty appointed by the Director, who shall arrange the courses to be taken by said students.

Students having chosen their course or subjects are not allowed to change or to drop any of them, except upon petition to, and by vote of the Faculty, and failure to observe this rule will subject the student to discipline.

The rank of each student is reported to himself, or, if he is a minor, to his parents or guardian, after the close of each term.

With this are reported all absences, whether excused or not, and such other information concerning the student as it may be considered advisable to report.

Entrance conditions are to be made up in accordance with the regulation announced previously under the heading *Requirements for Admission.*

Special regulations are made concerning the conditions received during the various terms, owing to the nature of the work and to the special arrangement of the terms in this institution, as follows:

Conditions received in any laboratory work can be made up only by a repetition of the work at a time when the laboratory is open for work in the same subject. This also applies to shop-practice, drawing (excluding topographical drawing) and to all field, mine or mill work.

Conditions received in work (not included under the general head of laboratory work) are to be made up as follows:

Conditions received during the fall term in Algebra, Trigonometry, Calculus, Physics, Graphical Statics, Mechanics of Materials, Mechanical and Electrical Engineering, Chemistry, Stoichiometry, Ore Dressing, Metallurgy, Physical and Economic Geology, are to be made up at the commencement of the winter term following.

Conditions received during the winter term, in Trigonometry, Analytical Geometry, Physics, first year Chemistry, Mine Surveying and Mining, are to be made up at the commencement of the spring term following.

Conditions received during the winter term, in Plane Surveying, Topographical Drawing, Hydraulics, Mechanism, Properties of Materials, Stratigraphical Geology, Economic Geology, Ore Dressing, Metallurgy, third year Mining, and Mechanical and Electrical Engineering, are to be made up at stated times in the summer term following.

Conditions received during the winter term, in Calculus, Analytical Mechanics, and in second year Chemistry are to be made up at the commencement of the fall term following.

Conditions received during the spring term, in Analytical Geometry, and Electricity and Magnetism, are to be made up at the commencement of the fall term following.

Conditions received in the summer term, in the Theoretical work in Surveying, are to be made up at the commencement of the winter term following.

The dates upon which examinations in the above subjects will be held will be assigned by the Faculty at the opening of each term.

In case of failure on the part of any student to remove his conditions at the specified time, he will have to take the course in that subject over again. If he fails then at the regular examination, he will not be allowed to repeat the subject again.

No student shall take any course, to the successful prosecution of which a previous course in which he is conditioned is considered essential, except upon his petition for this privilege to the Faculty, and its authorization by that body.

A student who absents himself from any examination, without reasons satisfactory to the Faculty, shall be considered as having failed in such examination, and the following rule will then cover his case:

A student who, in any subject, obtains a rank of fifty or less, in either term work or examination, shall, at the discretion of the Faculty, be debarred from further examination and required to repeat the work.

Any student having more than six conditions at any one time will either be dropped from the School or assigned to special work, as in the judgment of the Faculty seems to be best for him.

Any of the general regulations of the school may be suspended by the Faculty, in behalf of special students of age and experience, to aid them in their work, if such suspension seems advisable.

All students are required to observe proper decorum, and to refrain from any conduct that disturbs others, or is injurious to the School.

The attempt of any student to falsify in any of his school relations is regarded as a most serious offence, and renders the offender liable to suspension or even to expulsion.

Each instructor shall have power to take such action as he may see fit in case he detects any illegitimate work in the class room, but a second offense on the part of the same student or any illegitimate work of any kind during an examination shall be reported to the Faculty for action, and may be punished by summary dismissal.

LOCATION.

The school is located at Houghton, the county seat of Houghton county. The twin towns of Houghton and Hancock lie in the sheltered valley of Portage Lake, an arm of Lake Superior. The climate is bracing and healthful. Although Houghton is in a high latitude, yet one is far less inconvenienced by the cold here than he is much further south along the Atlantic coast, or in the immediate vicinity of the Great Lakes. This is due to the dryness of the Houghton climate, a climate which is free from any malaria, hay fever, etc. In general, students coming from localities further south have found health and strength improved by the change. The town has an abundant supply of pure spring water. Houghton is easily reached by rail from Detroit, Chicago, Milwaukee, St. Paul, Superior and Duluth (a descriptive pamphlet showing the routes to Houghton can be obtained from the General Passenger Agent, D., S. S. & A. R'y., Minneapolis, Minn.); and by steamer from all the important ports on the chain of the Great Lakes. Within the State, half-fare rates are given to the students of the Mining School by the Duluth, South Shore & Atlantic Railway.

While the School itself is situated in the Portage Lake copper district, the access to the Keweenawan copper district on the north is easy, and there lie within comparatively short distances the Ontonagon copper district, and the iron mining regions of Marquette, Menominee and Gogebic.

In the immediate vicinity of the Mining School are located the Quincy, Atlantic, Franklin and Huron copper mines, while within a distance of fifteen miles are situated the Calumet and Hecla, Tamarack, Osceola and other copper mines, with their machine shops, smelting works, rolling and stamp mills, etc. In the iron mining regions lie numerous great iron mines, prominent among which are the Cleveland, Jackson, Lake Superior, Lake Angeline, Champion, Republic, Chapin, Vulcan, Cyclops, Colby and Norrie.

In addition to copper and iron, among the mineral products of the state are numbered gold, silver, gypsum, building stones, slate, coal, salt, etc.

Some idea of the vastness of the mining operations in the Lake Superior district can be gathered from the following statistics: It contains over sixty-five copper mines, which have produced, up to 1890, one billion three hundred and twenty-seven million seven hundred and ninety-nine thousand four hundred and twenty pounds of copper, valued at two hundred and forty-three million seven hundred and six thousand eight hundred and nine dollars. The cost sheet of one mine alone is some four millions yearly, mainly expended in this region. One mine alone has paid over forty millions of dollars in dividends, or over three times as much as any other mine now working in the United States, except one, and over twice as much as that one.

In the iron mining districts about Lake Superior, in Michigan, there were produced in 1890 seven million one hundred and eighty-five thousand one hundred and seventy-five tons of iron ore, or nearly one-half of all the iron ore produced in the United States.

The Michigan iron mines have produced since their discovery over fifty millions of tons of iron ore.

Michigan is credited by the Director of the Mint with producing in 1889 gold to the amount of seventy thousand dollars, and silver amounting to seventy-seven thousand five hundred and seventy-five dollars.

The State of Michigan is also the chief producer of salt and gypsum in the United States.

The Michigan Mining School has been located in the Upper Peninsula of Michigan for the same reason that a medical school should be in the vicinity of large hospitals, in order that it should be associated with the objects about which it treats.

From this location the student of the Michigan Mining School is placed in a mining atmosphere, in which all his surroundings and associations are in conformity with his present and future work. He is thus enabled to see in actual operation some of the most successful and extensive mining operations now conducted anywhere.

The Calumet and Hecla mine is now worked at a depth on the lode of over 4,500 feet, with an extent in length of about two and one-half miles. This mine is operated by fourteen shafts, one of which is a six-compartment shaft, now sunk to a perpendicular depth of about 3,500 feet; when completed, it will be upwards of 5,000 feet deep. The aggregate power of the steam plant in use and under construction is some 37,-500 horse power, including one engine of 4,700 horse power and eleven other engines of an average of 2,000 horse power each. The stamp mills of this mine contain 18 improved Ball steam stamps, making from 95 to 98 blows per minute, and crushing about 4,500 tons of rock in· twenty-four hours. Three of the pumping engines have an aggregate capacity of 50,000,000 gallons in twenty-four hours, while another triple expansion pumping engine has alone the capacity of 60,000,000 gallons in twenty-four hours. Beside the two sand wheels forty feet in diameter capable of lifting some 16,000,000 to 18,000,000 gallons of water and 1,600 tons of sand per day, there is now completed another wheel fifty-four feet in diameter capable of lifting 30,000,000 gallons of water and 3,000 tons of sand per day.

The smelting works of this mine contain sixteen refining furnaces with an aggregate capacity of 224 tons in twenty-four hours. They also contain two blast and two blister furnaces, etc. All the other appliances of this remarkable mine are commensurate with those above given.

The Tamarack mine has two perpendicular shafts, one over 4,700 feet and the other over 4,500 feet in depth.

The other mines, mills, smelting works, etc., are all well equipped for their work, and every assistance is given by their officers and men to aid the students of the Mining School in studying the various appliances, under the direction of the Faculty of the School.

EXPENSES.

Under the act of organization, the Board of Control have made the school entirely free, no charge being made for tuition or incidentals, whether the student was a resident of the State of Michigan, or of the United States, or not; all has been made free to the students from every land. Owing to the fact that the expenses of providing a thorough technical education in any branch, particularly in Mining Engineering, are much greater than those attendant upon a literary education, it is possible that after a few more years, the same tuition fee will be charged non-resident students that is now charged students in most of the technical schools in other States, while there will also be charged to all students the amount allowed for incidentals, as specified in the act of organization. Should this change be made, due and full notice will be given. The supplies in the chemical and allied laboratories are furnished the students, and they are required to pay for materials, re-agents, etc., and for the use and breakage of apparatus.

In order partially to insure the State against damage and loss to its school property, every student is required to deposit with the Treasurer the sum of twenty-five dollars ($25). This sum shall not be withdrawn by the student until he closes his connection with the School; and if any portion is required by the School as a refund for damages, the part withdrawn shall be at once replaced by the student, or he shall be dismissed from the school.

Charges for apparatus, chemicals and other supplies from

the store room, as well as for repairs of damages to school property, and also fines, shall be deducted from coupons procurable from the Clerk upon payment of five dollars each, but no portion of the twenty-five dollars above mentioned shall be used for the purchase of these coupons.

The permanent deposit of twenty-five dollars together with any balance equivalent to the unused portion of a coupon shall be returned to the student when he closes his connection with the school, but not before. Each student is required to present to the Director his certificate of deposit from the Treasurer, at the commencement of each school year, or at such time thereafter as he may present himself at the School for work. The Director may then issue an annual certificate of membership to the student, subject to the subsequent approval of the Faculty.

No student shall be considered a member of the School or allowed to join in any of the exercises, or to take any apparatus, chemicals, books, etc., until he shall have presented to the Instructor, Librarian, and Dispensing Clerk, his certificate of membership for that school year.

It shall be the duty of the Treasurer to have printed such coupons as are needed. These shall be deposited with the Clerk, the Treasurer taking his receipt therefor. The Clerk shall pay over to the Treasurer all money received from the student in payment for the coupons, taking his receipt therefor. The accounts of the Clerk shall be audited every year, at which time the Clerk shall show to the Auditing Committee Treasurer's receipts and unused coupons amounting in value to all the coupons deposited with him by the Treasurer, before the Clerk's accounts shall be adjusted.

There are no dormitories connected with the School.

Arrangements can be made by those who desire to do so, to obtain board and rooms in private families, and in boarding houses, in Houghton and Hancock, at prices varying from twenty to twenty-five dollars per calendar month. Twenty-two to twenty-three dollars per month is understood to be the standard average price. This is to include the room, heat and lights, as well as board. Board alone can be obtained at from eighteen to twenty dollars per calendar month.

The necessary expenses of the students are estimated by them as follows for each year :

Board, etc., 10½ months at $20.00 to $25.00..	$210 00 to	$262 50
Apparatus, Chemicals, etc.	20 00 to	40 00
Books and Drawing Materials	25 00 to	50 00
Traveling Expenses (Excursions, Field work, etc.)	10 00 to	50 00
Washing	20 00 to	30 00
Total	$285 00	$432 50

EMPLOYMENT.

The question is often asked the officers of the Mining School if they can promise employment to students on graduation. The only answer is, that neither the Mining School nor any other self-respecting institution can make any such promises. The question of employment depends on too many factors to be promised three or four years in advance. It depends on the demand and the supply, which are liable to vary from year to year, and it also very largely depends on a student's personal "equation." Thus far the demand for suitable men has been greater than the supply, but how it will be in the future can not be told. A thorough, hard working student, with the ability to command the respect of men and to manage them, and to work harmoniously with his fellow officers, will hardly ever fail of obtaining the choicest positions that are open to him, especially after having had the practical work and experience about the mines that the graduates of this school have.

Education and training do not give qualities to any man; they simply sharpen and develop those natural abilities that he possesses; hence, if he is not by nature fitted for a certain position, he ought not, and will not be likely, to obtain it. On the other hand, whatever may be a man's natural abilities, he will not be likely to obtain a position of any high grade unless he has been educated for it, either in school or outside—the outside education being by far the most expensive kind of education that can be obtained.

Slothful, lazy, careless, and inefficient students will not naturally obtain places as readily as the hard-working ones, other things being equal. They certainly will not be recommended by the officers of the Mining School, since a man who cannot be trusted to attend faithfully to his work when engaged in obtaining his professional training is not one whom it is safe to trust with important business and mining interests.

Students should remember that their conduct, from the day they enter the Mining School until they leave it, has an all important bearing upon their future position and standing, since almost every one on leaving has obtained his position through its officers or its graduates.

The Director of the Mining School makes one invariable rule, *i. e.*, that all persons desiring students or graduates of this School shall be informed of the defects, as well as of the virtues of the candidates, so far as he knows them, believing that such a course is the only one that is just either to the employer, to the student, or to the School. When information is fully given concerning the position and desired qualities of the person to fill it, pains are taken to select the student who is believed to be most suitable for the position.

In order to secure the best future for themselves, students are urged to neglect no opportunities, even beyond those afforded by the School, to inform themselves in the practical work of mining.

The graduates are also urged to turn their attention to a field in which success is almost sure, to men of ability and energy; to enter the mines or works as miners, foremen, or in some other subordinate capacity, and thoroughly master every detail from the lowest to the highest work.

It is men who have had a thorough education, both in the theoretical and practical mining, and who have worked in every grade of work, that are even now sought to take charge of our mines and their allied industries. The future is for the man who is willing to commence at the bottom of his profession, and who is conscious of the truth, that on graduation he is only just prepared to begin his work.

The graduates of the school are urged to keep the Director constantly informed concerning their positions, salaries, etc., and also what their desires are, in order that they may be assisted to advance if opportunity offers.

Officers of mines and others desiring surveyors, engineers, draughtsmen, foremen, chemists, assayers, etc., etc., are requested to make their wants fully known to the Director of the Mining School, who will then recommend suitable candidates to them, if he knows of any.

The inquiry is frequently made by persons intending to become students, if they can attend to their school work and earn enough to pay their way at the same time. Such a course is not practicable, as the regular school work, if it is done as it should be, requires the entire available time of any student, however strong and able he may be. As a special student, taking only a few studies, one might be able to procure sufficient work to pay one's way. The better way for the needy student is either to attend to his school and to his labor in alternate years, or else to borrow the means to continue his education, repaying through his increased earning power after graduation.

The salaries obtained upon graduation have been from $540.00 to $1,500.00, averaging about $900.00 per year.

9

The lower salaries were obtained by students who had less practical experience with men and with the world in general; these were obliged to spend some time in acquiring a special kind of knowledge that the Mining School cannot give.

So far as known, the salaries have increased after a varied time from $900.00 to even $2,000.00 or more per year, averaging about $1,200. All this, however, is dependent upon the demand and supply, the state of the mining industries at any time, as well as upon other factors too numerous to be mentioned.

PRIZES AND SCHOLARSHIPS.

THE LONGYEAR PRIZES.

Through the liberality of J. M. Longyear, Esq., of Marquette, the following prizes have been offered, as stated in his letter making the offer, which is here appended:

Marquette, Michigan, Nov. 9, 1887.

CHARLES E. WRIGHT, ESQ., MARQUETTE:

DEAR SIR—I wish to offer three first prizes of seventy-five dollars ($75) each, and three second prizes of fifty dollars ($50) each, to be competed for by the members of the senior class of the Michigan Mining School. The competition to be by means of papers on three subjects, written by members of the class and submitted to the Board of Control for examination, in such a manner and at such a time as the Board may determine. I desire subjects selected with a view of producing papers which will be of practical use in developing the mineral resources of the state of Michigan. I should like something which would be of service to the average woodsman or explorer, and suggest the subjects of Practical Field Geology, and the use of the Dial and the Dip Compass in explorations, leaving the selection of the third subject to the judgment of the Board. If this offer is accepted and there are two or more papers on each subject submitted, I will pay seventy-five dollars to each of the writers of the three papers which may be awarded the first prize, and fifty dollars to each of the writers of the three papers which may be awarded the second prizes.

I would suggest, however, that in case only two papers are submitted, that the Board reserve the right of awarding only one prize, in case such action should seem advisable. In case only one paper should be submitted, I should like the Board to exercise its judgment in awarding a prize. It is my desire to publish the papers under the writer's names, in pamphlet form, for distribution among miners, explorers, land owners, and others.

Yours very truly,

J. M. LONGYEAR.

In conformity with the above letter, the Board of Control have decided upon the following subjects and conditions:

SUBJECTS.

1. Field Geology; its Methods and their Applications.
2. The Dial and the Dip Compass and their Uses.
3. The Diamond Drill and its Uses.

CONDITIONS.

The conditions under which the prizes are awarded are as follows:

The papers are to be presented by September 30th, for each year.

A student may present a paper upon each of the three subjects, which will entitle him to three prizes, if his papers are found worthy.

The dissertations must be written in a clear, legible hand, or type-written, on letter paper, quarto size. The sheets are to be securely fastened together, written on one side only, and a margin of not less than one inch left all around, in order that the dissertation may be bound if desired.

The title page is to have upon it an assumed name, and each dissertation is to be accompanied by a sealed envelope bearing the same name. This envelope must contain the writer's true, as well as assumed, name, and his address, and it will not be opened until the awards have been made.

No prizes will be awarded, unless the papers are judged by the committee to whom they are referred, to be of a sufficiently high standing to be entitled to a prize; hence there may be awarded all, part, or none of the prizes, as the case may be.

These prizes can now be competed for by any students of the school, whether special or regular, without restriction to the graduating class, as was originally specified.

THE CHARLES E. WRIGHT SCHOLARSHIP.

The Charles E. Wright Scholarship has been founded by Mrs. Carrie A. Wright, of Ann Arbor, in accordance with the conditions expressed in the letter given below:

To the Honorable Board of Control of the Michigan Mining School:

GENTLEMEN:—In memory of my husband, the late Charles E. Wright, and as a token of the deep interest he had in the Michigan Mining School, I desire to give to said school the sum of one thousand dollars.

If said gift shall be accepted, it is to be held under the following conditions, to-wit: It is to be invested as a permanent fund by the Board of Control, to form the nucleus of a scholarship to be known as the Charles E. Wright Scholarship. The income is to be given to some indigent student, by vote of the Board of Control, with the advice and consent of the faculty of said school.

The award is to be made during the first term of the year to some student who has a satisfactory record during the entire preceding year in the Michigan Mining School, and who intends to devote himself to the profession of Mining Engineering or Geological work. The income is to be divided into three equal parts, to be paid during the three terms of the year, and if at any time the conduct or standing of the student receiving the award should become unsatisfactory, the portion then remaining unpaid should be withheld from him and given to some other student, in accordance with the terms of this gift.

(Signed)   CARRIE A. WRIGHT.

THE NORRIE SCHOLARSHIP.

This scholarship has been founded, and will be awarded, in accordance with the conditions and requirements stated below:

Know all men by these presents, That I, A. Lanfear Norrie, of the city of New York, hereby give, grant, assign and set over unto the Michigan Mining School, of Houghton, Michigan, and to Peter White, D. H. Ball and J. M. Longyear, of Marquette, Michigan, as trustees, the sum of five thousand dollars ($5,000), lawful money of the United States.

The conditions of this gift, and upon which this fund is to be taken, are, that the said trustees shall invest the same upon bond and mortgage in the village of Marquette, or in the city of Detroit, in the State of Michigan, or in the city of Milwaukee, in the State of Wisconsin, or in the city of Chicago, in the State of Illinois, upon unencumbered improved real estate.

That one-half of the income of said sum of $5,000 shall be paid yearly by said trustees unto the Board of Control for the support of some student whose father has worked in, or in some way been connected with mining operations in the Upper Peninsula of Michigan, who shall be designated by the faculty of said school; and the remainder of said income shall be accumulated and invested as said principal shall be invested, and that this fund with its accumulations shall be the basis of a larger fund to be obtained from other contributions, amounting to at least one hundred thousand dollars ($100,000), to be used for the erection of a dormitory building for the use of such students as shall be designated by said faculty, which building, when erected, shall be under the exclusive control of the corporation or Board of Control of the said Michigan Mining School.

This gift is to the said trustees and their successors forever, for the benefit of the said Mining School. In case of the death of either of the said trustees, the survivors or survivor shall appoint a successor or successors.

When the erection of said building shall be commenced, after the said fund of one hundred thousand dollars is obtained, the sum hereby given, with all its accumulations, shall be paid over to the said Mining School, for the purpose aforesaid.

Witness my hand, the 30th day of January, 1890.

                                        A. LANFEAR NORRIE.

Witness, T. E. O. M. STETSON.

We, Peter White, D. H. Ball and J. M. Longyear, the persons named in the above instrument, accept the trust therein granted, in all respects, and agree to comply with the conditions thereof. Witness our hands, the 1st day of February, 1890.

PETER WHITE,
D. H. BALL,
J. M. LONGYEAR.

THE LONGYEAR FUND.

This is a fund of $500.00 given for the year 1892–93 by Mr. J. M. Longyear, of the Board of Control, to be the property of the Mining School, to be loaned to students of said school that may be designated by the Treasurer and Director, said students being unable to maintain their connection with the school without such aid. This money is not to be.a gift to the student, but he is to pay it back as soon as practicable after graduation. After his graduation, interest will be charged him for the first three years at 5 per cent, and for the following two years at 7 per cent. The money and the interest are to go to the fund, to aid other students in the same way. This method, it is believed, will lead the student to a more manly feeling than a gift outright would produce in him, since it gives him the means of paying for his own education, assists him when he most needs assistance, and enables him to return the money to aid others, at a time when he can best do so. It is believed that it would be better if all funds given to the School for investment and use, should be accompanied by some proviso that a certain portion, at least, of the income shall be paid or set aside, to increase the principal until it shall attain a limit either fixed or left to the proper authorities to determine. Such a method would enable the institution in the future to do much more good than it would if the income were to be spent entirely each year.

The School is in great need of funds to aid students who would otherwise be unable to attend this institution. Aid of this kind is frequently sought by able and worthy young men, and all is done that can be with the limited means at the command of the School to aid them.

The Longyear Fund has been continued for three years, and now amounts to $1,500.00.

DEGREES AND GRADUATE INSTRUC-
TION.

Students who have graduated in the former two years' course of the school with the degree of Bachelor of Science may obtain the degree of Mining Engineer by returning to the school and completing the course given at the time of such return; or else they may receive it upon application to the Board of Control and Faculty, and upon presentation of satisfactory evidence of two years' successful practical work, and of a suitable thesis in some line co-ordinate with their course of study in this school.

Five years' successful practical work of an advanced grade will be required after September, 1894.

The thesis must be an original investigation undertaken in Mining, Mechanical or Electrical Engineering, Chemistry, Metallurgy, Petrography, Geology, or in some allied subject that shall belong within the objects of this institution; and it must be approved by the Faculty.

Students who complete the present course of three years. and present a satisfactory thesis, will receive the degree of Mining Engineer, or Engineer of Mines (E. M.). The thesis must conform to the requirements given above, and must be completed and approved by the Faculty before that body will recommend that the degree of Mining Engineer, or Engineer of Mines, be conferred upon the student.

Students who complete the first three years of the four years' course will have conferred upon them the degree of Bachelor of Science, if they so desire; those who complete the fourth year of that course will receive the degree of Mining Engineer.

Students who are graduates of this, or of other institutions, will be admitted as special students to take any study taught in this school, or to take special graduate instruction.

Those who wish to become candidates for a higher degree will enter under the following conditions:

Students who are graduates of this institution, or of others of similar grade, whose course shall be approved by the Faculty, will be admitted as candidates for the degree of Doctor of Philosophy. In order to attain this degree they must pursue for at least two years an advanced course of study in subjects germane to the undergraduate course in this institution, which course of study is to be approved by the Faculty.

One of the years of study may, in special cases, be spent elsewhere, and the work accepted, on sufficient proof of its thoroughness and high character, as the equivalent of one year's work spent here. But under no condition will the degree be given, unless one year at least is spent as a resident worker at this institution.

Students who are graduates both of this, or of an equivalent professional school, and also of some college or university whose course of study is accepted by the Faculty, may be admitted to the degree of Doctor of Philosophy, after having taken for at least one year an approved course of study at this institution.

The degree of Doctor of Philosophy will be given only in case the student shall have shown marked ability and power for original investigation, shall have passed a satisfactory oral public examination, and presented a thesis embodying the result of original investigation that shall be approved by the Faculty.

Students who are graduates of this or of other institutions having a satisfactory equivalent course, and who shall have pursued here according to the above regulations, a successful course of study, for the degree of Doctor of Philosophy, may at the same time receive the degree of Mining Engineer, if said degree has not been conferred at their previous graduation.

COLLECTIONS.

For purposes of illustration and study, a number of collections have been provided for the use of the students.

Crystal Models	2,304
Natural Crystals	1,800
General Mineral Collection	27,310
Emerson Collection of Minerals	550
Exhibition Collection of Minerals	1,000
Collection of Thin Sections (1893)	2,500
General Rock Collections	11,575
Stratigraphical and Illustrative Collections	500
Collection of the State Geological Survey, Rocks	6,250
Collection of the Geological Survey, Thin Sections	6,293
Zoölogical Collection	1,000
Paleontological Collections	2,600
	63,682

Beside the above there are collections of paleontological charts, metallurgical, geological, and petrographical diagrams, geological models, maps, etc.

Collections of slags, metallurgical products, materials for illustration in economic geology, as well as some exhibition collections, have been commenced, and all persons who can are urged to contribute to the school collections of minerals, rocks, veinstones, ores, slags, metallurgical products, samples of building stones, machinery, tools, etc., and models, photographs and prints of the same, etc.

In the case of the mineral products used in arts and manufactures, it is desired to procure specimens showing the various stages in the processes of manufacture. It is especially important for the School to receive and preserve sets of cores from drill holes, samples of ores from every mine, with specimens of the associated gangue minerals and rocks, as well as of the walls and associated country rocks.

LIBRARY.

The Library of the School contains at present 8,095 volumes, besides numerous pamphlets, and additions are constantly made to it. It is proposed to have not only a good reference library for student work, but also one that shall be as complete as possible upon the subjects taught in the school. It is especially desired to have a full set of all reports and works relating to the mining and other mineral industries of the districts bordering on Lake Superior. The library is now valuable for reference, both for practical and scientific men; and it is freely open to all who desire to consult it.

In addition to the school library, the scientific library of the Director is deposited in the school building, and can be used by students and others. This library is especially devoted to Crystallography, Mineralogy, Petrography and General and Economic Geology.

Contributions of pamphlets, papers, maps and books, on subjects germane to those taught in this institution are solicited for the Mining School Library. Plans, drawings and engravings, relating to mines, mining machinery and metallurgy are desired.

It is hoped to make the Library very full in files of the different journals published throughout the country, especially in the mining regions; contributions of present and past numbers of such journals are solicited for the library, to aid in making it a complete depository of literature relating to the progress and industries of the country as well as of the Lake Superior region.

READING ROOM.

Connected with the Library is a Reading Room which is well supplied with scientific periodicals, technical journals, and the transactions and proceedings of scientific societies. The importance of periodical literature as a means of bringing before the student the results of scientific investigations is fully realized, and the collection is made as complete as possible for this reason. Below is given a full list of the journals on file, numbering in all one hundred and fifty-four.

Contributions of journals for the Reading Room are earnestly solicited throughout the State and country.

American Chemical Journal, Baltimore.

American Geologist, Minneapolis.

American Journal of Mathematics, Baltimore.

American Journal of Science, New Haven.

American Machinist, New York.

American Naturalist, Philadelphia.

Annalen der Physik und Chemie, Leipzig.

Annalen der Physik und Chemie, Beiblätter, Leipzig.

Annales de Chimie et de Physique, Paris.

Annales de la Société, Géologique de Belgique, Liège.

Annales des Mines, Paris.

Annales des Ponts et Chaussées, Paris.

Annales des Sciences Géologiques, Paris.

Annals of the New York Academy of Science, New York.

Annals of Mathematics, University of Virginia.

Berg-und Hüttenmaennische Zeitung, Leipzig.

Berg-und Hüttenmaennisches Jahrbuch, Vienna.

Berichte der deutschen chemischen Gesellschaft, Berlin.

*Brickmaker, Chicago.

Builder, London.

*Bulletin of the American Iron and Steel Association, Philadelphia.

Bulletin of the Essex Institute.

Bulletin of the Geological Society of America, Rochester, New York.

Bulletin of the New York Mathematical Society, New York.

Bulletin of the Philosophical Society, Washington.

Bulletin de la Société Chimique de Paris.

Bulletin de la Société Francaise de Minéralogie, Paris.

Bulletin de la Société Géologique de France, Paris.

*Calumet Conglomerate, Red Jacket.

*Calumet and Red Jacket News, Calumet.

Chemical News and Journal of Physical Science, London.

Chemiker Zeitung, Cöthen, Germany.

Chemische Industrie, Berlin.

Civilingenieur, Leipzig.

Colliery Engineer, Scranton, Pennsylvania.

Comptes Rendus, Hebdomadaires des Séances de l'Académie des Sciences, Paris.

Connecticut Academy of Arts and Sciences, Transactions, New Haven.

*Current, Norway.

*Daily Mining Journal, Marquette.

Dingler's Polytechnisches Journal, Stuttgart.

*Diamond Drill, Crystal Falls.

Electrical Engineer, New York.

Electrical Engineer, London.

*Gift of the Publishers.

Electrical World, New York.

Electrician, London.

Elektrotechnische Zeitschrift, Berlin.

Engineer, New York.

Engineer, London.

Engineering, London.

Engineering Magazine, New York.

Engineering Mechanics, New York.

Engineering and Mining Journal, New York.

Engineering News and American Railway Journal, New York.

Essex Institute Bulletin.

*Florence Mining News, Florence, Wisconsin.

Génie Civil, Paris.

Geological Magazine, London.

Industries, London.

Iron Age, New York.

*Iron Spirit, Bessemer.

*Iron Ore, Ishpeming.

Jahres-Bericht der chemischen Technologie, Leipzig.

Jahresbericht über die Fortschritte der Chemie, Braunschweig, Germany.

Jahrbuch für das Berg-und Hüttenwesen, Freiberg.

Jahrbuch der kaiserlich-königlichen geologischen Reichsanstalt, Vienna.

Jahrbuch der königlich preussischen geologischen Landesanstalt und Bergakademie, Berlin.

*Johns Hopkins University Circulars, Baltimore.

Journal of Analytical and Applied Chemistry, Easton, Pa.

Journal of the Association of Engineering Societies, Chicago.

Journal of the Chemical Society, London.

*Gift of the Publishers.

10

Journal of Education, Boston.

Journal of the Franklin Institute, Philadelphia.

Journal of the Iron and Steel Institute, London.

Journal des Mathématiques Pures et Appliquées, Paris.

Journal de Pharmacie et de Chimie, Paris.

Journal für praktische Chemie, Leipzig.

Journal of the Society of Arts, London.

Journal of the Society of Chemical Industry, London.

Justus Liebig's Annalen der Chemie, Leipzig.

Kritischer Vierteljahresbericht über die Berg-& Hüttenmännische und verwandte Literatur, Freiberg.

*Lake Superior Herald, Weekly, Ishpeming.

*Lake Superior Herald, Daily, Ishpeming.

*L'Anse Sentinel, L'Anse.

London, Edinburg and Dublin Philosophical Magazine and Journal of Science, London.

Lumière Électrique, Paris.

Manufacturer and Builder, New York.

Mathematical Magazine, Washington.

Mathematical Visitor, Washington.

Memoirs of the American Academy of Arts and Sciences, Boston.

Memoirs of the Boston Society of Natural History.

*Michigan Copper Journal, Hancock.

Michigan School Moderator, Lansing.

Mineralogical Magazine and Journal of the Mineralogical Society, London.

Mineralogische und petrographische Mittheilungen, Vienna.

Mining and Scientific Press, San Francisco.

*Mining and Scientific Review, Denver.

Nature, London.

---

* Gift of the Publishers.

Neues Jahrbuch für Mineralogie, Geologie und Palae-
ontologie, Stuttgart.

*News-Record, Ironwood.

*Oakland County Post, Pontiac.

Oesterreichische Zeitschrift für Berg-und Hüttenwesen,
Vienna.

*Official Gazette of the U. S. Patent Office, Washington.

*Ontonagon Herald, Ontonagon.

*Ontonagon Miner, Ontonagon.

Petermann's Mittheilungen aus Justus Perthes' geographischer Anstalt, Gotha.

Philosophical Transactions of the Royal Society of
London.

*Pick and Axe, Bessemer.

Popular Science Monthly, New York.

*Portage Lake Mining Gazette, Houghton.

*Printer's Ink, New York.

Proceedings of the Academy of Natural Sciences,
Philadelphia.

Proceedings of the American Academy of Arts and
Sciences, Boston.

Proceedings of the American Association for the
Advancement of Science, Salem, Massachusetts.

Proceedings of the Boston Society of Natural History,
Boston.

Proceedings of the Institution of Civil Engineers,
London.

Proceedings of the Institution of Mechanical Engineers,
London.

Proceedings of the Geologists' Association, London.

Proceedings of the London Mathematical Society.

*Gift of the Publishers.

Proceedings of the Royal Geographical Society and Monthly Record of Geography, London.

Proceedings of the Royal Society of London.

Publishers' Weekly, New York.

Quarterly Journal of the Geological Society, London.

Quarterly Journal of Pure and Applied Mathematics, London.

Railroad and Engineering Journal, New York.

Report of the British Association for the Advancement of Science, London.

Revue Universelle des Mines, de la Métallurgie, etc., Paris.

School of Mines Quarterly, New York.

Science, New York.

Scientific American, New York.

Scientific American Supplement, New York.

Sitzungsberichte der kaiserlichen Akademie der Wissenschaften, Vienna.

Sitzungsberichte der königlich-preussischen Akademie der Wissenschaften zu Berlin.

Stahl und Eisen Düsseldorf.

* Stone, Indianapolis.

Technologiste, Paris.

* Torch Lake Times, Lake Linden.

* Transactions of the American Institute of Mining Engineers, New York.

Transactions of the American Society of Civil Engineers, New York.

Transactions of the American Society of Mechanical Engineers, New York.

Transactions of the Federated Institute of Mining Engineers, Newcastle-on-Tyne.

---

* Gift of the Publishers.

Transactions of the Manchester Geological Society, Manchester.

Transactions of the Royal Society of Canada, Montreal.

Transactions of the Royal Society of Edinburgh.

Transactions of the Academy of Science, St. Louis.

Verhandlungen der k. k. geologischen Reichsanstalt, Vienna.

Washington Philosophical Society, Bulletin.

Zeitschrift für analytische Chemie, Wiesbaden.

Zeitschrift für anorganische Chemie, Leipzig.

Zeitschrift für das Berg-, Hütten-, u. Salinen-wesen, Berlin.

Zeitschrift der deutschen geologischen Gesellschaft, Berlin.

Zeitschrift für Krystallographie und Mineralogie, Leipzig.

Zeitschrift für physikalische Chemie, Leipzig.

---

*Gift of the Publishers.

TEXT BOOKS.

In 1891–1892 the following text books were used:

Olney's University Algebra.

Wentworth's Plane and Spherical Trigonometry.

Wentworth's Analytical Geometry.　Last Ed.

Wentworth and Hill's Logarithmic Tables.

Peck's Practical Calculus.

Peck's Analytical Mechanics.

Olmsted's Natural Philosophy, revised by Sheldon.

Johnson's Theory and Practice of Surveying.

Davies's Elements of Surveying, revised by Van Amringe.

Searle's Field Engineering.

Merriman's Hydraulics, 1890.

Merriman's Mechanics of Materials.　Last Ed.

Goodeve's Elements of Mechanism.

Warren's Elementary Projection Drawing.

Greene's Trusses and Arches, Part I.

Slingo and Brooker's Electrical Engineering.

Holmes's The Steam Engine.

E. S. Dana's Text Book of Mineralogy.

A. Geikie's Text Book of Geology.

Smith and Keller's Experiments for Students in General Chemistry.

Richter's Inorganic Chemistry.

Elliot and Storer's Qualitative Analysis.

Fresenius's Qualitative Analysis.

Fresenius's Quantitative Analysis.

Greenwood's Steel and Iron.

Peters's Modern Copper Smelting.　Second Ed.

In 1892–1893 the following text books are being used:

Olney's University Algebra.

Wentworth's University Algebra.

Wentworth's Plane and Spherical Trigonometry.

Wentworth's Analytical Geometry. Last Ed.

Wentworth and Hill's Logarithmic Tables.

Peck's Practical Calculus.

Peck's Analytical Mechanics.

Olmsted's Natural Philosophy, revised by Sheldon.

Johnson's Theory and Practice of Surveying.

Searle's Field Surveying.

Merriman's Hydraulics, 1890.

Merriman's Mechanics of Materials. Last Ed.

Goodeve's Elements of Mechanism.

Angell's Practical Plane and Solid Geometry.

Greene's Trusses and Arches. Part I.

Slingo and Brooker's Electrical Engineering.

Holmes's The Steam Engine.

James D. Dana's System of Mineralogy. Sixth Ed.

LeConte's Elements of Geology. Third Ed.

Smith and Keller's Experiments for Students in General Chemistry.

Richter's Inorganic Chemistry.

Elliot and Storer's Qualitative Analysis.

Fresenius's Qualitative Analysis.

Fresenius's Quantitative Analysis.

Greenwood's Steel and Iron.

Peters's Modern Copper Smelting. Third Ed.

SAMPLE EXAMINATION QUESTIONS FOR ADMISSION TO THE MINING SCHOOL.

ARITHMETIC.

1. (1). Draw a line a decimeter long and divide it into centimeters.

    (2). What is the fundamental unit of length in the metric system?

2. (1). Describe the units of capacity and of weight in the metric system.

    (2). Draw a cubic centimeter; a cubic decimeter.

3. (1). Multipl $\frac{4}{5}$ by $\frac{1}{8}$ and explain the process.

    (2). Divide   by $\frac{5}{16}$ and explain the process.

4. Change the common fractions to decimals in question 3, and perform the operations there required.

5. (1). B lost 5 per cent by selling a hektoliter of turpentine which cost $15. For what did he sell it a liter?

    (2). If A buys copper for 30 cents per kilogram, and on selling it makes 40 per cent on the cost, after deducting 10 per cent from his asking price, what was the asking price?

6. (1). Having sold a consignment of goods on 3 per cent commission, the agent was instructed to invest the proceeds, after deducting his commission of 2 per cent. His whole commission was $265. What amount did he invest?

(2). If copper stock pays 8 per cent on the par value, at what price must it be purchased to pay 10 per cent on the cost?

7. (1). What is the interest of $16,941.20 for 1 yr. 7 mo. and 28 days at 4¼ per cent?

(2). What sum of money, invested at 6½ per cent, will produce $279,815.00 in 1 yr. and 6 mo.?

8. (1). A ship's chronometer, set at Greenwich, points to 5 h. 40 min. 20 sec. P. M. when the sun is on the meridian; what is the ship's longitude?

(2). A steamer arrives at Halifax, 63° 36' west at 4 h. 30 min. P. M ; the fact is telegraphed to New York without loss of time. The longitude .of New York being 74° 1' west, what is the time of the receipt of the telegram?

9. Extract the square root of 58.140625, of .0000316969.

10. Extract the cube root of 10460353203, of .000148877.

ALGEBRA.

1. Add a—2b + c, 4—3b—c + 2d, 4d—3c—a, 7c—a—d; and substract c—2b+a from their sum.

2. (1). Multiply $x^4 + x^3 y - x^2 y^2 + xy^3 + y^4$ by $x^2 - xy + y^2$.

(2). Divide $y^8 - 2b^4 y^4 + b^8$ by $y^3 + by^2 + b^2 y + b^3$.

3. (1). Find the factors of $324\ a^4 b^2 - 64 b^6$, of $y^3 + y^2 - y - 1$ and of $y^7 + 1$.

(2). Prove that $x^m - 1$ is exactly divisible by $x - 1$, m being a positive integer.

4. (1). What is the sum of $\dfrac{x}{(x-y)\ (x-z)}$, $\dfrac{y}{(y-z)\ (y-x)}$ and $\dfrac{z}{(z-x)\ (z-y)}$.

(2). **Extract** the square root of $4 a^2 + 9 b^2 + 16 c^2 - 12ab$ $- 24 bc + 16ac$.

5. (1). **Extract** the square root of $30 + 12 \sqrt{6}$.

(2). **Solve** $\dfrac{y-5}{2} - \dfrac{y-3}{4} + \dfrac{y+3}{5} - \dfrac{y+5}{6} = 0$, and explain the transformations necessary for the solution.

.6 (1). Solve $x^2 + px + q = 0$ and give the conditions under which the roots are real and *unequal*, real and *equal*, and imaginary; also when are they equal *numerically* with opposite signs.

(2). What is the sum of the two roots of the preceding equation? What is their product? •

7. (1). Solve $\sqrt{x-3} + \sqrt{3x+4} + \sqrt{x+2} = 0$. .

(2). Find the values of x and y in the independent, simultaneous equations $x + y = 27$ and $x^2 + y^2 = 5103$.

8.   Find the 6th and the 15th terms of $(x-y)^{23}$, reducing the numerical results to their prime factors and not performing the multiplications.

9. (1). Prove that, if the corresponding terms of two proportions be multiplied together or divided by each other, the result, in either case, is a proportion.

(2). If $a:b = x:y = z:q$, Prove that $a:b = \dfrac{x+z}{y+q}$.

10. (1). Find the sum of ten terms of the series 1, 3, 5, 7, etc.: also the sum of the entire series, 27, 9, 3, 1, $\frac{1}{3}$, etc.

(2). Under the influence of a force g, assumed to be constant, a body falls to the earth from a height *h* and rebounds one-half this distance; it then falls again to the earth and again rebounds one-half the last distance fallen, and so continues its motion; find the entire distance fallen and the time of falling this distance.

PLANE GEOMETRY.

Demonstrate the following propositions:

1. The sum of the angles of any plane triangle is equal to two right angles.
2. Show that each angle of an equiangular pentagon is $\frac{4}{5}$ of a right angle.
3. In the same or in equal circles, angles at the center have the same ratio as their intercepted arcs. (Two cases.)
4. An inscribed angle is measured by one-half the intercepted arc. (Three cases.)
5. Two triangles are similar when an angle of the one is equal to an angle of the other, and the sides including these angles are proportional.
6. When a line is divided in extreme and mean ratio, the greater segment is one side of a regular decagon inscribed in a circle whose radius is the given line.
7. Similar polygons are to each other as the squares described on their homologous sides.
8. The square described upon the hypothenuse of a right triangle is equivalent to the sum of the squares described upon the other two sides.
9. (Problem). Given the perimeters of a regular inscribed and a similar circumscribed polygon, to com-

pute the perimeters of regular inscribed and circumscribed polygons of double the number of sides.

10. (Problem). To compute the ratio of the circumference of a circle to its diameter.

SOLID AND SPHERICAL GEOMETRY.

Demonstrate the following propositions:

1. If a straight line is perpendicular to each of two
straight lines at their intersection, it is perpendicular
to their plane.

2. If two triedral angles have the three face angles of
the one equal, respectively, to the three face angles of
the other, the corresponding diedral angles are equal.

3. Two triangular pyramids having equivalent bases and
equal altitudes are equivalent.

4. The frustum of a triangular pyramid is equivalent
to the sum of three pyramids whose common altitude
is the altitude of the frustum, and whose bases are the
lower base, the upper base and a mean proportional
between the bases of the frustum.

5. In two polar triangles, each angle of one is measured
by the supplement of the side lying opposite to it in
the other.

6. The sum of the angles of a spherical triangle is
greater than two and less than six right angles.

7. The area of a spherical triangle, expressed in spherical degrees, is numerically equal to the spherical excess
of the triangle.

8. The area of a zone is equal to the product of its
altitude by the circumference of a great circle,

9. (Problem). To find the volume of a spherical segment.

10. (Problem). To find the volume of that part of a sphere lying outside of a chord revolved parallel to its diameter and at a constant distance from it.

ELEMENTARY PHYSICS.

1. (1). Upon what property do most of the characteristic properties of matter depend.

   (2). Name three general and five characteristic properties of matter.

2. (1). Name and define the three states of matter.

   (2). Give Newton's laws of motion.

3. (1). Define work and energy: give the formula for the calculation of kinetic energy from weight and velocity.

   (2). Give the laws of freely falling bodies.

4. (1). How prove that the atmosphere has weight?

   (2). What is the object of experiments in the study of physics?

5. (1). Diagram, and explain the operation of the hydrostatic press.

   (2). Define specific gravity and describe the experiments necessary to determine the specific gravity of an irregular solid. If the specific gravity of copper is 8.9 what is the volume in cubic centimeters, of a mass of this metal which weighs 3.2 pounds?

6. (1). What is the mechanical equivalent of heat? To what is the heat of a body due?. Do the atoms

or the molecules of a body set either themselves
or one another in motion?

(2). Give your idea of force. What is sound? What
are the properties of a musical note? Diagram
and explain the phonograph and the telephone.

7. (1). Explain the ways in which heat may be transmitted.   Give some of its principal sources and
effects. Change —40° F., to C. Upon what does
the boiling point depend?

(2). Define light. What constitutes the difference
between light and heat? Between the different
colors? What is the velocity of light? Of sound
in the air, at the temperature 0° C?

8. (1). Give the laws of magnets.   Give the laws of
currents of electricity. Explain Ampère's theory
of the magnet. How may magnets be made?

(2). Describe the experiments and the results obtained
by the use of a galvanometer, a primary coil, a
secondary coil, a battery and a magnet. Tabulate
the results.

9. (1). Give Ohm's law. Define ohm, volt, ampère.
Draw diagrams showing how to connect cells in
series and in multiple arc or abreast.   If a Bunsen cell has an electromotive force of 1.8 volts and
internal resistance of .9 ohm, show how to connect ten such cells to get the greatest current, the
external resistance being 100 ohms?

(2). Give some of the principal uses of electric currents. Explain how such currents are produced
by a dynamo?

10. (1). What constitutes the difference between the
operation of a dynamo and that of an electro-
motor?

(2) In charging a storage battery, what is stored up in it? What is meant by "the conservation of energy?"

ASTRONOMY.

1. What is the general structure of the Solar System, and what is the physical constitution of the sun and its surroundings?
2. What are the physical constitution and special characteristics of the inner group of planets, including the moon?
3. What are the physical constitution and characteristics of the outer group of planets?
4. What are the aspects, forms and physical constitution of the comets, meteors and shooting stars?
5. What are nebulæ; new, variable and double stars, and upon what evidences are the views concerning them based?
6. How are stars located in the heavens? What are the declination, right ascension, hour angle, latitude, longitude; and what are the six parts of the Polar triangle?
7. Describe the four kinds of time and give the maximum variations between them. How is the longitude of a place determined?
8. What is the general structure of the universe?
9. State clearly the Nebular Hypothesis, and give the evidence upon which it is based?
10. Give the general phenomena of the tides, their causes and laws.

BOOK-KEEPING.

1. Explain the use of day-book, journal and ledger, and state the rules for entering transactions in them.
2. What is a trial balance, and what is the process of making one?
3. Is a trial balance an absolute check? State reasons for your answer.
4. State the rules for crediting and debiting bills payable and bills receivable.

In addition to questions of the above character, a record of supposed transactions is given to the candidate to enter in the proper manner in the different books, and he is required to make his own rulings.

BUILDINGS.

The main building now occupied by the Mining School was completed by the State in 1889, at a cost of $75,000. The building is constructed of Portage Entry sandstone, with a tile roof. It is heated and ventilated by steam, having two large boilers for heating, and an extra boiler for driving machinery.

The larger part of the site and grounds was donated to the School by the Honorable Jay A. Hubbell, to whom the establishment of the school is chiefly due. The building has a large and independent supply of spring water, sufficient for all its present needs.

The main building is 109 feet by 53 feet, with a wing 37 feet by 25 feet. The interior portion of the building has been arranged so as to save the greatest amount of space possible for the laboratories and working rooms, consistent with safety to the structure and proper light. The halls have been reduced to a minimum. The plans of the four floors are appended: The basement floor is used for a Boiler Room, Weighing Room, Metal and Wood-Working Shops, and Assaying Laboratory. The first floor contains the Director's Room, Reading Room, Library, and Laboratories of General and Economic Geology, Petrography and Mineralogy. On the second floor are situated the Mathematical and other Recitation Rooms, together with the Laboratories for Physics, Drawing, Surveying and Mining Engineering. The third floor is devoted to the Chemical Laboratories,

11

Chemical Lecture Room, Chemical Supply Room, Balance Room, etc.

During the Spring of 1891 the Legislature of the State of Michigan appropriated $62,000 for the further equipment and expenses of the school for 1891 and 1892.

A well appointed Stamp Mill and Ore Dressing Works, a small Metallurgical building, etc. complete the structures belonging to the Mining School.

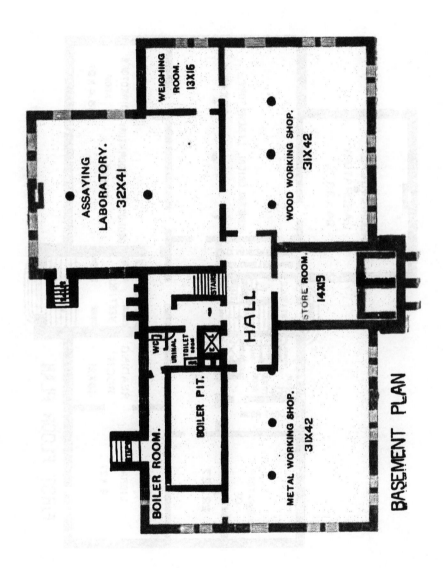

BASEMENT PLAN

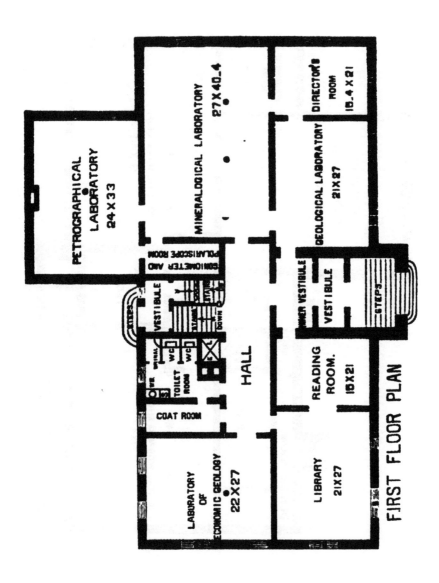

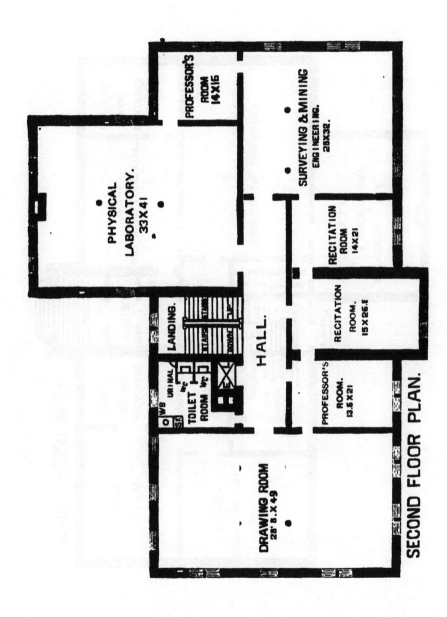

SECOND FLOOR PLAN.

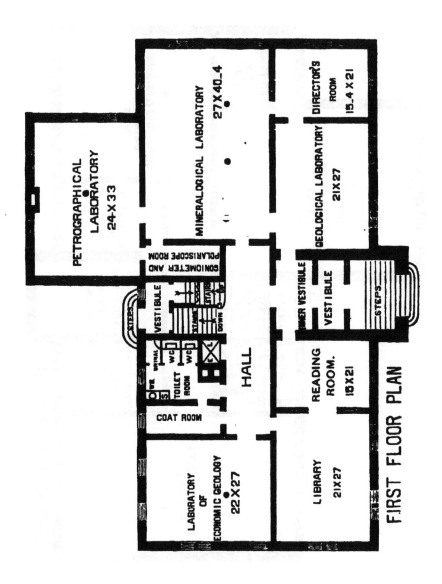

FIRST FLOOR PLAN

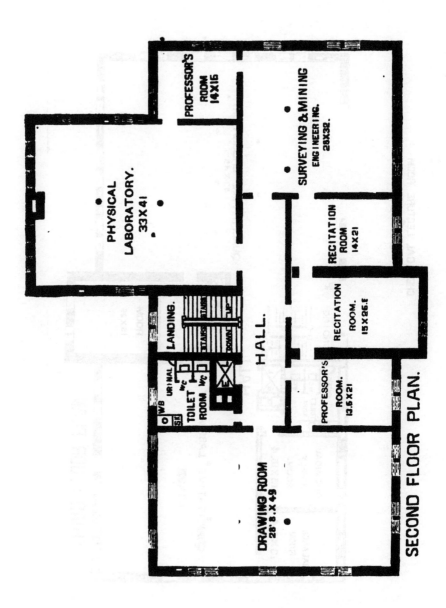

PROFESSOR'S
ROOM
14X16

SURVEYING & MINING
ENGINEERING.
26X32.

PHYSICAL
LABORATORY.
33X41

RECITATION
ROOM
14X21

LANDING.

RECITATION
ROOM.
15X26.½

HALL.

WB

URINAL
wc
wc

TOILET
ROOM

PROFESSOR'S
ROOM.
13.6X21

DRAWING ROOM
28' 8.X 49

SECOND FLOOR PLAN.

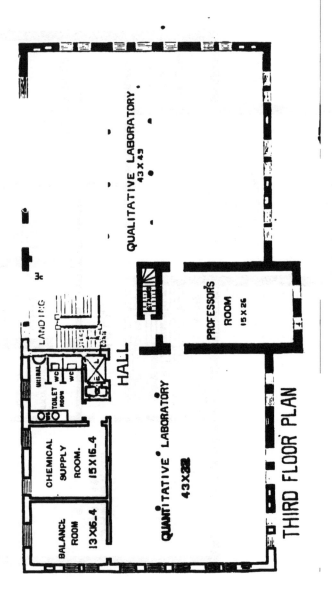

CHEMICAL LECTURE ROOM
24 X 33

QUALITATIVE LABORATORY
43 X 43

PROFESSOR'S ROOM
15 X 26

CHEMICAL SUPPLY ROOM.
15 X 16–4

BALANCE ROOM
13 X 16–4

LANDING

URINAL W.C. W.C. TOILET ROOM W.C.

HALL

QUANTITATIVE LABORATORY
43 X 32

THIRD FLOOR PLAN

GRADUATES, 1888.

NAME.	RESIDENCE AND OCCUPATION.
HARRIS, JOHN LUTHER, S. B.	Quincy.
	Mining Engineer, Quincy Mine.
LONGYEAR, EDMUND JOSEPH, S. B.	Merritt, Minnesota.
	Superintendent of the J. M. Longyear explorations on the Mesabi Range.
PARNALL, SAM'L ALEXANDER, S. B.	Ishpeming.
	Chief Mining Engineer, Cleveland and Iron Cliffs Mining Company.
PARNALL, WILLIAM EDWARD, S. B.	Ithaca.
	Electrical Engineering, Cornell University.
REID, WILLIAM JOSEPH, S. B.	Romeo.
SEAGER, JAMES BENJAMIN, S. B.	Hancock.
	Civil and Mining Engineer, Lake Superior Redstone Company.
UREN, WILLIAM JOHN, S. B.	Hancock.
	Civil Engineer, Mineral Range and Hancock and Calumet Railroads, and County Surveyor, Houghton County.

GRADUATES, 1889.

NAME.	RESIDENCE AND OCCUPATION.
CROZE, WALTER WILFRED JOS., S. B...	Negaunee.
	Chief Mining Engineer, Jackson Iron Company.
FARWELL, PAUL, S. B.	Anaconda, Montana.
	Assistant Chemist, Anaconda Mining Company.
*FESING, HERMAN WILLIAM, S. B.	Everett, Washington.
	Civil and Mining Engineer.
*HAAS, JACOB, S. B.	Everett, Washington.
	Civil and Mining Engineer.
HOATSON, JOHN, S. B.	Butte City, Montana.
	Mining Captain, Silver Bow Mine.
PRYOR, REGINALD CHAPPLE.	Houghton.
	Civil and Mining Engineer.

* See Graduates of 1890 for the second degree.

GRADUATES, 1890.

NAME.	RESIDENCE AND OCCUPATION.

DANIELL, JOSHUA, S. B................Great Falls, Montana.

> Assayer, Boston and Montana Consolidated Copper and Silver Mining Company.

DRAKE, FRANK, S. B..................Iron Mountain.

> Chief Mining Engineer, Chapin Mining Company.

FESING, HERMAN WM., S. B., E. M.....Everett, Washington.

> Civil and Mining Engineer.

HAAS, JACOB, S. B., E. M............Everett, Washington.

> Civil and Mining Engineer.

HODGSON. WILLIAM ADAMS, S. B.......Houghton.

SUTTON, LINTON BEACH, S. B..........Palmer.

> Mining Engineer and Chemist, Volunteer Mine.

WAKEFIELD, ARTHUR ALBERT, S. B....Hurley, Wisconsin.

> Civil and Mining Engineer.

GRADUATES, 1891.

NAME.	RESIDENCE AND OCCUPATION.

BOSSERT, OTTO HENRY, E. M.........Freiberg, Saxony.
> Mining Engineering, Bergakademie.

DENGLER, THEODORE, E. M............Houghton.
> Sub-Inspector Portage Lake Canal Improvement, United States Corps of Engineers.

FINK, EDWARD, E. M..................Milwaukee, Wisconsin.
> Chemist and Metallurgist, Geo. W. Goetz & Co.

LAWTON, NATHAN OLIVER, S. B.......Ironwood.
> Chief Mining Engineer, the Penokee and Gogebic Development Company.

CLASS OFFICERS.

CLASS OF 1893.

President....................ERWIN HUNTINGTON MCDONALD.
Vice President..............SAMUEL REED TRENGOVE.
Secretary and Treasurer...DONALD GILLIES.

CLASS OF 1894.

President....................BURTON TYNDALL SEELEY.
Vice President..............JOSEPH STRINGHAM, JR.
Secretary...................FREDERICK PECK BURBALL.
Treasurer...................FREDERICK JOSEPH BRULÉ.

CLASS OF 1895.

President....................ROYCE ELWIN BARLOW.
Vice President..............ROBERT JOHN WOOD.
Secretary...................JOHN NELSON ESSELSTYN.
Treasurer...................CARL RAYMOND DAVIS.

OFFICERS OF MICHIGAN MINING SCHOOL YOUNG MEN'S CHRISTIAN ASSOCIATION.

President....................JOHN ALEXANDER KNIGHT.
Vice President..............ELMER WHIPPLE DURFEE.
Recording Secretary.......JAMES FISHER.
Corresponding Secretary...WILLIAM WRAITH.
Treasurer...................ROYCE ELWIN BARLOW.

A "Hand Book of Useful Information for New Students" entering the Michigan Mining School is published by the Y. M. C. A., and may be had from the Secretary, Mr. William Wraith, by addressing him at Houghton. This Hand Book gives information regarding rooms, boarding houses, churches, societies, examinations, and all other points of interest to the new student, and will be of considerable service to him.

OFFICERS OF THE ATHLETIC ASSOCIATION.

President......................BURTON TYNDALL SEELEY.
Vice President...............AI ARTHUR ABBOTT.
Secretary....................WILLIAM WRAITH.
Treasurer....................DONALD CAMERON.

ADVISORY COMMITTEE.

Faculty......................PROF. FRED FRALEY SHARPLESS.
Class of 1893...............DONALD GILLIES.
Class of 1894...............LOUIS EDWARD RIEDINGER.

HOLDERS OF SCHOLARSHIPS, ETC.

THE NORRIE SCHOLARSHIP.

1891-1892....................DONALD GILLIES.
1892-1893....................DONALD GILLIES.

THE LONGYEAR FUND.

1890-1891.................... { GEORGE BATCHELOR CHURCH.
                             { ARTHUR PARKS SILLIMAN.
1891-1892.................... { GEORGE BATCHELOR CHURCH.
                             { ARTHUR PARKS SILLIMAN.
1892-1893....................GEORGE BATCHELOR CHURCH.

OFFICERS OF THE ALUMNI ASSOCIATION.

President...............SAMUEL ALEXANDER PARNALL, '88·
First Vice President....FRANK DRAKE, '90·
Second Vice President..EDWARD FINK, '91.
Secretary...............LINTON BEACH SUTTON, '90·
Treasurer...............WALTER WILFRED JOSEPH CROZE, '89·
Director, First Year....JOHN LUTHER HARRIS, '88·
Director, Second Year..OTTO HENRY BOSSERT, '91·
Director, Third Year....EDWARD VOSE PALMER, '92·

CALENDAR.

1893–1894.

Winter Term commences Monday morning, January 9, 1893.
Winter Term ends Friday evening, April 14, 1893.

Recess of nine days.

Spring Term commences Monday morning, April 24, 1893.
Spring Term ends Friday evening, June 2, 1893.

Summer Recess.

Summer Course in Surveying commences Monday morning, June 26, 1893.

Summer Course in Surveying ends Wednesday evening, September 6, 1893.

Summer Shop Practice begins Monday morning, July 17, 1893.

Summer Shop Practice ends Wednesday evening, September 6, 1893.

Summer Course in Assaying and Ore Dressing begins Monday morning, June 26, 1893.

Summer Course in Assaying and Ore Dressing ends Friday evening, August 4, 1893.

Summer Course in Field Geology begins Monday morning, August 7, 1893.

Summer Course in Field Geology ends Friday evening, September 1, 1893.

Commencement Exercises, Thursday and Friday, September 7 and 8, 1893.

    Thursday—Field Day—all classes, 9 A. M. and 2 P. M.

Commencement Exercises—*Continued.*
> Friday—Meeting of Alumni, 10 A. M.
>> Graduation Exercises, 2 P. M.
>> Alumni Dinner, 8 P. M.
>> Recess of five days.

Fall Term commences Thursday morning, September 14, 1893.

Examinations for admission and advanced standing commence Thursday morning at 9 A. M., and continue through Thursday and Friday.

Examinations for making up conditions commence on Thursday at 9 A. M., and will be continued through Thursday, Friday and Saturday.

Regular work for all classes commences Monday, September 18, 1893, at 9 A. M.

Thanksgiving Recess, November, Wednesday noon until Monday morning.

Fall Term ends Friday evening, December 22, 1893.

> Recess of two weeks.

Winter Term commences Monday morning, January 8, 1894.

Winter Term ends Friday evening, April 13, 1894.

CALENDAR 1893.

	S	M	T	W	T	F	S		S	M	T	W	T	F	S
JAN.	1	2	3	4	5	6	7	**JULY.**	..	..	..	..	..	..	1
	8	9	10	11	12	13	14		2	3	4	5	6	7	8
	15	16	17	18	19	20	21		9	10	11	12	13	14	15
	22	23	24	25	26	27	28		16	17	18	19	20	21	22
	29	30	31	..	..	..	..		23	24	25	26	27	28	29
									30	31	..	..	..	..	..
FEB.	..	..	..	1	2	3	4	**AUG.**	..	..	1	2	3	4	5
	5	6	7	8	9	10	11		6	7	8	9	10	11	12
	12	13	14	15	16	17	18		13	14	15	16	17	18	19
	19	20	21	22	23	24	25		20	21	22	23	24	25	26
	26	27	28	..	..	..	..		27	28	29	30	31	..	..
MAR.	..	..	..	1	2	3	4	**SEPT.**	..	..	..	..	..	1	2
	5	6	7	8	9	10	11		3	4	5	6	7	8	9
	12	13	14	15	16	17	18		10	11	12	13	14	15	16
	19	20	21	22	23	24	25		17	18	19	20	21	22	23
	26	27	28	29	30	31	..		24	25	26	27	28	29	30
APRIL.	..	..	..	..	..	..	1	**OCT.**	1	2	3	4	5	6	7
	2	3	4	5	6	7	8		8	9	10	11	12	13	14
	9	10	11	12	13	14	15		15	16	17	18	19	20	21
	16	17	18	19	20	21	22		22	23	24	25	26	27	28
	23	24	25	26	27	28	29		29	30	31	..	..	..	..
	30	..	..	..	..	..	..								
MAY.	..	1	2	3	4	5	6	**NOV.**	..	..	..	1	2	3	4
	7	8	9	10	11	12	13		5	6	7	8	9	10	11
	14	15	16	17	18	19	20		12	13	14	15	16	17	18
	21	22	23	24	25	26	27		19	20	21	22	23	24	25
	28	29	30	31	..	..	..		26	27	28	29	30	..	..
JUNE.	..	..	..	..	1	2	3	**DEC.**	..	..	..	..	..	1	2
	4	5	6	7	8	9	10		3	4	5	6	7	8	9
	11	12	13	14	15	16	17		10	11	12	13	14	15	16
	18	19	20	21	22	23	24		17	18	19	20	21	22	23
	25	26	27	28	29	30	..		24	25	26	27	28	29	30
									31	..	..	..	..	..	..

CATALOGUE

OF THE

MICHIGAN MINING SCHOOL.

1892-1894.

ANNOUNCEMENTS.

1895-1896.

HOUGHTON, MICHIGAN.

HOUGHTON, MICHIGAN.
PUBLISHED BY THE MINING SCHOOL.
1894.

CATALOGUE

OF THE

MICHIGAN MINING SCHOOL.

1892-1894.

WITH STATEMENTS CONCERNING THE INSTITUTION AND ITS COURSES OF INSTRUCTION FOR 1895-1896.

HOUGHTON, MICHIGAN.

HOUGHTON, MICH., U. S. A.
PUBLISHED BY THE MINING SCHOOL.
JULY, 1894.

MINING JOURNAL PRINT,
MARQUETTE, MICH.

Index.

TABLE OF CONTENTS.

	PAGE.
To the Public	1, 2
Board of Control	3
Board of Visitors	4
Officers of the Michigan Mining School and Geological Survey	5, 6
Officers of the Michigan Mining School	7, 9
Faculty of the Michigan Mining School	10
Register of Students, 1892–1893	11–20
Register of Students, 1893–1894	21–29
Summaries	30–32
Requirements for Admission	33–40
The Course of Instruction	41–45
Departments of Instruction	46–48
Outline of the Courses of Study	49–78
Number of Hours in the Courses	79
Departments of Instruction	80–140
Mathematics	80–82
Physics	82–86
Mechanics	86, 87
Hydraulics	87
Drawing	88–94
Chemistry	94–100
General Chemistry	94–97
Qualitative Analysis	97, 98
Quantitative Analysis	98, 99
Synthetic Chemistry	99, 100
Assaying	100, 101
Metallurgy	101, 102
Metallurgical Designing	102

Drawing and Manual Instruction 151, 152

Education 153–157

School Board of the 158, 159

Composition 160

Library 161

Reading Room 162–169

PAGE.

Text-Books.. 170–172
Examination Questions for Admission.................. 173–180
Buildings... 181–186
    Basement Plan,   Science Hall................... 183
    First Floor Plan,   "   "   184
    Second Floor Plan, "   "   185
    Third Floor Plan,   "   "   186
Location. 187–202
Employment.. 203–207
Calendar 208–214

Tables and Plates:

    Frontispiece—Science Hall.

    Table I.—Three Years Course, facing page 48.

    Table II.—Four Years Course, facing page 64.

    Table III.—Old Three Years Course, facing page 72.

    Tables IV-X.—Showing Required Work in Mineralogy, facing page 136.

    Table XI.—Showing Required Work in Lithology, facing page 136.

    Table XII.—Lecture Scheme in Economic Geology, facing page 136.

    Table XIII.—Lecture Scheme in Economic Geology, Second Series, facing page 136.

    Map of the Portage Lake Mining District, facing page 200.
    Engineering Hall. page 215.

TO THE PUBLIC.

Although this Catalogue is for the years 1892–1894, its statements and calendar also apply to 1894–1895, and 1895–1896.

This Catalogue does not follow entirely the usual form of such a publication, but it has been prepared to answer each and every question that has been asked the Director concerning the institution for nearly seven years. Hence all persons seeking for information concerning this School are requested to look in the Table of Contents for the title under which their subject naturally falls, and then examine the statements made upon the pages referred to.

If the information can not be found, then application should be made in person or by letter to the Director, stating what points are not understood, or upon what subjects information is desired. Experience, however, has shown that for the past three years hardly any questions have been asked, that have not been more fully answered in the Catalogue than it is possible to do in a letter. The Director is the proper officer to apply to for catalogues, for all matters relating to the courses of study, admission qualifications, blank certificates, and in short, for anything relating to the educational side of the School; while all communications concerning purchases, bills and financial matters should be addressed to the Treasurer of the Mining School. All parties writing for catalogues or information, are particularly requested to see that their names and addresses are legibly and accurately given, for however familiar one may be with his own signature, the party to whom application is made for the Catalogue is not.

Very frequently catalogues and letters are returned to the School, owing to the parties asking for them having given an imperfect or incorrect address. In case of failure of any one to receive the Catalogue or information required, he should write again; as all requests of either kind that reach the Director are promptly attended to, and the information or Catalogue sent.

BOARD OF CONTROL OF THE MINING SCHOOL.

———

1892—1894.

Term Expires.

Hon. John Monroe Longyear, Marquette...........June 9, 1895.
Alfred Kidder, Marquette.........................June 9, 1895.
James Renrick Cooper, Hancock...................June 9, 1897.
Preston Carpenter Firth West, Calumet...........June 9, 1897.
Hon. Jay Abel Hubbell, Houghton.................June 9, 1899.
Hon. Thomas Bree Dunstan, Hancock..............June 9, 1899.

———

OFFICERS OF THE BOARD OF CONTROL.

———

PRESIDENT OF THE BOARD OF CONTROL,
HON. JAY ABEL HUBBELL.

SECRETARY OF THE BOARD OF CONTROL,
ALLEN FORSYTH REES.

DIRECTOR OF THE MINING SCHOOL,
MARSHMAN EDWARD WADSWORTH.

TREASURER AND PURCHASING AGENT OF THE MINING SCHOOL,
ALLEN FORSYTH REES.

BOARD OF VISITORS TO THE MINING SCHOOL.

———

September 5th, 1892, to September 4th, 1893.

Prof. MORTIMER ELWYN COOLEY, Ann Arbor, *Chairman.*

EDWARD LEROY PARMENTER, Vulcan.

HUGH BROWN, Lansing.

OFFICERS OF THE MICHIGAN MINING SCHOOL AND OF THE STATE GEOLOGICAL SURVEY.

1892–1893.

MARSHMAN EDWARD WADSWORTH, A. B. (Bowdoin College),
A. M., Ph. D. (Harvard University),
DIRECTOR AND STATE GEOLOGIST,
Professor of Mineralogy, Petrography and Geology.

GEORGE AUGUSTUS KOENIG, M. E. (Polytechnikum, Karlsruhe),
A. M., Ph. D. (University of Heidelberg),
Professor of Chemistry, and Chemist on the Geological Survey.

LUCIUS LEE HUBBARD, A. B. (Harvard University), LL. B.
(Boston University), A. M., Ph. D. (University of Bonn).
Assistant in Mineralogy, and on the Geological Survey.

ARTHUR EDWARD HAYNES, M. S., M. Ph. (Hillsdale College),
Professor of Mathematics and Physics.

HORACE BUSHNELL PATTON, A. B. (Amherst College),
Ph. D. (University of Heidelberg),
Instructor in Mineralogy and Petrography, and Assistant on
the Geological Survey.

ALFRED CHURCH LANE, A. M., Ph. D. (Harvard University),
Instructor in Petrography and Geology, and Assistant on the
Geological Survey.

EDGAR KIDWELL, A. M. (Georgetown University),
M. E. (University of Pennsylvania),
Professor of Mechanical and Electrical Engineering.

FRED FRALEY SHARPLESS, S. B. (University of Michigan),
Professor of Metallurgy, and Chemist on the Geological Survey.

FRED WARNER DENTON, C. E. (Columbia College School of Mines),
Professor of Civil and Mining Engineering.

WALTER JOHN BALDWIN, S. B. (University of Michigan),
Assistant in Surveying.

AI ARTHUR ABBOTT, S. B. (Michigan Agricultural College),
Assistant in Physics.

CARROLL LIVINGSTON HOYT, M. E. (Cornell University),
Instructor in Mechanical Engineering and Drawing.

ARTHUR EDMUND SEAMAN,
Assistant in Mineralogy, and on the Geological Survey.

MILO SMITH KETCHUM,
Assistant in Surveying.

ROBERT IRWIN REES,
Librarian and Clerk.

JOHN BONE WATSON,
Draughtsman for the Geological Survey.

JAMES WILTON SHIELDS,
Assistant in the Machine Shops.

———

HENRY GIBBS,
Janitor and Supply Clerk.

PATRICK ROBERT DILLON,
Engineer and Assistant Janitor.

MISS KATE KILLIAN,
Stenographer and Typewriter for the Mining School.

MISS HELEN MARY RYAN,
Stenographer and Typewriter for the Geological Survey.

JOHN BRIMACOMBE,
Janitor's Assistant.

OFFICERS OF THE MICHIGAN MINING SCHOOL.

1893–1894.

MARSHMAN EDWARD WADSWORTH, A. B. (Bowdoin College),
A. M., Ph. D. (Harvard University),
DIRECTOR,
Professor of Mineralogy, Petrography and Geology.

GEORGE AUGUSTUS KOENIG, M. E. (Polytechnikum, Karlsruhe)
A. M., Ph. D. (University of Heidelberg),
Professor of Chemistry.

EDGAR KIDWELL, A. M. (Georgetown University),
M. E. (University of Pennsylvania),
Professor of Mechanical and Electrical Engineering.

*FRED FRALEY SHARPLESS, S. B. (University of Michigan),
Professor of Metallurgy.

†FRED WARNER DENTON, C.E. (Columbia College School
of Mines),
Professor of Civil and Mining Engineering.

FRED WALTER McNAIR, S. B. (University of Wisconsin),
Professor of Mathematics and Physics.

ARTHUR EDMUND SEAMAN,
Instructor in Mineralogy and Geology.

AI ARTHUR ABBOTT, S. B. (Michigan Agricultural College),
E. M. (Michigan Mining School).
Instructor in Mechanical Engineering, Drawing and Surveying.

---

*Resigned, to take effect September 14th, 1894.
†Resigned, to take effect June 2nd, 1894.

MISS FRANCES HANNA,
Librarian and Secretary.

ROBERT IRWIN REES,
In charge of the preparation of the Library Catalogue.

JAMES WILTON SHIELDS,
Assistant in the Machine Shops.

HORACE TRAITON PURFIELD,
Assistant in the Machine Shops.

RUSSELL TEAL MASON,
Assistant in Physics.

CARLTON FRANKLIN MOORE,
Assistant in Chemistry.

CARL RAYMOND DAVIS,
Assistant in Surveying.

———

HENRY GIBBS,
Supply Clerk and Janitor of Science Hall.

PATRICK ROBERT DILLON,
Engineer and Janitor of Engineering Hall.

MISS KATE KILLIAN,
Stenographer and Typewriter.

JOHN BRIMACOMBE,
Janitor's Assistant.

APPOINTMENTS FOR 1894-1895.

CARLTON FRANKLIN MOORE,
Instructor in Mechanical Engineering and Drawing.

BURTON TYNDALL SEELEY,
Assistant in Chemistry.

CARL RAYMOND DAVIS,
Assistant in Physics.

LOUIS ALDRO WRIGHT,
Assistant in Mineralogy.

Assistant in Chemistry.

2

FACULTY OF THE MINING SCHOOL.

MARSHMAN EDWARD WADSWORTH, A. M , Ph. D.. DIRECTOR,
Professor of Mineralogy, Petrography and Geology.

GEORGE AUGUSTUS KOENIG, M. E., A. M., Ph. D.,
Professor of Chemistry.

EDGAR KIDWELL, A. M., M. E.,
Professor of Mechanical and Electrical Engineering.

FRED FRALEY SHARPLESS, S. B.,
Professor of Metallurgy.

FRED WARNER DENTON, C. E.,
Professor of Civil and Mining Engineering.

FRED WALTER MCNAIR, S. B.,
Professor of Mathematics and Physics, Secretary of the Faculty.

REGISTER OF STUDENTS

FOR THE SCHOOL YEAR 1892–1893.

GRADUATE STUDENTS.

Name.	Residence.	Room.
DRAKE, FRANK, S. B., (Michigan Mining School), Chemistry, Mechanical and Electrical Engineering, Mineralogy, Petrography and Geology.	*Portland, Oregon.*	Keweenaw Club.
HARRIS, HERBERT EUGENE, S. B. (University of Wisconsin,) Shop Practice.	*Waupun, Wis.*	Mr. Kroll's.
KAMPE, WESLEY EDWARD, A. B., S. B. (Hanover College), Chemistry.	*Madison, Ind.*	Butterfield House.
NICOL, WILLIAM, M. A., (Queen's University), Assaying and Ore Dressing.	*Kingston, Ontario.*	Mrs. Brimacombe's.
SILLIMAN, ARTHUR PARKS, B. L., (University of Wisconsin), Mathematics, Chemistry, Electrical Engineering and Geology.	*Hudson, Wis.*	Mrs. Burrows's.

CLASS OF 1893.

Name.	Residence.	Room.
ABBOTT, AI ARTHUR, S. B. (Michigan Agricultural College),	*Holt.*	Mrs. C. Didier's.
CHURCH, GEORGE BATCHELOR,	*Flint.*	Mrs. Alford's.
CRANSON, ROBERT EDWARD,	*St. John's.*	Mr. Cranson's.
FISHER, JAMES,	*Hancock.*	Mr. Fisher's, Hancock.
GILLIES, DONALD,	*Lake Linden.*	Mrs. Alford's.
HARRINGTON, FREDERICK LUCE,	*Port Huron.*	Mrs. E. M. Hoar's.
HONNOLD, WILLIAM LINCOLN,	*Camp Point, Ill.*	Keweenaw Club.
KIRK, MARCUS EUGENE,	*Cincinnati, Ohio.*	Mrs. Rice's.
McDONALD, ERWIN HUNTINGTON,	*Lyon Mountain, N. Y.*	Butterfield House.
McDONALD, WILLIAM NEAL,	*Houghton.*	Mr. McDonald's.
ROPES, LEVERETT SMITH,	*Ishpeming.*	Mrs. Douglas's.
TOWER, LOUIS LOVELL,	*Ionia.*	Mrs. Rice's.
TRENGOVE, SAMUEL REED,	*Lake Linden.*	Mrs. Brimacombe's.
WATERS, ALBERT LATCHA, S. B. (Michigan Agricultural College),	*Spring Lake.*	Keweenaw Club.

CLASS OF 1894.

Name	Residence.	Room.
BRULÉ, FREDERICK JOSEPH,	*Lake Linden.*	Miss Kelly's.
BURRALL, FREDERICK PECK,	*Battle Creek.*	Mr. Cameron's.
CAMERON, DONALD,	*St. Louis.*	Mr. Davey's.
CORRIGAN, JOHN ALEXANDER,	*Cleveland, Ohio.*	Dallmeyer Block.
DURFEE, ELMER WHIPPLE,	*Grand Rapids.*	Mr. Hummel's.
EBY, JOHN HENRY, B. A., (Franklin and Marshall College),	*Lancaster, Pa.*	Mr. Hummel's.
JONES, MAURICE LINDLEY,	*Benton Harbor.*	Mrs. E. M. Hoar's.
KIRCHEN, JOHN GEORGE,	*Lake Linden.*	Dallmeyer Block.
KNIGHT, JOHN ALEXANDER,	*Ionia.*	Miss Jones's, Hancock.
MASON, CLARENCE GEORGE,	*Hancock.*	Mr. Mason's.
MASON, RUSSELL TEEL,	*Boulder, Colo.*	Mrs. C. Didier's.
McCAULEY, JAMES,	*Hancock.*	Mr. McCauley's, Hancock.
McCORMICK, EDWARD PATRICK,	*Calumet.*	Mrs. Burrows's.
McFARLANE, GEORGE CAMPBELL,	*Bay City.*	Mrs. Beard's.
McGRATH, MICHAEL,	*Hancock.*	Mr. McGrath's, Hancock.
MOORE, CARLTON FRANKLIN,	*Marquette.*	Mr. Sparling's.
NEWTON, LEE LUKE,	*Lake Linden.*	Miss Kelly's.
PARKS, HENRY JAMES,	*Lake Linden.*	Dallmeyer Block.

Name.	Residence.	Room.
PEIFFER, PHILIP,	*Lake Linden.*	
		Mrs. C. Didier's.
RIDLEY, FREDERICK WILLIAM,	*Newcastle-on-Tyne, England.*	
		Mrs. E. M. Hoar's.
RIEDINGER, LOUIS EDWARD,	*Marquette.*	
		Mrs. Rice's.
ROURKE, JERRY,	*Hancock.*	
		Mr. Rourke's, Hancock.
SEELEY, BURTON TYNDALL.	*Genessee Township.*	
		Mr. Sparling's.
STRINGHAM, JOSEPH, JR.,	*Saginaw.*	
		Mr. Stringham's.
WILLIAMS, BERT HENRY,	*Champion.*	
		Mr. Ormsby's, Hancock.
WRAITH, WILLIAM,	*Newcastle, Colo.*	
		Mrs. Dallmeyer.

CLASS OF 1895.

——

Name.	Residence.	Room.
BARLOW, ROYCE ELWIN,	*Hastings.*	Mrs. Trim's.
BARSTOW, GEORGE MITCHELL,	*Detroit.*	Mrs. Beard's.
BATES, ARMAND WALTER,	*Ironwood.*	Mrs. Dallmeyer's.
BEARD, WILLIAM HENRY, Jr.,	*Stafford, Eng.*	Mr. Livermore's.
BEEN, JOHN THEODORE,	*Skanee.*	Mr. Lang's.
CALHOUN, CHARLES ANDREW,	*Albert Mines, Albert Co., N.B.*	Mrs. Mitchell's.
CAMERON, WILLIAM,	*St. Louis.*	Mr. Davey's.
CHANDLER, MARION INEZ,	*Hancock.*	Mr. Chandler's. Hancock.
CLARK, GEORGE CLOUGH,	*Springfield, Mo.*	Mrs. Brimacombe's.
COLEMAN, MILTON WATSON,	*Calumet.*	Hartman Block.
CORGAN, WILL JOHN,	*Ontonagon.*	Mr. Chapell's.
CROZE, LAWRENCE LUDGER,	*Houghton.*	Mr. Croze's.
DAVIS, CARL RAYMOND,	*Helena, Mont.*	Mr. Lange's.
DOCKERY, LOVE,	*Love, Miss.*	Mrs. Rashleigh's.
DUBOIS, WILBUR FISK,	*Mobile, Ala.*	Mr. Cameron's.
EMLAW, HARLOW STIGAND,	*Grand Haven.*	Mr. Lord's.
ESSELSTYN, JOHN NELSON,	*Lansing.*	Mr. J. Edward's.
GREENE, FRED TURRELL,	*Berlin, Ontario.*	Mr. Thomas's.

Name.	Residence.	Room.
HOLBERT, HENRY HOFFMAN,	St. Clair.	
		Mrs. Trim's.
HOOPER, JAMES KNIGHT,	Crystal Falls.	
		Mrs. Brimacombe's.
KENT, BAMLET,	Calumet.	
		Hartman Block.
MARTIN, NICHOLAS JOHN,	Bessemer.	
		Mr. Sparling's.
McDONALD, DONALD,	Calumet.	
		Mrs. Brimacombe's.
McINTYRE, CHARLES,	Lake Linden.	
		Miss Jones's, Hancock.
MONROE, WILLIAM DEARBORN,	Bath.	
		Mrs. Cameron's.
MURRAY, ROBERT, JR.,	Lake Linden.	
		Miss Kelly's.
ORR, JOHN FOREST,	L'Anse.	
		Mr. J. McCurdy's.
PAULL, STEPHEN, JR.,	Calumet.	
		Mr. J. McCurdy's.
RASHLEIGH, WILLIAM JOHN.	Houghton.	
		Mrs. Rashleigh's.
ROSE, ROBERT SELDON.	Fond du Lac, Wis.	
		Keweenaw Club.
ROWE, DAVID PRESCOTT,	Chicago, Ill.	
		Mrs. Dallmeyer's.
SCHUMANN, ADOLPH ENRIQUE,	Santiago de Cuba, Cuba.	
		Mrs. Mitchell's.
SLOCK, GEORGE,	Houghton.	
		Mr. Slock's.
SWEET, ROY WILLIAM,	Iron Mountain.	
		Miller's Hotel.
UPHAM, WILLIAM ERASTUS,	Duluth, Minn.	
		Mrs. Burrows's.
WEARNE, WILLIAM, JR.,	Red Jacket.	
		Mr. McCurdy's.
WEBB, FREDERICK MERKLEE,	River Edge, N. J.	
		Mr. Lange's.
WOOD, ROBERT JOHN,	Cleveland, Ohio.	
		Dallmeyer Block.
WRIGHT, LOUIS ALDRO,	Villa de Musquiz, Coahuila, Mexico.	
		Keweenaw Club.
WYCKOFF, FRED CARLTON,	Jacobsville.	
		Mr. Chandler's.

SPECIAL STUDENTS.

Name.	Residence.	Room.
BEELER, HENRY CHRISTIAN. Field Geology.	*Denver, Colo.*	Butterfield House.
BENSON, JOHN SYDNEY, Chemistry and Mineralogy.	*Wardner, Idaho.*	Mr. Livermore's.
BURTON, WARREN EDWARD, Chemistry.	*Geneva Lake, Wis.*	Douglass House.
CROCKARD, FRANK HEARNE, Surveying.	*Wheeling, W. Va.*	Keweenaw Club.
CROZE, CHARLES EDWARD, Shop Practice.	*Houghton.*	Mr. Croze's.
CRUSE, JAMES ALFRED, Mathematics and Drawing.	*Red Jacket.*	Mrs. Brimacombe's.
GOODELL, HORATIO STEWART, Shop Practice.	*Houghton.*	Mr. Goodell's.
GOODING, LOUIS EBENEZER, Surveying.	*Berkeley, California.*	Mrs. Brimacombe's.
JAMES, HOUGHTON EDWARD, Chemistry.	*Duluth, Minnesota.*	Mrs. Healy's.
MAGINN, JOHN BIGLIN, Surveying.	*Germantown, Philadelphia, Pennsylvania.*	Mr. J. Edwards.
OPPEN, WILLIAM ADOLPH, Chemistry.	*Milwaukee, Wis.*	Mr. Livermore's.
ROSS, GEORGE EDWARD, Chemistry.	*Hancock.*	Mr. Ross's.

Name.	Residence.	Room.
SEAMAN, ARTHUR EDMUND, Petrography.	*Houghton.*	Mr. Seaman's.
SILLIMAN, HENRY DICKINSON, Mathematics and Chemistry.	*Hudson, Wis.*	Mrs. Burrows's.
STEVENS, ROBERT CLARK, Surveying.	*Malone, N. Y.*	Mr. C. Brand's.
WATSON, JOHN BONE, Geology.	*Opechee.*	Mrs. Brimacombe's.

REGISTER OF STUDENTS

1893–1894.

GRADUATE STUDENTS.

Name.	Residence.	Room.

BALDWIN, WALTER JOHN, S. B.
(University of Michigan),
Chemistry, Mineralogy and Petrography.

Houghton.

Keweenaw Club.

HARRIS, HERBERT JEAN, S. B.
(University of Wisconsin),
Chemistry, Ore Dressing, Mechanical and Electrical Engineering and Mineralogy.

Waupun, Wis.

Mr. Kroll's.

WILLIAMS, HERBERT BALDWIN,
S. B. (University of Illinois),
Chemistry, Metallurgy, Mineralogy, Petrography and Graphical Statics.

Streator, Ill.

Mrs. Dallmeyer's.

CARPENTER, ALVIN BACON, Ph. B.
(Beloit College), Surveying.

Beloit, Wis.

Mr. John Edwards's,

CLASS OF 1894.

Name.	Residence.	Room.
BURRALL, FREDERICK PECK,	*Battle Creek.*	Club of '94.
CAMERON, DONALD,	*St. Louis.*	Mrs. P. Didier's.
CRANSON, ROBERT EDWARD,	*St. Johns.*	Club of '94.
DURFEE, ELMER WHIPPLE,	*Grand Rapids.*	Mrs. Alford's.
EBY, JOHN HENRY, A. B. (Franklin and Marshall College),	*Lancaster, Pa.*	Mrs. Alford's.
JONES, MAURICE LINDLEY,	*Benton Harbor.*	Mr. Kroll's.
KIRCHEN, JOHN GEORGE,	*Lake Linden.*	Mr. Kroll's.
KNIGHT, JOHN ALEXANDER,	*Ionia.*	Miss Jones's, Hancock.
McDONALD, WILLIAM NEAL,	*Houghton.*	Mr. McDonald's.
McFARLANE, GEORGE CAMPBELL,	*Bay City.*	Mrs. Beard's.
MASON, CLARENCE GEORGE,	*Hancock.*	Mr. W. H. Mason's, Hancock.
MASON, RUSSELL TEEL,	*Boulder, Colo.*	Mrs. C. Didier's.
MOORE, CARLTON FRANKLIN,	*Marquette.*	Mr. Sparling's.
RIDLEY, FREDERICK WILLIAM,	*Newcastle-on-Tyne, Eng.*	Mrs. E. M. Hoar's.
ROURKE, JERRY,	*Hancock.*	Mr. Rourke's, Hancock.
SEELEY, BURTON TYNDALL,	*Genessee Township.*	Mr. Sparling's.
STRINGHAM, JOSEPH, JR.,	*Saginaw.*	Club of '94.
TOWER, LOUIS LOVELL,	*Ionia.*	Mrs. Rice's.
WATSON, JOHN BONE,	*Opechee.*	Mrs. Brimacombe's.
WRAITH, WILLIAM,	*Newcastle, Colo.*	Mrs. Dallmeyer's.

CLASS OF 1895.

Name.	Residence.	Room.
BARLOW, ROYCE ELWIN,	*Hastings.*	
		Mr. James Thomas's.
BARSTOW, GEORGE MITCHELL,	*Detroit.*	
		Mrs. Beard's.
BATES, ARMAND WALTER,	*Ironwood.*	
		Mr. Schnitzer's.
BEEN, JOHN THEODORE,	*Skanee.*	
		Mr. Cameron's.
CAMERON, WILLIAM,	*St. Louis.*	
		Mr. C. Mills's.
COLEMAN, MILTON WATSON,	*Calumet.*	
		Dallmeyer Block.
DAVIS, CARL RAYMOND,	*Helena, Montana.*	
		Mr. C. Pryor's.
DOCKERY, LOVE,	*Love, Miss.*	
		Mr. Cameron's.
DUBOIS, WILBUR FISK,	*Mobile, Alabama.*	
		Mr. C. Brand's.
EMLAW, HARLAN STIGAND,	*Grand Haven.*	
		Mr. C. Brand's.
HARDENBURG, LOUIS MARTIN, A. B. (Hillsdale College),	*Tecumseh.*	
		Mrs. Burrows's.
HOLBERT, HENRY HOFFMAN,	*St. Clair.*	
		Club of '94.
KENT, BAMLET,	*Houghton.*	
		Dallmeyer Block.
MARTIN, NICHOLAS JOHN,	*Bessemer.*	
		Mrs. Dallmeyer's.
MUNROE, WILLIAM DEARBORN,	*Bath.*	
		Mr. Cameron's.
MURRAY, ROBERT, JR.,	*Lake Linden.*	
		Miss Kelly's.
ORR, JOHN FOREST,	*L'Anse.*	
		Mrs. Burrows's.
ROSE, ROBERT SELDEN,	*Fond du Lac, Wis.*	
		Keweenaw Club.

3

SCHUMANN, ENRIQUE ADOLPHO,   *Santiago de Cuba, Cuba.*
  Mr. James Thomas's.

SLOCK, GEORGE,   *Houghton.*
  Mr. Slock's.

UPHAM, WILLIAM ERASTUS,   *Duluth, Minn.*
  Mr. James Thomas's.

WEARNE, WILLIAM, JR.,   *Red Jacket.*
  Mrs. Burrows's.

WEBB, FREDERICK MERKLEE,   *River Edge, N. J.*
  Mr. Lange's.

WRIGHT, LOUIS ALDRO,   *Villa de Musquiz,*
  Coahuila, Mexico.
  Keweenaw Club.

WYCKOFF, FRED CARLTON,   *Jacobsville.*
  Mr. Schnltzer's.

FRESHMAN CLASS..

ALDRICH, WILLIAM IRVING,   *Coldwater.*
         Butterfield House.

BEARD, WILLIAM HENRY,   *Stafford, England.*
         Mr. Harrington's.

CROZE, LAWRENCE LUDGER,   *Houghton.*
         Mr. J. Croze's.

FIGUEROA, CAMILO, A. B.   *Saltillo, Coahuila,*
    (St. Mary's College),   *Mexico.*
         Mr. Livermore's.

HOAR, FREDERIC WALPOLE,   *Houghton.*
         Mr. R. M. Hoar's.

HOULE, ALBERT JOSEPH,   *Negaunec.*
         Mr. Pummervillo's.

McDONALD, DONALD,   *Calumet.*
         Mrs. Brimacombe's.

PATRICK, JOHN CUTHBERT,   *Detroit.*
         Mrs. Brimacombe's.

RASHLEIGH, WILLIAM JOHN,   *Houghton.*
         Mrs. Rashleigh's.

RUSSELL, EDWARD FRANCIS,   *Yonkers, N. Y.*
         Mr. C. Brand's.

SMITH, WILLARD JOSEPH,   *Allouez.*
         Mrs. Livermore's.

SWEET, ROY WILLIAM,   *Iron Mountain.*
         Mr. Pfeiffer's.

TRETHEWEY, JAMES HENRY,   *South Lake Linden.*
         Butterfield House.

WALKER, ELTON WILLARD,   *Detroit.*
         Mrs. Brimacombe's.

SPECIAL STUDENTS.

Name.	Residence.	Room.
BOYD, FREDERICK JAMES, 　Physics and Surveying.	*Dollar Bay, Mich.*	Mr. Berg's.
CALHOUN. CHARLES ANDREW, 　Mathematics, Drawing, Chemistry, Metallurgy and Petrography.	*Albert Mines,* 　*Albert Co., N. B.*	Dallmeyer Block.
COGGIN, FREDERICK GRISWOLD, JR., 　Chemistry, Metallurgy, Ore Dressing and Mineralogy.	*Denver, Col*	Mr. Coggin's, Lake Linden.
CROCKARD, FRANK HEARNE, 　Physics, Metallurgy, Mineralogy, Mechanical and Electrical Engineering.	*Wheeling, W. Va.*	Keweenaw Club.
CROZE, CHARLES EDWARD, 　Shop Practice.	*Houghton.*	Mr. Croze's.
ESSELSTYN, JOHN NELSON, 　Drawing, Chemistry and Mineralogy.	*Lansing.*	Mr. J. Edwards's.
FESING, ERNEST, 　Shop Practice.	*Houghton.*	Mr. Fesing's.
FLOETER, ALBERT HENRY CHRISTOPHER, 　Mathematics, Physics, Drawing and Chemistry.	*Menominee.*	Mr. Peiffer's.
HOOPER, JAMES KNIGHT, 　Mathematics, Drawing and Chemistry.	*Crystal Falls.*	Mr. C. Brand's.

JEFFERS, FRED ALFRED,
Mineralogy.
Atlantic Mine.
Mr. Peter Thomas's.

JAMES, HOUGHTON EDWARD.
Chemistry.
Duluth, Minn.
Mrs. James Healey's.

KNOX, JOHN,
Chemistry.
Hamilton, Ontario.
Mr. Shafer's.

LEE, ROBERT ERWIN,
Mathematics, Drawing,
Chemistry and Surveying.
Rock Island, Ill.
Mr. Lange's.

McCORMICK, EDWARD PATRICK,
Drawing, Graphical Statics,
Chemistry, Metallurgy, Ore
Dressing and Electrical En-
gineering.
Calumet.
Mrs. Burrow's.

NEWTON, LEE LUKE,
Mineralogy, Graphical Statics,
Assaying, Ore Dressing and
Mechanical and Electrical En-
gineering.
Lake Linden.
Mrs. Kelly's.

PARKS, HENRY JAMES,
Chemistry, Metallurgy and
Mineralogy.
Lake Linden.
Mr. Kroll's.

TRUETTNER, IRVING WILLARD,
Mathematics, Physics, Drawing,
and Chemistry.
Bessemer.
Mrs. Dallmeyer's.

VAN ORDEN, FRANK LYON,
Shop Practice.
Houghton.
Mr. W. Van Orden's.

WEBB, FRANCIS JOHN,
Physics.
Calumet.
Mr. Charles Retallic's.

SUMMARY, 1892-1893.

Graduate Students...................... 5
Class of 1893................................. 14
Class of 1894................................. 26
Class of 1895................................. 40
Special Students........................... 16
                                               101

BY COUNTRIES AND STATES.

Alabama.................................... 1
California.................................. 1
Canada..................................... 2
Colorado................................... 3
Cuba....................................... 1
England.................................... 2
Idaho...................................... 1
Illinois................................... 2
Indiana.................................... 1
Mexico..................................... 1
Michigan { Upper Peninsula.........44 } 64
          { Lower Peninsula.........20 }
Minnesota.................................. 2
Mississippi................................ 1
Missouri................................... 1
Montana 1
New Brunswick.............................. 1
New Jersey................................. 1
New York................................... 2
Ohio....................................... 8
Oregon..................................... 1
Pennsylvania............................... 2
West Virginia.............................. 1
Wisconsin 6
                                               101

SUMMARY, 1893-1894.

Graduate Students	4
Class of 1894	20
Class of 1895	25
Class of 1896	14
Special Students	19
	82

BY COUNTRIES AND STATES.

Alabama		1
Canada		1
Colorado		3
Cuba		1
England		2
Illinois		2
Mexico		2
Michigan	{ Upper Peninsula.........38 } { Lower Peninsula.........20 }	58
Minnesota		2
Mississippi		1
Montana		1
New Brunswick		1
New Jersey		1
New York		1
Pennsylvania		1
West Virginia		1
Wisconsin		3
		82

AVERAGE AGE OF STUDENTS.

1892—1893.

Special Students.......... ....24½ years.
Class of 1895............ ....22 years.
Class of 1894 ....22 vears.
Class of 1893........ ....23½ years.
Graduate Students............................ ....27 years.
Average Age of all Students...........................23 years.

1893—1894.

Special Students......................................23 years.
Freshman Class....... ... .21 years.
Class of 1895...21 years.
Class of 1894...22 years.
Graduate Students....................................27 years.
Average Age of all Students........ ....22 years.

REQUIREMENTS FOR ADMISSION.

Students entering the Michigan Mining School are divided into three classes as follows:

1. **Graduate Students.** { Enter by presentation of their Diplomas.

2. **Regular Students.**
   1. Enter through examination at the Mining School.
   2. Enter by presentation of special certificate of admission.

3. **Special Students.** { Enter upon presentation of evidence that they are prepared to do the work they desire to take.

The special details for entrance are given below under these three divisions.

GRADUATE STUDENTS.

Graduates of any high grade Scientific or Technical School, College, or University will be admitted on the presentation of their diplomas, to take special graduate instruction; but they must satisfy the Faculty that their previous course has been of a grade entitling them to the privileges they seek.

Those graduates who desire to enter upon the regular

undergraduate work of the Mining School, for the purpose
of obtaining the degree of Bachelor of Science, or that of
Mining Engineer, at this institution, will have their diplomas
received for admission to the first year. Such studies as
these graduates have taken in other institutions will then
be allowed them, in lieu of the same studies in the undergraduate course here; provided that each graduate presents
a certificate from the institution from which he has graduated, that he has taken these studies, giving the rank he
obtained in each study; but credit will be allowed for those
parts only that the Faculty are satisfied are the real equivalents of the work in the Mining School.

The Mining School courses having been arranged expressly to prepare students to do their subsequent professional
work, it is believed that the institution offers unusual facilities for advanced and graduate students to obtain such professional training as they wish; and the School will take
extra pains to encourage and assist such students.

REGULAR STUDENTS.

Admission by Examination.

All students (not graduates) who desire to enter the regular undergraduate courses of the Mining School by examination, will be examined in the following subjects:

ARITHMETIC AND METRIC SYSTEM: either Wentworth's
High School, Ray's Higher, Olney's Practical, Robinson's
Practical, or an equivalent.

ALGEBRA, THROUGH QUADRATIC EQUATIONS: either Wentworth's School, Olney's Complete, Robinson's Elementary,
Loomis's Elements, Van Velzer and Slichter's School, or
an equivalent.

GEOMETRY—PLANE, SOLID AND SPHERICAL: either
Davies's Legendre revised by Van Amringe, Wentworth's

New, Olney's Revised, Chauvenet's revised by Byerly, Peck's Manual, or an equivalent.

BOOK-KEEPING: Elements of Single and Double Entry: either Bryant and Stratton's, Mayhew's, or an equivalent.

ELEMENTARY PHYSICS: either Gage's or Avery's Elements, or an equivalent.

ELEMENTS OF ASTRONOMY: either Newcomb's Popular or School, Young's High School, or an equivalent.

Conditions in Book-keeping and Astronomy are allowed in these requirements when necessary.

Entrance by Presentation of Certificate.

Candidates who desire to enter by certificate are divided into two divisions *1st*, those eighteen years of age and upwards; and *2nd*, those under eighteen years of age.

1st. A candidate eighteen years of age or over may present a certificate from the superintendent or principal of any high school, academy or seminary in good standing, certifying that the candidate has studied not less than one year in that institution; has been examined under the direction of the superintendent or principal who has signed the certificate; and that the candidate has passed in *Arithmetic; Metric System; Algebra, through quadratic equations; Plane, Solid and Spherical Geometry; Book-keeping; Elementary Physics;* and *Elements of Astronomy;* with a rank of not less than eighty-five on a scale of one hundred, in each and every study required for admission.

Conditions in Book-keeping and Astronomy are allowed when necessary.

2nd. Candidates for admission by certificate, who are under eighteen years of age, must present a certificate from the superintendent or principal of some reputable high school, academy or seminary, that they have completed one of the *regular courses* of study in that school and *have graduated,* obtaining a rank of not less than eighty-five in

a scale of one hundred in each and every subject required
for admission to the Mining School, and that the candidate's
rank in all other studies in the school's prescribed course is
not less than seventy-five for each and every one.

Conditions in Book-keeping and Astronomy are allowed
when necessary.

All pupils admitted on certificate will be placed on probation, and afterwards dropped from the course, if on trial,
they shall be found to be not properly qualified; and no
certificate will be accepted afterwards from the teachers
and schools improperly recommending such pupils.

The certificates to be presented shall be in the form given
here, and blanks can be obtained on application to the
Director, by letter or otherwise.

Students desiring to enter on certificate, instead of by
examination, *must see* that their certificates conform to the
one required here, as only certificates which do so conform
will be received in place of an examination.

If the rank is given in some other form than the decimal
scale, then it will be necessary for the officer signing the
certificate to state what his marks are equivalent to in the
decimal scale, if he wishes the certificate to be received at
the Mining School.

CERTIFICATE FOR ADMISSION TO THE MICHIGAN MINING SCHOOL.

Of Mr. ....

Age of candidate... ....

Name of school ....

Name of principal or superintendent ....

Course taken.................................. ....

    I certify that Mr. .... graduated in the.... ....school under my charge; that he was examined in the following studies under my direction and that he obtained the marks set opposite each subject. I further certify that the examinations, to the best of my knowledge and belief, have been conducted fairly and honorably. I also certify that Mr. ....is of good moral character, that his attention to his duties has been ...., and that his conduct has been ....

    I also send with this a catalogue or schedule which will show the course of study taken by Mr. .... in this institution.

        (Signed) ....

	Subjects.	Rank.
	Arithmetic	....
	Metric System	....
Required Studies.	Algebra, through Quadratics...	....
	Geometry, Plane..................	....
	Geometry, Solid	....
	Geometry, Spherical	....
	Astronomy	....
	Book-keeping	....
	Physics..........................	....

Other studies taken to be given here, with the rank obtained: .

-------------------- ----------------------- ---- --------------------------

----------- ----------   ------------   ------ ---- --- ---- --- ---- --- --- -

----

UNDERGRADUATES OF OTHER INSTITUTIONS.

Undergraduates of any high grade Scientific and Technical School, College, or University, will be admitted to the regular course in the Mining School, on the presentation of a certificate from the proper officers of that institution, stating that said undergraduates have been regularly admitted to said school, etc.; that they have pursued their studies there for a specified length of time; that they have passed upon entrance or subsequently in the school in all the subjects required for admission to the Mining School; that their standing in the institution in question is good, and that they have been honorably dismissed at their own request.

If these undergraduates will also present proper certificates showing the ranks obtained in their respective institutions in such subjects as they have taken there, all studies which shall be found to be the real equivalents of the studies of the Mining School course will be accepted in lieu of the corresponding studies here, if the certificates presented shall show that they obtained a satisfactory rank not less than 75 per cent in those studies; provided that the application for the acceptance of their past work, as an equivalent for work in the Mining School, shall be made at the time that the students in question join the Mining School.

The examination for acceptance of work done in other institutions is not generally formal, but is of such a nature as enables the Faculty to ascertain if the work done is the equivalent of the work here, and that the student is sufficiently advanced to be allowed the credit he seeks.

Conditions in Astronomy and Book-keeping are allowed when necessary.

ENTRANCE CONDITIONS.

No student will be admitted as a regular student with conditions in any other subjects than Astronomy and Book-keeping. The condition in Astronomy must be made up at the commencement of the winter term after entrance, and the condition in Book-keeping by the commencement of the winter term of the third year.

In case of failure on the part of the student, without satisfactory excuse, to make up his conditions as required, he will be dropped from the school and not allowed to continue his work here until the conditions shall have been removed.

It is necessary for those who are preparing to take the regular course in the Mining School to give special attention to the Mathematics and Physics required for entrance, since a thorough working knowledge of the elements of these subjects is not only indispensable for entry upon the advanced work in them, but is very important in its relation to most of the other subjects taken, as Mathematics and Physics form a large part of the required preparation for successful work in the other studies of the course.

SPECIAL STUDENTS.

Persons of suitable age will be admitted as special students to take such studies as they may be found qualified to pursue, but they will be required to take sufficient work to occupy all the time that is at their disposal for school duties. This regulation will be departed from only for good and sufficient reasons in the case of persons of age and experience. In case any of these special students intend hereafter to take the full course and graduate, they should present, so far as practicable, the same certificates as those entering the regular course.

When these special or partial students are sufficiently advanced, so that they are enabled to do most of the work of a certain class, and expect shortly to become regular students and candidates for a degree, their names are generally given for convenience in the catalogue with those of the members of the class to which they most properly belong; the same as is done with the regular students who, owing to failure in one or more subjects, will not be able to graduate with the class with which they entered.

THE COURSE OF INSTRUCTION.

The Michigan Mining School offers two courses of study in Mining Engineering:

1st. One three years in length leading to the degree of Bachelor of Science.

2nd. The other four years in length, leading to the degree of Engineer of Mines.

The first course covers the ordinary work of a Mining Engineer, while the second course is intended to prepare one for the higher and more specialized work in Engineering.

The former three years' course will be discontinued in 1895, except so far as it may be necessary to continue some portions of it in 1896, to enable some students to graduate who entered with the class of 1895, but who from sickness or other causes have been obliged to fall behind. No new students will be allowed to take this course, unless they are fully prepared to enter and graduate with the class of 1895.

The first three years of the new three and four years' courses are identical, enabling the student to graduate at the end of his third or fourth year, at his option, without loss of time.

The Michigan Mining School is not a college, nor an undergraduate school—it is kept strictly as a *professional* school of high grade, in which it is intended to give instruction to graduates and to others who desire a professional education.

The Michigan Mining School, like Theological, Law and

Medical schools, assumes that the student's preparatory and literary education has been completed prior to his entering upon his professional studies; and that he has taken up the work here for the purpose of preparing himself for his future life work. Like other professional schools, the Michigan Mining School urges all students intending to take their professional studies here to obtain previously an education of the broadest and most liberal character. This is necessary if the student wishes fully to profit by his studies here, and desires to take that high professional rank that should be the ultimate aim of every graduate.

Although not required, the student is advised to obtain before entering the school a reading knowledge of some of the important modern languages, as German, French, Swedish, and Spanish, and to have thoroughly studied subjects that will give him the requisite training in habits of close, accurate and logical reasoning, together with a good command of language, e. g., Psychology, Logic, Rhetoric, Literature, etc. Experience has shown that of two students of equal ability, the one that can give the time to obtain the best preparation, will in the end pass far beyond the one that has had the inferior training.

While it is preferred that students entering should have a liberal education, for their own advantage, the Mining School will not repel, but invites and will try to assist in every possible way, all those who have not been so fortunate, if they have the requisite knowledge and ability to profit by the course, and in conformity with this idea, it has confined its requirements for admission, in the case of those of sufficient age, to those subjects that are absolutely essential as a preparation for the required course, the same as is done in Law, Theological and Medical schools. So, too, the course of instruction is restricted to those subjects that are considered essential to the practical work of a Mining Engineer, since the school does not concern itself with anything except its legitimate business—*professional or technical education.*

In preparing the course of instruction, the effort has been made to contribute somewhat to the solution of one of the greatest educational problems of the age—properly to combine scientific or theoretical knowledge with practical training. In pursuance of this object it is intended that the student shall be well grounded in the principles or in the science of all the subjects he studies, while it is further proposed that he shall also obtain experience and practice in every subject taught, so far as the means and time at the disposal of the School will permit. That is, the student shall have an opportunity to observe and to verify in the laboratory, field, mill or mine, whatever he shall have learned in the class room.

Further, it is intended that the practical work shall here be carried to such an extent that the pupil can make use of it subsequently in his profession.

To this end, the course of instruction has been made as practical as possible, embodying as it does not only the experience of other Mining Schools, but also that of various leading practical mining men, who have been freely consulted concerning the things that they wish men to know in mining work.

·The work in the course is extended and difficult, and requires a man's ability to accomplish it satisfactorily in the given time, as it is so strongly professional. In case, however, one is not able to do the work in the required time, he can readily arrange his work so as to take one or two more years for it.

In general, the instruction will be given by means of lectures, recitations, and laboratory and field practice, including the inspection of mills, mines and smelting works. Each student will receive individual instruction in the laboratories, and those qualified will be advised and directed in original investigations.

Every facility will be given to special and graduate students who desire to pursue any particular subject or subjects taught in the schools, provided they enter during the time when that subject or subjects are taught in their regular order.

In Mathematics, Physics, Drawing, Chemistry, Mineralogy, Petrography, Geology, etc., the instruction is so given that any one who desires a knowledge of any of these subjects, as a matter of general education, or as a preparation for teaching, or for some other profession than Mining Engineering, can profitably study here.

The amount of labor is so great in accomplishing the necessary work of the regular course in this institution in the given time, that every student needs to present himself promptly at the opening of the school year and remain until its close. Every regular student is required to spend seven hours a day for five days each week in laboratory or field work, or in recitation or lecture. He prepares for his recitations in time taken outside of these seven hours a day. When the work is of such a nature that comparatively little outside preparation is required, then eight or ten hours a day may be required in the shop, mill, field or laboratory, at the discretion of the instructor.

In order to enable such students, as can do the work in the required time, to graduate as soon as possible, and to give them the requisite amount of laboratory, shop and field practice, the course is extended over forty-five weeks a year. This can be readily done owing to the cool summer climate, and thus give in three or four years as much instruction as other institutions, having shorter years, can do in four or five years. This saves for the pupils of the Mining School one year of their time. As stated before, any man can extend his course over a longer period of time, if he desires, and in practice many do, since the daily work taxes fully the capacity of our best college and university graduates.

Since the instruction is largely personal, the maximum amount of work that can be done by each student is limited only by his time and ability, while in most of his studies he can advance as far and as rapidly as he is able to do consistently with good work.

Various excursions are taken to the mines, mills and smelting works in the vicinity, on Saturdays or on other days, as occasion may require. Some of these excursions are required and some are voluntary, and all students who join in them are under the direction of the instructor in charge, and are subject to discipline, the same as when in the laboratories of the school.

The laboratories and buildings are closed at 4 P.M. on Saturdays, and at 6 P.M. on other week days.

It is advised that no student should endeavor to enter the Mining School unless he is interested in the subjects taught, and intends to attend strictly to his business, since under these conditions alone will he be allowed to remain.

THE DEPARTMENTS OF INSTRUCTION.

———

I. MATHEMATICS AND PHYSICS.
   Professor McNair and Mr. Davis.
   A.   Mathematics.
        1, Advanced Algebra.
        2, Trigonometry, Plane and Spherical.
        3, Analytical Geometry.
        4. Calculus, Differential and Integral.
   B.   Physics.
        1, Mechanics.
        2, Heat.
        3, Light.
        4, Electricity.
        5, Magnetism.
        6, Laboratory Work.
   C.   Mechanics.
   D.   Hydraulics.

II. CHEMISTRY AND METALLURGY.
    Professor Koenig, Mr. _____ and Mr. Seeley.
    A.   Chemistry.
         1, General Chemistry.
         2, Blowpipe Analysis.
         3, Qualitative Analysis.
         4, Quantitative Analysis.
         5, Assaying.
         6, Synthetic Chemistry.
    B.   Metallurgy.
         1, Theoretical Metallurgy.
         2, Metallurgical Experimentation.
         3, Metallurgical Engineering Designing.

III. MECHANICAL AND ELECTRICAL ENGINEERING.
Professor Kidwell and Mr. Moore.

A. Drawing.
1, Descriptive Geometry.
2, Topographical Drawing.
3, Isometric and Cabinet Projection.
4, Free-hand Sketching.

B. Mechanical Engineering.
1, Properties of Materials
2, Mechanism.
3, Mechanics of Materials.
4, Engineering Appliances.
5, Steam Engineering.
6, Shop Practice.
7, Testing of Materials of Engineering.
8, Mechanical Engineering Designing.

C. Electrical Engineering.
1, Electrical Instruments and Measurements.
2, Electrical Engineering.
3, Laboratory Practice.

IV. CIVIL AND MINING ENGINEERING.
Professor _ _ _ _ _ _ _. and Mr. Abbott.
1, Plane Surveying.
2, Railroad Surveying.
3, Mine Surveying.
4, Mining.
5, Mine Accounts.
6, Mining Engineering.
7, Engineering Construction.
8, Mining Engineering Designing.
9, Ore Dressing.
10, Practical Work (Mines, Mill and Field).

V. MINERALOGY, PETROGRAPHY AND GEOLOGY.
Director Wadsworth, Mr. Seaman and Mr. Wright.

A. Mineralogy.
1, Crystallography.
2, Physical Mineralogy.
3, Chemical Mineralogy.
4, Determinative Mineralogy.
5, Laboratory Practice.

B. Petrography.
  1, Microscopic Mineralogy.
  2, Macroscopic Lithology.
  3, Microscopic Lithology.
  4, Petrology.
  5, Laboratory Practice.

C. Biology.
  1, Botany.
  2, Zoology.
  3, Paleontology.
  4, Laboratory Practice.

D. Geology.
  1, Stratigraphical Geology.
  2, Physical Geology.
  3, Chemical Geology.
  4, Economic Geology.
  5, Field Geology.

OUTLINE OF THE THREE YEARS COURSE OF STUDY FOR THE DEGREE OF BACHELOR OF SCIENCE.

FIRST, OR FRESHMAN, YEAR.

Fall Term—Fourteen Weeks.

MATHEMATICS: Higher Algebra. Lectures and Recitations. Five hours a week.

Professor McNair.

MATHEMATICS: Plane Trigonometry. Lectures and Recitations. Two hours a week.

Professor McNair.

PHYSICS: Elementary Mechanics and Heat. Lectures, Recitations and Laboratory Work. Eight hours a week.

Professor McNair and Mr. Davis.

DRAWING: Drawing-instruments and Materials, Plane Geometrical Problems, Projection, Development, Intersection of Lines, Surfaces and Solids, Tinting, Lettering, Round Writing. Lectures and work in Drawing Room. Twelve hours a week.

Mr. Moore.

CHEMISTRY: General Principles and Non-metals. Lectures, Recitations and Laboratory work. Eight hours a week for eight weeks. Five hours a week for six weeks.

Professor Koenig, Mr. __ ____ and Mr. Seeley.

SURVEYING: Lectures and Recitations. Three hours a week for six weeks.

Professor ____ __.

Winter Term—Fourteen Weeks.

MATHEMATICS: Spherical Trigonometry. Lectures and Recitations. Two hours a week.

Professor McNair.

MATHEMATICS: Analytic Geometry. Recitations. Five hours a week.

Professor McNair.

PHYSICS: Light, Electricity and Magnetism. Lectures, Recitations and Laboratory work. Eight hours a week.

Professor McNair and Mr. Davis.

DRAWING: Topographical Drawing; Making Scales, Platting, Topographical Signs. Lectures and work in the Drawing Room. Ten hours a week.

Professor _____ and Mr. Moore.

SURVEYING: Lectures and Recitations. Three hours a week.

Professor _____.

CHEMISTRY: General Principles and Elements. Lectures, Recitations and Laboratory work. Seven hours a week.

Professor Koenig, Mr. Seeley and Mr. _____.

Summer Term—Seventeen Weeks.

MATHEMATICS: Higher Algebra. Lectures and Recitations. Five hours a week for six weeks.
Professor McNair.

MATHEMATICS: Analytic Geometry. Recitations. Five hours a week for six weeks.
Professor McNair.

PHYSICS: Electricity and Magnetism. Lectures, Recitations and Laboratory work. Ten hours a week for six weeks.
Professor McNair and Mr. Davis.

CHEMISTRY: Blowpipe Analysis. Introduction to Qualitative Analysis. Lectures, Recitations and Laboratory work. Twenty hours a week for six weeks.
Professor Koenig, Mr. Seeley and Mr._____.

SURVEYING: Plane, Topographical and Railroad Surveying. Lectures, Recitations, and Practical work in the Field and Drawing Room. Forty-five hours a week for eleven weeks.
Mr. Abbott and Mr. Davis.

SECOND, OR SOPHOMORE, YEAR.

Fall Term—Fourteen Weeks.

MATHEMATICS: Differential and Integral Calculus. Lectures and Recitations. Five hours a week.

Professor McNair.

DRAWING: Descriptive Geometry, Lettering and Construction Drawing from Rough Sketches and Models. Lectures, and work in Drawing Room. Four hours a week.

Mr. Moore.

CHEMISTRY: Qualitative Analysis. Recitations and Laboratory work. Eight hours a week.
Professor Koenig, Mr. Seeley and Mr._____.

BOTANY: Lectures and Recitations. Two hours a week for eight weeks.

The Director.

ZOÖLOGY: Lectures and Recitations. Two hours a week for eight weeks.

Mr. Seaman.

PROPERTIES OF MATERIALS: Wrought and Cast Iron, Steel, Copper, Tin, Zinc, Antimony, Bismuth, Alloys, Timber, Brick, Mortar, Cements, etc. Lectures and Recitations. Two hours a week.

Mr. Moore.

MINING AND MINE SURVEYING: Lectures and Recitations. Four hours a week for six weeks.

Professor _____.

MINERALOGY: Crystallography, Physical and Determinative Mineralogy. Lectures, Recitations and Laboratory work. Twelve hours a week.
The Director, Mr. Seaman and Mr. Wright.

Winter Term—Fourteen Weeks.

MATHEMATICS: Integral Calculus. Lectures and Recitations. Three hours a week.
Professor McNair.

MECHANICS: Analytical Mechanics. Lectures and Recitations. Four hours a week.
Professor McNair.

DRAWING: Machine Drawing, Tracing, Blue Printing, Making Drawings from Models. Lectures and work in Drawing Room. Four hours a week.
Mr. Moore.

CHEMISTRY: Qualitative and Quantitative Analysis. Lectures, Recitations and Laboratory work. Eight hours a week.
Professor Koenig, Mr. _____ and Mr. Seeley.

MINING AND MINE SURVEYING: Lectures and Recitations. Four hours a week.
Professor _____ ____.

MINERALOGY: Physical and Determinative Mineralogy. Lectures, Recitations and Laboratory work. Twelve hours a week.
The Director, Mr. Seaman and Mr. Wright.

Summer Term—Seventeen Weeks.

MINING AND MINE SURVEYING: Practical work in the Mines. Forty-five hours a week for six weeks. Professor ———— and Assistant.

ASSAYING: Lectures and Practical work. Forty-five hours a week for one week.

SHOPWORK: Practical work in Pattern and Machine Shops. Forty-five hours a week for ten weeks. Professor Kidwell, Mr. Shields and Mr. Purfield.

THIRD, OR JUNIOR, YEAR.

Fall Term—Fourteen Weeks.

MECHANICS: Analytical Mechanics. Recitations. Two hours a week.
Professor McNair.

CHEMISTRY: Quantitative Analysis. Lectures, Recitations and Laboratory work. Ten hours a week.
Professor Koenig, Mr.—— ——— and Mr. Seeley.

METALLURGY: Fuel, Refractory Materials, Iron, Steel and Aluminum. Lectures and Recitations. Five hours a week.
Professor Koenig.

MECHANISM: Laws of Motion, Linkwork, Cams, Teeth of Wheels, Aggregate Motion, etc. Lectures and Recitations. Three hours a week.

Mr. Moore.

MECHANICS OF MATERIALS: Application of Principles of Statics to Rigid Bodies, Elasticity and Resistance of Materials, Discussion of Beams, Columns and Shafts, Combined Stresses, Testing of Materials. Lectures and Recitations. Three hours a week.

Professor Kidwell.

MINING ENGINEERING: Lectures and Recitations. Four hours a week for six weeks.

Professor _____.

PALEONTOLOGY: Lectures, Recitations and Laboratory Work. Four hours a week for eight weeks.

Mr. Seaman.

PETROGRAPHY: Microscopic Mineralogy, Determinative Lithology. Lectures, Recitations and Laboratory work. Six hours a week.

The Director and Mr. Seaman.

PHYSICAL GEOLOGY: Lectures and Recitations. Two hours a week.

The Director.

Winter Term—Fourteen Weeks.

DRAWING: Lectures and work in Drawing Room. Four hours a week.

Professor Kidwell.

DRAWING: Graphical Statics; Analysis of Roof Trusses of various standard designs. Lectures and work in Drawing Room. Three hours a week.
Professor _____ and Mr. Moore.

METALLURGY: Copper, Lead, Silver and Gold. Lectures and Recitations. Three hours a week.
Professor Koenig.

MECHANICAL ENGINEERING, continued: Lectures and Recitations. Four hours a week.
Professor Kidwell.

ELECTRICAL ENGINEERING: Batteries, Ammeters, Orthometers, Electrical Measurements, Magnets, Electro-Magnetic Induction and Theory of the Dynamo. Lectures and Recitations. Three hours a week.
Professor Kidwell.

MINING ENGINEERING AND MINE ACCOUNTS: Lectures and Recitations. Four hours a week.
Professor_ _____.

PETROGRAPHY: Microscopic Mineralogy, Determinative Lithology, Petrology. Lectures, Recitations and Laboratory work. Six hours a week.
The Director and Mr. Seaman.

STRATIGRAPHICAL GEOLOGY: Lectures, Recitations and Laboratory work. Five hours a week.
Mr. Seaman.

PHYSICAL GEOLOGY: Lectures and Recitations. Three hours a week.
The Director.

Summer Term—Seventeen Weeks.

CHEMISTRY: Quantitative Analysis. Lectures, Recitations and Laboratory work. Forty-five hours a week for six weeks.
Professor Koenig, Mr. _____ and Mr. Seeley.

ASSAYING: Practical work in the Laboratory with Lectures and Recitations. Forty-five hours a week for two weeks.
Professor Koenig, Mr. _____ and Mr. Seeley.

MECHANICAL ENGINEERING: Practice in the Testing Laboratory. Forty-five hours a week for three weeks.
Professor Kidwell and Mr. Moore.

FIELD GEOLOGY: Practical work in the Field. Forty-five hours a week for six weeks.
The Director and Mr. Seaman.

GRADUATION.

5

OUTLINE OF THE FOUR YEARS COURSE OF STUDY FOR THE DEGREE OF ENGINEER OF MINES.

FIRST, OR FRESHMAN, YEAR.

Fall Term—Fourteen Weeks.

MATHEMATICS: Higher Algebra. Lectures and Recitations. Five hours a week.

Professor McNair.

MATHEMATICS: Plane Trigonometry. Lectures and Recitations. Two hours a week.

Professor McNair.

PHYSICS: Elementary Mechanics and Heat. Lectures, Recitations and Laboratory Work. Eight hours a week.

Professor McNair and Mr. Davis.

DRAWING: Drawing-instruments and Materials, Plane Geometrical Problems, Projection, Development, Intersection of Lines, Surfaces and Solids, Tinting, Lettering, Round Writing. Lectures and work in Drawing Room. Twelve hours a week.

Mr. Moore.

CHEMISTRY: General Principles and Elements. Lectures, Recitations and Laboratory Work. Eight hours a week for eight weeks. Five hours a week for six weeks.

Professor Koenig, Mr. Seeley and Mr.————.

SURVEYING: Lectures and Recitations. Three hours a
week for six weeks.

Professor ———.

Winter Term—Fourteen Weeks.

MATHEMATICS: Spherical Trigonometry. Lectures and
Recitations. Two hours a week.

Professor McNair.

MATHEMATICS: Analytic Geometry. Recitations. Five
hours a week.

Professor McNair.

PHYSICS: Light, Electricity and Magnetism. Lectures,
Recitations and Laboratory work. Eight hours
a week.

Professor McNair and Mr. Davis.

DRAWING: Topographical Drawing; Making Scales, Platting, Topographical Signs. Lectures and work
in the Drawing Room. Ten hours a week.

Professor ——— and Mr. Moore.

SURVEYING: Lectures and Recitations. Three hours a
week.

Professor ———.

CHEMISTRY: General Principles and Elements. Lectures,
Recitations and Laboratory work. Seven hours
a week.

Professor Koenig, Mr. ——— and Mr. Seeley.

Summer Term—Seventeen Weeks.

MATHEMATICS: Higher Algebra. Lectures and Recitations. Five hours a week for six weeks.
Professor McNair.

MATHEMATICS: Analytic Geometry. Recitations. Five
hours a week for six weeks.
Professor McNair.

PHYSICS: Electricity and Magnetism. Lectures, Recitations and Laboratory work. Ten hours a week
for six weeks.
Professor McNair.

CHEMISTRY: Blowpipe Analysis. Introduction to Qualitative Analysis. Lectures, Recitations and
Laboratory work. Twenty hours a week for
six weeks.
Professor Koenig, Mr.————— and Mr. Seeley.

SURVEYING: Plane, Topographical and Railroad Surveying. Lectures, Recitations, and Practical work
in the Field and Drawing Room. Forty-five
hours a week for eleven weeks.
Mr. Abbott and Mr. Davis.

SECOND, OR SOPHOMORE, YEAR.

Fall Term—Fourteen Weeks.

MATHEMATICS: Differential and Integral Calculus. Recitations. Five hours a week.

Professor McNair.

DRAWING: Descriptive Geometry, Lettering and Construction Drawing from Rough Sketches and Models. Lectures, and work in Drawing Room. Four hours a week.

Mr. Moore.

CHEMISTRY: Qualitative Analysis. Recitations and Laboratory work. Eight hours a week.
Professor Koenig, Mr. ————— and Mr. Seeley.

BOTANY: Lectures and Recitations. Two hours a week for eight weeks.

The Director.

ZOÖLOGY: Lectures and Recitations. Two hours a week for eight weeks.

Mr. Seaman.

PROPERTIES OF MATERIALS: Wrought and Cast Iron, Steel, Copper, Tin, Zinc, Antimony, Bismuth, Alloys, Timber, Brick, Mortar, Cements, etc. Lectures and Recitations. Two hours a week.

Mr. Moore.

MINING AND MINE SURVEYING: Lectures and Recitations. Four hours a week for six weeks.

Professor ——— ———.

MINERALOGY: Crystallography, Physical and Determinative Mineralogy. Lectures, Recitations and Laboratory work. Twelve hours a week.
The Director, Mr. Seaman and Mr. Wright.

Winter Term—Fourteen Weeks.

MATHEMATICS: Integral Calculus. Lectures and Recitations. Three hours a week.
Professor McNair.

MECHANICS: Analytical Mechanics. Lectures and Recitations. Four hours a week.
Professor McNair.

DRAWING: Machine Drawing, Tracing, Blue Printing, Making Drawings from Models. Lectures and work in Drawing Room. Four hours a week.
Mr. Moore.

CHEMISTRY: Qualitative and Quantitative Analysis. Lectures, Recitations and Laboratory work. Eight hours a week.
Professor Koenig, Mr. _____ ___ and Mr. Seeley.

MINING AND MINE SURVEYING: Lectures and Recitations. Four hours a week.
Professor _____ ___.

MINERALOGY: Physical and Determinative Mineralogy. Lectures, Recitations and Laboratory work. Twelve hours a week.
The Director, Mr. Seaman and Mr. Wright.

Summer Term—Seventeen Weeks.

MINING AND MINE SURVEYING: Practical work in the Mines. Forty-five hours a week for six weeks.
Professor _____ and Assistant.

ASSAYING: Lectures and Practical work. Forty-five hours a week for one week.
Professor Koenig and Mr. Seeley.

SHOPWORK: Practical work in Pattern and Machine Shops. Forty-five hours a week for ten weeks.
Professor Kidwell, Mr. Shields and Mr. Purfield.

THIRD, OR JUNIOR, YEAR.

Fall Term—Fourteen Weeks.

MECHANICS: Recitations. Two hours a week.
Professor McNair.

CHEMISTRY: Quantitative Analysis. Lectures, Recitations and Laboratory work. Ten hours a week.
Professor Koenig, Mr. __ ___ __ and Mr. Seeley.

METALLURGY: Fuel, Refractory Materials, Iron, Steel and Aluminum. Lectures and Recitations. Five hours a week.
Professor Koenig.

MECHANISM: Laws of Motion, Linkwork, Cams, Teeth of Wheels, Aggregate Motion, etc. Lectures and Recitations. Three hours a week.

Mr. Moore.

MECHANICS OF MATERIALS: Application of Principles of Statics to Rigid Bodies, Elasticity and Resistance of Materials, Discussion of Beams, Columns and Shafts, Combined Stresses, Testing of Materials. Lectures and Recitations. Three hours a week.

Professor Kidwell.

MINING ENGINEERING: Lectures and Recitations. Four hours a week for six weeks.

Professor Denton.

PALEONTOLOGY: Lectures, Recitations and Laboratory Work. Four hours a week for eight weeks.

Mr. Seaman.

PETROGRAPHY: Microscopic Mineralogy, Determinative Lithology. Lectures, Recitations and Laboratory work. Six hours a week.

The Director and Mr. Seaman.

PHYSICAL GEOLOGY: Lectures and Recitations. Two hours a week.

The Director.

Winter Term—Fourteen Weeks.

DRAWING: Lectures and work in Drawing Room. Four hours a week.

Professor Kidwell and Mr. Moore.

DRAWING: Graphical Statics; Analysis of Roof Trusses of various standard designs. Lectures and work in Drawing Room. Three hours a week.
Professor ————— and Mr. Moore.

METALLURGY: Copper, Lead, Silver and Gold. Lectures and Recitations. Three hours a week.
Professor Koenig.

MECHANICAL ENGINEERING: Lectures and Recitations. Four hours a week.
Professor Kidwell.

ELECTRICAL ENGINEERING: Batteries, Ammeters, Orthometers, Electrical Measurements, Magnets, Electro-Magnetic Induction and Theory of the Dynamo. Lectures and Recitations. Three hours a week.
Professor Kidwell.

MINING ENGINEERING AND MINE ACCOUNTS: Lectures and Recitations. Four hours a week.
Professor ——————.

PETROGRAPHY: Microscopic Mineralogy, Determinative Lithology, Petrology. Lectures, Recitations and Laboratory work. Six hours a week.
The Director and Mr. Seaman.

STRATIGRAPHICAL GEOLOGY: Lectures, Recitations and Laboratory work. Five hours a week.
Mr. Seaman.

PHYSICAL GEOLOGY: Lectures and Recitations. Three hours a week.
The Director.

Engineering Apparatus. Pumps, Compressors, Laboratories. Safety Valves, Fuel Heaters, etc. Lectures and Recitations. One hour a week.

Mr. Moore.

ELECTRICAL.

Junior.

Dynamo-Electric Machinery.—Library and Laboratory work. Twenty-three hours a week.

Professor Koenig.

Metallurgical Drawings.—Work in the Drawing Room. Seven hours a week.

Professor Koenig and Mr. Moore.

Electrical Engineering.—Motors and their applications. Storage Batteries, Arc and Incandescent Lamps. Wiring, Electrical Fittings, etc., continued. Lectures and Recitations. Two hours a week.

Professor Kidwell.

Mineral Exploring or Prospecting. Designing Shaft Houses, Rock Houses, Mine Plants, Laying out Locations, etc. Work in the Drawing Room. Nine hours a week.

Professor _____ and Mr. Moore.

Economic Geology. Lectures and Recitations. Five hours a week.

The Director.

ENGINEERING APPLIANCES: Pumps, Gauges, Lubricators. Safety Valves. Fuel Heaters, etc. Lectures and Recitations. One hour a week.

Mr. Moore.

ELECTIVE,

Either

SYNTHETIC CHEMISTRY: Library and Laboratory work. Twenty-three hours a week.

Professor Koenig.

Or

METALLURGICAL DESIGNING: Work in the Drawing Room. Seven hours a week.

Professor Koenig and Mr. Moore.

ELECTRICAL ENGINEERING: Motors and their applications. Storage Batteries, Arc and Incandescent Lamps. Wiring, Electrical Fittings, etc., continued. Lectures and Recitations. Two hours a week.

Professor Kidwell.

MINING ENGINEERING DESIGNING: Designing Shaft Houses, Rock Houses, Mine Plants, Laying out Locations, etc. Work in the Drawing Room. Nine hours a week.

Professor ___ ____ and Mr. Moore.

ECONOMIC GEOLOGY. Lectures and Recitations. Five hours a week.

The Director.

Summer Term—Seventeen Weeks.

METALLURGICAL EXPERIMENTATION: Laboratory work. Forty-five hours a week for seven weeks. Professor Koenig, Mr._____ and Mr. Seeley.

ORE DRESSING: Practical work in the Stamp Mill. Forty-five hours a week, four weeks.
Professor_____ and Assistant.

MECHANICAL ENGINEERING: Practice in the Testing Laboratory. Forty-five hours a week, six weeks.
Professor Kidwell and Mr. Moore.

THESIS.

GRADUATION.

OUTLINE OF·THE COURSE OF STUDY FOR THE CLASS OF 1895 FOR THE DEGREE OF ENGINEER OF MINES.

FIRST YEAR.

Fall Term—Fourteen Weeks.

MATHEMATICS: Higher Algebra. Lectures and Recitations. Five hours a week.

> Professor McNair.

MATHEMATICS: Plane Trigonometry. Lectures and Recitations. Two hours a week.

> Professor McNair.

PHYSICS: Elementary Mechanics and Heat. Lectures and Recitations. Three hours a week.

> Professor McNair.

DRAWING: Drawing Instruments and Materials, Plane Geometrical Problems, Projection, Development, Round Writing. Lectures and work in Drawing Room. Ten hours a week.

> Mr. Abbott.

CHEMISTRY: General Principles and Non-Metals, Blowpipe Analysis. Lectures, Recitations and Laboratory work. Four hours a week.

> Professor Koenig.

MINERALOGY: Crystallography and Determinative Mineralogy. Lectures, Recitations and Laboratory work. Eleven hours a week.

> The Director and Mr. Seaman.

Winter Term—Fourteen Weeks.

MATHEMATICS: Spherical Trigonometry. Lectures and Recitations. Two hours a week.

> Professor McNair.

MATHEMATICS: Analytic Geometry. Recitations. Five hours a week.

> Professor McNair.

PHYSICS: Light, Electricity and Magnetism. Lectures and Recitations. Three hours a week.

> Professor McNair.

DRAWING: Intersection of Lines, Surfaces and Solids, Tinting, Lettering, Round Writing. Lectures and work in the Drawing Room. Eight hours a week for six weeks.

> Mr. Abbott.

DRAWING: Topographical Drawing, Making Scales, Platting, Topographical Signs. Lectures, and work in the Drawing Room. Eight hours a week for eight weeks.

> Professor Denton and Mr. Abbott.

CHEMISTRY: Metals. Lectures, Recitations and Laboratory work. Four hours a week.

> Professor Koenig

SURVEYING: Lectures and Recitations. Two hours a week.

Professor Denton.

MINERALOGY, DETERMINATIVE: Lectures, Recitations and Laboratory work. Eleven hours a week.

The Director and Mr. Seaman.

Spring Term—Six Weeks.

MATHEMATICS: Analytic Geometry. Recitations. Five hours a week.

Professor McNair.

PHYSICS: Recitations and Practical Laboratory work. Fifteen hours a week.

Professor McNair.

CHEMISTRY: Introduction to Qualitative Analysis. Recitations and Laboratory work. Fifteen hours a week.

Professor Koenig and Mr. Moore.

Summer Term—Eleven Weeks.

SURVEYING: Plane, Topographical and Railroad Surveying. Lectures, Recitations and practical work in the Field and Drawing Room. Five days a week.

Mr. Abbot and Mr. Davis.

SECOND YEAR.

Fall Term—Fourteen Weeks.

MATHEMATICS: Differential and Integral Calculus. Lectures and Recitations. Five hours a week.
Professor McNair.

DRAWING: Descriptive Geometry, Lettering and Construction Drawing from Rough Sketches and Models. Lectures, and work in Drawing Room. Six hours a week.
Mr. Abbott.

CHEMISTRY: Qualitative Analysis. Recitations and Laboratory work. Twelve hours a week.
Professors Koenig and Sharpless.

METALLURGY: Fuel, Refractory Materials, Iron, Steel and Aluminum. Lectures and Recitations. Four hours a week.
Professor Sharpless.

PETROGRAPHY: Optical and Microscopic Mineralogy, Determinative Lithology. Lectures, Recitations and Laboratory work. Eight hours a week.
The Director.

Winter Term—Fourteen Weeks.

MATHEMATICS: Integral Calculus. Lectures and Recitations. Two hours a week.
Professor McNair.

MECHANICS, ANALYTICAL: Recitations. Five hours a week.
Professor McNair.

6

DRAWING: Machine Drawing, Tracing, Blue Printing, Making Drawings from Models. Lectures and work in Drawing Room. Four hours a week.

Mr. Abbott.

CHEMISTRY: Qualitative and Quantitative Analysis. Recitations and Laboratory work. Ten hours a week.

Professors Koenig and Sharpless.

PROPERTIES OF MATERIALS: Wrought and Cast Iron, Steel, Copper, Tin, Zinc, Antimony, Bismuth, Alloys, Timber, Brick, Mortar, Cements, etc. Lectures and Recitations. Two hours a week.

Mr. Abbott.

MECHANISM: Laws of Motion, Linkwork, Cams, Teeth of Wheels, Aggregate Motion, etc. Lectures and Recitations. Three hours a week.

Mr. Abbott.

MINING AND MINE SURVEYING: Lectures and Recitations. Four hours a week.

Professor Denton.

STRATIGRAPHICAL GEOLOGY AND PALEONTOLOGY: Lectures, Recitations and Laboratory Work. Five hours a week.

Mr. Seaman.

Summer Term—Seventeen Weeks.

MINE SURVEYING AND MINING: Practical work in the Mines. Five days a week for six weeks.

Professor Denton and Mr. Abbott.

SHOPWORK: Practical work in Pattern and Machine Shops. Forty-five hours a week for eleven weeks.
Professor Kidwell, Mr. Shields and Mr. Purfield.

THIRD YEAR.

Fall Term—Fourteen Weeks.

DRAWING: Graphical Statics; Analysis of Roof Trusses of various standard designs. Lectures, and work in Drawing Room. Four hours a week.
Mr. Abbott.

CHEMISTRY: Quantitative Analysis. Lectures, Recitations and Laboratory work. Ten hours a week.
Professor Koenig.

METALLURGY: Copper and Lead. Lectures and Recitations. Three hours a week.
Professor Sharpless.

ORE DRESSING: Lectures and Recitations. One hour a week.
Professor Sharpless.

MECHANICS OF MATERIALS: Application of Principles of Statics to Rigid Bodies, Elasticity and Resistance of Materials, Discussion of Beams, Columns and Shafts, Combined Stresses, Testing of Materials. Lectures and Recitations. Three hours a week.
Professor Kidwell.

MECHANICAL ENGINEERING: The Steam Engine and Allied Subjects. Lectures and Recitations. Five hours a week.
Professor Kidwell.

ELECTRICAL ENGINEERING: Batteries, Ammeters, Orthometers, Electrical Measurements, Magnets,
Electro-Magnetic Induction and Theory of
the Dynamo. Lectures and Recitations. Four
hours a week.
Professor Kidwell.

PHYSICAL GEOLOGY: Lectures and Recitations. Five
hours a week.
The Director.

Winter Term—Fourteen Weeks.

DRAWING: Designing, Floors, Trestles, Flumes, Steam
Piping, Arrangement of Steam Plants. Lectures, and work in the Drawing Room. Four
hours a week.
Professor Kidwell.

CHEMISTRY: Metallurgical Analysis. Recitations and
Laboratory work. Seven hours a week.
Professors Koenig and Sharpless.

METALLURGY: Lead, Silver and Gold. Lectures and Recitations. Two hours a week.
Professor Sharpless.

ORE DRESSING: Lectures and Recitations. One hour a
week.
Professor Sharpless.

MECHANICAL ENGINEERING: The Steam Engine continued, Steam Boilers, Fuel, Steam Pumps. Lectures and Recitations. Four hours a week.
Professor Kidwell.

ENGINEERING APPLIANCES: Gauges, Lubricators, Safety Valves, Fuel Heaters, etc. Lectures and Recitations. One hour a week.

Mr. Abbott.

ELECTRICAL ENGINEERING: ·Motors and their Applications, Storage Batteries, Arc and Incandescent Lamps, Wiring, Electrical Fittings, etc. Lectures and Recitations. Four hours a week.

Professor Kidwell.

MINING ENGINEERING AND MINE ACCOUNTS: Lectures and Recitations. Four hours a week.

Professor Denton.

HYDRAULIC AND STRUCTURAL ENGINEERING: Lectures and Recitations. Three hours a week.

Professor Denton.

ECONOMIC GEOLOGY. Lectures and Recitations. Five hours a week.

The Director.

Summer Term—Seventeen Weeks.

PREPARATION OF THESIS.

ASSAYING: Practical work in the Laboratory, with Lectures and Recitations. Forty-five hours a week for two weeks.

Professors Koenig and Sharpless and Mr. Trengove.

ORE DRESSING: Practical work in the Stamp Mill. Forty-five hours a week, four weeks.

Professor Sharpless.

FIELD GEOLOGY: Practical work in the Field. Forty-five
hours a week, six weeks.
The Director, Mr. Seaman and Mr. Burrall.

GRADUATION.

TABLE SHOWING NUMBER OF HOURS IN THE COURSES.

SUBJECTS.	Three Years Course.	Four Years Course.		Three Years Course.		Four Years Course.			
		Division 1.	Division 2.	Theoretical Work.	Practical Work.	Division 1		Division 2	
						Theoretical Work.	Practical Work.	Theoretical Work.	Practical Work.
Mathematics.............	452	452	452	452	....	452	....	452	....
Physics	284	284	284	68	216	68	216	68	216
Drawing	476	476	476	....	476	....	476	....	476
Chemistry	946	946	1268	270	676	270	676	298	970
Assaying.................	135	135	135	....	135	....	135	....	185
Metallurgy...............	112	707	609	112	....	221	486	207	402
Mechanical Engineering..	753	1199	1199	168	585	434	765	434	765
Electrical Engineering....	42	202	174	42	....	112	90	84	90
Surveying................	555	555	555	75	480	75	480	75	480
Mining Engineering......	472	598	472	160	312	160	438	160	312
Hydraulics	....	56	56	....	....	56	....	56	....
Ore Dressing.............	....	222	222	....	....	62	160	62	160
Botany...................	16	16	16	16	....	16	....	16	....
Zoölogy	16	16	16	16	....	16	....	16	....
Mineralogy	336	336	336	52	284	52	284	52	284
Petrography..............	168	168	168	28	140	28	140	28	140
Geology.................	442	582	512	118	324	258	324	188	824
Total..........	5205	6950	6950	1577	3628	2280	4670	2196	4754

DEPARTMENTS OF INSTRUCTION.

MATHEMATICS.

PROFESSOR McNAIR.

As will be seen by a detailed examination of the following pages of this Catalogue, the subjects of this department form the necessary foundation for a great part of the student's subsequent work in his course; and they are taken as a preparation for this work, as well as for their value in actual engineering practice, and in affording mental discipline.

It is the intention, therefore, to give the instruction in this department in such a manner as will give prominence to those subjects or portions of subjects which will be of actual use to the student, and, later, to the engineer. It follows that many things, of interest only to the specialist in mathematics, are entirely omitted.

The value of the study of mathematics in developing the power to do vigorous and logical thinking is not lost sight of, but it is thought that the effort to master the logic of the subjects necessary to the engineer will afford the student ample opportunity to develop this power.

Every effort is made to see that the student takes advantage of the opportunity thus offered. At each step of his progress he is required to think. The ability to describe a given method, or to correctly quote a given formula, and to apply either to a given case, is in no instance accepted as sufficient. The student is required to logically derive the method or formula, and to rigidly demonstrate its correctness.

Attention is again called to the entrance requirements in this department. The intending student, whether he expects to enter on certificate from High School or not, is asked to pay particular attention to the subjects of Factoring, Fractions, Quadratic Equations, Radicals and Indices in Algebra, and to make sure of his understanding of and familiarity with each of them.

The work in mathematics is distributed as shown below:

ALGEBRA. *First Year*—Fall term, five hours a week. Summer term, five hours a week for six weeks.

The course includes the Theory of Limits, Logarithms, Progressions, Arrangements and Groups, and Binomial Theorem, in the Fall term. Undetermined Coefficients, Series, and the Solution of Higher Equations, are treated in the summer term.

Wentworth's College Algebra is used in '93-'94 as the text-book.

TRIGONOMETRY. *First Year*—Fall and winter terms, two hours a week.

The ratio system is used exclusively, and considerable prominence is given to the solution of trigonometric equations, and the transformation of trigonometric expressions.

Most of the time is devoted to *Plane Trigonometry.*

The Algebra of the fall term must precede or be taken along with this subject.

Wheeler's Plane and Spherical Trigonometry is used as the text-book.

ANALYTIC GEOMETRY. *First Year*—Winter term, five hours a week. Summer term five hours a week for six weeks.

The usual course is given, including the straight line and conic sections, with the transformation of co-ordinates, general equation of the second degree, and an introduction to higher plane curves and geometry of three dimensions.

The text-book is Wentworth's Analytic Geometry.

This subject must be preceded by the Algebra and Trigonometry of the fall term.

CALCULUS.　*Second Year.*—Fall term, five hours a week. Winter term, three hours a week.

The *Differential Calculus* is developed with a rate as its fundamental notion.　Throughout the course an effort is made to give the student a logical basis for his formulas, as well as a working knowledge of the subject.　Applications to Expansion in Series, Indeterminate Forms, Maxima and Minima, Tangents, Normals, etc., are treated.

The *Integral Calculus* is from the start treated as a method of summation.　Applications to problems of area, volume, etc., are taken up as soon as possible and their treatment is carried along with that of methods of integration.

The Calculus is given partly by lectures, with printed notes, and partly from Taylor's "Elements of the Calculus".

The Calculus must be preceded by the mathematics of the first year.

PHYSICS.

PROFESSOR McNAIR.

FIRST YEAR.—Fall and winter terms, eight hours a week; spring term, ten hours a week.

What is said above of the work in Mathematics, might, to a large extent, be repeated about that in the department of *Physics.*　The aim is to select such subjects as have, directly or indirectly, a bearing on the practical work of the Mining Engineer.

The instruction is given by the laboratory method.　The

student goes at once into the laboratory, and there, under the direction of the instructors, investigates for himself, experimentally, the laws of *Mechanics, Heat, Light, and Electricity.* The experiments are mostly quantitative, and he is required to measure and give a definite account of the quantity with which he is dealing.

As far as possible, mere mechanical following of directions is excluded, and intelligent thinking is made necessary to the accomplishment of the work. Every effort is made to have the student clearly develop and fix in his mind the principles of *Physics* which he will afterward use, and also to lay the foundation for that skill in accurate determination of quantity, and care of delicate apparatus, which are needed by the practical engineer. Accuracy and order are insisted on from the first. Each student receives individual attention, and, with the exception of a few experiments requiring more than one observer, he does his work independently of all other students.

The laboratory work is accompanied by illustrated lectures, and by such text-book and recitation work as is found necessary.

Below is given a partial list of the equipment of this department for lecture illustration and laboratory work. Besides the apparatus here listed, the department possesses the usual outfit of battery cells, magnets, lenses, thermometers, and other minor apparatus.

Physical Apparatus.

2 sets of Apparatus for experimental demonstration of the laws of composition and resolution of forces.

12 Vernier Calipers.

12 Micrometer Calipers.

12 small Spherometers.

1 large Spherometer.

1 Cathetometer.

1 Atwood Machine.

1 large Gyroscope.

1 set Compound Pendulums.

1 Whirling Table and Accessories.

1 "Swiftest Descent" Apparatus.

6 sets Apparatus for determining Modulus of Elasticity.

6 Kohlbusch Balances.

1 Becker Balance.

1 Springer Torsion Balance.

6 Troemner Balances.

5 Jolly Balances.

1 Hydrostatic Balance.

4 Mohr-Westphal Specific Gravity Balances.

24 Specific Gravity Bottles.

6 Nicholson's Hydrometers.

4 Baume Hydrometers.

1 Ritchie's Rotary Air Pump and Accessories.

1 Lever Air Pump.

1 Fortin's Barometer.

2 Aneroid Barometers.

2 Marriotte's Law Apparatus.

2 Condensing and Exhausting Pumps.

1 Condensing Pump and Cylinder.

1 Anemometer.

7 Sonometers.

6 Vibrating Forks and Resonators.

1 Savart's Toothed Wheel Apparatus.

1 Lissajous Apparatus.

1 set Singing Flame Apparatus.

12 sets Apparatus for Velocity of Sound.

12 sets Apparatus for Calibrating Thermometer and Determining Specific Heats.

1 Pyrometer.

1 set Natterer Tubes.

1 Maximum and Minimum Thermometer.

1 Standard Centigrade Thermometer.

12 Calorimeters.

2 Glass Prisms, 8 in. and 6 in.

1 Achromatic Prism.

8 Spectra-Goniometers (Geneva).

12 Prisms for same.

1 Rowland Plane Grating.

1 Pair Tourmaline Tongs.

1 Table Polariscope.

1 Combined Projecting Microscope and Polariscope.

1 Newton's Rings Apparatus.

1 Bunsen Photometer.

3 Bradley's Marine Sextants.

1 Sextant with Artificial Horizon (Heath & Co.).

4 small Reading Telescopes with Stands and Scales.

8 large Reading Telescopes and Scales (Geneva).

1 Electro Magnet.

1 Electrophorus.

1 Toepler-Holtz Machine.

1 Gold Leaf Electroscope.

6 Leyden Jars.

4 Copper Voltameters.

6 Volume Voltameters.

4 sets Geissler Tubes.

1 Clamond's Thermo-Battery.

2 Thermopiles.

7 Astatic Galvanometers.

12 Calorimeters with Resistance Coils, for Determination of Galvanometer Constant.

4 Mirror Galvanometers, with interchangeable Coils of High and Low Resistance.

4 Mirror Galvanometers of High Resistance.

8 Dead-Beat Mirror Galvanometers (Hartman and Braun).

1 Reflecting D'Arsonval Galvanometer.

1 set of Shunts for same.

1 Reflecting D'Arsonval Differential Galvanometer.

DRAWING

PROFESSOR KIDWELL AND MR. MOORE.

In planning the course in Drawing given in this school, the object kept constantly in view was to give special prominence to such branches of the subject as are of most value to the engineer; hence perspective, shades and shadows, etc., have been excluded, and more than the usual proportion of time is devoted to Mechanical Topographical Drawing.

Drawings that are not satisfactory are returned, and at the option of instructor, must be made up outside of the regular class hours.

The following schedule shows the distribution of work during the successive years:

First Year.—Fall term, twelve hours a week.

Description, preparation and testing of drawing instruments and materials: graphical solution of geometrical problems. Descriptive Geometry. Projections on right and oblique planes; intersections of lines, surfaces and solids; plans, elevations and sections. Soennecken's system of Round Writing.

Angel's "Practical Plane and Solid Geometry" is used as the text book in Descriptive Geometry, and the other subjects are taught by lectures in conjunction with the practical work in the draughting room.

Every attempt is made to prevent mere copying. Accuracy, neatness, and a thorough understanding of the work in progress are insisted upon at all times, and no sheet will be accepted that would not pass in the average drafting room. The subject of lettering receives considerable attention during the entire course, as nothing more effectually spoils a good drawing or map than injudiciously selected or poorly executed lettering.

No student having conditions in Plane, Solid, or Spherical Geometry may take this term's work in Drawing.

WINTER TERM, ten hours a week.

TOPOGRAPHICAL DRAWING: Making scales, methods of plotting surveys, by protractor and rectangular co-ordinates; topographical signs. This branch of Drawing is under the personal supervision of the Professor of Civil and Mining Engineering, and is arranged with special reference to the practical work in *Plane and Mine Surveying.* The first sheets are devoted to the making of scales, and to the different methods of plotting survey lines, the student having previously made the necessary computations from field notes furnished him. These sheets are followed by practice in making topographical signs and in filling in the details of a survey. This course gives the student sufficient skill to plot his own surveys, and assists him in the making of these surveys, by teaching him what data are necessary for plotting.

SECOND YEAR.—Fall and winter terms, four hours a week.

DESCRIPTIVE GEOMETRY: Continuation of work of preceding year, until subject is completed. After principles given in text-book have been mastered, special problems prepared by instructor are given for solution.

LETTERING: Roman, Italic, Gothic, block and free hand lettering. Tinting.

ISOMETRIC AND CABINET PROJECTION: Construction drawing, dimensioning, lettering, and the shading of working drawings; conventional methods of hatching and tinting sections, tracing, blue printing, and use of bond paper; production of complete working drawings of separate pieces from the model, or rough sketches furnished by the instructor. Lectures, and work in Drawing Room.

7

FREE-HAND SKETCHING: Making working sketches, with all necessary views, sections, dimensions, etc., of pieces of machinery or timber constructions assigned by the instructor. This work must be done by the student outside of the class hours, in a book of sectioned paper to be devoted exclusively to this subject, and turned in for inspection on the date set by the instructor.

Students having conditions in the Fall term of the first year in Drawing cannot take this course.

THIRD YEAR.—Winter term, four hours a week.

CONSTRUCTION DRAWING AND FREE-HAND SKETCHING: Continuation of work of preceding term. Production of complete assembled drawings of machines in laboratory and work shops.

No student may take this course who has conditions in the preceding courses in Drawing, or in Shop Practice.

THIRD YEAR.—Winter term, three hours a week.

GRAPHICAL STATICS: Analysis of roof and the simple forms of bridge trusses of various designs (Greene's "*Roof Trusses*", supplemented with lectures). This subject will be given under the direction of the Professor of Civil and Mining Engineering.

While the text book will serve as a guide, the scope of the instruction will not be confined to it. The course is designed to teach the theory of the graphical analysis of stresses in structures, and leads up to the course in designing given in the succeeding year.

No student may take this course who has conditions in any part of the previous courses in Drawing or Analytical Mechanics.

FOURTH YEAR.—Fall term, nine hours a week.

DESIGNING: Lectures and work in Drawing Room.

Prominence is given in this course to the designing of girders, columns, shafts, floors for heavy loads, framing, trestles, etc. Special attention is also given to designs for long lines of steam pipe, line and counter shafting for various duties, etc. No design is accepted unless accompanied by complete working drawings and bill of materials.

No student may take this course who has conditions in any part of the previous work in Drawing, Analytical Mechanics, Properties of Materials, Graphical Statics, Mechanism, Mechanics of Materials, or Steam Engineering.

The Three Years Course for Degree of Mining Engineer.

The schedule of studies for the three years course taken by students who entered previous to the Fall of 1893, will not be followed in the future, except by the classes to graduate in 1894 and 1895. A detailed statement of this course can be found in the catalogue for 1891-92. The following condensed schedule shows such parts of this course as will be given during the year 1894-1895:

SECOND YEAR.—Fall term, six hours a week; winter term, four hours a week. Lectures, and work in draughting room.

CONSTRUCTION DRAWING: Dimensioning, lettering, shading and tinting working drawings; tracing and blue printing. Isometric and Cabinet Projections. Freehand sketching from the model.

THIRD YEAR.—Fall term, four hours a week.

GRAPHICAL STATICS: Of Roof and Bridge trusses (*Green's Roof Trusses*).

THIRD YEAR.—Winter term, four hours a week.

Designing of girders, columns, shafts, floors, framing miscellaneous constructions in wood and metal. Lectures, and work in draughting room.

In addition to the regular instruction in Drawing, r merous applications of the subject are obtained in con'-15. tion with the other courses; the students are requir

make plats of all their field work in *Plane Surveying*, to
prepare working plans and sections of a mine from their
own survey, make a map and profile of a railroad surveyed by themselves, and to draw sections, diagrams, maps,
etc., in their geological field work.

Much personal instruction is given during the entire
course. In addition to the regular lectures and recitations,
the instructors are present in the Drawing Room during
the hours prescribed for practical work, to give advice and
personal instruction to those who need it.

Whenever students desire the privilege of working in
the Drawing Room on Saturdays or other holidays, during
the fall and winter terms, arrangements may usually be
made with the instructor, the day before, by which such
privilege can be granted.

Special Students in Drawing.

Those who desire to enter as special students to take the
course in Drawing only, or in Drawing in conjunction with
some other subject, may do so, provided the professor in
charge of the course is convinced of their competency to
profit by the instruction. To pursue the course in Drawing with success, *Plane, Solid and Spherical Geometry*
of two dimensions should have been well mastered. In
case these subjects have not been completed, the professor
in charge will prescribe as a necessary part of the student's
work, the courses in mathematics which should precede
the work in Drawing.

Equipment.

This Department is well equipped for every branch of
the work it professes to teach. The more expensive or
rely used instruments are in stock, and are used by the
dents as occasion may demand. The drawing tables
gira been so planned that each student has a private

drawer or locker for his instruments and materials and a rack for his drawing board. A printing frame capable of making a blue print 3x4 feet, several frames of smaller capacity, a slate vat for developing prints, and a drying rack, having been recently added to the equipment.

New Draughting Room.

In the new building now in course of erection for the Department of Mechanical and Mining Engineering, provision has been made for a draughting room 25x97 feet, with an annex 28x34 feet to contain instructor's office, dark room, blue printing outfit, etc. This room will be ready for use by September, 1894, and will provide accommodations for a largely increased attendance, and enable more efficient work to be done than is possible in the present quarters.

Instruments Needed by Students.

Each student, upon entrance, will provide himself with the following instruments and materials, a list of which is given for those who may desire to purchase before coming to Houghton:

One 5-inch Alteneder improved right line pen.

One 5½ inch Alteneder dividers (pivot joint) with hair spring, pen, pencil points, and extension bar.

One 2½-inch Alteneder bow pen.

One 2½-inch bow pencil.

One 2½-inch bow dividers.

One 8-inch horn protractor.

One 12-inch triangular scale, divided into twelfths.

One T-square, 36-inch blade.

One 8-inch 30-x60- rubber triangle.

One 8-inch 45- rubber triangle.

One each K. & E. curves, Nos. 1820-6; 1820-11; 1820-15.

One dozen German silver thumb tacks, ⅜ diam.

One bottle W. and N. or Higgins's prepared India ink.

One Faber's pencil form wood-cased rubber.

One rubber stamp.

One piece Artist's gum, $\frac{1}{2}$x$\frac{1}{2}$x3 inches.

Two each Faber's artist's 6H and 4H pencils.

One bottle mucilage (or paste) with brush.

One medium sized sponge, fine quality.

One Arkansas stone, about $\frac{1}{2}$x$\frac{3}{4}$x3 inches.

Two cabinet saucers, about 1$\frac{3}{4}$ inches diameter.

One piece chamois skin, not less than 12 inches square.

One Soennecken Round Writing Copy Book, and box of selected pens.

A black enameled tin box, 13x8x4 inches, with lock, in which instruments can be kept, is strongly recommended.

A drawing board and two sable brushes will also be required. *Owing to liability of getting sizes that will not answer, these latter should be purchased in Houghton.*

The articles called for in this list are necessary for a proper prosecution of the course, and care should therefore be taken to get the exact instruments specified, or others of *equal grade. Instruments not up to standard will not be allowed in the Drawing Room,* as they will not give satisfaction, and will waste the time of both instructors and students.

CHEMISTRY.

GENERAL CHEMISTRY.

PROFESSOR KOENIG, MR.——————— AND MR. SEELEY.

FIRST YEAR.—Fall term, eight hours a week for eight weeks, and five hours a week for six weeks. Winter term, seven hours a week. Summer term, twenty hours a week for six weeks.

This course in general chemistry is planned from the standpoint that all engineering resolves itself ultimately into a change of matter, either in form or in substance. More especially is this the case with metallurgical engineering. Not only a knowledge and habit of experimentation, but also a love and enthusiasm for it, are to be acquired by the student. It is thought that theoretical considerations should not form the basis of such a course. The system adopted may be called the historical system. The student does not start with a table of elements and atomic weights, nor thermo-chemical notions, nor the periodic harmony of the elements. He begins with the commonest bodies, to the handling of which he has been accustomed from childhood, although he may have never had a thought or query arising in his mind, concerning them. No re-agents are used in the usual meaning of this term; heat is the only force used, charcoal and water the agents. In the course of his work the student discovers everything himself, and is made to draw his conclusions from every observation he records. It has been found possible to so arrange the series of experiments that no term or symbol need be used before the student can fully understand its meaning. At the end of the course, six lectures give a recapitulation of the main observations, and evolve out of them the present notions concerning the chemical nature of matter, and the systems of notation. In regard to apparatus, the greatest simplicity is observed, so that the students may make it themselves, even for elaborate experiments. The lectures are intended to show how to experiment; and experiments for effect are avoided. Everything must be for a purpose, nothing for mere show.

The guiding thread followed in the work is the professor's full notes, issued to the students in mimeograph copies. It is not found advisable to use any book of reference, because all those that are worthy of recommendation follow a very different plan to the one outlined above, and

and thus confusion must result.   At the end of the course, however, the students will be in a condition to take up and read understandingly any book on chemistry.

Following is a synopsis of the course:

Fall Term.

(1).   The metals: iron, copper, lead, tin, and their behaviour when heated; discovery of oxydation and the composition of the air; oxygen-azote.   Action of water on the metals at red heat; discovery of hydrogen.   The weights of azote and hydrogen compared.   The notion of mass-units or atomic weights.   Electrolytic decomposition of water.   Atomic weight of oxygen, and chemical symbols or formulæ.

(2).   The behavior of copperas when heated; discovery of a powerful agent, the oil of vitriol, which the students distill.   The connection between this substance and sulphur is traced.

(3).   Experiments with common salt and Varec salt. Discovery of the spirits of salt, of chlorine, and of chlorides generally; also bromides and iodides.

(4).   Potash and soda ash.   Discovery of potassium and sodium.   The students are made to distill these metals from the ash and charcoal.

(5).   Nitre and Chili nitre.   Discovery of the oxides of nitrogen, of nitrogen itself, of its identity with azote, and of ammonium and its compounds.

Winter Term.

(6).   Limestone.   Discovery of carbon in the limestone gas, by its action on sodium.   Identity of this body with charcoal, mineral coal.   Gas analysis, distillation of wood and coal, of petroleum.   The nature of fats (animal and vegetal).   Alcohol, ether, albuminoid bodies.   Discovery of cyanogen.

(7). Study of sulphur and combinations.
(8). Bone ash; the discovery of Phosphorus.
(9). Discovery of Fluorine.
(10). Borax and quartz, Boron, Silicon.

Summer Term.

As all the principal agents and reagents have now been found by the student, and prepared by him, it is not very material in what sequence the combinations of the metals are treated. The larger part of the time is occupied by a course in Blowpipe analysis, which is so united with reactions in the humid way, that it forms a limited course in Qualitative analysis.

The Professor's notes are the guide in this work. Students recite two hours a week during all three terms.

QUALITATIVE ANALYSIS.

PROFESSOR KOENIG, MR.——————— AND MR. SEELEY.

SECOND YEAR.—Fall term, eight hours a week; winter term, eight hours a week, seven weeks.

This course is an amplification of the *Blowpipe Course*, in the direction of humid reactions, more particularly in small quantities of an element, when admixed with a large excess of other elements or combinations. A. Elliot's textbook of qualitative analysis is followed. The spectroscope is used in all cases where it promises to be serviceable. The students recite on their work, on the reaction of elements generally. They are drilled in the writing and balancing of chemical equations. The class will generally have acquired proficiency enough to pass an examination in the middle of the winter term. They are then promoted to the quantitative laboratory. Those not proficient in equation writing and in recitation work, must take the course over. Those behind only in the solving of unknowns, can be permitted to attend the lectures on quantitative methods.

QUANTITATIVE ANALYSIS.

PROFESSOR KOENIG, MR.———————— AND MR. SEELEY.

SECOND YEAR.—Winter term, eight hours a week, seven weeks.

THIRD YEAR.—Fall term, ten hours a week; summer term, forty-five hours a week for seven weeks.

Lectures two hours a week. Recitation one hour or two hours. Professor Koenig's Notes. For reference and amplification are recommended: Fresenius's "Qualitative Analysis", Am. Edit.; Edgar F. Smith's Electro-chemical Analysis; Fresenius's Zeitschrift; American Journal of Analytical Chemistry; etc.

For the purpose of introducing the student at once to all operations of analysis, and more especially that he may form his judgment as regards rapidity of work and accuracy, the students prepare chemically pure, crystallized copper sulphate, and determine the copper by gravimetry (as $Cu_2 S$ after Rose); by electrolysis; by titration with K Cy; by colorimetry in the ordinary way, and spectroscopically after Vierordt.

(2). Analysis of an iron ore containing Fe, Mn, Al, Ti, Si, P, S, Ca, Mg.

(3). Analysis of Pig iron containing Fe, Mn, C, P, S, Si.

(4). Analysis of steel containing Fe, Mn, C, P, S, Si, W.

(5). Analysis of an ore, containing As, Sb, Sn, Ag, Cu, Bi, Pb, Fe, Zn, S; also analysis of quartz and fluorite.

(6. Titration of silver, lead and zinc.

In the recitation work the principal drill consists in making the students apply to special cases those methods which they have acquired in working on the complicated mixtures, as time will not allow them to make all the separations. Accuracy is aimed at first, rapidity second.

SYNTHETIC CHEMISTRY.

PROFESSOR KOENIG.

FOURTH YEAR.—Winter term, 23 hours a week (elective).

The principal aim of the fourth year course is to direct the student how to go to work in a new field of chemical research, whether theoretical, analytical, or practical. There is no end to this kind of work, but if left to chance and untrained exertion, its cultivation is not apt to be remunerative. On the other hand, if a man has been trained under experienced direction his efforts have all chances in favor of success. It is not possible to outline a course of this kind, since each specialty is more or less independent. But some idea may be derived from the following.

First, the idea. The student may have the idea himself, either from attentive reading of the technical periodicals, from a lecture, or from observation in a mill or factory. In the majority of cases it will be a suggestion of the professor's. Now, after discussing the probable or possible scope of the investigation, the student must master all the available literature in journals, proceedings of associations, patent reports, encyclopædias, etc. When this is collected it will be possible to pronounce on the chances of success or failure in reaching the desired end. The student will be led to see where and why others have failed, consequently where the new experiments will have to be started from; and accordingly he sets at work or goes over to another idea. The results obtained will form the subject of the thesis of each student electing this course.

Instead of lecturing, the professor will hold a seminar of two hours each week. For each week a student will be assigned to the preparation of a report or synopsis of some technical subject. .After the reading of the report, the professor will discuss it, and may be interrupted by the students for questions, as in a general debating assembly.

Such special students as prefer to perfect themselves in the technical use of certain methods of analysis, rather than to investigate new fields and new methods, have permission to follow their choice, and will have all advantages which the professor's experience may afford.

The laboratories and store-rooms of the school are sufficiently provided with apparatus to prosecute studies of the above character.

ASSAYING.

PROFESSOR KOENIG, MR. ... ___ AND MR. SEELEY.

SECOND YEAR.—Summer term; forty-five hours a week, one week.

THIRD YEAR.—Summer term; forty-five hours a week, two weeks.

Instruction is given in the fire assay of gold, silver, lead and copper ores, gold and silver coin, bullion, copper "mineral", and slags.

The assay laboratory contains ten large crucible furnaces and eighteen muffle furnaces of the Brown pattern, and sixteen crucible and muffle gasoline furnaces (Hoskins's), the intention being to provide a muffle for each student, and so avoid the inconvenience of making one furnace do for two or more persons. The laboratory is provided with a Blake and a Gates crusher, laboratory size, to be run by power; large buck plates, large and small mortars, sets of sieves, etc. The weighing room is supplied with six pulp scales and five button balances, of Troemner's and Becker's make, for use in this department.

Of the three weeks devoted to assaying, almost all the time is spent in the laboratory; lectures and recitations form a minor portion of the work. One hundred and twenty-five to one hundred and fifty assays are made, upon samples differing as widely as possible in composition, and consequently, in methods of treatment.

METALLURGY.

PROFESSOR KOENIG.

THIRD AND FOURTH YEARS.—Third year: Fall term, five hours a week; winter term, three hours a week. Fourth year: Fall term, five hours a week.

Instruction in Metallurgy is given, during the third and fourth years, in lectures and recitations, supplemented when possible by the use of text-books and visits to the metallurgical works. The object of the course is to give the student a through foundation in the fundamental principles of the different metallurgical processes. In studying each of the metals, special attention is paid to the properties of the commercial forms, and to the effects of impurities upon their value for engineering purposes. During the third year, fuel, refractory materials, iron, steel and aluminum are discussed; the various ores of iron; the properties of cast iron, wrought iron and steel; the methods by which objectionable elements in the ore may be kept out of the finished product, or their effects neutralized; theory and description of blast furnace and puddling process; puddled, blistered, and crucible steel; acid and basic Bessemer steel; and open-hearth steel processes.

During the fourth year the metallurgy of copper, lead, silver and gold is studied by lectures and frequent references to the library. It is the aim of these courses to acquaint the student with the best modern American methods in sufficient detail to enable him to make an intelligent choice for the treatment of any particular ore, and also to familiarize him with the modern metallurgical literature.

In connection with these courses frequent visits are made to the smelting works in the vicinity, and each student is required to report upon the observations made by him.

Students taking either of the courses in Metallurgy must have taken the first year's course in Chemistry and the second year's course in Mineralogy.

METALLURGICAL DESIGNING.

PROFESSOR KOENIG.

This course is divided into two parts:

First Part.—The student is directed to analyze sectional drawings of furnaces, in regard to number, shape and dimensions of parts, to calculate or estimate the dimensions required for a given daily production and to make working drawings for the parts.

Second Part.—Designing of a complete plant for the reduction of a given ore. Estimation of the required power, arrangement of the machinery, economy of space, placing of the apparatus in such manner that the successive operations require a minimum of handling. Estimated cost of the plant.

METALLURGICAL EXPERIMENTATION.

PROFESSOR KOENIG.

This course is essentially a part of the course in Synthetic Chemistry, except in so far as it deals with well established methods chiefly, and finds its originality in adapting such methods to peculiar ore combinations, or metal combinations.

The special subjects, among which the student may choose, are:

(1). Gold ores to be treated either by amalgamation, by the cyanide process, by chlorination, or by smelting, in order to insure complete extraction.

(2). Silver ores similar to gold ores.

(3). Electrolysis of ores or secondary products, either in aqueous or igneous liquefaction.

(4). Studying the influence of small quantities of negative elements upon the physical properties of metals and the metallic alloys.

(5). Microscopic study of metals.

MECHANICAL ENGINEERING.

PROFESSOR KIDWELL AND MR. MOORE.

The instruction in Mechanical Engineering has been made sufficiently full to give the student proper preparation for actual work, and to point out the studies subsequently to be pursued, should he desire to continue the subject after graduation. Following is a detailed statement of the course:

SECOND YEAR.—Fall term, two hours a week.

PROPERTIES OF MATERIALS OF ENGINEERING.—General qualities of metals; cast and wrought iron; steel; copper, brass and bronzes; lime, concrete and brick; paints, etc.; timber; and cordage. *South Kensington Notes on Building Construction, Vol. III.*

The course includes a discussion of methods of manufacture of the more important materials (except such information as comes within the province of the course in Metallurgy), forms in which they appear in the market, their adaptation to the purposes of the engineer, methods of preserving materials from corrosion and decay, etc. The course is supplemented with practical work in testing, for details of which see section on *Mechanics of Materials.*

No student may take this course who has conditions in Physics.

THIRD YEAR.—Fall term, three hours a week.

MECHANISM.—Laws of motion; linkwork; cams; teeth of wheels, with ·use of odontograph; wheels in trains; aggregate motion; miscellaneous problems in Applied Mechanics, with applications. Power-transmitting machinery, pulleys, belting, hangers, shafting, clutches, etc., and determination of proper sizes for particular duties. Taught partly from lectures, partly from Goodeve's *Elements of Mechanism* as a text-book.

No student may take this course who has conditions in Mathematics, Analytical Mechanics, or Mechanical Drawing.

THIRD YEAR.—Winter term, four hours a week.

STEAM ENGINEERING.—Description and discussion of the various details of engines; mechanics of the steam engine, and determination of proper proportions for its most important parts. Taught partly by lectures, and partly from Holmes' "*The Steam Engine*".

No student may take this course who has conditions in Mathematics, Mechanism, Properties of Materials, or Shop Practice.

FOURTH YEAR.—Fall term, three hours a week for six weeks; two hours a week for eight weeks.

STEAM ENGINEERING.—An elementary course in thermodynamics, and its application to steam and air engines, rock drills, etc.; the steam engine indicator; interpretation and methods of working up indicator diagrams; injectors, ejectors; surface, jet and ejector condensers; jacketing; distribution of steam in compound cylinders. Holmes' *The Steam Engine*, supplemented with lectures.

Fall term, two hours a week for six weeks, three hours a week for eight weeks.

VALVES AND VALVE GEARS.—Kinematics of the plane slide valve, link motions, double valve gears, radial and drop cut-off gears. Peabody's *Valve Gears for Steam Engines.*

These courses are not open to any student having conditions in the preceding work in Steam Engineering or Mechanical Drawing.

Winter term, two hours a week.

STEAM ENGINEERING.—Boilers. General description of the various kinds of modern boilers. Determination of proper proportions for heating surface, grate surface, flues, etc. Boiler appurtenances, settings, proportions for boiler chimneys. Care and management of boilers, boiler testing. Heating value of fuels. Wilson's *Treatise on Steam Boilers.*

Winter term, two hours a week.

STEAM ENGINEERING.—Pumps and pumping machinery. Discussion of typical forms of pumps, and their adaptation to various duties. Methods of testing pumps.

Winter term, one hour a week.

8

ENGINEERING APPLIANCES.—Steam gauges; lubricators; safety valves; reducing valves; steam traps; feed heaters and purifiers; steam separators; damper regulators; the various styles of patent grates; steam pipe and fittings; boiler and pipe coverings; rubber, leather and cotton belting, etc. Instruments and appliances used in engine and boiler testing, such as dynamometers, planimeters, speed counters, pyrometers, calorimeters, etc. Taught partly by lectures, and partly from the various manufacturers' trade circulars.

None of these courses are open to any student having conditions in the preceding term's work in Steam Engineering, or Mechanical Drawing.

Summer term, forty-five hours a week for four weeks.

PRACTICAL WORK IN TESTING LABORATORY.—Use of steam engine indicator, Prony brake, and other dynamometers, testing of engines and boilers, gauges, steam pumps, etc.

This course is not open to any student having conditions in Physics, Mechanics of Materials, or the preceding term's work in Steam Engineering.

•

MECHANICS OF MATERIALS.

PROFESSOR KIDWELL.

THIRD YEAR.—Fall term, three hours a week.

APPLICATION OF THE PRINCIPLES OF STATICS TO RIGID BODIES; elasticity and resistance of materials; cantilevers; simple, restrained and continuous beams; bodies of uniform strength; riveting; torsion of shafts; combined stresses; computation of proper sizes and proportions of beams, columns, and shafts. (Merriman's *Mechanics of Materials*, supplemented with lectures.)

No student may take this subject who has conditions in Analytical Mechanics, Mathematics, or Properties of Materials.

THIRD YEAR.—Summer term, forty-five hours a week for three weeks.

TESTING OF MATERIALS OF ENGINEERING.—Such as wrought and cast iron, steel, brick, cement, stone and slate. Each student makes a series of tests in tension, compression, torsion, shearing, and cross breaking, on laboratory testing machines.

SHOP PRACTICE.

PROFESSOR KIDWELL, MR. SHIELDS AND MR. PURFIELD.

SECOND YEAR. Summer term, five days a week for ten weeks.

The entire summer term of the second year of the course is devoted to shop work. In the Machine Shop, instruction is given in chipping, filing, scraping, general vise work, pipe fitting, and use of machine tools. In the Pattern Shop, a course in bench work, making joints, turning, etc., precedes actual practice in pattern making. To familiarize the student with the use of actual working drawings, nearly all work done in both shops is to blue prints made in the Drawing Room. In order that the students may learn actual shop methods, as used at the present day, the instructors who assist the professor in charge will be men who have had a number of years' practical experience in the kind of work they are expected to teach here.

The shop work is planned with reference to the needs

of the School as well as of the students; and models of valves, link motions, mechanical movements, etc., for lecture purposes, pedestals, hangers, and part of the smaller machine tools needed in the shops, will be made by the students.

The equipment of the shops has been carefully selected. The Machine Shop as now planned contains work benches for twelve students, a 24-inch by 16-foot New Haven Tool Co. engine lathe, a 12-inch by 5-foot Prentice engine lathe, two hand lathes, a 34-inch automatic feed Blaisdell drill press, a 20-inch Lodge and Davis drill press, a 16-inch Gould and Eberhardt shaper, a Whitcomb planer, of capacity 8x2x2 feet, a Brainard No. 4 Universal milling machine, one wet and two dry emery grinders, and several smaller machine tools.

A 20"x20"x4 foot Seller's planer, a 14"x6 foot Lodge and Davis engine lathe, with power cross-feed, a 13"x5 foot Putnam engine lathe, and a 10" Boynton & Plummer traverse shaper, have also been ordered, and will be available for use during the summer term of 1894.

The assortment of chucks, taps, drills, reamers and general tools is very complete. For practice in pipe fitting a separate bench has been provided, and a complete set of pipe tools and fittings up to two inches inclusive is in stock. The present Pattern Shop contains two Clement wood lathes, a 33-inch Fay band saw, Beach jig saw, emery wheels and grindstones, Pedrick and Ayer gouge grinder, a very complete assortment of hand tools and appliances, and work benches for eighteen students. Each student, in each shop, has a separate work bench, locker and set of hand tools, for which he will he held responsible. Any damage to tools, or other part of the equipment, beyond wear and tear by legitimate use, will be charged to the student accountable for it.

The check system of accounting for tools is used in both shops, thus familiarizing the student with its operation by actual practice. Both shops are lighted with electricity furnished by a No. 4 Edison dynamo in the testing room. Power for shops is supplied by a 9x9-inch New York Safety vertical high speed engine, arranged to take steam either from the boilers in the building, or from the boiler in the Stamp Mill.

To familiarize the student with the operation and care of machinery; each one will be detailed from time to time to fire the boiler, run the engine, clean and oil the machinery, and to perform such other duties as the instructor in charge may assign him.

No students having conditions in Drawing, Elementary Mechanics, or Properties of Materials, may take this course, except those who enter for shop work only.

Special Students in Shop Work.

Those who desire to take shop work only, and devote all their time to it, may be admitted as special students on presentation of evidence that they can pursue the course with profit. Such special students must be of the age prescribed for entrance, and should have the equivalent of a high school course. Application should be made to the Professor in charge of the work not later than one week before the course opens in the summer term. *Such special students will be subject to all the usual rules of discipline in this school, and must be regular in their attendance or they will be dropped from the course.*

No student will be allowed to enter the course after the first week of the summer term.

THE THREE YEARS COURSE FOR THE DEGREE OF MINING ENGINEER.

The classes to graduate in 1895, will follow the regular three years' course laid down for all students who entered previous to the fall of 1893. The following is an outline of the work they will follow in this department in 1894-95.

SECOND YEAR.—Winter Term, two hours a week.

PROPERTIES OF MATERIALS:—*South Kensington Notes on Building Construction, Vol. III.*

Winter Term three hours a week.

MECHANISM:—Goodeve's *Elements of Mechanism.*

THIRD YEAR.—Fall Term, five hours a week; Winter Term four hours a week.

STEAM ENGINES AND BOILERS:—Holmes' *The Steam Engine*, supplemented with lectures.

Winter Term, one hour a week.

ENGINEERING APPLIANCES:—Taught by lectures.

Fall Term, three hours a week.

MECHANICS OF MATERIALS:—Merriman's Mechanics of Materials, supplemented with lectures.

Equipment.

The Mining School is well provided with instruments and machinery necessary for practical demonstration of the subjects taught in the class room. There are now in stock, one Tabor indicator, one Crosby indicator, one Hine and Robertson indicator, eight polar planimeters, three varieties of steam calorimeters, ten of Greene's standard thermometers for calorimetric work, Heath stop watch, Tabor speed counter, Schaeffer and Budenburg tachometer, lazy tongs, Hine and Robertson reducing motion, two draught gauges, Ashcroft boiler test pump and gauge, gauges for use with water or steam, one Shaw's standard mercurial column gauge tester, Ashcroft pyrometer, Bristol recording gauge, a number of working injectors with cut models of same, etc. For indicator practice, there are now available the 9x9 New York Safety engine in the shops, an 8x12 Buckeye engine in Stamp Mill, and a 5x5 high speed engine to be used for driving the testing machines.

The School is provided with a 100,000 lb. machine fitted for tests in tension, compression, cross-breaking and shearing, a Thurston autographic torsion machine, an Olsen 2,000 lb. cement tester, appliances for testing the shearing strength of wood, and an Ashcroft oil testing machine. There are also on hand a Henning electric-contact micrometer for measurement of extension, an Olsen electric contact compression micrometer; a deflectometer, a Brown and Sharp Vernier caliper, and several screw micrometers.

Those having materials to be tested should make application to the professor in charge of the department, and make definite arrangements with him for the precise work they desire to have done.

New Building and Equipment.

Owing to the increasing attendance, and the extension of the work of this department, due to the adoption of the Four Years Course, it has become necessary to make a material increase in the equipment, and provide larger and better planned laboratories than those now in use in the main building. To meet this need there is now nearly completed a new building, in which provision has been made for ample laboratory space. The additional instruments and machinery necessary for proper equipment of the new laboratory will be added at once.

The machine and Pattern Shops, temporarily located in the main building, will, after August 17th, 1894, be removed to the new building, which is especially designed for shop and laboratory purposes. This building will contain the following-named rooms;

BASEMENT.

Machine Shop	97x24 feet.
Engine Room	34x17 feet.
Electrical Laboratory	34x27 feet.
Lavatory	28x10 feet.

FIRST FLOOR.

Pattern Shop	97x25 feet.
Lecture Room	28x26 feet.
Professor's Office	18x 9 feet.
Tool Room	11x 8 feet.
Lavatory	12x12 feet.
Paint Shop	16x13 feet.
Model Room	18x 9 feet.
Storage Battery Room	15x11 feet.

SECOND FLOOR.

Drawing Room	97x25 feet.
Blue Print Room	12x 8 feet.
Lecture Room	35x28 feet.
Assistant's Office	12x11 feet.
Office of Mining Department	16x15 feet.
Map Room	15x12 feet.
Lavatory	11x11 feet.

An annex contains a Fuel Room 16x34 feet, and a Boiler Room 29x34 feet. In the latter will be located three boilers, two of which are to be used for heating purposes. To enable the student to become practically familiar with water tube boilers, a 58 HP Stirling water tube boiler will be used to supply steam to shop and laboratory engines.

As soon as the building is ready for occupation, a material increase in both shop and laboratory equipment will be made. The number of machines, hand tools and appliances, work benches, testing apparatus, etc., will be increased sufficiently to provide accommodations for from seventy to eighty students at work at one time. Both engines now in use will be retained, and to them will be added a new 8"x24" Corliss engine fitted with surface condenser, and all attachments needed for complete engine tests.

Owing to the danger and inconvenience of gas in the shops, it has been decided to light the whole building with electricity.

ELECTRICAL ENGINEERING.

PROFESSOR KIDWELL.

The use of electricity in mining, both as an illuminant, and as a motive power for hauling, pumping, and operating portable machinery, requires of the mining engineer a working knowledge of Electrical Engineering; hence an elementary course in that subject is prescribed for all regular students in this institution.

The instruction is made as comprehensive as the time available will permit, and special care is taken to familiarize the student with the fundamental principles of the science. Sufficient ground is covered to enable him to understand the electrical machinery, appliances, and processes in general use, and give him a good foundation for more advanced work, should he desire to devote himself more particularly to Electrical Engineering after graduation.

The preparatory instruction in Electricity given in Physics is supplemented with the following course:

THIRD YEAR.—Winter term, three hours a week.

FOURTH YEAR.—Fall term, three hours a week; winter term two hours a week (elective).

ELECTRICAL INSTRUMENTS AND MEASUREMENTS: Primary batteries, the various forms of ammeters, voltmeters, bridges, resistance sets, etc., and the method of using them in making measurements of current, electro motive force, insulation resistance, and in determining faults, etc. Power and measurement.

ELECTRICAL ENGINEERING: Theory of dynamo, both direct and alternating current, with description and discussion of the typical forms in general use; motors and their applications; transformers: stage batteries; wiring; fittings; etc.   (Slingo and Brookers' *Electrical Engineering*, and Badt's *Incandescent Wiring Handbook*.

Summer term, forty-five hours a week for two weeks.

PRACTICAL WORK IN ELECTRICAL LABORATORY: Measurements of current, electro motive force, resistance, calibration of instruments, etc., determination of efficiency of dynamos and motors.   Practice in running dynamos for arc and incandescent lighting.

This course is not open to any student having conditions in Mathematics, Physics, Analytical Mechanics, Mechanical Drawing, or Steam Engineering.

Equipment.

In the new Engineering building now erected an *Electrical Laboratory* has been provided for, and it will be thoroughly equipped with the machinery and apparatus necessary to give the student a practical acquaintance with electrical light and power work. The equipment will include incandescent dynamos, both direct and alternating current, and an arc light machine, with complete switch boards, current and pressure indicators, regulators, transformers, etc. While the laboratory is running the current necessary for lighting the building will be supplied from the dynamo room.

The dynamos will be driven by a separate high speed automatic engine.

The instruments necessary for electrical testing will also be provided, as well as a battery of not less than twenty-five storage cells, to furnish current for measurements, lecture demonstrations, and electric projecting lantern.

Until this laboratory can be fitted up, the instruction will be given mainly by lectures; but in connection with the shop course some practical work in dynamo running will be given. A 12 K Edison dynamo has been fitted up complete, with switch board, regulator, etc., and is wired to light the shops and mechanical laboratory. There are also a 2 HP Sprague motor, arranged to drive some of the testing machinery, several Ayrton and Perry ammeters and voltmeters, Edison ammeter, storage cells, and other instruments for electrical work.

PLANE SURVEYING.

PROFESSOR ————.

FIRST YEAR.—Fall term, three hours for six weeks; Winter term, three hours a week.

The course in surveying is designed to be practical and complete as far as regards the ordinary wants of a mining or civil engineer. The course begins in the winter term of the first year. This part of the course is devoted exclusively to the study of the computations necessary in plane surveying, and to the making of maps and scales.

Johnson's *Theory and Practice of Surveying* is used as a text-book. The Topographical Drawing, which is in charge of the same instructor, is arranged with special reference to this course, and the two subjects are made to harmonize, and to prepare the student to perform the practical work of the summer course in surveying with facility.

Understanding the computations and the methods of plotting, the student is able to appreciate the different methods of collecting data, and can devote his whole attention to them and to the practical work. *To take this course the regular student must have passed in all the preceding Mathematics.*

FIELD WORK IN SURVEYING.

MR. ABBOTT AND MR. DAVIS.

FIRST YEAR.—Summer term, forty-five hours a week for eleven weeks.

During eleven weeks of each summer a special course of surveying will be conducted. Attendance upon this course is obligatory for all regular students who intend to complete the first year. The object of this summer course is two fold:

First, to give the regular students more thorough and extended practice in the field than it is possible to do when they are attending to other school work. Second, to provide a thorough, practical course in surveying for persons, other than regular students, who may be desirous of becoming surveyors, or who may wish to obtain practical experience in the subject. There is perhaps no course of study which can be offered by an institution, that will give such quick and profitable returns for the money and time expended by the pupil, as a thorough, practical course in surveying, since employment at a fair salary can almost always be obtained by a competent surveyor.

In this summer course study and practical work are combined.

Johnson's *Theory and Practice of Surveying* (last edition) is used as a text-book, being supplemented when necessary with lectures. Generally the first hour of the day is devoted to class-room work and the remainder of it to field work.

The subjects studied comprise the use and adjustment of surveying instruments, and methods of surveying.

For field work the students are generally divided into squads of two men each. Each squad is required to make a certain number of surveys, and each member of the squad has to make, from the work done, a full set of notes, computations and maps.

The field work consists of:

1. Exercises in pacing, with a detailed survey of a field by pacing.

2. Practice in chaining distances, and in laying off right angles and parallel lines with the chain.

3. Practice in ranging lines with sight poles under different conditions.

4. Exercises in reading compass bearings.

5. Detailed survey of a farm, made by means of solar compass and chain.

6. Adjustment of the hand level, and practice in its use.

7. Topographical survey on the rectangular plan, with compass, chain and hand level.

8. Adjustment of the transit, and exercises in reading the angles of a triangle by the repetition method.

9. Determination of the true meridian by observations

on Polaris and on the sun, and by means of solar attachments to the transit.

10. Running a close traverse, the angles being determined by repetition, the distances measured with a steel tape, and afterwards corrected for inclination, catenary, and temperature.

11. Running an azimuth traverse around a polygon, the distances being measured by stadia.

12. City surveying, laying out lots and streets, and determining the position of house and fence lines.

13. Adjustment of the Wye level, and running a line of levels about one mile in length.

14. Survey of a mining claim, with transit, according to government regulations.

15. Retracing and subdividing of a section of land in accordance with the United States Government field notes.

16. Topographical survey with the plane table, based upon a system of triangulation with the transit.

17. Topographical survey with transit and stadia.

15. Railroad survey. About one mile of road is located, slope stakes set, profiles, maps and cross sections made, and the cuttings and embankments calculated.

The equipment for instruction comprises the following set of instruments: One plane table from Buff and Berger; nine transits, three from Buff and Berger, three from Heller and Brightly, two from Fauth, one from Gurley; five Burt solar compasses; five magnetic compasses; six Wye levels, one from Buff and Berger, three from Heller and Brightly, and two from Gurley: fifteen Locke hand levels. In addition to these more expensive instruments, the School owns the necessary number of mining lamps, chains, steel tapes, poles, rods, etc.

Two of the transits are provided with three tripod outfits for mine surveying, and all the transits are adapted to mine as well as surface work.

Persons who wish to join the Summer course only, are required to prepare themselves upon the first two books of Davies's Surveying revised by Van Amringe, in the subjects of Plane Trigonometry, Logarithms and Mensuration.

Those attending the Summer Course should provide themselves with Johnson's *Theory and Practice of Surveying* (last edition), a pair of six-inch dividers with pen and pencil attachments, a right line pen, a decimal scale, a large triangle, a T square, medium and hard pencils, and a twenty-five foot steel pocket tape graduated to feet and tenths. These articles are indispensable, but additional drawing instruments will be found convenient.

The furnishing of the surveying apparatus by the Mining School is a considerable expense to the institution, and while losses due to ordinary and legitimate wear and tear of the instruments are borne by the school, any injuries due to carelessness on the part of the student must be made good by him.

The summer course in surveying will commence each year about the first of June, and all persons who desire to attend are requested to send in their names early to the professor in charge of the course, or to the Director of the Mining School, in order that proper provision may be made for them. This course, like all others in the School, is free to any one who is properly qualified, whether a resident of the State of Michigan or not. The course is given in Houghton.

Regular students, in order to take this course, must have passed in all the preceding Mathematics and Plane Surveying.

MINE SURVEYING.

PROFESSOR ————.

SECOND YEAR.—Fall term, one hour a week for six weeks: Winter term, one hour a week; Summer term, forty-five hours a week for two weeks.

Instruction in Mine Surveying is given to the second year students by means of text-books, lectures and recitations. Many practical problems are assigned the students, to be solved by them.

The field survey conducted in the first year largely prepares the student for the mine surveying. The first two weeks of the spring term, preceding the four weeks given to practical mining, are spent in making a complete survey of some mine or portion of a mine. In the survey, lines are transferred underground, shaft lines are established, and courses are run in cross-cuts. Drifts, stopes, rooms and stations located, and cross and longitudinal sections made. Plans and elevations are made of the mine surveyed.

Regular students taking this field work must have passed in the preceding work in Mine Surveying and in the Plane Surveying.

MINING.

PROFESSOR ————.

SECOND YEAR.—Fall term, three hours a week for six weeks; Winter term, three hours a week; Summer term, forty-five hours a week for four weeks.

THIRD YEAR.—Fall term, four hours a week for six weeks; Winter term, four hours a week.

FOURTH YEAR.—Winter term, nine hours a week (elective).

This course is given in lectures and text-book work, supplemented with drawings, photographs and the actual examination of mines, and extends through the second, third and fourth years.

In general, instruction is given in excavation, prospecting, mine development, underground operations, mine ventilation, mine lighting, mine surveying, designing shaft and rock houses, location of the various parts of a mine plant relative to one another and to the underground workings, mine accounts and mine management.

The entire working day for six weeks of the spring term of the second year is given to mine surveying and the study of mines and mining operations.

Instruction in Mining Engineering is given in the fourth year.

More in detail the course is as follows:

(1) EXCAVATIONS OF EARTH AND ROCK. Method of removing material; machines and tools used in loosening and handling material; explosives used in loosening rocks; and drainage of pit excavated.

(2) TUNNELLING. Excavating tunnels; timbering tunnels; removing of excavated material; ventilation and location of tunnel; examination and survey of mineral property and making reports on work done.

(3) QUARRYING. Formations quarried to advantage; methods used depend on geological formation; open quarrying; underground quarrying; explosives, charges; block splitting and dressing.

(4) PROSPECTING. Various methods. Importance of doing work well.

(5) MINE DEVELOPMENT. Location and sinking of shafts, test pits and winzes, and driving of cross-cuts, drafts and adits.

(6) DRILLING. Various operations in which drills are

9

used; machine drills for deep holes; machine drills for shallow holes; drilling in shafts, winzes, stopes and drifts. and placing holes under various conditions.

(7) BLASTING. Theory of blasting; conditions that will admit of blasting; explosives used in blasting; charging: detonators; methods of firing blasts; ventilation; removal of stuff.

(8) HAULAGE. Various conditions met with in haulage: loading tram cars; use of sledges, wheel barrows and carts. in getting material moved to tram-cars; tram cars, their form, size, shape, and material of construction; motive power for tram-cars, and the various ways in which it is applied; inclined planes, gradients, and level roads; junctions, stations, and curves.

(9) HOISTING. Power to be used; transmission of power by wire rope, compressed air, steam, water and electricity: conical and cylindrical drums and reels; ropes, girders, cages, kibbles, safety devices, and signalling.

(10) EXPLOSIVES. Nitro-glycerine: various explosives prepared with nitro-glycerine; other high explosives: fulminates; directions for using and methods of firing.

(11) DRAINAGE. Sources of water found in mines: keeping of water out of mines; natural drainage; drainage by means of mechanical devices and pumping machinery.

(12) VENTILATION. Causes of bad air in mines; natural ventilation; winter and summer currents; artificial ventilation; furnaces, blowing machines and fans; conditions to be observed in distribution of air currents and testing of foul air.

(13) LIGHTING. Candles, air lamps, coal gas, and electric lighting; distribution of lights; various safety devices used in lighting and expense of lighting.

(14) TIMBERING. Timbering in shafts, cross cuts, winzes, drafts and stopes; handling timber; kinds of timber used in mines; preservation of timber; cost of timber; saving
ꞌer resulting from the use of caving and filling

(15) HYDRAULIC MINING. Physical conditions; methods of placer mining; some of the properties of water; construction of dams; waterways and sluices.

(16) COAL MINING. Exploring for coal; tools used in coal mining; methods of working coal; ventilation of coal mines; timbering; haulage and the more important operations connected with coal mining.

(17) DEEP WELLS AND DEEP BORINGS. Where employed; various methods of making borings and making wells.

(18) AIR COMPRESSORS AND ROCK DRILLS. Mechanism of rock drills and compressors; testing efficiency of machines and comparison of various makes of machines.

(19) ACCIDENTS. Accidents from explosives and from falls of roof and sides; accidents from other causes; means of guarding against accidents; legislation regarding the preventing of accidents.

(20) SURFACE PLANTS. Consideration of various conditions to be met; surface equipment; location of power houses, boiler houses, rock houses, drys, shops, tramways and railroads.

(21) MINE ACCOUNTS. Books to be found in most mine offices; entering and balancing accounts; cost sheets; reports made to mine officials and stockholders. Each student taking this subject is given a set of books in which to enter and balance accounts. Costs and estimates of mine supplies are an important consideration in connection with mine accounts, as here given.

(22) MINE MANAGEMENT. Mine officials and their duties; some of the questions to be answered by the officials; place of business of mine officials; salaries and wages; work done by contract, and on company account; tribute working and its results.

YEAR IN PRACTICAL MINING.

... given in the course, comprehends ... ments and mining operations in ... Excursions are made under the in... of instructors during the fall and winter ... and the copper mines in the ... ... The student is early made ... the general working of copper mines; ... in the entire year to persons ... the knowledge of mines and their ...

... the second year, the entire ... given to the study of iron ... at a large mine. ... in metal tools and ma... ... blasting and timber... ... which are turned ... ... examined. ... ... the mine ... ... that was ... This and is followed ... ... made ... ... examine ... ... at the School ...

trestles, shaft and rock houses, and timber construction for underground service. Complete working, drawings are made of the constructions designed.

BOTANY.

THE DIRECTOR.

SECOND YEAR.—Fall term, two hours a week for eight weeks.

Instruction in this subject is given by lectures, with recitations upon the same. It is intended in these lectures to give a brief review of botanical classification, the special characters of important plants economically, and their various uses. The object is to prepare the student for his subsequent work in *Engineering, Paleontology and Geology.*

ZOÖLOGY.

MR. SEAMAN.

SECOND YEAR.—Fall term, two hours a week for eight weeks.

This course is given by lectures and recitations, and its object is to give a general knowledge of the fundamental principles of *Zoology.* The work is given as a preface to the work in *Paleontology,* and particular attention will be given to those orders of animals which furnish the more common and characteristic fossils. Their structure and habitat will be briefly described, and the phylogenetic significance of ontogenetic facts will be pointed out. Attention will be called to the modes of life, habits, and

peculiarities of animals, including their relation to man
and his works.

Students will be given references to such books upon
the subject, as their personal tastes may require.

PALEONTOLOGY.

MR. SEAMAN.

THIRD YEAR.—Fall term, four hours a week for eight
weeks.

This course is given as an elementary one. The work,
however, will be made as practical as possible, much of
the time being spent in laboratory practice. The method
of working will not differ materially from that pursued in
Mineralogy. While much detail is left out, care will be
taken to point out the principal characteristics by which
fossils may be recognized and determined. A personal
handling of the forms of living species will be insisted upon, so that the knowledge will be real as far as it goes.
Special attention will be given to certain groups that yield
common and characteristic fossils, and these will be treated more in detail. The manner of entombment, and the
conditions under which organisms are preserved will be
discussed. The relative importance of land and marine
fauna, and flora, in determining the chronological sequence
of the rocks of the earth's crust, will be considered. There
is a working collection of nearly two thousand specimens,
especially selected to cover the entire geological column.
These will be used to drill the students in recognizing fossils in different states of preservation, in assigning them to
their general orders, and in certain cases giving their generic names. The specimens are arranged unlabeled in
drawers, for the students to work upon; and pains will be
taken to train the eye to recognize resemblances and differences. There is also a small type collection of living and

fossil forms, arranged zoölogically in accordance with the system of Nicholson's New "Manual of Palæontology;" and a larger one of fossils, containing over a thousand specimens, arranged mainly according to geological horizons. Students have free access to all collections. The text-books used are Wood's "Elementary Palæontology," supplemented by lecture notes, and Archibald Geikie's "Text Book of Geology", book V.

Regular students taking this course must have passed in the preceding courses in Botany and Zoology.

CRYSTALLOGRAPHY,

THE DIRECTOR, MR. SEAMAN AND MR. WRIGHT.

SECOND YEAR.—Fall term, twelve hours a week, five weeks.

Instruction in this subject is given by means of lectures and laboratory practice in determining the forms and planes of glass and wooden crystal models, and natural crystals, with recitations and examinations upon the same. The instruction is given in connection with the course in Mineralogy, and therefore is confined to training the student in that practical knowledge of crystal forms which he needs in his Determinative Mineralogy and Petrography. For purposes of instruction in this subject the laboratory is supplied with the following collections:

Crystal Models in Glass........................ 151
Crystal Models in Wood and Plaster............. 2,153
Natural Crystals............................... 1,800

                                                4,104

Regular students taking this work must have passed in all the preceding work in Physics and in Analytic Geometry of Three Dimensions.

MINERALOGY.

THE DIRECTOR, MR. SEAMAN AND MR. WRIGHT.

SECOND YEAR.—Fall term, twelve hours a week for nine weeks; winter term, twelve hours a week.

The work in *Determinative Mineralogy* is preceded by the course in *Crystallography* and by instruction in general *Physical* (including *Optical*) *Mineralogy*, although part of the instruction in these subjects is given as needed in connection with the *Descriptive Mineralogy*.

It is intended to give in the *Optical Mineralogy* all instruction necessary to precede the subsequent work in *Petrography*.

For *Determinative Mineralogy* there is provided a typical set of all the important minerals, special attention being paid to those of economic value, as well as to those occurring as gangue, or rock-forming minerals. Special collections are arranged showing the physical characters of minerals, their pseudomorphs, etc.

These minerals are arranged in drawers, labeled, and are at all times freely accessible to the student.

Besides the typical collection of minerals, there are placed in drawers a large number of specimens of the same mineral species. These are arranged in convenient groups, but are unlabeled. These specimens are selected so as to represent as great a variety of form, appearance and locality as possible, in order that the student may be familiar with all the types that he will be likely to meet with in his professional practice. Drawers of these unlabeled minerals are assigned to each student, who is required to determine them and to recite upon them. He is required to do that which the practical mineralogist does; to determine his minerals by the shortest method possible, consistent with accuracy; the method to vary according to the specimen. To this end every method of determination short of quantitative analysis is employed; that is, in each case the crystal form and other physical characters are used, as well as the blowpipe and wet tests, so far as they may be needed.

After the student has studied and recited upon the specimens contained in a sufficient number of drawers of one group, he is then assigned to drawers containing the unlabeled minerals of another group, which have mixed with them specimens of the preceding group or groups. In this way each student is required to determine in his course from 3,000 to 6,000 different mineral specimens, belonging to the 302 selected species.

The instruction is based on the sixth edition of Professor James D. Dana's *System of Mineralogy*, revised by Professor Edward S. Dana, 1892, and every student is expected to provide himself with a copy. In addition, or supplementary, to this work, there is given a series of lectures and notes by the Director, in which the characteristic features of each mineral, its uses, and the practical methods employed to distinguish each one, are pointed out. Especial attention is given to the methods needed in the field and mine, when one can not have recourse to a chemical laboratory. Every effort is made to train the student to close, accurate observation, to reason correctly upon what he sees, and to exercise good judgment in his decisions.

The result of this work is such that a student not only knows how to proceed, in order to determine any mineral that he may meet, but he is also enabled to recognize at sight, or by simple tests, the great majority of specimens belonging to the three hundred and two mineral species that he is required to study in his course.

During the summer term of 1892 the entire mineral collection was rearranged to correspond to the sixth edition of Dana's *System of Mineralogy*, with the exception of some modifications that, it was thought, would enable the

student to do his determinative work in an easier and
better way, (see Tables IV–X).

Beside the collections given under the head of Crystallography there are the following for use in the laboratory
work in Mineralogy:

Collections illustrating Physical Properties, Pseudo- morphs, Optical Properties, etc.		485
Lecture Collection		10,000

| Practice Collection | First Series.......... 2,500
Second Series....... 2,100
Third Series......... 1,275
Fourth Series........ 3,225
Fifth Series.......... 1,525
Sixth Series.......... 1,850
Seventh Series....... 1,425
Review Series....... 3,125 | 17,025 |

27,510

In order that the special mineralogical work done in this
institution may be better understood by persons seeking
information upon this point, and in addition to serve as a
guide to the pupil in referring to the lecture specimens,
the appended tables IV-X are given of the species to be
studied in the laboratory work in this course. The system of
numbering is that adopted by Professors Brush, of Yale,
and Cooke, of Harvard; the original-collection numbers increase by ten each time, in order to allow of interpolations
of new specimens without having to re-number those
already in the lecture collection.

The tables only show the numbers of the specimens belonging to the species upon which laboratory work is
given, and not those of the other species represented in
the lecture collection.

*Regular students taking this course must have passed in
the Chemistry and Physics of the first year, and the preceding Crystallography.*

PETROGRAPHY.

THE DIRECTOR AND MR. SEAMAN.

THIRD YEAR.—Fall and winter terms, six hours a week.

In this course the student is taught to use the microscope as a simple instrument, and also as a piece of optical apparatus for the determination of minerals and rocks.

The work is incidentally divided into three parts: *Microscopic Mineralogy, Lithology,* and *Petrology.*

Microscopic Mineralogy: Under this head is treated the various optical and other characters of minerals as revealed by the microscope. Their alterations are especially studied owing to the importance of these in the subject of Economic Geology.

In this elementary course the student is expected to do sufficient laboratory work to enable him to distinguish globulites, trichites, microlites, spherulites, aggregates, twinned crystals, fluid, glass and stone inclusions, isotropic and anisotropic bodies, uniaxial and biaxial crystals, positive and negative uniaxial and biaxial crystals; and to determine the axis of elasticity in a crystal plate, the extinction line of crystals, and the crystal system of plates in parallel polarized light. He is required to know the conditions necessary for the determination of uniaxial and biaxial crystals in converging polarized light; also pleochroism, how determined and for what use; the use of Newton's scale of colors and the use of the gypsum and mica plates, quartz wedge, and the Bertrand lens. He should be able to determine the following minerals, and give the characters that distinguish each one from the others: Graphite, pyrite, quartz (chalcedony), hematite, ilmenite, spinel (picotite), magnetite, chromite, rutile, zircon, opal, calcite, dolomite, orthoclase, microcline, plagioclase, leucite, enstatite (bastite), hypersthene, pyroxene (diallage, omphacite, and augite), amphibole (tremolite, actinolite and hornblende), glaucophane, nephelite (elaeolite), sodalite, haüynite, noselite, garnet, chrysolite (olivine), andalusite (chiastolite), sillimanite (fibrolite), tourmaline, staurolite, titanite, muscovite, biotite, chlorotoid (ottrelite), chlorite, serpentine (chrysotile), talc, kaolinite, apatite and gypsum.

For the purpose of instruction there is used as a text book and laboratory manual, Rosenbusch's "Microscopical Physiography", translated by Joseph P. Iddings, Third Edition, 1893.

This is supplemented by a series of lectures given by the Director.

For the purpose of giving the above elementary, as well as graduate, instruction, the department is supplied, amongst other things, with the following apparatus:

Twenty-nine Bausch and Lomb's Petrographical Microscopes, made expressly for the Michigan Mining School; with Micrometer Eyepieces, Bertrand's Lenses, Quartz Wedges, Undulation Plates, etc.

Four Beck's Petrographical Microscopes with Accessories.

One Fuess's Largest Petrographical Microscope, of the latest pattern, with all the Accessories; made expressly for this institution.

One Nachet's Largest Petrographical Microscope, with all the Accessories.

One Dick's Petrographical Microscope, with Swift's Objectives and other Accessories.

One projection Microscope.

One Nachet's Inverted Chemical Microscope.

One Spectroscope.

One Spectropolarizer.

One Sorby's Apparatus for observing the four images given by biaxial bodies.

Two Calderon's Oculars.

Three Bertrand Oculars.

One Spectroscope Ocular.
One Goniometer Ocular.
One Babinet's Compensator Ocular.
One Michel-Levy's Comparateur.
One Axial Angle Apparatus for measurements in oil.
Two Axial Angle Apparatuses.
One Periscope Eyepiece.
One Filar Micrometer.
One Cross-hair Micrometer.
Three Micrometers.
Four Camera Lucidas.
Two Abbé's Camera Lucidas.
One Bausch and Lomb's One-inch Microphotographic
Objective.
One Mica Plate Nose Piece.
Many Extra Eyepieces, Objectives, etc.
One Condenser.
One Condenser with Iris Diaphragm.
One Jannettaz's Thermal Apparatus.
One Latterman's Apparatus.
One Fuess's Polariscope with Accessories.
One Groth's Universal Apparatus, with Goniometer.
One Fuess's Application Goniometer for dull crystals.
One Fuess's Reflection Goniometer.
One Hirschwald's Microscope Goniometer.
One Linhof's Reflection Goniometer.
One Total Reflectometer Attachment.
Fourteen Miller's Goniometers.
One Stage Goniometer.
One Bertrand's Micro-goniomoter with Special Stage.
One Flask for measuring Index of Fluids.
One Pyroelectric Duster.
One Streng's Chest and Apparatus, for Microchemical
Reactions, etc, etc.
3752 Thin Sections of Rocks and Minerals.

Lithology: The instruction in this branch of *Petrography* comprises both macroscopic and microscopic study of rocks.

For this work large and complete collections of rock specimens, with numerous thin sections, are arranged for the use of the student. The course of instruction here is similar to that followed in the course in Mineralogy. Lectures are given upon the specimens of the typical collection, the method of classification explained, and the distinguishing characters of the different groups, species, and varieties pointed out. Special attention is called to the variations and alterations in rocks, and to their local modifications due to their special mode of occurrence in the field.

The object of the course is to give the student that training in the practical determination of rocks that will enable him to know them in the field and mine, as well as to observe their alterations and modifications—subjects that have a very important bearing upon the vital questions relating to ore deposits.

After the study of a sufficiently large number of types has been had, the student has assigned to him drawers containing unlabeled specimens of these rocks, which he is expected to determine and recite upon, as he has done in his study of the minerals. The course is thus made thorough and practical, and adapted to the needs of the miner and geologist, giving them a training which they can make use of in their future work.

The student is drilled at the same time upon both the microscopic and macroscopic characters of the rocks he is studying.

Besides between three and four thousand thin sections for microscopic work, for macroscopic work there are the following collections of rocks available for use in this course:

Lecture Collection.. 3,800
Practice Collection.. 6,500
Rosenbusch Collection...................................... 1,000
Collection of Michigan Rocks............................. 275
_____
11,575

The subjoined classification of rocks, Table XI, will show the scope of the laboratory work and lectures, as the instruction in *Lithology* is given entirely by lectures and laboratory practice.

Petrology: Under this subdivision of *Petrography*, the various questions relating to the origin, modes of occurrence, relations and alterations of rocks, as observed in the field, are considered.

This subject is further considered under the head of *Physical Geology.*

Regular students taking this course must have completed the course in Mineralogy, Physics and the preceding General and Qualitative Chemistry.

STRATIGRAPHICAL GEOLOGY.

MR. SEAMAN.

THIRD YEAR.—Winter term, five hours a week.

This course will consist of recitations and laboratory work, and will be given in continuation of the course in Paleontology. The object of the course will be to familiarize the student with the life history, lithological characters, mode of formation, and distribution in time and space, of the formations which compose the earth's crust.

In the laboratory the student will be drilled in determining the fossils in hand specimens, and in assigning the fossils so determined to their proper geological system. For this purpose there are available, the Paleontological collections of three thousand specimens, three small collec-tions—one European and two American—containing specimens arranged stratigraphically, and over one thou and specimens of sedimentary rocks belonging to th lithological collection. If time permits, there will be exercises in determining horizons, with the aid of paleon-tological literature, with which the library is well supplied.

In addition to the above, some time will be given to sur-face geology, in which the present contours of the land will be explained. The text-book is Dr. Archibald Geikie' "Text-Book of Geology," books VI and VII.

Regular students taking this course must have complet the preceding courses in Botany, Zoölogy, Paleontology and Physical Geology.

PHYSICAL GEOLOGY.

THE DIRECTOR.

THIRD YEAR.—Fall term, two hours a week, winter term, three hours a week.

The instruction in *Physical Geology* is intended to be especially adapted to the needs of the explorer, the engi-neer, the petrographer, the geologist, the miner, the quarryman, and of all others who desire to understand the connection and the structural relations that rock masses have to one another and to the valuable deposits which they may contain. It is intended to treat of the origin and alterations of rocks, of general volcanic and earthquake action, metamorphism, jointing, faulting, cleavage, moun-tain building, eruptive rocks and crystalline schists; the

TABLE VI. THIRD SERIES.—SEVENTEEN SPECIES.

Divis-ions.	Subdivisions.	Group.	Species.	Varieties.	Pages in Dana's System.	No. of Drawer.	First and last numbers of the Specimens.	No. of Speci-mens.
Carbonates.	Anhydrous Carbonates.	Calcite	Calcite	Dog-Tooth Spar. Iceland Spar. Satin Spar. Marble. Limestone. Chalk. Oolite. Pisolite. Stalactite. Stalagmite. Mexican Onyx. Calc Sinter. Calc Tufa. Travertine.	262–271	80–82	28040–29000	114
			Dolomite.		271–273	92, 93	29020–30270	37
			Magnesite.	Breunnerite.	274, 275	94	30460–30640	49
			Siderite.	Spherosiderite. Clay-Ironstone.	276–278	94–96	30650–31440	60
			Rhodochrosite.	Manganocalcite. Manganosiderite.	278, 279	96, 97	31450–31780	38
			Smithsonite.		279, 280	97, 98	31790–32300	58
		Aragonite	Aragonite.	Stalactite. Stalagmite. Coralloidal or Floss-Ferri.	281–283		32310–32970	97
			Witherite.		284, 285		33010–33220	25
			Strontianite.		285, 286		33230–33470	25
			Cerussite.		286–289		33475–34040	64
		Barytocalcite	Barytocalcite.		289		34050–34090	8
	Hydrous Carbonates.	Malachite	Malachite.		294, 295		34110–34900	90
			Azurite.		295–298		34910–35650	82
			Hydrozincite.		299		35670–35815	20
			Natron.		301		35830–35960	4

Division	Subdivisions	Group	Species	Varieties	Pages in Dana's System	No. of Drawer	First and last numbers of the Specimens	No. of Specimens
Carbonates	Anhydrous Carbonates	Calcite	Calcite	Dog-Tooth Spar, Iceland Spar, Satin Spar, Marble, Limestone, Chalk, Oolite, Pisolite, Stalactite, Stalagmite, Mexican Onyx, Calc Sinter, Calc Tufa, Travertine	262-271	80-92	29040-29000	114
			Dolomite, Magnesite	Breunnerite	271-273	92, 93 / 93, 94	29920-30270 / 30460-30640	37 / 40
			Siderite	Spherosiderite, Clay-Ironstone	276-278	94-96	30850-31440	60
			Rhodochrosite	Manganocalcite, Manganosiderite	278-279	96, 97	31450-31780	38
			Smithsonite		279-280	97, 98	31790-32300	58
		Aragonite	Aragonite	Stalactite, Stalagmite, Coralloidal or Floss-Ferri	281-283	98-100	32310-32970	97
			Witherite		284, 285	101	33010-33220	25
			Strontianite		285, 286	101, 102	33230-33470	25
			Cerussite		286-289	102, 103	33475-34040	64
		Barytocalcite	Barytocalcite		289	103	34050-34090	8
	Hydrous Carbonate	Malachite	Malachite		294, 295	104, 105	34110-34900	80
			Azurite		295-299	106, 107	34910-35650	82
			Hydrozincite		301	107	35670-35815	20
			Natron		301	107	35830-35960	4
			Hydromagnesite		304, 305	107	36400-35980	9
			Zaratite		305	108	36070-36100	7

TABLE IX.   SIXTH SERIES.—THIRTY-SIX SPECIES.

Divisions.	Subdivisions.	Group.	Species.	Varieties.	Pages in Dana's System.	Number of Drawer.	First and last Numbers of the Specimens.	No. of Specimens.

TABLE X.   SEVENTH SERIES.—THIRTY-SIX SPECIES.

CLASSIFICATION OF UTILITES OR USEFUL GEOLOGICAL PRODUCTS BASED ON THEIR USES.

TABLE XIII.

Utilites

- Erites, or Metallites .... } Ores, or Metalliferous Materials.

- Non-erites, or Memetallites, or Non-metalliferous Materials.

Tectonites.................. }	Construction Materials, or Building and Road Materials.
Cosmites................. }	Decorative Materials, or Ornamental Stones and Gems.
Pyrolites................. }	Refractory, or Fire-resisting Materials.
Chalicites................ }	Binding Materials, or Limes, Mortars, Cements, etc.
Ceramites................ }	Fictile, or Ceramic Materials.
Rholites................. }	Smelting Materials, or Fluxes.
Vitrites................. }	Vitrifying Materials, or Glass, etc.
Tribolites................ }	Abrasives, or Attrition Materials.
Thermites................ }	Fuels or Burning Materials, or Carbonites.
Grapholites............... }	Graphic, or Illustrative Materials.
Lubricites................ }	Lubricants, or Friction Materials.
Chromatites............... }	Color Materials, or Paints, Pigments, etc.
Coprites................. }	Fertilizers, or Mineral Manures.
Salites.................. }	Salts and Saline Materials.
Ignites.................. }	Pyrotechnic Materials.
Pharmacites............... }	Mineral Medicines.
Chemites................. }	Chemical Materials.

action of air, surface and underground waters, and life; the interior condition of the earth, etc., especially in their relations to the problems that the economic geologist, miner and quarryman have to meet. The student has brought before him constantly the various problems that arise in the practical work and their methods of solution.

The course is given by lectures and by recitations based upon the lectures and upon Dr. Archibald Geikie's *Text Book of Geology,* third edition, 1893, books I, II (part I), III and IV.

Regular students who take this course must have completed the preceding work in Physics, Chemistry and Mineralogy.

ECONOMIC GEOLOGY.

THE DIRECTOR.

FOURTH YEAR.—Fall term, five hours a week; winter term, five hours a week (elective).

In the old three years' course, the instruction is confined to the winter term of the third year, and is given in an abbreviated form. In 1893-1894 Kemp's "Ore Deposits" was used as the text book, but was supplemented by numerous lectures. In the four years' course, the instruction will take up the geology of the useful, or economic, mineral products in two different ways.

1st, Their origin and modes of occurrence.

2nd, Their uses.

The general ground covered by lectures relating to the modes of occurrence of products treated in the course of Economic Geology is shown in Table XII; while that

10

covered by the lectures relating to the uses of these products is shown in a general way by Table XIII.

Special attention is given to the instruction of the student in Mineralogy, Petrography and Geology, in order that he may in after years understand the nature of the deposits upon which he may be at work; since disastrous mistakes probably occur in the practice of a mining engineer oftener through ignorance of the petrographical and geological relations of the ore deposits in question, than from a lack of engineering or metallurgical skill.

The location of the school affords special advantages for the study of Petrography and General and Economic Geology. It is situated in the midst of the vast and ancient lava flows and conglomerates generally known as the Copper-bearing or Keweenawan series, and near the Eastern or Potsdam Sandstone. In the immediate vicinity are to be solved some of the most important and fundamental problems of petrographical and geological science, e. g. the metamorphism, or alteration of rocks; the true age of the so-called Keweenawan series; the relation of the so-called Huronian and Laurentian series; the origin of the iron ore, etc.; while almost every problem of Geology finds its illustration in some portion of the Upper Peninsula.

The instruction in the various departments under the charge of the Director is intended to be given so that all those who wish to obtain a knowledge of the subjects as a matter of general information, or to prepare themselves to be teachers or investigators, can attend with advantage.

Regular students who take this course must have completed the preceding work in Physics, Elementary Chemistry, Qualitative Analysis, Mineralogy, Petrography and Geology.

FIELD WORK IN GEOLOGY.

THE DIRECTOR AND MR SEAMAN.

THIRD YEAR.—Summer term, forty-five hours a week, six weeks.

Part of the summer term of the third year is spent in the field and about the mines, in the practical study of various questions in General and Economic Geology, Mineralogy and Petrography.

In order to increase the usefulness of the Mining School, by enabling persons to take some of its courses of instruction, the summer work in *Geology, Shop Practice, Ore Dressing, Assaying, and Surveying*, is open to all properly prepared persons. All candidates for a degree in this institution are required to take all this work, as it is a part of the regular course. The summer course in Geology will commence early in July and continue for six weeks. The course consists essentially in the examination and discussion of observed phenomena of the sedimentary and eruptive rocks, whether metamorphic or not, as well as of the associated ores to be seen in the Upper Peninsula of Michigan. The work, for the most part, will be done in the vicinity of the mines, and students will be expected to make maps, notes, sections, diagrams, etc.

Special instruction is given in geological wood craft and surveying, like finding quarter posts, tracing section lines, finding and locating outcrops, tracing dikes and veins, distinguishing geological formations, their distribution and relations, etc.

For purposes of instruction, this department is well supplied with dial and dip compasses and barometers.

During the summer of 1893, the class worked in the Marquette, Menominee and Gogebic Iron districts, and in 1894 the work will be done along the shore of Lake Superior and in the Marquette Iron district, as this region offers the most varied and extended problems of almost any district of its size in the world.

The student of geology can study within the limits of the Upper Peninsula of Michigan the following stratigraphical formations, commencing in the list with the oldest:

Azoic or Archaean System..............	Laurentian (?) Period	Cascade Formation.
	Huronian (?) Period..	Republic Formation. Mesnard Formation.
	Michigan Period.......	Holyoke Formation. Negaunee Formation.
Paleozoic System....	Cambrian Period..	Potsdam Formation. [Keweenawan Formation.] Calciferous Formation.
	Silurian Period.... ...	Trenton Formation. Hudson River Formation. Niagara Formation. Onondaga Formation. Lower Helderberg Formation.
	Devonian Period.	Upper Helderberg Formation.
Anthropozoic or Anthozoic System.....	Quaternary Period....	Pleistocene Formation. Recent Formation.

THESES.

Every student who is a candidate for the degree of Mining Engineer in the four years course is required to present to the Faculty a satisfactory thesis giving the results of original work in some subject related to the studies of the course, before he can be recommended to receive his degree. Students who intend to graduate in any year are required to select their subjects and present them to the Faculty for approval during the fall term of that school year.

The theses are required to embody the results of some investigation, followed under the direction of one or more of the teachers in the school; and to be accepted, they need to possess considerable merit, and to give evidence to thorough work.

Candidates for the degree of Bachelor of Science are not required to present any thesis.

ORGANIZATION..

The Michigan Mining School is an Institution established and supported by the State of Michigan, in accordance with that liberal educational policy which has placed the University of Michigan amongst the foremost educational institutions of America.

The Mining School is organized under the authority of an Act, approved May 1, 1885, portions of which are as follows:

"SECTION 1.   The people of the State of Michigan enact: That a school shall be established in the Upper Peninsula of the State of Michigan, to be called the Michigan Mining School, for the purpose and under the regulations contained in this Act.

"SEC. 2.   The said school shall be under the control and management of a board of six members, not less than four of whom shall be residents of the Upper Peninsula of the State of Michigan, who shall be known as the 'Board of Control of the Michigan Mining School,' and who shall be appointed by the Governor of the State of Michigan, by and with the consent of the Senate, (* * * *) and who shall serve without compensation.

"SEC. 5.   The course of instruction shall embrace geology, mineralogy, chemistry, mining and mining engineering, and such other branches of practical and theoretical knowledge as will, in the opinion of the board, conduce to the end of enabling the students of said Institution to obtain a full knowledge of the science, art and practice of mining, and the application of machinery thereto. Tuition shall be free in said Institution, to all bona fide residents of this State, but a reasonable charge for incidental expenses, not less than ten dollars nor exceeding thirty dollars per year, may be made against any student, if deemed necessary, and the board shall not be obliged to furnish books, apparatus, or other materials for the use of students.

"SEC. 6. The course of study, the terms, and the hours of instruction, shall be regulated by the board, who shall also have power to make all such rules and regulations concerning admission, control and discipline of students, and such others, as may be deemed necessary for the good government of the Institution and the convenience and transaction of its business.

"SEC. 7. No debt shall be contracted beyond or apart from the actual means at the disposal of the Institution. The board may dispose of, or lease any property donated to the State for said School, or which may be acquired in payment of debts, except of such as is necessary for the accommodation of the school.   *   *   *   *   *   *   "

In conformity with the above act, the Michigan Mining School was first opened to students September 15, 1886, and has been made free to students from every land. All are received on the same conditions, no matter where their residence may be.

EXPENSES.

Under the act of organization, the Board of Control have made the school entirely free, no charge being made for tuition or incidentals, whether the student was a resident of the State of Michigan, or of the United States, or not; all has been made free to the students from every land. The supplies in the chemical and allied laboratories are furnished the students, and they are required to pay for materials, re-agents, etc., and for the use and breakage of apparatus.

All students working in the Chemical Laboratories are required to pay ten dollars a year, which general charge covers all chemicals, gas, use of balances, etc. Students taking the course in Assaying are required to pay four dollars for the first year, and eight dollars for the second year.

In order partially to insure the State against damage and loss to its school property, every student is required to deposit with the Treasurer the sum of twenty-five dollars ($25). This sum shall not be withdrawn by the student until he closes his connection with the School; and if any portion is required by the School as a refund for damages, the part withdrawn shall be at once replaced by the student, or he shall be dismissed from the school.

Charges for apparatus, chemicals and other supplies from the store room, as well as for repairs of damages to school property, and also fines, shall be deducted from coupons procurable from the Clerk upon payment of five dollars each, but no portion of the twenty-five dollars above mentioned shall be used for the purchase of these coupons.

The permanent deposit of twenty-five dollars, together with any balance equivalent to the unused portion of a coupon, shall be returned to the student when he closes his connection with the school, but not before.

Each student is required to present to the Director his certificate of deposit from the Treasurer, at the commencement of each school year, or at such time thereafter as he may present himself at the School for work. The Director may then issue an annual certificate of membership to the student, subject to the subsequent approval of the Faculty.

No student shall be considered a member of the School, or allowed to join in any of the exercises, or to take any apparatus, chemicals, books, etc., until he shall have presented to the Instructor, Librarian and Dispensing Clerk, his certificate of membership for that school year.

It shall be the duty of the Treasurer to have printed such coupons as are needed. These shall be deposited with the Clerk, the Treasurer taking his receipt therefor. The Clerk shall pay over to the Treasurer all money received from the student in payment for the coupons, taking his receipt therefor. The accounts of the Clerk shall be audited every year; at which time the Clerk shall show to the Auditing Committee, Treasurer's receipts and unused coupons amounting in value to all the coupons deposited with him by the Treasurer, before the Clerk's accounts shall be adjusted.

There are no dormitories connected with the School. Arrangements can be made by those who desire to do so, to obtain board and rooms in private families, and in boarding houses, in Houghton and Hancock, at prices varying from twenty to twenty-five dollars per calendar month. Twenty-two to twenty-three dollars per month is understood to be the standard average price. This is to include the room, heat and lights, as well as board. Board alone can be obtained at from seventeen to twenty dollars per calendar month.

The necessary expenses of the students are estimated by them as follows, for each year:

Board, etc., 10½ months at $20.00 to $25.00	$210 00	to	$262 50
Apparatus, Chemicals, etc.	20 00	to	40 00
Books and Drawing Materials	25 00	to	50 00
Traveling Expenses (Excursions, Field-work, etc.)	10 00	to	50 00
Washing	20 00	to	30 00
Total	$285 00		$432 50

PRIZES AND SCHOLARSHIPS.

THE LONGYEAR PRIZES.

Through the liberality of Hon. J. M. Longyear, of Marquette, the following prizes have been offered, as stated in his letter making the offer, which is here appended:

Marquette, Michigan, Nov. 9, 1887.

CHARLES E. WRIGHT, ESQ., MARQUETTE:

DEAR SIR—I wish to offer three first prizes of seventy-five dollars ($75) each, and three second prizes of fifty dollars ($50) each, to be competed for by the members of the senior class of the Michigan Mining School. The competition to be by means of papers on three subjects, written by members of the class, and submitted to the Board of Control for examination, in such a manner and at such a time as the Board may determine. I desire subjects selected with a view of producing papers which will be of practical use in developing the mineral resources of the State of Michigan. I should like something which would be of service to the average woodsman or explorer, and suggest the subjects of Practical Field Geology, and the use of the Dial and Dip Compass in explorations; leaving the selection of the third subject to the judgment of the Board. If this offer is accepted, and there are two or more papers on each subject submitted, I will pay seventy-five dollars to each of the writers of the three papers which may be awarded the first prizes, and fifty dollars to each of the writers of the three papers which may be awarded the second prizes.

I would suggest, however, that in case only two papers are submitted, that the Board reserve the right of awarding only one prize, in case such action should seem advisable. In case only one paper should be submitted, I should like the Board to exercise its judgment in awarding a prize. It is my desire to publish the papers under the writers' names, in pamphlet form, for distribution among miners, explorers, land owners, and others.

Yours very truly,
. J. M. LONGYEAR.

In conformity with the foregoing letter, the Board of Control have decided upon the following subjects and conditions:

SUBJECTS.

1. Field Geology; its Methods and their Applications.
2. The Dial and the Dip Compass and their Uses.
3. The Diamond Drill and its Uses.

CONDITIONS.

The conditions under which the prizes are awarded are as follows:

The papers are to be presented by September 30th, for each year.

A student may present a paper upon each of the three subjects, which will entitle him to three prizes, if his papers are found worthy.

The dissertations must be prepared in the same manner as the theses, the regulations for which can be procured on application to the Secretary of the School.

The title page is to have upon it an assumed name, and each dissertation is to be accompanied by a sealed envelope bearing the same name. This envelope must contain the writer's true, as well as assumed, name, and his address, and it will not be opened until the awards have been made.

No prizes will be awarded, unless the papers are judged by the committee to whom they are referred, to be of a sufficiently high standing to be entitled to a prize; hence there may be awarded all, part, or none of the prizes, as the case may be.

These prizes can now be competed for by any students of the school, whether special, graduate or regular, without restriction to the graduating class, as was originally specified.

THE CHARLES E. WRIGHT SCHOLARSHIP.

The Charles E. Wright Scholarship has been founded by Mrs. Carrie A. Wright, of Ann Arbor, in accordance with the conditions expressed in the letter given below:

To the Honorable Board of Control of the Michigan Mining School:

GENTLEMEN:—In memory of my husband, the late Charles E. Wright, and as a token of the deep interest he had in the Michigan Mining School, I desire to give to said school the sum of one thousand dollars.

If said gift shall be accepted, it is to be held under the following conditions, to-wit: It is to be invested as a permanent fund, by the Board of Control, to form the nucleus of a scholarship to be known as the Charles E. Wright Scholarship. The income is be given to some indigent student, by vote of the Board of Control, with the advice and consent of the faculty of said school.

The award is to be made during the first term of the year, to some student who has a satisfactory record during the entire preceding year in the Michigan Mining School, and who intends to devote himself to the profession of Mining Engineering or Geological work. The income is to be divided into three equal parts, to be paid during the three terms of the year, and if at any time the conduct or standing of the student receiving the award should become unsatisfactory, the portion then remaining unpaid should be withheld from him, and given to some other student, in accordance with the terms of this gift.

(Signed) CARRIE A. WRIGHT.

THE NORRIE SCHOLARSHIP.

This scholarship has been founded, and will be awarded, in accordance with the conditions and requirements stated below:

Know all men by these presents, That I, A. Lanfear Norrie, of the city of New York, hereby give, grant, assign, and set over unto, the Michigan Mining School, of Houghton, Michigan, and to

Peter White, D. H. Ball and J. M. Longyear, of Marquette, Michigan, as trustees, the sum of five thousand dollars ($5,000), lawful money of the United States.

The conditions of this gift, and upon which this fund is to be taken, are, that the said trustees shall invest the same upon bond and mortgage in the village of Marquette, or in the city of Detroit, in the State of Michigan, or in the city of Milwaukee, in the State of Wisconsin, or in the city of Chicago, in the State of Illinois, upon unencumbered improved real estate.

That one-half of the income of said sum of $5,000 shall be paid yearly by said trustees unto the Board of Control, for the support of some student whose father has worked in, or in some way been connected with, mining operations in the Upper Peninsula of Michigan, who shall be designated by the faculty of said school; and the remainder of said income shall be accumulated and invested as said principal shall be invested, and that this fund with its accumulations shall be the basis of a larger fund, to be obtained from other contributions, amounting to at least one hundred thousand dollars ($100,000), to be used for the erection of a Dormitory Building, for the use of such students as shall be designated by said faculty; which building, when erected, shall be under the exclusive control of the corporation or Board of Control of the said Michigan Mining School.

This gift is to the said trustees and their successors forever, for the benefit of the said Mining School. In case of the death of either of said trustees, the survivors or survivor shall appoint a successor or successors.

When the erection of said building shall be commenced, after the said fund of one hundred thousand dollars is obtained, the sum hereby given, with all its accumulations, shall be paid over to the said Mining School, for the purpose aforesaid.

Witness my hand, the 30th day of January, 1890.

A. LANFEAR NORRIE.

Witness, T. E. O. M. STETSON.

We, Peter White, D. H. Ball and J. M. Longyear, the persons named in the above instrument, accept the trust therein granted, in all respects, and agree to comply with the conditions thereof.

Witness our hands, the 1st day of February, 1890.

PETER WHITE,
D. H. BALL,
J. M. LONGYEAR.

THE LONGYEAR FUND.

This is a fund of $500.00, given for the year 1892-93, by Mr. J. M. Longyear, of the Board of Control, to be the property of the Mining School, to be loaned to students of said school who may be designated by the Treasurer and Director, said students being unable to maintain their connection with the school without such aid. This money is not to be a gift to the student, but he is to pay it back as soon as practicable after graduation. After his graduation, interest will be charged him for the first three years at 5 per cent, and for the following two years at 7 per cent. The money and the interest are to go to the fund, to aid other students in the same way. This method, it is believed, will lead the student to a more manly feeling than a gift outright would produce in him, since it gives him the means of paying for his own education, assists him when he most needs assistance, and enables him to return the money to aid others, at a time when he can best do so.

It is believed that it would be better if all funds given to the School for investment and use, should be accompanied by some proviso that a certain portion, at least, of the income shall be saved or set aside, to increase the principal until it shall attain a limit, either fixed, or left to the proper authorities to determine. Such a method would enable the institution in the future to do much more good, than it would if the income were to be spent entirely each year.

The School is in great need of funds to aid students who would otherwise be unable to attend this institution. Aid of this kind is frequently sought by able and worthy young men, and all is done that can be, with the limited means at the command of the School, to aid them.

The Longyear Fund has been continued for three years, and now amounts to $1,500.00, but no part of it is available in 1893-1895.

DEGREES AND GRADUATE INSTRUCTION.

Students who have graduated in the former two years course of the school with the degree of Bachelor of Science, may obtain the degree of Mining Engineer, by returning to the school and completing the course given at the time of such return; or else they may receive it upon application to the Board of Control and Faculty, and upon presentation of satisfactory evidence of five years' successful practical work, and of a suitable thesis in some line co-ordinate with their course of study in this school.

The thesis must be an original investigation undertaken in Mining, Mechanical or Electrical Engineering, Chemistry, Metallurgy, Petrography, Geology, or in some allied subject that shall belong within the objects of this institution; and it must be approved by the Faculty.

Students who complete the old course of three years, and present a satisfactory thesis, will receive the degree of Mining Engineer, or Engineer of Mines (E. M.). The thesis must conform to the requirements given above and must be completed and approved by the Faculty before that body will recommend that the Degree of Mining Engineer, or Engineer of Mines, be conferred upon the student.

Students who complete the new three years course and graduate, will have conferred upon them the degree of Bachelor of Science.

Students who complete the four years course and present a satisfactory thesis will receive the degree of Mining Engineer.

Students who are graduates of this, or of other institutions of high grade, will be admitted as special students to take any study taught in this school, or to take special graduate instruction.

Those who wish to become candidates for a higher degree will enter under the following conditions:

Students who are graduates of this institution, or of others of similar grade, whose course shall be approved by the Faculty, will be admitted as candidates for the degree of Doctor of Philosophy. In order to attain this degree they must pursue for at least two years an advanced course of study in subjects germane to the undergraduate course in this institution, which course of study is to be approved by the Faculty.

One of the years of study may, in special cases, be spent elsewhere, and the work accepted, on sufficient proof of its thoroughness and high character, as the equivalent of one year's work spent here. But under no condition will the degree be given, unless one year at least is spent as a resident worker at this institution.

Students who are graduates both of this, or of an equivalent professional school, and also of some college or university whose course of study is accepted by the Faculty, may be admitted to the degree of Doctor of Philosophy, after having taken for at least one year an approved course of study at this institution.

The degree of Doctor of Philosophy will be given only in case the student shall have shown marked ability and power for original investigation, shall have passed a satisfactory oral public examination, and presented a thesis, embodying the result of original investigation, that shall be approved by the Faculty.

Students who are graduates of this or of other institutions having a satisfactory equivalent course, and who shall have pursued here, according to the above regulations, a successful course of study for the degree of Doctor of Philosophy, may at the same time receive the degree of Mining Engineer, if said degree has not been conferred at their previous graduation.

GRADUATES, 1888.

NAME.	RESIDENCE AND OCCUPATION.

HARRIS, JOHN LUTHER, S. B......Quincy.

Mining Engineer, Quincy Mine.

LONGYEAR, EDMUND JOSEPH. S.B..Hibbing, Minnesota.

Superintendent of the Longyear and Bennett Explorations.

PARNALL, SAMUEL ALEXANDER, S. B.
Ishpeming.

In charge of Installation, Electric Haulage Plant, Cleveland and Iron Cliffs Mining Company.

PARNALL, WILLIAM EDWARD, S.B..Ishpeming.

Electrical Engineer, Cleveland and Iron Cliffs Mining Company.

REID, WILLIAM JOSEPH, S. B......Romeo.

SEAGER, JAMES BENJAMIN, S. B...Hancock.

Superintendent of the Lake Superior Redstone Company.

UREN, WILLIAM JOHN, S. B......Hancock.

Civil Engineer, Mineral Range and Hancock and Calumet Railroads, and County Surveyor, Houghton County.

11

GRADUATES, 1889.

| NAME. | RESIDENCE AND OCCUPATION. |

CROZE, WALTER WILFRED JOSEPH, S.B.
Houghton.
Mining Engineer.

FARWELL, PAUL, S. B.............Denver, Colo.
Chemist.

*FESING, HERMAN WILLIAM, S.B..Crystal Falls.
Civil and Mining Engineer.

*HAAS, JACOB, S. B...............Marcus, Washington.
Mining Engineer, Skylark Mine.

HOATSON, JOHN, S. B............Butte City, Montana.
Mining Engineer, Butte and
Boston Mining Company.

PRYOR, REGINALD CHAPPLE......Houghton.
Civil and Mining Engineer.

* See Graduates of 1890 for the second degree.

GRADUATES, 1890.

NAME.	RESIDENCE AND OCCUPATION.

DANIELL, JOSHUA, S. B............**Great Falls, Montana.**
Blast Furnace Foreman, Boston
and Montana Consolidated
Copper and Silver Mining Company.

DRAKE, FRANK, S. B.............**Boston.**
Metallurgy and Ore Dressing.
Mass. Institute of Technology.

FESING, HERMAN WILLIAM, S.B., E.M.
Crystal Falls.
Civil and Mining Engineer.

HAAS, JACOB, S. B., E. M.........**Marcus, Washington.**
Mining Engineer Skylark Mines.

HODGSON, WILLIAM ADAMS, S. B...**Houghton.**
Thomson and Hodgson Company,
Stephens, Ark.

SUTTON, LINTON BEACH, S. B......**Gould, Mont.**
Mining Engineer, Tremont Gold
Mining and Milling Company.

WAKEFIELD, ARTHUR ALBERT, S.B.   **Velardena, Durango, Mexico.**
Mining Engineer.

OFFICERS OF THE YOUNG MEN'S CHRISTIAN ASSOCIATION.

President......................WILLIAM WRAITH.
Vice-President.....................BAMLET KENT.
Treasurer..............MILTON WATSON COLEMAN.
Recording Secretary.....ELMER WHIPPLE DURFEE.
Corresponding Secretary........JOHN FORREST ORR.

CLASS OFFICERS.

CLASS OF 1894.

President............ ......FREDERICK PECK BURRALL.
Vice-President........CARLTON FRANKLIN MOORE.
Secretary and Treasurer...JOHN GEORGE KIRCHEN.

CLASS OF 1895.

President..........................LOVE DOCKERY.
Vice-President....... ......ROBERT SELDEN ROSE.
Secretary..............MILTON WATSON COLEMAN.
Business Committee..⎰ WILLIAM WEARNE.
⎱ MILTON WATSON COLEMAN.
⎱ CARL RAYMOND DAVIS.

FRESHMAN CLASS.

President................WILLIARD JOSEPH SMITH.
Vice-President.........WILLIAM IRVING ALDRICH.
Secretary...............ELTON WILLARD WALKER.

OFFICERS OF THE ATHLETIC ASSOCIATION.

President .... CARL RAYMOND DAVIS.
Vice-President .... HENRY HOFFMAN HOLBERT.
Secretary and Treasurer... ELTON WILLARD WALKER.

HOLDERS OF SCHOLARSHIPS.

THE NORRIE SCHOLARSHIP.

1893-1894 .... ROBERT MURRAY, JR.

THE WRIGHT SCHOLARSHIP.

1893-1894 .... JOHN ALEXANDER KNIGHT.

OFFICERS OF THE ALUMNI ASSOCIATION.

President .... WILLIAM JOHN UREN, '88.
Vice-President.... ...... JOHN LUTHER HARRIS, '88.
Secretary and Treasurer,
         WALTER WILFRED JOSEPH CROZE, '89.

COLLECTIONS.

For purposes of illustration and study, a number of collections have been provided for the use of the students.

Crystal Models...............................	2,304
Natural Crystals.............................	1,800
General Mineral Collection...................	27,310
Emerson Collection of Minerals..............	550
Exhibition Collection of Minerals............	1,000
Collection of Thin Sections..................	3,500
General Rock Collections....................	11,575
Stratigraphical and Illustrative Collections..	500
Collection of Economic Geology..............	1,000
Zoölogical Collection........................	1,000
Paleontological Collections..., ...	2,600
	53,139

Besides the above, there are collections of paleontological charts, metallurgical, geological, and petrographical diagrams, geological models, maps, etc.

Collections of slags, metallurgical products, materials for illustration in economic geology, as well as some exhibition collections, have been commenced, and all persons who can are urged to contribute to the school collections of minerals, rocks, veinstones, ores, slags, metallurgical products, samples of building stones, machinery, tools, etc., and models, photographs and prints of the same, etc.

In the case of the mineral products used in arts and manufactures, it is desired to procure specimens showing the various stages in the process of manufacture. It is especially important for the School to receive and preserve sets of cores from drill holes, samples of ores from every mine, with specimens of the associated gangue minerals and rocks, as well as of the walls and associated country rocks.

LIBRARY.

The Library of the School contains at present 10,159 volumes, besides numerous pamphlets; and additions are constantly made to it. It is proposed to have not only a good reference library for student work, but also one that shall be as complete as possible upon the subjects taught in the school. It is especially desired to have a full set of all reports and works relating to the mining and other mineral industries of the districts bordering on Lake Superior. The library is now valuable for reference, both for practical and scientific men; and it is freely open to all who desire to consult it.

In addition to the school library, the scientific library of the Director is deposited in the school building, and can be used by students and others. This library is especially devoted to Crystallography, Mineralogy, Petrography and General and Economic Geology.

Contributions of pamphlets, papers, maps and books, on subjects germane to those taught in this institution, are solicited for the Mining School Library. Plans, drawings and engravings, relating to mines, mining machinery, and metallurgy, are desired.

It is hoped to make the Library very full in files of the different journals published throughout the country, especially in the mining regions; contributions of present and past numbers of such journals are solicited for the library, to aid in making it a complete depository of literature relating to the progress and industries of the country, as well as of the Lake Superior region.

READING ROOM.

Connected with the Library is a Reading Room, which is well supplied with scientific periodicals, technical journals, and the transactions and proceedings of scientific societies. The importance of periodical literature as a means of bringing before the student the results of scientific investigations is fully realized, and the collection is made as complete as possible for this reason. Below is given a full list of the journals on file, numbering in all two hundred and nine.

Contributions of journals for the Reading Room are earnestly solicited from publishers throughout the State and country.

*Alpena Pioneer, Alpena.

American Chemical Journal, Baltimore.

American Engineer and Railroad Journal, New York.

†American Geologist, Minneapolis.

American Journal of Mathematics, Baltimore.

†American Journal of Science, New Haven.

American Machinist, New York.

†American Naturalist, Philadelphia.

*American School Commissioner, Saginaw.

Annalen des K. K. Naturhistorischen Hofmuseums, Wien.

†Annalen der Physik und Chemie, Leipzig.

†Annalen der Physik und Chemie, Beiblätter, Leipzig.

†Annalen der Physik und Chemie (Electrotechnische Bibliographie), Leipzig.

Annalen de Chimie et de Physique, Paris.

†Annales de la Société Géologique de Belgique, Liège.

*Gift of Publishers.
†A complete set of this Publication is in the Library.

†Annales des Mines, Paris.
Annales des Ponts et Chaussées, Paris.
Annales des Sciences Géologiques, Paris.
Annals of the New York Academy of Science, New York.
Annals of Mathematics, University of Virginia.
*Ann Arbor Argus, Ann Arbor.
*Arbetaren, Cadillac.
*Belleville Enterprise, Belleville.
*Bellevue Gazette, Bellevue.
Berg-und Hüttenmaennisches Jahrbuch, Vienna.
†Berg-und Hüttenmaennisches Zeitung, Leipzig.
†Berichte der Deutschen Chemischen Gesellschaft, Berlin.
*Boyne Falls News, Boyne Falls.
*Brickmaker, Chicago.
*Brick Roadways, Chicago.
*Bronson Journal, Bronson.
*Brown City Banner, Brown City.
Builder, London.
†Bulletin of the Essex Institute.
†Bulletin of the Geological Society of America, Rochester, N. Y.
Bulletin of the New York Mathematical Society, New York.
†Bulletin of the Philosophical Society, Washington.
Bulletin de la Société Chemique de Paris.
Bulletin de la Société Francaise de Minéralogie, Paris.
Bulletin de la Société Géologique de France, Paris.
*Calumet Conglomerate, Calumet.
*Calumet and Red Jacket News, Calumet.
*Canadian Mining Review.
*Capac Journal, Capac.
*Cass City Enterprise, Cass City.
†Cassier's Magazine, New York.
*Century Magazine, New York.
Chemical News and Journal of Physical Science, London.
Chemiker Zeitung, Cöthen, Germany.

†Chemische Industrie, Berlin.

Civilingenieur, Leipzig.

Colliery Engineer, Scranton, Pennsylvania.

†Comptes Rendus, Hebdomadaires des Séances de l'Académie des Sciences, Paris.

Copper Country Evening News, Calumet.

*Current, Norway.

*Daily Mining Journal, Marquette.

*Detroit Free Press, Detroit.

*Detroit Journal, Detroit.

*Diamond Drill, Crystal Falls.

†Dingler's Polytechnisches Journal, Stuttgart.

Electrical Engineer, New York.

†Electrical World, New York.

Electrician, London.

Electrotechnische Zeitschrift, Berlin.

Engineer, London.

†Engineering, London.

†Engineering Magazine, New York.

Engineering Mechanics, New York.

†Engineering and Mining Journal, New York.

Engineering News and American Railway Journal, New York.

*Ely Times, Ely, Minnesota.

*Escanaba Iron Port, Escanaba.

*Evening Journal, Flint.

*Evening News, Detroit.

*Florence Mining News, Florence, Wisconsin.

*Forum, New York.

Génie Civil, Paris.

Geographical Journal, London.

†Geological Magazine, London.

*Gogebic Iron Spirit, Bessemer.

*Good Health, Battle Creek.

*Grand Traverse Herald, Grand Traverse.

*Harper's Magazine, New York.

*Harvard University Bulletin, Cambridge, Mass.
*Imlay City Record, Imlay City.
*Industries and Iron.
*Ingham County Republican, Leslie.
 Iron Age, New York.
*Iron Ore, Ishpeming.
*Ironwood News Record, Ironwood.
*Ironwood Times, Ironwood.
†Jahres-Bericht der chemischen Technologie, Leipzig.
†Jahresbericht über die Fortschritte der Chemie, Braunschweig, Germany.
 Jahrbuch für das Berg-und Hüttenwesen, Freiberg.
†Jahrbuch der kaiserlich-königlichen geologischen Reichsanstalt, Vienna.
†Jahrbuch der königlich preussischen geologischen Landesanstalt und Bergakademie, Berlin.
†Journal of Analytical and Applied Chemistry, Easton, Pa.
†Journal of the Association of Engineering Societies, Chicago.
†Journal of the Chemical Society, London.
 Journal of Education, Boston.
 Journal of the Franklin Institute, Philadelphia.
†Journal of Geology, Chicago.
 Journal of the Iron and Steel Institute, London.
 Journal für praktische Chemistry, Leipzig.
 Journal of the Society of Arts, London.
 Journal of the Society of Chemical Industry, London.
 Justus Liebig's Annalen der Chemie, Leipzig.
 Kritischer Vierteljahresbericht über die Berg-& Hüttenmännische und verwandte Literatur, Freiberg.
 L'Anse Sentinel, L'Anse.
 Lapeer Clarion, Lapeer.
 Library Journal, New York.
†Library Notes, Boston, Mass.
*Literary News, New York.

†London, Edinburgh and Dublin Philosophical **Magazine**
and Journal of Science, London.

Lumière Electrique, Paris.

*Lyons Herald, Lyons.

*Manistique Semi-Weekly Pioneer, Manistique.

Manufacturer and Builder, New York.

*Maple Rapids Dispatch, Maple Rapids.

Mathematical Magazine, Washington.

Mathematical Visitor, Washington.

†Memoirs of the American Academy of Arts and Sciences,
Boston.

†Memoirs of the Boston Society of Natural History,
Boston.

*Menominee Democrat, Menominee.

*Michigan Copper Journal, Hancock.

Michigan School Moderator, Lansing.

*Michigan State Democrat, Cadillac.

*Milan Leader, Milan.

Mineralogical Magazine and Journal of the Mineralogical
Society, London.

Mineralogische und petrographische Mittheilungen,
Vienna.

Mining and Scientific Press, San Francisco.

*Mining and Scientific Review, Denver.

*Native Copper Times, Lake Linden.

†Nature, London.

†Neues Jahrbuch für Mineralogie, Geologie und Palæontologie, Stuttgart.

*Newaygo County Democrat, Newaygo.

*North American Review, New York.

*Northwest Mining Review, Spokane, Washington.

*Oakland County Post, Pontiac.

†Oesterreichische Zeitschrift für Berg-und-Hüttenwesen,
Vienna.

*Official Gazette of the U.S. Patent Office, Washington.

*Ontonagon Herald, Ontonagon.

*Ontonagon Miner, Ontonagon.

*Owosso Press, Owosso.

*Peninsular Record, Ishpeming.

†Petermann's Mittheilungen aus Justus Perthes' Geographisches Anstalt, Gotha.

†Philosophical Transactions of the Royal Society of London, London.

*Physician and Surgeon, Ann Arbor.

*Pick and Axe, Bessemer.

*Pontiac Gazette, Pontiac.

†Popular Science Monthly, New York.

*Portage Lake Mining Gazette, Houghton.

*Port Huron Weekly Times, Port Huron.

Power, New York.

†Proceedings of the Academy of Natural Sciences, Philadelphia.

†Proceedings of the American Academy of Arts and Sciences, Boston.

†Proceedings of the American Association for the Advancement of Science, Salem, Massachusetts.

†Proceedings of the Boston Society of Natural History, Boston.

†Proceedings of the Institution of Civil Engineers, London.

†Proceedings of the Institution of Mechanical Engineers, London.

Proceedings of the Geologists' Association, London.

Proceedings of the London Mathematical Society.

Proceedings of the Royal Geographical Society and Monthly Record of Geography, London.

†Proceedings of the Royal Society of London.

†Publishers' Weekly, New York.

†Quarterly Journal of the Geological Society, London.

Quarterly Journal of Pure and Applied Mathematics, London.

*Quincy Herald, Quincy.

†Report of the British Association for the Advancement of Science, London.

*Review of Reviews, New York.

Revue Universelle des Mines, de la Métallurgie, etc., Paris.

*Sault Ste. Marie News, Sault Ste. Marie.

*Scribner's Magazine, New York.

*St. Andrew's Cross, New York.

*St. Clair Republican, St. Clair.

*St. Johns News, St. Johns.

†School of Mines Quarterly, New York.

†Science, New York.

Scientific American, New York.

†Scientific American Supplement, New York.

†Sitzungsberichte der kaiserlichen Akademie der Wissenschaften, Vienna.

†Sitzungsberichte der königlich-preussischen Akademie der Wissenschaften zu Berlin.

*Soo Democrat, Sault Ste. Marie.

Stahl und Eisen, Düsseldorf.

*State Republican, Lansing.

*†Stone, Chicago.

†Techniker, New York.

†Transactions of the Academy of Science, St. Louis.

Transactions of the American Institute of Electrical Engineers, New York.

*†Transactions of the American Institute of Mining Engineers, New York.

†Transactions of the American Society of Civil Engineers, New York.

†Transactions of the American Society of Mechanical Engineers, New York.

†Transactions of the Connecticut Academy of Arts and Sciences, New Haven.

†Transactions of the Federated Institute of Mining Engineers, Newcastle-on-Tyne.

Transactions of the Manchester Geological Society, Manchester.

†Transactions of the Royal Society of Canada, Montreal.

*Vassar Times, Vassar.

†Verhandlungen der k. k. Geologischen Reichsanstalt, Vienna.

*Workman, Grand Rapids.

*Ypsilantian, Ypsilanti.

†Zeitschrift für analytische Chemie, Wiesbaden.

†Zeitschrift für anorganische Chemie, Leipzig.

†Zeitschrift für das Berg.-Hütten-und Salinenwesen, Berlin.

†Zeitschrift der deutschen geologischen Gesellschaft, Berlin.

†Zeitschrift für Krystallographie und Mineralogie, Leipzig.

†Zeitschrift für physikalische Chemie, Leipzig.

†Zeitschrift für praktische Geologie, Berlin.

TEXT BOOKS.
1893–1894.

FIRST YEAR.

College Algebra.—1891.   G. A. Wentworth.
 Ginn and Company, Boston.
Plane and Spherical Trigonometry.—1893. H. N. Wheeler.
 Ginn and Company, Boston.
Logarithmic Tables.—1892.   G. W. Jones.
 G. W. Jones, Ithaca, N. Y.
Analytic Geometry.—1887. Last Edition. G. A. Wentworth.
 Ginn and Company, Boston.
Elementary Treatise on Physics.—1893.   14th Edition.
  Ganot, translated by Edmund Atkinson.
 Wm. Wood and Company, New York.
Practical, Plane and Solid Geometry.   Last Edition.
        Henry Angel.
 William Collins and Sons, Glasgow.
Manuscript Notes on General Chemistry.—1893.
       George A. Koenig.
Manuscript Notes on Experimental Chemistry.   1893.
       George A. Koenig.
Descriptive Mineralogy.—1892.   Sixth Edition.
   James D. Dana and Edward S. Dana.
 John Wiley and Sons, New York.
Theory and Practice of Surveying.—1892. Tenth Edition.
       J. B. Johnson.
 John Wiley and Sons, New York.
Field Engineering.—1893.   Sixteenth Edition.
       William H. Searle.
 John Wiley and Sons, New York.

SECOND YEAR.

Elements of the Calculus.—1891. James M. Taylor.
Ginn and Company, Boston.

Mechanics of Engineering. Irving P. Church.
(Sixth Edition of Statics and Dynamics.)
Wiley and Sons, New York.

Qualitative Analysis.—1893. Arthur H. Elliot.
Arthur H. Elliot, New York.

South Kensington Notes on Building Construction. 1889.
Vol. 3. Rivington, London.

Elements of Mechanism.—1888. Second Edition.
T. M. Goodeve.
Longmans, Green and Company, London.

Steel and Iron.—1892. Fifth Edition.
Wm. Henry Greenwood.
Cassell and Company, London.

The Determination of Rock-Forming Minerals.—1891.
Second Edition.
Dr. Eugene Hussak, Translated by Erastus G. Smith.
John Wiley and Sons, New York.

Text Book of Geology.—1893. Third Edition.
Archibald Geikie.
Macmillan and Company, New York.

Manuscript Notes in Lithology. 1892—1893.
M. E. Wadsworth.

THIRD YEAR.

Quantitative Analysis.   Dr. C. Remigius Fresenius.
        John Wiley and Sons.

Modern American Methods of Copper Smelting.—1892.
                Edward D. Peters.
    Scientific Publishing Company, New York.

Metallurgy of Lead.—1892.   H. O. Hofman.
    Scientific Publishing Company, New York.

Manual of Assaying.—1892.   Walter Lee Brown.
    E. H. Sargent and Company, Chicago.

Manual of Assaying.—1889.
        Bodeman and Kerl, translated by W. Goodyear.
        John Wiley and Sons, New York.

Hydraulics.—1890.   Mansfield Merriman.
    John Wiley and Sons, New York.

Trusses and Arches. Part I.—1892.   Third Edition.
                Charles E. Greene.
    John Wiley and Sons, New York.

Electrical Engineering.—1891.   Slingo and Brooker.
    Longmans, Green and Company, London.

The Steam Engine.—1893. Fifth Edition. G.C.V.Holmes.
    Longmans, Green and Company, London.

Mechanics of Materials.—1893.   Second Edition.
                Mansfield Merriman.
    John Wiley and Sons, New York.

Elements of Geology.—1892.   Third Edition.
                Joseph LeConte.
    D. Appleton and Company, New York.

The Ore Deposits of the United States.—1893.
                James F. Kemp.
    Scientific Publishing Company, New York.

SAMPLE EXAMINATION QUESTIONS FOR ADMISSION TO THE MINING SCHOOL.

ARITHMETIC.

1. (1). Draw a line a decimeter long and divide it into centimeters.

    (2). What is the fundamental unit of length in the metric system.

2. (1). Describe the units of capacity and of weight in the metric system.

    (2). Draw a cubic centimeter; a cubic decimeter.

3. (1). Multiply $\frac{3}{4}$ by $\frac{1}{8}$ and explain the process.

    (2). Divide $\frac{7}{8}$ by $\frac{5}{16}$ and explain the process.

4. Change the common fractions to decimals in question 3, and perform the operations there required.

5. (1). B lost 5 per cent by selling a hektoliter of turpentine, which cost $15. For what did he sell it a liter?

    (2). If A buys copper for 30 cents per kilogram, and on selling it makes 40 per cent on the cost, after deducting 10 per cent from his asking price, what was the asking price?

6. (1). Having sold a consignment of goods on 3 per cent commission, the agent was instructed to invest the proceeds, after deducting his commission of 3 per cent. His whole commission was $265. What amount did he invest?

    (2). If copper stock pays 8 per cent on the par value, at what price must it be purchased to pay 10 per cent on the cost?

7. (1). What is the interest of $16,941.20 for 1 yr. 7 mo. and 28 days, at $4\frac{3}{4}$ per cent?

(2). What sum of money, invested at $6\frac{1}{2}$ per cent, will produce $279,815.00 in 1 yr. and 6 mo. ?

8.   (1). A ship's chronometer, set at Greenwich, points to 5 h. 40 min. 20 sec. P. M. when the sun is on the meridian; what is the ship's longitude?

    (2). A steamer arrived at Halifax, 63° 36' west at 4 h. 30 min. P. M.; the fact is telegraphed to New York without loss of time. The longitude of New York being 74° 1' west, what is the time of the receipt of the telegram?

9.   Extract the square root of 58.140625, of .0000316969.

10.   Extract the cube root of 10460353203, of .000148877.

ALGEBRA.

1.   (a) Multiply $x^6 + x^5y - x^3y^3 + xy^5 + y^6$ by $x^2 - xy + y^2$.

    (b) Divide $y^8 - 2b^4y^4 + b^8$ by $y^3 + by^2 + b^2y + b^3$.

2.   Resolve into its factors $16x^4 - 81y^8$, also $a^6 - 1$, also $x^4 + x^2y^2 + y^4$, also $y^3 + y^2 - y + 1$.

3.   (a) Simplify $\dfrac{x}{(x-y)(x-z)} + \dfrac{y}{(y-z)(y-x)} + \dfrac{z}{(z-x)(z-y)}$

    (b) Simplify $\left(\dfrac{x^4 - y^4}{x^2 - y^2} \div \dfrac{x+y}{x^2 - xy} \right) \div \left(\dfrac{x^2 + y^2}{x - y} \div \dfrac{x+y}{xy - y^4} \right)$

4.   (a) Multiply $x^2 + xy^{-1} + y^{-2} + x^{-1}y^{-3}$ by $x^{-2} - y^2$.

    (b) Simplify $\left[(a^m)^{m - \frac{1}{m}} \right]^{\frac{1}{m+1}}$ also $\left(\dfrac{x^{p+q}}{x^p} \right)^p \left(\dfrac{x^q}{x^q - p} \right)^{-(p-q)}$

5.   (a) Extract the square root of $30 + 12\sqrt{6}$.

    (b) Solve $\dfrac{y-5}{2} - \dfrac{y-3}{4} + \dfrac{y+3}{5} - \dfrac{y+5}{6} = 0$, and explain the transformations necessary for the solution.

6. (a) Simplify $\sqrt{\dfrac{a^4c}{b^3}} - \sqrt{\dfrac{a^3c^3}{bd^2}} - \sqrt{\dfrac{a^2cd^3}{bm^2}}$

(b) Simplify $\left(\dfrac{10\sqrt[3]{a^2}}{\sqrt[4]{5b^{11}}}\right)\left(\dfrac{5a\sqrt[3]{a^2}}{4b \cdot \sqrt[5]{a^2}}\right)$

7. (a) Solve $x^2 + px + q = 0$, and give the conditions under which the roots are real and *unequal*, real and *equal*, and imaginary; also when are they equal *numerically* with opposite signs.

(b) What is the sum of the two roots of the preceding equation? What is their product?

8. (a) Solve $\sqrt{x-3} + \sqrt{3x+4} \cdot \sqrt{x+2} = 0$.

(b) Find the values of x and y in the independent, simultaneous equations $x + y = 27$ and $x^3 + y^3 = 5103$.

9. Find the 6th and the 15th terms of $(x-y)^{23}$, reducing the numerical results to their prime factors and not performing the multiplications.

10. (a) Prove that, if the corresponding items of two proportions be multiplied together or divided by each other, the result, in either case, is a proportion.

(b) If $a:b=x:y=z:q$, Prove that $a:b=\dfrac{x+z}{y+q}$.

––––––––––

PLANE GEOMETRY.

Demonstrate the following propositions:

1. The sum of the angles of any plane triangle is equal to two right angles.

2. Show that each angle of an equiangular pentagon is $\frac{6}{5}$ of a right angle.
3. In the same or in equal circles, angles at the center have the same ratio as their intercepted arcs.   (Two cases.)
4. An inscribed angle is measured by one-half the intercepted arc.   (Three cases.)
5. Two triangles are similar when an angle of the one is equal to an angle of the other, and the sides including these angles are proportional.
6. When a line is divided in extreme and mean ratio, the greater segment is one side of a regular decagon inscribed in a circle whose radius is the given line.
7. Similar polygons are to each other as the squares described on their homologous sides.
8. The square described upon the hypothenuse of a right triangle is equivalent to the sum of the squares described upon the other two sides.
9. (Problem).   Given the perimeters of a regular inscribed and similar circumscribed polygon, to compute the perimeters of regular inscribed and circumscribed polygons of double the number of sides.
10. (Problem).   To compute the ratio of the circumference of a circle to its diameter.

SOLID AND SPHERICAL GEOMETRY.

Demonstrate the following propositions:
1. If a straight line is perpendicular to each of two straight lines at their intersection, it is perpendicular to their plane.
2. If two triedral angles have the three face angles of the one equal, respectively, to the three face angles of the other, the corresponding diedral angles are equal.

3. Two triangular pyramids having equivalent bases and equal altitudes are equivalent.

4. The frustum of a triangular pyramid is equivalent to the sum of three pyramids whose common altitude is the altitude of the frustum, and whose bases are the lower base, the upper base and a mean proportional between the bases of the frustum.

5. In two polar triangles, each angle of one is measured by the supplement of the side lying opposite to it in the other.

6. The sum of the angles of a spherical triangle is greater than two and less than six right angles.

7. The area of a spherical triangle, expressed in spherical degrees, is numerically equal to the spherical excess of the triangle.

8. The area of a zone is equal to the product of its altitude by the circumference of a great circle.

9. (Problem). To find the volume of a spherical segment.

10. (Problem). To find the volume of that part of a sphere lying outside of a chord revolved parallel to its diameter and at a constant distance from it.

ELEMENTARY PHYSICS.

1. (1). Upon what property do most of the character-istic properties of matter depend.

(2). Name three general and five characteristic properties of matter.

2. (1). Name and define the three states of matter.

(2). Give Newton's laws of motion.

3. (1). Define work and energy; give the formula for

the calculation of kinetic energy from weight and velocity.

(2). Give the laws of freely falling bodies.

4. (1). How prove that the atmosphere has weight?

(2). What is the object of experiments in the study of physics?

5. (1). Diagram, and explain the operation of the hydrostatic press.

(2). Define specific gravity and describe the experiments necessary to determine the specific gravity of an irregular solid. If the specific gravity of copper is 8.9 what is the volume in cubic centimeters, of a mass of this metal which weighs 3.2 kilograms?

6. (1). What is the mechanical equivalent of heat? To what is the heat of a body due? Do the atoms or the molecules of a body set either themselves or one another in motion?

(2). Give your idea of force. What is sound? What are the properties of a musical note? Diagram and explain the phonograph and the telephone.

7. (1). Explain the ways in which heat may be transmitted. Give some of its principal sources and effects. Change —40° F., to C. Upon what does the boiling point depend?

(2). Define light. What constitutes the difference between light and heat? Between the different colors? What is the velocity of light? Of sound in the air, at the temperature 0° C?

8. (1). Give the laws of magnets. Give the laws of currents of electricity. Explain Ampère's theory of the magnet. How may magnets be made?

(2). Describe the experiments and the results obtained by the use of a galvanometer, a primary coil, a secondary coil, a battery and a magnet. Tabulate the results.

9. (1) Give Ohm's law. Define ohm, volt, ampère. Draw diagrams showing how to connect cells in series and in multiple arc or abreast. If a Bunsen cell has an electromotive force of 1.8 volts and internal resistance of .9 ohm, show how to connect ten such cells to get the greatest current, the external resistance being 100 ohms.

(2). Give some of the principal uses of electric currents.

10. (1). What constitutes the difference between the operation of a dynamo and that of an electro-motor?

(2) In charging a storage battery, what is stored up in it? What is meant by "the conservation of energy"?

ASTRONOMY.

1. What is the general structure of the Solar System, and what is the physical constitution of the sun and its surroundings?

2. What are the physical constitution and special characteristics of the inner group of planets, including the moon?

3. What are the physical constitution and characteristics of the outer group of planets?

4. What are the aspects, forms and physical constitution of the comets, meteors and shooting stars?

5. What are nebulæ; new, variable and double stars, and upon what evidences are the views concerning them based?

6. How are stars located in the heavens? What are the declination, right ascension, hour angle, latitude, longitude; and what are the six parts of the Polar triangle?

7. Describe the four kinds of time and give the maximum variations between them. How is the longitude of a place determined?
8. What is the general structure of the universe?
9. State clearly the Nebular Hypothesis, and give the evidence upon which it is based?
10. Give the general phenomena of the tides, their causes and laws.

BOOK-KEEPING.

1. Explain the use of day-book, journal and ledger, and state the rules for entering transactions in them.
2. What is a trial balance, and what is the process of making one?
3. Is a trial balance an absolute check? State reasons for your answer.
4. State the rules for crediting and debiting bills payable and bills receivable.

In addition to questions of the above character, a record of supposed transactions is given to the candidate to enter in the proper manner in the different books, and he is required to make his own rulings.

BUILDINGS.

SCIENCE HALL, or the main building now occupied by the Mining School, was completed by the State in 1889, at a cost of $75,000. The building is constructed of Portage Entry sandstone, with a tile roof (see Frontispiece).

The larger part of the site and grounds was donated to the School by the Honorable Jay A. Hubbell, to whom the establishment of the School is chiefly due. The building has a large and independent supply of spring water, sufficient for all its present needs.

The main building is 109 feet by 53 feet, with a wing 37 feet by 25 feet. The interior portion of the building has been arranged so as to save the greatest amount of space possible for the laboratories and working rooms, consistent with safety to the structure and proper light. The halls have been reduced to a minimum. The plans of the four floors are appended: The basement floor is used for a Boiler Room, Weighing Room, Metal and Wood-Working Shops and Assaying Laboratory. The first floor contains the Director's Room, Reading Room, Library, and Laboratories of General and Economic Geology, Petrography and Mineralogy. On the second floor are situated the Mathematical and other Recitation Rooms, together with the Laboratories for Physics, Drawing, Surveying and Mining Engineering. The third floor is devoted to the Chemical Laboratories, Chemical Lecture Room, Chemical Supply Room, Balance Room, etc.

ENGINEERING HALL will be ready for occupancy in August, 1894. This building was provided for by the Legislature of 1893, and it will contain the following rooms:

BASEMENT.

Machine shop...97x24 feet.
Engine Room..34x17 feet.
Electrical Laboratory............................34x27 feet.
Lavatory ....28x10 feet.

FIRST FLOOR.

Pattern Shop...97x25 feet.
Lecture Room.......................................28x26 feet.
Professor's Office..................................18x9 feet.
Tool Room...11x8 feet.
Lavatory ....12x12 feet.
Paint Shop..... ....16x13 feet.
Model Room...18x9 feet.
Storage Battery Room......:.....................15x11 feet.

SECOND FLOOR.

Drawing Room......................................97x25 feet.
Blue Print Room...................................12x8 feet.
Lecture Room.......................................35x28 feet.
Assistant's Office..................................12x11 feet.
Office of Mining Department....................16x15 feet.
Map Room...15x12 feet.
Lavatory ....11x11 feet.

An annex contains a Fuel Room 16x34 feet, and a Boiler Room 29x34 feet. In the latter will be located three boilers, two of which are to be used for heating purposes. To enable the student to become practically familiar with water tube boilers, a 58 HP Stirling water tube boiler will be used to supply steam to shop and laboratory engine.

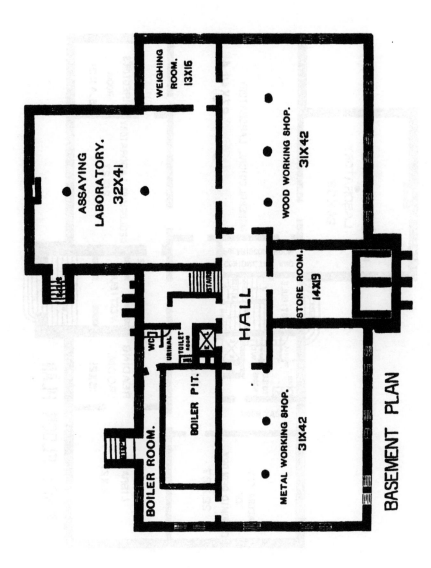

WEIGHING ROOM. 13X16

ASSAYING LABORATORY. 32X41

WOOD WORKING SHOP. 31X42

STORE ROOM. 14X19

HALL

WC
URINAL
TOILET ROOM

BOILER ROOM.

BOILER PIT.

METAL WORKING SHOP. 31X42

BASEMENT PLAN

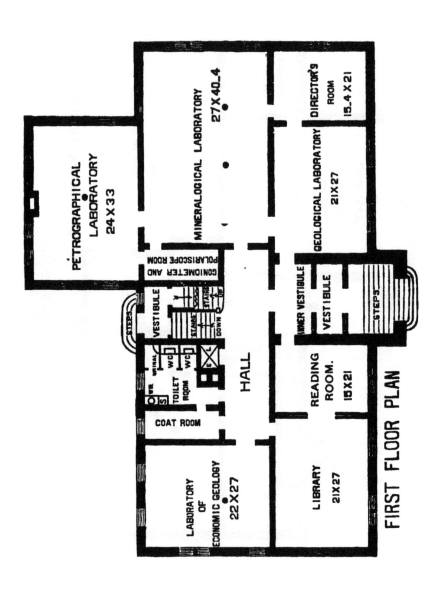

FIRST FLOOR PLAN

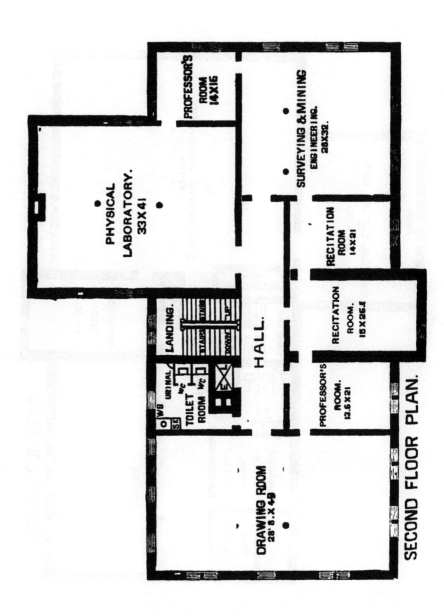

SECOND FLOOR PLAN.

13

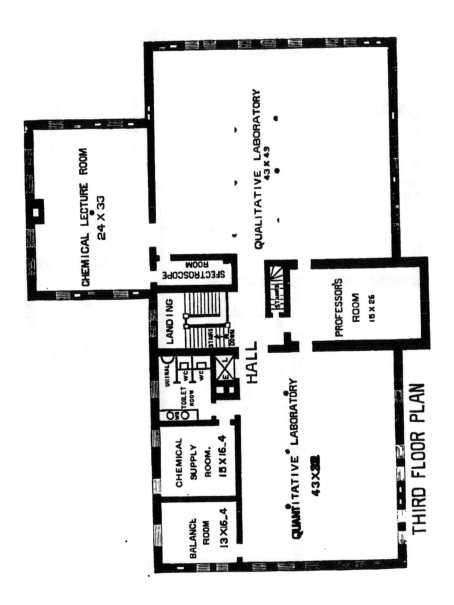

CHEMICAL LECTURE ROOM 24 X 33

QUALITATIVE LABORATORY 43 X 49

SPECTROSCOPE ROOM

LANDING

STAIRS

DOWN

STAIRS

HALL

PROFESSORS ROOM 15 X 26

URINAL

WC
WC

TOILET ROOM

CHEMICAL SUPPLY ROOM. 15 X 16_4

BALANCE ROOM 13 X 16_4

QUANTITATIVE LABORATORY 43 X 32

THIRD FLOOR PLAN

LOCATION.

The School is located in the village of Houghton (Portage Township), the county seat of Houghton county. The twin villages of Houghton and Hancock lie in the sheltered valley of Portage Lake, an arm of Lake Superior. The climate is bracing and healthful. Although Houghton is in a high latitude, yet one is far less inconvenienced by the cold here than he is much further south along the Atlantic coast, or in the immediate vicinity of the Great Lakes. This is due to the dryness of the Houghton climate, a climate which is free from any malaria, hay fever, etc. In general, students coming from localities further south have found health and strength improved by the change. The town has an abundant supply of pure spring water. Houghton is easily reached by rail from Detroit, Chicago, Milwaukee, St. Paul, Superior and Duluth; and by steamer from all the important ports on the chain of the Great Lakes. Within the State, half-fare rates are given to the students of the Mining School by the Duluth, South Shore & Atlantic Railway and its associated railroads.

In answer to various questions asked, some of the routes are here designated: From Detroit one travels by the Michigan Central Railway to Mackinaw City, via Bay City. At Mackinaw City the cars of the Duluth, South Shore & Atlantic Railway are taken direct to Houghton. Time from Detroit about twenty-four hours. From Sault Ste. Marie, the Duluth, South Shore & Atlantic Railway carries its passengers direct to Houghton, time about thirteen hours. The same railway is taken from Duluth and Superior to reach the Mining School. Passengers from

Chicago and Milwaukee take either the Chicago, Milwaukee & St. Paul Railway, via Champion; or the Chicago & Northwestern Railway, via Negaunee and Ishpeming; at which places, on both routes, the passengers transfer to the Duluth, South Shore & Atlantic Railway for Houghton. Time from Chicago to Houghton, about seventeen hours.

Students desiring to reach Houghton by boat, can take steamers of the Lake Michigan and Lake Superior Transportation Company, at Chicago or Milwaukee, taking about three days from Chicago. From Buffalo, Cleveland and Detroit, one can take the steamers of The Western Transit Company, and The Erie and Western Transportation Company. Time from Buffalo about five days, Cleveland four days, and Detroit three days.

Any of these lines can be taken from Duluth.

Special information, descriptive pamphlets, time tables and rates can be obtained from the General Passenger Agents of the various companies by writing to their respective offices, as follows:

Duluth, South Shore & Atlantic Railway, Marquette, Michigan.

Michigan Central Railway, Monadnock Block, Chicago, Ill.

Chicago, Milwaukee & St. Paul Railway, Chicago, Ill.

Chicago & Northwestern Railway, Chicago, Ill.

The Lake Michigan & Lake Superior Transportation Co., Rush and North Water Streets, Chicago, Ill.

The Western Transit Co., No. 47 Main Street, Buffalo, N. Y.

The Erie & Western Transportation Co., Atlantic Dock, Buffalo, N. Y.

Houghton County is the third wealthiest county in Michigan, being surpassed only by Wayne (Detroit) and Kent (Grand Rapids) Counties. The population of the county, with its various townships and villages, is here given according to the latest returns.

The official census returns for Houghton County, as approved by the Board of Supervisors, are as follows:

		1890.	1894.
Adams Township			1,675
Calumet	"	12,529	16,709
Chassell	"	680	993
Duncan	"	680	984
Franklin	"	2,687	2,685
Hancock	"	2,737	4,345
Laird		159	231
Osceola	"	3,630	4,712
Portage	"	3,531	8,417
Quincy	"	1,490	1,490
Schoolcraft	"	3,325	3,908
Torch Lake	"	2,904	3,055
	Total	35,089	45,398
			35,089
	Increase in 3 years		10,309

The population of the villages is as follows:

	1894.
Atlantic Mine	1,675
Calumet	2,192
Chassell	554
Crystal Lake	55
Gregoryville	320
Hancock	1,662
Houghton	2,178
Kenton	113
Kitchie	75
Lake Linden	2,448
Mills' Station	794
Osceola	1,514
Oskar	171
Perkinsville	520
Quincy Mill	151
Quincy Mine	1,490
Red Jacket	3,242
Sidnaw	344
Tamarack and North Tamarack	1,402
Withey	184

The accompanying map (facing page 200) will give a fair idea to the prospective student of the location of the Mining School and the adjacent mines.

While the School itself is situated in the Portage Lake copper district, the access to the Keweenawan copper district on the north is easy; and there lie within comparatively short distances the Ontonagon copper district, and the iron mining regions of Marquette, Menominee and Gogebic.

In the immediate vicinity of the Mining School are located the Quincy, Atlantic, Franklin and Huron copper mines; while within a distance of fifteen miles are situated the Calumet and Hecla, Tamarack, Osceola and other copper mines, with their machine shops, smelting works, rolling and stamp mills, etc. In the iron mining region lie numerous great mines, prominent among which are the Cleveland, Jackson, Lake Superior, Lake Angeline, Champion, Republic, Chapin, Vulcan, Cyclops, Colby and Norrie.

In addition to copper and iron, among the mineral products of the state are numbered gold, silver, gypsum, building stones, slate, coal, salt, etc.

Some idea of the vastness of the mining operations in the Lake Superior district in Michigan alone, can be gathered from the following statistics: Its copper mines have produced, up to 1890, one billion seven hundred and sixty-four million five hundred and twenty-six thousand five hundred and thirty-nine pounds of copper. One mine alone has paid over forty millions of dollars in dividends.

In the iron mining districts about Lake Superior, in Michigan, there were produced in 1892 seven million five hundred and forty-three thousand five hundred and forty-four tons of iron ore, or nearly one-half of all the iron ore produced in the United States.

The Michigan iron mines have produced since their discovery over sixty-eight million tons of iron ore.

Michigan is credited with producing, in 1892, gold and silver amounting to one hundred and forty-five thousand dollars.

The State of Michigan is also the chief producer of gypsum in the United States; and in its salt production is second to New York only. It produced in 1892 one hundred and thirty-nine thousand five hundred and fifty-seven tons of gypsum; and during the same year, three million eight hundred and twelve thousand and fifty-four barrels of salt. Its coal product was in 1893, one hundred and four thousand six hundred and twenty tons.

The Michigan Mining School has been located in the Upper Peninsula of Michigan for the same reason that a medical school should be in the vicinity of large hospitals, in order that it should be associated with the objects about which it treats.

From this location the student of the Michigan Mining School is placed in a mining atmosphere, in which all his surroundings and associations are in conformity with his present and future work. He is thus enabled to see in actual operation some of the most successful and extensive mining operations now conducted anywhere.

Some little idea of the work of a few of the numerous mines of the Lake Superior district can be gathered from the following statements. That for the Calumet and Hecla is taken from a report published in 1893, while for the others, the information is taken from personal letters sent to the Director of the Mining School, by the agents or other officers of the mines:

CALUMET AND HECLA MINING COMPANY.

"Beginning on the shore of Lake Superior, we have there the Lake Superior Water Works, Pump House, and Boiler House, containing one Worthington high pressure compound condensing pump with cylinders of 19¼ inches and 33¼ by 24 inches, and plungers 9 by 24 inches. Two spare Worthington pumps with cylinders 10 by 18 inches, and two boilers 64 inches diameter by 17 feet long, of 300 horse power, and one locomotive boiler 54 inches diameter, of 100 horse power. When fully equipped, the capacity of these works will be 2,000,000 gallons a day. The water is taken from a pipe 18 inches in diameter, and extending 1200 feet into Lake Superior. It is pumped through a 12-inch wrought-iron pipe line 4½ miles in length, to an altitude of more than 700 feet, to the mine, where it is distributed over the whole location.   *   *   *   *

"The real estate of the Company consists of 2599 $\frac{13}{100}$ acres of mineral land in Houghton County, and 20,352 $\frac{44}{100}$ acres of timber lands in Keweenaw, Houghton, and Ontonagon Counties. At the Stamp Mill there are 988 $\frac{19}{100}$ acres.

"There are 698 houses belonging to the Company, of which 570 are on the mine location, 106 at the lake, and 22 at the Smelting Works. On leased lots, our men own 782 houses at the mine, and 159 at the lake.

"There are 20 churches on the property of the Company, the greater number of which have been materially assisted by the Company at some time in their history.

"There are, on land of the Company, six schools at the mine and lake, built partly at the cost of the Company and partly by the school district. The Company also owns a hotel.

"There are at the mine, for cutting sets of timber used underground, a timber building, a large machine shop 225 by 250 feet, with a full complement of tools. We have also at the mine three blacksmith's shops, two warehouses,   *   *   *   two carpenter shops, and a paint shop.   *   *   *   *

"The Calumet Engine House is a building of brick and stone, 146 by 62 feet. It contains: the compound engine 'Superior', with cylinders of 40 inches, and 70 by 72 inch stroke, of 4700 horse power; the Corliss engine 'Rockland', used as a spare, of 600 horse power; the Leavitt engine 'Baraga', 40 by 60 inches, also a spare, of 2000 horse power; one pair 32 by 48 inch Rand Compressors, with a capacity of 26 air drills; and one pair 36 by 60 inch Rand Compressors, with a capacity of 41 air drills. There are four drums 20 feet 6½ inches in diameter by 8 feet 4 inches face, to hoist from a depth of 4000 feet from shafts Nos. 2, 4 and 5 Calumet, and No. 3 Hecla. By winding over and not increasing the load we may reach 6000 feet.

"The Boiler House is of stone 77 by 60 feet. It contains five boilers, two of 84 inches in diameter by 35 feet long, made by Kendall and Roberts: three of 90 inches diameter by 34 feet 6⅛ inches long, made by the Dickson Manufacturing Company, the Southwark Foundry, and the I. P. Morris Company; total horse power, 2780. The stack is 5 feet 6 inches bore, and 150 feet high.

"The Hecla Engine House is a brick building 80 by 47 feet, with an ell 44 by 17 feet 5 inches, and contains the compound engine 'Frontenac', 27⅜ and 48 by 72 inches, of 2000 horse power; the Corliss engine 'La Salle', 30 by 72 inches, used as a spare, of 900 horse power; and the Corliss engine 'Perrot', 30 by 48 inches, also a spare engine, of 600 horse power; in addition, the two pair of compressors, water plunger type, 42 by 60 inches, with a capacity of 144 air drills, 72 drills for each set; one pair of Rand Compressors, 28 by 48 inches, of a capacity of 31 air drills.

"The Boiler House is of brick, 80 by 58 feet, and contains three boilers made by Kendall and Roberts, 84 inches by 32 feet 10⅜ inches, and two boilers made by the Dickson Manufacturing Co., 90 inches by 34 feet 4 inches, with a total of 1690 horse power. The brick stack is 4 feet 6 inches in diameter and 120 feet high.

"On the Hecla, another Hoisting Engine and Boiler House contains the triple expansion hoisting engines 'Gratiot', 'Houghton', and 'Seneca', of 2000 horse power each, having cylinders 18 and 27⅜ inches, and 48 by 90 inches, fitted with conical hoisting drums to reach a depth of 5500 feet. The engine house is of stone, 112 by 78 feet. The boiler house of the same material, is 76 by 68 feet. There are five boilers, of 505 horse power each, 90 inches in diameter by 34 feet 6 inches long, built by the Dickson Manufacturing Company, of Scranton, Penn., and the I. P. Morris Co., of Philadelphia, Penn. The brick stack is 9 feet 4 inches in diameter, and 200 feet high. * *

"The Engine House for Hecla shafts Nos. 7 and 8 contains the triple-expansion engines 'Hancock' and 'Pewabic', each of 2000 horse power; each operating by spur gearing its own drum, which is 25 feet in diameter by 8 feet 2⅜ inches face, having a rope capacity of 5500 feet, of 1⅜ inch diameter. The cylinders are 20⅜ and 31⅜ inches and 50 by 48 inches. The maximum speed is 92 revolutions per minute, which is 3⅜ revolutions to one of the drums. The house is 122 feet long, and 50 feet wide; it is built of stone.

"The Boiler House will eventually hold ten boilers; it now contains three. They are 90 inches in diameter by 34 feet 6 inches long, and 505 horse power each. The house is 150 feet long and 65 feet wide. The stack is 12 feet 6 inches inside diameter, and 250 feet high.

"Shafts Nos. 9 and 10 Hecla, are operated from a Hoisting Engine House built of stone, 75 by 46 feet. It contains two compound hoisting-engines, the 'Detroit' and 'Onota', of 1000 horse power combined, having cylinders 18 and 32 by 48 inches stroke, built by George H. Corliss These engines drive by spur gearing two hoisting drums, formerly located at the Superior Engine House, each 20 feet in diameter by 8 feet 4 inches face, and will wind 4000 feet of 1¼ inch rope. The drums make one revolution for every three revolutions of the engine.

"In the Hoisting Engine House operating shafts Nos. 11 and 12 Hecla, there is a pair of Woodruff and Beach engines built in 1869, of 20 inches diameter by 48 inches stroke, with two drums of 8 feet diameter and 6 feet face.   As one of the man-shaft engines, we use a vertical engine 26 inches in diameter by 36 inch stroke, built in 1867.   *   *   *   *

"We have eight new shaft-rock houses, extending from Calumet No. 5 to Hecla No. 12, a total length on the surface of 9000 feet; the copper shute having in all a length of something over two miles underground, say 10,630 feet. There are eight shaft-rock houses at Hecla and at Calumet shafts, each containing a Westinghouse Driving engine of 60 horse power, and two 'Blake' crushers; each rock house with a bin capacity of about 1500 tons.   Both at No. 5 Calumet and at No 4 Hecla, there is a fan for underground ventilation; these are 30 feet in diameter, with a capacity of about 100,000 cubic feet per minute.   There are man-hoist buildings at five of the Hecla and three of the Calumet shafts; each contains a pair of engines and a drum, used only for taking men up and down.   Twenty-eight men can ride on one of the cars; they are especially constructed for that use. Three of the houses contain each a pair of 20 by 30 inch engines, with drums to wind 4000 feet of 1¼ inch rope; the other five, one pair of engines 20 by 36 inches, with drums to wind 6000 feet of 1¼ inch rope.

"The Electric Light and Power House is built of stone, 74 by 74 feet; it contains a Porter-Allen engine, 18 inches in diameter by 36 inch stroke, of 400 horse power. A Westinghouse compound engine 23 and 40 by 20 inches, and 740 horse power, will be installed in this house.

"There are two electric light dynamos for 1000 sixteen candle power lights each; three Brush arc-light dynamos for 74 lights; five Brush generators 120 horse power each, with electric lines leading to the principal buildings, and to the three underground electric pumps at the Hecla end.   Each pump has three double acting plungers 5¼ inches in diameter by 18 inch stroke, to run 50 revolutions per minute. At the Calumet end in No. 4 shaft, there are to be five electric pumps, each with three double acting plungers 5¼ inches in diameter by 18 ihch stroke, to run 50 revolutions per minute. These pumps are placed 800 feet apart, having a vertical lift of 600 feet; the pump column is 8 inches in diameter. We have at Calumet Nos. 4 and 5 shafts two spare steam Worthington pumps, with cylinders 10 and 18 inches by 18 inches, of a capacity of over 500,000 gallons per 24 hours.

"The six-compartment Red Jacket Vertical Shaft has reached a depth of 3050 feet. It will intersect the Calumet lode at a depth of 3300 feet, and will reach the bottom of our territory at a depth of 5000 feet.

"It is equipped with a sinking-engine house of stone, 69 by 36 feet, containing a pair of horizontal tandem Corliss engines, with cylinders 16 and 32 inches in diameter by 48-inch stroke, with tail-rope house, and has the Whiting drum system.

"The main hoisting-engine house, built of stone, 220 by 70 feet, contains two pair of triple expansion engines, of 3000 horse power per pair, having cylinders 20¼, 31¼, and 50 inches in diameter by 72 inch stroke, to run 60 revolutions per minute, and fitted with the Whiting drum system, arranged to hoist ten tons per load, at a speed of 60 feet per second. The tail house for the fleet gear is 412 by 32 feet, and is placed on the north end of the engine house. The sheave house is placed at the south end; it is 43 by 32 feet. These engines are calculated to hoist from a maximum vertical depth of 5000 feet.

"The Boiler House is built of stone, 150 by 68 feet, and will contain ten boilers, each 90 inches in diameter by 34 feet 6 inches long, and adapted to a working pressure of 185 pounds, at which they will each furnish steam for 1000 horse power. There are at present six boilers in the house. The stack is of brick, 12¼ feet inside diameter, and 250 feet high. * * * * *

"The water used by our condensing engine is supplied from the Calumet Pond Water Works, where we have a main pond of a capacity of 60,000,000 gallons, at five feet depth, and an auxiliary pond of a capacity of 30,000,000 gallons, at 2¼ feet; both ponds are, when filled, of a capacity of say 100,000,000 gallons.

"The Water Works Building consists of an engine and boiler house of brick, 100 by 45 feet; it contains a Leavitt pumping engine, of a capacity of 5,000,000 gallons per day, steam cylinders 11¼ inches, and plungers 17 by 24 inches. In addition, there are two Worthington pumping-engines, of a capacity of 14,000,000 gallons per day; one pump with steam cylinders 14 and 24 by 36 inches, and 20 by 36 inch plungers, of a capacity of 4,000,000 gallons: and two others with steam cylinders 21 and 42 by 36 inches, and 29 by 36 inch plungers, of a capacity of 10,000,000 gallons. The boiler house contains three boilers, Kendall & Roberts make, of 603 horse power, two of 54 inches by 26 feet 10 inches; and one of 84 inches by 35 feet. A pipe-line 16 and 24 inches in diameter, runs to the Superior Engine House, and from there north and south along the line of the lode.

"The length of all the shafts sunk below the average level of the stopes is over two miles, and the length of all the drifts run below the average level of the stopes is $13\frac{6}{10}$ miles.   *   *   *   *

"At Torch Lake are located the Stamp Mills, the Calumet Mill containing eleven Leavitt heads with steam cylinders of 14 and 21½ by 24 inches stroke, with a complete equipment of washers, Huntington and Haberle grinding-mills, and slime tables.

"As spare power, we have a Westinghouse driving-engine of 200 horse power. At the Hecla Stamp Mill we have made an addition of four heads, which gives us there now eleven Leavitt heads, with steam cylinders 14 and 21½ by 24 inch stroke, and an equipment similar to that of the Calumet mill. We are also preparing to place solid anvils under all the stamps.

"The Stamp Mills and Water Works Boiler House contains eleven boilers, four of 80 inches diameter by 32 feet long, and seven of 90 inches diameter by 34 feet 6 inches long, made by Kendall & Roberts, the Dickson Manufacturing Company, the Southwark Foundry, and the I. P. Morris Co., aggregating 4730 horse power, commercial standard.

"The three boilers now running the pumping house, of 1515 horse power, will be removed to the main stamp-mill boiler house, which will be enlarged to accommodate twenty-two boilers.   *   *   *   *

"Torch Lake Water Works, which supply the Stamp Mills, consist of the triple-expansion pumping engine 'Michigan', of a capacity of 60,000,000 gallons daily, with the following engines as spare pumps: The compound pumping engine 'Erie', with a capacity of 10,000,000 gallons daily; the compound pumping engine 'Ontario', with a capacity of 20,000,000 gallons daily; the geared pumping engine 'Huron', with a capacity of 20,000,000 gallons daily.

"The compound driving engine 'Wabeek', 22½ and 38 by 60 inch stroke, of 728 horse power, operates the washing machinery, the stamp steam-valve gear, and the sand wheels, by means of wire rope transmission. The stamped sand is distributed by four sand wheels: the Calumet 40-foot sand wheel, with a capacity of 18,000,000 gallons, and of 1,600 tons of sand: the Calumet 50-foot sand wheel, with a capacity of 30,000,000 gallons and of 3,000 tons of sand. As a spare engine for the Calumet wheel, we have a high-pressure engine 24 by 48 inch stroke, of 250 horse power. The Hecla 40- and 50-foot sand wheels have the same capacity as the Calumet sand wheels of the same dimensions. The spare engine for the Hecla wheels is a duplicate of the Calumet. * *

"The horse power of the boilers at the mine, commercial standard, is 13,765; the horse power of the boilers at the Lake Superior Water Works is 400; the horse power of the boilers at the Stamp Mills is 6,235; the horse power of the boilers now building is 2,022; and the total horse power, commercial standard, is 22,422. The aggregate horse power which can be developed by the engines belonging to the Company is 40,000.

"The Smelting Works at Torch Lake occupy nearly thirty acres; they are connected with the Stamp Mills by a short line of Railway, over which our mineral trains handle the daily product, which is there stored in the mineral houses.

"The plant consists of four stone furnace buildings 80 by 130 feet each, with four furnaces, boshes, cranes, and all the ordinary equipment; one blister furnace building, of stone, 50 by 70 feet, with two furnaces; one cupola building containing two furnaces, with the necessary engines, blowers, and boilers; machinists' and blacksmiths' outfits, electric light plant, etc. Mineral building No. 1 has a bin capacity of 2,000 tons, and mineral building No 2 and its addition has a capacity of about 9,000 tons; and there are two wharves of a length of over 1,000 feet, with the necessary hoisting apparatus for coal and limestone."

ALLOUEZ MINING COMPANY.

"The mine is opened by three shafts. No. 1 is about 1300 feet; No. 2, 1700 feet; and No. 3, 1200 feet, in depth. The bed or lode mined is the 'Allouez Conglomerate'. It has a thickness of from 18 to 28 feet. The copper rock usually makes in several layers from foot to hanging wall, with layers of barren rock between them. Two 'Knowles' pumps, operated with compressed air, and stationed at the 13th and 18th levels, No. 2 shaft, pump the water to the 7th level, where it flows through the level to No. 1 shaft, into a sump at the 8th level, and is from there forced to surface by a Gordon & Maxwell steam pump. The Mine equipment consists of two hoisting engines, capable of hoisting from 700 to 800 tons of rock per day.   Two 'Rand Air Compressors', with a capacity for thirty-four No. 3 Rand Drilling Machines.

"The rockhouse is furnished with driving engine, two 18x24 inch, and three 9x15 inch Blake type rock crushers; also drop hammer for breaking the larger size of rock.   Six fire box crown flue boilers, of about 100 hundred horse power each, furnish steam for all the mine plant.   Machine, Blacksmith, and Carpenter shops are provided with the necessary tools to do all ordinary repair work.

"The Stamp Mill is situated about 2¼ miles to the north of the mine.   It contains three 15-inch cylinder 'Balls' steam stamps, capable of crushing 500 tons rock per day.   The crushed material is dressed by 'Collom' Jiggers.   Steam is supplied by four 100 horse power boilers of the fire box crown flue type.   Two loco-motives are on hand, one of which ordinarily is used to transport the rock from the mine to the mill, over a three-foot gauge track, laid with 50 pound steel rails.   The mine, when in full operation, employes about 300 men."

Pittsburgh and Lake Angeline Mining Company.

"The Lake Angeline mine workings are a little over 5,000 feet in length.   The depth is 500 feet.   There are four shafts: A, 450 feet deep; C, 500 feet deep: D, 350 feet deep; and E, 210 feet deep.

"There are eight boilers and mine engines; two Cornish plunger pumps, and four steam pumps.   There are six hundred and fifty men employed, and the capacity of the mine is a little over five hundred thousand tons per year."

The Volunteer Iron Company.

"The ore in the mine extends for about 2,500 feet in length, and the mine is about 600 feet deep.   There are four shafts, A, B, C, and D.   The capacity of the mine is about 300,000 tons per year.   Three boilers; five engines."

Winthrop Iron Company.

"There are two shafts at the 'Mitchell', 'A' and 'D'.   'A' shaft is 555 feet deep, and the workings are about 350 feet long. 'D' shaft is 300 feet deep.

"A continuation of the 'Mitchell' to the west is the 'Win-throp', which is owned in fee by the Winthrop Iron Co.   We had two shafts on the north side of the dioryte; No. 1, which is now owned by the Lake Superior Iron Co., being 420 feet deep, and No. 4, which is 560 feet deep.   We have one other shaft on

Winthrop land, on the south side of the dioryte No. 2 shaft, which is 480 feet deep, and the workings are about 500 feet in length.

"We have in use ten boilers, two hoisting engines, one 18x30 Rand Compressor, and one 15x25x10x24 Duplex Worthington Pump, with which we handle all of our water from the mine."

SAGINAW IRON MINING CO.

"Depth of mine, 318 feet; length of mine, 120 feet; number of shafts, one; number of boilers, 72"x18', three; number of hoisting engines, one; number of air compressors, one; number of pumps, 14x12x10, three; number of Rand drills (No. 3) five; number of men employed, fifty-three."

ARAGON MINING COMPANY.

"This mine has produced, since mining was commenced in the latter part of 1889, until June, 1894, 530,314 tons of ore. We are mining three grades, viz: *Castile*, guaranteed to run 65½ per cent Iron and not above .010 P; *Aragon*, Fe 64, P .030; and *Granada*, Fe 64, P .125. The ore now produced is mostly non-bessemer.

"The ore deposit is very much folded and broken.

"The size of the productive area has increased from level to level, being 37,400 square feet at a depth of 500 feet. On the 7th level—650 feet deep—which is still undeveloped, we have now 34,400 square feet of ore.

"The ore is hoisted through one incline shaft, equipped with skips, and one vertical cage shaft. The hoisting engines are of the portable type, having five and six foot drums respectively.

"Compressed air is furnished to 30 Rand drills, by one 18x30 inch duplex Rand compressor, and one 14x16 compound Norwalk compressor. A 15x25x10x24 compound condensing Worthington pump lifts 500 gallons water per minute, from the 500 feet level to the surface. The bottom level is unwatered by two No. 10 Cameron pumps, throwing water from the 650 to the 500 feet level. The surface water, from the swamps overlaying the mine, is taken care of by low-service Cameron pumps.

"There are eight horizontal return tubular boilers, and one vertical tubular, of a combined capacity of 960 horse power.

"300 men are employed, producing 15,000 tons per month."

MASTODON IRON COMPANY.

"Depth of main shaft, 400 feet (2 cages); length of mine, 250 feet. Two boilers, 6x18 feet. Open pit has skip road and

Rochester double hoisting engine, 10x14. Hoisting engine of Marinette manufacture, 18x24-inch cylinder. Two six-foot drums. Two No. 10 Cameron pumps, only one being in use at a time. Number of men employed, about fifty. One Merritt Duplex Air Compressor, 12x24. Three Rand drills; two No. 2, one No. 3. One Diamond drill outfit. Width of ore deposit, 75 feet."

ASHLAND IRON MINING CO.

"The Ashland has six working shafts, of depth and length as follows, respectively:

Shaft No.	3	4	5	6	7	8
Length	926	944	862	935	999	940
Depth	843	859	778	818	909	819

"Boilers: Seven return tubular, 600 horse power capacity; two Stirling water tube, 300 horse power capacity.

"Hoisting Engines: One Webster, Camp & Lane hoisting plant, duplex, cylinders 26½x48, Brown cut off, five drums 10 feet diameter. One Marinette hoist, 18x24, two drums 6 feet diameter. Several small hoists.

"One Ingersoll-Sergeant Duplex Air Compressor, 18x30; engines are Cooper Corliss, with No. 7 Worthington Independent Condenser; rated capacity, 25 drills. Two Ingersoll-Sergeant Right Line Air Compressors, 20x24, Myers' cut off; capacity of each, 12 drills. One Cornish Pumping Plant (E. P. Allis), Corliss Engine, 22x48 inch, two plungers, 14 inches; 9 ft. stroke.

"Electric Light Plant: Two U. S. dynamos; capacity, 300 incandescent lamps 16 c. p., 110 volts. Two Westinghouse Junior engines 9x8, 35 horse power each.

"One Worthington Duplex Compound Plunger Pump, 15x25x-9½x24 inches; capacity, 700 gallons under pressure of 300 lbs. per square inch. Eighteen Cameron pumps, sizes No. 7 to No. 10.

"Machine Shop has: One Blaisdell Engine Lathe, 26" swing, 14' long; one Bickford Drill Press, 38" table; one Gray Planer 30x30", 8' table; one Curtis & Curtis pipe machine, 2½ to 6 inches.

"One Bucyrus Steam Shovel.

"Mine working capacity, 400 men. Have mined and shipped since 1883, 1,700,000 tons of ore, of average analysis, 63.5 Fe, .044 Phos.

BROTHERTON IRON MINING COMPANY.

"There are three working shafts at a depth of 400 feet; two hoisting engines; four boilers; and six No. 10 Cameron pumps.

Two hundred and ten men employed. The annual output is about 120,000 tons of ore."

NEWPORT MINING COMPANY.

"Location comprises N. ¼ of Section 24, Twp. 47 N., Range 47 W.

"On N. W. ¼ are four producing shafts as follows: No. 4, on North Vein; depth 359 feet. 'A', on South Vein footwall; depth 473 feet. 'B', on South Vein footwall; depth 517 feet. 'C', on South Vein footwall; depth 489 feet.

"The pumps in these shafts are as follows: 'A', No. 5 Cameron pump. 'B', No. 5 Cameron pump. 'C', No. 5 Cameron pump. 'C', No. 9 Cameron pump.

"The No. 5 pumps all pump up to the No. 9, which throws all the water from these shafts to surface. These shafts are all connected, and are about 400 feet apart. C. is also connected with them by a cross cut.

"The power house on this location has one tubular boiler, 72"x16'; one tubular boiler 60"x16'; and one Sterling Boiler. One Bullock Corliss Engine of 150 horse power; and one Webster, Camp & Lane Engine of about 100 horse power; and four 6-foot drums for hoisting.

"On the N.E. ¼ is one producing shaft, 504 feet deep, called "K", not connected with any other shaft, and is on footwall. Pumps in this shaft: One No. 10 Cameron special; one No. 10 Cameron.

"The power house on this location has one tubular boiler 72"x16'; two tubular boilers 48"x16'; and one Marinette engine, double, of about 50 horse power, with a 6-foot drum. Boilers are all return tubular, except Sterling.

"Shafts are all measured for depth on inclination of footwall, which makes an angle of about 65° with the horizontal.

"Number of men employed varies. When all the shafts are running, about 250."

GREAT WESTERN MINE.

"Our workings are 760 feet long, reached by two shafts, 535 and 550 feet deep respectively, at the present time.

"The mine is equipped with: One 100 horse power Hoisting Engine, with three 7-foot drums; one 80 horse power Hoisting Engine, with two 4-foot drums; one 8x10 Duplex Hoisting Engine, with two 4-foot drums; one 12x36 in. Duplex Air Compressor; twenty-one No. 2 Rand Rock Drills; three No. 3 Rand Rock

14

Drills: two 100 horse power Steel Boilers: two 80 horse power Steel Boilers: one 60 horse power Steel Boiler. Machine Shop fully equipped.

"We employ about two hundred men."

ROPES GOLD & SILVER COMPANY.

"Our shaft No. 1 (or Curry) is 800 feet deep: No. 2 (or Ely) shaft is 100 feet in depth. Are using three boilers, three engines, eight pumps, forty stamps, twelve vanners: and employing forty men."

EMPLOYMENT.

The question is often asked, if the Mining School can promise employment to students, on graduation. The only answer is, that neither the Mining School nor any other self-respecting institution can make any such promises. The question of employment depends on too many factors to be promised three or four years in advance. It depends on the demand and the supply, which are liable to vary from year to year; and it also very largely depends on a student's personal "equation". Prior to 1893, the demand for suitable men was greater than the supply; and. such will be the case again, on the revival of business. People are prone to forget the general laws of Political Economy, as shown in periods of prosperity, and in business depressions and panics. The student is apt to think that because at any one time there is a depression in the profession he is proposing to follow, that therefore there is no future in it; overlooking the fact that such depressions are shown by history to be incident to every occupation, and that prosperity follows stagnation as surely as the latter will succeed a period of marked business activity. The cycle may be formulated as, "a state of quiescence,—next improvement,— growing confidence,— prosperity, — excitement, — over-trading,— convulsion,— pressure,—stagnation,—distress,—ending again in quiescence", when the cycle is again repeated. Thus it follows, that a pupil entering upon his preparation for his future occupation in a time of prosperity is less sure of employment on graduation than one who starts upon this preparation during a time of distress.

The following table taken from Thom's Edition of

Juglar's "Brief History of Panics", will indicate that these periods of depression are not confined to any one country or business, but are widespread, if not universal—and are dependent upon some general periodic law:

DATE OF COMMERCIAL CRISES.

FRANCE.	ENGLAND.	UNITED STATES.
1804	1803	. . . .
1810	1810	. . . .
1813–14	1815	1814
1818	1818	1818
1825	1825	1826
1830	1830	1829 31
1836–39	1836 39	1837–39
1847	1847	1848
1857	1857	1857
1864	1864–66	1864
. . . .	1873	1873
1882	1882	1884
1893	1890–91	1893

The periodic time is variable, but latterly it appears to be from eight to ten years in length, roughly divided as follows: "Prosperity, for five to seven years; panic, a few months to a few years; and liquidation about a few years". The past three panics have been followed by strikes in 1877, 1885-86 and 1894, that greatly retarded the advancing tide of prosperity. The signs of the times, are that already the current has changed, and that in from one to three years business activity will be the rule, and our mineral industries will prove no exception. The natural law is to prepare in dull times to take advantage of the active years, and this applies to mining as well as to all other occupations.

The success of a graduate depends very much upon himself, and it will be evident from the positions now occupied by the class that graduated during the panic of 1893, that those who went out and searched for employment found it.

A thorough, hard working student, with the ability to command the respect of men and to manage them, and to work harmoniously with his fellow officers, will hardly ever fail of obtaining the choicest positions that are open to him; especially after having had the practical work and experience about the mines that the graduates of this school have.

Education and training do not give qualities to any man; they simply sharpen and develop those natural abilities that he possesses; hence, if he is not by nature fitted for a certain position, he ought not, and will not be likely, to obtain it. On the other hand, whatever may be a man's natural abilities, he will not be likely to obtain a position of any high grade unless he has been educated for it, either in school or outside—the outside education being by far the most expensive kind of education that can be obtained.

Slothful, lazy, careless, and inefficient students will not, naturally, obtain places as readily as the hard-working ones, other things being equal. They certainly will not be recommended as different from what they are by the Director of the Mining School; since a man who cannot be trusted to attend faithfully to his work when engaged in obtaining his professional training is not one whom it is safe to trust with important business and mining interests.

Students should remember that their conduct, from the day they enter the Mining School until they leave it, has an all important bearing upon their future position and standing.

The Director of the Mining School makes one invariable rule, *i. e.*, that all persons desiring students or graduates of this School shall be informed of the defects, as well as of the virtues, of the candidates, so far as he knows them; believing that such a course is the only one that is just either to the employer, to the student, or to the school. When information is fully given concerning the position and desired qualities of the person to fill it, pains are taken to select the student who is believed to be most suitable for the position.

In order to secure the best future for themselves, students are urged to neglect no opportunities, even beyond those afforded by the School, to inform themselves in the practical work of mining.

The graduates are also urged to turn their attention to a field in which success is almost sure, to men of ability and energy; to enter the mines or works as miners, foremen, or in some other subordinate capacity, and thoroughly master every detail, from the lowest to the highest work, since only men who have had this experience are apt to obtain the highest positions.

It is men who have had a thorough education, both in the theoretical and practical mining, and who have worked in every grade of work, that are even now sought to take charge of our mines and their allied industries. The future is for the man who is modest and willing to commence at the bottom of his profession, and who is conscious of the truth, that on graduation he is only just prepared to begin his work.

The graduates of the school are urged to keep the Director constantly informed concerning their positions, salaries, etc., and also what their desires are, in order that they may be assisted to advance, if opportunity offers.

Officers of mines, and others, desiring surveyors, engineers, draughtsmen, foremen, chemists, assayers, etc., are requested to make their wants fully known to the Director of the Mining School, who will then recommend suitable candidates to them, if he knows of any.

The inquiry is frequently made by persons intending to become students, if they can attend to their school work and earn enough to pay their way at the same time. Such a course is not practicable, as the regular school work, if it is done as it should be, requires the entire available time of any student, however strong and able he may be. As a special student, taking only a few studies, one might be able to procure sufficient work to pay one's way. The better way for the needy student is either to attend to his school and to his labor in alternate years, or else to borrow the means to continue his education, repaying through his increased earning power after graduation.

The salaries obtained upon graduation have been from $500.00 to $1,800.00, averaging about $900.00 per year. The lower salaries were obtained by students who had less practical experience with men and with the world in general; these were obliged to spend some time in acquiring a special kind of knowledge that the Mining School cannot give.

So far as known, the salaries have increased, after a varied time from $900.00 to even $2,000.00 or more per year, averaging about $1,200. All this, however, is dependent upon the demand and supply, the state of the mining industries at any time, as well as upon other factors too numerous to be mentioned.

The Mining School has several positions that are expected to be open every year, paying various sums up to $500.00, that are available for students of a suitable grade to give a certain amount of instruction, and to pursue their studies in certain lines. For graduates and others who have a taste for such work, it opens an excellent opportunity for study and self discipline preparatory to their future occupation.

CALENDAR.

1894-1897.

SUMMER TERM commences Monday morning, April 23, and ends Friday evening, August 17, 1894.

Field Work in Surveying commences Monday morning, June 4, and ends Wednesday evening, August 15, 1894.

Shop Practice begins Monday morning, June 11, and ends Wednesday evening, August 15, 1894.

Practical Work in Assaying begins Monday morning, May 28, and ends Friday evening, June 8, 1894.

Practical Work in Ore Dressing begins Monday morning, June 11, and ends Friday evening, July 6, 1894.

Field Geology begins Monday morning, July 9, and ends Wednesday evening, August 15, 1894.

Commencement Exercises, Thursday and Friday, August 16 and 17, 1894.

Thursday—Field day, all classes, 9 A.M. and 2 P.M.

Reception for the Graduating Class, by the Board of Control and Faculty, 9 P.M.

Friday—Annual Meeting of the Board of Control, 10 A.M.

Graduation Exercises, 2 P.M.

Meeting of the Alumni Association, 4 P.M.

Alumni Dinner, 8:30 P.M.

Recess of Four Weeks.

———

FALL TERM commences Friday morning, September 14, 1894.

Examinations for admission and advanced standing commence Friday at 9 A.M., and continue through Friday and Saturday.

Examinations for making up conditions commence on Friday at 9 A.M., and will continue through Friday and Saturday.

Regular work for all classes commences Monday, September 17, 1894, at 9 A.M.

Thanksgiving Recess, November, Wednesday noon until Monday morning.

Fall Term ends Friday evening, December 21, 1894.

Recess of Two Weeks.

WINTER TERM commences Monday morning, January 7, and ends Friday evening, April 12, 1895.

Recess of Nine Days.

SUMMER TERM commences Monday morning, April 22, 1895, and ends Friday evening, August 16, 1895.

Field Work in Surveying commences Monday morning, June 23, and ends Wednesday evening, August 14, 1895.

Shop Practice begins Monday morning, June 10, and ends Wednesday evening, August 14, 1895.

Practical Work in Assaying begins Monday morning, May 27, and ends Friday evening, June 7, 1895.

Practical Work in Ore Dressing commences Monday morning, June 10, and ends Friday evening, July 5, 1895.

Field Geology begins Monday morning, July 8, and ends Wednesday evening, August 14, 1895.

Commencement Exercises, Thursday and Friday, August 15 and 16, 1895.

Thursday—Field day, all classes, 9 A.M. and 2 P.M.

            Reception for the Graduating Class, by the Board of Control and Faculty, 9 P.M.

Friday—Annual Meeting of the Board of Control, 10 A.M.

            Graduation Exercises, 2 P.M.

            Meeting of the Alumni Association, 4 P.M.

            Alumni Dinner, 8:30 P.M.

            Recess of Four Weeks.

FALL TERM commences Friday morning, September 13, 1895.

Examinations for admission and advanced standing commence Friday morning, at 9 A.M., and continue through Friday and Saturday.

Examinations for making up conditions commence on Friday, at 9 A.M., and will be continued through Friday and Saturday.

Regular work for all classes commences Monday, September 16, 1895, at 9 A.M.

Thanksgiving recess, November, Wednesday noon until Monday morning.

Fall Term ends Friday evening, December 20, 1895.

            Recess of Two Weeks.

WINTER TERM commences Monday morning, January 6, and ends Friday evening, April 10, 1896.

Recess of Nine Days.

SUMMER TERM commences Monday morning, April 20, 1896, and ends Friday evening, August 14, 1896.

Field Work in Surveying commences Monday morning, June 1, and ends Wednesday evening, August 12, 1896.

Shop Practice begins Monday morning, June 8, and ends Wednesday evening, August 12, 1896.

Practical Work in Assaying begins Monday morning, June 1, and ends Friday evening, June 12, 1896.

Practical work in Ore Dressing commences Monday morning, June 8, and ends Friday evening, July 3, 1896.

Field Geology begins Monday morning, July 6, and ends Wednesday evening, August 12, 1896.

Commencement Exercises, Thursday and Friday, August 13 and 14, 1896.

Thursday—Field Day—All classes, 9 A.M. and 2 P.M.

Reception for the Graduating Class by the Board of Control and the Faculty.

Friday—Annual Meeting of the Board of Control, 10 A.M.

Graduation Exercises, 2 P.M.

Meeting of the Alumni Association, 4 P.M.

Alumni Dinner, 8:30 P.M.

FALL TERM commences Friday morning, September 11, 1896.

Examinations for admission and advanced standing commence Friday morning, at 9 A M., and continue through Friday and Saturday.

Examinations for making up conditions commence on Friday at 9 A.M., and continue through Friday and Saturday.

Regular work for all classes commences Monday, September 14, 1896, at 9 A.M.

Thanksgiving Recess, November, Wednesday noon until Monday morning.

Fall Term ends Friday evening, December 18, 1896.

Recess of Two Weeks.

WINTER TERM commences Monday morning, January 4, 1897, and ends Friday evening, April 9, 1897.
Recess of Nine Days.

SUMMER TERM commences Monday morning, April 19, and ends Friday evening, August 13, 1897.
Recess of Four Weeks.

FALL TERM commences Friday morning, September 10, 1897, and ends Friday evening, December 17, 1897.

CALENDAR, 1894.

	S	M	T	W	T	F	S
JAN.	..	1	2	3	4	5	6
	7	8	9	10	11	12	13
	14	15	16	17	18	19	20
	21	22	23	24	25	26	27
	28	29	30	31			
FEB.					1	2	3
	11	12	13	14	15	16	17
	18	19	20	21	22	23	24
	26	27	28	..			
MARCH.	..				1	2	3
	4	5	6	7	8	9	10
	11	12	13	14	15	16	17
	18	19	20	21	22	23	24
	25	26	27	28	29	30	31
APRIL.	1	2	3	4	5	6	7
	8	9	10	11	12	13	14
	15	16	17	18	19	20	21
	22	23	24	25	26	27	28
	29	30	..				
MAY.	..	..	1	2	3	4	5
	6	7	8	9	10	11	12
	13	14	15	16	17	18	19
	20	21	22	23	24	25	26
	27	28	29	30	31	..	
JUNE.	..	..	..	..	..	1	2
	3	4	5	6	7	8	9
	10	11	12	13	14	15	16
	17	18	19	20	21	22	23
	24	25	26	27	28	29	30

	S	M	T	W	T	F	S
JULY.	1	2	3	4	5	6	7
	8	9	10	11	12	13	14
	15	16	17	18	19	20	21
	22	23	24	25	26	27	28
	29	30	31	..	..	..	..
AUG.	..	..	..	1	2	3	4
	5	6	7	8	9	10	11
	12	13	14	15	16	17	18
	19	20	21	22	23	24	25
	26	27	28	29	30	31	..
SEPT.	..	..	..	..	..	..	1
	2	3	4	5	6	7	8
	9	10	11	12	13	14	15
	16	17	18	19	20	21	22
	23	24	25	26	27	28	29
	30						
OCT.	..	1	2	3	4	5	6
	7	8	9	10	11	12	13
	14	15	16	17	18	19	20
	21	22	23	24	25	26	27
	28	29	30	31	..	..	
NOV.	..	..	..	..	1	2	3
	4	5	6	7	8	9	10
	11	12	13	14	15	16	17
	18	19	20	21	22	23	24
	25	26	27	28	29	30	..
DEC.	..	..	..	..	..	..	1
	2	3	4	5	6	7	8
	9	10	11	12	13	14	15
	16	17	18	19	20	21	22
	23	24	25	26	27	28	29
	30	31	..	..	..	..	..

CALENDAR, 1895.

	S	M	T	W	T	F	S		S	M	T	W	T	F	S
Jan.	..	..	1	2	3	4	5	**July.**	..	1	2	3	4	5	6
	6	7	8	9	10	11	12		7	8	9	10	11	12	13
	13	14	15	16	17	18	19		14	15	16	17	18	19	20
	20	21	22	23	24	25	26		21	22	23	24	25	26	27
	27	28	29	30	31	..	..		28	29	30	31	..	..	..
Feb.	..	..	..	..	..	1	2	**Aug.**	..	..	..	..	..	1	2	3
	3	4	5	6	7	8	9		4	5	6	7	8	9	10
	10	11	12	13	14	15	16		11	12	13	14	15	16	17
	17	18	19	20	21	22	23		18	19	20	21	22	23	24
	24	25	26	27	28	..	..		25	26	27	28	29	30	31
March.	..	..	..	..	..	1	2	**Sept.**	1	2	3	4	5	6	7
	3	4	5	6	7	8	9		8	9	10	11	12	13	14
	10	11	12	13	14	15	16		15	16	17	18	19	20	21
	17	18	19	20	21	22	23		22	23	24	25	26	27	28
	24	25	26	27	28	29	30		29	30	..	..	..	..	..
	31	..	..	..	..	..	..		..	..	..	..	..	..	..
April.	..	1	2	3	4	5	6	**Oct.**	..	..	1	2	3	4	5
	7	8	9	10	11	12	13		6	7	8	9	10	11	12
	14	15	16	17	18	19	20		13	14	15	16	17	18	19
	21	22	23	24	25	26	27		20	21	22	23	24	25	26
	28	29	30	..	..	..	..		27	28	29	30	31	..	..
May.	..	..	..	1	2	3	4	**Nov.**	..	..	..	..	..	1	2
	5	6	7	8	9	10	11		3	4	5	6	7	8	9
	12	13	14	15	16	17	18		10	11	12	13	14	15	16
	19	20	21	22	23	24	25		17	18	19	20	21	22	23
	26	27	28	29	30	31	..		24	25	26	27	28	29	30
June.	..	..	..	..	..	..	1	**Dec.**	1	2	3	4	5	6	7
	2	3	4	5	6	7	8		8	9	10	11	12	13	14
	9	10	11	12	13	14	15		15	16	17	18	19	20	21
	16	17	18	19	20	21	22		22	23	24	25	26	27	28
	23	24	25	26	27	28	29		29	30	31	..	..	..	..
	30	..	..	..	..	..	..		..	..	..	..	..	..	..

CALENDAR. 1896.

	S	M	T	W	T	F	S			S	M	T	W	T	F	S

JAN.

JULY

FEB.

AUG.

MAR.

SEPT.

APRIL

OCT.

MAY

NOV.

JUNE	1	2	3	4	5	6
	7	8	9	10	11	12	13
	14	15	16	17	18	19	20
	21	22	23	24	25	26	27
	28	29	30				

DEC.			1	2	3	4	5
	6	7	8	9	10	11	12
	13	14	15	16	17	18	19
	20	21	22	23	24	25	26
	27	28	29	30	31		

Engineering Hall

CATALOGUE

OF THE

MICHIGAN MINING SCHOOL

1894-1896.

WITH STATEMENTS CONCERNING THE INSTITUTION
AND ITS COURSES OF INSTRUCTION
FOR 1896–1898.

HOUGHTON, MICHIGAN.

HOUGHTON, MICH., U. S, A.
PUBLISHED BY THE MINING SCHOOL.
JUNE, 1896.

CATALOGUE

OF THE

MICHIGAN MINING SCHOOL

1894-1896.

WITH STATEMENTS CONCERNING THE INSTITUTION AND ITS COURSES OF INSTRUCTION FOR 1896–1898.

HOUGHTON, MICHIGAN.

HOUGHTON, MICH., U. S. A.
PUBLISHED BY THE MINING SCHOOL.
JUNE, 1896.

PRESS OF
ROBERT SMITH PRINTING CO.,
LANSING, MICH.

TABLE OF CONTENTS.

	PAGE
Table of Contents	iii–v
Note of Explanation	vi
To the Public	1, 2
The Michigan Mining School: Its Purposes and History	3–9
Property of the Michigan Mining School	10, 11
Board of Control of the Mining School	12
Officers of the Michigan Mining School	13–16
Faculty of the Mining School	17
Graduates of the Michigan Mining School and their past and present occupations	19–31
Present Location of Graduates	31
Requirements for Admission	33–52
Admission by Diploma	35–49, 52
Courses of Study, High School	36–39
Text-Books, High School	39–45
Methods of Instruction, High School	45–49
Admission by Certificate	49, 50
High School Preparatory, Two Years	50
Admission by Examination	50
Special Students	51
Preparatory Studies in the Mining School	51
Courses of Instruction	53–59
Choice of Electives	57–59
Outline List of the Courses of Instruction	61–73
Departments of Instruction	77–156
Mathematics	77–79
Physics	79–85
Mechanics	85
Chemistry	85–90
Metallurgy	91–94
Drawing	94–99
Mechanical Engineering	99–107

PAGE

Electrical Engineering........................... 107–110
Civil Engineering............................... 110–113
Mining Engineering............................. 113–116
Ore Dressing................................... 116
Biology 117, 118
Mineralogy.................................... 118–121
Petrography 121–131
Geology....................................... 131–154
Thesis.. 154
Preparatory Subjects.......................... 155, 156

Degrees... 157, 158
Text-Books.. 159–164
Advisory Elective Schedules....................... 165–172
Entrance Examination Questions.................... 173–176
Library 177–186
    Periodicals................................... 178–185
    Regulations of the Library.................... 185, 186

Collections....................................... 187, 188
Prizes and Scholarships........................... 189–193
    The Longyear Prizes.......................... 189, 190
    The Charles E. Wright Scholarship............ 190, 191
    The Norrie Scholarship....................... 191, 192
    The Longyear Fund............................ 192, 193
    Beneficiaries of Scholarships and Funds....... 193, 194

Buildings... 194–200
Deposits, Tuition and other Expenses.............. 201–203
Organization and Goverment....................... 204, 205
Employment....................................... 206–211
Location and Routes.............................. 212–216
Mineral Industries............................... 217–223
Copper District.................................. 224–239
    Portage Lake Division........................ 224–239
    Keweenaw Division............................ 239
    Ontonagon Division........................... 239
Iron Ranges...................................... 240–245
    Marquette Range.............................. 240–242
    Menominee Range.............................. 242, 243
    Gogebic Range................................ 244
    Ore Docks.................................... 245

CONTENTS.

	PAGE
Building Stone, etc.	246–250
Coal	250, 251
Salt	251, 252
Register of Students	253–271
Officers of Athletic Association	272
Alumni Association	272
Calendars	273–280
Index	281–283

PLATES AND TABLES:

Science Hall—Frontispiece.

Table I. Schedule showing number of hours given to each subject each week in each term.

Two Years—1896–1898—Facing page 48.

Table II.—Schedule, Fall and Winter Terms, facing page 64.

Table III.—Summer Term, facing page 80.

Tables IV–X—Classification and Required Work in Mineralogy, facing page 128.

Table XI.—Classification of Rocks, facing page 128.

Tables XII and XIII.—Engineering Hall, finis.

EXPLANATION.

.. of this and of the past catalogues of the
.ing School, that relate to each department
.ared by the heads of the several departments.
. parts have always been prepared by the
.ed in the clerical work by the Librarian. The
'.. been greatly aided by the advice and assist-
members of the Faculty. Professor Kidwell
devoted much time and labor to the revision
..pt and to the reading of the proof, never
If when any good was to be accomplished.
..de range of subjects, materials, tables and
. .remption from typographical errors can
..el in a work which necessarily passes through

TO THE PUBLIC.

Although this Catalogue is for the years 1894-1896, its statements and calendar also apply to 1896-1897 and 1897-1898.

The Catalogue does not follow entirely the usual form of such a publication, since it has been prepared to answer each and every question that has been asked the Director concerning the institution for nearly nine years. Hence all persons seeking information concerning this School are requested to look in the Table of Contents for the title under which the subject of their inquiry naturally falls, and then read carefully the statements thus found.

If the desired information can not be found, application should then be made to the Director, in person or by letter, stating what points are not understood, or upon what subject information is desired. Experience, however, has shown that for the past four years hardly any questions have been asked, that have not been answered in this Catalogue more fully than is possible in a letter.

All requests for Catalogues, for information concerning all matters relating to the course of study, admission qualifications, blank certificates, and in short, for anything relating to the educational side of the school should invariably be addressed to the DIRECTOR; while all communications concerning purchases, bills and financial matters should be addressed to the TREASURER of the Mining School, or, in certain cases, to heads of departments seeking information concerning material to be used in their work.

All parties writing for catalogues or information, are particularly requested to see that their names and addresses are legibly written and accurately stated, for however familiar any one may be with his own signature, the party to whom application is made for the Catalogue is not usually acquainted with it. Very frequently catalogues and letters mailed from the school are returned because the party asking for them gave a deficient or incorrect address. Any one who fails to receive within a reasonable time an answer to his request, or inquiry, should write again, as all communications which reach the Director receive prompt attention, and the Catalogue, or information desired, is forwarded at once.

THE MICHIGAN MINING SCHOOL: ITS PURPOSES AND HISTORY.

The Michigan Mining School was established as the fourth and last of the institutions of Michigan, which are devoted to higher education. From the moment of its inception its single object has been to send out men who are qualified to take an active part in the development of the mineral wealth of our State and Nation; and any subject of study which is essential to this end will not be found wanting in its courses of instruction.

The school has been singularly happy in its location. It is an axiom of modern education that any school, which is to obtain the greatest return for the money and energy spent in establishing it, must be situated in a region which shall from its very nature serve free of all expense, as a part of the real equipment of that school. This can be so only when the district presents for the daily observation of the student the most extensive and "up-to-date" practical applications of the subjects which are taught in the school,—a district in which the student is inspired with a strong appreciation of, and interest in, his future work, by being brought into frequent contact with able men whose lives have been devoted to the same profession. The location must be such that the body of the people regard the institution as a co-worker with them in the main business of their daily life, and naturally take far more interest in it, than in a school whose object and officials have little in common with them. The student thus lives in an atmosphere which harmonizes with his work and his attention and energies are not distracted and wasted by making digressions into matters which have no bearing on his real future.

On this account, medicine, law, theology and cognate subjects are best taught in large cities whose hospitals, libraries, courts, churches,

societies, and meetings of congresses devoted to such subjects, all
furnish material indispensable for the proper teaching of these
branches of knowledge; mechanical and electrical engineering can
be most advantageously studied only in a locality containing machine
works, manufactures, mills, lighting and power plants; and civil
engineering can be most thoroughly acquired in a school which has
in its immediate vicinity numerous examples of modern constructions in the form of bridges, railways and their appurtenances, large
buildings and establishments which design and produce the material
for them. Similarly, mining engineering can be most efficiently
taught only in a district containing numerous mines which are
worked on the largest scale and in which scientific and economical
considerations are given full sway.

From this point of view the Michigan Mining School has, more
than any other school of mines in America, been fortunate in its
location. Within a radius of eleven miles from its doors are situated several of the largest, deepest and most successful mines in the
world. The most powerful and stupendous machinery ever employed in mining is here in constant use and always open to the
inspection of the student. The aggregate horse power of the engines
used by only two of these mining companies exceeds the grand total
of all the engines used in the gold and silver mines in the United
States in the halcyon days of 1889; or far more than double all those
employed in the grandest spectacle this earth has ever seen—the
World's Columbian Exposition in 1893.

The mines of the Marquette, Menominee and Gogebic iron ranges
are within a few hours' ride of the school, and furnish a most efficient means of illustrating a large part of its teachings. The output
of the various mines and other mineral industries in the Upper Peninsula is so enormous that its yearly value is about $70,000,000, and
places Michigan, among the States of the Union, second only to
Pennsylvania in the value of its mineral products.

The further development of this vast industry requires men who
are thoroughly trained for this special work, and to meet this requirement the Michigan Mining School was established. It was
fortunate for the School that its Founders realized at the start that,
to fulfill its mission, it must not, as is so frequently and unfortu-
nely done, waste its energies in the vain attempt to teach branches
n to the object of the institution, and which were already well

taught by other schools maintained by the State. In consequence they determined that this School should confine its attention wholly to *mining and the subjects relating thereto:* hence the course is designed to teach the student to conduct explorations in the forest and field; to distinguish the useful minerals and rocks; to understand the geological principles that govern the formation and association of useful mineral products, and to determine approximately their values; to study ores, building stones, limes, mortars, cements, coal, salt, gypsum, petroleum, natural gas, clays, fertilizers, gems, and useful vegetable products; to survey, map, and lay out the ground, the railroads, tramways, and towns; to select or design hoisting, transportation, power, and light plants; to design the mills, furnaces, docks, dams, bridges, shaft and rock houses, and other structures; to determine in each case which is the most suitable method for opening and conducting a quarry or mine, and of timbering, ventilating and draining it; to assay, concentrate and smelt ores; to investigate the strength and other properties of engineering materials, that designs may be intelligently worked out; to make working drawings to illustrate fully these designs; to understand the most economical methods of generating and using steam; to study in detail engines, pumps, boilers, and other machinery, and the methods of operating, testing and repairing them; to master the principles of electricity and its generation, storage, transmission, and use as an illuminant and source of motive power; to study hydraulics, and its various applications in civil affairs and hydraulic mining; to understand mine management and accounts; in short, to train men to be of real use in any line of work connected with the winning and reduction of mineral products.

Such work naturally arranges itself along various clearly defined lines in each of which the training may proceed to almost any length; hence the branches of study which here most naturally resolve themselves into specialties are drawing, chemistry, metallurgy, mechanical, civil, electrical and mining engineering, ore dressing and geology. In consequence, the men educated at the Mining School are now engaged as surveyors, mining, civil, electrical and mechanical engineers, woodsmen, explorers, railroad men, chemists, assayers, mill men, quarrymen, manufacturers, stock raisers, farmers, teachers, etc. It therefore appears that the Mining School has fulfilled its mission and educated its students to be useful and efficient

men, who are daily adding to the world's material wealth and to its
stock of knowledge.

The range of subjects bearing on the mineral industry is extremely
wide; this, coupled with the fact that all men are endowed with a
natural aptitude for some lines of work, while wholly unfitted for
others; and the further fact that circumstances beyond control frequently force men into particular occupations and deprive them of
the opportunity to prosecute a full course of training, all conspire to
demonstrate the correctness of the modern educational view, that a
rigid set course of instruction in higher education is now out of date,
and that the student must have some liberty in selecting the studies
which are to enable him to cope with his life work. This fact has
been long recognized here, and the Mining School has squarely met
the issue by adopting an elective system so designed that while the student is allowed to choose the main lines of his work, he is compelled
by the *proper sequence* of studies to take up such subjects as are essential to a broad and thorough engineering training.

Further, in the effort to save the valuable time of young men, the
school work is continued during forty-five weeks a year instead of
thirty to thirty-six as in most institutions. This enables the student
who so wishes, to accomplish as much in three years as he would
ordinarily do elsewhere in four.

The instruction given at the Mining School is intended to be
strictly professional and practical, and the school considers that to
give a general educational training is as little in keeping with its
legitimate functions as would be the case in schools devoted to law,
medicine and theology. Such general training is already fully provided for by other institutions maintained by the State, and to
attempt it here would cause a serious detriment in the quality of
the engineering instruction, and add only a source of needless
expense to the State. It is therefore clear that the Michigan Mining
School in no way encroaches on the work which legitimately belongs
to any other of our institutions of learning; indeed, it really assists
them by offering an education which no one of them, by reason of its
location, can possibly give in the way it is given here.

The mineral industries adjacent to the Mining School are the
most efficient portions of its equipment. Without a similar advantage no school can properly teach mining, and any attempt to do so
—'ll result in an inferior engineering training, no matter if millions

of dollars be spent in equipping that school. The Pennsylvania Railway Company wisely recognized this principle when it established its school at Altoona. It wanted railroad men, and it very properly trains them at a place where all the matters pertaining to railways are directly under the eye of the student.

The Mining School forces its students to do thorough work, and also to acquire some practical knowledge of the subjects they are studying. The day has passed when engineering students could be properly trained through an equipment of lecture rooms, teachers and books; this school has therefore ever been mindful of the wise observation of Seneca: "Long is the way through precept, short and effective through examples," * hence it tries to make its students not only hear, but see, and to act with their own hands as well as their minds. In this fact and in it only, can be found the reason why its graduates have been signally successful in practice, and that they have rarely been attracted into a line of work different from that which they pursued at this School.

The Mining School was established by an act of the Legislature approved May 1st, 1885, and was opened for the reception of students on September 15th, 1886. Its inception, establishment, and to a great extent its appropriations have been due to the foresight, energy and executive ability of Hon. Jay A. Hubbell of Houghton. He has spared no labor in endeavoring to accomplish everything he considered essential to the success and prosperity of the institution.

In 1886, Albert Williams, Jr., a graduate of the College of New Jersey, was elected principal, and had charge of the school until he resigned during the summer of 1887. M. E. Wadsworth, a graduate of Bowdoin and post graduate of Harvard, was then chosen as Director, and still retains that position.

The first classes were taught in rooms located on the top floor and in the basement of the "fire engine house" of the village of Houghton. Four additional rooms in the Oldfellows Building were secured in September, 1887, but the continued growth of the school made it necessary to vacate the latter quarters during the summer of 1888, and to replace them by others obtained in the Roller Rink Building, now the Armory Opera House.

In May, 1889, the school was moved into the building now known as Science Hall. This was erected by the State on land donated

---

* " *Longum est inter per præcepta, breve et efficax per exempla.*"

by Judge Hubbell, but even then it was well known that the building
was too small for the necessary work of the school. In 1890, ore
dressing works were constructed, and there was added in 1892 a
small structure containing a furnace for roasting ores. As the
school grew faster than its most sanguine friends had any reason to
hope, further buildings became necessary, and during 1894-95 the
State erected another large one to accommodate the departments of
drawing and mechanical and electrical engineering, and the offices
and lecture rooms of the department of civil and mining engineering.

The equipment of the institution has also been increased so far as
its funds have permitted, and the total school property, as inven-
toried in August, 1895, amounted to $219,666.79.

In 1886, a course of instruction of two years duration was
announced, but its details were not worked out; indeed, the educational side of the school was not regularly organized until the academic year, 1887-88. Since then the curriculum has been steadily broad-
ened and perfected in detail. In 1889 a three years course was
adopted, and in 1893 this was changed to four years. The full
elective system went into successful operation in 1895, and has
proven entirely satisfactory to both instructors and students alike.

No Mining School in America has ever had such a phenomenal
growth as this one, whether viewed from the standpoint of attendance of students in mining engineering; in the thorough and practical nature of the education given; or in the standing the school has
won at home and abroad. Since 1890 it has been recognized as one
of the leading institutions of its kind in the world, and it will ever
strive to retain this position by hard work and true merit, if those
for whose benefit it was established will do their duty toward it.

The number of new students who entered; the total enrollment;
and the number of graduates sent out for each year of the school's
existence are as follows:

Year	'86-7.	'87-8.	'88-9.	'89-90.	'90-1.	'91-2.	'92-3.	'93-4.	'94-5.
New students	23	15	16	15.	46	40	45	17	49
Total attendance	23	29	40	35	61	78	01	82	94
Graduates	....	7	6	5	4	0	8	17	32—69

These students were from twenty-four different states of the
and from the following foreign countries: Canada, Cuba,

England, Germany, Japan, Mexico, New Brunswick, Peru and the South African Republic. The large majority of the students came from Michigan, as would naturally be expected from the magnitude of the mining interests of our state.

The Legislature has made for the school appropriations as follows:

	1885.	1887.	1889.	1891.	1893.	1895	Total.
Current expenses........	$25,000	$17,500	$14,000	$57,600	$75,000	$80,000	$299,100
Building and Equipment .	....	75,000	60,000	15,000	35,000	....	185,000

Through the exercise of rigid economy in the use of its funds the institution has saved and put into equipment much of the money intended for current expenses, and so well has this been done that the average annual expense per student since the school was established has been somewhat less than $400 00. No other leading school has ever been able to do work of equal grade for so small a sum.

PROPERTY OF THE MICHIGAN MINING SCHOOL.

August, 1895.

MATHEMATICS AND PHYSICS.

Mathematics	$175 00	
Physics	7,580 22	
		$7,755 22

CHEMISTRY AND METALLURGY.

Qualitative Laboratory	$2,090 00	
Quantitative Laboratory	2,778 00	
Photographic Laboratory	532 95	
Assay Laboratory	2,319 91	
Metallurgy	1,242 00	
		$8,962 86

MECHANICAL AND ELECTRICAL ENGINEERING.

Drawing	$1,308 00	
Pattern Shop	1,858 00	
Machine Shop	6,433 10	
Testing Laboratory	3,057 00	
Steam Plant	2,910 00	
Electrical Engineering	3,641 00	
		$19,217 10

CIVIL AND MINING ENGINEERING.

Engineering Equipment	$6,646 15	
Dressing Plant	3,461 57	
		$10,107 72

MINERALOGY AND GEOLOGY.

Mineralogy	$8,373 50	
Petrography	7,523 88	
General Geology	3,630 10	
Economic Geology	823 00	
		$20,350 48
LIBRARY		23,465 06
ADMINISTRATIVE DEPARTMENT		426 75
SUPPLY ROOMS		6,231 73
BUILDINGS AND GROUNDS		123,159 82
Total		$219,666 79

MICHIGAN MINING SCHOOL.

BOARD OF CONTROL OF THE MINING SCHOOL.

1894—1896.

	Term Expires
...ger Hancock	June 9, 1897
...irth West, Calumet	June 9, 1897
...well, Houghton	June 9, 1899
...Dunstan, Hancock	June 9, 1899
...Longyear, Marquette	June 9, 1901
Marquette	June 9, 1901

OFFICERS OF THE BOARD OF CONTROL.

PRESIDENT OF THE BOARD OF CONTROL,
HON. JAY ABEL HUBBELL.

DIRECTOR OF THE MINING SCHOOL,
FREEMAN EDWARD WADSWORTH.

SECRETARY OF THE BOARD OF CONTROL,
ALLEN FORSYTH REES.

AND PURCHASING AGENT OF THE MINING SCHOOL,
ALLEN FORSYTH REES.

OFFICERS OF THE MICHIGAN MINING SCHOOL
1894–1895.

MARSHMAN EDWARD WADSWORTH, A. B., A. M. (Bowdoin College),
A. M., Ph. D. (Harvard University),
DIRECTOR,
Professor of Mineralogy, Petrography and Geology.

GEORGE AUGUSTUS KOENIG, M. E. (Polytechnikum, Karlsruhe),
A. M.. Ph. D. (University of Heidelberg),
Professor of Chemistry and Metallurgy.

FREDERICK WILLIAM SPERR, E. M. (Ohio State University).
Professor of Civil and Mining Engineering.

EDGAR KIDWELL, A. B., A. M. (Georgetown University),
M. E. (University of Pennsylvania),
Professor of Mechanical and Electrical Engineering.

FRED WALTER McNAIR, S. B., (University of Wisconsin),
Professor of Mathematics and Physics.

ARTHUR EDMUND SEAMAN,
Instructor in Mineralogy and Geology.

CARLTON FRANKLIN MOORE, E. M. (Michigan Mining School),
Instructor in Mechanical Engineering and Drawing.

MISS FRANCES HANNA,
Librarian and Secretary.

JAMES WILTON SHIELDS
Assistant in the Machine Shop.

GEORGE WASS,
Assistant in the Pattern Shop.

BURTON TYNDALL SEELEY, E. M. (Michigan Mining School)
Assistant in Chemistry.

MICHIGAN MINING SCHOOL.

IRA PECK BURRALL, E. M. (Michigan Mining School).
Assistant in Chemistry.

ROBERT IRWIN REES.
Assistant in Physics.

LOUIS ALDRO WRIGHT.
Assistant in Mineralogy.

HENRY GIBBS,
Supply Clerk, and Janitor of Science Hall.

PATRICK ROBERT DILLON,
Engineer, and Janitor of Engineering Hall.

MISS KATE KILLIAN,
Stenographer and Typewriter.

JOHN BRIMACOMBE,
Janitor's Assistant.

OFFICERS OF THE MICHIGAN MINING SCHOOL.

1895—1896.

MARSHMAN EDWARD WADSWORTH, A. B., A. M. (Bowdoin College),
A. M., Ph. D. (Harvard University),
DIRECTOR,
Professor of Mineralogy, Petrography and Geology.

GEORGE AUGUSTUS KOENIG, M. E. (Polytechnikum, Karlsruhe),
A. M., Ph. D. (University of Heidelberg),
Professor of Chemistry and Metallurgy.

FREDERICK WILLIAM SPERR, E. M. (Ohio State University),
Professor of Civil and Mining Engineering.

EDGAR KIDWELL, A. B., A. M. (Georgetown University),
M. E. (University of Pennsylvania),
Professor of Mechanical and Electrical Engineering.

FRED WALTER MCNAIR, S. B. (University of Wisconsin),
Professor of Mathematics and Physics.

ARTHUR EDMUND SEAMAN, S. B. (Michigan Mining School),
Assistant Professor of Mineralogy and Geology.

CARLTON FRANKLIN MOORE, E. M. (Michigan Mining School),
Instructor in Mechanical Engineering and Drawing.

MISS FRANCES HANNA,
Librarian and Secretary.

JAMES WILTON SHIELDS,
Instructor in the Machine Shop.

GEORGE WASS,
Instructor in the Pattern Shop.

BURTON TYNDALL SEELEY, E. M. (Michigan Mining School).
Assistant in Chemistry.

FREDERICK PECK BURRALL, E. M. (Michigan Mining School),
Assistant in Chemistry.

JAMES FISHER, E. M. (Michigan Mining School),
Assistant in Mathematics and Physics.

WILLIAM JOHN SUTTON,
Assistant in Mineralogy and Geology.

JOHN KNOX,
Assistant in Physics.

FREDERICK WALPOLE HOAR,
Assistant is Surveying and Mining.

GEORGE SLOCK, S. B. (Michigan Mining School,)
Assistant in Drawing.

HENRY GIBBS,
Supply Clerk, and Janitor of Science Hall.

PATRICK ROBERT DILLON,
Engineer, and Janitor of Engineering Hall.

MISS KATE KILLIAN,
Stenographer and Typewriter.

JOHN BRIMACOMBE,
Janitor's Assistant.

HERMANN RUMPH,
Engineer's Assistant.

FACULTY OF THE MINING SCHOOL.

MARSHMAN EDWARD WADSWORTH, A. M., Ph. D., DIRECTOR,
Professor of Mineralogy, Petrography and Geology.

GEORGE AUGUSTUS KOENIG, M. E., A. M., Ph. D.,
Professor of Chemistry and Metallurgy.

FREDERICK WILLIAM SPERR, E. M.,
Professor of Civil and Mining Engineering.

EDGAR KIDWELL, A. M., M. E.,
Professor of Mechanical and Electrical Engineering.

FRED WALTER MCNAIR, S. B.,
Professor of Mathematics and Physics.

ARTHUR EDMUND SEAMAN, S. B.,
Assistant Professor of Mineralogy and Geology.

MISS FRANCES HANNA, LIBRARIAN,
Secretary of the Faculty.

2

GRADUATES

OF THE

MICHIGAN MINING SCHOOL

AND THEIR

PAST AND PRESENT OCCUPATIONS.

GRADUATES.

1888.

NAME.   OCCUPATION.   PRESENT RESIDENCE.

HARRIS, JOHN LUTHER, S. B.,

Surveyor, Quincy and Torch Lake Railroad. Special Course, Massachusetts Institute of Technology, Boston, Mass. Assistant, and later, Chief Mining Engineer, Quincy Mine, Hancock, Mich.

Quincy Mine, Hancock, Mich.

LONGYEAR, EDMUND JOSEPH, S. B.,

Assistant, Michigan Geological Survey. Explorer, Mesabi Range, Minn. Superintendent of the Longyear and Bennet Explorations on the Mesabi Range, Minn.

Hibbing, Minn.

PARNALL, SAMUEL ALEXANDER, S. B.,

Mining Engineer, Cleveland Iron Mining Co. Mining Engineer, Cleveland Iron Mining Co. and Iron Cliffs Mining Co , Ishpeming, Mich. Superintendent Old Dominion Copper Mining and Smelting Co., Globe, Arizona.   *Globe, Arizona.*

PARNALL, WILLIAM EDWARD, S. B.,

Superintendent, Stamp Mill, National Mine, Ontonagon, Mich. Mining Engineer and Chemist, Champion Mine, Beacon, Mich. Electrical Engineering Courses in Cornell University, Ithaca, N. Y.; and Massachusetts Institute of Technology, Boston, Mass. In charge of the Installation of the Electric Haulage Plant, Cleveland and Iron Cliffs Mining Co., Ishpeming, Mich. In charge of Installation work for the Morgan Gardner Electric Co., Chicago, Ill.   *Huntington, W. Va.*

NME.	OCCUPATION.	PRESENT RESIDENCE.

WILLIAM, S. B.,
Miner, Champion Mine, Beacon, Mich. Miner, Lake
Superior Mine, Ishpeming, Mich. With R. J. Hosmer,
Romeo Door Hanger Co.. Romeo, Mich. Conductor,
West End St. Ry.. Boston, Mass. Farmer, Lawtey,
Florida. Clerk, Baltimore Dairy Lunch Co., Boston,
Mass.   *Boston, Mass.*

R. JAMES BENJAMIN, S. B.,
Mining Engineer and Chemist, Tyler's Forks Mine, Wis.,
and Excelsior Red Stone Co., Jacobsville, Mich. Super-
intendent of Excelsior Red Stone Co., Jacobsville, Mich.
General Manager, Mackolite Fire Proofing Co., Chicago,
Ill.   *Chicago, Ill.*

. WILLIAM JOHN, S. B.
Surveyor, Northern Michigan Railroad. Civil Engineer, Mineral Range and Hancock and Calumet Railroads. County Surveyor, Houghton County. Sub-Inspector, United States Engineers, Portage Lake Ship
Canals. Draughtsman Lake Superior Iron Works, Hancock, Mich.   *Hancock, Mich.*

1889.

. WALTER WILFRED JOSEPH, S. B.
Assistant Mining Engineer, Cleveland Mine, Ishpeming,
Mich. Chief Mining Engineer, Jackson Iron Co.,
Negaunee, Mich. Mining Engineer, Houghton, Mich.
Mining Engineer, Canton Mine, Biwabik, Minn. Super-
intendent of work on Magnolia Claim, Cripple Creek,
Colo. Consulting Mining Engineer (Crose and Dengler),
Denver, Colo.   *Cripple Creek, Colo.*

ELL, PAUL, S. B.
Draughtsman, Colorado and Northwestern Railway, Pueblo, Colo. Assistant Chemist, Philadelphia Smelting and
Refining Company, Pueblo, Colorado. Assistant Chemist,
Anaconda Mining Company, Anaconda, Mont. Assayer
and Chemist, Santa Rosa Consolidated Mining and Smelting Co., Musquiz, Coahuila, Mexico. Civil Engineer, Denver and Rio Grande Railroad. Assayer, A. M. Donaldson
and Co.. Denver, Colo. Assayer in charge, Assay Office
of M. D. Currigan, Denver, Colo.   *Denver, Colo*

NAME. OCCUPATION. PRESENT RESIDENCE.

FESING, HERMAN WILLIAM, S. B., E. M. (1890).
Assistant City Engineer, Iron Mountain, Mich. Mining Engineer and Chemist, Hamilton Ore Co., Iron Mountain, Mich. Civil and Mining Engineer, Everett, Washington. Fee-Owner's Agent, Dunn, Crystal Falls and Columbia Mines, Crystal Falls, Mich. Chemist in charge of the Experimental Laboratory of John T. Jones, Iron Mountain, Mich. Assistant Superintendent, Manufacture and Introduction of Explosives, Summit, Ill. Mining Engineer, Dallas, Texas. *Dallas, Texas.*

HASS, JACOB, S. B , E. M. (1890).
Civil Engineer, Penokee and Gogebic Consolidated Mining Co., Ironwood, Mich. Assistant Mining Engineer, Cleveland and Iron Cliffs Mining Co., Ishpeming, Mich. Mining Engineer, Skylark Mines, Marcus, Washington. Mining Engineer and Assayer, Midway, B. C. Mining Engineer, Midway, B. C. *Midway, B. C.*

HOATSON, JOHN, S. B.
Assistant Mining Engineer and Chemist, Champion Mine, Beacon, Mich. Mining Captain, Silver Bow Mine, Silver Bow, Mont. Mining Engineer, Butte and Boston Mining Co. *Butte City, Mont.*

PRYOR, REGINALD CHAPPLE, S. B.
Assistant Civil Engineer, Isle Royale Land and Exploration Co., Isle Royale, Mich. Civil and Mining Engineer, Houghton. *Houghton, Mich.*

1890.

DANIELL, JOSHUA, S. B.
Assistant Mining Engineer, Tamarack, Osceola and Kearsarge Mines, Opechee, Mich. Assayer, Boston and Montana Consolidated Copper and Silver Mining Co., Great Falls, Mont. Blast Furnace Foreman, Boston and Montana Consolidated Copper and Silver Mining Co. *Great Falls, Mont.*

NAME.   OCCUPATION.   PRESENT RESIDENCE.

DRAKE, FRANK, S. B.

Assistant Mining Engineer, Chapin Mining Co., Iron
Mountain, Mich. Mining Engineer, Buffalo Mining Co.,
Negaunee, Mich. Graduate Student, Michigan Mining
School. Mining Engineer, Chapin Mining Co. Student,
Massachusetts Institute of Technology, Boston, Mass.
Mining Engineer, Taylor and Brunton, and H. P. Cow-
enhoven and Co., Aspen, Colo. Superintendent of the
Russian-American Manufacturing Co.'s Mines in Russia.

St. Petersburg, Russia.

HODGSON, WILLIAM ADAMS, S. B.

Manufacturer of General Cooperage, Stephens, Arkansas. Graduate Student, Michigan Mining School.

Houghton, Mich.

SUTTON, LINTON BEACH. S. B.

Mining Engineer and Chemist, Volunteer Mine, Palmer,
Mich. Chemist, Chapin Mining Co.. Iron Mountain,
Mich. Mining Engineer, Tremont Gold Mining and
Milling Co., Gould, Montana. Mining Engineer and
Chemist, Chapin Mining Co.   *Iron Mountain, Mich.*

WAKEFIELD, ARTHUR ALBERT, S. B.

Mining Engineer, Fronteriza Silver Mining and Milling
Co., Velardena, Mexico. Mining Engineer, Hurley, Wis.
Mining Engineer. Velardena, Mexico.

Velardena, Durango, Mexico.

1891.

BOSSERT, OTTO HENRY, E. M.

Student at the Bergakademie, Freiberg. Saxony. Assay-
or, Bingham Canyon, Utah.   *Bingham Canyon, Utah.*

DENGLER, THEODORE, E. M.

Mining Engineer, Millie Iron Mine, Iron Mountain,
Mich. Sub-Inspector, United States Engineers, Portage Lake Ship Canals, Houghton, Mich. Mining and
Civil Engineer, Atlantic Mine, Mich. Consulting Mining Engineer (Croze and Dengler), Denver, Colo.

Denver, Colo.

FINK, EDWARD, E. M.

Chemist and Metallurgist, with George W. Goetz and
Co., Milwaukee, Wis. Organic and Technical Chemistry,
Polytechnische Hochschule, Charlottenburg, Prussia.
Chemist and Metallurgist with George W. Goetz and
Co., Milwaukee, Wis.   *Milwaukee, Wis.*

NAME. OCCUPATION. PRESENT RESIDENCE.

LAWTON, NATHAN OLIVER, S. B.
Chief Mining Engineer, the Penokee and Gogebic Development Co., Ironwood, Mich. Chief Mining Engineer and Chemist, Aurora Iron Mining Co., and City Engineer, Bessemer, Mich. *Bessemer, Mich.*

1893.

ABBOTT, A. ARTHUR, S. B., (Mich. Agricultural College), E. M.
Instructor in Drawing, Surveying, and Mechanical Engineering, Michigan Mining School. Draughtsman, S. E. Cleaves and Son, Hancock, Mich. Civil and Mining Engineer, Coulterville, Cal.
Coulterville, Mariposa Co., Cal.

CHURCH, GEORGE BATCHELOR, E. M.
Civil Engineer, Chicago, Ill. Miner, Comstock Silver Mine, Park City, Utah. Mining Engineer and Foreman, Comstock Silver Mine. Mining Engineer and Chemist, Daly West Mine, Park City, Utah. U. S. Deputy Surveyor. *Park City, Utah.*

FISHER, JAMES, E. M.
Instructor in Drawing, Y. M. C. A., Hancock, Mich. Assistant in Mathematics and Physics, Michigan Mining School. *Quincy Mine, Hancock, Mich.*

GILLIES, DONALD, E. M.
Assistant Assayer of the Parrot Mining and Smelting Co., Butte City, Mont. Assistant Assayer and Draughtsman, Montana Ore Purchasing Co., Butte City, Mont. Assayer, Lost River Mining Co., Cliffs, Custer Co., Idaho. Surveyor and Assistant Superintendent, W. A. Clark's Properties, Butte City, Mont. *Butte City, Montana.*

KIRK, MARCUS EUGENE, E. M.
Mining Engineer and Prospector, Aurania, Lumpkin Co., Georgia. Electrical Engineer, Missouri and Kansas Telephone Co., Kansas City, Mo. *Kansas City, Mo.*

McDONALD, ERWIN HUNTINGTON, E. M.
Professor of Mining Engineering, College of Montana, Deer Lodge, Mont. U. S. Deputy Mineral Surveyor, Deer Lodge, Mont. Machinist, Anaconda Concentrator, Mont. *Anaconda, Mont.*

TRENGOVE, SAMUEL REED, E. M.
City Engineer, Red Jacket, Mich. Assayer, Tremont
Gold Mining and Milling Co., Gould, Mont. Assayer, Diamond Hill Mining Co., St. Louis, Mont. Mining Engineer
and Assayer, Office of Larsen and Greenough.   *Willan, Idaho.*

WATERS, ALBERT LATCHA, S. B. (Mich. Agricultural College), E. M.
Superintendent Smelting and Concentrating Works,
Blue Springs Mining Co., Blue Springs, Tenn. Assayer,
Silver Creek Mining Co., Cooney, New Mexico. Night
Stamp Mill Foreman, Silver Creek Mining Co. Assistant
Mine Superintendent and Mining Engineer, Silver Creek
Mining Co. Supply Clerk, Old Dominion Copper Mining
and Smelting Co., Globe, Arizona. Timberman, Old Dominion Copper Mining and Smelting Co.   *Globe, Arizona.*

1894.

BURRALL, FREDERICK PECK, E. M.
Topographer, Michigan Geological Survey, Houghton,
Mich. Assistant in Chemistry, Michigan Mining School.
Houghton, Mich.

COLWELL, ALFRED BUNDY, E. M.
Assistant Mining Engineer, Lake Angeline Mining Co.,
Ishpeming, Mich. Chemist, Buffalo Mining Co., Negaunee, Mich. Mining Engineer, Winthrop Iron Co.,
Ishpeming, Mich. Mining Engineer, Cripple Creek,
Colo. Draughtsman, Surveyor General's Office, Denver,
Colo. Superintendent, Goldfield Mining and Milling
Co., Tin Cup, Colo.   *Tin Cup, Colo.*

DURFEE, ELMER WHIPPLE, E. M.
Concentrating Mill, R. E. Lee Silver-Copper Mine, Lordsburg, New Mex. Superintendent, Concentrating Mill,
R. E. Lee Silver-Copper Mine.   *Lordsburg, New Mex.*

EBY, JOHN HENRY, E. M.
Civil Engineer and Draughtsman for Pennsylvania Traction Co., Lancaster, Pa. Draughtsman for Shaymaker
and Henderson, Civil Engineers, Lancaster, Pa. Mining Engineer, Minnesota Mine of the Minnesota Iron Co.,
Soudan, Minn.   *Soudan, Minn.*

HARRIS, HERBERT JEAN, S. B. (University of Wisconsin), E. M.
Engineer, Illinois and Mississippi Canal. Engineer
Double Track Work, Madison Division, Chicago and
Northwestern Railway.   *Chicago, Ill.*

JONES, MAURICE LINDLEY, E. M.
Transit-man for Government Engineers, Eastern Division, Hennepin Canal, Bureau, Ill. Inspector, Illinois and Mississippi Canal. *Bureau, Ill.*

KIRCHEN, JOHN GEORGE, E. M.
Assistant Surveyor, Trap Rock River Railroad. Assistant Mining Engineer, Quincy Mine, Hancock, Mich.
Hancock, Mich.

KNIGHT, JOHN ALEXANDER, E. M.
Chemist, Illinois Steel Company, Chicago, Ill.
9057 Commercial Avenue, Chicago, Ill.

MCDONALD, WILLIAM NEAL, E. M.
Practical Mining, National Mine, Ontonagon, Mich. Sub-Inspector, United States Engineers, Portage Lake Ship Canals, Houghton, Mich. Assistant Mining Engineer, Cleveland and Iron Cliffs Mining Co., Ishpeming, Mich. Assistant Surveyor, Isle Royale Co., Isle Royale, Mich. Assistant Surveyor, Atlantic and Salmon Trout River Railroad, Atlantic Mine, Mich. Assistant Surveyor, with J. P. Edwards, C. E., Houghton, Mich. Sub-Inspector, United States Engineers, Portage Lake Ship Canals. *Houghton, Mich.*

MCFARLANE, GEORGE CAMPBELL, E. M.
Mining Engineer, Lemhi Mining Co.
Gibbonsville, Lemhi Co., Idaho.

MASON, CLARENCE GEORGE, E. M.
Assistant Inspector, United States Engineers, Portage Lake Ship Canals. Chemist and Engineer, Jackson and Negaunee Mines, Negaunee, Mich. *Negaunee, Mich.*

MASON, RUSSELL TEAL, E. M.
Assistant in Physics, Michigan Mining School. Secretary of the University of Colorado, Boulder, Colo. Assistant in Mining and Surveying, Michigan Mining School. Assistant, Michigan Geological Survey, Houghton, Mich. *Houghton, Mich.*

MOORE, CARLTON FRANKLIN, E. M.
Assistant in Chemistry, Michigan Mining School. Instructor in Mechanical Engineering and Drawing, Michigan Mining School. *Houghton, Mich.*

RIDLEY, FREDERICK WILLIAM, E. M.
> Assistant Mining Engineer, Calumet and Hecla Mining
> Co., Ca'umet, Mich. Mechanical Engineer, in charge of
> Experimental Work, Calumet and Hecla Mining Co.
> > *Lake Linden, Mich.*

ROURKE, JERRY, E. M.
> Civil and Mining Engineer, Hancock, Mich. Civil
> Engineer, Cripple Creek, Colo. Mining Engineer,
> Michigan Gold Mining and Milling Co., Cripple Creek,
> Colo. Mining Engineer, Cripple Creek Gold Mining and
> Development Co. *Dubois, Colo.*

SEELEY, BURTON TYNDALL, E. M.
> Assistant in Chemistry, Michigan Mining School.
> > *Houghton, Mich.*

WRAITH, WILLIAM, E. M.
> Resident Engineer for Canon City Coal Co., Rockvale,
> Colo. Engineer for Vulcan Fuel Co., at Newcastle,
> Colo. *Rockvale, Colo.*

1895.

BARLOW, ROYCE ELWIN, S. B., E. M.
> Assistant Electrical Engineer, Chicago Traction Co.
> > *No. 1259 Unity Building, Chicago, Ill.*

CAMERON, WILLIAM MCCALLUM, S. B., E. M.
> Assistant Engineer, with Union Leasing and Mining Co.,
> Leadville, Colo. Mining Engineer, Small Hopes Consol-
> idated Mining Co., Leadville, Colo. *Leadville, Colo.*

CLOSE, FRED BAGLEY, S. B.
> Engineering Office, Hancock, Mich. Assistant in office
> of C. B. Davis, C. E., Chicago, Ill. Engineer, West Bluff
> Sewer System, Peoria, Ill. Assistant Chief Engineer of
> Calumet and Blue Island R. R., Chicago. Civil Engi-
> neer, Chicago Heights' Land Association, Chicago, Ill.
> > *Chicago, Ill.*

COLEMAN, MILTON WATSON, S. B., E. M.
> Chemist, Ropes Gold and Silver Mining Co., Ishpeming,
> Mich. *Ishpeming, Mich.*

DYER, HOLMES HAYWARD, E. M.
> Inspecting Engineer, Ishpeming Sewer System. Assist-
> ant Mining Engineer, Cleveland and Iron Cliffs Mining
> Co's., Ishpeming, Mich. Electrical Engineer and Super-
> intendent of Public Works, Stanton, Mich. Assistant
> Mining Engineer, Cleveland and Iron Cliffs Mining Co.'s
> Mining Engineer, Old Dominion Copper Mining and
> Smelting Co., Globe, Arizona. *Globe, Arizona.*

| NAME. | OCCUPATION. | PRESENT RESIDENCE. |

EMLAW, HARLAN STIGAND, S. B., E. M.
Draughtsman, Midland Terminal Railway, Cripple Creek, Colo. Transit man with U. S. Deputy Mineral Surveyor. *Cripple Creek, Colo.*

HOLBERT, HENRY HOFFMAN, S. B., E. M.
Mining Engineer, Low Moor Iron Co., Low Moor, Va.
Low Moor, Va.

HONNOLD, WILLIAM LINCOLN, E. M.
Assistant Superintendent, Mahoning Ore Co., Hibbing, Minn. *Hibbing, Minn.*

MARTIN, NICHOLAS JOHN, S. B., E. M.
Oiler and Lighter, Drake and Stratton, Oliver Mine, Virginia, Minn. Conductor on Stripping Train, Oliver Mine. Time Keeper, Canton Mine, Biwabik, Minn. Assistant Engineer to City Engineer and to Engineer for Consolidated Mining Co. on Mesabi Range, Minn.
Virginia, Minn.

McDONALD, RONALD H., S. B.
Assistant Surveyor, Quincy and Torch Lake R. R., Hancock, Mich. Assistant County Surveyor, Houghton County. Assayer and Chemist, Tamarack-Osceola Manufacturing Co., Dollar Bay, Mich. Chemist and Assayer, Lake Superior Smelting Co., Hancock, Mich.
Dollar Bay, Mich.

MURRAY, ROBERT, JR., S. B., E M.
Mining Engineer, Loretto Iron Co., Loretto, Mich.
Loretto, Mich.

PALMER, EDWARD VOSE, E. M.
Transit-Man, Duluth, Mesabi and Northern R. R., Minn. Assistant Mining Engineer, Queen Iron Mining Co., Negaunee, Mich. Mining Engineer and Chemist, Queen Iron Mining Co. Secretary and Superintendent, Tenderfoot Hill Tunnel Gold Mining and Milling Co., Cripple Creek, Colo. *Cripple Creek, Colo.*

ORR, JOHN FORREST, S, B., E. M.
Mining Engineer, El Concheño, Mexico.
El Concheño, Mexico.

ROPES, LEVERETT SMITH, S. B.
Explorer for Corundum, Messrs. Hamlin and Kline, Detroit, Mich. Mining Engineer, American Corundum, Co., Franklin, N. C. *Franklin. N. C.*

ROSE, ROBERT SELDEN, S. B.

Mining Engineer, El Conchefio, Mexico. Assistant Engineer, D., S. S. and A. Railway, Superior, Wis. Supt. of Erection of Ore Docks, L. S. and I. Ry., Marquette, Mich.   *Marquette, Mich.*

SCOTT, DUNBAR DOOLITTLE, S. B.

Assistant Cashier, Chapin Mine, Iron Mountain, Mich. Cashier and Mining Engineer, Millie Mine, Iron Mountain. Mining Engineer, Ludington Mine, Iron Mountain. Assistant Mining Engineer, Penokee and Gogebic Consolidated Mines, Bessemer, Mich. Material Agent, Metropolitan Iron and Land Co., Ironwood, Mich. Agent, Comet Mine, for Keweenaw Association, Limited, of Marquette, Bessemer, Mich. Chemist and Engineer, Montreal Mine, Hurley, Wis. Manager, Shores Mining Co., Iron Belt, Wis.   *Iron Belt, Wis.*

SEAMAN, ARTHUR EDMUND, S. B.

Assistant State Geologist, Michigan Geological Survey, Marquette, and Houghton, Mich. Assistant in Mineralogy and Geology, Michigan Mining School. Instructor in Mineralogy and Geology, Michigan Mining School. Assistant Professor of Mineralogy and Geology, Michigan Mining School.   *Houghton, Mich.*

SLOCK, GEORGE, S. B.

Assistant in Drawing, Michigan Mining School. Inspector, L. S. and I. Ry., Marquette, Mich.

Houghton, Mich.

STRINGHAM, JOSEPH, JR., S. B., E. M.

Examiner and Reporter of Gold Mines, Algoma District, Ontario, Canada. Bridge Builder on the Cleveland, Lorain and Wheeling R. R., Toledo Bridge Co., Toledo, Ohio. Mining Engineer, Cripple Creek, Colo.

Cripple Creek, Colo.

TOWER, LOUIS LOVELL, E. M.

Sub-Inspector on Dredge, United States Engineers, Grosse Point, Mich. Mining Engineer, Cook's Inlet, Alaska.   *Cook's Inlet, Alaska.*

UPHAM, WILLIAM ERASTUS, S. R., E. M.

Engineer and Chemist, Canton Iron Co., Biwabik, Minn. Engineer, Mining Department, Kansas City Smelting and Refining Co., Sierra Mojada, Coahuila, Mexico.

Sierra Mojada, Coahuila, Mexico.

| NAME. | OCCUPATION. | PRESENT RESIDENCE. |

WATSON, JOHN BONE, S. B., E. M.
    Assistant Engineer and Chemist, Tamarack and Osceola
    Mines, Calumet, Mich.   *Opechec, Mich.*

PRESENT LOCATION OF GRADUATES.

STATES AND COUNTRIES.

Alaska	1
Arizona	3
British Columbia	1
California	1
Colorado	10
Idaho	2
Illinois	6
Massachusetts	1
Mexico	3
Michigan	22
Minnesota	3
Missouri	1
Montana	4
New Mexico	1
North Carolina	1
Russia	1
Texas	1
Utah	2
Virginia	2
West Virginia	1
Wisconsin	2
	69

REQUIREMENTS

FOR

ADMISSION.

3

REQUIREMENTS FOR ADMISSION.

1897-1898.

Students may enter in 1896, under the conditions published in the calalogue for 1892-1894, which will be sent on request.

Students who desire to enter as candidates for degrees, or to pursue special studies are admitted under the elective system through examination, exhibition of diploma, special certificate, or on presentation of evidence that they are prepared to follow with profit the special studies they elect. Detailed conditions for each of these cases are subjoined.

ADMISSION BY DIPLOMA.

A graduate of a high school or academy will be admitted upon presentation of his diploma, provided the school from which he received it, conforms to the following conditions: The school in question is to give a course of instruction, including all subjects embraced in the Mining School's requirements for admission through examination, in addition to such other studies as that school may consider it desirable for its students to follow. The principal or superintendent is to send to the Director of the Mining School a copy of the course of study, list of text-books employed, and copies of examination papers actually used in the school examinations. If these are satisfactory the school will, upon request, be placed upon the accredited or diploma list of the Michigan Mining School, which is hereafter to be published.

The authorities of all schools included in this list must send to the Director of the Mining School prompt notice of any subse quent changes of principals, superintendents or courses of study, otherwise their diplomas will not be accepted as fulfilling the requirements for entrance to this school.

If it shall subseqently be found that any student admitted upon the presentation of his diploma, was imperfectly prepared, he will excluded from the Mining School until his deficiencies are made up; and the school responsible for such deficiencies shall be stricken from the diploma list.

To indicate to the high schools the courses of study which the Mining School deems most advantageous, the following courses have been prepared:

COURSE OF STUDY, HIGH SCHOOL.

NINTH YEAR OR GRADE.

First Half Year. { English Composition and Literature, Arithmetic (Advanced and Commercial), Zoology, French.

Second Half Year. { English Composition and Literature, Physiology, Book-keeping and Business Law, French.

TENTH YEAR OR GRADE.

First Half Year. { Rhetoric, Algebra, General History, French.

Second Half Year. { Logic, Algebra, General History, French.

ELEVENTH YEAR OR GRADE.

First Half Year. { Civil Government, Geometry, Political Economy, German.

Second Half Year. { Botany, Geometry, Political Economy, German.

TWELFTH YEAR OR GRADE.

First Half Year. { Physics, Trigonometry, Physical Geography, German.

Second Half Year. { Physics, Astronomy, Physical Geography, German.

If it should be deemed more convenient for the school to mass its language work in the first two years, and the mathematics and science in the next two, the following course is recommended:

COURSE OF STUDY, HIGH SCHOOL.

(Two Years Languages, Two Years Science and Mathematics.)

NINTH YEAR OR GRADE.

First Half Year. { English Composition and Literature, Arithmetic (Advanced and Commercial), French, German.

Second Half Year. { English Composition and Literature, Civil Government, French, German.

TENTH YEAR OR GRADE.

First Half Year. { Physiology, General History, French, German.

Second Half Year. { Book-keeping and Business Law, General History, French, German.

ELEVENTH YEAR OR GRADE.

First Half Year. { Rhetoric, Algebra, Geometry, Zoology.

Second Half Year. { Logic, Algebra, Geometry, Botany.

TWELFTH YEAR OR GRADE.

First Half Year { Physics, Trigonometry, Physical Geography, Political Economy.

Second Half Year. { Physics, Astronomy, Physical Geography, Political Economy.

The courses of study just given are published simply to point out clearly the work which experience has demonstrated students should take before matriculating at the Mining School. That a student may be admitted to full standing the Mining School finds it essential to demand that he shall have a thorough knowledge of Arithmetic, Metric System, Book-keeping and Commercial Law, Algebra, Plane, Solid and Spherical Geometry, Physics, Astronomy and English Composition.

These branches excepted, it leaves to the judgment of the local school authorities the arrangement of the course and the selection of the studies to be taught in the school. It does not concern itself with the number or nature of these studies but asks how efficiently they are taught; it wishes to know if the student has gone *through* them instead of *over* them. Instruction in the common branches, including Arithmetic and United States History, is expected to precede the entrance to the high school. Any other languages, ancient or modern, except English, can be substituted for the French and German. It is, however, especially requested that instruction in Chemistry and Geology be entirely omitted when preparing pupils for the Michigan Mining School, as it is found that much better results are obtained if the student, previous to entering this school, devotes all his time to the other branches already enumerated.

If students are to achieve success here, it is imperative that they be able to collate facts, reduce them to order, draw sound conclusions from them, and use with facility the knowledge thus gained. All subjects of study, whether taught here or required for entrance, are regarded by the Mining School as merely so many tools which the student, in proportion to the excellence of his training, can use to advantage in shaping his future. The necessity for a daily drill in reasoning out fully, and applying through varied methods, the fundamental principles of each subject of study cannot be too strongly impressed upon teachers; without it no educational results of sterling value can be obtained. The Mining School has frequently found that its matriculates knew a little of everything, but very little of any one thing; they knew facts but no explanation of these facts. Their knowledge was almost valueless, because they lacked the training which could enable them to use it. These evils are not more common to graduates of high schools than of colleges and universities, and they demonstrate that the failure to teach men to *reason critically* is the chief defect of American education. Students are literally stuffed with facts gathered from all departments of knowledge, and by the time this heterogeneous mass has been swallowed no energy is left to digest it; hence but little development of the intellectual or reasoning faculties is possible, and the very object of all education is defeated. The Mining School considers such teaching a great evil, and urges all who are preparing students for it to see that fewer subjects than usual are taught, but that the instruction in them is such that memorizing is prevented, while the intellect is strengthened and sharpened by constant exercises.

The following text books will give a fair idea of the grade of work desired. In many cases, several books are recommended because conditions vary in different schools, and a work that is suitable for one institution is often ill adapted to the needs of another.

Other books in this list are named because they are considered to be the best works available for the use of those schools which, either through necessity or choice, have not introduced the modern laboratory method of instruction.

ALGEBRA.

Smith's Elementary Algebra, Irving Stringham.

Macmillan & Co., New York.

Hall and Knight's Elementary Algebra, or Algebra for Beginners, F. L. Sevenoak.

Macmillan & Co., New York.

School Algebra, College Algebra or Higher Algebra, G. A. Wentworth.

Ginn & Co., Boston.

Higher Algebra, George Lilley.

Silver, Burdett & Co., Boston.

Text Book of Algebra, Joseph V. Collins.

Albert, Scott & Co., Chicago.

School Algebra or University Algebra, Van Velzer and Slichter.

Tracy, Gibbs & Co., Madison, Wis.

Jones' Drill Book in Algebra, Geo. W. Jones.

Ithaca, New York.

ARITHMETIC.

Robinson's New Higher Arithmetic.

American Book Company, New York.

Smith's Arithmetic, C. L. Harrington.

Macmillan & Co., New York.

High School Arithmetic, Wentworth and Hill.

Ginn & Co., Boston.

ASTRONOMY.

Lessons in Astronomy, Charles A. Young.

Ginn & Co., Boston.

BOOK-KEEPING AND BUSINESS LAW.

Practical Business Book-Keeping, Manson Seavy.

D. C. Heath & Co., Boston.

Manual of Business Book-Keeping, A. L. Gilbert.

Albert, Scott & Co., Chicago.

Complete Practical Book-Keeping.

The Practical Text Book Co., Cleveland.

Business Law, Alonzo R. Weed.

D. C. Heath & Co., Boston.

BOTANY.

Introduction to Botany, Volney M. Spalding.

D. C. Heath & Co., Boston.

Lessons and Manual of Botany, Asa Gray.

American Book Company, New York.

CIVIL GOVERNMENT.

Civil Government in the United States, John Fiske.

Houghton, Mifflin & Co., Boston.

The American Civil Government, B. A. Hinsdale.

The Werner Co., Chicago.

The American Citizen, Charles F. Dole.

D. C. Heath & Co., Boston.

Young's Government Class Book, Salter S. Clark.

Maynard, Merrill & Co., New York.

Our Government, Jesse Macy.

Ginn & Co., Boston.

The Government of the United States, W. J. Cocker.

Harper & Brothers, New York.

The Government of the People of the United States; or A Course in Civil Government. Francis Newton Thorpe.

Eldridge & Brothers, Philadelphia.

CIVIL GOVERNMENT, MICHIGAN.

The Government of the People of the State of Michigan, Julia Anne King.

Eldridge & Brothers, Philadelphia.

Elements of Civil Government of the State of Michigan, Andrew C. McLaughlin.

Silver, Burdett & Co., Boston.

Civil Government of Michigan, H. R. Pattengill.

Robert Smith, Lansing, Michigan.

CIVIL GOVERNMENT, BRITISH EMPIRE.

How We Are Governed, W. J. Gordon.

Frederick Warne & Co., New York.

COMPOSITION.

English Composition, Barrett Wendell.

Charles Scribner's Sons, New York.

Hand-Book of English Composition, J. M. Hart.

Eldridge & Brothers, Philadelphia.

Also see Rhetoric.

FRENCH.

French Grammar, A. P. Huguenet.

Hirschfield Brothers, New York.

French Grammar, A. Hjalmar Edgren.

D. C. Heath & Co., Boston.

Selected readings, particularly of "Scientific French,".

GEOMETRY.

Plane and Solid Geometry, VanVelzer and Shutts.

Tracy, Gibbs & Co., Madison, Wis.

Plane and Solid Geometry, Beman and Smith.

Ginn & Co., Boston.

Elements of Geometry, G. C. Edwards.

Macmillan & Co., New York.

Chauvenet's Geometry, W. E. Byerly.

J. B. Lippincott Co., Philadelphia.

White's Elements of Geometry, John Macnie.

American Book Company, New York·

GENERAL HISTORY.

General History, P. V. N. Myers.

Ginn & Co., Boston.

Studies in General History, Mary D. Sheldon.

D. C. Heath & Co., Boston.

GERMAN.

Eysenbach's German Grammar, William C. Collar.

Ginn & Co., Boston.

German Grammar, C. Brenkmann.

Hirschfield Brothers, New York.

Meissner's German Grammar, Edward S. Joynes.

D. C. Heath & Co., Boston.

German Science Reader, J. Howard Gore.

D. C. Heath & Co., Boston.

Course in Scientific German, H. B. Hodges.

D. C. Heath & Co., Boston.

HISTORY OF THE UNITED STATES.

History of the United States, John Fiske.

Houghton, Mifflin & Co., Boston.

American History, D. H. Montgomery.

Ginn & Co., Boston.

History of the United States, Allen C. Thomas.

D. C. Heath & Co., Boston.

The United States, Alexander Johnston.

Charles Scribner's Sons, New York.

LITERATURE.

Masterpieces of British Literature.

Houghton, Mifflin & Co., Boston.

Masterpieces of American Literature.

Houghton, Mifflin & Co., Boston.

A Century of American Literature, Huntington Smith.

Thomas Y. Crowell & Co., New York.

Introduction to English Literature, F. V. N. Painter.

Leach, Shewell & Sanborn, Boston.

Essential Studies in English and American Literature, James Baldwin.
> John E. Potter & Co., Philadelphia.

A Hand Book of Literature, Esther J. Tremble.
> Eldridge & Brother, Philadelphia.

Studies in English and American Literature, Albert N. Raub.
> Raub & Co., Philadelphia.

LOGIC.

The Principles of Science, W. Stanley Jevons.
> Macmillan & Co., New York.

Elementary Lessons in Logic, W. Stanley Jevons.
> Macmillan & Co., New York.

Logic, Inductive and Deductive, William Minto.
> Charles Scribner's Sons, New York.

Logic and Ontology, or General Metaphysics, Walter S. Hill.
> John Murphy & Co., Baltimore.

PHYSICAL GEOGRAPHY.

Elementary Physical Geography, Ralph S. Tarr.
> Macmillan & Co., New York.

The Realm of Nature, Hugh Robert Mill.
> Charles Scribner's Sons, New York.

The Elements of Physical Geography, Edwin J. Houston.
> Eldridge & Brothers, Philadelphia.

Complete Geography, Alex. Everett Frye.
> Ginn & Co., Boston.

Maury's Physical Geography, Mytton Maury.
> University Publishing Co., New York·

PHYSICS.

A Text Book of Physics, Hall and Bergen.
> Henry Holt & Co., New York.

Principles of Physics, or, Introduction to Physical Science, A. P., Gage.
> Ginn & Co., Boston.

Elements of Physics, Carhart and Chute.
> Allyn & Bacon, Boston.

Physical Laboratory Manual, H. N. Chute.

D. C. Heath & Co., Boston.

Elements of Physics, S. P. Meads.

Silver, Burdett & Co., Boston.

Physics by Experiment, Edward R. Shaw.

Maynard, Merrill & Co., New York.

PHYSIOLOGY.

The Essentials of Health, Charles H. Stowell.

Silver, Burdett and Co., Boston.

Physiology for Beginners, Foster & Shore.

Macmillan & Co., New York.

An Academic Physiology and Hygiene, Brands and Gieson.

Leach, Shewell & Sanborn, Boston.

Comprehensive Physiology, John C. Cutter.

J. B. Lippincott Co., Philadelphia.

Physiology and Hygiene, Joseph C. Hutchinson.

Maynard, Merrill & Co., New York.

Human Physiology, John Thornton.

Longmans, Green & Co., New York.

POLITICAL ECONOMY.

Outlines of Economics, Richard T. Ely.

Hunt & Eaton, New York.

Political Economy for Beginners, Millicent Garrett Fawcett.

Macmillan & Co., New York.

Political Economy for American Youth, Jacob Harris Paton.

A. Lovell & Co., New York.

RHETORIC.

Foundations of Rhetoric, A. S. Hill, with Practical Exercises in
English, Huber Gray Buehler.

Harper & Brothers, New York.

A Text-Book on Rhetoric, Brainard Kellogg.

Maynard, Merrill & Co., New York.

Elementary Composition and Rhetoric, William Edward Mead.

Leach, Shewell & Sanborn, Boston.

Composition and Rhetoric, William Williams.

D. C. Heath & Co., Boston.

Practical Rhetoric and Composition, Albert N. Raub.

Raub & Co., Philadelphia.

Exercises in Rhetoric and Composition, G. R. Carpenter.

Macmillan & Co., New York.

TRIGONOMETRY.

Plane Trigonometry, S. L. Loney.

Macmillan & Co., New York.

Elementary Trigonometry, Hall and Knight.

Macmillan & Co., New York.

Plane and Spherical Trigonometry, H. N. Wheeler.

Ginn & Co., Boston.

Elements of Trigonometry, Edwin S. Crawley.

J. B. Lippincott & Co , Philadelphia.

ZOOLOGY.

Orton's Comparative Zoology, Charles Wright Dodge.

Harper & Brothers, New York.

Introduction to the Study of Zoology, B. Lindsay.

Macmillan & Co., New York.

METHODS OF INSTRUCTION.

Since experience shows that certain methods of instruction yield better results than others, and that a practical education demands a much more intimate acquaintance with some parts of subjects than with others, some suggestions regarding the teaching of many high school studies are here given.

ASTRONOMY.

Preparatory work in Astronomy is desired for two purposes. One: For use in Surveying and other engineering work. Two: As a rational foundation for a philosophical treatment of geological problems.

The pupils should be thoroughly prepared in all subjects given in Young's Lessons in Astronomy, paying particular attention to those studied in chapters I., III., IV., V., VI., VII., VIII., IX., X., XI., XII , and XIV.

BOOKKEEPING AND BUSINESS LAW.

The pupil should master the principles of single and double entry, business forms, the laws of contracts, and such general principles as

he must use in everyday life, in mine accounts, drawing up specifications, letting engineering contracts, etc. The foundation laid in
the high school should be so broad and deep that an ample structure
can be built upon it during some of the subsequent studies in the
Mining School.

BOTANY.

In Botany it is desired that the instruction shall cover the classification of plants, as a preparation for the subsequent study of Economic Botany and Palæontology.

The student should also be made acquainted with as many as practicable of the useful trees and other plants growing in the locality
where he is making his studies.

CIVIL GOVERNMENT.

In this subject the pupil should be thoroughly taught the principles which underlie our municipal, state and national governments,
and his duties and rights as a law-abiding citizen. The principles of
government are desired, rather than special details of their construction in laws and constitutions.

ENGLISH LITERATURE, COMPOSITION AND RHETORIC.

The student's success in meeting the ever increasing competition
of our modern civilization demands of him an ability not only to
produce ideas, but to state them briefly, forcibly and clearly; teachers are therefore urged to give special attention to the above named
subjects.

Through literature the pupil should gather a knowledge of the
methods of expression employed by the best writers; the training in
composition and rhetoric should then be conducted with a view of
making him proficient in applying these methods, when discussing,
either orally or in writing, the things that play a part in his daily
life. On no account should the pupil have as a subject for an exercise anything, concerning which he lacks either knowledge or interest, since such an exercise only wastes his time, and cultivates in
him a forced and unnatural literary style.

FRENCH AND GERMAN.

It is particularly desired that the instruction in these subjects
should look entirely to teaching the student to read the language,

instead of speaking it; when practicable the reading of scientific texts should form an integral part of his course.

LOGIC.

It is not necessary that the pupil follow a formal course in logic, but he must be so taught as to be able to perceive whether a given conclusion correctly follows from the premises supplied. He must know the nature of a syllogism, even though he has never heard the name of it. The teacher can easily select from Jevons' Principles of Science, edition of 1892, such parts as are adapted to his needs.

MATHEMATICS.

Efficient teaching of geometry requires of the instructor more patience and skill than does any other mathematical subject of a high school course, hence it is in this subject that candidates for entrance are found most deficient. It is therefore necessary to reiterate that the prime object of a course in geometry is not to furnish the student with facts, but to quicken his intellect, and train him to think rapidly and logically. The acquisition of facts will then follow as a natural consequence. The teacher is advised to lay out a short course embracing the facts essential to the student's future studies, and select such text-books and class room methods that the pupil shall be unable to memorize any demonstration.

During the preparation in Algebra special stress should be laid on Factoring, Fractions, Quadratic Equations, Radicals, and Indices. The course in Trigonometry, to be satisfactory, must be based on the ratio system; particular attention should be given to solution of trigonometric equations, transformation of trigonometric expressions, solution of triangles, and the theory and use of logarithms, excluding their *computation*.

PHYSICAL GEOGRAPHY.

Physical Geography should be taught in connection with, or after, Physics; and not, as is so commonly done, in the more elementary portions of the high school course, otherwise the pupil cannot acquire the broad and comprehensive knowledge of the subject which is here desired. If properly taught, Physical Geography can and ought to replace the Geology given in many of the high schools.

Tarr's Physical Geography shows well the ground that should be covered.

8.

PHYSICS.

Much has been said of the necessity of teaching Physics by "laboratory method"; while it is generally admitted that this is the only logical and thoroughly efficient one, its agitation some teachers to gather the impression that simply because a is manipulating apparatus in conformity with some set he is in consequence learning Physics. Such ideas are erroneous; mere motions of the hands without corresponding of the thinking faculties can no more produce intellectual frui laboratory than in a corn field. If the course is to be of valu student must be compelled to record every experiment whether by the teacher or by himself, in a neatly written and arranged report covering the objects of the experiment, employed, methods of procedure with reasons therefor, the tions made, the computations together with all the figuring, and clude with a succinct statement of the laws verified, or quan determined.

No matter how limited the facilities at his command, every er is urged to require *some* laboratory work of his students. T are numerous laboratory manuals abounding in suggestions wh will help the inexperienced to gain much valuable knowled through the thoughtful use of material in the possession of ev home.

PHYSIOLOGY.

In connection with this subject, it is desired that special stress laid on a full discussion of the laws of health, habits of perso neatness and order, the use, and the abuse of narcotics and stimulants, since high school graduates appear, as a rule, to have but little knowledge of these and other such subjects which have so great a bearing on their future well being.

POLITICAL ECONOMY.

As the students of the Michigan Mining School are educated for the purpose of becoming active producers in increasing the wealth of the country, it is considered highly important that they should be instructed in the principles and laws of production, exchange, distribution, and consumption of valuable materials, and the relations of governments thereto; while special attention should be given to questions pertaining to the employé, the employer, and finance.

		SUMMER TERM.													Dura-tion.	Totals.
	e.			July.				August.					Sept.			
		40	41	42	43	44	45	46	47	48	49	50	51	52		
		......	......	......	......	......	......	......	......	......	......	......	......	......		
		......	......	......	......	......	......	......	......	......	......	......	......	......		
		......	......	......	......	......	......	......	......	......	......	......	......	......		
		......	......	......	......	......	......	......	......	......	......	......	......	......		
		......	......	......	......	......	......	......	......	......	......	......	......	......		
	1	......	......	......	......	......	......	......	......	......	......	......	......	......		
		......	......	......	......	......	......	......	......	......	......	......	......	......		
		......	......	......	......	......	......	......	......	......	......	......	......	......		

PHYSICS.

Much has been said of the necessity of teaching Physics by "laboratory method"; while it is generally admitted that this met is the only logical and thoroughly efficient one, its agitation has some teachers to gather the impression that simply because a stud is manipulating apparatus in conformity with some set instructio he is in consequence learning Physics. Such ideas are who erroneous; mere motions of the hands without corresponding exerc of the thinking faculties can no more produce intellectual fruit ii laboratory than in a corn field. If the course is to be of value, student must be compelled to record every experiment whether mi by the teacher or by himself, in a neatly written and systemati arranged report covering the objects of the experiment, appar employed, methods of procedure with reasons therefor, the obse tions made, the computations together with all the figuring, and clude with a succinct statement of the laws verified, or quanti determined.

No matter how limited the facilities at his command, every teac er is urged to require *some* laboratory work of his students. The are numerous laboratory manuals abounding in suggestions whi will help the inexperienced to gain much valuable knowled through the thoughtful use of material in the possession of eve home.

PHYSIOLOGY.

In connection with this subject, it is desired that special stress laid on a full discussion of the laws of health, habits of personal neatness and order, the use, and the abuse of narcotics and stimulants, since high school graduates appear, as a rule, to have but little knowledge of these and other such subjects which have so great a bearing on their future well being.

POLITICAL ECONOMY.

As the students of the Michigan Mining School are educated for the purpose of becoming active producers in increasing the wealth of the country, it is considered highly important that they should be instructed in the principles and laws of production, exchange, distribution, and consumption of valuable materials, and the relations of governments thereto; while special attention should be given to questions pertaining to the employé, the employer, and finance.

98.

		SUMMER TERM.										Vaca-tion.		Totals.
e.			July.				August.					Sept.		
	40	41	42	43	44	45	46	47	48	49	50	51	52	
														102
														42
														24
														80
														102
														24
														408
														72

ZOOLOGY.

In Zoology, special attention should be paid to the classification and relationships of animals, in order to prepare properly the pupil for his subsequent work in Palæontology and Stratigraphical Geology.

In conformity with the general policy of the Mining School to give every aid and support it can to the cause of education in the public schools, its instructors will be pleased to afford help to teachers who desire it, in arranging their courses, or in assisting them through the free use of the school's laboratories, apparatus and collections.

ADMISSION BY CERTIFICATE.

In many cases young men have engaged in mining operations or in other business until they have arrived at the age of 18 to 25 years, when they desire to better their condition by obtaining an education that will be of practical benefit to them; but are not able to spend the time necessary to graduate in the usual high school course. Such men prove to be among the best of students, since they realize the necessity of an education and the value of time. In order to help them and at the same time to benefit the high schools, (since otherwise these pupils would never return to them), the Mining School will admit from the high schools persons who are 19 years of age or over, upon the presentation of a certificate from the high school superintendent or principal, certifying that the pupil has satisfactorily completed a two year's course in his school, provided this course shall be the equivalent of the one given below. If any of these students are subsequently found to be not qualified they will be dropped from the Mining School and the names of the schools which sent them be stricken from the approved list.

4

TWO YEARS HIGH SCHOOL, PREPARATORY.

(Pupils, Nineteen Years of Age or Over.)

FIRST YEAR.

First Half Year. { English Composition and Literature, Arithmetic and the Metric System, Algebra, Geometry.

Second Half Year. { English Composition and Literature, Bookkeeping and Commercial Law, Algebra, Geometry.

SECOND YEAR.

First Half Year. { Physics, Physical Geography, Botany and Zoology, Political Economy.

Second Half Year. { Physics, Physical Geography, Astronomy, Political Economy.

ADMISSION BY EXAMINATION.

All students who desire to enter the regular undergraduate work of the Mining School by examination, must pass in the following subjects:

ENGLISH COMPOSITION.—The candidate will be required to write upon some subject selected from Physics or Astronomy.

ARITHMETIC AND METRIC SYSTEM.

BOOKKEEPING AND COMMERCIAL LAW.

ALGEBRA, THROUGH QUADRATIC EQUATIONS.

GEOMETRY—PLANE, SOLID AND SPHERICAL.

PHYSICS.

ELEMENTS OF ASTRONOMY.

Conditions in Book-keeping and Astronomy are allowed when necessary, owing to the fact that many of the high schools do not give instruction in these subjects. The condition in Astronomy must be made up at the commencement of the winter term after entrance, and the condition in Book-keeping by the commencement of the fall term of the year after entrance.

For text-books to be used in this preparation, see the list given on preceding pages.

SPECIAL STUDENTS.

Persons of suitable age will be admitted without examination as special students to take such studies as they may be found qualified to pursue.

Since its organization the Mining School has had many students of ages* varying up to nearly 60 years enter for special work. They do not ask to receive a degree, but desire to study certain subjects which they consider will be useful in their subsequent work. Such students have proved themselves excellent and valuable workers, and the Mining School extends a most cordial welcome to all such and will give them every advantage that lies in its power. It has aided in this way numerous practical and active business men who have had many years of previous experience, and it is desirous of continuing a work from which such valuable results have been obtained in the past—a work which it will ever take pride in doing.

The Michigan Mining School especially desires to aid those who in their younger days have not had the opportunity of obtaining the higher education that their subsequent work demands, since it is well known at this school that the zeal and experience of such men more than overbalance the defects in their early training.

PREPARATORY STUDIES IN THE MINING SCHOOL.

Since its organization the Michigan Mining School has has spared no labor to aid the high schools to hold their students until they had graduated. Circumstances beyond its control compelled the Mining School in 1895–96 to temporarily and reluctantly take up part of the preparatory work in Algebra, Geometry, Book-keeping, Physics and Astronomy.

Since then arrangements have been perfected with the Houghton High School whereby every facility practicable will be given in that institution to pupils desiring to prepare for the Mining School. Should this plan prove satisfactory in 1896–97, the Mining School intends to abandon all its preparatory work after the opening of the summer of 1897, and all pupils desiring to take such work will be turned over to the Houghton and such other high schools as make satisfactory arrangements.

---

* The average age is from 24 to 39 years,

Details have so far been perfected that hereafter the diplomas and certificates of the Houghton, Calumet and Lake Linden high schools will enable their possessors to enter the Michigan Mining School without examination.

COURSES

OF

INSTRUCTION.

COURSES OF INSTRUCTION.

The Michigan Mining School has been the first technical school in the United States to adopt a full and free elective system for its engineering instruction.

Concerning the elective system, it may be said that in this country two systems have been chiefly followed in the higher educational institutions—the fixed and the elective. The latter was introduced first in this country by President Wayland, of Brown University, and it has since been systematized and developed with remarkable skill and success by President Eliot, of Harvard. Indeed, the system has proved to be so well adapted to the needs of modern times and to be so popular that it has made its way in the face of strenuous opposition, until all or nearly all of our colleges and universities have employed it for their work in general or literary, and scientific education.

In technical or engineering education the case has been different, since even those schools which have a most liberal elective system for general education, have still only a partially modified form of the rigid system in the engineering or technical courses. The rigid system is disguised in most institutions in their technical work under the head of election between various fixed courses, which may or may not have a few options, or it masquerades under an elective dress to which it has but little, if any, right.

The elective system, proper, in any of the higher institutions, giving general education, consists of two features: First, the Essential Studies; second, the Sequence of Studies. The first is composed of those studies which are considered in each institution as necessary, or essential to maintain the scholarship or traditions of the school in question, and in engineering schools, the required and essential studies as a rule constitute the chief amount of the entire course in any of the engineering branches. In the case of general or literary education, the number of studies that are considered essential usu-

ally rapidly diminishes according to the experience and number of
the Faculty until only a few studies are required and in time this
feature will be fully eliminated.

Regarding the second, or "Sequence of Studies," but little public
attention is called to it in any statements relating to electives in any
institution, although it is the keynote of them all. No school can
maintain any efficient system of any sort above a kindergarten or
primary grade without carefully considering the question of the
natural sequences. It is the universal law that no student can
take Calculus who has not previously prepared himself in Algebra,
nor can he study Petrography without any knowledge of Mineralogy.

Hence, on account of the natural sequence of studies every instructor in the Mining School, not only has the right, but also is
obliged, to demand that each student, before being admitted into
his class, must have completed every preparatory subject essential
to the work of that class. This is a necessary and fundamental part
of the elective system.

The Michigan Mining School's province is to train men to assist in
the development of the mineral wealth of the country. To do this
it has attempted to apply to technical or engineering education the
same methods that are used in the elective systems of the various
higher literary and scientific institutions of the country. In
accomplishing this it has tried to reduce to a minimum all studies
to be taken by every student, to conserve the sequence, and to obtain thorough work by the business method of individual responsi-
bility.

The only studies required of all the students are the "Elementary
Principles of Geology" and the "Elementary Principles of Mining"—
these are asked for because it is believed that in any institution dealing with the problems relating to the mineral wealth of the country,
the student should have some knowledge of Geology and of mining
methods and also because the Director desires to come into personal
contact with every student in the school, early in his course. The
above mentioned studies require, altogether, the student's presence
in the class room only three times a week for twenty-eight weeks.

Outside of the Elementary Geology and Mining the student is
allowed unrestricted freedom of choice in his studies, the same as he
is in the literary, but not in engineering, work in any other of our
colleges or universities; observing, of course, the proper sequences.

In the elective system of the Michigan Mining School, the unit of work is taken as three hours a week in the class room or nine hours a week in the laboratory for thirty-four weeks, and this amount of work is called a course or a full course, while any subject scheduled for less time is taken for its proportionate part of a full course. The student, to obtain the degree of Bachelor of Science, must complete eighteen full courses, and to obtain that of Mining Engineer, twenty-two full courses, which in both cases include the subjects of Elementary Geology and Mining.

Owing to the fact that the regular work in the Michigan State Mining School extends through forty-five weeks of the year, a good student can obtain his degree in three or in four years, depending upon the question of whether he remains during the forty-five weeks each year, or for only the first thirty-four weeks; and, also, whether he wishes his course to be largely of practical or of theoretical work.

CHOICE OF ELECTIVES.

Duplicate written lists of the electives chosen for each year are to be handed to the Secretary by every student intending to remain during the subsequent year, by the Saturday before the preceding commencement.

Students joining the school at the beginning of, or during the year are to present at the time of entrance their choice of electives for the year in which they enter.

The full courses can be made up of studies which form a complete subject, i. e., any subject numbered in the list of electives, but no partially completed or broken study will be accepted for any part of a full course or receive any credit.

Table I. shows the time in the year that each subject is taught, commencing with the opening of the school year, about the middle of September, and numbering the weeks around to September again. The number of hours given shows the time expected to be taken by the student in the class room, laboratory, etc., but does not include the time needed to be spent in preparation for the exercise.

Tables II. and III give the days of the week and the hours of the day that the student is to set apart for meeting the instructor in the class or lecture room.

In selecting his electives the three tables should be used together, in order to prevent a conflict owing to two subjects elected coming at the same hours and weeks.

Certain subjects consuming a large amount of time for laboratory work have been scheduled as more than nine hours a week but are not necessarily rated in the courses in proportion to the hours taken.

After the electives have been chosen for the year, a student can change, drop or take up any study only in the following manner. He is to hand to the Secretary a written request addressed to the Director, stating the change desired and the reasons therefor. This petition before it is placed in the Secretary's list is to bear the written approval of each and every instructor affected by the proposed change. If it shall then be approved by the Director the change may be made, and the Secretary shall so inform the instructors and student interested. Further, the work already done in the elective from which the change is made, will not be counted, but the student will be obliged to complete the required work in the subject to which he is transferred, as if the latter subject had been originally chosen.

Any student failing to hand in to the Secretary his choice of studies by the time specified, or who drops or takes up any study, except in the manner here stated, will be considered as having withdrawn from the school, and will stand suspended from all exercises in the institution until he is reinstated by the Director.

If at any time the Director shall consider that any student is taking too few studies to properly occupy his time, he may require that student to take additional subjects: again, if the student has elected more work than he can properly perform the Director may require him to drop such studies as may be thought best.

Since the majority of the electives require other studies to precede them as preparatory work, the student when making choice of studies must be guided by the sequence as given in the list of electives. In very exceptional cases a student may be allowed by the Director with the approval of the instructor concerned, to take a subject out of its order, but when the work is so taken, no credit will be given for it, until the required preparatory work has been fully made up.

Each instructor is the sole judge of the fitness of every student electing his subjects; he may refuse to admit into his class any student found deficient in preparation, or dismiss from his courses at any time a student whose work is unsatisfactory.

OUTLINE

LIST OF

THE COURSES OF

INSTRUCTION.

A. MATHEMATICS.

PROFESSOR McNAIR AMD MR. FISHER.

A 1. ALGEBRA. Three times a week, thirty-four weeks. To count for a full course.   Mr. Fisher.

A 2. PLANE TRIGONOMETRY. Three times a week, fourteen weeks. To count as a two-fifths course. To be preceded by or accompanied with subject A 1 (Algebra).

                                      Mr. Fisher.

A 3. SPHERICAL TRIGONOMETRY. Four times a week, six weeks. To count as a one-fifth course. To be preceded by subject A 2 (Plane Trigonometry).   Mr. Fisher.

A 4. ANALYTIC GEOMETRY. Four times a week, twenty weeks. To count as a four-fifths course. To be preceded by subject A 2 (Plane Trigonometry).   Mr. Fisher.

A 5. DIFFERENTIAL AND INTEGRAL CALCULUS. Four times a week, twenty-eight weeks. To count as a full course. To be preceded by subjects A 1 (Algebra), A 2 (Plane Trigonometry), and A 4 (Analytic Geometry).

                                 Professor McNair.

A 6. INTRODUCTION TO DIFFERENTIAL EQUATIONS. Four times a week, six weeks. To count as a one-fifth course. To be preceded by subjects A 5 (Calculus) and C 1 (Analytic Mechanics).   Professor McNair.

B. PHYSICS.

PROFESSOR McNAIR AND MR. KNOX.

B 1. PHYSICS. Twelve hours a week, thirty-four weeks. To count for a full course. Must be preceded by, or accompanied with, subjects A 1 (Algebra), and A 2 (Plane Trigonometry).   Professor McNair and Mr. Knox.

B 2. PHYSICAL MEASUREMENTS. Twelve hours a week, six weeks. To count as a one-fifth course. Must be pre‐ ceded by subject B 1 (Physics).

Professor McNair and Mr. Knox.

B 3. ELECTRICAL MEASUREMENTS. Three times a wee thirty-four weeks. To count as a full course. To be p ceded by subjects B 1 (Physics) and C 1 (Analytic Mechanics

Professor McNair.

C. MECHANICS.

PROFESSOR McNAIR.

C 1. ANALYTIC MECHANICS. Three times a week, four‐ teen weeks. To count as a two-fifths course. To be p ceded by, subject B 1 (Physics), and preceded by, or accom‐ panied with, subject A 5 (Calculus). Professor McNair.

C 2. ANALYTIC MECHANICS. Three times a week, four‐ teen weeks. To count as a two-fifths course. To be pre‐ ceded by subject C 1 (Analytic Mechanics).

Professor McNair.

F. CHEMISTRY.

PROFESSOR KOENIG AND MR. BURRALL.

F 1. GENERAL EXPERIMENTAL CHEMISTRY. Nine hours a week, twenty-eight weeks. To count as a four-fifths course.

Professor Koenig and Mr. Burrall.

F 2. BLOWPIPE ANALYSIS. Twelve hours a week, six weeks. To count as a one-fifth course. To be preceded by subject F 1 (General Experimental Chemistry).

Professor Koenig and Mr. Burrall.

F 3. QUALITATIVE ANALYSIS. Nine hours a week, twenty eight weeks. To count as a four-fifths course. To be pre‐ ceded by subjects F 1 (General Experimental Chemistry) and F 2 (Blowpipe Analysis).

Professor Koenig and Mr. Burrall.

F 4. QUANTITATIVE ANALYSIS. Twelve hours a week,

Winter Terms.

THURSDAY.

Cálculus.
Electrical Engineering.
Principles of Mining.
Elementary Algebra.

Plane Trignometry.
Analytic Geometry.
Mechanical Engineering.

Qualitative Analysis.
Electricity and Magnetism
Elementary Physics.

Algebra.
Quantitative Analysis.
Mine Ventilation.

Metallurgy.
Machine Design.
Geometry.

Mechanical Drawing.
Petrography.

Topographical Drawing.
Economic Geology.
Book-keeping.
Astronomy.

Electrical Engineering.
Mine Management.
Economic Botany.

Principles of Geology.
Physical Geology.

thirty-four weeks. To count for a full course. To be preceded by subject F 3 (Qualitative Analysis).

> Professor Koenig and Mr. Burrall.

F 5. Advanced Quantitative Analysis. Twelve hours a week, thirty-four weeks. To be preceded by, or accompanied with, subject F 4 (Quantitative Analysis).

> Professor Koenig and Mr. Burrall.

F 6. Synthetic Chemistry. Three times a week, thirty-four weeks. To be preceded by subjects F 4 (Quantitative Analysis), F 5 (Advanced Quantitative Analysis), and W 2, (Mineralogy). Professor Koenig.

G. METALLURGY.

PROFESSOR KOENIG AND MR. BURRALL.

G 1. Assaying. One hundred and forty-four hours. To count as a two-fifths course. To be preceded by subject F 3, (Qualitative Analysis).

> Professor Koenig and Mr. Burrall.

G 2. Metallurgy. Three times a week, thirty-four weeks. To be preceded by subjects F 3 (Qualitative Analysis), and preceded by, or accompanied with, subjects F 4 (Quantitative Analysis) and W 2 (Mineralogy).

> Professor Koenig.

G 3. Metallurgical Experimentation. Three times a week, thirty-four weeks. To be preceded by subjects F 4 (Quantitative Analysis), G 1 (Assaying), G 2 (Metallurgy), and W 2 (Mineralogy). Professor Koenig.

G 4. Metallurgy and Metallurgical Designing. Nine hours a week, thirty-four weeks. To be preceded by subjects F 4 (Quantitative Analysis), G 2 (Metallurgy), L 4 (Graphical Statics), M 3 (Mechanism), M 5 (Mechanical Engineering), and W 3 (Mineralogy).

> Professor Koenig and Mr. Burrall.

5

L. DRAWING.

PROFESSORS KIDWELL AND SPERR, AND MESSRS. MOORE
AND HOULE.

L 1. MECHANICAL DRAWING. Eighteen hours a week for
eight weeks, and nine hours a week for twenty-six weeks.
To count for a full course.   Mr. Moore.

L 2. TOPOGRAPHICAL DRAWING. Twelve hours a week,
six weeks. To count as a one-fifth course.

Professor Sperr and Mr. Houle.

L 3. TOPOGRAPHICAL DRAWING (Mapping). Twelve
hours a week, six weeks. To count as a one-fifth course. To
be preceded by Q 1 (Surveying).

Professor Sperr and Mr. Houle.

L 4. GRAPHICAL STATICS. Nine hours a week, fourteen
weeks. To count as a two-fifths course. To be preceded
by subjects C 2 (Analytic Mechanics) and L 1 (Mechanical
Drawing).   Mr. Houle.

L 5. ENGINEERING DESIGN AND CONSTRUCTION. Nine
hours a week, twenty weeks. To count as a three-fifths
course. To be preceded by subjects L 4 (Graphical Statics),
M 5 (Mechanical Engineering), and R 4 (Mining Engineering).   Professor Sperr and Mr. Houle.

L 6. MACHINE DESIGN. Twelve hours a week, twenty-
six weeks. To count as a full course. To be preceded by
subjects M 5 (Mechanical Engineering), M 6 (Testing Materials of Engineering), and accompanied with subjects M 7
(Valve Gears), and M 8 (Thermodynamics).

Professor Kidwell and Mr. Moore.

M.—MECHANICAL ENGINEERING.

PROFESSOR KIDWELL, AND MESSRS. MOORE, SHIELDS AND
WASS.

M 1. PROPERTIES OF MATERIALS. Three times a week,
twenty weeks. To count as a three-fifths course. To be

preceded by subjects B 1 (Physics), and F 1 (General Chemistry.) Mr. Moore.

M 2. SHOP PRACTICE. Forty-five hours a week, eleven weeks. To count for two full courses. To be preceded by subjects L 1 (Mechanical Drawing), and M 1 (Properties of Materials), except in the case of pupils who enter for Shop Practice alone.

Professor Kidwell, Mr. Shields and Mr. Wass.

M 3. MECHANISM. Three times a week, fourteen weeks. To count as a two-fifths course. To be preceded by subjects C 1 (Analytic Mechanics), and L 1 (Mechanical Drawing), and preceded by, or accompanied with, subject C 2 (Analytic Mechanics). Mr. Moore.

M 4. MECHANICS OF MATERIALS. Three times a week, thirty-four weeks. To count as a full course. To be preceded by subjects C 1 (Analytic Mechanics) and M 1 (Properties of Materials), and preceded by, or accompanied with, C 2 (Analytic Mechanics). Mr. Moore.

M 5. MECHANICAL ENGINEERING. Three times a week, thirty-four weeks. To count as a full course. To be preceded by subjects L 1 (Mechanical Drawing) and M 2 (Shop Practice), and preceded by, or accompanied with, subjects C 2 (Analytic Mechanics), M 3 (Mechanism) and M 4 (Mechanics of Materials). Mr. Moore.

M 6. TESTING MATERIALS OF ENGINEERING. Forty-five hours a week, five weeks. To count as a full course. To be preceded by subject M 4 (Mechanics of Materials).

Professor Kidwell and Mr. Moore.

M 7. VALVE GEARS. Twice a week, twenty-six weeks. To count as a one-half course. To be preceded by subject M 5 (Mechanical Engineering) and accompanied with L 6 (Machine Design), and M 8 Thermodynamics.

Professor Kidwell.

M 8. THERMODYNAMICS. Twice a week, twenty-six weeks. To count as a one-half course. To be preceded by subject M 5 (Mechanical Engineering).   Professor Kidwell.

M 9. MECHANICAL ENGINEERING—EXPERIMENTAL WORK IN THE MECHANICAL LABORATORY. Forty-five hours a week, eleven weeks. To count as two full courses. To be preceded by subjects L 6 (Machine Design), M 7 (Valve Gears) and M 8 (Thermodynamics).   Professor Kidwell.

For further subjects belonging to this department see

L 1. Mechanical Drawing.

L 6. Machine Design.

N. ELECTRICAL ENGINEERING.

PROFESSOR KIDWELL AND MR. MOORE.

N 1. ELECTRICAL ENGINEERING. Three times a week, twenty-six weeks. To count as a four-fifths course. To be preceded by, or accompanied with, subjects B 3 (Electrical Measurements), C 2 (Analytic Mechanics), and M 5 (Mechanical Engineering).   Professor Kidwell.

N 2. ELECTRICITY AND MAGNETISM. (Mathematical Theory.) Three times a week, twenty-six weeks. To count as a four-fifths course. To be preceded by subjects B 3 (Electrical Measurements) and N 1 (Electrical Engineering), and to be accompanied with N 3 (Electrical Engineering).

Professor Kidwell.

N 3. ELECTRICAL ENGINEERING. Two times a week, twenty-six weeks. To count as one-half a course. To be preceded by subjects B 3 (Electrical Measurements), and N 1 (Electrical Engineering) and accompanied with N 2 (Electricity and Magnetism).   Professor Kidwell.

N 4. ELECTRICAL ENGINEERING—LABORATORY PRACTICE. Forty-five hours a week, eleven weeks. To count as two full courses. To be preceded by subjects M 7 (Valve

Gears), N 2 (Electricity and Magnetism) and N 3 (Electrical Engineering).   Professor Kidwell.

Q. CIVIL ENGINEERING.

PROFESSOR SPERR AND MR. HOAR.

Q 1. SURVEYING, (Theory and Practice). Forty-five hours a week, eleven weeks. To count as two full courses. To be preceded by subjects A 3 (Spherical Trigonometry) and L 2 (Topographical Drawing), except for those who enter for this work alone, who need to be prepared in Logarithms, Plane Trigonometry and Mensuration.

Professor Sperr and Mr. Houle.

Q 2. HYDRAULICS. Three times a week, twenty weeks. To count as a three-fifths course. To be preceded by subjects A 5 (Calculus), B 1 (Physics), C 1 (Analytic Mechanics), and R 1 (Principles of Mining), and preceded by, or accompanied with, subject C 2 (Analytic Mechanics).

Professor Sperr.

For further subjects belonging to this department see

L 2. Topographical Drawing.

L 3. Topographical Drawing (Mapping).

L 4. Graphical Statics.

L 5. Engineering Design and Construction.

R. MINING ENGINEERING.

PROFESSOR SPERR AND MR. HOULE.

R 1. PRINCIPLES OF MINING. Three times a week, twenty weeks. To count as a three-fifths course. Must be preceded by subject Y 1 (Principles of Geology). Excursions to the mines, etc., required as extras. This subject is required of all candidates for the S. B. and E. M. degrees.

Professor Sperr.

R 2. MINE SURVEYING AND MINING. Two times a week, twenty weeks. To count for two-fifths of a course. To be preceded by L 3 (Topographical Drawing), Q 1 (Surveying), R 1 (Principles of Mining), and Y 1 (Principles of Geology).

Professor Sperr.

R 3. MINE SURVEYING AND MINING (PRACTICAL WORK). Forty-five hours a week, six weeks. To count as a full course. To be preceded by subject R 2 (Mine Surveying and Mining), except for students who enter for this study alone, who are required to be prepared in Algebra, Geometry, Trigonometry, and in the use of the transit and level.

Professor Sperr and Mr. Houle.

R 4. MINING ENGINEERING. Three times a week, twenty weeks. To count as a three-fifths course. To be preceded by subjects C 2 (Analytic Mechanics), M 3 (Mechanism), R 3 (Mine Surveying and Mining), and Q 2 (Hydraulics.

Professor Sperr.

R 5. MINE MANAGEMENT AND ACCOUNTS. Six hours a week, twenty weeks, to count as a two-fifths course. To be preceded by subjects R 1 (Principles of Mining), and R 3 (Mine Surveying and Mining).

Professor Sperr.

R 6. MINE VENTILATION. Twice a week for twenty weeks. To count as a two-fifths course. To be preceded by M 5 (Mechanical Engineering), and Q. 2 (Hydraulics).

Professor Sperr.

S.—ORE DRESSING.

PROFESSOR SPERR AND MR. BURRALL.

S 1. ORE DRESSING, (THEORY AND PRACTICE). Forty-five hours a week, five weeks. To count as a full course. To be preceded by subjects G 1 (Assaying), M 2 (Shop Practice), Q 2 (Hydraulics), and W 2 (Mineralogy).

Professor Sperr and Mr. Burrall.

V. BIOLOGY.

THE DIRECTOR, ASSISTANT PROFESSOR SEAMAN AND
MR. SUTTON.

V 1. Botany (General and Economic). Three times a week, eight weeks. To count as a one-fifth course.

The Director.

V 2. Zoology and Palæontology. Nine hours a week, fourteen weeks. To count as a two-fifths course.

Assistant Professor Seaman and Mr. Sutton.

W. MINERALOGY.

THE DIRECTOR, ASSISTANT PROFESSOR SEAMAN AND
MR. SUTTON.

W 1. Crystallography. Twelve hours a week, eight weeks. To count as a one-fifth course.

Assistant Professor Seaman and Mr. Sutton.

W 2. Mineralogy. Twelve hours a week, twenty-eight weeks. To count as a full course. To be preceded by subjects B 1 (Physics), F 1 (General Chemistry), F 2 (Blowpipe Analysis), W 1 (Crystallography), and Y 1 (Principles of Geology).   Assistant Professor Seaman and Mr. Sutton.

X. PETROGRAPHY.

THE DIRECTOR AND MR. SUTTON.

X 1. Petrography (Lithology and Petrology). Three times a week, thirty-four weeks. To be preceded by subjects B 1 (Physics), F 1 (General Chemistry), Y 1 (Principles of Geology), and W 2 (Mineralogy).

The Director and Mr. Sutton.

Y. GEOLOGY.

THE DIRECTOR, ASSISTANT PROFESSOR SEAMAN AND MR.
SUTTON.

Y 1. Elements of Geology. Three times a week, eight weeks. To count as a one-fifth course. No student will be allowed to take this subject who has an entrance condition in Astronomy. This subject is required of all candidates for S. B. and E. M. degrees.   The Director.

Y 2. STRATIGRAPHICAL GEOLOGY. Three times a week, fourteen weeks. To count as a two-fifths course. To be preceded by subjects B 1 (Physics). F 1 (General Chemistry), V 1 (Botany, after 1896–1897), V 2 (Zoology and Palæontology), Y 1 (Principles of Geology, and preceded by, or accompanied with, W 2 (Mineralogy).

Assistant Professor Seaman and Mr. Sutton.

Y 3. PHYSICAL AND CHEMICAL GEOLOGY. Three times a week, fourteen weeks. To count as a two-fifths course. To be preceded by B 1 (Physics), F 1 (General Chemistry). W 2 (Mineralogy) and Y 2 (Stratigraphical Geology), and preceded by, or accompanied with, subject X 1 (Petrography).
The Director.

Y 4. GEOLOGICAL FIELD WORK. Forty-five hours a week, six weeks. To count as a full course. To be preceded by subjects Q 1 (Surveying), L 3 (Topographical Drawing). W 2 (Mineralogy), X 1 (Petrography), Y 2 (Stratigraphical Geology), and Y 3 (Physical Geology), except for those who enter for this study alone.

Assistant Professor Seaman and Mr. Sutton.

Y 5. ECONOMIC GEOLOGY. Three times a week, twenty-eight weeks. To count as four-fifths of a course. To be preceded by subjects R 1 (Principles of Mining). X 1 (Petrography), Y 3 (Physical Geology), and Y 4 (Geological Field Work).   The Director.

J. THESIS.

THE FACULTY.

J 1. THESIS. Nine hours a week, thirty-four weeks. To count as a full course. The subject of the thesis is to be selected at the same time that the other electives are chosen. The work is to be done under the direction and with the approval of some instructor or instructors, and both the subject and thesis must be approved by the Director.

The student must have taken all the necessary preparatory work that is required to enable him to properly handle his subject, or it will not be approved by the Director. The instructor or instructors under whom the thesis work is done must have presented to the Secretary a written statement certifying that the student is properly prepared and able in their judgment to accomplish the work specified. This statement is to accompany the elective schedule.

PREPARATORY SUBJECTS.

September, 1895, to June, 1897.

I. ELEMENTARY ALGEBRA.   Three times a week, thirty-four weeks.   Mr. Fisher.

II. GEOMETRY, PLANE, SOLID AND SPHERICAL.   Three times a week, thirty-four weeks.   Mr. Fisher.

III. ELEMENTARY PHYSICS, WITH LABORATORY WORK. To be preceded by or accompanied with subjects I (Elementary Algebra) and II (Geometry).   Three times a week, thirty-four weeks.   Mr. Knox.

IV. BOOK-KEEPING. Three time a week, fourteen weeks.
                                                  Mr. Fisher.

V. ASTRONOMY.   Three times a week, twenty weeks.   To be preceded by or accompanied with subjects II (Geometry) and III (Elementary Physics).   Mr. Fisher.

DEPARTMENTS OF INSTRUCTION.

DEPARTMENTS OF INSTRUCTION.

A. MATHEMATICS.

PROFESSOR McNAIR AND MR. FISHER.

As will be seen by a detailed examination of the following pages of this catalogue, the subjects of this department form the necessary foundation for a great part of the student's subsequent work; and they are given as a preparation for this work, as well as for their value in actual engineering practice, and in affording mental discipline.

It is the intention, therefore, to give the instruction in this department in such a manner as will place in prominence those subjects or portions of subjects which will be of actual use to the student, and later, to the engineer. It follows that many things, of interest only to the specialist in mathematics, are entirely omitted.

The value of the study of mathematics in developing the power to do vigorous and logical thinking is not lost sight of, but it is thought that the effort to master the logic of the subjects necessary to the engineer will afford the student ample opportunity to develop this power.

Every effort is made to see that the student takes advantage of the opportunity thus offered. At each step of his progress he is required to think. The ability to describe a given method, or to correctly quote a given formula, and to apply either to a given case, is in no instance accepted as sufficient. The student is required to logically derive the method or formula, and to demonstrate its correctness.

Attention is again called to the entrance requirements in this department. The intending student is asked to pay particular attention to the subjects of Factoring, Fractions, Quadratic Equations, Radicals and Indices in Algebra, and to make sure of his understanding of, and familiarity with, each of them.

The courses offered in mathematics are the following:

A 1.—*Algebra.*

MR. FISHER.

The course includes the Theory of Limits, Logarithms, Progressions, Arrangements and Groups, Binomial Theorem, Undetermined Co-efficients, Series, and the Solution of Higher Equations.

Wentworth's College Algebra is used in '95–'96 as the text-book.

Three times a week, thirty-four weeks, to count as a full course.

A 2.—*Plane Trigonometry.*

MR. FISHER.

The ratio system is used exclusively, and prominence is given to the solution of trigonometric equations, and the transformation of trigonometric expressions.

The fall term's work in subject A 1 (Algebra) must precede or be taken along with this course.

Wheeler's Plane and Spherical Trigonometry is used as the text-book.

Three times a week, fourteen weeks, fall term. Counts as two-fifths of a course.

A 3.—*Spherical Trigonometry.*

MR. FISHER.

The solution of Right and Oblique spherical triangles given from the same text-book as is used in subject A 2 (Plane Trigonometry).

Four times a week, first six weeks of the summer term. Counts as one-fifth of a course. Must be preceded by subject A 2 (Plane Trigonometry).

A 4.—*Analytic Geometry.*

MR. FISHER.

The course covers the straight line, conic sections, a few higher plane curves, transformation of co-ordinates, general equation of the second degree, and an introduction to geometry of three dimensions.

The object is to familiarize the student with methods rather than with any set of curves.

Given partly by lectures and partly from Wentworth's Analytic Geometry.

Four times a week, twenty weeks, winter term and first six weeks of the summer term. Counts as four-fifths of a course.

Must be preceded by course A 2 (Plane Trigonmetry) and preceded by, or accompanied with, course A 1 (Algebra).

A 5.—*Differential and Integral Calculus.*

PROFESSOR McNAIR.

The *Differential Calculus* is developed from a rate as its fundamental notion. The *Integral Calculus* is from the beginning treated as a method of summation.

The object of the course is to give the student a thorough working knowledge of the subject—to put him in possession of a tool of which he can afterward make efficient use. It is believed that this can best be accomplished by giving him a rigorously logical basis for his methods and formulas, and the attempt to do this is therefore made.

Applications of differentiation to Expansion in Series, Indeterminate Forms, Maxima and Minima, etc., are treated; while problems of Area, Volume, Work, etc., introduce the subject of integration, and their treatment is carried along simultaneously with that of methods.

The Calculus is given partly by lectures, with printed notes, and partly from Taylor's Elements of the Calculus.

Four times a week, twenty-eight weeks, fall and winter terms. Counts as a full course.

Must be preceded by course A 4 (Analytic Geometry).

A 6.—*Introductory Differential Equations.*

PROFESSOR McNAIR.

An introduction to Differential Equations which will include the treatment of those special equations which the student will meet in his study of Mechanics and Electricity.

The course is given by lectures and recitations.

Four times a week, first six weeks of the summer term. Counts as one-fifth of a course.

Open to those who have credit for course A 5 (Calculus).

B.—PHYSICS.

PROFESSOR McNAIR AND MR. KNOX.

The aim in the department of *Physics* as in that of *Mathematics* is to select such subjects as have, directly or indirectly, a bearing on the practical work of the mining engineer, and to treat these in as practical a manner as possible.

The instruction is given by the laboratory method. The student goes at once into the laboratory and there, under the direction of the instructors, experiments for himself. The experiments are mostly quantitative, he being required to measure and give a definite account of the quantity with which he is dealing.

As far as possible, mere mechanical following of directions is excluded, and intelligent thinking is made necessary to the accomplishment of the work. Every effort is put forth to have the student clearly develop and fix in his mind the principles of Physics which he will afterward use, and also to lay the foundation for that skill in accurate determination of quantity, and care of delicate apparatus, which are needed by the practical engineer. Accuracy and order are insisted on from the first. Each student receives individual attention, and, with the exception of a few experiments requiring more than one observer, he does his work independently of all other students.

The work of the laboratory is accompanied by illustrated lectures, and by such text-book and recitation work as is found necessary.

Below is given a partial list of the equipment of this department for lecture illustration and laboratory work. Besides the apparatus here listed, the department possesses the usual outfit of battery cells, magnets, lenses, thermometers, and other minor apparatus.

Physical Apparatus.

Four sets of apparatus for experimental verification of the laws of composition and resolution of forces.

Twelve Vernier Calipers.
Twelve Micrometer Calipers.
Twelve small Spherometers.
One large Spherometer.
One Cathetometer.
One Atwood Machine.
Two sets Pendulums.
One Whirling Table and Accessories.
One "Swiftest Descent" Apparatus.
Two sets Moment of Inertia Apparatus.
One Clock Electrically Recording Seconds.

WEEKS—JUNE, JULY.	SCHEDULE: SIX WEEKS—JULY, AUGUST.
RS—8–12; 1–6.	HOURS—8–12; 1–6.
ractice. Materials. ical Laboratory. al Laboratory. ng. essing.	M 2. Shop Practice. M 9. Mechanical Laboratory. N 4. Electrical Laboratory. Q 1. Surveying. Y 4. Field Geology.
ractice. Materials. ical Laboratory. al Laboratory. ng. essing.	M 2. Shop Practice. M 9. Mechanical Laboratory. N 4. Electrical Laboratory. Q 1. Surveying. Y 4. Field Geology.
ractice. Materials. ical Laboratory. al Laboratory. ng. essing.	M 2. Shop Practice. M 9. Mechanical Laboratory. N 4. Electrical Laboratory. Q 1. Surveying. Y 4. Field Geology.
ractice. Materials. ical Laboratory. al Laboratory. ng. essing.	M 2. Shop Practice. M 9. Mechanical Laboratory. N 4. Electrical Laboratory. Q 1. Surveying. Y 4. Field Geology.
ractice. Materials. ical Laboratory. al Laboratory. ng. essing.	M 2. Shop Practice. M 9. Mechanical Laboratory. N 4. Electrical Laboratory. Q 1. Surveying. Y 4. Field Geology.

Six sets Apparatus for Determining Modulus of Elasticity.
Six Kohlbusch Balances.
One Becker Balance.
One Springer Torsion Balance.
Six Trœmner Balances.
Five Jolly Balances.
One Hydrostatic Balance.
Four Mohr-Westphal Specific Gravity Balances.
Twenty-four Specific Gravity Bottles.
Six Nicholson's Hydrometers.
Four Baume Hydrometers.
One Ritchie's Rotary Air Pump and Accessories.
One Lever Air Pump.
One Fortin's Barometer.
Two Aneroid Barometers.
Two Mariotte's Law Apparatus.
Two Condensing and Exhausting Pumps.
One Anemometer.
Seven Sonometers.
Six Vibrating Forks and Resonators.
One Savart's Toothed Wheel Apparatus.
One Lissajous' Apparatus.
One Set Singing Flame Apparatus.
Twelve Sets Apparatus for Velocity of Sound.
Twelve Sets Apparatus for Calibrating Thermometers and Deter-
mining Specific Heats.
One Pyrometer.
One Set Natterer Tubes.
One Maximum and Minimum Thermometer.
Thirty Calorimeters.
One Achromatic Prism.
Eight Geneva Spectra-Goniometers.
Twelve Prisms for same.
One Plane Rowland Grating with Mounting.
One Glass Grating for Projection of Spectra.
One pair Tourmaline Pincets.
One Table Polariscope with Convergent Ring System.
One Single Electric Projection Lantern.
One Combined Microscope and Polariscope fitted to same.

6

One Newton & Co's Bi-Unial Optical Lantern, complete with gas jets and arc lamp.

One Wright's Projecting Polariscope by Newton & Co.

One set Specimens for projecting Polariscope.

One Projecting Micro Polariscope by Newton & Co.

One Wright's Refraction Tank for Optical Lantern.

One Wright's Wave Apparatus for Optical Lantern.

One Moore's Wave and Beat Apparatus for Optical Lantern.

One Huyghen's Apparatus for Optical Lantern.

One Newton's Ring Apparatus for Projection.

One Bunsen's Photometer.

Three Bradley's Marine Sextants.

One Heath & Co.'s Sextant with Artificial Horizon.

Twelve Plain Reading Telescopes with Scales.

Eight Geneva Reading Telescopes with Scales.

One Lamp and Scale.

One Electromagnet.

One Electrophorus.

One Toepler-Holtz Machine.

One Gold-Leaf Electroscope.

One Elliot Brothers' Quadrant Electrometer.

Six Leyden Jars.

Six Copper Voltameters.

Six Volume Voltameters.

Four Sets Geissler Tubes.

One Clamond's Thermo-Battery.

Two Thermopiles.

Twelve Calorimeters with Resistance Coils.

Seven Astatic Pointer Galvanometers.

Four Mirror Galvanometers with Interchangeable Long and Short Coils.

Four Mirror Galvanometers with Long Coils.

Twelve Tangent Galvanometers with Long and Short Coils.

Three Tangent Galvanometers, Helmholtz-Gaugain form.

One Single Ring Tangent Galvanometer.

One Focault Apparatus.

Four sets Primary and Secondary Coils.

One small Induction Coil.

One large Induction Coil.

Five Earth Inductors.
One small Hand Dynamo.
Five small Electro-Motors.
One Continuous Rheostat, Lord Kelvin's Form.
One Kohlrausch Universal Rheometer.
Seven Meter Bridges.
Eight Box Wheatstone Bridge and Resistance Sets, range 1-100 to 11,110 ohms.
One Portable Testing Apparatus, range 0.0002 to 555555 ohms.

The courses offered by the department of Physics are as follows:

B 1.—*General Physics.*

PROFESSOR McNAIR AND MR. KNOX.

An elementary course including Mechanics, Heat, Light, Magnetism, and Electricity. Lecture, recitation, and laboratory work proceed together throughout the course.

Text-books are Lock's Mechanics for Beginners, Glazebrook's Heat and Light, Thompson's Electricity and Magnetism, Sabine's Laboratory Manual, and printed lecture notes. The geometrical side of Light is developed mostly in the laboratory, the wave theory and polarization in the lecture room with the optical lantern and the arc light.

Twelve hours a week, thirty-four weeks. To count as a full course. Must be preceded by, or accompanied with, subjects A 1 (Algebra), and A 2 (Plane Trigonometry).

B 2.—*Physical Measurements.*

PROFESSOR McNAIR AND MR. KNOX.

A more advanced course in measurements of precision, open to those who have taken subjects A 5 (Calculus), and B 1 (Physics).

The work offered will be mainly in the determination of densities, moments of inertia, calorimetry and photometry.

Each student will work independently of all others, and to a considerable extent the choice of the line of work he is to pursue will lie with him.

Text-books are Nichol's Manual of Laboratory Physics, and Stewart & Gee's Elementary Practical Physics, Vols. I and III.

Twelve hours a week, first six weeks of the summer term. Counts as one-fifth of a course.

B 3.—*Electrical Measurements.*

PROFESSOR McNAIR.

The increasing use of electricity in mining and related industries has caused the Michigan Mining School to enlarge somewhat its facilities for giving instruction in this subject.

The course in Electrical Measurements is offered to those who are making Electrical Engineering their principal subject, those who intend taking up Electrolytic or Electro-metallurgical work, and to any others who wish to become familiar with those modern methods of electrical measurement necessary wherever there is made any practical application of this agent.

In the course are included the measurement of Current, Resistance, Potential Difference, Electromotive Force, Quantity, Capacity, Mutual and Self Induction, Strength of Field, etc.

In the lecture room the theory of a given measurement is taken up; then the construction and calibration of the instrument used in the measurement are studied, the instrument being at hand for inspection; and finally, in the laboratory, the student calibrates, if necessary, and uses the instrument in making the measurement.

Examples of all of the principal instruments used in modern electrical methods are owned by this institution, and are available for the work of this course. Among them may be mentioned a Kelvin Composite Balance; a Siemens Electrodynamometer; a Weston Portable Ammeter; a vertical Magnet D'Arsonval Galvanometer with Shunt Box; a Differential D'Arsonval Galvanometer; a Queen Horizontal Magnet D'Arsonval Galvanometer; eight Kohlrausch Differential Galvanometers by Hartman and Braun; a Willyoung Thomson Astatic Galvanometer; a Willyoung Ballistic Galvanometer; two Rowland D'Arsonval Galvanometers with Ballistic Systems by Willyoung & Co.; an Ayrton Shunt Box; a Special Meter Bridge by Willyoung & Co.; a Queen Anthony Bridge and Resistance Set; two Standard B. A. Units by Elliot Brothers; a Crompton Potentiometer, station class, with Standard Resistances for Current Measurement, by Crompton & Co.; a Weston Portable Direct Voltmeter; a Weston Portable Alternating Current Voltmeter; a Marshall Standard One Microfarad Condenser; a variable Standard of Self Induction; and a Double Deflector Magnetometer.

The Text-books are Carhart and Patterson's Electrical Measurements, and Nichol's Laboratory Manual.

Three times a week, thirty-four weeks.   To count as a full course. Must be preceded by subjects B 1 (Physics) and C 1 (Analytic Mechanics).

MECHANICS.

PROFESSOR McNAIR.

An attempt is made in Mechanics to develop the essential principles, and to render the student proficient in applying them to practical rather than theoretical problems.   To this end a large number of problems are solved, which, so far as possible, are selected from machines or structures with which the student is already familiar, or the study of which he is subsequently to take up.

C 1.—Analytic Mechanics.

PROFESSOR McNAIR.

Church's Mechanics of Engineering, Parts I and II, Statics and Dynamics, is made the basis of this and the following course.

Subject C 1 is given three times a week for fourteen weeks, in the winter term.   Counts as two-fifths of a course.

It must be preceded by subject B 1 (Physics), and preceded by or accompanied with, subject A 5 (Calculus).

C 2.—Analytic Mechanics.

PROFESSOR McNAIR.

Subject C 2 continues the work begun in subject C 1 and is given three times a week, fourteen weeks, in the fall term.   Counts as two-fifths of a course.

It must be preceded by subject C 1 (Analytic Mechanics).

CHEMISTRY.

PROFESSOR KOENIG AND MR. BURRALL.

The instruction in chemistry is designed to excite in the student a love for experimentation and to train him in inductive thinking.   If this aim can be reached, or if it can only be approximated, it is believed that the gain to the student will be great, much greater than the accumulation of any num-

ber of facts might be to him.   For all the modern advancement in the subjugation of Nature's forces is owing to experiment, and we know from the autobiographical statements of
many inventors of genius, that they lost the labor of years
through the lack of training in properly correlating the
results of their experiments.

In carrying out the plan of this course it has been found necessary
and useful to abandon the use of text books altogether.   For no matter how such a text-book be written and arranged it will present to
the beginner the science of chemistry as a finished edifice, very
wonderful and very intricate in its details.   The study of it thus becomes of necessity mechanical ; the memory is loaded with facts
and figures, and the thinking faculties become numbed rather
than quickened.   Experience of years has shown, that even a set of
notes will have a similar effect on the student.   The best results are
obtained when the teacher builds up the science from experiment, by
making suggestions leading the student to experiment on similar
bodies in his own way.   In this course there are no definitions to
start with of atoms, molecules and structural formulæ.   By
means of a proper selection of common bodies, the student not only
discovers the qualitative and quantitative relations of matter, the
simple and compound bodies, but he reveals his very reagents as
he goes along; he comes to compare and correlate the phenomena;
he finally classifies the phenomena, and works up to the evolution of
their laws.   It is not claimed that any and all brain organizations
will become thinking instruments under this system.   But it is
claimed that it will greatly stimulate and improve existing faculties.

F 1.—General Experimental Chemistry.

PROFESSOR KOENIG AND MR. BURRALL.

Nine hours a week for twenty-eight weeks; one recitation, two
lectures, and six hours of laboratory work each week; to count as a
four-fifths course.

The instruction in this subject covers the following ground :

First. Experiments with the common metals, their action when
heated in air, and when heated in the absence of air; discovery of
the composite nature of air: a life sustaining part (ozone); a life des-
troying part (azote).   Specific gravity of azote by direct weight and

of ozone by calculation. The increase in weight of metals when heated in air, discovery of ozonites (oxides). Ratio of increase. Burning of sulphur in air, discovery of a gaseous sulphur ozonite possessing an acid taste; change of the name ozone into oxygen. Restoration of the original metals from the ozonites by the action of charcoal; hence the notion of elements or simple bodies. Action of the common metals at a red heat upon steam, the forming of bodies similar to the oxides and of an inflammable gas; discovery of hydro· gen and its properties. Proving the identity of water-oxides with air oxides, hence the conclusion that water is a combination of oxy· gen with hydrogen.

Second (1.) The study of copperas or vitriol. Under the action of heat it yields an oily liquid—the oil of vitriol. Correlation of this body with the sulphur oxide. With the oil of vitriol the student has gained now a powerful reagent, but he does not know, and should not be told at this stage of his development, that this oil of vitriol is $H^1 SO^4$. The body is for his purposes simply oil of vitriol for which the symbol O^v may stand.

(2.) Study of potash, soda ash, limestone. Their action with heat, with heat and charcoal, with oil of vitriol. Their action upon each other; of burnt lime upon potash. Discovery of potassium, sodium, calcium, and of caustic soda, caustic potash and of a non life-sus· taining, heavy, slightly sour gas, lime gas (not CO^2). Alkaline re· action, acid reaction; the notion of hydroxides, of acid hydroxides and of basic hydroxides.

(3.) Study of common salt, the mother-liquor salt and the varec salt. The spirits of salt. Decomposition into a green gas and hydro· gen. Chlorine probably a simple body. Bromine, iodine, fluorine. Action of chlorine upon hydrogen in equal volumes. The theory of combinations by volumes; the notion of *molecules* and *atoms:* of molecular weights and atomic weights. The action of chlorine upon the common metals—the chlorides, their properties. Reproduction of salt by acting with spirits of salt upon soda-ash—hence the identity of the metal in salt and soda-ash. Atomic weight of sodium and potassium by experiment.

(4.) The study of nitre. Action in heat. Yields a gas which sus· tains combustion and animal breathing. Identification of this gas with the ozone or oxygen of the air. The notion of super or per· oxides. The spirits of nitre. Its action upon the metals. Discovery

of nitrogen and identification of this gas with the azote of the air.
The several oxides of nitrogen. Nitrogen chloride. Action of zinc·
and caustic potash upon nitre. Discovery of a gaseous alkaline body.
Ammonia. Study of its properties and combinations; ammonium
salts.

(5.) The study of sulphur. The oxides and chlorides of sulphur.
The manufacture of hydrogen sulphate.

(6.) Discovery of carbon by decomposing the limestone gas with
sodium. Identification of this body with the substance of charcoal,
of mineral coal, of plant and animal structures. The mineral oils,
the natural gases. The fats, alcohols, ethers, albumenoid bodies.
Discovery of cyanogen and its principal compounds.

(7.) The study of bone-ash and discovery of phosphorus-oxides and
hydroxides of phosphorus.

(9.) The study of borax and quartz; boron and silicon.

(10.) Theoretical deductions. Electrolysis. Thermo-chemistry.
Structural and stereographic formulæ.

The students are required to take notes during the lectures, and
they must keep a detailed account of their own observations and deductions in the laboratory. The term standing is derived from these
notes and from the recitations, which are held once a week.

F 2.—*Blowpipe Analysis.*

PROFESSOR KOENIG AND MR. BURRALL.

Twelve hours per week for six weeks. Two lectures, one recitation and nine hours of laboratory work each week. To count for
one-fifth of a course.

This is a short course in Qualitative Analysis in which preference
is given to reactions in the igneous way, so that students may be
enabled to take the course in Mineralogy with full benefit.

Brush's tables and Landauer's small treatise are referred to.

To be preceded by subject F 1 (General Chemistry).

F 3.—*Qualitative Analysis.*

PROFESSOR KOENIG AND MR. BURRALL.

Nine hours a week for twenty-eight weeks. Two lectures, one
recitation, and six hours of laboratory work each week.

To count for four-fifths of a course.

This course comprises the chemistry of the metals. The students are to make the salts of the metals and then compare the differences existing in the same classes, whereby they are enabled to understand the reasons upon which the schemes for separation are based. The use of the spectroscope is introduced. More intricate blowpipe reactions than those taken in subject F 2 (Blowpipe Analysis), such as the separation of manganese, iron, cobalt, nickel and copper, in the form of arsenides, are studied.

Elliott's tables are used as a guide.

Must be preceded by F 1 (General Chemistry), and F 2 (Blowpipe Analysis).

F 4.—*Quantitative Analysis.*

PROFESSOR KOENIG AND MR. BURRALL.

Twelve hours a week for thirty-four weeks. Two lectures, one recitation, and seven hours of laboratory work a week. To count as a full course.

The course opens with volumetric analysis: acidimetry, alkalimetry and permanganate methods. volumetric analysis of limestones. Analysis of copper ores: gravimetric, volumetric, colorimetric and electrolytic methods. Analysis of iron ores. In the soluble portion there are determined volumetrically, the elements iron, manganese, phosphorus. In the insoluble portion there are determined gravimetrically: SiO^2, TiO^2, Cr^2O^3, Al^2O^3, Fe^2O^3, MnO^2, CaO, MgO. The material for this analysis is prepared and mixed artificially so that all the bodies appear in weighable proportions. In separate portions are determined sulphur (by fusion with nitre and sodium carbonate), carbon dioxide and water. It will be seen that the analysis covers all the operations of silicate analysis, except the alkalies, and therefore a separate analysis of furnace slag is not needed, to teach its methods.

Analysis of a matte containing arsenic, antimony, tin, bismuth, silver, copper, lead, cadmium, zinc, iron and sulphur. Analysis of pig iron for graphite, combined carbon, manganese, phosphorus and sulphur.

Analysis of steel. Determination of carbon by the copper, ammonium chloride, wet and dry combustion, and colorimetry process; manganese by colorimetry; phosphorus by molybdic solution and titration with permanganate solution; sulphur by bromine method; and finally determination of silicon. The lectures [cover a more extended range of analytical methods, but the students are not required to complete any work aside from that given above. Fresenius's Quantitative Analysis is used as a book of reference. Professor Koenig's notes also are followed in the work.

Must be preceded by F 3 (Qualitative Analysis).

F 5.—*Advanced Quantitative Analysis.*

PROFESSOR KOENIG.

Twelve hours a week for thirty-four weeks. One lecture, one recitation and eight hours of laboratory work a week. To count as one full course.

This course embraces: the analysis of fats, oils and soaps; the extraction and estimation of poisons; the analy-is of fertilizers. the analysis of explosives; the estimation and separation of the rare elements in minerals; analysis of samarskite; nitrometry, and oxygenometry. Theoretical chemistry.

Must be preceded by, or accompanied with, F 4 (Quantitative Analysis).

F 6.—*Synthetic Chemistry.*

PROFESSOR KOENIG.

Eighteen hours a week for thirty-four weeks. To count as two full courses. Candidates must have completed subjects F 4 (Quantitative Analysis), F 5 (Advanced Quantitative Analysis) and W 2 (Mineralogy).

This course is intended as an amplification of the course in General Chemistry, or to cultivate the field of original discovery and invention, or to produce with known reactions a desired commercial result. Students who wish to take this course must have shown by their previous work that they possess the required originality of mind and practical sense. To all others it is a waste of time. The students are required to read much chemical literature and to discuss their reading in a seminar to be appointed from time to time. The subjects of experimentation may either originate with the student or may be suggested by the professor.

The student must keep a minute account of all his work, in arranging the apparatus, as well as in the actual experiment, whether the latter be a failure or a success,

G. METALLURGY.

PROFESSOR KOENIG AND MR. BURRALL.

G 1.—*Assaying.*

PROFESSOR KOENIG AND MR. BURRALL.

One hundred and forty-four hours as follows:

Twenty-four lectures, once a week, and one hundred and twenty hours of laboratory work.

To count as two-fifths of a course.

The laboratory work may be done at any time during the winter term or during the first six weeks of the summer term, provided that the student puts in at least four hours a day of consecutive work.

The furnace assaying comprises: silver ores by scorification and crucible methods; gold ores by roasting and crucible fusion, by nitre in crucible fusion, by lead oxide in crucible fusion; lead ores by iron precipitation and by roasting; native copper concentrates and slimes, by crucible fusion; tin ores by German method; by potassium cyanide method; by Professor Koenig's method (reduction in hydrogen and the loss of weight giving percentage of tin, after having previously removed all reducible and volatile bodies by roasting and extraction with boiling hydrogen chloride).

The assaying in the humid way comprises: bullion assaying; titration according to Gay-Lussac, and Volhard; parting by quartation; zinc ores by the potassium ferrocyanide method; lead ores by Professor Koenig's universal method.

The ore samples used in this assay work are mostly artificial mineral mixtures most carefully prepared, so that the difficulties and losses which are inherent in the different methods may be fully comprehended by the student.

Must be preceded by subject F 3 (Qualitative Analysis).

G 2.—*Metallurgy.*

PROFESSOR KOENIG.

Three times a week for thirty-four weeks, or two lectures and one recitation a week. To count as one full course.

It is the intention that the student acquire in this course the principles and practice of modern methods in the extraction of the technically useful metals. For those who intend to follow metallurgy as

a specialty it is to be the broad foundation upon which to raise their
further education.   Others will through it be enabled to read understandingly the technical advances in the current literature.

The instruction covers the following subjects:

(1.) Fuel: gas versus oils and solid coal, its technical and economical
aspects; essential and unessential parts in gas generator; smokeless
combustion.   Coking.   The physical and chemical qualtities of pig
iron.   Relations between the compostion of iron ores and the resulting pig iron.   The chemistry of the blast furnace.   Calculation of
cinder or slag compositions.   Influence of the profile, cross sections
and height of the blast furnace upon the qualtities and quantity of
the product.

(2.) Dry puddling.   The Bessemer process.   The Thomas-Gilchrist
process.

(3.) Wet puddling;   the common puddling furnace; the rotary
puddlers; the open hearth process.   Washing out of phosphorus.
Washing out of sulphur by manganese.   Crucible steel; cement steel;
Mushet steel, chrome steel; phosphor steel.   Theory of the temper-
ing process   Malleable cast iron.   Ferro-silicon in steel-casting.
The Harvey process.   Aluminum in melting and casting wrought
iron.

(4.) The metallurgy of lead, copper, silver, gold.   The Muldener-
Huette Process.   Desilverization of work lead by zinc and aluminum.
Cupellation.   The refining of copper matte.   Separation of copper,
silver and gold by electrolysis of the matte, or of the black copper
by Ziervogel's process.

(5.) The leaching process: sulphate leaching; brine leaching;
copper—sodium hyposulphite leaching, potassium cyanide leaching
and other chemical possibilities.   Chlorination in the dry way by
Stettefeldt's furnace; by Bruckner's furnace and its modifications.
In the wet way according to Plattner, Meass and Koenig.   Amalgamation.   Refining of crude bullion; parting of gold and silver.

The metallurgy of zinc and aluminum.

To be preceded by F 3 (Qualitative Analysis) and preceded by, or
accompanied with, F 4 (Quantitative Analysis) and W 2 (Mineralogy).

G 3.—*Metallurgical Experimentation.*

PROFESSOR KOENIG.

Nine hours a week for thirty-four weeks. To count as one full course. There are no lectures in this course; the work is wholly experimental. Students must have completed subjects F 4 (Quantitative Analysis) G 1 (Assaying), G 2 (Metallurgy), and W 2 (Mineralogy).

The student may choose among the following subjects:

(1). Comparative extraction of gold ores by amalgamation, by chlorination, and by the smelting process; that is to say, to prove by experiment which of the foregoing methods will yield the highest percentage of gold from a given gold ore.

(2). Comparative extraction of silver ores by amalgamation or leaching.

(3). Electrolysis of ores or secondary products either in aqueous or igneous liquefaction.

(4). The influence of small quantities of negative elements upon the physical properties of metals and metallic alloys.

(5). Microscopic study of metals and alloys.

After the student has chosen the subject of his investigation, he will be required to read all the more recent literature upon the subject, and to extract, condense and digest the same. The Professor will discuss the methods of investigation with the student and a plan will be fixed upon as to the kind and sequence of the experiments. The experience which a student may gain in this work is of great value to him in conducting a testing laboratory and in taking upon himself the superintendence of any metallurgical plant.

G 4.—*Special Metallurgy and Metallurgical Designing.*

PROFESSOR KOENIG AND MR. BURRALL.

Nine hours a week for thirty-four weeks. To count a full course.

Candidates for this course must have completed subjects F 4 (Quantitative Analysis), G 1 (Assaying), G 2 (Metallurgy), L 4 (Graphical Statics), M 3 (Mechanism), M 5 (Mechanical Engineering), and W 2 (Mineralogy).

One lecture a week on special metallurgical subjects. The practical part of the work comes under two heads:

1. The student is directed to analyze sectional drawings of fur-

naces, in regard to number, shape and dimensions of parts, and their relation to the temperature and chemical action of the solids and gases which come in contact with them.

2. Designing of a complete plant for the reduction of a given ore and certain topographical features of the locality. Estimation of the required power; arrangement of the machinery as to economy of space and economy of manual labor in the successive operations; estimated cost of the plant.

L. DRAWING.

PROFESSORS KIDWELL AND SPERR AND MR. MOORE AND MR. HOULE.

The instruction in Drawing is designed to give special prominence to such branches of the subject as are of most value to the engineer, hence perspective, shades and shadows, etc., are excluded, and all the time is devoted to mechanical and topographical drawing, and their applications. The following schedule shows details of courses:

L 1.—*Mechanical Drawing.*

MR. MOORE.

(a). DESCRIPTION, PREPARATION AND TESTING OF DRAWING INSTRUMENTS AND MATERIALS: Graphical solution of geometrical problems. Descriptive Geometry. Projections on right and oblique planes; intersections of lines, surfaces, and solids; plans, elevations and sections; isometric and cabinet projection.

Anthony's Elements of Mechanical Drawing.

Lettering; Soennecken's system of round writing. Roman, Italic, Gothic, block, and free hand lettering.

(b). CONSTRUCTION DRAWING: Making of complete working drawings of various details of machine work and timber construction, from rough sketches, or from the model. Tracing and blue printing.

Anthony's Machine Drawing is used as a text-book.

(c). FREE-HAND SKETCHING: Making working sketches, with all necessary views, sections, dimensions, etc., of pieces of machinery or timber constructions assigned by the instructor. This work must be done by the student outside of the class hours, in a book of sectioned paper devoted exclusively to this subject, and turned in for inspection on the date set by the instructor.

Eighteen hours a week for eight weeks and nine hours a week for twenty-six weeks. Subject L 1 must be taken as a whole, and counts as one full course.

Instruments and Materials Needed by Students.

For the convenience of those who desire to purchase their drawing outfit before coming to Houghton, the following list has been prepared.

The articles called for in this list are necessary for a proper prosecution of the course, and care should therefore be taken to get the exact instruments specified, or others of *equal grade*. Those without experience in judging such material are strongly advised to adhere strictly to these lists. Experience has shown that almost invariably when the list has been disregarded the result has been that inferior instruments have been purchased, at a greater cost than necessary to obtain the quality here called for. *Instruments not up to standard will not be allowed in the Drawing Room*, as they will not give satisfaction, and will waste the time of both instructors and students.

Instruments to be got by those who wish to take the work in Mechanical Drawing, and the subsequent course in Machine Design.

One 5-inch Alteneder improved right line pen, or No. 695, Keuffel-Esser 5¼-inch drawing pen.

One 5¼-inch Alteneder dividers (pivot joint) with hair spring, pen, pencil, points, and extension bar.

One 3-inch Alteneder bow pen, or No. 486 Keuffel and Esser 3¼-inch bow pen and needle point.

One 3-inch bow pencil, or No. 487 Keuffel and Esser 3¼-inch spring bow pencil and needle point.

One 3-inch bow dividers, or No. 485 Keuffel and Esser spring bow dividers.

One 6-inch brass protractor.

One 12-inch triangular scale, divided into twelfths.

One T square, 30-inch blade.

One 8-inch 30 x 60 degree rubber or amber triangle.

One 8-inch 45 degree rubber or amber triangle.

One K. & E. curve, No. 1820–20.

One dozen German silver thumb tacks, ⅜ diam,

One bottle Keuffel and Esser's Columbia indelible black drawing ink.

One bottle Keuffel and Esser's Columbia indelible carmine drawing ink.

Two rubber *pencil* erasers.

One piece Artist's gum ¼ x ¼ x 3 inches.

Three Faber's artist's 6H pencils.

One bottle paste with brush.

One medium-sized sponge, fine quality.

One Arkansas stone, about ¼ x ¼ x 3 inches.

Six cabinet saucers, about 2½ inches diameter.

One piece chamois skin, about 12 x 18 inches.

One Soennecken Round Writing Copy Book, and a box of selected pens, with holder.

One-half pan each, moist colors, as follows: Prussian blue, carmine, gamboge, Payne's gray.

Three dozen No. 1 Spencerian pens, with holder.

A black enameled tin box, 13 x 8 x 4 inches, with lock, in which instruments can be kept, is strongly recommended.

A drawing board and two sable brushes will also be required.

Owing to liability of getting sizes that will not answer, these latter should be purchased in Houghton.

L 2.—*Topographical Drawing.*

PROFESSOR SPERR AND MR. HOULE.

This subject precedes the work in Surveying, and is designed to teach the student by means of lectures and practical work the art of lettering, plotting by protraction and rectangular co-ordinates, making scales and topographical signs.

Twelve hours a week, for six weeks. To count as a one-fifth course.

L 3.—*Topographical Drawing (Mapping).*

PROFESSOR SPERR AND MR. HOULE.

This subject follows the work in Surveying, and the student makes his maps from the notes taken in the field by himself.

Twelve hours a week, for six weeks. To count as a one-fifth course. To be preceded by Q 1 (Surveying).

Instruments to be procured by those who wish to take Topographical Drawing.

One 5-inch Alteneder improved right line pen.

One Alteneder swivel curve pen.

One 5⅝-inch Alteneder dividers (pivot joint) with hair spring, pen, pencil points, and extension bar.

One 3-inch Alteneder bow pen.

One 3-inch bow pencil.

One 3-inch bow dividers.

One 6-inch brass protractor.

One 12-inch triangular, decimal scale.

One T-square, 30-inch blade.

One 8-inch, 30 x 60 degree rubber or amber triangle.

One 8-inch, 45 degree rubber or amber triangle.

One K. & E. Curve, No. 1820 1–6.

One dozen German silver thumb tacks, 3–8 diam.

One bottle Higgin's waterproof carmine ink.

One bottle Higgin's waterproof India ink,

Two rubber pencil erasers.

One piece artist's gum 1-2 x 1-2 x 3 inches.

Three Faber's artist's 6H pencils.

One Arkansas stone, about 1-4 x 3-4 x 3 inches.

One piece chamois skin, about 12 x 18 inches.

One-half pan moist Prussian blue.

Three dozen No. 1 Spencerian pens, with holder.

A black enameled tin box, 18 x 8 x 4, with lock, in which instruments can be kept, is strongly recommended.

A drawing board and two sable brushes will also be required. *Owing to liability of getting sizes that will not answer, these latter should be purchased in Houghton.*

L 4.—*Graphical Statics.*

MR. HOULE.

Nine hours a week for fourteen weeks. To count as two-fifths of a course.

This subject is designed to teach the theory of the graphical analysis of stresses in structures, and leads up to the subject of Engineering Design and Construction (L 5). The instruction is given by lectures, following Greene's Roof Trusses, although the principal part of the time is spent in the Drawing Room analyzing trusses, using the lectures and text-book as guides.

This subject must be preceded by L 1 (Mechanical Drawing) and by C 2 (Analytic Mechanics).

7

L 5.—*Engineering Design and Construction.*

PROFESSOR SPERR.

The work in designing is applied to the shaft head-frames, rock houses, engine and boiler houses, bridges, trestles, etc., of the mining plants considered under the subject R 4 (Mining Engineering).

A general outline of the work is as follows:

1. The general requirements of the structure.
2. Drawing the general plans.
3. The materials best adapted to the various purposes.
4. Strength of materials.
5. Methods of construction.
6. Making detailed drawings, bills of material, and estimates of cost.
7. Synopsis of the law of contracts.
8. Drawing up specifications.
9. Letting contracts.
10. Superintending the construction.

Nine hours a week, twenty weeks. To count as three-fifths of a course. To be preceded by subjects L 4 (Graphical Statics) and R 4 (Mining Engineering).

L 6.—*Machine Design.*

PROFESSOR KIDWELL AND MR. MOORE.

Determination of proper proportions for various minor machine details, such as screws, bolts, nuts, keys, and cotters. Pipes and joints, for gas, water and steam. Power-transmitting machinery:—shafts, pulleys, clutches, hangers; belt, rope, and wire rope gearing; toothed gearing. Designing of engine and boiler details, thereby applying in actual design the principles laid down in subjects M 5, M 7 and M 8. Low and Bevis' Manual of Machine Drawing and Design, and Unwin's Machine Design. One hour lecture, and eleven hours in Drawing Room, per week, twenty-six weeks. To count as one full course. To be preceded by subjects M 5 (Mechanical Engineering) and M 6 (Testing Materials of Engineering) and accompanied with subjects M 7 (Valve gears) and M 8 (Thermodynamics).

———

In addition to the regular courses in Drawing and Designing, numerous applications of the subject are obtained in connection with the other courses; the students are required to prepare w orking plans and sections of a mine from their own survey, make a map and profile of a railroad surveyed by themselves, and to draw sections, diagrams, maps, etc., in their geological field work.

Much personal instruction is given in connection with all the above mentioned courses. In addition to the regular lectures and recitations the professors or some of their assistants are present in the Drawing Room during the hours prescribed for practical work, to give advice and personal instruction to those who need it.

Those who desire to enter as special students to take Drawing only. or Drawing in conjunction with some other subject, may do so, provided the professor in charge of the course is convinced of their competency to profit by the instruction. To take up Drawing with success, *Plane, Solid and Spherical Geometry* should have been mastered. In case these subjects have not been completed, the professor under whose direction the student is working will prescribe as a necessary part of the work, the courses in Mathematics which should precede the work in Drawing.

Draughting Room and Equipment.

The Draughting Room is located in the new Engineering Hall, and is 25 x 97 feet, with a 28 x 84 foot annex containing instructors' offices, blue print room, lavatory, etc. The room is on the north side of the building, thereby insuring perfect freedom from shadows at any part of the day. It is provided with electric lights so arranged as to permit night work with the minimum of discomfort. The drawing tables have been so planned that each student has private lockers for his materials, and a rack for his board and T-square. There are two blue printing frames, capacity 3 x 4 feet, a number of smaller frames, for both tracings and photographic negatives, two large vats for developing prints, drying rack, etc. There are also cut models of pumps, injectors, valve gears, structural material, wire ropes, drawings of machinery, buildings, models of trestles and docks, etc., used as illustrative material in the various courses.

M. MECHANICAL ENGINEERING.

PROFESSOR KIDWELL AND MR. MOORE.

Since the successful and economical operation of any mine depends so largely upon the judicious selection, proper de-

73641

sign, and skilful operation of its power plant and general
machinery, the Mining School offers a course in Mechanical
Engineering which covers all the ground necessary fully to
prepare the student to take up such work.   But as the fundamental principles of Mechanical Engineering are the same,
whether the application be made to Mining, or any other industry, it has been possible so to design the course that it
gives the student a thorough preparation, and points out to
him the methods of study and observation to be followed
after graduation, should he decide to take up *any* branch of
Mechanical Engineering as his specialty.

Throughout the whole course the attempt is made to present
clearly the theory underlying each part of the subject, and then to
fix the theory by practical exercises, either in the Mechanical Laboratory, or in the course in Designing.   The following subjects are
now offered:

M 1.—*Properties of Materials of Engineering.*

MR. MOORE.

General qualities of metals; cast and wrought iron, steel, copper,
brass and bronzes; lime, cement, concrete and brick; paints, etc.;
timber, and cordage.

Three times a week, twenty weeks, to count as a three-fifths
course.   To be preceded by subjects B 1 (Physics) and F 1 (General
Chemistry).

The course includes a discussion of methods of manufacture of the
more important materials (except such information as comes within
the province of the course in Metallurgy); forms in which these
materials appear in the market; their adaptation to the purposes of
the engineer; methods of preserving materials from corrosion and decay; etc.   South Kensington Notes on Building Construction, Vol.
III.   The course is supplemented with practical work in testing, for
details of which see subject M 6 (Testing Materials of Engineering).

M 2.—*Shop Practice.*

MR. WASS AND MR. SHIELDS.

Forty-five hours per week, eleven weeks.   To count as two full
courses.   To be preceded by subjects L 1 (Mechanical Drawing) and

M 1 (Properties of Materials), except in case of pupils who enter for this course alone.

The classes meet every week day, Saturday excepted, and work nine hours per day, including lectures and practical work. The entire shop practice is to be taken as a whole and no credit can be given for the completion of any part of it alone.

Instruction.—The instruction is largely personal, and each student is advanced according to his proficiency, irrespective of the progress made by other members of the class. In the Machine Shop, practice is given in chipping, filing, scraping, general vise work, pipe fitting, and use of machine tools. In the Pattern Shop, a course in bench work, making joints, turning, etc., precedes actual practice in pattern making. To familiarize the student with the use of actual working drawings, nearly all work done in both shops is to blue prints made in the drawing room. In order that the students may learn real shop methods, as used at the present day, the instructors who assist the professor in charge are men who have had a number of years' practical experience in the work they are expected to teach here.

The instruction here followed is calculated to teach the student, from the very start, the necessity of close and accurate work. Each man, as soon as he has had a little preliminary practice, is put on some piece of work *intended for actual use*, and held responsible for the results. This plan is here considered superior to the others in common use, whereby the work is confined to practice pieces which end up in the scrap pile. No man will take extra care in fitting such pieces, nor does a student regard it as a matter of any consequence whether the work is got out to exact size or not, if it is to be thrown away in the end.

To familiarize the student with the operation and care of machinery, each one will be detailed from time to time to fire the boiler, run the engine, clean and oil the machinery, and to perform such other duties of this nature as the instructor in charge may assign him.

All work done in the shops is considered as the property of the school. No student is allowed to take up any work not assigned to him by the instructor.

Shop Equipment.—The equipment of the shops has been carefully selected. The machine shop contains in addition to the necessary work benches, a 24-inch by 16-foot New Haven Tool Co.'s engine lathe with power cross-feed and compound rest, a 12-inch by 5-foot Prentice engine lathe, a 14-inch by 6-foot Lodge and Davis engine lathe with power cross-feed, a 13-inch by 5-foot Putnam engine lathe, two hand lathes, a 34-inch automatic feed Blaisdell drill press, a 20-inch Lodge and Davis drill press, a 16-inch Gould and Eberhardt shaper, a 10-inch Boynton and Plummer traverse head shaper, a Whitcomb planer, of capacity 8x2x2 feet, a 20x20-inch x 4-foot planer, by Wm. Sellers & Co., a Brainard No. 4 Universal milling machine, one wet and two dry emery grinders, a challenge buffer, a Q. and C. power hack saw, and several smaller machine tools.

The assortment of chucks, taps, drills, reamers and general tools is very complete. For practice in pipe fitting a separate bench has been provided; a complete set of pipe tools, and a supply of pipe and fittings up to two inches inclusive are in stock.

The pattern shop contains two Clement wood lathes, one Reed wood lathe, three wood lathes built in the shops, a pattern maker's lathe to swing five feet, a 33-inch Fay band saw, Beach jig saw, emery wheels and grindstones, Pedrick and Ayer gouge grinder, steam glue heaters, a very complete assortment of hand tools and appliances, and the necessary work benches and vises.

Each student, in each shop, has a separate work bench, set of hand tools, and locker, for which he will be held responsible. Any damage to tools, or other part of the equipment, beyond wear and tear by legitimate use, is charged to the student accountable for it, and must be paid for at once.

Each shop has its own separate tool room, in which the check system of accounting for tools is used, thus familiarizing the student with its operation by actual practice.

Power for the shops is furnished by an 8 x 24 Reynolds Corliss engine, taking steam from the Stirling boiler. Both shops are lighted with electricity, the current being obtained from the school plant, or from the mains of the local Electric Co., when the school dynamos are not in operation.

Charges.—There are no tuition charges, but each student is required to purchase one machinist's hammer, all hand files, emery cloth, a two-foot boxwood rule, waste, and to pay for stock used whenever any work has been spoiled through neglect to obey the orders of the instructor.

Engineering Hall.—The work shops, mechanical laboratories, electrical engineering laboratories, and draughting room, are now located in Engineering Hall, a new building especially designed for shop and laboratory purposes. It is fully equipped with lavatories, lockers, and everything necessary for the students' convenience and comfort when at work. It is lighted throughout with electricity.

Special Students.—Those who desire to take shop work only, and devote all their time to it, are admitted as special students on the following conditions. No student shall be less than 17 years of age. Students between the age of seventeen and twenty must present evidence of having spent at least two years in some reputable high school or academy. Persons 20 years of age or over may be admitted as special students, without having attended a high school, provided they give evidence of being able to follow the work with profit. Those desiring admission as special students should apply directly to Professor Kidwell, and at the earliest possible date, so that due provision can be made for them. Special students have to make the regular $25.00 deposit, the return of which is subject to the following regulations: *No person will be admitted as a special student in shopwork, except with the distinct understanding that in addition to being subject to all the general regulations of the school, he must be in attendance up to the close of the course, otherwise his $25.00 deposit shall be forfeited. Students who are suspended or expelled are included in this rule.* Those who take the entire course will be allowed to withdraw their deposit when the shop work is completed. The course is free to all who are qualified to take it, and in pursuance of its general policy the Mining School is glad to admit, and assist all who are competent, and seriously determined to avail themselves of its advantages; those who fail to apply themselves diligently to the work, and who show that their presence here is of no advantage to themselves, or injurious to others, will be promptly excluded from the course.

Such a special course cannot be credited to any student who later on decides to work for a degree, unless courses L 1 (Mechanical Drawing) and M 1 (Properties of Materials) preceded the shop work.

M 3.—*Mechanism.*

MR. MOORE.

Laws of motion, linkwork, cams, teeth of wheels, wheels in trains, aggregate motion, miscellaneous problems in applied mechanics. Goodeve's Elements of Mechanism. Three times a week, fourteen weeks. To count as a two-fifths course. To be preceded by subjects C 1 (Analytic Mechanics) and L 1 (Mechanical Drawing), and preceded by, or accompanied with, subject C 2 (Analytic Mechanics).

M 4.—*Mechanics of Materials.*

MR. MOORE.

Application of the principles of statics to rigid bodies; elasticity and resistance of materials; cantilevers; simple, restrained and continuous beams; bodies of uniform strength; riveting; torsion of shafts; combined stresses; resilience; apparent and true stresses, computation of proper sizes and proportions of beams, columns, shafts, flat plates, etc. Merriman's Mechanics of Materials. Three times a week, thirty-four weeks. To count as one full course. To be preceded by subject M 1 (Properties of Materials) and preceded by, or accompanied with, C 2 (Analytic Mechanics).

M 5.—*Mechanical Engineering.*

MR. MOORE.

Three times a week, thirty-four weeks. To count for a full course. The instruction is divided as follows:

(a) The STEAM ENGINE.—Description of the various styles and types of engines, such as ordinary slide valve, Corliss, Westinghouse, Willans, etc.; description of compound, triple, and quadruple expansion engines. General arrangement of parts, and discussion of various engine details, such as cylinders, piston and rods; stuffing boxes, cross heads, cranks and crank shafts, etc. Elementary course, leading up to subjects L 6 (Machine Designs), M 7 (Valve Gears) and M 8 (Thermodynamics). Text-book used: Whitham's Constructive Steam Engineering, together with manufacturer's trade circulars. Three hours a week, five weeks.

(b) STEAM BOILERS. Fuel and combustion; representative types of boilers, with description and discussion of leading exponents of each type: proportions of boilers, heating surface, grate surface, tube area, strength of shell heads, stays, etc.; boiler details, grate bars, mechanical stokers, settings, breechings, chimneys, etc. Leads up to subject L 6 (Machine Design). Whitham's Constructive Steam

Engineering, together with lectures. Three hours a week, thirteen weeks.

(c) ENGINEERING APPLIANCES. Steam gauges; lubricators; safety valves; reducing valves; steam traps; feed heaters and purifiers; steam separators; grease extractors; damper regulators; surface, jet, and ejector condensors; steam pipe and fittings; boiler and pipe coverings; etc. Taught principally from manufacturer's catalogues. Three hours a week five weeks.

(d) PUMPS AND PUMPING MACHINERY. Discussion of pump details such as pistons; plungers, and methods of packing them; size of suction and delivery pipes, air and vacuum chambers, etc. Types of pump, hydraulic, force pump, crank and fly wheel, direct acting, duplex, compound and triple expansion pumps. Fire, mine, rotary, centrifugal, and high duty pumps. Duty trials of pumps. Barr's Pumping Machinery, and Whitham's Constructive Steam Engineering. Three hours a week, eleven weeks.

Subject M 5 must be taken as a whole, and counts as one full course. To be preceded by subjects L 1 (Mechanical Drawing) and M 2 (Shop Practice), and preceded by or accompanied with subjects M 3 (Mechanism) and M 4 (Mechanics of Materials).

M 6.—Testing Materials of Engineering.

PROFESSOR KIDWELL AND MR. MOORE.

Tensile, compressive, transverse, torsional, and impact tests of metals and timber. Tensile tests of cordage, and iron and steel wire rope. Transverse, compressive, and absorption tests of stone and brick. Tensile, compressive, cross breaking, and specific gravity tests of cement, also tests for fineness, time of setting, and constancy of volume. Tests of lubricating oils, including density, viscosity, fire test, cold test, wearing qualities and coefficient of friction under various speeds and loads on journal. Lectures and mimeographed notes. Forty-five hours a week, or five hours class room and thirty hours laboratory work a week, five weeks. To count as a full course. To be preceded by subject M 4 (Mechanics of Materials).

Laboratory for Testing of Materials.—The equipment of this laboratory is as follows: One 100,000 lb. Riehlé Machine, fitted for making tensile, compressive, cross breaking, and shearing tests, (special appliances have also been provided to enable this machine to make shearing tests on wood, and transverse tests on specimens up to nine feet in length); an autographic torsional testing machine, an Ashcroft oil tester driven by a separate electro-motor, a 2,000 lb. Olsen cement testing machine, with tools for tensile, compressive and transverse tests; a Henning electro-contact micrometer for measurement of extension, an Olsen electric-contact compression micrometer; a deflectometer, a Brown and Sharp Vernier caliper, and several screw micrometers; two Troemner balances, viscosometers, etc.

Those having materials to be tested should make application to the professor in charge of the department, and make definite arrangements with him for the precise work they desire to have done.

M 7.— *Valve Gears.*

PROFESSOR KIDWELL.

Kinematics of the plain slide valve, link motions, double valve gears, radial and drop cut-off gears. Peabody's Valve Gears for the Steam Engine. Twice a week, twenty-six weeks. To count as a one-half course. Must be preceded by subject M 5 (Mechanical Engineering) and accompanied with subject L 6 (Machine Design).

M 8. — *Thermodynamics.*

PROFESSOR KIDWELL.

Its application to steam, gas and air engines; air compressors, rock drills, and refrigerating machines. Tabulation and discussion of steam engine and boiler tests. Peabody's Thermodynamics of the Steam Engine. Twice a week, twenty-six weeks, to count as one-half a course. To be preceded by subject M 5 (Mechanical Engineering.)

M 9.—*Mechanical Engineering: Laboratory Practice.*

PROFESSOR KIDWELL AND ASSISTANTS.

Experimental work in the Mechanical Laboratory; determination of heating value of fuels; quality of steam; use of steam engine indicator, Prony brake, and other dynamometers; standardizing of indicators, steam gauges, etc.; complete tests of engines, boilers and pumps. Peabody's Thermodynamics of the Steam Engine, Barr's Pumping Machinery, and mimeographed notes and forms. Five hours recitation and thirty hours laboratory work per week, eleven weeks. To count as two full courses. Must be preceded by subjects

L 6 (Machine Design), M 7 (Valve Gears) and M 8 (Thermodynamics).

This course is intended to give the student ample opportunity to verify practically the principles laid down in the preceding courses. Each student will be required to set up his own apparatus, and in many cases to design and build appliances for any special work on hand.

Equipment.—The power plant contains one 58 H. P. Stirling water-tube boiler, two 40 H. P. steel return tubular boilers, one 8x24 Reynolds Corliss Engine in shops, an 8x12 Buckeye engine in dynamo room, a 9x9 N. Y. safety vertical slide valve engine in the stamp mill, a 5x5 horizontal slide valve engine in laboratory for testing materials, and one 50 H. P. Wheeler surface condenser, with Worthington air and circulating pump. Of the minor apparatus there is now in stock one Tabor indicator, one Crosby indicator, one Hine and Robertson indicator, eight polar planimeters, ten of Greene's standard thermometers for calorimetric work, calorimeters of the following kinds—barrel, continuous, superheating, throttling, and separator,— Heath's stop-watch speed counter, Tabor speed counter, Schaeffer and Bundenburg tachometer, lazy tongs, Hine and Robertson reducing motion, draught gauges, Ashcroft boiler test pump and gauge, gauges for use with water or steam, one Shaw's standard mercurial column gauge tester, one gauge tester of the Ashcroft pattern, with cylinder and plunger made by Pratt and Whitney, Ashcroft pyrometer, Bristol recording gauge, one Hancock ejector, a number of working injectors, with cut models of same, Buffalo scales of several patterns, Worthington water meter; Worthington, Davidson and Prescott pumps, Prony brakes, 8½-inch Leffel turbine, 28 H P Van Duzen gas engine, Deane and Marsh pumps cut to show the interior mechanism, parts of various sectional boilers, etc.

For further subjects belonging to the department of Mechanical Engineering, see

L 1. Mechanical Drawing.

L 6. Machine Design.

N.   ELECTRICAL ENGINEERING.

PROFESSOR KIDWELL.

The use of electricity in mining, as an illuminant; a motive power for hauling, pumping, and operating portable machinery; and as a means of economically transmitting power over long distances, requires of the mining engineer a working knowledge of Electrical Engineering, and to meet this requirement the Mining School at an early date introduced a course in Electrical Engineering. The course is limited to electric light and power work, and does not include telegraphy and telephony.

The instruction is made as comprehensive as the time available will permit, and special care is taken to familiarize the student with the fundamental principles of the subject. In no department of science is this more necessary than in electrical engineering, if the object of the course is to fit the student to be an *engineer*, rather than to spend his time wholly on applications whose details are continually changing, and thereby in the end give him only a smattering of the subject, and prepare him to be a mere starter and stopper. Sufficient ground is covered to enable the student to understand the electrical machinery, appliances, and processes in general use, but in all the work the idea kept steadily in view is to give him a solid foundation for advanced work, should he desire to devote himself particularly to Electrical Engineering after graduation. Details of the courses are as follows:

N 1.—*Electrical Engineering.*

PROFESSOR KIDWELL.

Electrical instruments and measurements considered from an engineering standpoint; accumulators and storage of electrical energy; the arc and incandescent lamps; photometry; methods of wiring, and wiring calculations; electrical fittings; etc. Introductory course, designed to give the student some acquaintance with the practical side of electrical engineering, and thereby prepare him to grasp fully the bearings of the mathematical course in subject N 2 (Electricity and Magnetism). Slingo and Brooker's Electrical Engineering, and Badt's Incandescent Wiring Handbook. Three hours a week, twenty-six weeks. To count as a four-fifths course. To be preceded by or accompanied with subjects B 3 (Electrical Measurements), C 2 (Analytic Mechanics) and M 5 (Mechanical Engineering).

N 2.—*Electricity and Magnetism*.

PROFESSOR KIDWELL.

Mathematical Discussion of the fundamental principles of electricity and magnetism, embracing potential, electrostatics, capacity magnetism, steady currents, variable currents, alternating currents, and electrical units. Nipher's Electricity and Magnetism. Three hours per week, twenty-six weeks. To count as a four-fifths course. Must be preceded by subjects B 3 (Electrical Measurements) and N 1 (Electrical Engineering). This course is intended to teach the principles which lie at the bottom of the science of Electricity, and which must be thoroughly mastered by the student if he is to obtain other than a superficial knowledge of the subject. It is to be taken in connection with subject N 3 (Electrical Engineering).

N 3.—*Electrical Engineering*.

PROFESSOR KIDWELL.

Practical application of principles laid down in the preceding course, covering the dynamo, for direct and alternating currents; motors, and their adoption to various duties and conditions; static and motor transformers; electric meters; switchboard work; transmission of electrical energy. Slingo and Brooker's Electrical Engineering, Nipher's Electricity and Magnetism, and Snell's Electric Motive Power. Twice a week, twenty-six weeks. To count as one-half a course. To be preceded by subjects B 1 (Electrical Measurements) and accompanied with subject N 2 (Electricity and Magnetism).

N 4.—*Electrical Engineering—Laboratory Practice*.

PROFESSOR KIDWELL AND ASSISTANTS.

Practical work in the Electrical Engineering laboratory. Testing of dynamos, motors, transformers, meters, etc. Photometric tests of arc and incandescent lamps. Testing of electrical engineering apparatus and materials. Forty-five hours a week, or five hours lecture work, thirty hours laboratory a week, eleven weeks. To count as two full courses. To be preceded by subjects N 2 (Electricity and Magnetism) and N 3 (Electrical Engineering). (Subject N 4 will not be given in 1897–98).

Equipment.—In the new engineering building now erected an

Electrical Laboratory has been provided for, and it will be thoroughly equipped with the machinery and apparatus necessary to give the student a practical knowledge of the principles taught in the class room. The equipment will include incandescent dynamos, both direct and alternating current, and an arc light machine, with complete switch boards, current, and pressure indicators, regulators, transformers, etc.

The dynamos will be driven by a separate Buckeye 8x12 automatic engine.

At present writing, this equipment has not been completed. The Buckeye engine, and line shafting, etc., for the dynamo room, are in place. There are on hand one No. 4 Edison dynamo, with all switchboard instruments, a 5 H. P. Excelsior constant current motor, one 2 H. P. Sprague motor, one T. H. recording meter, several Ayrton and Perry ammeters and voltmeters, German silver and iron wire resistance frames, etc. During the past year the laboratory has through the liberality of Hon. J. M. Longyear of Marquette, been further provided with one 200 light National compound wound dynamo; one 28 H. P. Van Duzen gas engine, and a battery of fifty-six Bradbury-Stone storage cells, together with all switchboard instruments necessary for operating them. The remainder of the equipment will be provided as soon as an appropriation therefor has been made by the legislature. Until this equipment is provided, subject N 4 (Electrical Engineering—Laboratory Practice) will not be given.

Q. CIVIL ENGINEERING.

PROFESSOR SPERR AND MR. HOULE.

Q 1.—*Surveying, Theory and Practice.*

PROFESSOR SPERR AND MR. HOULE.

Summer term, forty-five hours a week for eleven weeks. To count for two full courses.

During eleven weeks of each summer term a course of surveying is conducted. The object of this course is two-fold:

First, to give the regular students more thorough and extended practice in the field than it is possible to do when they are attending to other school work. Second, to provide a thorough, practical course in Surveying for persons, other than regular students, who may be desirous of becoming surveyors, or who may wish to obtain practical experience in the subject. There is perhaps no course of study which can be offered by an institution, that will give such quick and profitable returns for the money and time expended by the student, as a thorough, practical course in Surveying, since employment at a fair salary can almost always be obtained by a competent surveyor.

Study and practical work are combined in this course.

Johnson's Theory and Practice in Surveying, edition of 1895, and Searle's Field Engineering are used as text-books.

One or more hours of each working day will be taken for lecture and recitation work, while the remainder of the time will be given to field practice. The course treats for the most part of the adjustment of instruments and practice in typical kinds of surveying work ordinarily required to be done by, or under the supervision of, a civil or mining engineer.

The vicinity of the school affords opportunity for laying out this work as may be required for a large mining enterprise. A certain mining location is taken as a base for operations, and the work is laid out as follows:

1. A preliminary topographical map is made by means of pacing and the hand level.

2. A survey is made of the location with chain and sight poles.

3. The farms are surveyed with solar compass and chain.

4. A meridian line is established by observations on Polaris.

5. A town site is laid out with transit and steel tape.

6. An azimuth traverse is run around an adjoining piece of land with transit and stadia.

7. Lines of leveling are run from Portage Lake to establish permanent bench-marks upon the location.

8. An adjoining section of land is retraced and sub-divided according to United States Land Office regulations.

9. The mines are considered as claims under the United States laws governing mineral lands, and surveys for patents are made according to government regulations.

10. A base line is measured for a system of triangulation connecting points on the opposite shores of Portage Lake.

11. Signals are erected and the angles of the triangulation system are measured with the transit.

12. A topographical survey is made of the included area with the transit and stadia.

13. A topographical survey of a certain area is made with the plane table.

14. A line of railroad two or three miles in length, is surveyed from the mines to some point on the Lake. This survey includes (1) a preliminary survey with compass, chain, hand level and Y level; (2) permanent location with transit, steel tape and Y level; (3) establishment of grade line on profile sheet; (4) cross-section leveling; (5) computations of excavations and embankments from cross-section sheets; (6) location of bridge abutments and piers; (7) laying in frogs and switches.

The class is divided into squads, each kind of work being divided and apportioned to the different squads. Each member of a squad is required to make a full set of notes of the work done, and to carry out the computations. From these notes maps are made in the second course in Topographical Drawing (L 3). Facilities are given, however, to students who wish to do mapping work during the summer, if they are prepared to do so and can find the time.

The equipment for instruction comprises the following set of instruments: One plane table from Buff and Berger; nine transits,—three from Buff and Berger, three from Heller and Brightly, two from Fauth, one from Gurley; five Burt solar compasses; five magnetic compasses; six Wye levels, one from Buff and Berger, three from Heller and Brightly, and two from Gurley; fifteen Locke hand levels. In addition to these more expensive instruments, the school owns the necessary number of chains, steel tapes, poles, rods, etc.

Persons who wish to attend this summer course only, are required to prepare themselves upon the subjects of Plane Trigonometry, Logarithms, and Mensuration. They are to provide themselves with the text-books used, a 25 ft. steel pocket tape graduated to feet and tenths, and 5½ inch dividers, brass protractors, right line pen, decimal scale, T square, 8-inch triangle, thumb tacks, India ink, red ink, pencils and erasers, and drawing board, such as are required in Topographical Drawing.

The furnishing of the Surveying apparatus by the Mining School is a heavy expense to the institution, and while losses due to ordinary and legitimate wear and tear of the instruments are borne by the school, any injuries due to carelessness on the part of the student must be made good by him.

The summer course in Surveying will commence each year about the first of June, and all persons who desire to attend are requested to send in their names early to Professor Sperr or to the Director of the Mining School, in order that proper provision may be made for them. This course, like all others in the school, is free to anyone who is properly qualified, whether a resident of the State of Michigan or not. The course is given in Houghton.

Regular students, in order to take this course, must have passed in subjects A 3 (Spherical Trigonometry) and L 2 (Topographical Drawing).

Q 2.—*Hydraulics.*

PROFESSOR SPERR.

Merriman's Treatise on Hydraulics is used as a text-book and the subject is studied with special reference to its applications in mining, milling and metallurgical operations.

The subjects required to precede this are A 5 (Calculus), B 1 (Physics), C 1 (Analytic Mechanics), and R 1 (Principles of Mining), and preceded by, or accompanied with, subject C 2 (Analytic Mechanics).

For further work in the department of Civil Engineering, see

L 2. Topographical Drawing.

L 3. Topographical Drawing (Mapping).

L 4. Graphical Statics.

L 5. Engineering Design and Construction.

R. MINING ENGINEERING.

PROFESSOR SPEER AND MR. HOULE.

R 1.—*Principles of Mining.*

PROFESSOR SPERR.

This course is designed to cover the elementary principles of mining under the following general topics:

(1) Fluid Mining: Oil. Gas. Salt.

(2) Gravel Mining (Placer): River Mining. Drift Mining. Hydraulic Mining. "Dry Washing." Beach Mining.

(3) Ore Mining.

(4) Coal Mining.

(5) Rock Mining (Quarrying).

This year Ore and Stone Mining by C. LeNeve Foster, is used

8

as a text-book. On Wednesdays trips are made into the copper mines. These excursions are helpful to the student in enabling him to understand the nature of ore deposits and to comprehend the discussion of the various mining operations as applied to different kinds of mining.

This subject is required to be preceded by subject Y 1 (Principles of Geology); and to be taken by all candidates for the S. B. or E. M. degree.

R 2.—*Mine Surveying and Mining.*

PROFESSOR SPERR AND MR. HOULE.

Two hours a week for twenty weeks. To count for two-fifths of a course.

The classroom work in these subjects is divided into two parts: First: Mine Surveying. Second: Mining.

First: Surveying. This comprises the

(1) The adjustment and use of instruments employed in Mine Surveying.

(2) The methods of surveying the surface location.

(3) The connection of the surface survey with the underground workings.

    (a) By adit level.

    (b) By stope.

    (c) By vertical shaft.

    (d) By inclined shaft.

(4) Methods employed in surveying the various kinds of underground workings.

Full sets of notes of Mine Surveys are given to the students, which are employed by them in making maps as they would do in actual practice.

Second: Mining.

   (1) The laying out of different kinds of mines to obtain

    (a) The maximum output.

    (b) The greatest economy.

    (c) All the mineral.

The instruction is given from private notes and from references to professional papers to be found in the Mining School library. To be preceded by L 3 (Topographical Drawing), Q 1 (Surveying), R 1 (Principles of Mining) and Y 1 (Principles of Geology).

R 3.—*Mine Surveying and Mining: Practical Work.*

PROFESSOR SPERR AND MR. HOULE.

Forty-five hours a week for six weeks. To count as a full course.

The first three weeks are devoted to surveying and mapping a mine or some portion thereof, either in the "Copper Country" or in some one of the iron mining districts of Northern Michigan. The last three weeks are devoted to the examination of mining methods in the iron ore mines. Sketches are made (a), of the plans of the mines to show methods of laying out; (b), of cross-sections to show methods of stoping; (c), of timbers to show methods of framing; (d), of the timbers set up in drifts and stopes; (e), of the tramming, hoisting and general handling arrangements; (f), of ore schutes, ore pockets, etc.

This work must be preceded by subject R 2 (Theoretical Mine Surveying and Mining) except for students who enter for this subject alone, who are required to be prepared in Algebra, Trigonometry, and in the use of the transit and level.

R 4.—*Mining Engineering.*

PROFESSOR SPERR.

The instruction covers the theoretical study of laying out, designing, and equipping surface and underground works, employed in placer mining, and in gold, silver, copper, lead, zinc, tin, coal, iron and diamond mines.

Three times a week, twenty weeks. To count as three-fifths of a course, to be preceded by subjects, C 2 (Analytic Mechanics), M 3 (Mechanism) and Q 2 (Hydraulics). (Subject R 4 will not be given in 1896–1897.)

R 5.—*Mine Management and Accounts.*

PROFESSOR SPERR.

This course is designed for the study of the relations of employer and employé; the nature of contracts, leases, etc.; the questions relating to contract work, work on company account, and tribute work.

The student, having an elementary training in book-keeping, is required to make out pay rolls and other auxiliary books especially adapted to mining operations; make out cost sheets and reports to officials and stockholders.

This subject is to be preceded by subjects R 1 (Principles of Mining), and R 3 (Mine Surveying and Mining).

R 6.—*Mechanical Ventilation of Mines.*

PROFESSOR SPERR.

This subject is given to afford an opportunity for the discussion of Mechanical Ventilators to those who may wish to acquire a working knowledge of the subject and who are prepared to understand the theoretical principles involved. The general principles of Ventilation are given in courses R 1 (Principles of Mining), R 2 (Mine Surveying and Mining), and R 4 (Mining Engineering) and these subjects, with M 5 (Mechanical Engineering) and Q 2 (Hydraulics), are required to precede subject R 6.

(This subject will not be given in 1896–1897).

S. ORE DRESSING.

PROFESSOR SPERR AND MR. BURRALL.

S 1.—*Ore Dressing—Theory and Practice.*

PROFESSOR SPERR AND MR. BURRALL.

Forty-five hours a week, five weeks. Summer term. To count for a full course.

Most of the time is given to practical work in the stamp mill, taking a certain time each day for instruction in the theoretical principles involved in the operations.

The students do all the work in the mill, and each student is given an opportunity to become familiar with all the different kinds of work.

The students are required to take samples and ascertain by fire assay the degree of efficiency of the dressing operations which they are conducting.

Each student is required to spend some time each day in reading technical literature upon the subject, which is to be found in the library and to which references are given.

This subject is to be preceded by G 1 (Assaying), M 2 (Shop Practice), Q 2 (Hydraulics), and W 2 (Mineralogy).

V. BIOLOGY.

THE DIRECTOR, ASSISTANT PROFESSOR SEAMAN AND MR. SUTTON.

V 1.—*Botany, General and Economic.*

THE DIRECTOR.

First eight weeks of the fall term, three times a week. To count for one-fifth of a course.

Instruction in this subject is given by lectures with recitations upon the same. It is intended in these lectures to give a brief review of Botanical Classification, Fossil Botany and the special characters of plants, important economically, and their various uses. The object is to give the student such information about woods and other useful plants, and fossils, as he needs for subsequent work in Engineering, Paleontology and Geology. (This subject will not be given in the year 1896–1897.)

V 2.—*Zoology and Palæontology.*

ASSISTANT PROFESSOR SEAMAN AMD MR. SUTTON.

Fall term, nine hours a week, fourteen weeks. To count for two-fifths of a course.

An elementary course is given in these subjects in order that the students may better understand their later work in Geology.

As these subjects have been united in one course, the Zoology will be given more as a preface to the Palæontology, than as a full description of the various forms of animal life. The classes of animals whose structure is such that they are seldom, or never preserved as fossils will be mentioned but incidentally; while those classes, which, on account of their hard parts, yield common and characteristic fossils, will be described more in detail. In the Palæontology, will be considered the various means by which organisms are preserved, their manner of entombment, their habitat, zonal and areal distribution, etc.

It will be the aim of this course to train the student to close and accurate observation, and special care will be taken to point out those characters by which fossils may be recognized and determined. The student will be required to determine about one hundred genera which have been specially selected to cover the entire geological column. There is a working collection of nearly three thousand specimens. These will be used to drill the students in determining fossils in various states of preservation, and in assigning them to their proper class, order, or genera according to the perfection of the specimens. The specimens are arranged unlabeled in drawers and pains will be taken to train the eye to recognize resemblances and differences. Besides the working collection there is a small type collection, of living and fossil forms, arranged zoologically in accordance with Nicholson's New Manual of Palæontology, and a larger one of fossils containing over one thousand specimens arranged both zoologically, and according to geological horizons.

Wood's Elementary Palæontology, supplemented with lecture notes will be used as a laboratory guide.

W. MINERALOGY.

W 1.—*Crystallography.*

ASSISTANT PROFESSOR SEAMAN AND MR. SUTTON.

Nine hours a week for the first eight weeks of the Fall term.

To count for one-fifth of a course.

The instruction is given by means of lecture notes and laboratory practice in determining the crystal forms on wooden models and natural crystals.

As the student's future work in Mineralogy largely depends upon his knowledge of this subject, he is required to familiarize himself with the principles which it involves.

The law of symmetry is explained somewhat in detail, thus enabling the student to comprehend the derivation of hemihedral and tetartohedral forms, as well as to better understand those forms that are holohedral.   The formation of crystal aggregates are briefly considered, and the more common laws of twinning are explained and illustrated with models and natural crystals.

Cleavage is shown to conform with the law of symmetry, and the student is drilled in determining the crystal system, and symmetry of cleavage fragments.

The laboratory is provided with a working collection of two thousand one hundred and fifty wooden models, and two thousand two hundred natural crystals representing more than one hundred different mineral species.

Besides the above there are one hundred and fifty glass models for illustrative purposes.

W 1.—MINERALOGY.

ASSISTANT PROFESSOR SEAMAN AND MR. SUTTON.

Fall and winter terms, twelve hours a week for twenty-eight weeks. To count as a full course. The work in Determinative Mineralogy is preceded by the course in Crystallography and by instruction in Physical Mineralogy, although part of the instruction in these subjects is given as needed in connection with the Descriptive Mineralogy.

For Determinative Mineralogy there is provided a typical set of all the important minerals, special attention being paid to those of economic value, as well as to those occurring as gangue, or rock-forming minerals. Special collections are arranged showing the physical characters of minerals, their pseudomorphs, etc.

These minerals are in drawers, labeled, and are at all times freely accessible to the student.

Besides the typical collection of minerals, there are placed in other drawers a large number of specimens of the same mineral species. These are arranged in convenient groups, but are unlabeled. These specimens are selected so as to represent as great a variety of form, appearance and locality as possible, in order that the student may be familiar with all the types that he will be likely to meet in his professional practice. Numerous drawers of these unlabeled minerals are assigned to each student, who is to determine them and to recite upon them, not in a class, but singly with the instructor. He is required to do that which the practical mineralogist does; to determine his minerals by the shortest method possible, consistent with accuracy; the method to vary according to the specimen. To this end every method of determination short of quantitative analysis is employed; that is, in each case the crystal form and other physical characters are used, as well as the blow-pipe and wet tests, so far as they may be needed.

After the student has studied and recited upon the specimens contained in a sufficient number of drawers of one group, he is assigned to drawers containing the unlabeled minerals of another group, which have mixed with them specimens of the preceding group or groups. In this way each student is required to determine in his course from 3,000 to 6,000 different mineral specimens, belonging to the 287 selected species.

The instruction is based on the sixth edition of Professor James D.

Dana's System of Mineralogy, revised by Professor Edward S. Dana, 1892, and every student is expected to provide himself with a copy.

In addition, or supplementary to this work, there is given a series of lectures and notes prepared by the Director for use in his classes in 1876, and revised and enlarged from time to time since. In these notes the characteristic features of each mineral, its uses, and the practical methods employed to distinguish each one, are pointed out. Especial attention is given to the methods needed in the field and mine, where one cannot have recourse to a chemical laboratory. Every effort is made to train the student to close, accurate observation, to reason correctly upon what he sees, and to exercise good judgment in his decisions.

The result of this work is such that a student not only knows how to proceed, in order to determine any mineral that he may meet, but he is also enabled to recognize at sight, or by simple tests, the great majority of specimens belonging to the two hundred and eighty-seven mineral species that he is required to study in his course.

During the summer of 1892 the entire mineral collection was re-arranged to correspond to the sixth edition of Dana's System of Mineralogy, with the exception of such modifications in classification, as the Director thought would enable the student to do his determinative work in an easier and better way. (See Tables IV-X).

For purposes of instruction in this subject the laboratory is supplied with the following collections:

Crystal Models in Glass............................	151
Crystal Models in Wood and Plaster.................	2,153
Natural Crystals...................................	2,260
Collections illustrating Physical Properties, Pseudomorphs, Optical Properties, etc..................	485
Lecture Collection of Minerals.....................	10,000

	First Series.............. 2,500	
	Second Series............. 2,100	
	Third Series.............. 1,275	
Practice Collection	Fourth Series............. 3,225	
of Minerals.	Fifth Series.............. 1,525	
	Sixth Series.............. 1,850	
	Seventh Series............ 1,425	
	Review Series............. 3,125	
		—— 17,025
		—— 32,074

In order that the special mineralogical work done in this institution may be better understood by persons seeking information upon this point, and in addition to serve as a guide to the pupil in referring to the lecture specimens, the appended tables IV-X., prepared by the Director, with the aid of Professor Seaman, are given of the species to be studied in the laboratory work in this course as well as to show the classification followed. The system of numbering for the original or lecture collection numbers is to increase by ten each time, in order to allow of interpolations of new specimens without having to re-number those already in the lecture collection.

The tables show only the numbers of the specimens belonging to the species upon which laboratory work is given, and not those of the other species represented in the mineral collections.

This subject is to be preceded by B 1 (Physics), F 1 (General Chemistry), F 2 (Blowpipe Analysis) and W 1 (Crystallography).

X. PETROGRAPHY.

THE DIRECTOR AND MR. SUTTON.

XI.—*Petrography: Lithology and Petrology.*

THE DIRECTOR AND MR. SUTTON.

Fall and winter terms, twelve hours a week for twenty-eight weeks. To count for a full course.

In this subject the student is taught to use the microscope as a simple instrument, and also as a piece of optical apparatus for the determination of minerals and rocks.

The work is divided into three parts: *Microscopic Mineralogy, Lithology, and Petrology.*

A. *Microscopic (Optical) Mineralogy:* Under this head is treated the various optical and other characters of minerals as revealed by the microscope. Their alterations are especially studied owing to the importance of these in the subjects of Economic Geology and Lithology.

The lectures given by the Director are chiefly devoted to the description and use of the microscope as a simple instrument and as a piece of optical apparatus for the determination of minerals and rocks. This part of the work will comprise its use in common and in polarized light, both as a microscope, and as a polariscope; the chemical properties of minerals as determined under the microscope;

and the general description of the distinguishing characters of the important rock forming minerals.

These lectures are intended to give a clear and suitable introduction to the subject of Microscopic and Optical Mineralogy, that shall be adapted to the needs of the Geologist, the Civil and Mining Engineer, Chemist, Metallurgist, Teacher, Architect, and others who may need a good working or practical knowledge of the subject.

The lectures on Optical and Microscopic Mineralogy in general cover the following ground:

I. APPARATUS.

(a) Simple Microscope or Lens.

(b) Compound Microscope—
- Base or Foot.
- Arm.
- Body - { Simple. Binocular. }
- Objectives - { Dry, Immersion, } { Resolving Power. Flatness of Field. Penetration. Working Distance. Magnify'g Power. }
- Society Screw.
- Adaptor.
- Nose Piece.
- Eye Piece or Ocular - { Huygenian, Solid, Periscopic, } { Flatness of Field. Size of Field. Magnify'g Power. Cross Hairs. }
- Draw Tube.
- Collar.
- Coarse Adjustment.
- Fine Adjustment.
- Stage - { Fixed. Revolving. }
- Clips.
- Centering Screws.
- Mirror and Bar.
- Sub-stage and Bar.
- Diaphragm.
- Optical Axis.
- Use of Powers.
- Magnifying Power.
- Size of Object.
- Camera Lucida and Drawing.
- Shade.

(c) Accessory Apparatus—
- Table.
- Light.
- Use and Care of the Eyes.
- Slide.
- Cover Glass.
- Iron Plate for Grinding Sections.
- Grinding Machine.
- Cutting Machine.

II. PREPARATION OF MATERIALS.

(a) Preparation of Section......
- Breaking off the Chip.
- Cutting the Section.
- Grinding on one Side.
- Polishing on one Side.
- Canada or Fir Balsam.
- Cementing Chip to Glass Plate.
- Grinding the Second Side.
- Polishing the Second Side.
- Transference.
- Cover Glass.
- Cleaning Section.
- Labeling Section.
- Thinness of Section.

III. CHARACTER OF MINERALS.

(a) Crystal Form..
- Cleavage Plates.
- Splinters.
- Powder.
- Section.
- Normal.
- Abnormal.

(b) Crystalline Structure.
- Globulites.
  - Cumulites.
  - Margarites.
  - Longulites.
- Microlites.
  - Belonite.
  - Trichites.
- Skeletons.
- Deformed Crystals.
- Zonal Forms.

(c) Mineral Aggregates.

(d) Corrosion of Crystals.

(e) Inclusions in Minerals.
- Gas or Vapor Cavities.
- Vacuum Cavities.
  - Bubble.
  - Water.
- Fluid Inclusions.
  - Liquid Carbonic Acid.
  - Saline, etc.
- Glass Inclusions.
  - Bubbles.
- Stone Inclusions.
- Included Minerals.
- Arrangement of Inclusions.
- Determination of Inclusions.

(f) Cleavage.
- Octahedral.
- Cubic.
- Pyramidal.
- Prismatic.
- Pinacoidal.
- Slipping Planes.
- Pressure Planes,

IV. LIGHT.

(a) Vibration...... { Rectilinear.
Elliptical.
Circular.

(b) Refraction,

Single Refraction, { Isotropic, { Gas.
Fluid.
Amorphous Substances.
Isometric Minerals.

Double Refraction, { Anisotropic, { Tetragonal, } Two
Hexagonal, } Indices.
Orthorhombic, } Three
Monoclinic, } Indices.
Triclinic,

Index of Refraction, { Critical Angle.

Determination of Index, { Comparative Indices.
Sorby's Method.
Bertin's Method.
Total Reflectometer.

(c) Unmodified or Common Light, { Natural colors of the Mineral Plate.

(d) Polarized Light,

Comparison of Properties of Common and Polarized Light.

Means of Polarizing Light, { Reflecting Plate or Surface.
Bundle of Glass Plates.
Tourmaline Plate.
Nicol Prism.

Ordinary and Extraordinary Rays.

Plane of Polarization, { Longer Nicol { Horizontal
Diagonal, } Cross Hair.

Plane of Vibration, { Shorter Nicol { Vertical
Diagonal, } Cross Hair.

Polarizer.
Analyzer.

Optic Axes, {
Uniaxial, { Tetragonal.
Hexagonal.

Biaxial, { Orthorhombic.
Monoclinic.
Triclinic.

Bisectrics, { Acute.
Obtuse.

Solids of Elasticity, { Sphere.
Spheroid.
Ellipsoid.

Axes of Elasticity, { Least.
Mean.
Greatest.

Uniaxial Crystals, { Positive.
Negative.

Biaxial Crystals, { Positive.
Negative.

(e) Parallel Polarized Light.

- Extinction Lines
  - Always Dark,
    - Amorphous.
    - Isometric.
  - Always Parallel,
    - Tetragonal.
    - Hexagonal.
    - Orthorhombic.
  - Usually Oblique, { Monoclinic.
  - Always Oblique, { Triclinic.
  - Determination of Extinction Lines
    - Crossed Nicols Alone.
    - Calcite Plate.
    - Brezina Plate.
    - Quartz Plate.
    - Calderon's Plate.
    - Bertrand Ocular.
- Colors and Color Scale.
- Determination of Axes of Elasticity,
  - Mica Plate.
  - Gypsum Plate.
  - Quartz Wedge.
- Color with Polarizer only or Pleochroism,
  - Dichroic.
  - Trichroic.
  - Pleochroic Halos.

(f) Converging Polarized Light.........

- Sections Must be Cut in Special directions.
- Converging Lens.
- Observation of Axial Images,
  - Ocular Removed.
  - Elevation of the Eye.
  - Lens Above the Ocular.
  - Bertrand Lens.
- Uniaxial Images,
  - Cut Perpendicular,
    - Crossed Nicols.
    - Parallel Nicols.
  - Cut Oblique or Parallel
    - Crossed Nicols.
    - Parallel Nicols.
  - Circular Polarization.
  - Positive or Negative Character
    - Mica Plate.
    - Gypsum Plate.
    - Quartz Wedge.
- Bixial Images.
  - Cut Perpendicular,
    - Crossed Nicols.
    - Parallel Nicols.
  - Cut Oblique or Parallel,
    - Crossed Nicols.
    - Parallel Nicols.
  - Positive or Negative Character,
    - Mica Plate.
    - Gypsum Plate.
    - Quartz Wedge.
  - Orthorhombic,
    - $r < v.$
    - $r > v.$
  - Monoclinic,
    - Inclined Dispersion.
    - Horizontal Dispersion.
    - Crossed Dispersion.
  - Triclinic.
- Imperfect Axial Images.

V. TABLE FOR DETERMINING THE CRYSTAL SYSTEM OF MINERAL
PLATES IN THIN SECTIONS BETWEEN CROSSED NICOLS IN
PARALLEL AND IN CONVERGENT POLARIZED LIGHT.

VI. MINERAL AGGREGATES.

(a) { Aggregate Polarization.

(b) { Structure, { Concentric.
Radial, { Spherulite, { Cross.
Axiolites.
Granospherite.

VII. SPECIFIC GRAVITY.

(a) Solutions........ { Sonstadt.
Klein.
Rohrbach.
Brauns.

(b) Apparatus....... { Church.
Harada.
Thoulet.
Brogger.
Smeeth.
Sollas.
Wulfing.
Evans.
Westphal Balance.
Goldschmidt's Scale.
Hobbs' Scale.
The Derby Pan.

VIII. MICROCHEMICAL ANALYSIS.

(a) Methods, ... { Boricky's Method.
Streng's Method.
Behrens's Method.

(b) Etching.

(c) Staining.

(d) Testing for Aluminium, Calcium, Carbon, Chlorine, Chromium,
Cobalt, Copper, Gold, Iron, Lithium, Magnesium, Manganese,
Nickel, Potassium, Phosphorus, Silicon, Silver, Sodium, Titan-
ium, etc.

IX. SPECIAL MICROSCOPIC CHARACTERS OF ROCK FORMING MINER-
ALS.

(a) *Native Elements:*
Graphite, Iron.

(b) *Sulphides:*
Pyrrhotite, Pyrite.

(c) *Oxides:*

    Fluorite, Quartz, Tridymite, Corundum, Hematite, Ilmenite, Perofskite, Spinel, Magnetite, Chromite, Rutile, Zircon, Opal.

(d) *Carbonates:*

    Calcite, Dolomite, Magnesite, Aragonite.

(e) *Anhydrous Silicates:*

    Orthoclase, Microcline, Plagioclase, Leucite, Enstatite (Bastite), Hypersthene, Pyroxene, Wollastonite Anthophyllite, Amphibole, Glaucophane, Arfvedsonite, Iolite, Nephelite, Cancrinite, Sodalite, Haüynite, Noselite, Garnet, Chrysolite, Scapolite, Melilite, Vesuvianite, Andalusite, Sillimanite, Axinite, Tourmaline, Staurolite, Titanite.

(f) *Hydrous Silicates:*

    Prehnite, Analcite, Natrolite, Muscovite (Sericite), Paragonite, Lepidolite, Zinnwaldite, Biotite, Phlogopite, Lepidomelane, Chloritoid, (Ottrelite, Phyllite), Chlorite, Delessite, Serpentine, Talc, Kaolinite, Glauconite.

(g) *Phosphates:*

    Monazite, Apatite.

(h) *Sulphates:*

    Anhydrite, Gypsum, Alunite.

(i) *Hydrocarbons:*

    Carbonaceous Matter.

X. TABLE SHOWING ORDER AND METHODS OF WORK EMPLOYED IN THE STUDY OF ROCKS AND THEIR THIN SECTIONS.

The Director's lectures are supplemented by a special card catalogue which directs the student to the mineral sections, and indicates the plates that he needs to study in order to familiarize himself with the special optical and microscopic characters of minerals. It gives him, in a sufficient number of cases, particular directions how to proceed in his optical work on the selected sections, and informs him what results he may expect to obtain. A card catalogue like this saves a large amount of the time both of student and teacher.

Most of the thin sections of the minerals have been made at the Mining School from the specimens in the Lecture Collection of Minerals, enabling the student to study the microscopic and optical properties in connection with the cabinet specimens from which they were taken.

Besides the lectures there are used as text-books and laboratory manuals, Rosenbusch's Microscopical Physiography of the Rock-Making Minerals, translated by Joseph P. Iddings; Lévy and Lecroix's Tableau des Biréfringences; and Behrens's Manual of Microchemical Analysis.

For the purpose of giving the above elementary, as well as the subsequent graduate, instruction, the department is supplied, amongst other things, with the following apparatus:

Twenty-nine Bausch and Lomb's petrographical microscopes, made expressly for the Michigan Mining School; with micrometer eyepieces, Bertrand's lenses, quartz wedges, undulation plates, etc.

Four Beck's petrographical microscopes with accessories.

One Fuess's largest petrographical microscope, of the latest pattern, with all the accessories; made expressly for this institution.

One Nachet's largest petrographical microscope, with all the accessories.

One Dick's petrographical microscope, with Swift's objectives and other accessories.

One projection microscope.

One Nachet's inverted chemical microscope.

One spectroscope.

One spectropolarizer.

One Sorby's apparatus for observing the four images given by biaxial bodies.

Two Calderon's oculars.

Three Bertrand oculars.

One spectroscope ocular.

One goniometer ocular.

One Babinet's compensator ocular.

One Michel-Levy's comparateur.

One axial angle apparatus for measurements in oil.

One periscope eyepiece.

One Filar micrometer.

One cross-hair micrometer.

Three micrometers.

Four camera lucidas.

Two Abbé's Camera Lucidas.

One Bausch and Lomb's one-inch microphotographic objective.

One mica plate—nose piece.

Many extra eye pieces, objectives, etc,

SECOND SERIES—FORTY-SEVEN SPECIES.

Group	Species	Varieties	Nos.	Nos.	Syst.	Formula
Opal	Brookite		242, 243	55	IV	TiO^2.
	Pyrolusite		243, 244	55, 56	IV	MnO^2.
	Opal	Precious Opal, Fire Opal, Girasol, Common Opal, Resin Opal, Semi-Opal, Hydrophane, Cacholong, Opal-Agate, Menilite, Jasp-Opal, Wood Opal, Hyalite, Florite, Geyserite, Tripolite	194–197	56–58	VII	$SiO^2 + H^2O$.
Limonite	Turgite		245	59	VII	$2Fe^2O^3 + H^2O$.
	Diaspore		246, 247	59	IV	$Al^2O^3 + H^2O$.
	Göthite		247, 248	59, 60	IV	$Fe^2O^3 + H^2O$.
	Manganite		248, 250	60	IV	$Mn^2O^3 + H^2O$.
	Limonite	Yellow Ochre, Umber, Bog Ore, Pisolitic, Oolitic	250, 251	60–63	VII	$2Fe^2O^3 + 8H^2O$.
	Bauxite	Wocheinite	251	63	VII	$Al^2O^3 + 2H^2O$.
Brucite	Brucite	Nemalite	252, 253	63, 64	III	$MgO + H^2O$.
	Gibbsite		254, 255	64	IV	$Al^3O^3 + 3H^2O$.
	Hydrotalcite	Hydrargillite	255, 256	65	III	$3MgO + Al^2O^3 + 15H^2O$.
	Chalcophanite		256, 257	65	III	$(Mn\,Zn)O + 2H^2O$.
	Psilomelane	Houghite	257	65	VII	$(Mn\,Ba)O + H^2O$.
	Wad	Asbolite, Lampadite, Bog Manganese	257, 258	66	VII	$(Mn\,Ba\,Cu\,Co)O + H^2O$.

FOURTH SERIES.—FIFTY-FIVE SPECIES.

Nephelite

Cancrinite

427, 428   105   III | Al, Na, Ca + CH^2O^4.

TABLE VIII.

FIFTH SERIES.—FIFTY-FOUR SPECIES.

		Species	Sub-species				
Serpentines and Talc	Serpentine	Genthite	....	676	155	VII	Ni, Mg.
		Garnierite	{ Noumeite / Garnierite }	676, 677	156	VII	Ni, Mg.
		Talc	{ Talc / Steatite / Rensselaerite }	678–680	156–158	IV	Mg.
		Pyrophyllite	....	691, 692	158, 159	V	Al.
		Pinite	{ Pinite / Fahlunl / Chlorophyll / Gigantolite / Gieseckite / Liebenerite }	421, 621 / 431 / 421, 621 / 425, 621 / 360, 621 / 621, 691 / 622, 623	159	VII	Al, K, Fe, Mg, Na, Ca.
		Sepiolite	Meerschaum	680, 681	160	VII	Mg.
		Kaolinite	{ Kaolinite / Pholerite }	685–687	160, 161	V	Al.
Clays	Kaoln	Halloysite	{ Halloysite / Indianaite / Smectite / Fuller's Earth / Bole }	688, 689 / 696	161	VII	Al.
		Allophane	....	693, 694	162	VII	Al.
......	Chrysocolla	Chrysocolla	....	699, 700	162, 163	VII	Cu.
......	Hisingerite		{ Glauconite / Chloropal / Hisingerite / Neocite }	683, 684 / 701, 702 / 702, 703 / 704, 705	163 / 163 / 164 / 164	VII / VIII / VII / VII	Fe, Al, K, Mg. / Fe. / Fe. / Mn, Fe, Mg.

TABLE IX.

SIXTH SERIES.—THIRTY-FIVE SPECIES.

Divisions.	Subdivisions.	Group.	Species.	Varieties.	Pages in Dana's System.	Number of Degrees.	Total System.

TABLE X.   SEVENTH SERIES.—TWENTY-NINE SPECIES.

					Pages	Number

One condenser.

One condenser with iris diaphragm.

One Jannettaz's thermal apparatus.

One Latterman's apparatus.

One Fuess's polariscope with accessories.

One Groth's universal apparatus, with goniometer.

One Fuess's application goniometer for dull crystals.

One Fuess's reflection goniometer.

One Hirschwald's microscope goniometer.

One Linholf's reflection goniometer.

One total reflectometer attachment.

Fourteen Miller's goniometers.

One Stage goniometer.

One Bertrand's micro-goniometer with special stage.

One flask for measuring index of fluids.

One pyroelectric duster.

One Streng's chest and apparatus, for microchemical reactions, etc.

About two thousand mineral sections for the microscope.

B—*Lithology*. The instruction in this branch of Petrography comprises both the macroscopic and the microscopic study of rocks. For this work large and complete collections of rock specimens, with numerous thin sections, are arranged for the use of the student. The course of instruction here is similar to that followed in the course in Mineralogy. Lectures are given upon the specimens of the typical collection, the method of classification explained, and the distinguishing characters of the different groups, species, and varieties pointed out. Special attention is called to the variations and alterations in rocks, and to their local modifications due to their special mode of occurrence in the field. The student is to supply himself with the Director's mimeographed Notes on Petrography.

The object of the course is to give the student that training in the practical determination of rocks that will enable him to know them in the field and mine, as well as to observe their alterations and modifications—subjects that have a very important bearing upon the vital questions relating to ore deposits.

After the study of a sufficiently large number of types has been had, the student has assigned to him a large number of drawers containing unlabeled specimens of these rocks, which he is expected to

9

determine and recite upon, as he has done in his study of minerals. The course is thus made thorough and practical, and adapted to the needs of the miner, teacher and geologist, giving them a training which they can make use of in their future work.

The student is drilled at the same time upon both the microscopic and macroscopic characters of the rocks he is studying, as the thin sections of rocks for the most part have been made at the Mining School from the hand specimens in the Lecture Collection of Rocks. All practical students of Petrography will recognize the great advantage of this arrangement.

The subjoined original classification of rocks, prepared in 1878, and subsequently modified by the Director (Table XI), will show the scope of the laboratory work, lectures, and the arrangement of the Lecture Collection of Rocks.

C—*Petrology:* Under this subdivision of Petrography, the various questions relating to the origin, modes of occurrence, relations and alterations of rocks, as observed in the field, are considered, but since the chief portion of the students electing Petrography also elect Physical and Chemical Geology, the majority of the instruction in Petrology is given in connection with that subject.

The entire subject of Petrography is to be taken as a whole, and the student is required to have passed in B 1 (Physics), F 7 (General Chemistry), and W 2 (Mineralogy).

In the above course in Petrography the following collections are used:

I. THIN SECTIONS OF MINERALS AND ROCKS.

Sections of Minerals	2,000
Polariscope Sections	132
Sections of Lecture Rock Collection	2,895
Sections of Michigan Rocks	650
Sections of Rosenbusch Rock Collection	729
Miscellaneous Sections	361
Sections of Stratigraphical Rock Collection	206
	6,973

II. Hand Specimens of Rocks.

Lecture Collection of Rocks........ 3,800
Practice Collection of Rocks.......................... 6,500
Lecture Collection of Michigan Rocks................ 675
Practice Collection of Michigan Rocks................ 1,300
Rosenbusch Collection of Rocks...................... 1,000
Stratigraphical Collection of Rocks.................. 210

13,485

Y. GEOLOGY.

THE DIRECTOR, ASSISTANT PROFESSOR SEAMAN AND MR. SUTTON.

Y 1.—*Principles of Geology.*

THE DIRECTOR.

First eight weeks of the fall term: five times a week. To count as one-fifth of a course.

The instruction in this subject is intended as a preparation for the study of the Principles of Mining and the subsequent work in Mineralogy, Petrography, Geology and Mining Engineering. Previous work in Geology, unless taken as a college or as a university course of a satisfactory nature will not be accepted for this subject, which is required of all candidates for the S. B. or E. M. degrees.

The subject is taught by lectures supplemented by the use of Dr. A. Geikie's Class Book in Geology. This is used in order to save as much of the time of the student in taking notes as practicable.

The design of the course is to give a clear and philosophical, but brief and rapid view of the principles that lie at the basis of geological science. The outline scheme of the lectures is given below, but it will be varied from time to time as circumstances indicate.

Outline Course of Lectures on the Principles of Geology.

A. GEOLOGY.

 I. Physical Geology.
 II. Chemical Geology.
 III. Stratigraphical Geology.
 IV. Economic Geology.

Divisions I. and II.—Principles of Physical and Chemical Geology.

B. OPTICS.

I. Light......... { Prism.
Spectroscope.
Spectrum... { Incandescent Gasses.
White Hot Liquids.
White Hot Solids.
White Hot Substances surrounded by an atmosphere. }

C. UNIVERSE.

I. Nebulæ .... { Luminous Gas.
Gases under pressure, or incandescent Liquids or Solids. }

II. Sun.......... { Chromosphere.. { Prominences.
Photosphere.... { Sun Spots.
Main Body.
Corona.
Light.
Heat.
Chemical Elements. }

III. Stars........ { Variable.. { Continuous.
Irregular.
Temporary.
Periodic. }
Multiple.. { Double Clusters. }
Spectrum. { Hydrogen (White or Blue Stars).
Metallic (Sunlike Stars).
Carbon (Red and Variable Stars).
Banded (Small Red Stars). } }

D. SOLAR SYSTEM.

I. Exterior Planets.......... { Jupiter... { Physical Constitution (Red Spot).
Moons. }
Saturn.... { Rings.
Moons. }
Uranus.
Neptune.
Asteroids. }

II. Inner Planets. { Mars....... { Physical Characters.
Moons. }
Venus.
Mercury. }

II. Moon .... { Atmosphere.
Surface. }

IV. Comets........ {
Nucleus.
Coma.
Tail.
}

V. Meteors....... {
Meteorites.
Shooting Stars.
}

VI. Cosmogony -- {
Solar System, { Nebular Hypothesis.
Universe.
}

E. EARTH.

I. The Earth's Formation..... {
Gaseous Stage.
Liquid Stage.
Solid Stage.
}

II. The Earth's Interior ...... {
Precession and Nutation.
Tides.
Heat and Pressure.
Relation of Liquid and Hot Solid States of Matter.
Density.
Geological Evidences.
}

III. The Earth's Exterior.... { Original Crust.

IV. Eruptive Action, {

Flowing Lava. {
Through Fissures.
Over the Surface.
Contact with Subterranean Waters.
Contact with Surface Waters.
Quiet Eruptions.
Explosive Eruptions.
Eruptive Energy Diminishing.
Forming Dykes.
Forming Flows.
Forming Laccolites.
Forming Bosses or Masses.
}

Volcanoes..... {

Cone. {
Origin.
Form.
Structure,
}

Materials. {
Steam, { Water.
Gases.
Ashes, { Mud.
Stones.
Lava.
}

Mud Volcanoes.
Solfateras.
Geysers.
Submarine.

Cause of Volcanic Action. {
Davey.
Scrope.
Mallet.
Prestwich.
}

}

}

F. Earth Movements.

I. Tremors and Pulsations.

II. Elevation of Surface.
{ Animal and Plant Remains.
Sea Worn Caves.
Raised Beaches.
Historical Records.
Cause of Upheaval.

III. Subsidence of Surface......
{ Submerged Forests.
Fiords.
Historical Records.
Cause of Subsidence.

IV. Earthquakes..
{ Wave Motion...
{ Shock or Motion.
Sea Wave.
Earth Wave.
Velocity of Wave Motion.
Depth of Source.
Duration.
Area Affected.

Fissures or Master Joints.
Cause of Earthquakes.

G. Earth Alteration.

I. Metamorphism.
{ Causes..
{ Pressure.
Dry Heat.
Percolating Waters... { Hot. Cold.
Chemical Action.

Local.
Regional.

H. Principal Minerals Forming Eruptive Rocks.

I. Foreign or of Prior Origin to the Rock.

(a) *Native Elements:* Iron.

(b) *Oxides:* Quartz, Magnetite.

(c) *Anhydrous Silicates:* Orthoclase, Plagioclase, Leucite, Enstatite, Amphibole (Hornblende), Haüyenite, Noselite, Chrysolite, (Olivine), Biotite.

II. Indigenous or Original: Crystallizing out of the Magma.

(a) *Native Elements:* Graphite, Iron.

(b) *Sulphides:* Pyrrhotite.

(c) *Oxides:* Quartz, Hematite, Spinel (Picotite), Magnetite, Rutile, Zircon.

(d) *Anhydrous Silicates:* Orthoclase (Adularia, Sanidin), Microcline, Plagioclase, Leucite, Enstatite (Bronzite), Pyroxene (Diallage, Augite), Amphibole (Hornblende). Iolite, Nephelite, Chrysolite (Olivine), Titanite, Biotite. (In this case the Biotite is anhydrous.)

(e) *Phosphates:* Apatite.

III. Secondary Minerals or Alteration Products.

(a) *Sulphides:* Chalcopyrite, Pyrite.

(b) *Oxides:* Quartz (Chalcedony, Agate, Jasper), Hematite, Martite, Magnetite, Spinel, Chromite, Rutile, Zircon. Opal (Hyalite), Limonite.

(c) *Carbonates:* Calcite, Dolomite, Magnesite, Siderite.

(d) *Anhydrous Silicates:* Orthoclase (Microcline), Plagioclase, (Labradorite), Saussurite. Enstatite (Bronzite, Bastite), Pyroxene, (Salite, Diallage). Amphibole (Tremolite, Actinolite, Asbestus, Smaragdite, Uralite, Hornblende), Iolite, Nephelite, (Elaeolite), Cancrinite, Sodalite, Haüynite, Noselite, Epidote, Tourmaline, Titanite.

(e) *Hydrous Silicates:* Zeolites, Prehnite, Apophyllite, Heulandite, Stilbite, Laumontite, Chabazite, Analcite, Datolite, Natrolite, Thomsonite, Pectolite, Muscovite (Sericite), Biotite, Chlorite, Delessite, Serpentine (Chrysotile), Talc (Steatite), Pinite, Kaolinite.

(f) *Phosphates:* Apatite.

(g) *Sulphates:* Gypsum.

I. PRINCIPAL ERUPTIVE (INCLUDING METEORIC) ROCKS.

I. *Original Forms:*

Siderolite, Meteoric Iron, Pallasite, Peridotite; Basalt, Tachylite, Nephelinite or Nephelite Basalt, Leucitite or Leucite Basalt; Andesite, Pyroxene Andesite, Amphibole Andesite; Trachyte, Lassenite (Pumice); Rhyolite, Obsidian (Pumice, Pitchstone, Pearlite, Spherulite), Liparite, Granite; Tufa.

II. *Metamorphosed Massive Forms:*

Cumberlandite; Serpentine, Ophicalcite, Dolomite; Zirkelite, Melaphyr, Diabase, Gabbro, Norite, Diorite; Phonolite, Propylite, Minette, Syenite; Felsite, Microgranite, Granite; Porodite.

III. *Metamorphosed Schistose Forms:*

Serpentine, Talc Schist (Steatite), Amphibole Schist, Eclogite,
Epidosite, Chlorite Schist; Argillite, Granulite, Quartz
Schist, Mica Schist, Gneiss; Jaspilite, Halleflinta; Porodite.

J. DENUDATION OR DESTRUCTIVE AGENCIES.

I. Changes of Temperature.

II. Lightning..{ Fulgurites.

III. Air......... { Dry Air.
                  Wind. Tempests.

IV.—Surface Waters

{ Rain......{ Mechanical. { Impact.
                             Raindrop Impressions.
                             Movement of Fragments.
                             Earth Pillars.

Streams.. { Supply.
                Discharge.
                Flow........ { Upland.
                                Valley.
                                Plain.
                Erosion..... { Channel.
                                Pot Holes.
                                Valleys.
                                Gorges.
                                Canons.
                                Rapids.
                                Falls.
                Transportation.

Lakes .... { Changes of Level.
              Waves.
              Erosion..... { Beaches.
                               Cliffs.
              Transportation.

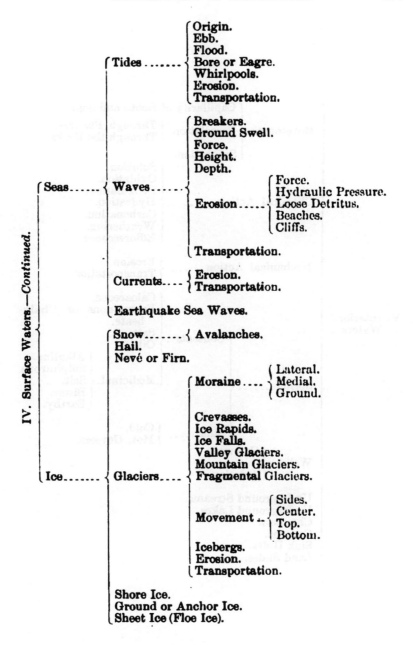

IV. Surface Waters.—*Continued.*

Seas
- Tides
  - Origin.
  - Ebb.
  - Flood.
  - Bore or Eagre.
  - Whirlpools.
  - Erosion.
  - Transportation.
- Waves
  - Breakers.
  - Ground Swell.
  - Force.
  - Height.
  - Depth.
  - Erosion
    - Force.
    - Hydraulic Pressure.
    - Loose Detritus.
    - Beaches.
    - Cliffs.
  - Transportation.
- Currents
  - Erosion.
  - Transportation.
- Earthquake Sea Waves.

Ice
- Snow
  - Avalanches.
- Hail.
- Nevé or Firn.
- Glaciers
  - Moraine
    - Lateral.
    - Medial.
    - Ground.
  - Crevasses.
  - Ice Rapids.
  - Ice Falls.
  - Valley Glaciers.
  - Mountain Glaciers.
  - Fragmental Glaciers.
  - Movement
    - Sides.
    - Center.
    - Top.
    - Bottom.
  - Icebergs.
  - Erosion.
  - Transportation.
- Shore Ice.
- Ground or Anchor Ice.
- Sheet Ice (Floe Ice).

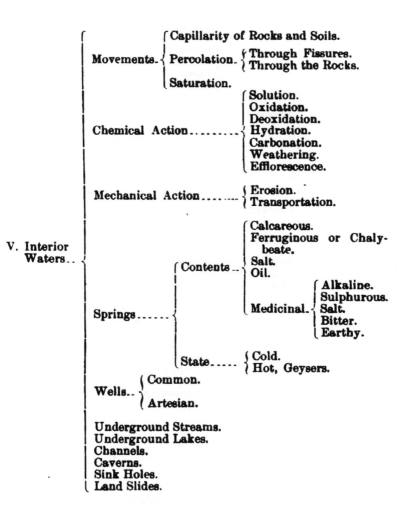

V. Interior Waters
- Movements
  - Capillarity of Rocks and Soils.
  - Percolation.
    - Through Fissures.
    - Through the Rocks.
  - Saturation.
- Chemical Action
  - Solution.
  - Oxidation.
  - Deoxidation.
  - Hydration.
  - Carbonation.
  - Weathering.
  - Efflorescence.
- Mechanical Action
  - Erosion.
  - Transportation.
- Springs
  - Contents
    - Calcareous.
    - Ferruginous or Chalybeate.
    - Salt.
    - Oil.
    - Medicinal.
      - Alkaline.
      - Sulphurous.
      - Salt.
      - Bitter.
      - Earthy.
  - State
    - Cold.
    - Hot, Geysers.
- Wells
  - Common.
  - Artesian.
- Underground Streams.
- Underground Lakes.
- Channels.
- Caverns.
- Sink Holes.
- Land Slides.

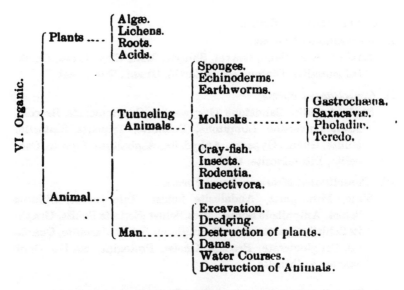

K. PRINCIPAL MINERALS FORMING SEDIMENTARY ROCKS.

(a) *Native Elements:* Graphite.

(b) *Sulphides:* Sphalerite (Blende) Pyrrhotite, Chalcopyrite, Pyrite, Arsenopyrite (Mispickel).

(c) *Chlorides-Oxides:* Halite, Sylvite, Quartz (Smoky Quartz, Chalcedony, Silicious Sinter, Flint, Jasper), Corundum (Emery), Hematite (Micaceous, Red Ochre), Martite, Ilmenite, Spinel, Magnetite, Rutile, Zircon, Opal, Limonite, (Yellow, Ochre, Umber, Bog Ore), Bauxite, Wad (Bog Manganese).

(d) *Carbonates:* Calcite (Limestone, Marble, Chalk, Oolite, Pisolite, Stalactite, Stalagmite), Dolomite, Magnesite, Siderite.

(e) *Anhydrous Silicates:* Orthoclase, Plagioclase, Saussurite, Anthopyllite, Amphibole (Tremolite, Actinolite, Asbestus, Hornblende), Glaucophane, Iolite, Garnet, Andalusite (Chiastolite), Sillimanite (Fibrolite), Cyanite, Epidote, Tourmaline, Staurolite, Titanite.

(f) *Hydrous Silicates:* Muscovite (Sericite), Biotite, Lepidomelane, Chloritoid, Ottrelite, Chlorite, Serpentine, Talc, Pinite, Kaolinite, Glauconite.

(g) *Phosphates:* Apatite (Phosphorite, Guano, etc.).

(h) *Sulphates:* Barite, Celestite, Anhydrite, Gypsum.

(i) *Hydrocarbons:* Asphaltum, Anthracite, Bituminosite, Caunelite, Lignite.

L. SEDIMENTARY ROCKS.

I. *Unconsolidated Forms.*

   Laxite: Mud, Sand, Gravel, Shingle, Marl, Clay, Loam, Chalk, Infusorialite (Diatomaceous Earth), Guano, Turf, Peat.

II. *Consolidated Forms.*

   Shale, Argillite, Sandstone (Graywacke), Conglomerate, Breccia, Marl, Travertine, Limestone, Dolomite, Tripolite, Sinterite, Millite, Guano, Gypsum, Anhydrite, Asphaltum, Lignite, Cannelite, Bituminosite, Coal.

III. *Consolidated Metamorphosed Forms.*

   Slate, Porcelanite, Andalusite Schist, Talc Schist, Chlorite Schist, Amphibole Schist, Mica Schist (Sericite Schist, Graphite Schist), Quartz Schist, Ferruginous Schist, Jaspilite, Quartzite, Conglomerate, Breccia, Gneiss, Protogine, Marble, Ophicalcite, Anthracite.

M. ROCK FORMING AGENCIES (NOT ERUPTIVE).

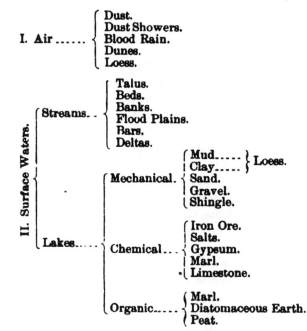

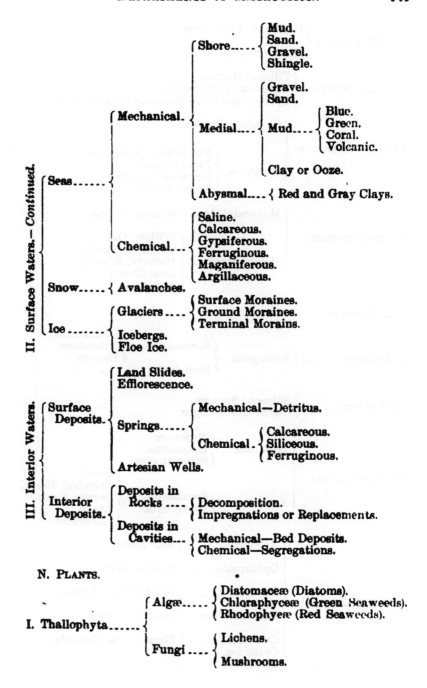

II. Surface Waters.—*Continued.*

Seas
- Mechanical.
  - Shore
    - Mud.
    - Sand.
    - Gravel.
    - Shingle.
  - Medial
    - Gravel.
    - Sand.
    - Mud
      - Blue.
      - Green.
      - Coral.
      - Volcanic.
    - Clay or Ooze.
  - Abysmal — Red and Gray Clays.
- Chemical
  - Saline.
  - Calcareous.
  - Gypsiferous.
  - Ferruginous.
  - Maganiferous.
  - Argillaceous.

Snow — Avalanches.

Ice
- Glaciers
  - Surface Moraines.
  - Ground Moraines.
  - Terminal Morains.
- Icebergs.
- Floe Ice.

III. Interior Waters.

Surface Deposits.
- Land Slides.
- Efflorescence.
- Springs
  - Mechanical—Detritus.
  - Chemical
    - Calcareous.
    - Siliceous.
    - Ferruginous.
- Artesian Wells.

Interior Deposits.
- Deposits in Rocks
  - Decomposition.
  - Impregnations or Replacements.
- Deposits in Cavities
  - Mechanical—Bed Deposits.
  - Chemical—Segregations.

N. PLANTS.

I. Thallophyta
- Algæ
  - Diatomaceæ (Diatoms).
  - Chloraphyceæ (Green Seaweeds).
  - Rhodophyeæ (Red Seaweeds).
- Fungi
  - Lichens.
  - Mushrooms.

II. Bryophyta.. $\begin{cases} \text{Hepaticæ (Liverworts).} \\ \text{Musci (Mosses).} \end{cases}$

III. Pteridophyta. $\begin{cases} \text{Filicinæ (Ferns).} \\ \text{Equisetaciæ (Horsetails).} \\ \text{Lycopodinæ (Club Mosses or Ground Pines).} \end{cases}$

IV. Gymnospermæ. $\begin{cases} \text{Cycadeæ (Cycads).} \\ \\ \text{Coniferæ.} \begin{cases} \text{Fir, Spruce, Hemlock,} \\ \text{Pine, Cypress,} \\ \text{Redwood, Juniper,} \\ \text{Larch, Cedar.} \end{cases} \end{cases}$

V. Angiospermæ... $\begin{cases} \text{Monocolyledons.} \{ \text{Grasses, Palms.} \\ \\ \text{Dicotyledons....} \begin{cases} \text{Willow, Oak,} \\ \text{Chestnut, Beech,} \\ \text{Hickory, Walnut,} \\ \text{Elm, Cherry,} \\ \text{Maple, etc.} \end{cases} \end{cases}$

O. ANIMALS.

I. Infusoria....... $\{$ Rhizopoda.. $\begin{cases} \text{Foraminifera,} \begin{cases} \text{Globigerina.} \\ \text{Numulites.} \\ \text{Eozoon.} \end{cases} \\ \text{Radiolaria.} \end{cases}$

II. Porifera....... $\begin{cases} \text{Siliceous Sponges.} \\ \text{Calcareous Sponges.} \end{cases}$

III. Coelenterata.. $\begin{cases} \text{Hydrozoa ..} \begin{cases} \text{Millepora.} \\ \text{Graptolites.} \\ \text{Stromatopora.} \end{cases} \\ \\ \text{Actinizoa...} \begin{cases} \text{Zoantharia....} \\ \text{Alcyonaria.} \end{cases} \begin{cases} \text{Coral.} \\ \text{Fringing Reefs.} \\ \text{Barrier Reefs.} \\ \text{Atolls.} \\ \text{Limestone.} \end{cases} \end{cases}$

IV. Echinodermata. $\begin{cases} \text{Asteroidea ....} \{ \text{Star Fishes.} \\ \text{Ophiuroide .....} \{ \text{Brittle Stars.} \\ \text{Echindea ....} \{ \text{Sea Urchins, Echini.} \\ \text{Holothuroidea.. } \{ \text{Sea Cucumbers.} \\ \text{Crinoidea.......} \{ \text{Stone Lilies, Crinoids.} \\ \text{Cystoidea.} \\ \text{Blastoidea.} \end{cases}$

V. Vermes..{ Annelida.{ Serpula.
Spirorbis.

VI. Moluscoida.{ Polyzoa.
Brachiopoda.

VII. Mollusca,

Lamellibranchiata ....{

Asiphonida . . {Oyster, Scallop.
Mussel, Lithodomus.
Unio.

Siphonida ....{Tridacna, Cockle.
Clam, Razor Shell,
Gastrochæna,
Saxicava, Pholas,
Teredo.

Gastropoda............ {Cone Shell, Cowries, Sea Snails,
Periwinkle, River Snails, Limpet,
Land Snails, Slugs, Pond Snails.

Scaphopoda............ { Dentalium (Tooth Shell.)

Cephalopoda.......... {

Tetrabranchiata... {Nautilus.
Orthocerata.
Ammonites.

Dibranchiata.... {Argonaut.
Octopus.
Squid, Cuttle Fish.

VIII. Arthropoda.

Crustacea...{

Entomostraca... {

Cirripedia .. {Acorn Shells
or Barnacles.

Trilobita.
Xiphosura.
Eurypterida.

Malacostraca ... { Decapoda... {Lobsters.
Cray Fishes.
Crabs.

Myriopoda.{ Millepedes, Centipedes.

Archnida..{ Mites, Ticks, Scorpions, Spiders.

Insecta...{

Neuroptera,{ Dragon Fly, May Fly, White Ants.

Orthoptera..{ Crickets, Locusts, Grasshoppers.
Cockroaches.

Hemiptera...{ Bed Bug, Louse, Plant Louse.

Coleoptera...{ Beetles.

Diptera..{ Flies.

Lepidoptera.{ Butterflies, Moths.

Hymenoptera.{ Bees, Wasps, Ants.

Tunicata { Ascidians.

Acrania.. { Amphioxus or Lancelet.

Pisces or Fishes
- Marsipobranchii .. { Lampreys, Hag Fish.
- Elasmobranchii... { Sharks. Rays.
- Ganoidei.......... { Sturgeon, Gar Pike, Mud Fish.
- Teleostei.......... { Salmon, Herring, Pike, Perch, Eel, Cat Fish, Cod.
- Dipnoi............ { Ceratodus, Protopterus, Lepidosiren.

Amphibia .... { Toads, Frogs, Salamanders, Newts, Mud Puppy.

Reptilia.........
- Ophida..... { Snakes.
- Lacertilia .. { Lizards. Chameleon. Iguana.
- Chelonia ... { Turtles. Tortoises.
- Crocodilia.. { Alligator. Crocodile. Gavial. Cayman.

Aves...........
- Ratitae ..... { Ostrich, Cassowary, Apteryx.
- Carinatae .. { Ducks, Gulls, Divers, Herons, Cranes, Hens, Turkeys, Hawks, Eagles, Owls, Doves, Crows, Swallows, Sparrows.

Mammalia ......
- Monotremata. { Duckbill, Echidna.
- Marsupialia. { Kangaroo, Opossum, Tasmanian Wolf, Tasmanian Devil.
- Edentata ... { Sloths, Ant-eaters, Pangolins, Armadillos.

IX. Vertebrata.

ABLE XII.—CLASSIFICATION OF UTILITES, OR USEFUL GEOLOGICAL PRODUCTS BASED O THEIR ORIGIN AND MODES OF OCCURRENCE.

BY M. E. WADSWORTH, 1882–1892.

- **Eruptive Deposits**
  - Non-Fragmental Deposits
    - Flow Deposits.
    - Dike Deposits.
    - Mass Deposits.
  - Fragmental Deposits
    - Bed (Placer) Deposits { Tufa Deposits. / Porodite Deposits.
    - Tufa De   its.

- **Chemical Deposits**
  - Impregnations..
    - ...posita ....{ Carbona Deposits.
  - Impregnations, or Replacement Deposits
    - Impregnations..
    - Fragmental Deposits ....
      - Bed Deposits.......{ Tufa Deposits. / Porodite Deposits.
      - Clasolite Deposits...{ Tufa Deposits. / Porodite Deposits.
    - Sedimentary Rock Impregnations..
      - Bed Deposits.......{ Fahlbands.
      - Clasolite Deposits.
  - Segregations, or Cavity Deposits
    - Pocket Deposits. / Chamber Deposits.
    - Vein Deposits......{ Gash Veins, / Segregated Veins. / Recticulated Veins, or Stockwork. / Fissure, or Fault Veins.

TABLE XIII.—CLASSIFICATION OF UTILITES OR USEFUL GEOLOGICAL PRODUCTS BASED ON THEIR USES.

BY M. E. WADSWORTH, 1893.

Utilites

Ærites, or Metallites .... { Ores, or Metalliferous Materials.

Non-ærites, or Mometallites, or Non-metalliferous Materials ..

Tectonites	Construction Materials or Building and Road Materials.
Cosmites	Decorative Materials, or Ornamental Stones and Gems.
Pyrolites	Refractory, or Fire-resisting Materials.
Challcites	Binding Materials, or Limes, Mortars, Cements, etc.
Ceramites	Fictile, or Ceramic Materials.
Rholites	Smelting Materials, or Fluxes.
Vitrites	Vitrifying Materials, or Glass, etc.
Tribolites	Abrasives, or Attrition Materials.
Thermites	Fuels or Burning Materials, or Carbonites.
Graphollites	Graphic, or Illustrative Materials.
Lubricites	Lubricants, or Friction Materials.
Chromites	Color Materials, or Paints, Pigments, etc.
Coprites	Fertilizers, or Mineral Manures.
Salites	Salts and Saline Materials.
Ignites	Pyrotechnic Materials.
Pharmacites	Mineral Medicines.
Chemites	Chemical Materials.

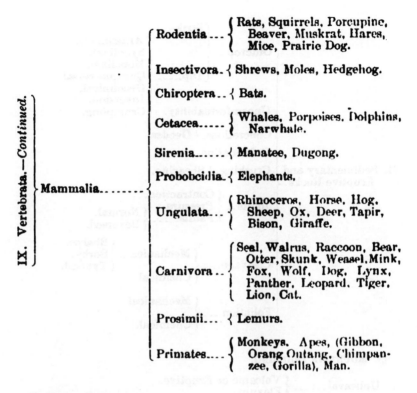

IX. Vertebrata.—*Continued.*

Mammalia.........

Rodentia ... { Rats, Squirrels, Porcupine, Beaver, Muskrat, Hares, Mice, Prairie Dog.

Insectivora. { Shrews, Moles, Hedgehog.

Chiroptera .. { Bats.

Cetacea..... { Whales, Porpoises, Dolphins, Narwhale.

Sirenia...... { Manatee, Dugong.

Probobcidia. { Elephants.

Ungulata... { Rhinoceros, Horse, Hog, Sheep, Ox, Deer, Tapir, Bison, Giraffe.

Carnivora .. { Seal, Walrus, Raccoon, Bear, Otter, Skunk, Weasel, Mink, Fox, Wolf, Dog, Lynx, Panther, Leopard, Tiger, Lion, Cat.

Prosimii... { Lemurs.

Primates.... { Monkeys, Apes, (Gibbon, Orang Outang, Chimpanzee, Gorilla), Man.

P. ROCK STRUCTURE.

I. Sedimentary Rocks... {

Laminæ.

Stratum.. { Current Bedding. Wind Drift Structure. Wave Marks. Ripple Marks. Rill Marks. Mud Flows. Sun Cracks. Rain Prints. Gas Pipes. Thickness. Extent Overlap.

Clasolite.

10

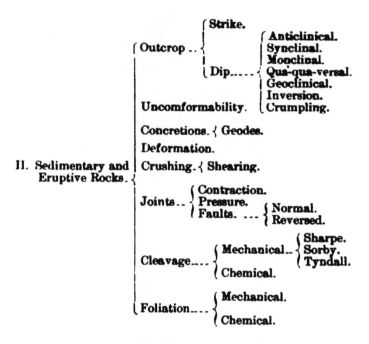

II. Sedimentary and Eruptive Rocks.
- Outcrop
  - Strike.
  - Dip
    - Anticlinical.
    - Synclinal.
    - Monclinal.
    - Qua-qua-versal.
    - Geoclinical.
    - Inversion.
    - Crumpling.
- Uncomformability.
- Concretions. { Geodes.
- Deformation.
- Crushing. { Shearing.
- Joints
  - Contraction.
  - Pressure.
  - Faults. { Normal. / Reversed.
- Cleavage
  - Mechanical
    - Sharpe.
    - Sorby.
    - Tyndall.
  - Chemical.
- Foliation
  - Mechanical.
  - Chemical.

Q. MOUNTAIN BUILDING.

I. Upheaval { Volcanic or Eruptive. / Flexure.

II. Denudation.

Division III.—Stratigraphical Geology.

R. GEOLOGICAL FORMATIONS.

I. Azoic or Archæan
- Laurentian. { Cascade.
- Huronian { Republic. / Mesnard.
- Michigan. { Holyoke. / Negaunee.

$$
\text{II. Palæozoic}
\begin{cases}
\text{Cambrian} \dots\dots \begin{cases} \text{Georgian.} \\ \text{Arcadian.} \\ \text{Potsdam.} \end{cases} \\[1em]
\text{Lower Silurian} \dots \begin{cases} \text{Canadian.} \\ \text{Trenton.} \end{cases} \\[1em]
\text{Upper Silurian} \dots \begin{cases} \text{Niagara.} \\ \text{Onondaga.} \\ \text{Lower Helderburg.} \end{cases} \\[1em]
\text{Devonian} \dots\dots \begin{cases} \text{Oriskany.} \\ \text{Corniferous.} \\ \text{Hamilton.} \\ \text{Chemung.} \end{cases} \\[1em]
\text{Carboniferous} \dots \begin{cases} \text{Subcarboniferous.} \\ \text{Carboniferous.} \\ \text{Permian.} \end{cases}
\end{cases}
$$

$$
\text{III. Mesozoic}
\begin{cases}
\text{Triassic} \dots\dots \begin{cases} \text{Vosgian.} \\ \text{Franconian.} \\ \text{Keuperian.} \\ \text{Rhaetic.} \end{cases} \\[1em]
\text{Jurassic} \dots\dots \begin{cases} \text{Liassic.} \\ \text{Oolitic.} \\ \text{Portlandian.} \end{cases} \\[1em]
\text{Cretaceous} \dots\dots \begin{cases} \text{Lower Cretaceous.} \\ \text{Upper Cretaceous.} \end{cases}
\end{cases}
$$

$$
\text{IV. Cenozoic} \begin{cases} \text{Tertiary} \dots\dots \begin{cases} \text{Eocene.} \\ \text{Oligocene.} \\ \text{Miocene.} \\ \text{Pliocene.} \end{cases} \end{cases}
$$

$$
\begin{matrix} \text{V. Anthozoic or} \\ \text{Anthropozoic.} \end{matrix} \Big\} \text{Quarternary} \dots \begin{cases} \text{Glacial.} \\ \text{Champlain.} \\ \text{Neitic or Recent.} \end{cases}
$$

Division IV.—Economic Geology.

S. UTILITES.

I. Definitions. Ore, Lode, Country Rock, Socialite (Associate or Comrade), Gangue or Veinstone.

II. Minerals Most Commonly Occurring as Socialites or Associates.

(a) *Sulphides:* Galenite, Sphalerite, Pyrite, Pyrrhotite, Arsenopyrite (Mispickel).

(b) *Fluorides and Oxides:* Fluorite, Quartz (Smoky), Hematite (Specular), Ilmenite, Magnetite, Rutile, Opal, Limonite.

(c) *Carbonates:* Calcite (Dog Tooth Spar), Dolomite, Magnesite, Siderite, Rhodochrosite, Aragonite (Floss-Ferri), Cerussite.

(d) *Anhydrous Silicates:* Orthoclase, Plagioclase, Saussurite, Wollastonite, Pyroxene (Coccolite), Amphibole (Tremolite' Actinolite, Asbestus, Hornblende), Nephelite, Garnet, Willemite, Scapolite, Vesuvianite, Epidote, Tourmaline, Titanite.

(e) *Hydrous Silicates;* Prehnite, Apophyllite, Stilbite, Laumontite, Chabazite, Analcite, Datolite, Natrolite, Thomsonite, Pectolite, Muscovite, Lepidolite, Zinnwaldite, Biotite, Chlorite, Serpentine, Talc, Pinite, Kaolinite.

(f) *Phosphates:* Apatite.

(g) *Sulphates:* Barite, Celestite, Anglesite, Anhydrite, Gypsum.

(h) *Tungstates:* Wolframite.

II. Principal Useful Minerals.

(a) *Native Elements:* Diamond, Graphite, Sulphur, Arsenic, Antimony, Bismuth, Gold, Silver, Copper, Mercury, Platinum.

(b) *Sulphides:* Realgar, Orpiment, Stibnite, Molybdenite, Argentite, Galenite, Chalcocite, Sphalerite (Blende), Cinnabar, Millerite, Niccolite, Pyrrhotite, Bornite, Chalcopyrite, Stannite, Pyrite, Smaltite, Cobaltite, Arsenopyrite (Mispickel), Bournonite, Pyrargyrite, Proustite, Tetrahedrite, Stephanite, Enargite.

(c) *Chlorides—Fluorides:* Halite, Sylvite, Cerargyrite (Horn Silver), Embolite, Fluorite, Cryolite, Atacamite, Carnallite.

(d) *Oxides:.* Quartz (Amethyst, Tiger's Eye, Chalcedony, Carnelian, Plasma, Blood Stone, Agate, Moss Agate, Onyx, Flint, Jasper, Silicfied Wood), Senarmontite, Cuprite, Zincite, Tenorite (Malconite), Corundum (Emery), Hematite (Specular, Columnar, Micaceous, Red Ochre), Martite, Ilmenite, Spinel, Magnetite, Franklinite, Chromite, Chrysoberyl, Cassiterite (Tin Stone), Rutile, Zircon, Pyrrhotite, Opal, Manganite, Limmonite (Yellow Ochre, Umber, Bog Ore), Bauxite, Psilomelane, Wad.

(e) *Carbonates:* Calcite (Iceland Spar, Mexican Onyx, Chalk, Limestone, Marble), Dolomite, Magnesite, Siderite, Rhodocrosite, Smithsonite, Willemite, Strontianite, Cerussite, Malachite, Azurite.

(f) *Anhydrous Silicates:* Orthoclase (Adularia), Plagioclase (Sunstone, Moonstone, Labradorite), Rhodonite, Amphibole (Asbestus), Beryl, Iolite, Garnet, Chrysolite (Olivine), Willemite, Topaz, Tourmaline.

(g) *Hydrous Silicates:* Calamine, Muscovite, Serpentine (Chrysotile), Garnierite, Talc, Sepiolite, Kaolinite, Halloysite (Fuller's Earth), Chrysocolla, Glauconite.

(h) *Phosphates:* Apatite (Phosphorite, Guano, etc.), Pyromophite, Mimetite.

(i) *Borates:* Boracite, Borax.

(j) *Uraninates:* Uranite.

(k) *Sulphates:* Glauberite, Barite, Celestite, Anglesite, Anhydrite, Gypsum (Selenite, Satin Spar, Alabaster), Aluminite, Alunite,

(l) *Tungstates:* Wolframite.

(m) *Hydrocarbons:* Ozocerite, Succinite (Amber), Petroleum, Asphaltum, Albertite, Uintahite, Anthracite, Bituminosite (Bituminous Coal), Cannelite (Cannel Coal), Lignite (Brown Coal, Jet).

III. Origin and Modes of Occurrence of Utilites, or Useful Geological Products.

1. Eruptive Deposits ....
   - Non-Fragmental Deposits,
     - Flow Deposits.
     - Dike Deposits.
     - Mass Deposits.
   - Fragmental Deposits, { Bed Deposits.

2. Organic Deposits ....
   - Vegetable Deposits, { Bed Deposits.
   - Animal Deposits, { Bed Deposits.

3. Mechanical Deposits ......
   - Unconsolidated Deposits, { Placer or Bed Deposits.
   - Consolidated Deposits, { Bed Deposits.

4. Chemical Deposits ....
   - Sublimations, or Vapor Deposits.
   - Water Deposits, { Bed Deposits.
   - Decomposition Deposits, { Bed Deposits.
   - Impregnations, or Replacement Deposits,
     - Eruptive Rock Impregnations. { Carbona Deposits
     - Sedimentary Rock Impregnations. { Bed Deposits.
   - Segregations, or Cavity Deposits,
     - Pocket Deposits.
     - Chamber Deposits.
     - Vein Deposits.
       - Gash Veins.
       - Segregated Veins.
       - Recticulated Veins, or Stockworks.
       - Fissure, or Fault Veins.

IV. Use of Geological Products—*See* Table XIII.

Y 2. *Stratigraphical Geology.*

ASSISTANT PROFESSOR SEAMAN AND MR. SUTTON.

Winter term, three hours a week, fourteen weeks. To count for two-fifths of a course.

The instruction in this subject will consist of recitations and laboratory work and will be given following V 2 (Zoology and Palaeontology). The main object of the course will be to familiarize the student with the life history of the earth, and with the lithological characters, mode of formation, order of superposition, times of upheaval, and distribution in time and space, of the formations which compose the earth's crust.

There will be laboratory drill in assigning fossils to their proper geological horizon. In this work the student will have access to palaeontological literature, with which the library is well supplied. The material at present accessible for the laboratory work consists of a palaeontological collection of four thousand specimens, three small rock collections, one European and two American, containing six hundred specimens arranged stratigraphically, and over one thousand specimens of sedimentary rocks belonging to the lithological collection.

In addition to the above, some time will be given to surface geology in which the present contours of the earth's surface will be discussed.

The text-book used is Dana's Manual of Geology, 4th Edition.

Y 3.—*Physical and Chemical Geology.*

THE DIRECTOR.

Winter term, three hours a week, fourteen weeks.

To count as a two-fifths course.

The instruction in Physical Geology is intended to be especially adapted to the needs of the explorer, the teacher, the engineer, the petrographer, the geologist, the miner, the quarryman, and all others who desire to understand the connection and the structural relations that rock masses have to one another and to the valuable deposits which they may contain. It treats of the origin and alterations of rocks, of general volcanic and earthquake action, metamorphism, jointing, faulting, cleavage, mountain building, eruptive rocks and crystalline schists; the action of air, surface and underground waters, and life; the interior condition of the earth, etc., especially in their relations to the problems that the economic geologist, miner and quarryman have to meet. The student has brought before him constantly the various problems that arise in practical work and the methods of their solution.

This course enlarges and completes much that is briefly touched upon in the Principles of Geology and in Petrography.

The instruction is given by lectures and by recitations based upon the lectures and upon Dr. Archibald Geikie's Text Book of Geology, third edition, 1893, books I, II (part I), III, IV and VII.

Students who take this subject must have completed subjects W 2 (Mineralogy), and Y 2 (Stratigraphical Geology), and must either have completed, or take in connection with this, X 1 (Petrography).

Y 4. *Geological Field Work.*

ASSISTANT PROFESSOR SEAMAN AND MR. SUTTON.

Forty-five hours a week for the last six weeks of the Summer term. To count as a full course. The instruction in this subject begins early in July, and consists of six weeks practical work in the field, mostly amongst the pre-Cambrian rocks of the Lake Superior region.

The first two weeks of the course are spent at compass work, in which the student is trained in pacing, and in the use of the dial and dip compass and aneroid barometer. This work consists of running section lines, meandering woods, roads and streams, running contour lines, platting outcrops, in fact making a complete map of the traverses. Specimens are collected, and must be located with reference to some section, corner or quarter post established by the United States linear survey. On this work the student plats all of his work in the field, keeping his latitude and departure by means of his compass course and pacing.

After the students become more or less adept at platting and compass work, they are given special small areas to map in detail, and to work out the relations of the rocks. They make sections and plans showing these relations, and are required to write descriptions of the specimens collected, and to explain the geological phenomena observed.

Considerable time is spent in the study of the older granites, gneisses, and hornblende schists with their varied accompaniment of basic and acid intrusives comprising what is termed the Cascade formation.

Next in order are studied the great series of clastics that rest non-conformably upon the Cascade formation. These clastics are found to be capable of division into a lower and an upper series termed respectively the Republic and Holyoke formations with both of which are associated large bodies of iron ore. These ore bodies are studied with reference to their origin, and maps and sections are made showing their mode of occurrence, and their relations to the associated rocks.

The last week of the course is devoted to the study of the interbedded sandstones and old lava flows of Keweenaw Point. These rocks are termed the Keweenawan formation. Lastly a day or two is spent along the contact line between the Keweenawan rocks and the Eastern sandstones, in studying their relative stratigraphical position.

The department is well supplied with the instruments necessary for this work, and note books with special ruling are furnished the student at cost.

All students entering the Mining School for instruction in this subject (Y 4) alone, should have a fair knowledge of Mineralogy, Lithology and General Geology if they wish to fully profit by the course.

The other students of the Mining School who elect this subject are required to have passed in Q 1 (Surveying), L 3 (Topographical Drawing), W 2 (Mineralogy), Y 2 (Stratigraphical Geology), and Y 3 (Physical Geology).

Y 5.—*Economic Geology.*

THE DIRECTOR.

Three times a week for twenty-eight weeks, during the fall and winter term. To count for four-fifths of a course.

In this subject, the instruction will take up the geology of the useful, or economic, mineral products considered from two different points of view.

1st. Their origin and modes of occurrence.

2d. Their uses.

The general ground covered by the lectures is shown by two orig. inal classifications—the first blocked out in 1882 and subsequently modified, and the second prepared in 1893. The first classification relating to the modes of occurrence of products, treated in the course of Economic Geology, is shown in Table XII; while that covered by the lectures relating to the uses of these products is shown in a general way by Table XIII.

Special attention is given to the instruction of the student in Mineralogy, Petrography and Geology, in order that he may in after years understand the nature of the deposits upon which he may be at work; since disastrous mistakes probably occur in the practice of a mining engineer oftener through ignorance of the petrographical and geological relations of the ore deposits in question, than from lack of engineering or metallurgical skill.

The location of the school affords special advantages for the study of Petrography and General and Economic Geology. It is situated in the midst of the vast and ancient lava flows and conglomerates generally known as the Keweenaw formation and the Eastern or Potsdam Sandstone. In the immediate vicinity are to be solved some of the most important and fundamental problems of petrographical and geological science, e. g , the metamorphism, or alteration of rocks; the true age of the so-called Keweenaw series, the origin of the iron ore, etc.; while almost every problem of Geology finds its illustration in some portion of the Upper Peninsula.

The student of geology can study within the limits of the Uppe-Peninsula of Michigan the following stratigraphical formations, commencing in the list with the oldest.

Azoic or Archaean System	Laurentian	Cascade.
	Huronian	Republic. Mesnard.
	Michigan	Holyoke. Negaunee.
Paleozoic System	Cambrian	Potsdam. (Keweenawan). Calciferous.
	Silurian	Trenton. Hudson River. Niagara. Onondaga. Lower Helderberg.
	Devonian	Upper Helderberg.
Anthropozoic or Anthozoic System,	Quaternary	Glacial. Champlain. Neitic or Recent.

The instruction in the various departments under the immediate charge of the Director is intended to be given so that all those who wish to obtain a knowledge of the subjects as a matter of general information, or to prepare themselves to be teachers or investigators, can attend with advantage. All those who expect to give any time to mine superintendence, should pay special attention to geology.

Subject Y 5 (Economic Geology) is open only to those who have passed in R 1 (Principles of Mining), X 1 (Petrography), Y 3 (Phy ical Geology), and Y 4 (Geological Field Work).

(Subject Y 5 will not be given in 1896-97).

J. THESIS.

THE FACULTY.

Properly qualified students who so desire may include in their list of electives a thesis which shall be considered equal in value to a full course. The object of this departure from the usual custom of engineering schools is to save the time wasted by so many students in preparing a thesis simply to obtain a degree, when they have no real interest in the subject about which they write, nor practical knowledge of it. Their time is much more profitably employed when spent in systematic study under regular instruction.

It is hoped and expected that by making the thesis elective, more valuable work and results, which shall be real contributions to knowledge, can be obtained.

J 1.—*Thesis.*

The time supposed to be given to this work is nine hours a week for thirty-four weeks, and the thesis, if accepted, is to count as a full course. The subject of the thesis is to be handed in simultaneously with the other electives. The work is to be done under the direction and with the approval of some instructor or instructors, and the subject and thesis must be approved by the Director.

The student must have taken all the necessary preparatory work that is required to enable him to properly handle his subject, or it will not be approved by the Director. The instructor or instructors under whom the thesis work is done must have presented to the Sec retary a written statement certifying that the student is properly prepared and able in their judgment to accomplish the work specified. This statement is to accompany the elective schedule.

The thesis must be completed by July 1st and submitted to the Faculty for examination and acceptance, but in no case will the thesis be accepted unless the instructor or instructors under whom the thesis work was done shall have attached to it a written statement that they approve the thesis and recommend its acceptance by the Faculty.

PREPARATORY SUBJECTS.

Work of this character was first introduced in September, 1895, owing to circumstances over which the Mining School had no control. Since then those circumstances have changed and it is intended to drop again all work of a preparatory nature after June, 1897. No general preparatory department has been added, but a few elective studies are given, to be taken by persons whose training is defective in certain of the required preparatory subjects.

These subjects are as follows :

I. *Elementary Algebra.*

MR. FISHER.

A course for beginners, covering the fundamental operations, factoring, fractions, equations, simple and quadratic roots and indices.

Van Velzer and Slichter's School Algebra is used as a text-book.

Three times a week for thirty-four weeks.

II. *Geometry.*

MR. FISHER.

This subject includes Plane, Solid and Spherical Geometry, and is given from Van Velzer and Schutz's Suggestive Geometry.

Three times a week for thirty-four weeks.

III. *Elementary Physics.*

MR. KNOX.

A course for beginners, covering the beginnings of Mechanics, Sound, Heat, Light, Magnetism, and Electricity. Qualitative experiments are freely used, though the greater part of the laboratory work is quantitative. Hall and Bergen's Text-Book of Physics and Carhart and Chute's Elements of Physics are the text-books.

Three times a week thirty-four weeks.

Must be preceded by, or accompanied with, subjects I (Elementary Algebra) and II (Geometry).

IV. *Bookkeeping.*

MR. FISHER.

This is a general course covering the requirements in this subject for admission to the Mining School. The instruction is intended to comprise the principles of single and double entry, business forms, laws of contracts, etc.

The Complete Practical Bookkeeping has been used as a text-book.

Three times a week for fourteen weeks during the fall term.

V. *Astronomy.*

MR. FISHER.

Three times a week for twenty weeks, during the winter term, and the first six weeks of the summer term.

The work in this subject comprises the elementary principles of Astronomy, using Young's Lessons in Astronomy.

Must be preceded by, or accompanied with, subjects I (Elementary Algebra), II (Geometry), and III (Elementary Physics).

DEGREES.

Three degrees are offered by the Mining School as follows:

BACHELOR OF SCIENCE, S. B.

MINING ENGINEER, E. M.

DOCTOR OF PHILOSOPHY, PH. D.

The conditions under which the first two will be given are as follows:

All candidates for the degree of S. B. are required to pass in eighteen full courses, including subjects R 1 (Principles of Mining) and Y 1 (Principles of Geology).

All candidates for the degree of Mining Engineer are required to pass in twenty-two full courses, including subjects R 1 (Principles of Mining) and Y 1 (Principles of Geology).

The degree of Ph. D. will be given under the following conditions:

Students who are E. M. graduates of this institution, or graduates of other institutions of similar grade, whose course shall be approved by the Faculty, will be admitted as candidates for the degree of Doctor of Philosophy. In order to attain this degree they must pursue, for at least two years, advanced studies in subjects allied to the work of this institution, which studies are to be approved by the Faculty.

One of the years may, in special cases, be spent elsewhere, and the work accepted, on sufficient proof of its thoroughness and high character, as the equivalent of one year's work done here. But under no condition will this degree, or any other degree, be given unless at least one year of thirty-four weeks of actual school work be spent as a resident student at this institution.

Students who are E. M. graduates of this, or of an equivalent professional school, and also A. B. graduates of some college or university whose course of study is accepted by the Faculty, may be admitted to the degree of Doctor of Philosophy, after having taken for at least one year of thirty-four weeks, an approved course of study at this institution.

The degree of Doctor of Philosophy will be given only in case the student shall have shown marked ability and power for original investigation, shall have passed a satisfactory oral public examination, and presented a thesis, which shall embody the result of original investigation, and receive the approval of the Faculty.

The degree of Mining Engineer will carry with it also the degree of Bachelor of Science, if the candidate for the degree of E. M. shall make application for the S. B. degree and pay the required fee, which until after August 1897 will be $5.00 for each degree for all students who entered the Mining School prior to commencement, 1895, and who graduate before September, 1897. All others will pay fees according to the following list, which after August, 1897, will apply to every candidate for a degree.

> Bachelor of Science $15 00
> Mining Engineer..................................... 25 00
> Doctor of Philosophy............................... 50 00

No degree will be conferred until the required fee has been paid, which payment must be made to the Treasurer prior to August first.

TEXT-BOOKS—1895-1897.

A.—*Mathematics.*

A 1. College Algebra, 1891. G. A. Wentworth.
Ginn & Co., Boston.

A 2 and 3. Plane and Spherical Trigonometry, 1893. N. H. Wheeler.
Ginn & Co., Boston.

A 2 and 3. Logarithmic Tables. Last Edition. G. W. Jones.
G. W. Jones, Ithaca, New York.

A 4. Analytic Geometry. Last Edition. G. A. Wentworth.
Ginn & Co., Boston.

A 5. Element of the Calculus. Last Edition. J. M. Taylor.
Ginn & Co., Boston.

A 5. Manuscript Notes on Calculus. 1893. F. W. McNair.

A 6. A Treatise on Ordinary and Partial Differential Equations. W.
W. Johnson. John Wiley & Sons, New York.

B. *Physics.*

B 1. Manuscript Notes in Physics. 1894–1895. F. W. McNair.

B 1. Laboratory Course in Physics. Last Edition. W. C. Sabine.
Ginn & Co., Boston.

B 1. Heat and Light. 1894. R. T. Glazebrook.
The Macmillan Co., New York.

B 1. Mechanics for Beginners. Last Edition. J. B. Lock.
The Macmillan Co., New York.

B 1. Electricity and Magnetism. 1895. S. P. Thompson.
The Macmillan Co., New York.

B 2 and 3. A Laboratory Manual of Physics and Applied Electricity.
E. L. Nichols. The Macmillan Co., New York.

B 2. Lessons on Elementary Practical Physics. Vols. I and II. Bal-
four Stewart and W. W. Haldane Gee.

B 3 Electrical Measurements, H. S Carhart and G. W. Patterson, Jr.
Allyn & Bacon, Boston.

C. *Mechanics.*

C 1 and 2. Mechanics of Engineering. I. P. Church.

John Wiley & Sons, New York.

F. *Chemistry.*

F 1. Manuscript Notes on General Chemistry. 1893. George A. Koenig.

F 1. Manuscript Notes on Experimental Chemistry. 1893. George A. Koenig.

F 2. Manual of Determinative Mineralogy. Thirteenth Edition. George J. Brush. John Wiley & Sons, New York.

F 2. Landauer's Blowpipe Analysis. 1892. Translated by James Taylor. The Macmillan Co., New York.

F 3. A System of Instruction in Qualitative Analysis. 1843. A. H. Elliott. A.H. Elliott, New York.

F 4. A System of Instruction in Quantitative Chemical Analysis. C. R. Fresenius. Tenth Edition. Edited by O. D. Allen and S. W. Johnson. John Wiley & Sons, New York.

F 4. Manuscript Notes in Quantitative Analysis. 1895–1896. G. A. Koenig.

G. *Metallurgy.*

G 1. Manuscript Notes in Assaying. 1895. George A. Koenig.

G 2. Metallurgy of Lead. 1892. H. O. Hofman.

Scientific Publishing Co., New York.

G 2. Modern American Methods of Copper Smelting. Seventh Edition. 1895. E. D. Peters.

Scientific Publishing Co., New York.

L. *Drawing.*

L 1. Copy Book of Round Writing (School Edition). F. Soennecken.

Keuffel & Esser Co., New York.

L 1. Elements of Mechanical Drawing. Last Edition. G. C. Anthony. D. C. Heath & Co., Boston.

L 1. Machine Drawing. Last Edition. G. C. Anthony.

D. C. Heath & Co., Boston.

L 4. Trusses and Arches. 1890–1891. Charles E. Greene.
John Wiley & Sons, New York.

L 5. Printed Notes on Construction. 1892–1893. Edgar Kidwell.

L 5. Manuscript Notes on Roof Truss Designing. 1892–1893. Edgar Kidwell.

L 5. Manuscript Notes on Railway Trestles. 1892–1893. Edgar Kidwell.

L 6. Manual of Machine Drawing and Design. 1893. D. A. Low and A. W. Bevis. Longmans, Green & Co., New York.

L 6. Elements of Machine Design. Last Edition. W. Cawthorne Unwin. Longmans, Green & Co., New York.

M. *Mechanical Engineering.*

M 1. South Kensington Notes on Building Construction. Vol. III. 1889. Rivingtons, London.

M 2. Pattern Maker's Assistant. Latest Edition. Joshua Rose.
D. Van Nostrand Co., New York.

M 2. Complete Practical Machinist. Last Edition. Joshua Rose.
D. Van Nostrand & Co., New York.

M 4. Text Book on the Mechanics of Materials. 1895. Fifth Edition. Mansfield Merriman. John Wiley & Sons, New York.

M 5. Constructive Steam Engineering. 1890. J. M. Whitham.
John Wiley & Sons, New York.

M 5 and 9. Pumping Machinery. 1893. W. M. Barr.
J. B. Lippincott Co., Philadelphia.

M 7. Valve Gears for Steam Engines. 1892. C. H. Peabody.
John Wiley & Sons, New York.

M 8 and 9. Thermodynamics of the Steam Engine and Other Heat Engines. 1889. C. H. Peabody. John Wiley & Sons, New York.

N. *Electrical Engineering.*

N 1 and 3. Incandescent Wiring Hand Book. Last Edition. F. B. Badt. Electrician Publishing Co., Chicago.

N 1 and 3. Electrical Engineering. Last Edition. W. Slingo and A. Brooker. Longmans, Green & Co., New York.

11

N 2 and 3. Electricity and Magnetism. 1895. Francis E. Nipher.
John L. Boland Book Co., St. Louis.

N 3. Electric Motive Power. Albion T. Snell.
Electrician Publishing Co., London.

Q. *Civil Engineering.*

Q 1. Theory and Practice of Surveying. Last Edition. J. B. Johnson.
John Wiley & Sons, New York.

Q 1. Field Engineering. Last Edition. William H. Searle.
John Wiley & Sons, New York.

Q 3. A Treatise on Hydraulics. Fourth Edition. Mansfield Merriman.
John Wiley & Sons, New York.

R. *Mining Enigneering.*

R 1. A Text-Book of Ore and Stone Mining. 1894. C. LeNeve Foster.
C. Griffin & Co., London.

R 2. Manuscript Notes in Mine Surveying and Mining. Revised 1895. F. W. Sperr.

R 4. Manuscript Notes of Mining Engineering. Revised, 1894–1895. F. W. Sperr.

R 5. Manuscript Notes on Mine Management and Accounts. Revised, 1895. F. W. Sperr.

R 5. Engineering Contracts and Specifications. 1895. J. B. Johnson.
Engineering News Publishing Co., New York.

S. *Ore Dressing.*

S 1. Manuscript Notes on Ore Dressing. 1895. F. W. Sperr.

V. *Biology.*

V 2. Elements of Zoology. Manuscript. 1889. M. E. Wadsworth.

V 2. Orton's Comparative Zoology. 1894. Charles Wright Dodge.
Harper & Brothers, New York.

V 2. Elementary Palæontology. 1893. H. Woods.
The Macmillan Co., New York.

V 2. Manuscript notes on Palæontology. 1893. A. E. Seaman.

W. *Mineralogy.*

W 1. Manuscript Notes on Crystallography. 1898. A. E. Seaman.

W 2. The System of Mineralogy. Sixth Edition. 1892. James D, Dana and E. S. Dana.   John Wiley & Sons, New York.

W 2. Practical Determination of Minerals—Manuscript. 1876-1893. M. E. Wadsworth.

X. *Petrography.*

X 1. Introduction to Optical and Microscopic Mineralogy—Manuscript. 1877-1893. M. E. Wadsworth.

X 1. Practical Determination of Rock Forming Minerals. Manuscript. 1877-1893. M. E. Wadsworth.

X 1. Microscopical Physiography of the Rock Making Minerals. Third edition. 1893. H. Rosenbusch. Translated by J. P. Iddings. John Wiley & Sons, New York.

X 1. A Manual of Microchemical Analysis. 1894. H. Behrens. The Macmillan Co., New York.

X 1. Tableau des Birefringences. 1888. A. Michel Levy and A. Lacroix.   Baudry et Cie, Paris.

X 1. Elements of Lithology—Manuscript. 1877-1893. M. E. Wadsworth.

Y.—*Geology.*

Y 1. Class Book of Geology. Second Edition. Archibald Geikie. The Macmillan Co., New York.

Y 1. Compend of Geology. Last Edition. Joseph LeConte. D. Appleton & Co., New York.

Y 1 and 3. Principles of Geology—Manuscript. 1880-1893.

Y 1 and 5. Introduction to Economic Geology—Manuscript. 1892. M. E. Wadsworth.

Y 2. Manual of Geology. Fourth Edition. 1895. James D. Dana. John Wiley & Sons, New York.

Y 3. Text-Book of Geology. Third Edition. Archibald Geikie. The Macmillan Co., New York.

Y 5. Building Stones—Manuscript. 1878. M. E. Wadsworth.

PREPARATORY STUDIES.

I. School Algebra, 1894. Van Velzer and Slichter.

                Tracy, Gibbs & Co., Madison, Wis.

II. Plane and Solid Geometry, 1895. Van Velzer and Schutz.

                Tracy, Gibbs & Co., Madison, Wis.

III. Principles of Physics, 1895. A. P. Gage.

                Ginn & Co., Boston.

IV. Complete Practical Book-Keeping.

                The Practical Text Book Co., Cleveland.

V. Lessons in Astronomy, 1895. C. A Young.

                Ginn & Co., Boston.

ADVISORY ELECTIVE SCHEDULES.

In electing his course of study the student is at liberty to select any subjects he desires, provided that his choice does not conflict with the natural sequence of studies, *i. e.*, he is not to take any study until he has properly prepared himself in the studies that lead up to the one selected. The effort to choose his studies judiciously and in order is a laborious one for a student just entering upon his professional preparation, therefore a series of advisory schedules has been made as guides to students in making their selections.

The student is at perfect liberty to follow any other of the numerous schedules that can readily be laid out, and each member of the Faculty will be pleased to assist anyone who wishes aid in arranging his scheme of studies.

The schedules here given assign to one year more work than can properly be accomplished in a year's time by any but the best and ablest students, and all are advised to choose fewer rather than more studies each year.

From six to eight full courses in one year of forty-five weeks are all that should be undertaken, while if the year is limited to thirty-four weeks, from four to seven is the limit. The student gains far more if he takes only what he can do expediently and thoroughly, and as a rule graduates sooner, than if he selects more subjects than he is able to carry.

The fourth year given is a graduate year in every case, since the student can obtain his degree in the first three years, if he is able to carry seven and two-fifths courses each year.

PRINCIPAL OBJECT—CHEMISTRY OR GEOLOGY.

First Year—Seven and Four-fifths Courses.

A 1. Algebra, 1. *
A 2. Plane Trigonometry, 2-5.
A 3. Spherical Trigonometry, 1-5.
A 4. Analytic Geometry, 4-5.
B 1. Physics, 1.
F 1. General Chemistry, 4-5.
F 2. Blowpipe Analysis, 1-5.
L 2. Topographical Drawing, 1-5.
Q 1. Surveying, 2.
R 1. Principles of Mining, 3-5.
V 1. Economic Botany, 1-5.
W 1. Crystallography, 1-5.
Y 1. Principles of Geology, 1-5.

Second Year—Seven and Four-fifths Courses.

F 3. Qualitative Analysis, 4-5.
L 1. Mechanical Drawing, 1.
L 3. Topographical Drawing, 1-5.
M 1. Properties of Materials, 3-5.
M 2. Shop Practice, 2.
R 2. Mine Surveying and Mining, 2-5.
R 3. Mine Surveying and Mining (Practice), 1.
V 2. Zoology and Palæontology, 2-5.
W 2. Mineralogy, 1.
Y 2. Stratigraphical Geology, 2-5.

Third Year—Seven and Four-fifths Courses

A 5. Calculus, 1.
B 2. Physical Measurements, 1-5.
C 1. Analytic Mechanics, 2-5.
F 4. Quantitative Analysis, 1.
F 5. Quantitative Analysis, 1.
G 1. Assaying, 2-5.
G 2. Metallurgy, 1.

---

* The numerals given after the name of the subject indicate the value of it in courses or parts of a course.

R 5. Mine Management and Accounts, 2-5.
X 1. Petrography, 1.
Y 3. Physical Geology, 2-5.
Y 4. Geological Field Work, 1.

Fourth Year—Seven and Four-fifths Courses.

B 3. Electrical Measurements, 1.
C 2. Analytic Mechanics, 2-5.
F 6. Synthetic Chemistry, 2.
G 3. Metallurgical Experimentation, 1.
M 3. Mechanism, 2-5.
Q 2. Hydraulics, 3-5.
R 3. Mining Engineering, 3-5.
S 1. Ore Dressing, 1.
Y 5. Economic Geology, 4-5.

PRINCIPAL OBJECT—METALLURGY.

First Year—Seven and Four-fifths Courses.

A 1. Algebra, 1.
A 2. Plane Trigonometry, 2-5.
A 3. Spherical Trigonometry, 1-5.
A 4. Analytic Geometry, 4-5.
B 1. Physics, 1.
F 1. General Chemistry, 4-5.
F 2. Blowpipe Analysis, 1-5.
L 2. Topographical Drawing, 1-5.
Q 1. Surveying, 2.
R 1. Principles of Mining, 3-5.
V 1. Economic Botany, 1-5.
W 1. Crystallography, 1-5.
Y 1. Principles of Geology, 1-5.

Second Year—Seven and Four-fifths Courses.

A 5. Calculus, 1.
C 1. Analytic Mechanics, 2-5.
F 3. Qualitative Analysis, 4-5.
L 1. Mechanical Drawing, 1.
· L 3. Topographical Drawing, 1-5.
M 1. Properties of Materials, 3-5.

M 2. Shop Practice, 2.
R 2. Mine Surveying and Mining, 2-5.
R 3. Mine Surveying and Mining (Practice), 1.
V 2. Zoology and Palæontology, 2-5.

Third Year—Eight Courses.

C 2. Analytic Mechanics, 2-5.
F 4. Quantitative Analysis, 1.
F 5. Quantitative Analysis, 1.
G 1. Assaying, 2-5.
G 2. Metallurgy, 1.
L 4. Graphical Statics, 2-5.
M 3. Mechanism, 2-5.
M 4. Mechanics of Materials, 1.
M 5. Mechanical Engineering, 1.
W 2. Mineralogy, 1.
Y 2. Stratigraphical Geology, 2-5.

Fourth Year—Eight Courses.

F 6. Synthetic Chemistry, 2.
G 3. Metallurgical Experimentation, 1.
G 4. Metallurgy and Designing, 1.
Q 2. Hydraulics, 3-5.
S 1. Ore Dressing, 1.
X 1. Petrography, 1.
Y 3. Physical Geology, 2-5.
Y 4. Geological Field Work, 1.

PRINCIPAL OBJECT—MECHANICAL ENGINEERING.

First Year—Seven and Four-fifths Courses.

A 1. Algebra, 1.
A 2. Plane Trigonometry, 2-5.
A 3. Spherical Trigonometry, 1-5.
A 4. Analytic Geometry, 4-5.
B 1. Physics, 1.
F 1. General Chemistry, 4-5.
F 2. Blowpipe Analysis, 1-5.
L 2. Topographical Drawing, 1-5.

Q 1. Surveying. 2.
R 1. Principles of Mining. 3-5.
V 1. Economic Botany. 1-5.
W 1. Crystallography, 1-5.
Y 1. Principles of Geology. 1-5.

Second Year—Seven and Four-Fifths

A 5. Calculus, 1.
C 1. Analytic Mechanics, 4-5.
F 3. Qualitative Analysis, 4-5.
L 1. Mechanical Drawing. 1.
L 3. Topographical Drawing. 1-5.
M 1. Properties of Materials, 3-5.
M 2. Shop Practice, 2.
R 2. Mine Surveying and Mining, 2-5.
R 3. Mine Surveying and Mining (Practice), 1.
V 2. Zoology and Palæontology, 2-5.

Third Year—Eight Courses.

B 3. Electrical Measurements, 1.
C 2. Analytic Mechanics, 2-5.
G 2. Metallurgy, 1.
L 4. Graphical Statics, 2-5.
M 3. Mechanism, 2-5.
M 4. Mechanics of Materials, 1.
M 5. Mechanical Engineering, 1.
M 6. Testing Materials of Engineering, 1.
N 1. Electrical Engineering, 4-5.
W 2. Mineralogy, 1.

Fourth Year—Eight Courses.

F 4. Quantitative Analysis, 1.
G 1. Assaying, 2-5.
L 6. Machine Design, 1.
M 7. Valve Gears, $\frac{1}{2}$.
M 8. Thermodynamics, $\frac{1}{2}$.
M 9. Mechanical Laboratory, 2.
N 2. Electricity and Magnetism, $\frac{1}{2}$.
N 3. Electrical Engineering, $\frac{1}{2}$.
Q 2. Hydraulics, 3-5.

R 4. Mining Engineering. 3-5.
Y 2. Stratigraphical Geology. 2-5.

PRINCIPAL OBJECT—ELECTRICAL ENGINEERING.

First Year—Seven and Four-fifths Courses.

A 1. Algebra, 1.
A 2. Plane Trigonometry. 2-5.
A 3. Spherical Trigonometry, 1-5.
A 4. Analytic Geometry, 4 5
B 1. Physics, 1.
F 1. General Chemistry. 4-5.
F 2. Blowpipe Analysis. 1-5.
L 2. Topographical Drawing. 1-5.
Q 1. Surveying. 2
R 1. Principles of Mining. 3-5
V 1. Economic Botany. 1-5.
W 1. Crystallography. 1-5.
Y 1. Principles of Geology. 1-5

Second Year—Seven and Four-fifths Courses.

A 5. Calculus. 1
C 1. Analytic Mechanics. 5-5.
F 8. Quantitative Analysis. 4-5.
L 1. Mechanical Drawing. 2
L 3. Topographical Drawing. 1-5
M 1. Properties of Materials. 5-5.
M 2. Shop Practice. 2
R 2. Mine Surveying and Mining 5-5
R 5. Mine Surveying and Mining Practice. 2
V 2. Zoology and Palæontology. 5-5

Third Year—Eight Courses

B 2. Electrical Measurements. 2
C 2. Analytic Mechanics. 5-5
G 2. Metallurgy. 2
L 4. Graphical Statics. 5-5
M 3. Mechanism. 5-5
M 4. Mechanics of Materials. 2
M 5. Mechanical Engineering. 2

M 6. Testing Materials of Engineering, 1.
N 1. Electrical Engineering, 4-5.
W 2. Mineralogy, 1.

Fourth Year—Eight Courses.

F 4. Quantitative Analysis, 1.
G 1. Assaying, 2-5.
L 6. Machine Design, 1.
M 7. Valve Gears, $\frac{1}{2}$.
M 8. Thermodynamics, $\frac{1}{2}$.
N 2. Electricity and Magnetism, $\frac{1}{2}$.
N 3. Electrical Engineering, $\frac{1}{2}$.
N 4. Electrical Engineering Laboratory, 2.
Q 2. Hydraulics, 3-5.
R 4. Mining Engineering, 3-5.
Y 2. Stratigraphical Geology, 2-5.

PRINCIPAL OBJECT—CIVIL OR MINING ENGINEERING.

First Year—Seven and Four-fifths Courses.

A 1. Algebra, 1.
A 2. Plane Trigonometry, 2-5.
A 3. Spherical Trigonometry, 1-5.
A 4. Analytic Geometry, 4-5.
B 1. Physics, 1.
F 1. General Chemistry, 4-5.
F 2. Blowpipe Analysis, 1-5.
L 2. Topographical Drawing, 1-5.
Q 1. Surveying, 2.
R 1. Principles of Mining, 3-5.
V 1. Economic Botany, 1-5.
W 1. Crystallography, 1-5.
Y 1. Principles of Geology, 1 5.

Second Year—Seven and Four-fifths Courses.

A 5. Calculus, 1.
C 1. Analytic Mechanics, 2-5.
F 3. Qualitative Analysis, 4-5.
L 1. Mechanical Drawing, 1.
L 3. Topographical Drawing, 1-5.

M 1. Properties of Materials, 3-5.
M 2. Shop-Practice, 2.
R 2. Mine Surveying and Mining, 2-5.
R 3. Mine Surveying and Mining (Practice), 1.
V 2. Zoology and Palæontology, 2-5.

Third Year—Seven and Four-fifths Courses.

C 2. Analytic Mechanics, 2-5.
F 4. Quantitative Analysis, 1.
L 4. Graphical Statics, 2-5.
M 3. Mechanism, 2-5.
M 4. Mechanics of Materials, 1.
M 5. Mechanical Engineering, 1.
M 6. Testing Materials of Engineering, 1.
Q 2. Hydraulics, 3-5.
R 4. Mining Engineering, 3-5.
W 2. Mineralogy, 1.
Y 2. Stratigraphical Geology, 2-5.

Fourth Year—Eight and One-fifth Courses.

B 3. Electrical Measurements, 1.
G 1. Assaying, 2-5.
G 2. Metallurgy, 1.
L 5. Engineering Design, 3-5.
N 1. Electrical Engineering, 1.
R 5. Mine Management and Accounts, 2-5.
R 6. Mine Ventilation, 2-5.
S 1. Ore Dressing, 1.
X 1. Petrography, 1.
Y 3. Physical Geology, 2-5.
Y 4. Geological Field Work, 1.

ENTRANCE EXAMINATION QUESTIONS.

ARITHMETIC.

1. Simplify $\frac{2}{3}$ of $\frac{4}{5}$ + $\frac{5}{11}$ and give reasons for each step in the process.

2. Simplify $\dfrac{\dfrac{2\frac{3}{4} - \frac{5}{7}}{3\frac{1}{4} + 1.25 - \frac{4}{15}}}{\dfrac{(\frac{11}{5} - \frac{4}{5}) + 1\frac{4}{5})}{\frac{3}{11} \times \frac{17}{8}}}$.

3. Extract the square root of 63.90684, and the cube root of .00016876.

4. Multiply thirty-seven and sixty-nine hundred thousandths by thirty hundredths and divide by thirteen ten thousandths. Explain the use of the decimal point in this case.

. 5. If one ton of ore containing $1\frac{1}{2}$ per cent copper is worth $3.30, what is the price of copper per kilogram.

6. Find the present worth of $600, due in two years, the rate of interest being six per cent.

7. Four men can do a piece of work in one hour which two women can do in three hours and six children in two hours. How long would one man, one women, and one child take to do the work? Give a full solution.

8. A bar of metal 6.3 meters long, 4 c. in. wide and $1\frac{1}{4}$ c. in. thick is cast into a cube, what is the length of one side of the cube? What would be the diameter if cast in the form of a sphere?

ALGEBRA.

1. (a) Add $\frac{1}{2}(\sqrt[3]{x^2} - y^{-\frac{1}{2}} + y^{-2})$ and $\frac{1}{2}(x^{\frac{2}{3}} + \frac{1}{\sqrt[3]{y}} - \frac{1}{z^2})$.

   (b) From $a + b + \sqrt{a-b}$ take $b + a - (a - b)^{\frac{1}{2}} + \sqrt{a\,b}$

2. Multiply $m^4 + n^4 + o^4 - m^2 n^2 - m^2 o^2$ by $m^2 + n^2 + o^2$.

   (a) Multiply $a^4 + a^3 y + a^2 y^2 - a y^3 + y^4$ by $a^2 + 2 a y - y^2$.

   (b) Divide $x + y + z - 3\sqrt[3]{x y z}$ by $x^{\frac{1}{3}} + y^{\frac{1}{3}} + z^{\frac{1}{3}}$.

3. Factor $m^4 - n^6$, $x^3 + a\,x + x + a$, $x^2 + 12\,x - 28$.

4. Simplify $\dfrac{\frac{a}{b^{\frac{2}{3}}} + \frac{b}{a^{\frac{2}{3}}}}{\frac{1}{a^2} - \frac{1}{ab} + \frac{1}{b^2}}$ also $\left[\dfrac{\sqrt[4]{a^3}\,\sqrt[3]{b^2}}{5\sqrt[4]{c^5}}\right]$ $\left[\dfrac{2\,b^{\frac{3}{4}}}{5\,a^{12}\sqrt[4]{b^9\,c^9}}\right]$ and explain steps in solution.

5. Solve $\dfrac{6\,x + 7}{3} - \dfrac{8}{t + 2} - (2\,x + \tfrac{1}{2}) = 0$.

GEOMETRY, PLANE.

Demonstrate the following propositions:

1. The sum of the angles of any plane triangle is equal to two right angles.

2. If two parallel lines are cut by a transversal, prove that the alternate exterior angles are equal.

3. If a line parallel to the base of a triangle bisects one side, it bisects the other side also.

4. In the same circle or equal circles, two angles at the center have the same ratio as the arcs which they subtend. (Two cases.)

5. The square on the hypothenuse of a right triangle is equivalent to the sum of the squares on the other two sides.

6. The area of a circle is equal to what? State and prove.

7. The ratio of the squares of the legs of a right triangle is equal to the ratio of the segments formed by dropping a perpendicular from the vertex of the right angle upon the hypothenuse.

8. Construct a rectangle the sum of whose base and altitude are equal to a given line, and whose area is equivalent to that of a given square.

GEOMETRY, SOLID AND SPHERICAL.

1. If a straight line is perpendicular to each of two other straight lines at their intersection, it is perpendicular to the plane of the two lines.

2. Every point in a plane which bisects a dihedral angle is equidistant from the faces of the angle.

3. The sum of any two face angles of a trihedral angle is greater than the third face angle.

4. The volume of a triangular pyramid is equal to one-third the product of the area of the base by the altitude.

5. The volume of a triangular pyramid is equal to one-third the volume of a triangular prism having the same base and altitude.

6. In two polar triangles each angle of one is measured by the supplement of the opposite side in the other.

7. The volume of a spherical pyramid is equal to the area of its base multiplied by one-third of the radius of the sphere.

8. A pyramid whose altitude is $^3\sqrt{16}$ feet is cut into two parts of equal volume by a plane parallel to the base. Find the distance of the cutting plane from the vertex.

PHYSICS.

1. What are the laws of liquid pressure? Explain the Hydrostatic Press.

2. What is density? Give some good method of finding the density of an iron nut.

3. A block of wood weighs 33.5 grams in air. A sinker weighs 22.8 grams in water. Both together weigh 15.7 grams in water. Find the specific gravity of the wood.

4. Find the resultant and equilibrant of a pair of forces of 3 lbs. and 4 lbs. at right angles to each other.

5. A pin is placed in front of a mirror. Illustrate by means of a diagram how you would find the position of the image.

6. Explain fully sound wave vibrations.

7. Explain the sympathetic vibrations and the interference of sound waves, and give an example of each.

8. How would you test a Centigrade mercury thermometer?

9. Given the value of the latent heat of fusion of ice as 80 g. cs., and that of steam as 537 g. cs , how many gram calories will be necessary to change 500 grams of ice at 0 degrees to steam at 100 degrees C.

10. State the laws of magnets and describe how you would set up a Daniell cell.

BOOK-KEEPING.

1. What are the principal methods of book-keeping? Name and state object of books used in each.

2. State rules for debiting and crediting, bills payable, bills receivable, interest.

3. What is a trial balance and a balance sheet? When may an account be omitted from the trial balance?

4. Jan. 4. Bought of Moore & Co., Detroit, 2,000 bbls. flour at

$5.25. Gave in payment our check on German-American Bank for $4,000, Preston & Co.'s note for $5,000, discount to maturity allowed to Moore & Co. and cash for balance.

(a) What debits and credits will you make for this transaction? Why?

(b) What entries will Moore & Co., make? Why?

(c) What entry will the German-American Bank make when check is paid?

(d) Give the form of Preston & Co.'s note as originally received by you.

(e) Give the form of check on German-American Bank on Jan. 4.

In addition to questions of above character a record of supposed transactions is given to the candidate to enter in the proper names in the different books, and he is required to make his own rulings.

ASTRONOMY.

1. How are stars located in the heavens? Give two methods, defining terms used.

2. What are nebulæ, new, variable and double stars, and upon what evidence are based the views concerning them?

3. Explain and illustrate by diagram what is meant by the radius vector passing over equal areas in equal time.

4. Define Parallax; and describe a process of finding the moon's approximate distance from the earth.

5. Explain the difference between the four kinds of time.

6. Give the method of locating the position of a ship at sea, in the daytime.

7. What is the distance from the sun of an asteroid having a period of eight years?

8. Explain one method of finding the velocity of light.

9. State clearly the Nebular Hypothesis and give the evidence upon which it is based.

10. What is the general law of Gravitation?

In applying this law to the relation of the earth to other bodies, what is taken as the unit of measure?

ENGLISH COMPOSITION.

Comets. Give a clear account of them, that shall be correct in punctuation, spelling and in the use of the English language.

Undulatory Theory of Light. Give a clear statement of this theory and the evidence in favor of it.

LIBRARY.

The Library of the School contains at present 11,353 volumes, and some 1,700 pamphlets, not including school catalogues. The 1,194 volumes added since the last issue of the Catalogue have been acquired as follows:

	GIFT.	PURCHASE.	BINDING.
1894-95	262	87	102
1895-96	233	238	272
Total	495	325	374

It will thus be seen that a large per cent of the accessions have been obtained through the courtesy of various societies. (books, etc.) Books added by purchase relate strictly to the technical subjects taught in the school, and the instructors find the library indispensable in presenting their subjects. Because of the use made of a library of this kind, it becomes a necessity. to have on hand records of the latest researches in science; hence an effort is made to secure books needed for the various departments as soon as they appear. This necessity is doubled when we remember that there is no other library in the town or vicinity to which those in search of such special literature can apply.

The library is intended to supplement class-room instruction throughout the school. Constant reference is made in classes to works contained in the library, and their study is encouraged.

The efficiency of the library depends largely upon the completeness of its files in important scientific and technical journals; to this end missing numbers and portions of sets which are lacking are supplied as fast as the school funds permit. It is especially desirable that the library should be rich in reports and works relating to Mining and the Mineral industry in this and other Mining regions of the world.

12

Contributions of books, pamphlets, maps, etc., bearing on the subjects taught are earnestly solicited and grateful acknowledgment is made of all such material received.

During the past year the library has been moved to the second floor of Science Hall, and occupies commodious, well-lighted quarters. The work on the card catalogue is continued.

A large collection of pamphlets, accumulated during past years, has been so arranged and classified as to be readily accessible, thereby greatly enhancing their value.

The library is open daily throughout the entire year, Sundays and legal holidays excepted, for the use of students and the public, under proper restrictions.

The Reading Room in connection with the library is supplied with the leading newspapers, scientific periodicals, journals, proceedings and transactions of societies. Heretofore all current publications of this kind were kept on file in the reading room, students having free access to them. The result was that great difficulty was experienced in keeping volumes complete for binding. This difficulty has been obviated and the school saved needless expense by placing on the library shelves all material intended for binding and preservation, and issuing such to the students only upon application.

A list of the publications received by the library, numbering 246 is appended.

PERIODICALS.

†Academische Revue, Munich.
 American Chemical Journal, Baltimore.
 American Engineer and Railroad Journal, New York.
†American Geologist, Minneapolis.
 American Journal of Mathematics, Baltimore.
†American Journal of Science, New Haven.
 American Machinist, New York.
†American Naturalist, Philadelphia.
*American Pythian, Grand Rapids.
†American School Commissioner, Chicago.
†Annalen der Chemie, Justus Liebig's, Leipzig.
†Annalen der Physik und Chemie, Leipzig.

---

†A complete set of this publication is in the library.
*Gift of publishers.

†Annalen der Physik und Chemie, Beiblätter, Leipzig.

Annalen des k. k. naturhistorischen Hofmuseums, Wien.

†Annales des Mines, Paris.

†Annals of Mathematics, University of Virginia.

*Ann Arbor Physician and Surgeon, Detroit.

Anthony's Photographic Bulletin, New York.

*Appleton (D.) & Co.'s Monthly Bulletin.

†Astrophysical Journal, Chicago.

Atlantic Monthly, New York.

Berg–und huettenmaennisces Jahrbuch, Vienna.

Berg-und huettenmaennische Zeitung, Leipzig.

†Berichte der deutschen chemischen Gesellschaft, Berlin.

*Book Reviews, The Macmillan Co., Mew York.

†Builder, London.

Bulletin of the American Mathematical Society, New York.

†Bulletin de la Société Chimique de Paris.

†Bulletin of the Essex Institute, Salem, Mass.

†Bulletin de la Société Française de Minéralogie, Paris.

Bulletin of the Geological Institute of the University of Upsala.

†Bulletin of the Geological Society of America, Rochester, New York.

†Bulletin de la Société Géologique de France, Paris.

†Bulletin of the University of California, Berkeley, California.

*Bulletins of the Helena Public Library, Helena, Mont.

†Bulletin of the University of Wisconsin, Madison, Wisconsin.

*Canadian Engineer, Toronto.

Canadian Mining Review, Ottawa.

†Cassier's Magazine, New York.

Century Magazine, New York.

Chemical News, London.

Chemiker Zeitung, Cöthen, Germany.

Die chemische Industrie, Berlin.

*Chicago Mining Review, Chicago.

Civilingenieur, Leipzig.

Colliery Engineer, Scranton, Penn.

Colliery Guardian, London.

Colliery Manager, London.

†Comptes Rendus, Paris.

Cosmopolitan, New York.

Der Technicker, New York.

†Dingler's polytechnisches Journal, Stuttgart.

Electrician, London.

†Electrical Engineer, New York.

Electrical World, New York.

Electrotechnische Zeitschrift, Berlin.

Engineer, London.

†Engineering, London.

†Engineering Magazine, New York.

Engineering Mechanics, New York.

†Engineering and Mining Journal, New York.

†Engineering News, New York.

Engineering Record, New York.

*Field Columbian Museum, Publications of, Chicago.

The Forum, New York.

†Geographical Journal, London.

†Geological Magazine, London.

*Good Health, Battle Creek.

Harper's Magazine. New York.

*Harvard University Bulletin, Cambridge, Mass.

*Helios: Export Journal for Electrical Industry.

*Hochschule Nachrichten.

*Home Study, Scranton, Pa.

Industries and Iron.

Iron Age, New York.

*Iron Trade Review, Cleveland.

†Jahrbuch der k. k. geologischen Reichsanstalt, Vienna.

†Jahrbuch für das Berg-und Hüttenwesen, Freiberg.

†Jahresbericht ueber die Fortschritte der Chemie, Braunschweig, Germany.

†Jahres-Bericht Ueber die Leistungen der chemischen Technologie (Wagner's), Leipzig.

*Johns Hopkins University Circulars, Baltimore.

Journal de Physique, Paris.

Journal für praktische Chemie, Leipzig.

Journal of Education, Boston.

†Journal of the Association of Engineering Societies, Chicago.

†Journal of the Chemical Society, London.

Journal of the Franklin Institute, Philadelphia.

†Journal of Geology, Chicago.

Journal of Pure and Applied Mathematics, London.

Journal of the Society of Arts, London.

Journal of the Society of Chemical Industry, London.

Journal of the Iron and Steel Institute, London.

†*Journal of the Western Society of Engineers, Chicago.

*Kritischer Vierteljahresbericht ueber die berg- & hüttenmännische und verwandte Literatur, Freiberg.

L'Eclairage Electrique, Paris.

Le Génie Civil, Paris.

Library Journal, New York.

†Library Notes. Boston.

*Literary News, New York.

†London, Edinburgh and Dublin Philosophical Magazine, London.

Mathematical Magazine, Washington.

†Memoirs of the American Academy of Arts and Sciences, Boston.

McClure's Magazine, New York.

Michigan School Moderator, Lansing.

Mineralogical Magazine and Journal of the Mineralogical Society, London.

*Mining, Spokane Falls, Wash.

Mining and Scientific Press, San Francisco.

†Nature, London.

†Neues Jahrbuch fur Mineralogie, Geologie und Palæontologie, Stuttgart.

Oesterreichische Zeitschrift für Berg-und-Hüttenwesen, Vienna.

*Official Gazette of the United States Patent Office, Washington.

†Petermann's Mittheilungen aus Justus Perthes' geographischer Anstalt, Gotha.

†Philosophical Transactions of the Royal Society of London.

Physical Education, Springfield, Mass.

†Physical Review, New York.

†Popular Science Monthly, New York.

Power, New York.

†Proceedings of the Academy of Natural Sciences, of Philadelphia.

†Proceedings of the American Academy of Arts and Sciences, Boston.

†Proceedings and Transactions of the American Society of Civil Engineers.

†Proceedings of the Boston Society of Natural History, Boston.

Proceedings of the Geologists' Association, London.

†Proceedings of the Institution of Civil Engineers, London.

†Proceedings of the Institution of Mechanical Engineers, London.

Proceedings of the London Mathematical Society, London.

*Proceedings of the Rochester Academy of Science, Rochester, New York.

†Proceedings of the Royal Society, London.

Publishers' Weekly, New York.

†Quarterly Journal of the Geological Society, London.

Review of Reviews, New York.

†Revue Universelle des Mines, de la Métallurgie, etc., Paris.

*St. Andrews' Cross, New York.

†School of Mines Quarterly, New York.

†Science, New York.

†Science Progress, London.

Scientific American, New York.

†Scientific American Supplement, New York.

Scribner's Magazine, New York.

†Sitzungsberichte der kaiserlichen Akademie der Wissenschaften, Vienna.

†Sitzungsberichte der königlich-preussischen Akademie der Wissenschaften zu Berlin.

Société Géologique de France, Compte Rendu, Paris.

Stahl und Eisen, Düsseldorf.

*Stone, Chicago.

†Transactions of the American Institute of Electrical Engineers, New York.

†Transactions of the American Institute of Mining Engineers, New York.

†Transactions of the American Society of Mechanical Engineers, New York.

*Transactions of the Canadian Institute, Toronto.

*Transactions of the Association of Civil Engineers of Cornell University, Ithaca, N. Y.

†Transactions of the Federated Institute of Mining Engineers, New-castle-on-Tyne, England.

Transactions of the Manchester Geological Society, Manchester, England.

†Transactions of the Wisconsin Academy of Arts, Sciences and Letters, Madison, Wis.
†Verhandlungen der k. k. geologischen Reichsanstalt, Vienna.
†Zeitschrift der deutschen geologischen Gesellschaft, Berlin.
†Zeitschrift für analytische Chemie, Wiesbaden.
†Zeitschrift für anorganische Chemie, Leipzig.
†Zeitschrift für das Berg-Hütten-und Salinenwesen, Berlin.
†Zeitschrift für Krystallographie und Mineralogie, Leipzig.
†Zeitschrift für physikalische Chemie, Leipzig.
†Zeitschrift für praktische Geologie, Berlin.

NEWSPAPERS.

* Alpena Pioneer.
*Ann Arbor Argus.
*Ann Arbor Courier.
*Bay City Tribune.
*Belleville Enterprise.
*Bellevue Gazette.
*Bessemer Herald.
*Boise City (Idaho) Statesman.
*Bronson Journal.
*Cadillac State Democrat.
*Calumet Conglomerate.
*Calumet Copper Country Evening News.
*Calumet and Red Jacket News.
*Capac Journal.
*Chicago Herald.
*Church Helper of Western Michigan.
*Coldwater Sun.
*Coldwater Weekly Courier.
*Crystal Falls Diamond Drill.
*Detroit Evening News.
*Detroit Free Press.
*Detroit Journal.
*Ely Times.
*Escanaba Iron Port.
*Escanaba Journal.
*Escanaba Mirror.

* Gift of the publishers.

*Ewen Recorder.
*Fife Lake Monitor.
*Flint Evening Journal.
*Florence Mining News.
*Grand Rapids Democrat.
*Grand Rapids Workman.
*Grand Traverse Herald.
*Hancock Semi-Weekly Copper Journal.
*Hancock Progress.
*Houghton Portage Lake Mining Gazette.
*Imlay City Record.
*Iron River Iron County Reporter.
*Ironwood News-Record.
*Ironwood Times.
*Ishpeming Iron Ore.
*Ishpeming Peninsular Record.
*Jackson Weekly Patriot.
*Kalamazoo Daily Telegraph.
*Kalkaskian.
*L'Anse Sentinel.
*Lake Linden Native Copper Times.
*Lansing Republican.
*Lapeer Clarion.
*Manistee Advocate.
*Manistee Daily News.
*Manistique Tribune.
*Manistique Semi-Weekly Pioneer.
*Maple Rapids Dispatch.
*Marquette Mining Journal.
*Menominee Democrat.
*Menominee Herald.
*Stephenson Menominee County Herald.
*Michigan Maccabee.
*Milan Leader.
*Negaunee Iron Herald.
*New York Times.
*Norway Current.
*Ontonagon Herald.
*Ontonagon Miner.

*Owosso Press.
*Petoskey Independent Democrat.
*Petoskey Record.
*Pontiac Gazette.
*Pontiac Oakland County Post.
*Port Huron Bee Hive.
*Port Huron Weekly Times.
*Romulus Roman.
*Saginaw Evening News.
*Saginaw Weekly Courier-Herald.
*Sault Ste. Marie Democrat.
*Sault Ste. Marie News.
*St. Clair Republican.
*St. Ignace News.
*Traverse Bay Eagle.
*Traverse City, Grand Traverse Herald.
*Vassar Times.
*Virginian.
*Virginia Enterprise.
*Willis Times.
*Youths' Instructor.
*Ypsilantian.

REGULATIONS OF THE LIBRARY.

1. *Hours:* The Library is open daily throughout the year except Sundays and legal holidays from 8 A. M. to 6 P. M.

2. *Access:* Students are not allowed access to the shelves except through special permission obtained from the Librarian.

3. *Reference Books:* Reference books are not to be taken from the building except by special permission from the Librarian.

4. *Time:* Books may be held by the students for two weeks, and renewed at the end of that time if desired, unless previously asked for by another.

5. *Ticket:* A ticket is to be deposited with the Librarian for every book and periodical taken from the Library.

6. *Books Lost or Injured:* Books lost or injured are to be replaced or repaired at the expense of the person to whom they were issued.

7. *Books Called in:* Books may be called in by the Librarian at any time.

8. *Fines:* Keeping books beyond the allotted time will entail a fine of five cents per day for each book overdue, and will forfeit the privilege of renewing or taking any other books, until the fines are paid.

9. *Use of Library:* Members of the Board of Control, officers of the State Geological Survey, the chief officers of mines, stamp mills and smelting works, superintendents and principals of graded schools, resident clergymen, and resident officers in the service of the State or the United States, and officers and students of the Mining School can take out books under the usual regulations herein provided. All other persons on the recommendation of the Director and Librarian, can take out books under the usual condition, after making a deposit of $5, with the Treasurer, or in case of books of special value, a deposit sufficient to cover the cost. The Treasurer's receipt is to be exhibited to the Librarian before any book is to be taken out by the party in question.

10. *Use in Reading Room:* Books may be taken out by any one for use in the Reading Room, at the discretion of the Librarian.

COLLECTIONS.

The distinctive purpose of the Mining School has been to arrange its collections for their value and use in teaching and not for exhibition or show. For this reason only minor portions of the materials belonging to the school are placed in exhibition cases for the benefit of the general public. Most of the collections are kept in drawers and cases, in the laboratories where the student has, as a rule, as free access to them as the instructors themselves. This is done in order that they shall be of the greatest benefit to the students, the parties in whose interests the Mining School was organized and for whose benefit it is conducted.

The collections now in the possession of the school for the purpose of illustration and study are the following:

Biological Collections	800
Palæontological Lecture Collections	790
Palæontological Practice Collection	3,100
Collection of Glass Crystal Models	151
Collection of Wooden Crystal Models	2,153
Collection of Natural Crystals	2,260
Collection Illustrative of Physical Properties of Minerals	485
Lecture Collection of Minerals	10,000
Practice Collection of Minerals	17,025
Exhibition Collection of Minerals	1,000
Emerson Collection of Minerals	550
Thin Sections of Minerals	2,000
Polariscope Sections of Minerals	132
Lecture Collection of Rocks	3,800
Practice Collection of Rocks	6,500
Rosenbusch Collection of Rocks	1,000

Lecture Collection of Michigan Rocks................   675
Practice Collection of Michigan Rocks..............   1,800
Stratigraphical Rock Collections.....................   210
Thin sections of Rocks...............................   4,973
                                                        ——————
                                                        66,014

Besides the above, there are collections of palæontological charts, metallurgical, geological, and petrographical diagrams, geological models, maps, metallurgical collections, etc.

Collections of slags, metallurgical products, materials for illustration in Economic Geology, as well as some exhibition collections, have been commenced and all persons, particularly former students and graduates of the school, who can, are urged to contribute to the school collections of minerals, rocks, veinstones, ores, slags, metallurgical products, samples of building stones, machinery, tools, etc., and models, photographs and prints of the same, etc.

In the case of mineral products used in arts and manufactures, it is desired to procure specimens showing the various stages in the process of manufacture. It is especially important for the School to receive and preserve sets of cores from drill holes, samples of ores from every mine, with specimens of the associated gangue minerals and rocks, as well as of the walls and associated country rocks.

If the graduates and other former students of the Mining School would see to it that the materials desired were sent to the school from their respective localities, they would do some little toward repaying the heavy debt that they owe to the State of Michigan in generously giving them their education free of charge.

PRIZES AND SCHOLARSHIPS.

THE LONGYEAR PRIZES.

Through the liberality of Hon. J. M. Longyear, of Marquette, the following prizes have been offered, as stated in his letter which is here appended:

Marquette, Michigan, Nov. 9, 1887.

CHARLES E. WRIGHT, ESQ., MARQUETTE:

DEAR SIR—I wish to offer three first prizes of seventy-five dollars ($75) each, and three second prizes of fifty dollars ($50) each, to be competed for by the members of the senior class of the Michigan Mining School. The competition to be by means of papers on three subjects, written by members of the class, and submitted to the Board of Control for examination in such a manner and a such a time as the Board may determine. I desire subjects selected with a view of producing papers which will be of practical use in developing the mineral resources of the State of Michigan. I should like something which would be of service to the average woodsman or explorer, and suggest the subjects of Practical Field Geology, and the use of the Dial and Dip Compass; in explorations leaving the selection of the third subject to the judgment of the Board. If this offer is accepted, and there are two or more papers on each subject submitted, I will pay seventy-five dollars to each of the writers of the three papers which may be awarded the first prizes, and fifty dollars to each of the writers of the three papers which may be awarded the second prizes.

I would suggest, however, that in case only two papers are submitted, that the Board reserve the right of awarding only one prize, in case such action should seem advisable. In case only one paper should be submitted, I should like the Board to exercise its judgment in awarding a prize. It is my desire to publish the papers under the writers' names, in pamphlet form, for distribution among miners, explorers, land owners, and others.

Yours very truly

J. M. LONGYEAR.

In conformity with the foregoing letter, the Board of Control have decided upon the following subjects and conditions:

Subjects.

1. Field Geology; its Methods and their Applications.
2. The Dial and the Dip Compass and their Uses.
3. The Diamond Drill and its Uses.

Conditions.

The conditions under which the prizes are awarded are as follows: The papers are to be presented by June 1st, for each year.

A student may present a paper upon each of the three subjects, which will entitle him to three prizes, if his papers are found worthy.

The dissertations must be prepared in the same manner as the theses, the regulations for which can be procured on application to the Secretary of the school.

The title page is to have upon it an assumed name, and each dissertation is to be accompanied by a sealed envelope bearing the same name. This envelope must contain the writer's true, as well as assumed, name, and his address, and it will not be opened until the awards have been made.

No prizes will be awarded, unless the papers are judged by the committee to whom they are referred, to be of a sufficiently high standing to be entitled to a prize; hence, there may be awarded all, part, or none of the prizes, as the case may be.

These prizes can now be competed for by any students of the school, whether special, graduate or regular, without restriction to the graduating class, as was originally specified.

THE CHARLES E. WRIGHT SCHOLARSHIP.

The Charles E. Wright Scholarship has been founded by Mrs. Carrie A. Wright, of Ann Arbor, in accordance with the conditions expressed in the letter given below:

To the Honorable Board of Control of the Michigan Mining School:

GENTLEMEN—In memory of my husband, the late Charles E. Wright, and as a token of the deep interest he had in the Michigan

Mining School, I desire to give to said school the sum of one thousand dollars.

If said gift shall be accepted, it is to be held under the following conditions, to-wit: It is to be invested as a permanent fund, by the Board of Control, to form the nucleus of a scholarship to be known as the Charles E. Wright Scholarship. The income is to be given to some indigent student, by vote of the Board of Control, with the advice and consent of the Faculty of said school.

The award is to be made during the first term of the year, to some student who has a satisfactory record during the entire preceding year in the Michigan Mining School, and who intends to devote himself to the profession of Mining Engineering or Geological work. The income is to be divided into three equal parts, to be paid during the three terms of the year, and if at any time the conduct or standing of the student receiving the award should become unsatisfactory, the portion then remaining unpaid should be withheld from him, and given to some other student, in accordance with the terms of this gift.

(Signed)   CARRIE A. WRIGHT.

THE NORRIE SCHOLARSHIP.

This scholarship has been founded, and will be awarded in accordance with the conditions and requirements stated below:

Know all men by these presents, That I, A. Lanfear Norrie, of the city of New York, hereby give, grant, assign, and set over unto, the Michigan Mining School, of Houghton, Michigan, and to Peter White, D. H. Ball and J. M. Longyear, of Marquette, Michigan, as trustees, the sum of five thousand dollars ($5,000), lawful money of the United States.

The conditions of this gift, and upon which this fund is to be taken, are that the said trustees shall invest the same upon bond and mortgage in the village of Marquette, or in the city of Detroit, in the State of Michigan, or in the city of Milwaukee, in the State of Wisconsin, or in the city of Chicago, in the State of Illinois, upon unencumbered improved real estate.

That one-half of the income of said sum of $5,000 shall be paid yearly by said trustees unto the Board of Control, for the support of some student whose father has worked in, or in some way been connected with, mining operations in the Upper Peninsula of Michigan, who shall be designated by the Faculty of said school; and the remainder of said income shall be accumulated and invested as said principal shall be invested, and that this fund with its accumulations shall be the basis of a larger fund, to be obtained from other contributions, amounting to at least one hundred thousand dollars ($100,000), to be used for the erection of a Dormitory Building, for the use of such students as shall be designated by said Faculty; which building, when erected, shall be under the exclusive control of the corporation or Board of Control of the said Michigan Mining School

This gift is to the said trustees and their successors forever, for the benefit of the said Mining School. In case of the death of either of said trustees, the survivors or survivor shall appoint a successor or successors.

When the erection of said building shall be commenced, after the said fund of one hundred thousand dollars is obtained, the sum hereby given, with all its accumulations, shall be paid over to the said Mining School, for the purpose aforesaid.

Witness my hand, the 30th day of January, 1890.

A. LANFEAR NORRIE.

Witness, T. E. O. M. STETSON.

We, Peter White, D. H. Ball and J. M. Longyear, the persons named in the above instrument, accept the trust therein granted, in all respects, and agree to comply with the conditions thereof.

Witness our hands, the 1st day of February, 1890.

PETER WHITE,
D. H. BALL,
J. M. LONGYEAR.

THE LONGYEAR FUND.

This is a fund of $500.00 a year given for several years by Hon. J. M. Longyear of the Board of Control, to be the property of the Mining School, to be loaned to students of said School who may be designated by the Director and Treasurer, said students being unable to maintain their connection with the School without such aid.

This money is not to be a gift to the student, but he is to pay it back as soon as practicable after graduation. After his graduation interest will be charged him for the first three years at 5 per cent, and for the following two years at 7 per cent. The money and the interest are to go to the fund, to aid other students in the same way. This method, it is believed, will lead the student to a more manly feeling than a gift outright would produce in him, since it gives him the means of paying for his own education, assists him when he most needs assistance, and enables him to return the money to aid others, at a time when he can best do so.

It is believed that it would be better if all funds given to the School for investment and use, should be accompanied by some proviso that a certain portion, at least, of the income shall be saved or set aside, to increase the principal until it shall attain a limit, either fixed, or left to the proper authorities to determine. Such a method would enable the institution in the future to do much more good, than it would if the income were to be spent entirely each year.

The School is in great need of funds to aid students who would otherwise be unable to attend its classes. Aid of this kind is frequently sought by able and worthy young men, and all is done that can be, with the limited means at the command of the School to assist them.

The Longyear Fund has been continued for four years, and now amounts to $2,000.00, and part of it is at present available.

BENEFICIARIES OF SCHOLARSHIPS AND FUNDS.

Norrie Scholarship.

Robert Murray, Jr................................1894–1895

Longyear Fund.

Arthur Walter Bates... 1895–1896
Appleton Richey..................................1895–1896
Ralph Clark Works...............................1895–1896

13

BUILDINGS.

SCIENCE HALL, or the main building now occupied by the Mining School, was completed by the State in 1889, at a cost of $75,000. The building is constructed of Portage Entry sandstone, with a tile roof (see Frontispiece).

The larger part of the site and grounds was donated to the School by the Honorable Jay A. Hubbell, to whom the establishment of the School is chiefly due. The building has a large and independent supply of spring water, sufficient for all its present needs.

The main building is 109 feet by 53 feet, with a wing 37 feet by 25 feet. The interior portion of the building has been arranged so as to save the greatest amount of space possible for the laboratories and working rooms, consistent with safety to the structure and proper light. The halls have been reduced to a minimum. The size of the rooms and their uses are here given:

SCIENCE HALL.

BASEMENT.

Students' Room......................................16x33 feet.
Gymnasium ....31x42 feet.
Store Room..14x19 feet.
Carpenter Shop.....................................31x42 feet.
Assaying Laboratory...............................32x41 feet.
Weighing Room.....................................13x16 feet.
Lavatory ....8x11 feet.

FIRST FLOOR.

Laboratory of Economic Geology..................22x27 feet.
Palæontological Laboratory.......................21x27 feet.
Professor's Room....................................15x21 feet.
Geological Laboratory ....21x27 feet.

Mineralogical Laboratory.... ....27x40 feet.
Petrographical Laboratory.....................24x33 feet.
Goniometer Room............................. 7x16 feet.
Lavatory....................................13x16 feet.
Coat Room.... .... 6x16 feet.

SECOND FLOOR.

Library.....................................29x49 feet.
Reading Room...............................14x21 feet.
Recitation Room............................15x26 feet.
Recitation Room............................14x21 feet.
Recitation Room............................28x32 feet.
Professor's Room...........................14x16 feet.
Physical Laboratory........................33x41 feet.
Lavatory...................................13x16 feet.

THIRD FLOOR.

Balance Room...............................13x16 feet.
Quantitative Laboratory....................43x32 feet.
Professor's Room...........................15x26 feet.
Qualitative Laboratory.....................43x49 feet.
Chemical Lecture Room......................24x33 feet.
Spectroscope Room.......................... 6x16 feet.
Chemical Supply Room.......................15x16 feet.
Chemical Supply Room.......................11x13 feet.

TOWER.

Professor's Room...........................15x26 feet.
Photographic Laboratory....................15x19 feet.

ENGINEERING HALL.

This building was erected in 1893–1894, and first occupied in the summer of the latter year. (See plate at the end of this catalogue.) The size of its rooms and their uses are subjoined:

BASEMENT.

Machine shop...............................97x24 feet.
Tool Room.................................. 5x17 feet.
Electrical Instrument Room ....34x17 feet.
Dynamo Room...............................34x27 feet.

Lavatory..28x10 feet.
Photometer Room..................................... 8x14 feet.

FIRST FLOOR.

Pattern Shop.......................................70x25 feet.
Lecture Room......................................28x26 feet.
Laboratory for Testing Materials..................27x25 feet.
Oil Testing Room..................................18x 9 feet.
Tool Room...11x 8 feet.
Lavatory..12x12 feet.
Professor's Office................................16x13 feet.
Stock Room..18x 9 feet.
Storage Battery Room..............................15x11 feet.

SECOND FLOOR.

Drawing Room......................................97x25 feet.
Blue Print Room...................................12x 8 feet.
Lecture Room......................................35x28 feet.
Assistant's Office................................12x11 feet.
Office of Mining Department.......................16x15 feet.
Map Room..15x12 feet.
Lavatory..11x11 feet.

An annex contains a Fuel Room 16x34 feet, and a Boiler Room 29x34 feet. In the latter are located three boilers, two of which are used for heating purposes. To enable the student to become practically familiar with water tube boilers, a 58 HP Stirling water tube boiler is used to supply steam to shop, laboratory and stamp mill engines.

Besides the two principal buildings the School has also erected for its use other structures as follows:

Ore Dressing Plant or Stamp Mill..................81x30 feet.
Roasting Furnace Building.........................28x28 feet.
Oil House...22x20 feet.
Storage House.....................................46x25 feet.

The floor plans of Science Hall are appended.

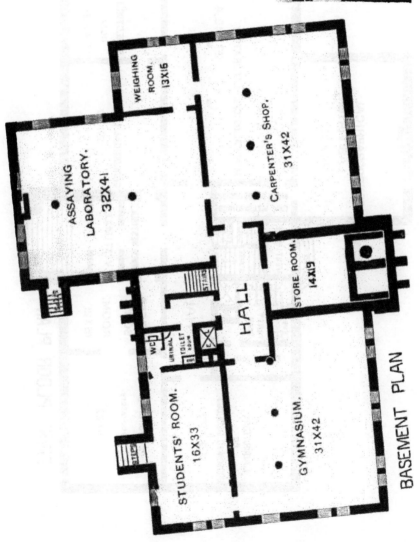

WEIGHING ROOM. 13X15

CARPENTER'S SHOP. 31X42

ASSAYING LABORATORY. 32X41

STORE ROOM. 14X19

STAIRS

HALL

W.C. URINAL TOILET ROOM

STUDENTS' ROOM. 16X33

GYMNASIUM. 31X42

BASEMENT PLAN

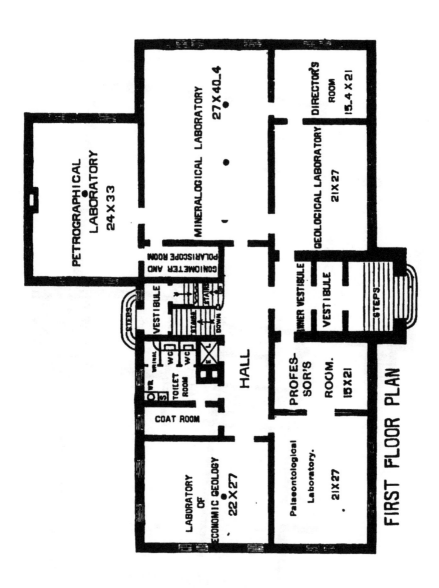

FIRST FLOOR PLAN

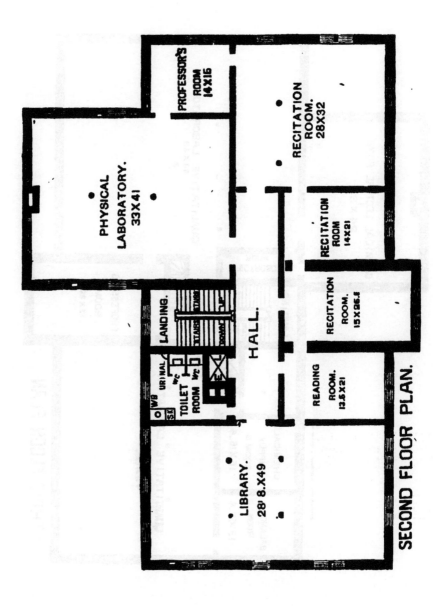

SECOND FLOOR PLAN.

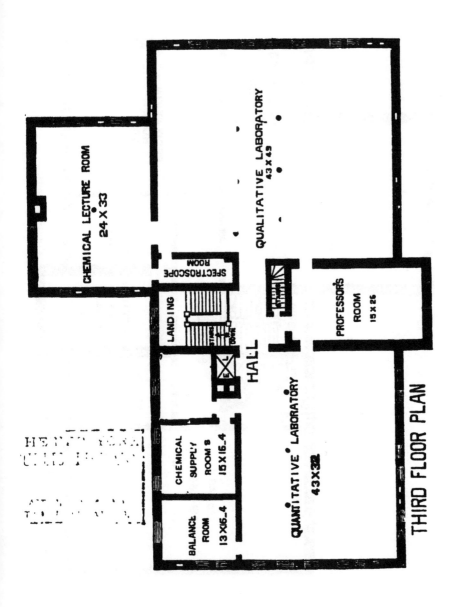

THIRD FLOOR PLAN

DEPOSITS, TUITION AND OTHER EXPENSES.

Under the act of organization, the Board of Control has made the school entirely free, no charge being made for tuition or incidentals, whether the student is a resident of the State of Michigan, or of the United States, or not; students from every land, under the broad, enlightened and liberal policy of the State, are cordially invited to make the fullest use of the educational advantage offered by this institution.

The supplies in the chemical and allied laboratories are furnished the students, and they are required to pay for materials, re-agents. etc., and for the use and breakage of apparatus, but there is no difference made between residents of the State and non-residents.

All students working in the Chemical Laboratories are required to pay ten dollars a year, which general charge covers all chemicals, gas, use of balances, etc. Students taking the course in Assaying are required to pay eight dollars for materials consumed.

In order partially to insure the State against damage and loss to its school property, every student is required to deposit with the Treasurer the sum of twenty-five dollars ($25). This sum shall not be withdrawn by the student until he closes his connection with the School; and if any portion is required by the School as a refund for damages, the part withdrawn shall be at once replaced by the student, or he shall stand dismissed from the institution.

Charges for apparatus, chemicals and other supplies from the store room, as well as for repairs of damages to school property, and also fines, shall be deducted from coupons procurable from the Clerk upon payment of five dollars each, but no portion of the twenty-five dollars above mentioned shall be used for the purchase of these coupons. The permanent deposit of twenty-five dollars, together with any balance equivalent to the unused portion of a coupon, shall be returned to the student when he closes his connection with the school, but not before.

There are no dormitories connected with the School. Arrangements can be made by those who desire to do so, to obtain board and rooms in private families, and in boarding houses, in Houghton and Hancock, at prices varying from twenty to twenty-five dollars per calendar month. Twenty-two or twenty-three dollars per month is understood to be the standard average price. This is to include the room, heat and lights, as well as board. Board alone can be obtained at from seventeen to twenty dollars per calendar month.

The expenses of course vary much with the taste and habits of the student, but when it is considered that he is given gratuitously instruction of a grade and with an equipment that he cannot obtain elsewhere except upon the payment of from $100.00 to $200.00 tuition fee, the average expenses seem very low.

Students have assured the Director that during the forty-five weeks in the school year their entire expenses were within $200.00. This small expense can of course be obtained only by self board or by boarding in clubs.

In averaging the expenses of the students the data given below have been furnished by the students to one of their own number who was interested in collecting the statistics. They can be relied upon, therefore, as being as accurate as it is possible to obtain. In comparing these expenses with those at other institutions, it is to be remembered three years of forty-five weeks at the Mining School are . the equivalent of the usual four years of most other institutions; while if a sudent remains here only the ordinary thirty-four weeks of a school year, he can proportionately diminish his expenses so that they will be only about two-thirds of the amounts given in the table of expenses.

ANNUAL EXPENSES OF STUDENTS IN THE MICHIGAN MINING SCHOOL FOR FORTY-FIVE WEEKS OF ACTUAL SCHOOL WORK.

EXPENSES FOR STUDENTS.	LOW.	MEDIUM.	HIGH
Board (Forty-five Weeks)..........	$175 00	$190 00	$225 00 +
Room (Eleven Months).............	11 00	55 00	65 00 +
Washing, etc. (Eleven Months)....	15 00	25 00	30 00 +
Books..........................	25 00	29 00	38 00 +
Laboratory Expenses.....	15 00	25 00	30 00 +
Incidental Expenses (Mining Trips, etc.).............................	10 00	13 00	25 00 +
Extra Expenses in Mining, Surveying, or Field Geology...........	10 00	50 00	65 00 +
Total Annual Expenses............	$261 00	$387 00	$478 00 +
Average Weekly Expenses	$5 80	$8 60	$10 62 +

ORGANIZATION AND GOVERNMENT.

The Michigan Mining School is an institution established and supported by the State of Michigan, in accordance with that liberal educational policy which has placed its educational institutions among the foremost of America.

The Mining School is organized under the authority of an Act, approved May 1, 1895, portions of which are as follows:

"SECTION 1. The people of the State of Michigan enact: That a school shall be established in the Upper Peninsula of the State of Michigan, to be called the Michigan Mining School, for the purpose and under the regulations contained in this Act.

"SEC. 2. The said school shall be under the control and management of a board of six members, not less than four of whom shall be residents of the Upper Peninsula of the State of Michigan, who shall be known as the Board of Control of the Michigan Mining School, and who shall be appointed by the Governor of the State of Michigan, by and with the consent of the Senate, * * * * and who shall serve without compensation.

"SEC. 5. The course of instruction shall embrace geology, mineralogy, chemistry, mining and mining engineering, and such other branches of practical and theoretical knowledge as will, in the opinion of the board, conduce to the end of enabling the students of said Institution to obtain a full knowledge of the science, art and practice of mining, and the application of machinery thereto. Tuition shall be free in said Institution, to all *bona fide* residents of this State, but a reasonable charge for incidental expenses, not less than ten dollars nor exceeding thirty dollars per year, may be made against any student, if deemed necessary, and the board shall not be obliged to furnish books, apparatus, or other materials for the use of students.

"Sec. 6. The course of study,]the terms, and the hours of instruction, shall be regulated by the board, who shall also have power to make all such rules and regulations concerning admission, control and discipline of students, and such others, as may be deemed necessary for the good government of the Institution and the convenience and transaction of its business.

"Sec. 7. No debt shall be contracted beyond or apart from the actual means at the disposal of the Institution. The board may dispose of, or lease any property donated to the State for said School, or which may be acquired in payment of debts except of such as is necessary for the accommodation of the school. * * * * "

In conformity with the above act, the Michigan Mining School was first opened to students September 15, 1886, and has been made free to students from every land. All are received on the same conditions.

Further, the school has never contracted any debt in advance of the means at its disposal, and has all its property clear.

The Board assumes general oversight over all expenses, all employees of the Institution, aud all its general interests; the Director has general charge of the course of instruction, change of electives, admission of students, discipline, general absences, etc.; while each professor and instructor has sole charge of his rooms, apparatus, classes, the instruction given in his department, and the admission, retention, passing, or disciplining of students in his classes. The heads of departments are made responsible to the Director and he to the Board, while the subordinates are directly responsible to the professor in charge of the department to which they belong.

EMPLOYMENT.

The question is often asked, if the Michigan Mining School can promise employment to students, on graduation. The only answer is, that neither the Mining School nor any other self-respecting institution can make any such promises. The question of employment depends on too many factors. to be promised three or four years in advance. It depends on the demand and the supply, which are liable to vary from year to year; and it also very largely depends on a student's "personal equation."

The Michigan Mining School does not seek to attract students through holding out any inducement except one, i. e., that owing to its location, to its specially prepared equipment, and its distinctive purposes it can give an education that is practical and adapted to assist the student in his future work. It endeavors at least to give him more in a shorter number of years and at a less expense than he will obtain elsewhere. Its principles and methods are original, distinct and independent; based only upon its location and its object of educating persons in all branches of knowledge that relate to the development of the mineral wealth of the country—since it is the only institution in the United States distinctively devoted to that purpose. It tries to meet the spirit and needs of this day and generation.

That the Mining School has succeded in giving an education that is practically available for "bread winning" purposes, the occupations of its graduates given earlier in the catalogue is sufficient proof.

The law of supply and demand will apply to the employment of the graduates of the Mining School as it does in every other case. Prior to 1893 the demands upon the Mining School was greater than it had suitable men to supply, and so far as now known all its grad-

·uates are employed, while this year a number of its students have been engaged prior to graduation.

People are prone to forget the general laws of Political Economy, as shown in periods of prosperity, and in business depressions and panics. The student is apt to think that because at any one time there is a depression in the profession he is proposing to follow, that therefore there is no future in it; overlooking the fact that such depressions are shown by history to be incident to every occupation, and that prosperity follows stagnation as surely as the latter will succeed a period of marked business activity. The cycle may be formulated as "a state of quiescence,—next improvement,—growing confidence,—prosperity,—excitement,—over-trading,—convulsion,—pressure,—stagnation,—distress,— ending again in quiescence", when the cycle is again repeated. Thus it follows, that a pupil entering upon his preparation for his future occupation in a time of prosperity is often less sure of employment on graduation than one who starts upon this preparation during a time of distress.

The following table indicates that these periods of depression are not confined to any one country or business, political party, or tariff, but are widespread, if not universal—and are dependent upon some general periodic law belonging in common to all the commercial nations of the globe.

DATES OF COMMERCIAL CRISES.*

FRANCE.	ENGLAND.	UNITED STATES.
1804	1803	......
1810	1810	......
1813–14	1815	1814
1818	1818	1818
1825	1825	1826
1830	1830	1829–31
1836–39	1836–39	1837–39
1847	1847	1848
1857	1857	1857
1864	1864–66	1864
	1873	1873
1882	1882	1884
1893	1890–91	1893

* A Brief History of Panics, Juglar and Thorn, pp. 19, 22.

The periodic time is variable, but latterly it appears to be from eight to ten years in length roughly divided as follows: "Prosperity, for five to seven years; panic, a few months to a few years; and liquidation about a few years." The past three panics have been followed by strikes in 1877, 1885-86 and 1894, that greatly retarded the advancing tide of prosperity. The natural law is to prepare in dull times to take advantage of the active years, and this applies to mining as well as to all other occupations.

The success of a graduate depends very much upon himself, and it is evident from the positions occupied by the graduates, that rarely if ever has a student's capacity been misjudged when engaged in his undergraduate work.

The most forcible law deduced from the career of the Mining School graduates is the necessity of avoiding catching that dangerous and almost incurable disease, self-conceit, which renders worthless so large a proportion of mankind for employment in any capacity.

Every graduate should bear in mind that his education has simply prepared him to begin, and that in three or four years of undergraduate study, he cannot expect to master work that takes a man's life time. He should be humble and modest and above all remember that "he that humbleth himself shall be exalted" if he has patience, and is found worthy and well qualified. More than one graduate of this institution has found his progress over a rough and rugged road, and has met with numerous obstructions simply and purely on account of his unwillingness or inability to learn the above lesson, and not on account of any deficiency in training or ability.

A thorough, hard working student, with the power to command the respect of men, to manage those under him, and to work harmoniously with his fellow officers, will hardly ever fail of obtaining the choicest positions that are open to him; especially after having had the practical work and experience about the mines that the graduates of this school have.

Education and training do not give qualities to any man; they simply sharpen and develop those natural abilities that he possesses; hence, if he is not by nature fitted for a certain position, he ought not, and will not be likely, to obtain it. On the other hand, whatever may be a man's natural abilities, he will not be likely to obtain a position of any high grade unless he has been educated for it, either in school or outside—the outside education being by far the most expensive kind of education, both for him and his employers, that can be obtained.

Slothful, lazy, careless, dissipated and inefficient students will not, naturally, obtain places as readily as the hard-working ones, other things being equal; since until they reform, business men do not wish to employ them and do not trust them. They certainly will not be recommended as different from what they are by the Director of the Mining School, since a man who cannot be trusted to attend faithfully to his work when engaged in obtaining his professional training. is not one in whose hands it is safe to place important business and mining interests, for obtaining a professional training in this institution, is an entirely different affair from getting the general education given in the literary departments of colleges and universities.

Students should remember that their conduct, from the day they enter the Mining School until they leave it, has an all important bearing upon their future position and standing, and the past history of its graduates most emphatically proves it.

The Director of the Mining School makes one invariable rule, i. e., that all persons desiring students or graduates of this School shall be informed of the defects, as well as of the virtues, of the candidates, so far as he knows them; believing that such a course is the only one that is just either to the employer, to the student, or to the School. When information is fully given to the Director concerning the position and desired qualities of the person to fill it, pains are taken to select the student who is believed to be the most suitable party.

In order to secure the best future for themselves, students are urged to neglect no opportunities, beyond those afforded by the School, to inform themselves in the practical work of mining.

The graduates are also urged to turn their attention to a field in which success is almost sure, to men of ability and energy; to enter the mines or works as laborers, miners, foremen, or in some other subordinate capacity, and thoroughly master every detail, from the lowest to the highest work, since only men who have had this experience are apt to obtain later the highest positions. There is a great dearth of educated men, who have had also sufficient practical experience, to place in charge of the important mineral interests of the country.

14

It is men who have had a thorough education, both in theoretical and practical mining, and who have worked in every grade and position, that are sought to take charge of our mines and their allied industries. The future is for the man who is modest and willing to commence at the bottom of his profession, and who is conscious of the truth, that on graduation he is only just prepared to begin his work.

The graduates of the school are urged to keep the Director constantly informed concerning their positions, salaries, etc., and also what their desires are, in order that they may be assisted to advance, if opportunity offers.

While the Director may not be able to serve them, yet whenever the time comes that he can assist them he must have the information at hand, since when men are wanted, they are desired without delay. Failure to keep the Director properly informed has cost many a graduate the loss of important positions—e. g., one a young graduate lost a position paying $2,000 a year to start on, simply because he had neglected to give his new address, and the letters and telegrams sent could not be delivered. The Director personally considers it his duty to aid every graduate when he can, the only question being the fitness of that graduate for the position. The Director has no time to pay attention to or to remember the past piques and prejudices of the graduate, whom he may have had to discipline when a student —he has only time to consider the commercial aspect of the case—is the graduate in question the man for the place? The character and ability of the man and not any personal likes or dislikes are the points to which the Director has and always must pay his attention.

Officers of mines, and others, desiring surveyors, engineers, draughtsmen, foremen, chemists, assayers, etc., are requested to make their wants fully known to the Director of the Mining School, who will then recommend suitable candidates to them, if he knows of any.

The inquiry is frequently made by persons intending to become students, if they can attend to their school work and earn enough to pay their way at the same time. Such a course is not practicable, as the regular school work, if it is done as it should be, requires the entire available time of any student, however strong and able he may be. As a special student, taking only a few studies, one might be able to procure work to pay his way. The location of the school in a village, however, offers but little of the irregular work that a student wishes to obtain. The better way for the needy student is either to attend to his school and to his labor in alternate years, or else to borrow the means to continue his education, repaying through his increased earning power after graduation.

The Mining School itself has more or less assistantships, that are open from year to year, which properly qualified undergraduate or graduate students can avail themselves of if they wish.

Likewise it is preferred to employ the graduates of this School, in preference to those of other institutions, in the various instructorships, since a man trained in the methods employed in any school, is more useful in subordinate positions in that school at first, than is one ignorant of the special duties required. This does not apply to professorships since continued "inbreeding" is disastrous to any educational institution.

The salaries obtained upon graduation have been from about $500 to $1,800, averaging about $900 per year. The lower salaries were obtained by students who had less practical experience with men and with the world in general; these were obliged to spend some time in acquiring a special kind of knowledge that the Mining School cannot give.

So far as known, the salaries have increased, after a varied time from $900 to even $6,000 or more per year. All this, however, is dependent upon the demand and supply, the state of the mining industries at any time, and upon other factors too numerous to be mentioned.

LOCATION AND ROUTES.

The State of Michigan is divided by the three great lakes and the straits of Mackinaw into two peninsulas, both of which form valuable portions of the State, and are especially distinguished for their productions.

The Lower Peninsula has great prominence from its fruit, grain and other agricultural products, its lumber, salt, gypsum, coal, building stones, etc.

The Upper Peninsula is noted for its production of copper, iron ore, building stones, and lumber, while its agricultural interests are rapidly increasing.

The Lower Peninsula is some 282 miles in extreme length and 198 miles in width, while the Upper Peninsula is some 347 miles in length and 165 miles in width, or much larger than the state of Massachusetts, while its climate is much like that of Maine.

The chief mining districts in the Upper Peninsula are known as the Marquette, Menominee and Gogebic Iron Ranges, and the Copper District.

This latter has three distinct divisions, respectively known as the Keweenaw, Portage Lake and Ontonagon Districts.

The chief cities and towns of the Upper Peninsula are Baraga, Bessemer, Calumet, Champion, Crystal Falls, Escanaba, Gladstone, Hancock, Houghton, Iron Mountain, Iron River, Ironwood, Ishpeming, L'Anse, Lake Linden, Laurium, Manistique, Menominee, Munising, Negaunee, Newberry, Norway, Ontonagon, Red Jacket, Republic, St. Ignace, Sault Ste. Marie and Wakefield.

The Michigan Mining School is located in the village of Houghton (Portage township). The twin villages of Houghton and Hancock lie in the sheltered valley of Portage Lake, an arm of Lake Superior. The climate is dry, bracing and healthful. Although Houghton is in a high latitude, yet one is far less inconvenienced by the cold here than he is much further south along the Atlantic coast, or in the immediate vicinity of the great lakes; and can generally wear lighter clothing in the winter. This is due to the dryness of the Houghton climate, a climate which is free from malaria, hay fever, etc. In general students coming from localities further south, even from Alabama, Mississippi, Texas and Mexico, have found health and strength improved by the change. The town has an abundant supply of excellent and pure spring water.

Houghton is easily reached by rail from Detroit, Chicago, Milwaukee, St. Paul, Superior and Duluth; and by steamer from all the important ports on the chain of the great lakes. Within the State half fare rates are given given to the students of the Mining School by the Duluth, South Shore & Atlantic Railway and its associated railroads. Application for a permit allowing the student to purchase half fare tickets is to be made to the Director a week or more before the student has occasion for its first use. The permit once obtained is good during that calendar year, if the party remains a student in the school.

Intending students frequently inquire concerning the routes they can take to reach the Mining School from various localities, and special information is here given:

By rail Houghton is distant from Ann Arbor 582 miles, Bessemer 144 miles, Calumet 14 miles, Champion 64 miles, Chicago 402 miles, Crystal Falls, 147 miles, Detroit 545 miles, Duluth 279 miles, Escanaba 145 miles, Hancock 1 mile, Iron Mountain 119 miles, Ironwood 150 miles, Ishpeming 80 miles, Lake Linden 10 miles, Lansing 513 miles, Laurium 14 miles, Manistique 231 miles, Marquette 95 miles, Menominee 209 miles, Milwaukee 327 miles, Negaunee 83 miles, Newberry 191 miles, Ontonagon 118 miles, Red Jacket 15 miles, Republic 73 miles, St. Ignace 246 miles, Sault Ste. Marie 250 miles, and Ypsilanti 575 miles.

From Detroit one travels by the Michigan Central Railway to Mackinaw City, via Bay City. At Mackinaw City the cars of the Duluth, South Shore & Atlantic Railway are taken direct to Houghton. Time from Detroit about twenty-one hours. From Sault Ste. Marie, the Duluth, South Shore & Atlantic Railway carries its pas-

sengers direct to Houghton, time about thirteen hours. The same
railway is taken from Duluth and Superior to reach the Mining
School.   Passengers from Chicago and Milwaukee take either the
Chicago, Milwaukee & St. Paul Railway, via Champion; or the Chicago & Northwestern Railway, via Negaunee and Ishpeming; at
which places, on both routes, the passengers transfer to the Duluth,
South Shore & Atlantic Railway for Houghton.   Time from Chicago
to Houghton, about fifteen hours.

Students desiring to reach Houghton by boat, can take the steamers
of the Lake Michigan and Lake Superior Transportation Company, at
Chicago or Milwaukee, taking about three days from Chicago.
From Buffalo, Cleveland and Detroit, one can take the steamers of
The Western Transit Company, The Erie and Western Trans-
portation Company, and others.   Time from Buffalo about five days,
Cleveland four days, and Detroit three days.

Any of these lines can be taken from Duluth.

Special information, descriptive pamphlets, time tables and rates
can be obtained from the General Passenger Agents of the various
companies by writing to their respective offices, as follows:

Duluth, South Shore & Atlantic Railway Co., Marquette, Michigan.

Michigan Central Railway Co., Chicago, Ill., or Detroit, Mich.

Chicago, Milwaukee & St. Paul Railway Co., Chicago, Ill.

Chicago & Northwestern Railway Co., Chicago, Ill.

The Lake Michigan & Lake Superior Transportation Co., Rush
and North Water Streets, Chicago, Ill.

The Western Transit Co , No. 47 Main Street, Buffalo, N. Y.

The Erie & Western Transportation Co., Atlantic Dock, Buffalo,
N. Y.

Houghton County is the third wealthiest county in Michigan,
being surpassed only by Wayne (Detroit) and Kent (Grand Rapids)
Counties; and has an assessed valuation of $40,000,000.   The popula-
tion of the county, with its various townships and villages, is here
given according to the State census of 1894.

	1890.	1894.
Adams Township,		1,675
Calumet "	12,529	16,709
Chassell "	680	993
Duncan "	680	984
Franklin "	2,687	2,685
Hancock "	2,737	4,315
Laird "	159	231
Osceola "	3,630	4,712
Portage "	3,531	3,417
Quincy "	1,490	1,490
Schoolcraft "	3,325	3,908
Torch Lake "	2,904	3,055
Total	35,389	45,398

Increase in 3 years	10,009
Increase in 14 years	22,925
Increase in 40 years	44,681

The population of the villages is as follows:

	1894.
Atlantic Mine	1,675
Calumet	2,192
Chassell	554
Crystal Lake	55
Gregoryville	320
Hancock	1,662
Houghton	2,178
Kenton	113
Kitchie	75
Lake Linden	2,443
Mills' Station	794
Osceola	1,514
Oskar	171
Perkinsville	520
Quincy Mill	151
Quincy Mine	1,490
Red Jacket	3,242
Sidnaw	344
Tamarack and North Tamarack	1,402
Withey	184

Within a radius of three miles some 8,000 inhabitants are located about Houghton.

The village of Houghton is the county seat, has many wealthy citizens, excellent society, and is the residence town of the county; while that portion in which the Mining School is situated is the equal in beauty to any New England town.

The accompanying map will give a fair idea to the prospective student of the location of the Mining School and the adjacent mines.

While the School itself is situated in the Portage Lake copper district, the access to the Keweenawan copper district on the north is easy; and there lie within comparatively short distances the Ontonagon copper district, and the iron mining ranges of Marquette, Menominee and Gogebic.

In the immediate vicinity of the Mining School are located the Quincy, Atlantic, Franklin and Huron copper mines; while within a radius of eleven miles are situated the Calumet and Hecla, Tamarack, Osceola and other copper mines, with their machine shops, smelting works, rolling and stamp mills, etc. In the iron mining regions lie numerous great mines, prominent among which are the Cleveland, Jackson, Lake Superior, Lake Angeline, Champion, Republic, Chapin, Vulcan, Cyclops, Colby and Norrie.

The Michigan Mining School has been located in the Upper Peninsula of Michigan for the same reason that a medical school should be in the vicinity of large hospitals, in order that it shall be associated with the objects about which it treats.

From this location the student of the Michigan Mining School is placed in a mining atmosphere, in which all his surroundings and associations are in conformity with his present and future work. He is thus enabled to see in actual operation some of the most successful and extensive mining operations now conducted anywhere.

MINERAL INDUSTRIES.

In order that some idea can be intelligently given concerning the location of the Michigan Mining School there are here collected some statistics concerning the country at large and that of Michigan in particular.

Owing to the Lake Superior basin being a unit in its mineral wealth and geological structure, it becomes very difficult to obtain statistics, that shall be separated by the state boundaries, so, in part, the productions of Northern Michigan, Wisconsin and Minnesota have to be considered together.

This causes the prolongation of the Gogebic range into Wisconsin to naturally fall with its component part in Michigan; and like manner the Vermilion and Mesabi ranges belong to the Lake Superior district and shipments.

There will first be given some general statistics regarding the mineral productions of the United States followed by a more specific description of the mining industries in the Upper Peninsula.

This material is gathered in part from the publications of the United States Census and Geological Survey reports, part from the Director's past publications, including the last catalogue of this institution, but chiefly from manuscript kindly provided by Hon. George A. Newett, the present able Commissioner of Mineral Statistics for Michigan, or taken from his very valuable report for 1895.

TOTAL MINERAL PRODUCTION. UNITED STATES.

1880	$350,319,000
1881	386,175,552
1882	435,895,259
1883	434,241,073
1884	395,489,105
1885	409,398,680

1886 445,786,594
1888 540,829,436
1889 .... *550,827,866
1890 619,506,161
1891 622,968,969
1892 648,616,954
1893 574,201,807
1894 527,655,562

MINERAL PRODUCTION OF MICHIGAN.

1889 .... $70,880,534

The States nearest are

Pennsylvania, 1889 .... $150,876,649
Colorado, 1889   41,126,610
Montana, 1889   33,737,775
Ohio, 1889   26,653,439

WORLD'S PRODUCTION OF IRON ORE, 1892.

United States .... 16,300,000 tons.
Germany and Luxemburg .... 11,400,000 tons.
Great Britain .... 11,850,000 tons.
Spain .... 5,850,000 tons.
France .... 3,650,000 tons.
Austro-Hungary .... 2,000,000 tons.
Russian Empire .... 1,500,000 tons.
Chinese Empire .... 1,500,000 tons.
Sweden .... 1,200,000 tons.
Other Countries .... 2,800,000 tons.
                                                ─────────────
        Total .... 57,050,000 tons.

---

* U. S. census gives $587,230,662.

PRODUCTION OF IRON ORE—UNITED STATES.

YEAR.	1880.	1889.	1890.	1891.	1892.	1893.	1894.
Lake Superior District—Tons	1,677,814	7,519,614	8,944,031	7,621,465	9,564,388	6,594,618	7,862,548
All Other Mines in United States—Tons	5,442,548	6,998,457	7,092,012	6,969,718	6,732,278	4,963,011	4,187,131
Total Product of United States—Tons	7,120,362	14,518,041	16,036,043	14,591,178	16,296,666	11,557,629	11,879,679
Value of Product, Michigan		$15,800,521			$16,587,521	$9,611,192	$5,844,995
Value of Product, Minnesota		$2,478,041			$3,090,942	$2,331,204	$2,166,802
Value of Product, Wisconsin		$1,840,908			$1,428,931	$394,094	$380,518
Value of Product, Pennsylvania		$3,063,534			$3,197,028	$1,374,313	$943,459
Value of Product, New York		$3,100,216			$2,879,267	$1,222,934	$996,456
Value of Product, New Jersey		$1,841,543			$1,888,575	$909,458	$968,066
Value of Product, Both Virginias		$935,290			$1,428,801	$1,030,977	$873,305
Value of Product, Alabama		$1,511,611			$2,422,515	$1,490,259	$1,240,895
Value of Product of United States		$33,351,978			$33,504,896	$19,295,978	$18,571,325

RELATIVE RANK OF THE EIGHT IRON ORE PRODUCING STATES.

No.	1850.	1860.	1870.	1880.	1889.	1896.
1	Pennsylvania.	Pennsylvania.	Pennsylvania.	Pennsylvania.	Michigan.	Michigan.
2	Ohio.	Ohio.	Michigan.	Michigan.	Alabama.	Alabama.
3	Maryland.	New York.	Ohio.	New York.	Pennsylvania.	Minnesota.
4	Tennessee.	New Jersey.	New York.	New Jersey.	New York.	Pennsylvania.
5	Kentucky.	Michigan.	Maryland.	Ohio.	Minnesota.	Virginia.
6	Virginia.	Kentucky.	Kentucky.	Missouri.	Wisconsin.	New York.
7	New Jersey.	Maryland.	Missouri.	Alabama.	Virginia.	Wisconsin.
8	New York.	Tennesse.	New Jersey.	Virginia.	Tennessee.	Tennessee.

IRON ORE SHIPMENTS, LAKE SUPERIOR DISTRICT.

Range.	1895.	Total to 1896.
Marquette Range (Michigan)	2,095,166 tons.	48,987,510 tons.
Menominee Range (Michigan)	1,094,804 tons.	18,578,827 tons.
Menominee Range (Wisconsin)	231,399 tons.	2,726,377 tons.
Gogebic Range (Michigan)	2,132,897 tons.	16,342,961 tons.
Gogebic Range (Wisconsin)	428,368 tons.	2,674,207 tons.
Mesabi Range (Minnesota)	2,778,296 tons.	5,192,504 tons.
Vermilion Range (Minnesota)	1,077,888 tons.	8,182,145 tons.
Total	10,488,268 tons.	97,586,581 tons.

GOLD MINING.

Production, California, 1889,................$12,586,722 00
"   Colorado,   " 3,883,859 00

SILVER MINING.

Production, Colorado, 1889, Coining Value..$23,757,751 00
"   Montana,' "   "   "   ... 17,468,960 00
"   Utah.   "   "   "   ... 9,057,014 00

GOLD AND SILVER (Combined) MINING.

Expenditures, Colorado, 1889,...............$13,834,332 00
"   California, " 12,506,555 00
"   Montana,   " 9,259,657 00
"   Nevada,   " 8,254,755 00

Wages, Colorado, 1889,...... ....   9,339,875 00
"   California, " 9,191,500 00
"   Montana,   " 5,881,500 00
"   Nevada,   " 3,522,280 00

Total Horse Power of all Engines in 1889 employed in Gold and Silver Mining, United States, 55,122.

COPPER MINING.

Expenditures, Michigan, 1889,............. ..$7,478,828 00
"   Montana,   " 3,204,455 00

Wages, Michigan, 1889,........................   3,174,363 00
"   Montana,   " 2,010,940 00

HORSE POWER OF ENGINES, COPPER MINING.

Michigan, 1889........ ....29,545 horse power.
Montana,   "   .... 3,530 horse power.

In 1896 the Calumet and Hecla Co. and the Tamarack and Osceola Co. alone have 60,000 horse power: Calumet and Hecla Co., 40,000, Tamarack and Osceola Co., 20,000.

CAPITAL INVESTED, COPPER MINING.

Michigan, 1889...............................$33,111,253 00
Montana,   " 23,395,000 00

LARGEST AMOUNTS OF DIVIDENDS PAID BY MINES ACTIVE AT PRESENT TIME.

Calumet and Hecla, Michigan.................$44,850,000 00

Belcher (Silver-Gold), Nevada................. 15,397,300 00

Ontario (Silver-Lead), Utah.................. 18,175,000 00

Granite Mountain (Silver), Montana.......... 12,120,000 00

Quincy (Copper), Michigan.................... 7,620,000 00

Total dividends paid by the copper mines of Michigan, $68,460,375.

POUNDS OF COPPER PRODUCED IN VARIOUS STATES AND IN THE UNITED STATES.

Year.	Michigan.	Montana.	Colorado.	Arizona.	Utah.	California.	United States.
1883	59,703,404	24,664,846	1,152,639	23,874,968	341,395	1,600,862	115,535,058
1884	69,358,202	48,063,054	2,018,125	26,734,345	295,526	876,166	144,946,653
1885	72,147,899	67,797,961	1,146,400	22,708,386	129,199	469,028	165,875,483
1886	80,918,460	57,611,621	409,306	16,657,035	500,000	430,210	157,763,048
1887	76,028,697	78,699,677	2,013,027	17,720,462	2,500,000	1,600,000	181,477,331
1888	86,472,034	97,897,966	1,621,100	31,797,300	2,181,047	1,570,021	229,881,466
1889	88,175,075	96,222,444	1,170,058	31,580,185	65,467	151,505	226,775,962
1890	101,410,277	112,980,896	3,555,091	34,706,689	1,036,686	28,347	259,763,092
1891	114,322,709	112,063,320	6,336,878	39,873,279	1,562,098	3,397,406	284,121,764
1892	123,198,460	163,205,128	7,593,647	89,436,099	2,202,428	2,980,944	344,996,679
1893	112,605,078	155,209,188	7,005,826	43,902,824	1,135,330	290,682	329,364,398
1894	114,808,870	188,072,156	6,491,418	44,514,564	1,147,570	120,000	354,188,374
1895	129,673,856	185,000,000	.....	48,000,000	.....	.....	385,578,856

COPPER DISTRICT.

PORTAGE LAKE DIVISION.

This division is the principal copper producing district of Michigan, and its territory is embraced in the map which is given in this catalogue and shows the location of the Michigan Mining School in its midst.

Calumet and Hecla Mine.

This famous mine has as its lode an old sea beach conglomerate which is underlaid by a lava flow, as well as overlaid by one; and the copper has been chemically deposited within this conglomerate by the percolating waters long subsequent to its formation, and after it was deeply buried under successive lava flows. Although many speak of the Calumet vein, neither that mine nor any other in the Portage Lake division is worked upon a vein or on anything that in the slightest degree approaches a vein in its character. All are bed mines—part conglomerate beds, part lava flows forming beds. The bed of the Calumet lode is inclined at an angle of about 39 degrees to the northwest, and averages about 16 feet in width.

From 6 to 30 pounds of copper are obtained from a ton of the sea beach rock, averaging about 9 pounds to the ton.

This mine has the largest machinery and the deepest shafts of any mine in the world.*

Beginning on the shore of Lake Superior, there are the Lake Superior Water Works, Pump House, and Boiler House, containing one Worthington high pressure compound condensing pump with cylinders of 19 1-4 inches and 33 3-8 by 24 inches, and plungers 9 by 24 inches.

Two spare Worthington pumps with cylinders 10 by 18 inches, and two boilers 64 inches diameter by 17 feet long, of 300 horse power,

---

*The following is mainly condensed from President Agassiz's Report for 1893, with some later additions.

XXXII   XXXVI

and one locomotive boiler 54 inches diameter, of 100 horse power. When fully equipped, the capacity of these works will be 2,000,000 gallons a day. The water is taken from a pipe 18 inches in diameter, and extending 1,200 feet into Lake Superior. It is pumped through a 12-inch wrought-iron pipe line 4½ miles in length, to an altitude of more than 700 feet, to the mine, where it is distributed over the whole location. A new water tower that will contain 520,000 gallons is in the course of construction.

The real estate of the Company consists of 2,599 25-100 acres of mineral land in Houghton county, and 20,352 35-100 acres of timber lands in Keweenaw, Houghton and Ontonagon counties. At the Stamp Mill there are 988 19-100 acres.

There are 698 houses belonging to the Company, of which 570 are on the mine location, 106 at the lake, and 22 at the Smelting Works. On leased lots the men own 782 houses at the mine, and 159 at the lake, while the Company employs some 3,456 men.

There are 20 churches on the property of the company, the greater number of which have been materially assisted by the Company at some time in their history.

There are, on land of the Company, six schools at the mine and lake, built partly at the cost of the Company and partly by the school district. The Company also owns a hotel.

There are at the mine, for cutting sets of timber used underground, a timber building, a large machine shop 225 by 250 feet, with a full complement of tools. Also at the mine three blacksmith's shops, two warehouses, two carpenter shops, and a paint shop.

The Calumet Engine House is a building of brick and stone, 146 by 62 feet. It contains: The compound engine "Superior," with cylinders of 40 inches, and 70 by 72 inch stroke, of 4,700 horse power; the Corliss engine "Rockland," used as a spare, of 600 horse power; the Leavitt engine "Baraga," 40 by 60 inches, also a spare, of 2,000 horse power; one pair 32 by 48 inch Rand Compressors, with a capacity of 26 air drills; and one pair 36 by 60 inch Rand Compressors, with a capacity of 41 air drills. There are four drums 20 feet 6¼ inches in diameter by 8 feet 4 inches face, to hoist from a depth of 4,000 feet from shafts Nos. 2, 4 and 5 Calumet, and No. 3 Hecla. By winding over and not increasing the load a depth of 6,000 feet may be reached.

15

The Boiler House is of stone 77 by 60 feet. It contains five boilers, two of 84 inches in diameter by 35 feet long, made by Kendall and Roberts; three of 90 inches diameter by 34 feet 6 5-8 inches long, made by the Dickson Manufacturing Company, the Southwark Foundry, and the I. P. Morris Company; total horse power, 2,780. The stack is 5 feet 6 inches internal diameter, and 150 feet high.

The Hecla Engine House is a brick building 80 by 47 feet, with an ell 44 by 17 feet 5 inches, and contains the compound engine "Frontenac," 27 3-4 and 48 by 72 inches, of 2,000 horse power; the Corliss engine "La Salle," 30 by 72 inches, used as a spare, of 900 horse power; and the Corliss engine "Perrot," 30 by 48 inches, also a spare engine, of 600 horse power; in addition, the two pair of compressors, water plunger type, 42 by 60 inches, with a capacity of 144 air drills, 72 drills for each set; one pair of Rand Compressors, 28 by 48 inches, of a capacity of 31 air drills.

The Boiler House is of brick, 80 by 58 feet, and contains three boilers made by Kendall and Roberts, 84 inches by 32 feet 10 3-4 inches, and two boilers made by the Dickson Manufacturing Co., 90 inches by 34 feet 4 inches, with a total of 1,690 horse power. The brick stack is 4 feet 6 inches inside diameter and 120 feet high.

On the Hecla, another Hoisting Engine and Boiler House contains the triple expansion hoisting engines "Gratiot," "Houghton," and "Seneca," of 2,000 horse power each, having cylinders 18 and 27 3-4 inches, and 48 by 90 inches, fitted with conical hoisting drums to reach a depth of 5,500 feet. The engine house is of stone, 112 by 78 feet. The boiler house of the same material, is 76 by 68 feet. There are five boilers, of 505 horse power each, 90 inches in diameter by 34 feet 6 inches long, built by the Dickson Manufacturing Company of Scranton, Penn., and the I. P. Morris Co., of Philadelphia, Penn. The brick stack is 9 feet 4 inches inside diameter, and 200 feet high.

The Engine House for Hecla shafts Nos. 7 and 8 contains the triple-expansion engines "Hancock" and "Pewabic," each of 2,000 horse-power; each operating by spur gearing its own drum, which is 25 feet in diameter by 8 feet 2 7-8 inches face, having a rope capacity of 5,500 feet, of 1 3-8 inch diameter. The cylinders are 20 1-8 and 31 3-4 inches and 50 by 48 inches. The maximum speed is 92 revolutions per minute, which is 3 3-4 revolutions to one of the drums. The house is 122 feet long, and 50 feet wide; it is built of stone.

The Boiler House will eventually hold ten boilers; it now contain three. They are 90 inches in diameter by 34 feet 6 inches long, and 505 horse power each. The house is 150 feet long and 65 feet wide. The stack is 12 feet 6 inches inside diameter, and 250 feet high.

Shafts Nos. 9 and 10 Hecla, are operated from a Hoisting Engine House built of stone, 75 by 46 feet. It contains two compound hoisting engines, the "Detroit" and "Onota," of 1,000 horse power combined, having cylinders 18 and 32 by 48 inches stroke, built by George H. Corliss. These engines drive by spur gearing two hoisting drums, formerly located at the Superior Engine House, each 20 feet in diameter by 8 feet 4 inches face, and will wind 4,000 feet of 1¼ inch rope. The drums make one revolution for every three revolutions of the engine.

In the Hoisting Engine House operating shafts Nos. 11 and 12 Hecla, there is a pair of Woodruff and Beach engines built in 1869, of 20 inches diameter by 48 inches stroke, with two drums of 8 feet diameter and 6 feet face. As one of the man-shaft engines, is used a vertical engine 26 inches in diameter by 36 inch stroke, built in 1867.

The company has eight new shaft-rock houses, extending from Calumet No. 5 to Hecla No. 12, a total length on the surface of 9,000 feet; the copper shute having in all a length of something over two miles underground, say 10,630 feet. There are eight shaft-rock houses at Hecla and at Calumet shafts, each containing a Westinghouse driving engine of 60 horse power, and two "Blake" crushers; each rock house with a bin capacity of about 1,500 tons. Both at No. 5 Calumet and at No. 4 Hecla, there is a fan for underground ventilation; these are 30 feet in diameter, with a capacity of about 100,000 cubic feet per minute. There are man-hoist buildings at five of the Hecla and three of the Calumet shafts; each contains a pair of engines and drum, used only for taking men up and down. Twenty-eight men can ride on one of the cars; they are especially constructed for that use. Three of the houses contain each a pair of 20 by 30 inch engines, with drums to wind 4,000 feet of 1¼ inch rope: the other five houses, one pair of engines 20 by 36 inches, with drums to wind 6,000 feet of 1¼ inch rope.

The Electric Light and Power House is built of stone, 74 by 74 feet; it contains a Porter-Allen engine, 18 inches in diameter by 36 inch stroke, of 400 horse power. A Westinghouse compound engine 23 and 40 by 20 inches, and 740 horse power, will be installed in this house.

There are two electric light dynamos for 1,000 sixteen candle power lights each; three Brush arc-light dynamos for 74 lights; five Brush generators 120 horse power each, with electric lines leading to the principal buildings, and to the three underground electric pumps at the Hecla end. Each pump has three double acting plungers 5¾ inches in diameter by 18 inch stroke, to run 50 revolutions per minute. At the Calumet end in No. 4 shaft, there are to be five electric pumps, each with three double acting plungers 5¾ inches in diameter by 18 inch stroke, to run 50 revolutions per minute. These pumps are placed 800 feet apart, having a vertical lift of 600 feet; the pump column is 8 inches in diameter. The company has at Calumet Nos. 4 and 5 shafts two spare steam Worthington pumps, with cylinders 10 and 18 inches by 18 inches, of a capacity of over 500,000 gallons per 24 hours.

The six-compartment Whiting Shaft has reached a depth of 4,900 feet. It intersected the Calumet lode at a depth of 3,300 feet, and will reach the bottom of the Company's territory at a depth of 5,000 feet.

It is equipped with a sinking-engine house of stone, 69 by 36 feet, containing a pair of horizontal tandem Corliss engines, with cylinders 16 and 32 inches in diameter by 48 inch stroke, with tail-rope house, and has the Whiting drum system.

The main hoisting-engine house, built of stone, 220 by 70 feet, contains two pair of triple expansion engines, of 3000 horse power per pair, having cylinders 20½ by 31¾, and 50 inches in diameter by 72 inch stroke, to run 60 revolutions per minute, and fitted with the Whiting drum system, arranged to hoist ten tons per load, at a speed of 60 feet per second. The tail house for the fleet gear is 412 by 32 feet, and is placed on the north end of the engine house. The sheave house is placed at the south end; it is 43 by 32 feet. These engines are calculated to hoist from a maximum vertical depth of 5000 feet.

The Boiler House is built of stone, 150 by 68 feet and will contain ten boilers, each 90 inches in diameter by 34 feet 6 inches long, and adopted to a working pressure of 185 pounds, at which they will each furnish steam for 1,000 horse power. There are at present six boilers in the house. The stack is of brick, 12½ feet inside diameter and 250 feet high.

The water used by the condensing engine is supplied from the Calumet Pond Water Works, where the Company has a main pond of a capacity of 60,000,000 gallons at five feet depth, and an auxiliary pond of a capacity of 30,000,000 gallons, at 2½ feet; both ponds are, when filled, of a capacity of say 100,000,000 gallons.

The Water Works Building consists of an engine and boiler house of brick, 100 by 45 feet; it contains a Leavitt pumping engine of a capacity of 5,000,000 gallons per day, steam cylinders 11¾ inches, and plungers 17 by 24 inches. In addition, there are two Worthington pumping-engines, of a capacity of 14,000,000 gallons per day; one pump with steam cylinders 14 and 24 by 36 inches, and 20 by 36 inch plungers, of a capacity of 4,000,000 gallons; and two others with steam cylinders 21 and 42 by 36 inches, and 29 by 36 inch plungers, of a capacity of 10,000,000 gallons. The boiler house contains three boilers, Kendall & Roberts make, of 603 horse power, two of 54 inches by 26 feet 10 inches; and one of 84 inches by 35 feet. A pipe-line 16 and 24 inches in diameter, runs to the Superior Engine House, and from there north and south along the line of the lode.

The length of all the shafts sunk below the average level of the stopes is over two miles, and the length of all the drifts run below the average level of the stopes is 13 6-10 miles.

At Lake Linden are located the Stamp Mills, the Calumet Mill containing eleven Leavitt heads with steam cylinders of 14 and 21¾ by 24 inches stroke, with a complete equipment of washers, Huntington and Hæberle grinding mills, and slime tables.

As spare power, the Company has a Westinghouse driving-engine of 200 horse power. At the Hecla Stamp Mill an addition has been made of four heads, which gives eleven Leavitt heads, with steam cylinders 14 and 21¾ by 24 inch stroke, and an equipment similar to that of the Calumet mill. The Company is placing solid anvils under all the stamps.

The Stamp Mills and Water Works Boiler House contains eleven boilers, four of 80 inches diameter by 32 feet long, and seven of 90 inches diameter by 34 four feet 6 inches long, made by Kendall & Roberts, the Dickson Manufacturing Company, the Southwark Foundry, and the I. P. Morris Co., aggregating 4,730 horse power, commercial standard. In 1895 an addition of 160x70 feet has been made to the boiler house, and two brick stacks erected, one 14 feet diameter by 250 feet high and the other 12 feet diameter by 185 feet high.

Torch Lake Water Works, which supply the Stamp Mills, consist of the triple-expansion pumping engine "Michigan," of a capacity of 60,000,000 gallons daily, with the following engines as spare pumps: The compound pumping engine "Erie," with a capacity of 10,000,000 gallons daily; the compound pumping engine "Ontario," with a capacity of 20,000,000 gallons daily; the geared pumping engine "Huron," with a capacity of 20,000,000 gallons daily.

The compound driving engine "Wabeek," 22¾ and 38 by 60 inch stroke, of 728 horse power, operates the washing machinery, the stamp steam-valve gear, and the sand wheels, by means of wire rope transmission. The stamped sand is distributed by four sand wheels; the Calumet 40-foot sand wheel, with a capacity of 18,000,000 gallons, and of 1,600 tons of sand; the Calumet 50-foot sand wheel, with a capacity of 30,000,000 gallons and of 3,000 tons of sand. As a spare engine for the Calumet wheel, the Company has a high-pressure engine 24 by 48 inch stroke, of 250 horse power. The Hecla 40- and 50-foot sand wheels have the same capacity as the Calumet sand wheels of the same dimensions. The spare engine for the Hecla wheels is a duplicate of the Calumet.

A new stone building in which an electric plant has recently been installed has been completed. There are three arc dynamos, Brush, each having a capacity of thirty 2,000 candle-power lights, and two Thompson Houston dynamos, incandescent, of similar power. These are driven by a Lake Erie Engine Works triple-expansion engine 7¼, 12 and 19-inch. In this same building is an artesian well 15 inches in diameter by 1,500 feet deep, which has recently been finished, making two at the mills. This provides water for the boilers. An air pipe is sent down the well to a distance of 200 feet, a little artificial assistance being necessary to send the water to surface. A tank located on the hill just back of the mill holds one million gallons of water, and gives a pressure at the mill of 150 lbs. per square inch. From these two wells 500,000 gallons of water are drawn daily.

The horse power of the boilers at the mine, commercial standard, is 13,765; the horse power of the boilers at the Lake Superior Water Works is 400; the horse power of the boilers at the Stamp Mills is 6,235; the horse power of the boilers now building is 2,022; and the total horse power, commercial standard, is 22,422. The aggregate horse power which can be developed by the engines belonging to the Company is 40,000.

The Smelting Works at Torch Lake occupy nearly thirty acres; they are connected with the Stamp Mills by a short line of railway, over which the mineral trains handle the daily product, which is there stored in the mineral houses.

The plant consists of four stone furnace buildings 80 by 130 feet each, with four furnaces, boshes, cranes, and all the ordinary equipment; one blister furnace building, of stone, 50 by 70 feet, with two furnaces; one cupola building containing two furnaces, with the necessary engines, blowers and boilers; machinists' and blacksmiths' outfits, electric light plant, etc. Mineral building No. 1 has a bin capacity of 2,000 tons, and mineral building No. 2 and its addition has a capacity of about 9,000 tons; and there are two wharves of a length of over 1,000 feet, with the necessary hoisting apparatus for coal and limestone.

Tamarack Mine.*

This is second only to the Calumet and Hecla, in the extent of its operations, and takes a second place to none other in the enterprise and skill displayed in the conducting of its mining and milling affairs. The company owns 29 forties in sections 10, 11, 12, and 15, these all being favored with the Calumet conglomerate lode, It is upon the latter that operations have thus far been principally confined by the company working upon an extension of the dip of the lode from a point where it leaves the western boundary of the Calumet and Hecla's property.

No. 1 shaft is located at the southeast corner of the company's property, and close to the south and west line of the Calumet and Hecla's lands, the latter surrounding this forty on three sides.

Like all the shafts of the company, No. 1 is vertical. It is to the 18th level, 3,234 feet from the surface.

No. 2 shaft is about 600 feet north of No. 1 and is to the 22d level, having been sunk from the 19th in 1895. The crosscut connecting with the lode is now just about completed, February 18, 1896. The lode having an inclination to the northwest of about 38 degrees, and the shaft being vertical, each added level finds the crosscuts connecting shaft and lode growing longer, so that at the 22d the distance is about 1,300 feet. Nos. 1 and 2 are 3-compartment shafts, two cageways and a timber way.

---

*The following is largely condensed and rearranged from Mr. Geo. A. Newett's report and manuscript.

No. 3 is north of No. 2 something like 4,200 feet, being located on section 11, and struck the lode on August 5, 1894, at a depth from surface of 4,185 feet.

The lode is very wide, something like 22 feet, nearly twice as thick as the conglomerate generally is.

No. 4 shaft is located about 700 feet north of No 3, reached the lode January 9, 1895, at a depth of 4,393 feet.

No. 5 shaft, the new one, has been located 3,300 feet south of No. 4. The work of clearing the ground, preparatory to beginning the sinking, was commenced on the 11th of August, 1895.

The company has erected a substantial shaft house, an engine and compressor house, and has installed hoisting and compressing machinery.

The shaft's dimensions are 27 ft. 5 in. x 7 ft. 2 in., and will contain five compartments, four cage-ways and a ladder and pipe way. It is expected it will strike the lode at a depth of about 4,600 feet.

In the sinking of the deep shafts Nos. 3 and 4, not a man was injured, which is a remarkable record considering that about 9,000 feet of sinking was done. It is the desire to sink No. 5 shaft at the rate of 100 feet per month.

At No. 3 shaft there are horizontal duplex engines, 34x48 inches, connected to a conical drum 12 feet at smallest diameter, 36 feet at largest, having a possible wind of 7,000 feet of rope. At places in the shaft the cages attain a maximum speed of 4,000 feet per minute. The cages at the different shafts are worked in balance. There is a fine new shaft and rock house at No. 3 that is conveniently arranged. There are breakers 18x24 inches, and the second size are 15x20 inches. There are also steam hammers for reducing extra large pieces so as to prepare them for the crushers. By their use something is saved in blockholing the large pieces in the mine. Electric lights have been put in, and water mains extended to this portion of the mine.

No. 2 shaft has direct-acting, double engines, 42x48 inch cylinders. Drum has 16-foot face and is 36 feet 6 inches in diameter. Each shaft has two hoisting engines, one for rock and men, and an auxiliary for handling timber, tools and men.

During the past few months small engines operated by air have been located on the 19th level to tram the cars to and from the shaft.

These are placed in the cross-cuts, and work on the endless rope system. Similar power trams will also be placed on the 20th and 21st levels. Five cars are handled at a time and a saving of fully 25 per cent is announced as compared to the hand-tramming. Cars hold 2 1-2 tons of rock each. In the hand-tramming three men are detailed to each car.

The company has a fine stamp milling plant, smelting works, rolling and wire mill at Dollar Bay. It also has an elaborate saw mill, and possesses valuable timber lands. It gives employment in mine and mills to 1,426 men.

Tamarack Junior Mine.

The Tamarack Junior Mine is on the same conglomerate lode as the Calumet and Hecla.

There are two shafts, No. 1 located on the most southerly forty and No. 2 on the forty next north.

A new shaft house has been erected at No. 2, and connection with No. 1 has been made by a trestle 1,000 feet long.

Osceola Mine.

The Osceola Mine is worked upon an old lava flow or melaphyr which like the conglomerate has been impregnated with copper, long subsequent to the successive series of flows and sea beach conglomerates, which piled one over the other, make up the Keweenawan formation.

There are three principal shafts, Nos. 3, 4 and 5, and No. 6, a new one, has been started.

No. 3, the most northern, is down to the 30th level.

No. 4 shaft is to the 32d level, two levels having been added in 1895.

No. 5 is to the 32d level, a distance vertically of 2,000 feet.

No. 6 was commenced in the spring of 1895, and has reached a depth on February 26, 1896, of 880 feet.

The mills of the company are located on Torch Lake and contain six heads of stamps, and an excellent general equipment.

The Wolverine Mine.

This is a melaphyr mine like the Osceola.

The lode is of a dull, brownish color, and much of the rock carrying the richest copper is a porous epidote of light green color.

There are four shafts. No. 1 is the most northern and is down to the 2d level. It is not in use, the ground being poor in that end of the mine.

No. 2, 400 feet south of No. 1, is to the 13th level. No. 3, 700 feet south of No. 2, is to the 11th.

No. 4 is a two-compartment shaft, recently commenced, and is 1,400 feet south of No. 3.

The number of men employed is 165 and the product of refined copper for 1895 was 1,815,831 lbs. The yield for 1894 was 1,656,255 lbs. The yield of copper per ton of rock treated is 21.08 lbs., or 1.05 per cent.

The Kearsarge Mine.

This is on the same lode as the Wolverine.

There is one shaft known as No. 2, a single-skip, that is down to the 17th level.

The yield of refined copper per cubic fathom of rock broken is 409 lbs.

The Tecumseh Mine.

This mine comprises 520 acres in sections 32 and 34 in town 33, range 56. At this point they are sinking a vertical shaft to find the Osceola amygdaloid.

The Franklin Junior Mine.

This tract, consisting of 1 359 acres, stretches two and one-half miles across the mineral range, and has a surface length on the trend of the formation of about 7,000 feet.

The property is crossed by the prominent copper bearing lodes of this district.

At the Pewabic shaft there is a new equipment of machinery, two boilers, a double cylinder hoisting engine and air compressor.

The Franklin Mine.

The company has reached the line of the Quincy mine in their shafts at a depth of 3,000 feet, and beyond this it cannot go. It is mining on the 32d, 34th, 35th and 36th levels in the lower portion of the mine, and in the 9th and 10th levels of the upper portion.

The Franklin is working upon the melaphyr lode upon which, immediately south, is located the Quincy mine. The dip of the lode is 52 degrees to the northwest. The company has developed it entirely across the property, and has two shafts now open to the bottom of the mine, these being inclined with the formation.

The rock is run by gravity from the shafts to a stamp mill located at the foot of the steep hill, on the north shore of Portage Lake, thus affording a ready and cheap means of transportation.

The Quincy Mine.

This is south of the Franklin, and its landed possessions surround the Franklin upon all sides excepting the east. It has been producing copper for the past forty years and has given substantial proof of its richness by distributing $7,670,000 in dividends, besides which it has credit for a surplus of $1,007,500.68

The Quincy is opened on a brownish, dark colored melaphyr belt, possessing a great width, probably nearly 200 feet, and in the mineralized portion of this the work of mining is prosecuted. There appear to be two belts of copper-bearing character in this formation, one being known as the "main vein," the other as the "east branch," the latter apparently occupying a position in the footwall. In the course of mining it is shown that there are many barren stretches of ground, and there is also considerable variation in the thickness of the copper-bearing material. In places it may be forty feet, and then may pinch to three or four. They simply take as much of the melaphyr belt as is profitably charged with copper.

The copper-bearing portion of the lode will probably average a thickness of twelve feet.

The mine is fortunate in the large amount of mass copper it produces, this running from the size of a man's fist to pieces weighing many tons.

The strike of the Quincy lode is a very regular one, being north of east and south of west. The lode dips to the northwest at an angle of about 50 degrees, the lower workings at some places in the mine showing a little flatter angle, but as there is considerable waving of the footwall, the dip may not vary as much as is commonly supposed. Sometimes the shafts are in the lode, at times on one side, and then again upon the other, due to the rolling of the formation. The shafts are located on the top of a hill that rises to a height of about 700 feet above the level of Portage lake. They are three in number, being sunk in the lode, following the inclination of the latter.

No. 4 shaft is the most southern and is 30 feet below the 47th level, one level having been added in 1895. It is east of the main lode and a cross-cut is now being driven to connect it with this portion of the mine.

No. 2 shaft is 600 feet north of No. 4, and is to the 48th level, having been sunk 30 feet below the 46th in 1895.

No. 6 shaft is 1,900 feet north of No. 2, and is 30 feet below the 45th level, having been sunk from the 43d level during the year.

The walls of the lode are generally so firm that no timber is needed to sustain them, but occasionally, where the lode is of extraordinary width, it is employed.

Nearly all the drilling is performed by machines, No. 3 Rand. A little hand drilling is done in places.

The rapid handling of the men at this property is one of the attractive features. Formerly they were sent into and out of the mine on the old-fashioned man engine; this required considerable time to take care of the men. Now they are lowered and raised in a man car, and the entire force underground, about 400 souls, can be gotten in or out of the mine in thirty minutes. The man car bears a close resemblance to a section of a flight of stairs, the under side of which is provided with wheels that rest upon the rails of the shaft track. There are banisters on this section of stairs to prevent the men from being crowded over the sides. They take their seats on the steps and are gently lowered into the earth a distance on the incline of about 4,000 feet. There is no jerking or jolting, no unpleasant sensation. Thirty men are carried at a load, and the different shafts are all equipped with this convenience. The change from the skips to the man cars is made at each shaft in less than two minutes. Two 5-ton cranes are located in each shaft, one on either side of the skip-way, and with these the skips are lifted off and the man cars substituted in the time given.

A new shaft house has just been completed at No. 4 shaft. It is 30x89 feet and 72 feet high. At this shaft the company has increased the size of the old engine house by an addition of 16 feet, and installed a second engine. The old drum is increased from 18 to 22 feet in diameter, and is now in shape to do hoisting from a depth of several hundred feet beyond the present lowest levels.

At No. 2 shaft there is a magnificent new hoisting plant. It consists of a pair of 48x84 inch engines connected to a steel drum 26 feet in diameter with 12 1-4 foot face, having capacity for 7,500 feet of 1 1-2 inch rope. The governor is regulated to prevent a speed of over 3,000 feet per minute, and the skip is prevented from going too high in the shaft house by an automatic arrangement that shuts off steam, reverses the engine and applies the brake. The plant is a substantial, sensible one, and is contained in a stone building 58x94 feet·

A new brownstone supply house has been erected at No. 2 shaft and additions made to machine and blacksmith shops. The latter are models of neatness, as, indeed, are all portions of the surface. The company builds its own skips, power drills, and has a complete machine and smithing equipment.

The Quincy Mining Company has credit for one of the finest stamp mills on the lakes. It is of modern construction, and a very economical arrangement for the treating of rock is possessed. There are five Allis heads. There are six miles of railway connecting the mine and mill, the track being narrow gauge. There are three mogul engines and fifty 17-ton cars. The location of the mill is on Torch Lake.

The average number of men employed during the year was 968, of which 836 were miners, who earned an average of $50 per month.

The number of tons of rock broken was 563,360; tons hoisted, 506,-058; stamp rock treated, 495,402 tons.

The product of mineral from stamp mill was 14,670,530 pounds; from rock houses, 5,062,440 pounds. The amount of refined copper was 16,304,721 pounds.

In 1894 a tract of 640 acres of mineral lands was purchased.

The Atlantic Mine.

The location of this mine is three miles southwest of Houghton on ground elevated several hundred feet above the lake's level. This mine has been one to which no little attention has been directed by reason of the excellent results achieved in its operation, it being credited with a net earning of about $900,000, this being won from a rock yielding an average of less than three-quarters of one per cent. of copper. For the year 1894 the yield was 14.06 pounds of copper per ton of rock, and the gross value of product per ton of rock treated was $1.3376. At this low yield, and with a low price for the product, the mine earned $48,762.95 in 1894. When it is considered that this rock has to be all drilled and blasted, the ground timbered, water pumped, the rock raised from a depth of over two thousand feet, put through crushers, run into cars and transported by railway nine miles, then to be stamped and otherwise treated in the mill, and all this for less than $1.84 per ton, none will dispute the fact that there must be an active management, and one well skilled in the different branches of the mining and milling business. In 1895 the percentage of copper per ton of rock was .78, and cost of mining, milling, etc., less construction account, was $1.2034 per ton.

The Atlantic is open on a melaphyr belt of dark-brown color, the mineralized portion of which has an average thickness of 15 feet. The copper in this is very evenly distributed. There are few barren stretches, and few rich bunches. There can be no selecting of the rock, and all the mineralized lode is sent to surface, no attempt at selection being made.

There are four shafts located on the lode, and the latter has been opened for a distance of 4,800 feet, No. 4 being the most southern. It has reached the 22d level. No. 1, the most northern, is to the 16th level; No. 2 is to the 20th; No. 3 to the 25th, 2,100 feet from surface.

What is known as the "New No. 3," is now to the 24th level.

The dip of the bed is about 55 degrees to the northwest, and the trend of the lode is more westerly than any of the lodes of this section.

At the mine there is a new boiler house, 88x66 feet. This contains a battery of eight boilers, of 100 horse-power each.   •

A new stamp mill has been built for the Atlantic Mine on the shore of Lake Superior at the mouth of Salmon Trout River.

Its dimensions are 151x284 feet, framed, with stone foundation and contains six heads of stamps, 18 inch, of the Ball's type, fifty-four iron Collun jigs, one 14x22 inch Reynolds-Corliss engine, a Gardner fire pump, lathes, pipe, bolt and nut cutters, planer, etc., making in all a fine equipment. There is a boiler house, 101x71 feet, containing three 16x6 foot Evans fire box boilers with Gardner duplex feed pumps, and a fire pump of same make. The smoke is conducted in a steel flue 175 feet long and 7 feet in diameter, that has been laid to a stone base on the hill back of the mill, which is surmounted by a smoke stack 30 feet high and 6 feet in diameter.

There is no pumping required to supply the water needed by the stamps. The water comes into the mill by gravity. A dam has been constructed across the Salmon Trout river, and the water from this is conveyed to the mill, a distance of 2,052 feet, being given a fall of 5 inches in each 100 feet. This dam cost the company over $30,000. It is constructed of timber, loose rock and earth. The main portion is crib work 53 feet thick at the bottom and 28 feet thick at the top, and 50 feet high. The length across the stream at the bottom is 51 feet, and at the top 228 feet. The crib work is of hewed flat timber 14 inches thick and bound together at the joints with inch square drift bolts. Loose rock was used for filling the cribs. The supply launder is 18x36 feet, which discharges into a steel tank 8 feet in diameter and 10 feet high, from which the water is conveyed to the stamps as needed. This water supply is a point of greatest importance to the company. When one considers that thirty tons of water are used in the washing of a single ton of rock, and that this company treats about 1,000 tons of rock daily, the value of the new plant can be readily recognized.

During 1895 the company stamped 331,058 tons of rock.

The mill is eight and one-half miles from the mine, and the company has connected the two by a standard-gauge railway. They have an ample equipment of locomotives and cars. There is one large consolidation engine, a Brooks, with four drivers, and weighing 90 tons, besides which there is a 45-ton Brooks, and two 20-ton locomotives. There are 32 flat cars and 127 rock cars, the latter having a capacity each of 5 1-4 tons.

The product of refined copper for 1895 amounted to 4,832,497 pounds, an increase over the production of the previous year of 605,-112 pounds. The total production of refined copper to date is 72,-048,632 pounds. The gross profit for 1895 was $110,559.47. The net surplus December 31, 1895, was $150,874.97. The number of men employed at mine and mill is 476.

KEWEENAW DIVISION.

The Central Mine.

This mine is worked upon a true fissure vein.

ONTONAGON DIVISION.

In this district there are working the Knowlton, Mass, Minnesota, National and Ridge.

This district is the first that was actively worked for copper and masses weighing 200, 300 and over 500 tons have been found.

IRON RANGES.

MARQUETTE RANGE.

Has a length of 40 miles by from 6 to 12 miles. Has shipped 43,937,510 tons, 2,095,166 in 1895.

BUFFALO MINES.—450 feet in depth. Use caving system and is a fine place to see it operated, 4 mines in fact; about 400,000 tons annually produced, fine machinery, underground haulage system, endless rope.

NEGAUNEE MINE —1 shaft 486 feet deep. Mine in square sets. A very interesting property to visit. Fine plan of ore sampling. New hoisting plant to be installed in 1896.

JACKSON MINE.—Oldest in the State, has 2 shafts 300 feet deep. Needs no timber. Hard and soft ores occur indiscrimately, a peculiar formation.

CAMBRIA MINE.—2 shafts 570 feet deep. Mine 40,000 tons annually. Use square sets. Formation rolls and twists erratically, and requires fine engineering to properly follow.

LILLIE MINE.—2 shafts 300 and 350 feet deep. Win the ore by caving the surface and slicing the ore off in horizontal sections. Have an 8 foot hoist. Three hundred men are employed.

LAKE SUPERIOR IRON CO.—Has been running since 1858, and has produced 6,734,472 tons of ore. It mines both hard and soft varieties and observes all the principal methods in its extraction. Its deepest workings are 920 feet. It has four mines, all of which are equipped with modern machinery.

THE PITTSBURG AND LAKE ANGELINE IRON CO.—The Lake Angeline mines, two in number, are interesting and important and enjoy a national reputation for the fine quality of their ores. The caving system of winning ores is employed in their soft hematite deposits. They mine both hard and soft ores. These mines were the first to introduce electric haulage machinery for the underground transportation of ore. They have an electric motor handling ten two-ton cars. Dynamo is 85 horse power. Voltage 500. A large territory has been opened up. Eight hundred men are employed, and the mine produced 850,000 tons in 1895, making a grand total of 3,352,561 tons. All portions of the mine are finely equipped with modern machinery.

The Cleveland Cliffs Iron Mining Co.'s.—The Cleveland mine is opened up under the bottom of Lake Angeline, the waters of which (800,000,000) gallons have been pumped out. On the ore deposit lies 40 feet of sand and overlying this is forty feet of mud. The latter has threatened the mine but it is effectively worked and the immense mass of mud successfully coped with. There are 76 rooms opened on the first level, a length of 2,760 feet. In the second level there are 72 rooms, in the third, which is but partly opened, 14 rooms. They work one level at a time, from the top down. An open pit 400 feet long by 80 feet wide is now worked. A new mine on the south side of the old lake basin is being opened up. There are two electric motors, one of thirty, the other of sixty-horse power. The electric generator is 4-pole, 100 kilowats, 220 volts, 600 revolutions per minute. This power operates the underground tramming railway, where there are about 5,000 feet of track. At the Lake Shaft mine is a new plant of machinery—cross-compound engines, 22 inches and 32x48 inches, Corliss condensing, with 12 foot first motion drum, equipped with hydraulic brake. Air compressors are Rand, 16x32 inches, duplex. The finest mill in the United States for framing mine timber is here. The operators of this also own and operate the Cliff Shafts, Moro and Incline Mines, yielding hard ore, and the Salisbury mine yielding soft ore.

Ore crushers weighing 82,000 pounds, with openings 18 inches by 24 inches are used. All mines of this company are thoroughly equipped and their annual product is 600,000 tons.

The furnace plant of the Cleveland Cliffs Co., located at Gladstone. Delta Co., Mich., are of the finest. Charcoal is the fuel used. The producing capacity is 130 tons daily. Bosh 12 feet, hearth 7 feet, stock line 8 feet, bell 5 feet. The stove plant has two Cowper stoves 16x70, each stove having 16,900 square feet heating surface. Casting house is 50 feet by 115 feet 2 inches. There are forty 65-cord kilns requiring 125 cords daily. A chemical plant for securing alcohol and other by-products from the consumption of wood is operated. The finest in America.

Excelsior blast furnace, Ishpeming, 60 tons daily, newly rebuilt.

Winthrop Mine—is working the longest open pit in this country

16

dislodging thousands of tons of ore at a single blast. Stripping drift with steam shovel.

REPUBLIC MINING CO.—The Republic mine, renowned for purity of its product, has been opened for a length of 3,000 feet. Has three shafts now working. Greatest depth 1,200 feet. Produces hard, specular, and magnetic ores. Power to operate machinery furnished by water power on Michigamme river. Has shipped 4,251,026 tons ore. Has four 14-foot drums at Nos 1 and 8 shafts. A " Cornish lift " takes care of the water.

THE CHAMPION MINING CO.—The Champion mine has 4 shafts, working on a lode 2,000 feet long, greatest depth 1,200 feet. Specular and magnetic ores produced. Has dike crossings, two lodes of ore, and is very interesting geologically. Two 55-ton ore crushers worked and another to be added. Openings of jaws 24 inches by 24 inches, and operated by manilla rope transmission on 10-foot pulleys. Ore going from shafts to crushers by gravity. Have four 14-foot drums, 7 foot face, and a compressing plant with 30x48 in air and 28x48 in steam cylinders. Fine shops.

ROPES GOLD MINE.—One shaft, 800 feet deep. Mine 760 feet in length worked on a series of segregated veins. Has produced $605,-056.95 worth of gold and silver. In the serpentine formation. Mill with 65 Cornish stamps. Frue vanners and perfect amalgamation plant.

———

MENOMINEE RANGE.

Has a length of 45 miles by from 4 to 15 miles—has sent out 18,528,827 tons, 1,694,804 in 1895.

VULCAN MINE.—Two shafts 1,000 feet deep. Very interesting geologically. Two strata of ore—much jaspilite. Rooms are rock-filled. Tramming rock done with mules. Worthington pump at 12th level, compound-condensing with 25 horse power high-pressure cylinders 43 3-10 inch low pressure, four 12 inch poles, 36 inch stroke. One thousand gallons per minute, in 1,000 feet left under 60 lbs. steam pressure.

ARAGON MINE.—Three shafts, to 7th level or 586 feet. The ore is mined in square sets, and the rooms filled with sand run in from the surface. New hoisting plant will be put in in 1896. The company is sinking a new shaft.

CHAPIN MINE.—Two thousand five hundred feet long, and 70 feet in thickness. Four principal working shafts, from 600 to 800 feet deep. Two lodes of ore. Produce 650,000 tons annually; 1,300 men employed. Caving system generally used but some square set work is done. At B and C shafts there is a pair Corliss engines 30x60 inches, with conical drums, with an average diameter of 12 1-2 feet, and capacity for 1,500 feet of 1 3-8 inch wire rope.

D shaft has a pair 24x48 inches Corliss engines operating two flat rope reels holding 1,500 feet of 1-2x4 inch steel rope. Pumping plant at D is one of largest mine pumps in world:—steeple compound—50 inch initial cylinders; 100-inch low preassure; 120-inch stroke; plunger 28 by 120 inches; capacity 3,000 gallons a minute with a 1,500 feet lift.

Hydraulic power is used to operate all the mine plant but the big pump. This power is obtained from falls on the Michigamme river some three miles from the mine where four large compressors are placed. Power trams are used underground, also 150 power drills. The mine has a saw-mill for framing timber, is lighted by electricity and also has fine shops. The Ludington and Hamiliton mines have been lately purchased by the Chapin Co. Hamiliton has a flat rope hoisting plant with 10 ton skips. The mine is 1,460 feet deep.

. PEWABIC MINE.—Three shafts, to 5th level; at each shaft are two 10-foot drums with direct acting engines 24 inches by 48 inches. The ore is mined on the square set plan but the company has a different system of slicing pillars than the other mines.

Finest underground pump in the country, a Worthington, triple expansion, cylinders, 15 inches, 23 inches and 38-inch by 12-inch plunger, 24-inch stroke. Supplied with surface condenser, capacity 1,500 gals. per min., 700 feet lift with 125 lbs. of steam. Fine system of sampling ores, with interesting occurrences of phosphorus and perplexing geological features. Produces the finest ore of any mine in the world—giving 68.60 per cent. iron, .007 per cent. phos.

ANTOINE ORE CO.—Mining high silicon—low iron ores, from open pits. Crushing ores. Crusher 30 inches by 30 inches.

COMMONWEALTH MINE.—Use no timber, hanging firm, hoisting from immense stopes 250 feet high—none other like it in the district.

DUNN MINE.—Use no timber, hanging firm; hoisting from sub-shafts from underground levels direct from surface plant by neat arrangement of pulleys, etc. Fine plant.

COLUMBIA MINE.—Two shafts—mine very wet, little or no timber used, two lodes of ore.

HEMLOCK MINE.—Has two shafts, 290 feet deep. Three modes of winning ore, large open stopes with no timber; drift sets and caving and on square sets.

GOGEBIC RANGE.

Has a length of 45 miles by 3 miles in width, has sent out 16,395,-375 long tons, 2,560,775 in 1895.

NORRIE MINING CO.—The Norrie Mine produces 800,000 gross tons iron ore annually—greatest iron mine in the world, Ore deposit one mile long, and reached by 12 shafts. Lode 60 feet to 300 feet wide, 800 feet deep at present. One thousand three hundred men employed, two hoisting stations 10 feet drums, Prescott pumps; electric signals and lighting, square set system of timbers.

AURORA MINE.—Two hundred and fifty thousand tons annually, 4 shafts 600 feet deep. Opened 2,500 feet long, caving pillars, 3 hoisting plants 8 feet drums, a 50 drill Ingersoll Compressor, and electric lights. Employs 845 men. Square set system of timbering.

ASHLAND MINE is opened for 2,500 feet in length, 8 shafts, caving pillars, well equipped.

PABST MINE.—Two hundred and twenty-five thousand tons annually, 5 shafts, opened 1,900 feet in length and from 60 to 300 feet in width. Five hundred feet deep. New hoisting plant with 24 inch by 48 inch engine connected by a 14 foot gear wheel to a pair of 10 feet hoisting drums made by Webster, Camp & Lane. Complete equipment with compressors, etc.

NEWPORT MINE.—Manganiferous iron ore, from 10 to 40 per cent. Six shafts. Deposits 2,000 feet long. Employs 200 men. One hundred and fifty-seven thousand eight hundred and twenty-one tons of ore produced in 1895. Timbering in square sets. Complete equipment.

TILDEN MINE.—Six shafts 700 feet deep. Mine 4,000 feet in length. Annual product 500,000 tons. Uses the "drawing" system of winning the ore. One 12 foot hoist, one of 6 feet, and has one 6-foot 60 drill air compressor. Employs the incandescent system lighting, and fine shops.

PALMS MINE.—Three shafts 500 feet deep.   Deposit 1,800 feet long. New 8-foot hoisting plant.

BROTHERTON MINE.—Three shafts 400 feet.   The mine secures the ore by the caving or "North of England" system.

ORE DOCKS.

MARQUETTE.—D., S. S. & A. Ry.   Three docks, 700 pockets, capacity 100 tons each.   Marquette, Lake Superior & Ishpeming Ry., 1 dock 1,200 feet long, 300 pockets, 100 tons each.

ASHLAND.—Three docks with capacity of 101,500 tons ore.

GLADSTONE.—One dock, 16,000 tons.

ESCANABA.—Five docks, capacity 151,218 tons.

Owing to lack of space only part of the mines, of the various districts have been enumerated, and most of them only briefly described.

BUILDING STONE, ETC.

Michigan contains a vast amount of sandstone suitable for building purposes, the finest varieties being found in the upper peninsula, on the shores of Lake Superior, near Keweenaw Bay. Here it can be readily quarried and transported to Chicago, Cleveland, Buffalo, and other distributing centers on the great lakes.

The varieties most popular with builders are the brown, rain-drop and red, these generally differing only in their markings. The brown is of the richest, and it has been principally secured from quarries at Marquette, Mich. The supply has steadily grown less, and but limited quantities can now be furnished. Some of the finest buildings in Michigan, as well as other states, are constructed of this stone.

THE KERBER-JACOBS REDSTONE COMPANY is one of the best known of the producers of sandstone in the State.

THE PORTAGE ENTRY QUARRIES COMPANY is one of the oldest sandstone producing concerns on the lakes. As indicated by their title, their principal quarrying is done at Portage Entry, where they have a complete plant for securing the stone rapidly. They also operate the Marquette quarries. The amount produced from the latter in 1895 was 38,014 feet, and from Portage Entry 181,511 feet, in all 219,525 feet.

THE EXCELSIOR REDSTONE COMPANY, is quarrying stone on the shores of Portage Lake, making their first shipment in 1894, the true sheet having been located after a years systematic exploration. The thickness of the marketable strata averages about 8 feet, and the quality of the stone is of the finest. The overlying burden varies in thickness according to location, showing about 21 feet at the present point of operations.

An average of 60 men are employed. The present equipment con_ sists of 3 steam pumps, 1 steam channeling machine, 2 steam drills, 1 steam hoister, 1 boiler 170-horse power, 1 derrick, 20 tons capacity. Besides this there is a well-equipped blacksmith shop, and three miles of railroad from the quarry to the lake shore, equipped with a locomotive and 30 flat cars.

The product in 1894 was 18,000 cubic feet, in 1895 45,000 feet.

THE L'ANSE BROWNSTONE COMPANY is a new one in the brown-stone producing business, having made its sample shipment of about 2,000 feet in 1894. Its quarry is at L'Anse, and it was worked in 1895 for five months and 23,000 cubic feet of stone quarried. The greater portion of this was of the brown variety. A force of 34 men was employed. The equipment consists of 1 two-power, 15-ton hoist geared for two derricks, 1 24-horse power engine, two Ingersoll-Sergeant steam drills, 1 bar channeler, 2 Wardwell channelers, 1 Worthington pump, 1 Lidgerwood double-drum hoist, 1 core drill, engine, boiler and fittings, 1 set Lidgerwood's friction drums worked by gravity for letting down cars from quarry to dock, a distance of 1,500 feet. The loaded car brings up the empty one. Another derrick is now being put up in the quarry.

THE TRAVERSE BAY REDSTONE COMPANY.—This company is operating in Houghton county, T. 56, R. 31, and has shown sandstone of excellent quality covering 120 acres. It has constructed eight miles of three-foot railroad, from the quarry to the bay, and has a dock 1,000 feet long at the latter place. The work of 1895 was devoted almost entirely to developing and equipping, 6,500 feet of stone being all that was quarried. There are two hoists with boilers, two derricks, and a full equipment of machinery for cutting stone.

Waverly Stone.

This stone is of a bluish-gray color, uniform in its appearance and texture, and makes a handsome stone for building purposes. It is found at Holland, Ottawa county, and takes its name from similar stone that is quarried in large quantities at Waverly, Ohio. The Michigan stone is free from iron stains that present such objectionable appearance in this stone from other places.

Grindstones.

Huron county has been a producer of grindstones and whetstones for more than forty years. The location of the quarries is at Grindstone City, on the shores of Lake Huron, twenty-four miles northeast of Bad Axe, the county seat, and ninety miles above Port Huron. Lake Huron blue stone is known in every market in the United States, and is also recognized abroad. In grindstones and scythe stones the supply is not equal to the demands of the trade.

Novaculite.

This stone, and of a very fine grain, suitable for hones, occurs in Marquette county, near the cities of Marquette and Negaunee.

Slate.

There are large deposits of slate in Baraga county, and considerable attention was given to its quarrying several years since.

Limestone.

Limestone is generously distributed throughout the entire State of Michigan. The manufacture of lime is carried on at several points, Bellevue being noted for its fine product. The stone is also used for building purposes.

Quartzite.

There are vast deposits of this rock in the northern portion of the state, gannister being quarried for the lining of blast furnaces.

Clay.

Clay is found in nearly every county in the State. Near Detroit a deposit suitable for the manufacture of pottery is operated. The manufacture of brick and tiling is conducted at many places, and provides employment to a large number of men.

Granite.

This stone exists in immense areas throughout the northern portion of Michigan, but at no point is it quarried. Near Marquette is a fine variety suited to building purposes.

Asbestus (Chrysotile).

Long ago the variety of serpentine known as chrysotile, which is used for asbestus, was found in association with the serpentine rocks north of Ishpeming, in Marquette county, on sections 29 and 30, town 48, range 27. It possesses a fine fibre of from one inch to one inch and a half long, and compares favorably with the Canadian product, which supplies the greatest portion of the amount of this mineral consumed in the United States.

Gypsum.

The principal gypsum producers of Michigan are now represented by the Michigan & Ohio Plaster Co.

The following concerns were active in 1895:

NAME.	LOCATION OF MILLS.
Alabastine Company...................	Grand Rapids Mich.
Grand Rapids Gypsum Works	" " "
Grand Rapids Plaster Co..............	" " "
F. Godfrey & Bro.....................	" " "
Gypsum Plaster and Stucco Co........	" " "
Loren Day...	" " "
Western Plaster Works...............	Alabaster, Mich., and South Chicago.

The product of the above named companies was as follows:

Calcined Plaster, tons................................	52,700
Land plaster, tons....................................	10,600
Gypsum rock, crude...................................	12,000

The gypsum product of Michigan is noted for its purity, and the supply is equal to meet the severest call that can be made upon it.

Talc.

This mineral is found in the serpentine range of Marquette county, and preparations are under way for its mining. Adjoining the property on which is located the Ropes gold mine, a large vein has been found, and can be cheaply worked.

Marble.

Michigan has only one marble quarry that is being operated at this time. The single quarry now showing activity is located in Dickinson county, on Sec. 26, 42, 28, and is operated by the Northern Michigan Marble Company.

The stone is a very bright, sparkling, crystalline carbonate of lime, hard and tenacious, making it desirable for building or monumental purposes. Some of it is pure white, some variegated, shading from white to pink, green, gray and purple, making beautiful slabs for wainscoting and interior work.

There is a pressing demand for the stone beyond anything the

company can supply, even the chips and small spals being disposed
of.

The Serpentines.

They are among the most beautiful of the rock creations when they
contain dolomite, the blending of the two forming what is known as
verde antique.

The Michigan serpentine outcrops at Presque Isle, near Marquette,
this being the most easterly point at which it is seen. It disappears
from view going west, and again is seen fifteen miles east on Sec. 27,
48, 27, a few miles north of Ishpeming. Prominent ridges show for
about four miles when it again sinks from view.

COAL.

Although several counties in the southern and central portions of
Michigan are underlaid by detached basins of the Central coal field,
there is but little being done in the way of coal mining.

The coal being mined is of a semi-bituminous character, is excellent for steaming and fuel purposes, and crude tests made of the
recently discovered beds in the Saginaw valley indicate it to be valuable for the manufacture of coke.

The Corunna Coal Co., whose mine is located near Corunna, Shi-
awassee county, worked part time during 1895, producing 12,241 tons.
About 60 men were employed. The mine can produce 150 tons per
day.

The Sebewaing Coal Co., located near Sebewaing, Huron county,
was the only one working continuously throughout the year, it sending out 38,523 tons, and giving employment to 75 men.

The Saginaw Bay Coal Co., closed their mines early in 1895 and are
not expecting to resume. The mines had been operated about four
years and produced about 10,000 tons annually.

The Bennett Sewer Pipe Co., of Jackson, has closed its mines, and
the New Coal Mining Company, of the same place, has also aban-
doned its workings.

Michigan reached its maximum output in 1882 when 135,339 tons
were produced, but in no year since has the output exceeded 81,500
tons.

The following is the total product of the State in tons of 2,000 pounds, for the past four years:

	1892	1893	1894	1895
Total product	77,990	45,979	43,780	50,764

SALT.

Michigan ranks first in the states in its production of salt. In 1895 there were made 3,529,342 barrels. For the year 1894 the United States produced 12,967,417, and the mineral is one very generally distributed throughout the Union.

The salt producing territory of Michigan is an immense one, and constant additions to the former salt-giving area are made.

Many of the salt works are operated in connection with saw mills, and the refuse from the manufacture of timber and shingles is used for fuel in evaporating the salt brine. Due to this practice the manufacturers have been enabled to make a small profit even at the very low price quoted for the salt which in 1895 was but 48 9-10 cents per barrel, this including the cost of the barrel.

The salt producing territory of the State is divided into nine districts, having manufacturing capacity as follows:

District No. 1, Saginaw county, has forty-two salt companies, with forty steam and three pan blocks and four thousand solar salt covers, having a manufacturing capacity of one million three hundred fifty thousand barrels of salt.

District No. 2, Bay county, has twenty-nine salt companies, with thiry-two steam blocks, one vacuum pan, and with a manufacturing capacity of one million three hundred thousand barrels of salt.

District No. 3, Huron county, has four salt companies, with one steam and three pan blocks and with a manufacturing capacity of three hundred thousand barrels of salt.

District No. 4, St. Clair county, has ten salt companies, with six steam and four pan blocks and with a manufacturing capacity of six hundred thousand barrels of salt.

District No. 5, Midland county, has two salt companies, with two steam blocks, having a manufacturing capacity of seventy-five thousand barrels of salt.

District No. 6, Iosco county, has six companies with six steam blocks having a manufacturing capacity of three hundred thousand barrels of salt.

District No. 7, Manistee county, has ten salt companies with nine steam and two pan blocks having a manufacturing capacity of one million two hundred fifty thousand barrels of salt.

District No. 8, Mason county, has four salt companies, with two steam and two pan blocks, having a manufacturing capacity of five hundred thousand barrels of salt.

District No. 9, Wayne county, has one salt company with one salt block, having a manufacturing capacity of one hundred fifty thousand barrels of salt.

REGISTER OF STUDENTS

1894–1895.

GRADUATE STUDENTS.

———

NAME.	RESIDENCE.	ROOM.
Abbott, Ai Arthur, S. B. (Michigan Agricultural College), E. M. (Michigan Mining School), Holt.		Mr. J. Edwards's.
Croze, Walter Wilfred Joseph, S. B. (Michigan Mining School), Houghton.		Mr. Jos. Croze's.

———

CLASS OF 1895.

Barlow, Royce Elwin,	Hastings.	Mrs. P. Didier's.
Been, John Theodore,	Skanee.	Mr. J. Edwards's.
Cameron, William,	St. Louis, Mich.	Mr. P. Didier's.
Coleman, Milton Watson,	Devizes, Ont.	Stroebel's Block.
Davis, Carl Raymond,	Helena, Mont.	Mr. T. Lange's.
Dockery, Love,	Love, Miss.	Mr. T. Lange's.
DuBois, Wilbur Fisk,	Mobile, Ala.	Mr. C. Brand's.
Emlaw, Harlan Stigand,	Grand Haven.	Mrs. Healey's.
Esselstyn, John Nelson,	Lansing.	Mr. J. Edwards's.

NAME.	RESIDENCE.	ROOM.
Graves, MacDowell,	Detroit.	Keweenaw Club.
Hardenburgh, Louis Martin, A. B. (Hillsdale College).	Hillsdale.	Mrs. Burrows's.
Holbert, Henry Hoffman,	St. Clair.	Mr. J. Edwards's.
Kent, Bamlet,	Forest, Ont.	Stroebel's Block.
Martin, Nicholas John,	Virginia, Minn.	Mr. Grignon's
Monroe, William Dearborn,	Bath.	Mr. C. Brand's.
Murray, Robert,	Lake Linden.	Miss Kelly's.
Orr, John Forrest,	L'Anse.	Mrs. Burrows's.
Rose, Robert Selden,	Fond du Lac, Wis.	Mr. Haas's.
Schumann, Enrique Adolpho,	Santiago, Cuba.	Keweenaw Club.
Slock, George,	Houghton.	Mr. Slock's.
Stringham, Joseph, Jr.,	Saginaw, E. S.	Mrs. Didier's.
Upham, William Erastus,	Duluth, Minn.	Mr. T. Lange's.
Watson, John Bone,	Opechee.	Mrs. Brimacombe's.
Wearne, William, Jr.,	Red Jacket.	Mrs. Burrows's.
Wright, Louis Aldro,	Villa de Musquiz, Coahuila, Mex.	Mr. A. Haas's.

CLASS OF 1896.

NAME.	RESIDENCE.	ROOM.
Cavazos, Amado,	Saltillo, Mex.	
		Mrs. Brimacombe's.
Figueroa, Camilo, A. B. (St. Mary's College),	Saltillo, Mex.	
		Miss Kelly's.
Greene, Fred Turrell,	Berlin, Ont.	
		Mrs. West's.
Hoar, Frederic Walpole,	Houghton.	
		Mr. R. M. Hoar's.
Houle, Albert Joseph,	Negaunee.	
		Mrs. Healy's.
McDonald, Donald William,	Calumet.	
		Miss Kelly's.
Rashleigh, William John,	Houghton.	
		Mr. Jos. Rashleigh's.
Russell, Edward Francis,	Yonkers, N. Y.	
		Mr. C. Brand's.
Smith, Willard Joseph,	Allouez.	
		Miss Kelly's.
Snow, Arthur Eugene,	St. George, Utah.	
		Mr. J. Ehler's.
Sweet, Roy William,	Iron Mountain.	
		Mr. J. B. Pfeiffer's.
Trethewey, James Henry,	Lake Linden.	
		Mr. J. Trethewey's.
Walker, Elton Willard,	Detroit.	
		Mr. J. Edwards's.
Zertuche, Ygnacio Maria.	Monterey, Mex.	
		Mrs. Brimacombe's.

CLASS OF 1897.

Blackwell, Frank,	Norway.	
		Mr. H. Hooper's.
Carpenter, Alvin Bacon, Ph. B. (Beloit College),	Beloit, Wis.	
		Mr. T. Lange's.
Daniell, John, Jr.,	Opechee.	
		Mrs. Brimacombe's.

17

NAME.	RESIDENCE.	ROOM.
Derr, Homer Munro,	Ann Arbor.	
		Mr. J. Ehler's.
Dykema, Frank Leonard.	Grand Rapids.	
		Mrs. Healy's.
Floeter, Albert Henry Christo-pher,	Menominee.	
		Mr. J. B. Pfeiffer's.
Haas, Frank William,	Houghton.	
		Mr. J. Haas's.
Haas, Nathan,	Houghton.	
		Mr. D. Haas's.
Harris, George Henry Ronald, C. E. (Royal Military College, Kingston, Ontario),	London, Ont.	
		Mr. Grignon's.
Hoar, John Mitchell,	Houghton.	
		Mrs. E. M. Hoar's.
Klein, William Louis,	Detroit.	
		Betzler's Hotel.
Knox, John, Jr.,	Hamilton, Ont.	
		Mrs. Healy's.
Minehan, Michael Matthias, A. B. (St. Mary's College),	Summerfield, Kan.	
		Mr. C. Brand's.
Remington, Charles Stevens,	Syracuse, N. Y.	
		Mr. C. Brand's.
Sarazin, William George,	Lake Linden.	
		Butterfield House.
Van Orden, Frank Lyon,	Houghton.	
		Mr. M. Van Orden's.
Walker, George Washington,	Walker, Ill.	
		Keweenaw Club.

SPECIAL STUDENTS.

Allen, Thomas,	Hancock.	
		Mr. W. H. Allen's.
Bates, Arthur Walter,	Gaylord.	
		Butterfield House.
Brand, William,	Houghton.	
		Mr. C. Brand's.

NAME.	RESIDENCE.	ROOM.
Brown, William Francis,	New York, N. Y.	
		Mr. C. Brand's.
Burnham, Guy Chynoweth,	Hancock.	
		Dr. Burnham's.
Calhoun, Charles Andrew.	Albert Mines,	
	Nova Scotia.	
		Stroebel's Block.
Gibbs, Frank Nicholson, C. E. (Royal Military College, Kingston, Ontario),	Port Arthur, Ont.	
		Mr. Grignon's.
Goodell, Horatio Stewart,	Houghton.	
		Mr. R. R. Goodell's.
Goudie, James Hunter, A. B. (Glasgow University),	Ironwood.	
		Butterfield House.
Hayen, Albert,	Hancock.	
		Mr. C. H. Hayen's.
Holmes, Edward Hyneman,	Flint.	
		Mr. T. Lange's.
Hooper, James Knight,	Crystal Falls.	
		Mr. C. Brand's.
Hosking, Charles,	Hancock.	
		Mr. G. Hosking's.
Hunt, Robert Courtney,	Houghton.	
		Mr. J. Hunt's.
Kennedy, John William,	Sharpsburg, Pa.	
		Mr. C. Brand's.
Martin, John Peter.	Houghton.	
		Mr. J. Martin's.
May, Albert Edward, A. B. (University of Minnesota),	Minneapolis, Minn.	
		Mr. A. Haas's.
McAskill, John Francis,	Hancock.	
		Mr. H. McAskill's
McElery, Frank Jerome,	New York, N. Y.	
		Mr. C. Brand's.
Merry, Thomas Woodward,	Low Moor, Va.	
		Mrs. E. M. Hoar's.
Nichols, John Lawrence Darvall,	Cheltenham, England.	
		J. B. Pfeiffer's.

NAME.	RESIDENCE.	ROOM.
Parker, Warren Downs, Jr.,	River Falls, Wis.	
		Keweenaw Club.
Parks, Henry James,	Lake Linden.	
		Mr. C. Brand's.
Penberthy, John Edward,	Houghton.	
		Mr. E. R. Penberthy's.
Penberthy, Samuel Roy,	Hancock.	
		Mrs. M. Penberthy's.
Raymond, John Chester,	Houghton.	
		Mrs. Raymond's.
Reynolds, Frederick Llewellyn,	Pasadena, Cal.	
		Mrs. Healy's.
Richey, Appleton,	Houghton.	
		Mr. A. R. Richey's.
Rioux, John Elisor,	Dollar Bay.	
		Mr. A. Rioux's.
Sanders, Nicholas,	Hancock.	
		Mrs. E. J. Sanders's.
Shields, Irving James,	Hancock.	
		Mr. Shields's.
Slock, Anthony,	Houghton.	
		Mr. Slock's.
Sturgis, James Bennett, Jr.,	Houghton.	
		Mr. J. B. Sturgis's.
Sutton, William John,	Victoria, B. C.	
		Betzler's Hotel.
Thomas, James Arthur,	Houghton.	
		Mr. William Thomas's.
Truettner, Irving Willard,	Bessemer.	
		Mr. Grignon's.

REGISTER OF STUDENTS.

1895–1896.

REGISTER OF STUDENTS, 1895–1896.

NAME.	RESIDENCE.	ROOM.
Baker, Franklin Jr., S. B. (Lehigh University),	Philadelphia, Pa.	
Bates, Arthur Walter,	Gaylord.	Butterfield House.
Been, John Theodore,	Skanee.	Mrs. West's.
Blackwell, Frank,	Norway.	Mr. H. Hooper's.
Blair, Arthur Eddlumund,	Marysville, Mont.	Mrs. West's.
Boyd, Frederick James,	Dollar Bay.	Mr. F. J. Boyd's.
Brand, William Jacob,	Houghton.	Mr. C. Brand's.
Brown, William Francis,	New York, N. Y.	Mr. C. Brand's.
Burnham, Mathew Howard,	Johannesburg, S. Africa.	Mr. M. H. Burnham's.
Carpenter, Alvin Bacon,	Beloit, Wis.	Mrs. West's.
Carpenter, Guy David,	Blissfield.	Mr. J. Edwards's.
Cavazos, Amado,	Saltillo, Mex.	Mrs. Brimacombe's.
Clark, Alonzo Webster, Jr.,	Detroit.	Keweenaw Club.
Colton, John Dudley, 2nd,	Longmeadow, Mass.	Mr. J. Thomas's.

NAME.	RESIDENCE.	ROOM.
Cooke, Harry Arthur,	Caspar, Wyo.	Mr. T. Lange's.
Cornell, Roscoe,	Dillon, Mont.	Mrs West's.
Croze, Charles Edward,	Houghton.	Mr. J. Croze's.
Cruse, Josiah Alfred,	Ripley.	Mr. J. Cruse's.
Curtis, George Doyle,	Butte City, Mont.	Mr. T. Lange's.
Daniell, John, Jr.,	Houghton,	Mr. J. Daniell's.
Daniell, Richard Ernest,	Houghton.	Mr. J. Daniell's.
DuBois, Wilbur Fisk,	Mobile, Ala.	Mrs. West's.
Duncan, William	Calumet.	Mr. John Duncan's.
Dunn, Bird Wallace,	Houghton.	Capt. W. Dunn's.
Edwards, Robert Leverich,	Houghton.	Mr. T. W. Edwards's.
Esselstyn, John Nelson,	Lansing.	Mrs. West's.
Farmer, Frank,	Georgetown, Colo.	Miss Kelly's.
Fay, Louis Douglas,	Chicago, Ill.	Mrs. E. M. Hoar's.
Fechheimer, Solomon,	Chicago, Ill.	Mrs. West's.
Fisher, Charles Gotfried,	Hancock.	Mr. Fisher's.
Floeter, Albert Henry Christopher,	Menominee.	J. B. Pfeiffer's.
Formis, Andre,	Stuttgart, Germany.	Keweenaw Club.

NAME.	RESIDENCE.	ROOM.
Gilbert, Edwin Gage,	Winnetka, Ill.	
		Mrs. West's.
Goulette, John,	Hancock.	
		Mr. Chas. Goulette's.
Graves, MacDowell,	Detroit.	
		Keweenaw Club.
Greene, Fred Turrell,	Berlin, Ont.	
		Mrs. West's.
Haas, Frank William,	Houghton.	
		Mr. J. Haas's.
Haas, George Allen,	Houghton.	
		Mr. A. Haas's.
Haas, Nathan,	Houghton.	
		Mr. D. Haas's
Hall, Edward John,	Central Mine.	
		Mrs. Didier's.
Hardenburgh, Louis Martin, A. B. (Hillsdale College),	Hillsdale.	
		Mrs. A. Burrows's.
Harris, George Henry Ronald, C. E. (Royal Military College, Kingston, Ontario),	London, Ont.	
		Mrs. West's.
Hartmann, William Frederick,	Houghton.	
		Mr. G. Hartmann's.
Hicks, William Charles.	Houghton.	
		Rev. W. C. Hicks's.
Hoar, Frederick Walpole,	Houghton.	
		Mr. R. M. Hoar's.
Hoar, John Mitchell,	Houghton.	
		Mrs. E. M. Hoar's.
Hodgson, Joseph, H.	Houghton.	
		Mr. J. Hodgson's.
Hodgson, William Adams, S. B. (Michigan Mining School),	Houghton.	
		Mr. J. Hodgson's.
Hooper, James Knight,	Crystal Falls.	
		Mr. C. Brand's.
Houle, Albert,	Negaunee.	
		Mrs. Healy's.

NAME   RESIDENCE   ROOM

Abbe, ...
                                      Mrs. Brimacombe's.

Aceee, George Henry,   Sault Ste. Marie.
                                      Mrs. A. Harris's.

Jenkins, ...   Bear Bay.
                                      Mr. . S. Jenkins's.

Keeler, James Edward,   Bothell.
                                      Mr. J. Edwards's.

Kent, Parmet,   Forest, Ont.
                                      Oriental House.

Knox, John, Jr.,   Hamilton, Ont.
                                      Mrs. Healy's.

McCurdy, William Alexander, Houghton.
                                      Mr. Wm. McCurdy's.

McDonald, Donald Wm.,   Calumet.
                                      Miss Kelly's.

McElhay, Frank Jerome,   New York, N. Y.
                                      Mr. C. Brand's.

Mercer, Harry Talman,   Ontonagon.
                                      Mrs. Brimacombe's.

Millard, James Harvey,   Bear Lake.
                                      Stroebel's Block.

Minehan, Michael Matthias, A.
   B. (St. Mary's College), Summerfield, Kan.
                                      Mr. J. Cameron's.

Munroe, William Dearborn,   Bath.
                                      Mrs. Trim's.

Ogorek, Leopold,   Scharley, Prussia.
                                      Mr. C. Brand's.

Oliver, Thomas,   Norway.
                                      Mr. H. Hooper's.

Osborne, Nathan Sanford,   Water Mill, N. Y.
                                      Mrs. A. Harris's.

Parker, Warren Downes, Jr., River Falls, Wis.
                                      Mrs. Healy's.

NAME.	RESIDENCE.	ROOM.
Peacock, Dan,	Chicago, Ill.	Mrs. A. Harris's.
Randall, Huntley Burnham,	Detroit.	Keweenaw Club.
Rashleigh, William John,	Houghton.	Mrs. A. Burrows's.
Reynolds, Fred Llewellyn,	Pasadena, Cal.	Mrs. Healy's.
Richey, Appleton,	Houghton.	Mr. A. R. Richey's.
Roberts, Frederick Charles, S. B. (Northwestern University),	Crystal Falls.	Mrs. McAllister's.
Russell, Edward Francis,	Yonkers, N. Y.	Mr. C. Brand's.
Sarazin, William George,	Lake Linden.	Oriental House.
Schumann, Enrique Adolpho,	Santiago, Cuba.	Keweenaw Club.
Shields, James Wilson,	Hancock.	Mr. Jas. W. Shields's.
Slock, George,	Houghton.	Mr. Slock's.
Smith, Willard Joseph,	Allouez.	Miss Kelly's.
Snell, Henry Vincent,	Lake Linden.	Mrs. A. Burrows's.
Snow, Arthur Eugene,	St. George, Utah.	Mrs. West's.
Spaulding, Charles Frank,	Rogers Park, Ill.	Mrs. West's.
Strickland, Roland Hugh, C. E. (Royal Military College, Kingston, Ontario),	Lakefield, Ont.	Mrs. West's.

NAME.	RESIDENCE.	ROOM.
Sutton, William John,	Victoria, B. C.	Stroebel's Block.
Taylor, William Wisner, Jr.,	Grand Rapids.	Mr. C. Brand's.
Thomas, James Arthur,	Houghton.	Mr. W. H. Thomas's.
Trethewey, James Henry,	Lake Linden.	Mr. Trethewey's.
Truettner, Irving Willard,	Bessemer.	Mr. J. Thomas's.
Van Orden, Frank Lyon,	Houghton.	Mr. M. VanOrden's.
Walker, Elton Willard,	Detroit.	Mrs. West's.
Wearne, William, Jr.,	Red Jacket.	Mrs. A. Burrows's.
Works, Ralph Clark,	Lima, N. Y.	Stroebel's Block.
Wright, Frederick Bennett,	Oberlin, Ohio.	Douglass House.
Zertuche, Ygnacio Maria,	Monterey, Mex.	Mr. A. Haas's.

SUMMARY, 1894–1895.

Graduate Students.................................. 2
Class of 1895..................................... 25
Class of 1896..................................... 11
Class of 1897..................................... 16
Special Students.................................. 40

94

BY COUNTRIES AND STATES.

Alabama... 4
British Columbia.................................. 4
California.. 1
Ontario... 5
Cuba.. 1
England... 4
Illinois.. 4
Kansas.. 1
Mexico.. 3
Michigan, { Upper Peninsula, 46 }
          { Lower Peninsula, 16 } 62
Minnesota... 3
Mississippi....................................... 1
Montana... 4
New Brunswick..................................... 4
New York.. 2
Pennsylvania...................................... 4
Texas... 2
Utah.. 4
Virginia.. 1
Wisconsin... 3

94

SUMMARY, 1895–1896.

Number of Students Enrolled............................ 94

BY COUNTRIES AND STATES.

Alabama......................	1
British Columbia......................................	1
California...	1
Ontario...	5
Colorado...	1
Cuba	1
Germany...	2
Illinois...	5
Indiana...	1
Kansas	1
Massachusetts...	1
Mexico...	2
Michigan, { Upper Peninsula, 46 } { Lower Peninsula, 12 }	58
Montana...	3
New York...	5
Pennsylvania..	1
Ohio...	1
South Africa...	1
Utah...	1
Wisconsin..	1
Wyoming...	1
	—
	94

AVERAGE AGE OF STUDENTS.

1894–1895.

Special Students	21 years.
Class of 1897	20 1-2 years.
Class of 1896	21 years.
Class of 1895	22 years.
Graduate Students	27 years.
Average Age of all Students	21 1-2 years.

1895–1896.

Average Age of Students	23 years.

OFFICERS OF THE ATHLETIC ASSOCIATION.

1894–1895.

President..............................EDWARD RUSSELL.
Vice President........................JOHN DANIELL.
Secretary...................... FREDERICK WALPOLE HOAR.
Treasurer........................... CAMILO FIGUEROA.

1895–1896.

President..............................JOHN DANIELL.
First Vice President ....ROLAND HUGH STRICKLAND.
Second Vice President.......WARREN DOWNES PARKER, JR.
Secretary......................ALONZO WEBSTER CLARK, JR.
Treasurer.............................DAN PEACOCK.

ADVISORY COMMITTEE.

DR. GEORGE AUGUSTUS KOENIG.
BURTON TYNDALL SEELEY, E. M.
GEORGE HENRY RONALD HARRIS, C. E.

MICHIGAN MINING SCHOOL ALUMNI ASSOCIATION.

President.................. ....J. FISHER.
First Vice President ....E. W. WALKER.
Second Vice President ....C. G. MASON.
Secretary................................. } J. B. ESSELSTYN.
Treasurer.................................. }
Director, One Year............................J. B. WATSON.
Director, Two Years...........................J. G. KIRCHEN.
Director, Three Years.........................W. J. UREN.

CALENDAR 1895–1896.

FALL TERM commences Friday morning, September 13, 1895.

Examinations for admission and advanced standing commence Friday morning at 9 o'clock, and continue through Friday and Saturday.

Regular work for all classes commences Monday, September 16, 1895, at 8 a. m., and all classes are expected to be fully prepared for work at that time.

Thanksgiving recess, November, Wednesday noon until Monday morning.

Fall term ends Friday evening, December 20, 1895.

WINTER TERM commences Monday morning, January 6, 1896, and ends Friday evening, April 10, 1896.

SUMMER TERM commences Monday morning, April 20, 1896, and ends Friday evening, August 14, 1896.

Practical Work in Mine Surveying and Mining begins Monday morning, April 20, and ends Friday evening, May 29, 1896.

Field Work in Surveying commences Monday morning, June 1, and ends Wednesday evening, August 12, 1896.

Shop Practice begins Monday morning, June 1, and ends Wednesday evening, August 12, 1896.

Practical Work in Ore Dressing and in Testing Materials of Engineering commence Monday morning, June 1, and end Friday evening, July 3, 1896.

Field Geology begins Monday morning, July 6, and ends Wednesday evening, August 12, 1896.

Commencement Exercises, Thursday and Friday, August 13 and 14, 1896.

Thursday—Field day, all classes, 9 A. M. and 2 P. M.

      Reception for the Graduating Class, by the Undergraduates, 9 P. M.

18

Friday—Annual Meeting of the Board of Control, 10 A. M.
　　　　Graduation Exercises, 2 P. M.
　　　　Meeting of the Alumni Association, 4 P. M.
　　　　Alumni Dinner, 8:30 P. M.

CALENDAR, 1896-1897.

FALL TERM commences Friday morning, September 18, 1896, and
　ends Thursday noon, December 24, 1896.

Examinations for admission and advanced standing commence
Friday at 9 A. M., and continue through Friday and Saturday.

Regular work for all classes commences Monday, September 21,
1896, at 8 A. M., and all students are expected to be fully prepared to
take up their work at that time.

Thanksgiving recess, November, Wednesday noon until Monday
morning.

WINTER TERM commences Monday morning, January, 11 and ends
　Friday noon, April 16, 1897.

SUMMER TERM commences Monday morning, April 26, 1897, and
ends Friday evening, August 20, 1897.

Practical Work in Mine Surveying and Mining begins Monday
morning, April 26, and ends Friday evening, June 4, 1897.

Surveying commences Monday morning, June 7, and ends Thursday evening, August 19, 1897.

Shop Practice begins Monday morning, June 7, and ends Thursday evening, August 19, 1897.

Ore Dressing and Testing Materials of Engineering commence
Monday morning, June 7, and end Friday evening, July 9, 1897.

Field Geology begins Tuesday morning, July 12, and ends Thursday evening, August 19, 1897.

Commencement Exercises, Friday, August 20, 1897.

Friday—Field Day—All classes.

　　　　Annual Meeting of the Board of Control, 2:30 P. M.
　　　　Meeting of the Alumni Association, 5 P. M.
　　　　Alumni Dinner, 5:30 P. M.
　　　　Graduation Exercises, 8 P. M.
　　　　Reception for the Graduating Class by the Undergradu-
　　　　　ates, 10 P. M.

CALENDAR, 1897–1898.

FALL TERM commences Friday morning, September 17, 1897, ends Friday noon, December 24, 1897.

Examinations for admission and advanced standing commence Friday at 9 A. M., and continue through Friday and Saturday.

Regular work for all classes commences Monday, September 20, 1897, at 8 A. M. Full work is to be taken up at this time.

Thanksgiving recess, November, Wednesday noon until Monday morning.

———

WINTER TERM commences Monday morning, January 10, and ends Friday noon, April 15, 1898.

———

SUMMER TERM commences Monday morning, April 25, 1898, and ends Friday evening, August 19, 1898.

Practical Work in Mine Surveying and Mining commences Monday morning, April 25, and ends Friday evening, June 3, 1898.

Field Work in Surveying commences Monday morning, June 6, and ends Thursday evening, August 18, 1898.

Shop Practice begins Monday morning, June 6, and ends Thursday evening, August 18, 1898.

Ore Dressing and Testing Materials of Engineering commence Monday morning, June 6, and end Friday evening, July 8, 1898.

Field Geology begins Monday morning, July 11, and ends Thursday evening, August 18, 1895.

Commencement Exercises, Friday, August 19, 1898.

Friday—Field day, all classes.

> Annual Meeting of the Board of Control, 2:30 P. M.
> Meeting of the Alumni Association, 5 P. M.
> Alumni Dinner, 5:30 P. M.
> Graduation Exercises, 8 P. M.
> Reception for the Graduating Class by the Undergraduates, 10 P. M.

———

CALENDAR 1898–1899.

FALL TERM commences Friday morning, September 16, 1898, ends Friday noon, December 23, 1898.

Examinations for admission and advanced standing commence

Friday morning at 9 o'clock, and continue through Friday and Saturday.

Regular work for all classes commences Monday, September 19, 1898 at 8 a. m. Full work is to be taken up at this time.

Thanksgiving recess, November, Wednesday noon until Monday morning

———

WINTER TERM commences Monday morning, January 9, and ends Friday noon, April 14, 1899.

———

SUMMER TERM commences Monday morning, April 24, 1899, and ends Friday evening, August 18, 1899.

Practical Work in Mine Surveying and Mining begins Monday morning, April 24, and ends Friday evening, June 2, 1899.

Surveying commences Monday morning, June 5, and ends Thursday evening, August 17, 1899.

Shop Practice begins Monday morning, June 5, and ends Thursday evening, August 17, 1899.

Ore Dressing and Testing Materials of Engineering commence Monday morning, June 5, and end Friday evening, July 7, 1899.

Field Geology begins Monday morning, July 10, and ends Thursday evening, August 17, 1899.

Commencement Exercises, Friday August 18, 1899.

Thursday—Field day, all classes, 9 A. M. and 2 P. M.

Friday—Annual Meeting of the Board of Control, 2:30 P. M.

　　　　Meeting of the Alumni Association, 5 P. M.

　　　　Alumni Dinner, 5:30 P. M.

　　　　Graduation Exercises, 2:30 P. M.

　　　　Reception for the Graduating Class, by the Undergraduates, 10 P. M.

CALENDAR, 1896.

S	M	T	W	T	F	S		JULY.	S	M	T	W	T	F	S
..	..	..	1	2	3	4			..	..	..	1	2	3	4
5	6	7	8	9	10	11			5	6	7	8	9	10	11
12	13	14	15	16	17	18			12	13	14	15	16	17	18
19	20	21	22	23	24	25			19	20	21	22	23	24	25
26	27	28	29	30	31	..			26	27	28	29	30	31	..

EB.

S	M	T	W	T	F	S		AUG.	S	M	T	W	T	F	S
..	..	..	..	..	..	1			..	..	..	..	..	..	1
2	3	4	5	6	7	8			2	3	4	5	6	7	8
9	10	11	12	13	14	15			9	10	11	12	13	14	15
16	17	18	19	20	21	22			16	17	18	19	20	21	22
23	24	25	26	27	28	29			23	24	25	26	27	28	29
									30	31	..	..	..	..	..

ARCH.

S	M	T	W	T	F	S		SEPT.	S	M	T	W	T	F	S
1	2	3	4	..	..	7			..	..	1	2	3	4	5
8	9	10	11	12	13	14			6	7	8	9	10	11	12
15	16	17	18	19	20	21			13	14	15	16	17	18	19
22	23	24	25	26	27	28			20	21	22	23	24	25	26
29	30	31	..	..	..	..			27	28	29	30	..	..	..

PRIL.

S	M	T	W	T	F	S		OCT.	S	M	T	W	T	F	S
..	..	..	1	2	3	4			..	..	..	..	1	2	3
..	..	..	8	9	10	11			4	5	6	7	8	9	10
12	13	14	15	16	17	18			11	12	13	14	15	16	17
19	20	21	22	23	24	25			18	19	20	21	22	23	24
26	27	28	29	30	..	..			25	26	27	28	29	30	31

AY.

S	M	T	W	T	F	S		NOV.	S	M	T	W	T	F	S
..	..	..	..	..	1	2			1	2	3	4	5	6	7
3	4	5	6	7	8	9			8	9	10	11	12	13	14
10	11	12	13	14	15	16			15	16	17	18	19	20	21
17	18	19	20	21	22	23			22	23	24	25	26	27	28
24	25	26	27	28	29	30			29	30	..	..	..	..	..
31	..	..	..	..	..	..									

UNE.

S	M	T	W	T	F	S		DEC.	S	M	T	W	T	F	S
..	1	2	3	4	5	6			..	..	1	2	3	4	5
7	8	9	10	11	12	13			6	7	8	9	10	11	12
14	15	16	17	18	19	20			13	14	15	16	17	18	19
21	22	23	24	25	26	27			20	21	22	23	24	25	26
28	29	30	..	..	..	..			27	28	29	30	31	..	..

CALENDAR, 1897.

	S	M	T	W	T	F	S			S	M	T	W	T	F	S
JAN.						1	2	JULY.						1	2	3
	3	4	5	6	7	8	9			4	5	6	7	8	9	10
	10	11	12	13	14	15	16			11	12	13	14	15	16	17
	17	18	19	20	21	22	23			18	19	20	21	22	23	24
	24	25	26	27	28	29	30			25	26	27	28	29	30	31
	31															
FEB.		1	2	3	4	5	6	AUG.		1	2	3	4	5	6	7
	7	8	9	10	11	12	13			8	9	10	11	12	13	14
	14	15	16	17	18	19	20			15	16	17	18	19	20	21
	21	22	23	24	25	26	27			22	23	24	25	26	27	28
	28									29	30	31				
MARCH.		1	2	3	4	5	6	SEPT.				1	2	3	4
	7	8	9	10	11	12	13			5	6	7	8	9	10	11
	14	15	16	17	18	19	20			12	13	14	15	16	17	18
	21	22	23	24	25	26	27			19	20	21	22	23	24	25
	28	29	30	31						26	27	28	29	30		
APRIL.					1	2	3	OCT.						1	2
	4	5	6	7	8	9	10			3	4	5	6	7	8	9
	11	12	13	14	15	16	17			10	11	12	13	14	15	16
	18	19	20	21	22	23	24			17	18	19	20	21	22	23
	25	26	27	28	29	30				24	25	26	27	28	29	30
										31						
MAY.							1	NOV.		1	2	3	4	5	6
	2	3	4	5	6	7	8			7	8	9	10	11	12	13
	9	10	11	12	13	14	15			14	15	16	17	18	19	20
	16	17	18	19	20	21	22			21	22	23	24	25	26	27
	23	24	25	26	27	28	29			28	29	30				
	30	31														
JUNE.			1	2	3	4	5	DEC.				1	2	3	4
	6	7	8	9	10	11	12			5	6	7	8	9	10	11
	13	14	15	16	17	18	19			12	13	14	15	16	17	18
	20	21	22	23	24	25	26			19	20	21	22	23	24	25
	27	28	29	30						26	27	28	29	30	31	

CALENDAR, 1898.

	S	M	T	W	T	F	S			S	M	T	W	T	F	S
JAN.	..	..	..	..	..	..	1	JULY.		..	..	..	..	..	1	2
	2	3	4	5	6	7	8			3	4	5	6	7	8	9
	9	10	11	12	13	14	15			10	11	12	13	14	15	16
	16	17	18	19	20	21	22			17	18	19	20	21	22	23
	23	24	25	26	27	28	29			24	25	26	27	28	29	30
	30	31	..	..	..	..	..			31	..	..	..	..	..	..
FEB.	..	..	1	2	3	4	5	AUG.		..	1	2	3	4	5	6
	6	7	8	9	10	11	12			7	8	9	10	11	12	13
	13	14	15	16	17	18	19			14	15	16	17	18	19	20
	20	21	22	23	24	25	26			21	22	23	24	25	26	27
	27	28	..	..	..	..	..			28	29	30	31	..	..	..
MARCH.	..	..	1	2	3	4	5	SEPT.		..	..	..	..	1	2	3
	6	7	8	9	10	11	12			4	6	6	7	8	9	10
	13	14	15	16	17	18	19			11	12	13	14	15	16	17
	20	21	22	23	24	25	26			18	19	20	21	22	23	24
	27	28	29	30	31	..	..			25	26	27	28	29	30	..
APRIL.	..	..	..	..	..	1	2	OCT.		..	..	..	..	..	..	1
	3	4	5	6	7	8	9			2	3	4	5	6	7	8
	10	11	12	13	14	15	16			9	10	11	12	13	14	15
	17	18	19	20	21	22	23			16	17	18	19	20	21	22
	24	25	26	27	28	29	30			23	24	25	26	27	28	29
										30	31	..	..	..	..	..
MAY.	1	2	3	4	5	6	7	NOV.		..	..	1	2	3	4	5
	8	9	10	11	12	13	14			6	7	8	9	10	11	12
	15	16	17	18	19	20	21			13	14	15	16	17	18	19
	22	23	24	25	26	27	28			20	21	22	23	24	25	26
	29	30	31	..	..	..	..			27	28	29	30	..	..	..
JUNE.	..	..	..	1	2	3	4	DEC.		..	..	..	..	1	2	3
	5	6	7	8	9	10	11			4	5	6	7	8	9	10
	12	13	14	15	16	17	18			11	12	13	14	15	16	17
	19	20	21	22	23	24	25			18	19	20	21	22	23	24
	26	27	28	29	30	..	..			25	26	27	28	29	30	31

CALENDAR, 1899.

	S	M	T	W	T	F	S			S	M	T	W	T	F	S
JAN.	1	2	3	4	5	6	7		JULY.							1
	8	9	10	11	12	13	14			2	3	4	5	6	7	8
	15	16	17	18	19	20	21			9	10	11	12	13	14	15
	22	23	24	25	26	27	28			16	17	18	19	20	21	22
	29	30	31							23	24	25	26	27	28	29
										30	31					
FEB.				1	2	3	4		AUG.			1	2	3	4	5
	5	6	7	8	9	10	11			6	7	8	9	10	11	12
	12	13	14	15	16	17	18			13	14	15	16	17	18	19
	19	20	21	22	23	24	25			20	21	22	23	24	25	26
	26	27	28							27	28	29	30	31		
MARCH.				1	2	3	4		SEPT.						1	2
	5	6	7	8	9	10	11			3	4	5	6	7	8	9
	12	13	14	15	16	17	18			10	11	12	13	14	15	16
	19	20	21	22	23	24	25			17	18	19	20	21	22	23
	26	27	28	29	30	31				24	25	26	27	28	29	30
APRIL.							1		OCT.	1	2	3	4	5	6	7
	2	3	4	5	6	7	8			8	9	10	11	12	13	14
	9	10	11	12	13	14	15			15	16	17	18	19	20	21
	16	17	18	19	20	21	22			22	23	24	25	26	27	28
	23	24	25	26	27	28	29			29	30	31				
	30															
MAY.		1	2	3	4	5	6		NOV.			1	2	3	4
	7	8	9	10	11	12	13			5	6	7	8	9	10	11
	14	15	16	17	18	19	20			12	13	14	15	16	17	18
	21	22	23	24	25	26	27			19	20	21	22	23	24	25
	28	29	30	31						26	27	28	29	30		
JUNE					1	2	3		DEC.						1	2
	4	5	6	7	8	9	10			3	4	5	6	7	8	9
	11	12	13	14	15	16	17			10	11	12	13	14	15	16
	18	19	20	21	22	23	24			17	18	19	20	21	22	23
	25	26	27	28	29	30				24	25	26	27	28	29	30
										31						

INDEX.

Admission, Requirements for, 35–52.
Admission by Certificate, 49, 50.
Admission, by Diploma, 35–49.
Admission, by Examination, 50.
Algebra, 39, 47, 63, 78.
Algebra, Elementary, 78, 155, 173, 174.
Alumni Association, 272.
Analytic Geometry, 63, 78.
Analytic Mechanics, 64, 85.
Antoine Ore Co., 243.
Aragon Mine, 242.
Arithmetic, 39, 173.
Asbestus, 248.
Ashland Mine, 244.
Assaying, 65, 91.
Astronomy, 40, 45, 78, 156, 176.
Athletic Association, 272.
Atlantic Mine, 237–239.
Attendance, 8.
Aurora Mine, 244.
Bachelor of Science, 157, 158.
Biology, 71, 117, 118, 162.
Blowpipe Analyses, 64, 88.
Board of Control, 12.
Book-keeping, 40, 45, 46, 78, 156, 175, 176.
Botany, 40, 46, 71, 117, 162.
Brotherton Mine, 244
Buffalo Mines, 240.
Building Stone, 246–250.
Buildings, 194–200.
Business Law, 40, 45, 46.
Calculus, 63, 79.
Calendars, 278–280.
Calumet and Hecla Mine, 224–231.
Cambria Mine, 240.
Catalogue, Character of, 2.
Central Mine, 239.
Champion Mining Co., 242.
Chapin Mine, 242, 248.
Chemistry, 64, 65, 85–90, 160, 166, 167.

Chemistry, General Experiment-al, 64, 86–88.
Chrysotile, 248.
Civil Engineering, 69, 110–118, 162, 171, 172.
Civil Government, 40, 41, 46.
Clay, 248.
Cleveland Cliffs Iron Mining Co.'s, 240, 241.
Coal, 250, 251.
Collections, 187, 188.
Columbia Mine, 243.
Commercial Crises, 206–208.
Commonwealth Mine, 243.
Composition, 41, 46.
Copper District, 224–239.
Copper Mining, 221.
Copper Produced, 228.
Courses of Instruction, 55–59.
Courses of Instruction, Outline of, 63–73.
Crystallography, 71, 118, 163.
Degrees, 157, 158.
Departments of Instruction, 77–156.
Deposits, 201, 202.
Differential Equations, 63, 79.
Director, 1, 58, 59.
Doctor of Philosophy, 157, 158.
Drawing, 66, 94–99, 160, 161.
Drawing Instruments, 95–97.
Dunn Mine, 243.
Electrical Engineering, 68, 69, 107–110, 161, 162, 170, 171.
Electrical Engineering Labora-tory, 68, 69, 109, 110.
Electrical Measurements, 64, 84 85.
Electricity and Magnetism, 68, 109.
Electives, Choice of, 57.
Elective Schedules, Advisory, 165–172.
Elective System, 55–59.
Employment, 206–211.

Engineering Design and Construction, 66, 98
Engineering Hall, 195, 196.
English Composition, 176.
Essential Studies, 55, 56.
Examination Questions, Entrance, 173–176.
Excelsior Redstone Company, 246.
Expenses, 201–208.
Expenses of the Mining School, 9.
Faculty, 17.
Franklin Junior Mine. 234.
Franklin Mine, 234, 235.
French, 41, 46, 47.
Geological Field Work, 72, 151, 152.
Geology, 71, 72, 131–154, 163, 166, 167.
Geology, Economic, 72, 172–154.
Geology, Elements of, 71, 72, 131–149.
Geology, Physical and Chemical, 72, 150, 151.
Geology, Stratigraphical, 72, 150.
General History, 42.
Geometry, 41, 47, 73, 155, 174, 175.
German, 42, 46, 47.
Gold Mining, 221.
Gogebic Range. 244.
Government, 204, 205.
Graduates, 8, 21–31.
Graduates, Occupation of, 21–31.
Granite, 248.
Graphical Statics, 66, 97.
Grindstones, 247.
Gypsum, 249.
Hemlock Mine, 243.
High School, Courses of Study, 36–87, 50.
History of the United States, 42.
Houghton, 214–216.
Hydraulics, 69, 113.
Inventory, 10, 11.
Iron Ore, Production of, 218–220.
Iron Ranges, 240–245.
Jackson Mine, 240.
Kearsarge Mine, 234.
Kerber-Jacobs Redstone Co., 246.
Keweenaw District, 239.
Lake Superior Iron Co., 240
L'Anse Brown Stone Co., 247.

Library, 177–186.
Lillie Mine, 240.
Limestone, 248.
Literature, 42, 43, 46.
Lithology, 71, 129, 130.
Location, 212–216.
Location of Graduates, 31.
Logic, 43, 47.
Longyear Fund, 192, 193.
Longyear Prizes, 189, 190.
Machine Design, 66, 98.
Marble, 249, 250.
Marquette Range, 240–242.
Mathematics, 47, 63, 77–79, 159.
Mechanical Engineering, 66–68, 99–107, 161, 168–170.
Mechanical Laboratory, 68, 106, 107.
Mechanics, 64, 85, 160.
Mechanics of Materials, 67, 104.
Mechanism, 67, 103, 104
Menominee Range, 242, 243.
Metallurgical Designing, 65, 93, 94.
Mechanical Drawing, 66, 94–96.
Metallurgical Experimentation, 65, 93.
Metallurgy, 65, 91–94, 160, 167, 168.
Michigan, Mineral Production, 218.
Mine Accounts, 70, 115, 116.
Mines, Dividends Paid, 222.
Mine Management, 70, 115, 116.
Mine Surveying and Mining, 69, 70, 114, 115.
Mine Ventilation, 70, 116.
Mineral Industries, 217–223.
Mineral Production, 217, 218.
Mineralogy, 71, 118–121, 163.
Mining Engineer, 157, 158.
Mining Engineering, 69, 70, 113–116, 162, 171, 172.
Mining, Principles of, 69, 113, 114.
Mining School, Purposes and History, 3–9.
Negaunee Mine, 240.
Newport Mine, 244.
Norrie Mining Co., 244.
Norrie Scholarship, 191, 192.
Novaculite, 248.
Officers, 13–16.
Ontonagon District, 239.

Ore Docks, 245.
Ore Dressing, 70, 116, 162.
Organization, 204, 205.
Osceola Mine, 233.

Pabst Mine, 244.
Palæontology, 71, 117, 118, 162.
Palms Mines, 244.
Periodicals, 178–185.
Petrography, 71. 121–131, 163.
Petrology, 71, 130. 131.
Pewabic Mine, 243
Physical Apparatus, 80–83.
Physical Geography. 43, 47.
Physical Measurements. 64, 83, 84.
Physics, 43, 48, 63, 64. 79–85, 159.
Physics, Elementary, 78, 155, 156, 175.
Physiology, 44, 48.
Pittsburg and Lake Angeline Iron Co., 240.
Political Economy, 44, 48.
Portage Entry Company, 246.
Portage Lake District, 224–239.
Preparatory Studies, 51. 52.
Preparatory Subject, 78, 155 ,156, 164.
Prizes and Scholarships, 189–193.
Properties of Materials, 66, 100.
Public, to the, 1.
Qualitative Analysis, 64, 88, 89.
Quantitative Analysis, 64, 65, 88, 89.
Quartzite. 248.
Quincy Mine, 235–237.
Regulations of the Library, 185, 186.
Republic Mining Co.. 241, 242.
Required Studies, 157.
Rhetoric, 44, 46.
Ropes Gold Mine, 242.

Routes, 212–214.
Salt, 251, 252.
Sandstone, 246, 247.
Science Hall, 194, 195, 197–200.
Serpentine, 248, 250.
Shop Practice, 67, 100–103.
Silver Mining, 221.
Slate, 248.
Students, Average Age of, 271.
Students, Register of, 253–268.
Students, Residence of, 8, 9.
Students, Special, 51.
Students, Summary of, 269, 270.
Studies, Sequence of, 55, 56.
Surveying, 69, 110–113.
Synthetic Chemistry, 65, 90.

Talc, 249.
Tamarack Junior Mine, 233.
Tamarack Mine, 231–233
Tecumseh Mine, 234.
Testing Materials of Engineering, 67, 105, 106.
Text Books, 159–164.
Topographical Drawing, 66, 96, 97.
Thermodynamics, 68, 108.
Thesis, 72, 73, 154, 155.
Tilden Mine, 244.
Traverse Bay Redstone Co., 247.
Treasurer, 1.
Trigonometry, Plane, 45, 63, 78.
Trigonometry, Spherical, 63, 78.
Tuition, 201, 202.

Valve Gears, 67, 106.
Vulcan Mine, 242.

Waverly Stone, 247.
Winthrop Mine, 241.
Wolverine Mine, 233, 234.
Wright Scholarship, 190, 191.

Zoology, 45, 49, 71, 117, 118, 162

ENGINEERING HALL

Lightning Source UK Ltd.
Milton Keynes UK
UKHW010331281218
334537UK00007B/207/P